Items should be returned to the library from which they
were borrowed on or before the date stamped above,
unless a renewal has been granted.   LM6.108.5

Wiltshire County Council

Library & Museum Service

HEADQUARTERS   BYTHESEA ROAD   TROWBRIDGE

THE OXFORD
ILLUSTRATED DICKENS

SKETCHES BY BOZ

THE OXFORD ILLUSTRATED DICKENS

Charles John Huffham Dickens was born on 7 February 1812 at Landport near Portsmouth, where his father was a Navy pay clerk. His family moved to London in 1815 and in 1817 to Chatham, where Dickens spent the happiest time of his boyhood. This was followed by a period of misery during which his father was imprisoned for debt in the Marshalsea and Dickens was withdrawn from school and, at the age of 12, sent to work in a blacking warehouse. These experiences deeply affected him and his future work. He returned to school, and left at 15 to become a clerk, a shorthand reporter in the law courts, and a reporter of debates in the Commons. In 1833 he began contributing articles to periodicals, which were later reprinted as *Sketches by Boz* (1836–7); these led to an approach from publishers, resulting in the creation of Mr Pickwick and the publication in monthly numbers of *The Posthumous Papers of the Pickwick Club* (1836–7). In 1836 he married Catherine Hogarth; they had ten children over the next 16 years. Dickens began to publish *Oliver Twist* in 1837 in *Bentley's Miscellany*, a periodical of which he was the first editor. *Nicholas Nickleby* followed in 1838–9. *The Old Curiosity Shop* (1840–1) and *Barnaby Rudge* (1841) were intended for *Master Humphrey's Clock*, a weekly written by Dickens, but he eventually abandoned 'Master Humphrey'.

Dickens's visit to America in 1842 resulted in *American Notes* (1842) and an American section in *Martin Chuzzlewit* (1843–4). He lost readership with the latter but regained it with 'A Christmas Carol' (1843), the first of his five *Christmas Books*. In 1844 he visited Italy, and contributed 'Pictures from Italy' (1846) to the *Daily News*, a paper he founded. *Dombey and Son* appeared in 1846–8 and *David Copperfield* in 1849–50. In 1850 Dickens began the weekly journal *Household Words*, incorporated in 1859 into *All The Year Round*, which he edited until his death. In these appeared essays later issued as *Reprinted Pieces* (1858) and *The Uncommercial Traveller* (1861), and his *Christmas Stories*. *A Child's History of England* was published in 1851–3, *Bleak House* in 1852–3, *Hard Times* in 1854, *Little Dorrit* in 1855–7, *A Tale of Two Cities* in 1859, *Great Expectations* in 1860–1, and *Our Mutual Friend* in 1864–5. In 1856 Dickens bought a country house, Gad's Hill Place, near Rochester, and in 1858 he and his wife separated. He threw himself into public readings of his works, which were greatly successful but draining. His last work, *The Mystery of Edwin Drood*, was left unfinished when he died suddenly on 9 June 1870.

SKETCHES
BY
BOZ

George Cruikshank

SKETCHES BY BOZ

ILLUSTRATIVE OF EVERY-DAY LIFE
AND EVERY-DAY PEOPLE

By
CHARLES DICKENS

With 55 Illustrations by
George Cruikshank and 'Phiz'
and an Introduction by
THEA HOLME

OXFORD   NEW YORK   TORONTO   MELBOURNE
OXFORD UNIVERSITY PRESS

Oxford University Press, Walton Street, Oxford OX2 6DP

Oxford New York Toronto
Delhi Bombay Calcutta Madras Karachi
Petaling Jaya Singapore Hong Kong Tokyo
Nairobi Dar es Salaam Cape Town
Melbourne Auckland

and associated companies in
Beirut Berlin Ibadan Nicosia

Oxford is a trade mark of Oxford University Press

The articles which make up *Sketches by Boz* were mostly contributed by Dickens to periodicals in the years 1833–6. Only a few additional sketches were written after *Pickwick Papers* began to appear in monthly parts in 1836. The First Series of *Sketches by Boz* was published in two volumes in 1836; the Second Series in one volume in 1837. The first octavo edition, bound up from an issue in monthly parts, with illustrations by George Cruikshank, appeared in 1839.

The 1839 edition comprised the bulk of the book as we now know it. The present edition also includes 'Sketches of Young Gentlemen' and 'Sketches of Young Couples', first published with illustrations by 'Phiz' (Hablot K. Browne) in 1838 and 1840 respectively, and 'The Mudfog and Other Sketches' which are drawn from *Bentley's Miscellany*, edited by Dickens in 1837–9. The last-named, with one exception, were first collected and published as 'The Mudfog Papers' in 1880; they contain additional illustrations by Cruikshank.

The Preface by Dickens, dated October 1850, was written for the first Cheap Edition.

In the Oxford Illustrated Dickens (known before 1966 as the New Oxford Illustrated Dickens) *Sketches by Boz* was first published in 1957, and reprinted in 1963, 1966, 1969, 1978, 1981, 1982, 1987.

Published in the United States by Oxford University Press, USA

This volume: ISBN 0 19 254518 3
21-volume set: ISBN 0 19 254522 1

Printed in the United States of America

INTRODUCTION

by THEA HOLME

ONE evening in the autumn of 1832 the manuscript of a fictional sketch entitled 'A Sunday out of Town' was dropped 'with fear and trembling into a dark letter-box in a dark office up a dark court in Fleet Street'. Its author, describing the event to a friend, gives a picture of the sequel. We see him in a Strand bookshop, hurriedly searching through a copy of *The Monthly Magazine*. He pauses, gazing at the page before him. His sketch—its name 'transmogrified' to 'A Dinner at Poplar Walk'—is there, 'in all the glory of print'. Thrusting his way through the crowded Strand, the young Charles Dickens hurries blindly towards Westminster Hall where he may pace in solitude—'my eyes so dimmed with pride and joy, that they could not bear the street, and were not fit to be seen'.

The delight of seeing his work in print was the only reward offered by *The Monthly Magazine*, whose Editor presently sent a 'polite and flattering communication' asking for more. He was duly supplied with 'Horatio Sparkins', 'The Bloomsbury Christening', and 'The Boarding House'. This last was the first sketch to bear the author's signature— 'Boz'. The pseudonym was, as he afterwards put it, 'the nickname of a pet child, a younger brother whom I had dubbed Moses, in honour of The Vicar of Wakefield; which, being facetiously pronounced through the nose, became Boses, and, being shortened, became Boz'.

The following year, Dickens, who was now twenty-one and earning five guineas a week as a reporter on *The Morning Chronicle*, was sent to review a new farce at the Adelphi Theatre. He found that the author, J. B. Buckstone, had unashamedly used the plot and many of the jokes from his own sketch, 'The Bloomsbury Christening'. Already he had been paid the doubtful compliment of plagiarism.

By now several influential men were becoming aware of young Boz, among them the successful author Harrison Ainsworth, who introduced him to his own publisher, Macrone. One night, after spending the evening at Ainsworth's house in Willesden, Dickens and Macrone walked back into the city together. The publisher declared that the *Sketches*, of which twenty or so had now appeared in *The Morning Chronicle* and other papers, were 'capital value'; and suggested their being collected into a volume for publication. Cruikshank the cartoonist, he added casually, might be the man to illustrate them. It is not difficult to imagine the enthusiasm with which this suggestion was received, or the eagerness with which Boz—in the spare time snatched from his travels as a parliamentary reporter in election time—was to fling himself into the production of a quantity of new sketches to complete the two volumes finally commissioned by Macrone. His mind was filled with ideas: he wrote with speed. In the end it was Cruikshank, not Dickens, who held up publication.

At last, on 7 February 1836, its author's twenty-fourth birthday, the First Series of *Sketches by Boz* was published. Its immediate success was almost immediately eclipsed; for some six weeks later the first number of *The Pickwick Papers* appeared. After a doubtful start this serial was to achieve, with the introduction of Sam Weller, a swift and enduring fame. By the time the Second Series of his *Sketches* appeared, Boz and *Pickwick* were household words.

'Perhaps', said *Cranford*'s Miss Jenkyns, 'the author is young. Let him persevere, and who knows what he may become if he will take the great Doctor for his model.' 'Doctor Johnson's style', she reiterated later—after listening 'with patient gravity' to a chapter of *Pickwick*—'Doctor Johnson's style is a model for young beginners.'

It is true that Mrs. Gaskell, in introducing Boz as a bone of contention between two of her characters, was incidentally paying a witty compliment to the Editor who had commissioned her work. But the fictitious Miss Jenkyns's attitude may well have had its counterpart in reality. The impact of Dickens upon the more reactionary of his readers must have been startling. After the rolling phrases, the remote philosophizing characters of Johnson; the exotic phantasmagoria of Gothic romance; even after the fastidious realism of Jane Austen—'Let other pens dwell on guilt and misery. I quit such odious subjects as soon as I can'—the contrast is remarkable. Here was Boz, reflecting a completely new outlook, the outlook of the man in the street;

setting down in his *Sketches* all the small events in the everyday life of common persons—bank clerks, shop assistants, omnibus drivers; laundresses, market women, and kidney-pie sellers: directing his powers of observation and description upon scenes and characters within the daily scope of any loiterer in London. 'I thought I knew something of the town', commented one of his fellow clerks in the law firm of Ellis and Blackmore; 'but after a little talk with Dickens I found that I knew nothing. He knew it all, from Bow to Brentford. . . . He could imitate, in a manner I never saw equalled, the low population of the streets of London in all their varieties.'

In these sketches we see a reflection of the tremendous social changes that were beginning to take place. On the one hand Dickens depicts in relentless detail the horrors of poverty, disease, and crime—legacy of eighteenth-century London; on the other the prosperous vulgarity of the rapidly rising middle class. The young Boz stood, as it were, between two worlds; and we are reminded that Dickens the Eminent Victorian was born in the reign of George the Third. Through his eyes we watch Hogarthian scenes of misery and despair, offset by brightly coloured pictures of mass jollification reminiscent of Frith's 'Derby Day'.

The heat is intense this afternoon, and the people, of whom there are additional parties arriving every moment, look as warm as the tables which have been recently painted, and have the appearance of being red-hot. What a dust and noise! Men and women—boys and girls—sweethearts and married people. . . . Gentlemen in alarming waistcoats, and steel watchguards, promenading about, three abreast . . . ladies, with great, long, white pocket-handkerchiefs like small table-cloths in their hands, chasing one another on the grass in the most playful and interesting manner, with the view of attracting the attention of the aforesaid gentlemen—husbands in perspective ordering bottles of ginger-beer for the objects of their affections, with a lavish disregard of expense; and the said objects washing down huge quantities of shrimps and winkles, with an equal disregard of their own bodily health and subsequent discomfort—boys, with great silk hats just balanced on the top of their heads, smoking cigars, and trying to look as if they liked them— gentlemen in pink shirts and blue waistcoats, occasionally upsetting either themselves, or somebody else, with their own canes.

I suppose it is almost inevitable that one should consider these sketches in terms of painting, for their writer is already a master of pictorial description. He lays on his colours boldly, giving us sharp contrasts of light and darkness in his 'Visit to Newgate', and bringing to life with vivid touches his portraits such as 'The Last Cab Driver' who is described as 'a brown-whiskered, white-hatted, no-coated cabman; his nose was generally red, and his bright blue eye not unfrequently stood out in bold relief against a black border of artificial workmanship'. His neck, we are told, 'was usually garnished with a bright yellow handkerchief. In summer he carried in his mouth a flower; in winter, a straw—slight, but, to a contemplative mind, certain indications of a love of nature, and a taste for botany.'

It is difficult to make a fair assessment of the literary value of these early sketches because, in doing so, one must temporarily forget the masterpieces of which they were the harbinger, and of which one is so frequently reminded by small inspired touches, or by the foreshadowing of characters as yet unborn. Dickens himself, years later, described his first book as 'often being extremely crude and ill-considered, and bearing obvious marks of haste and inexperience'. This may indeed be true of some of the 'Tales', such as 'Mr. Minns and His Cousin' (the original 'A Sunday out of Town'), which, after an amusing and carefully contrived start, ends with such suddenness that one wonders if the author had run out of paper; and also of the irritating humours of 'The Mudfog Association' in which the comic genius of Boz seems to have lost its way.

But as an example of what is now called 'documentary' the *Sketches* deserve a unique place in literature. It has been pointed out elsewhere that more than half this volume's contents are facts: facts observed with an astonishing precision and wealth of detail. But Boz is no objective reporter: the facts he presents are invested with his own reaction to them, and in some cases are lifted by his imagination into tragedy or fantasy. An example of this is to be found in 'Meditations in Monmouth Street', where, speculating upon the contents of a second-hand clothes shop, he creates the life story of a wastrel from some of the garments displayed; and then, 'by way of restoring the naturally cheerful tone of our thoughts', begins to fit 'visionary feet and legs into a cellar-board full

of boots and shoes'. With a swift stroke of invention he
brings to life a whole cast of characters, imagines their re-
lationships one with the other, and sets them before us in a
sort of comic ballet.

It is interesting to note that at the time of their publication, the two *Sketches* singled out for praise were concerned
with tragedy—'The Black Veil' and 'A Visit to Newgate'.
The former, which is included among the Tales, is a highly
dramatic, not to say melodramatic, story, of which the
theme is a recurrent one throughout the *Sketches*: the ruin
of a woman's life by the worthlessness of the man to whom
she has devoted it. In this case it is a mother whose fruitless
efforts to save her son from the gallows have driven her
insane. We are spared few of the horrors of this woeful tale;
there are moments when the dialogue is worthy of the
Radclyffian title.

'Who was he ?' inquired the surgeon.
'*My son*', rejoined the woman; and fell senseless at his feet.

But in contrast we find masterly passages such as that
describing 'the back part of Walworth'; and the 'corpulent
round-headed boy' at the opening might be a rough sketch
of the fat boy in *Pickwick*.

Dickens admitted that he found Newgate Prison 'a very
difficult subject'. There is little doubt that he found it a
heart-rending one. Reading this account one cannot fail to
be aware of the pity with which his imagination works upon
the mournful groups he describes: the women conversing
through the bars of 'a kind of iron cage . . . through which
the friends of the female prisoners communicate with them';
the three condemned murderers—one of them entertaining
some hopes of reprieve, and holding aloof from his two companions, who, as the turnkey intimated in a confident
undertone, 'were dead men'. After a pitiful description of
fourteen infant pickpockets 'drawn up in line for our inspection' in the prison school, he writes, 'There was not one redeeming feature among them—not a glance of honesty—
not a wink expressive of anything but the gallows and the
hulks, in the whole collection'; and concludes, 'We have
never looked upon a more disagreeable sight, because we
never saw fourteen such hopeless creatures of neglect, before.' Here, surely, is something greater than pity and

horror: the imaginative insight into the cause of crime which was later to inspire his relentless exposure of social evils. Already, it would seem, the foundations have been laid for *Oliver Twist*; and the images of Fagin and his gang have peered at their creator from out of the shadows of Newgate.

It is for the glimpses they afford us of their author that these sketches have a special fascination: not only in fore-shadowings of future greatness but in those touches which reveal the young Boz himself. In 'Making a Night of It' he gives us what is thought to be a self portrait. He is the romantic Smithers in his 'brown hat, very much turned up at the sides', who found his appreciation of a theatrical per-formance somewhat marred by the effects of Scotch whiskey and Havannah cigars. Young Boz must undoubtedly have met 'The Theatrical Young Gentleman' who is the subject of another sketch, and who called Drury Lane the lane, and the Victoria the vic. His own interest in theatrical matters is unquestionable; and in 'Private Theatres' it is clear that his knowledge of these places of entertainment extended backstage.

In the National Portrait Gallery there hangs a painting by Maclise, of which Thackeray declared, 'Here we have the real identical man, Dickens.' It shows a youthful figure seated in a crimson and gilt armchair before a writing desk, his left hand firmly placed upon a manuscript—an attitude which seems to suggest that he is playing, with enjoyment, the part of a famous writer. The pale smooth face is turned, like an actor's, full into the light. One observes the elegant folds of his black satin cravat, the neatness of his small well-polished boots. Then, drawing nearer, one becomes aware of the power and vitality in that face with its strong nose and sensuous, sensitive mouth—and the large brilliant eyes which, turned away from the artist, gaze thoughtfully out of the window. These are the eyes which observed the tragedy and comedy of life in such vivid detail; which saw and re-corded brutality and pathos, courage and despair, and all the innumerable absurdities of human behaviour.

This portrait was painted three years after the publication of *Sketches by Boz*, when its subject was assured of fame; but it is not difficult to recognize the author of these early works. It is in company with this same youthful, energetic figure

that, reading them, we walk the streets and visit the entertainments and institutions of the London of William the
Fourth. There are many rewarding discoveries for the ex-
plorer among these pages; many opportunities to exclaim in
echo of Thackeray, 'Here we have the real identical man,
Dickens!'

PREFACE

THE whole of these Sketches were written and published, one by one, when I was a very young man. They were collected and republished while I was still a very young man; and sent into the world with all their imperfections (a good many) on their heads.

They comprise my first attempts at authorship—with the exception of certain tragedies achieved at the mature age of eight or ten, and represented with great applause to over-flowing nurseries. I am conscious of their often being extremely crude and ill-considered, and bearing obvious marks of haste and inexperience; particularly in that section of the present volume which is comprised under the general head of Tales.

But as this collection is not originated now, and was very leniently and favourably received when it was first made, I have not felt it right either to remodel or expunge, beyond a few words and phrases here and there.

CONTENTS

OUR PARISH

SCENES

CHARACTERS

TALES

LIST OF ILLUSTRATIONS

By GEORGE CRUIKSHANK

CHARACTERS

OUR PARISH

THE THREE MISS BROWNS, members of various visitation committees.
MR. BUNG, a broker's man, candidate for the office of beadle.
MR. DAWSON, a surgeon.
FIXEM (*alias* SMITH), a broker; Bung's master.
MRS. JOHNSON PARKER, the founder of a Ladies' Society.
CAPTAIN PURDAY, a bluff, half-pay naval officer.
MR. ROBINSON, a gentleman in a public office.
SIMMONS, a parish beadle.
MR. THOMAS SPRUGGINS, defeated candidate for office of beadle.
MRS. SPRUGGINS, his wife.
WILLIAM, a young man who overtasks himself in supporting a widowed mother.
THE FOUR MISS WILLISES, four sisters who seem to have no separate existence.

SCENES

MR. WILLIAM BARKER, a waterman, afterwards an omnibus cad.
THE CAPTAIN, a spare, squeaking, drinking old man.
DANDO, a boatman.
MR. GREEN, an aeronaut at Vauxhall-gardens.
MR HENRY, a pawnbroker near Drury-lane.
JANE, the Hebe of " Bellamy's."
JEM LARKINS, an amateur actor in the genteel comedy line.
MR. LOGGINS, an amateur actor who takes the part of *Macbeth*.
MARY, a quarrelsome woman of the Seven Dials.
NICHOLAS, butler of "Bellamy's."
SARAH, a vixenish woman, who falls out with Mary.
THOMAS SLUDBERRY, a little red-faced, sly ginger-beer seller.
MR. SLUFFEN, a speaker at the May-day chimney-sweeps' dinner.
MR. SMUGGINS, a round-faced man, in the comic line.
HONEST TOM, a metropolitan member of the House of Commons.
MISS WOOLFORD, a circus-rider at Astley's.

CHARACTERS

BELLA, a young girl, forced into a life of crime.
SIGNOR BILLSMETHI, a dancing-master.
MISS BILLSMETHI, his daughter.

Mr. Augustus Cooper, a young man in the oil and colour business.

Mr. Dobble, a clerk in a public office.

Miss Julia Dobble, his daughter.

Mr. John Dounce, a retired glove and braces maker.

Mr. Ellis, a sharp-nosed man, with a soft voice.

Emily, a hardened and depraved young woman.

Miss Jemima Evans, a shoe-binder and straw-bonnet maker.

Mr. Harris, a law-stationer.

Mr. Jennings, a robe-maker.

Mr. Jones, a barrister's clerk.

Miss Amelia Martin, an ambitious milliner and dressmaker.

Mr. Thomas Potter, a clerk in the City.

Mr. Rogers, a "parlour orator" with a confident manner.

Mr. Smith, a poor clerk; a passive and enduring man.

Mr. Robert Smithers, a clerk in the City.

Mr. Tupple, a junior clerk.

Mr. Samuel Wilkins, a carpenter.

TALES

THE BOARDING-HOUSE

Mrs. Bloss, the wealthy widow of a cork-cutter.

Mr. Calton, a vain, selfish, superannuated beau.

Mr. John Evenson, a morose and discontented man.

Mr. Gobler, a lazy, selfish hypochondriac.

Mr. Septimus Hicks, a tall, white-faced, spectacled young man.

Mrs. Maplesone, a shrewd, enterprising, good-looking widow of fifty.

Miss Julia and Miss Matilda Maplesone, her daughters.

Mr. Frederick O'Bleary, a patriotic Irishman.

Mr. Simpson, an empty-headed young man.

Mr. Tibbs, a short man with a long face.

Mrs. Tibbs, his wife; mistress of the boarding-house.

Mr. Alfred Tomkins, clerk in a wine-house.

Mr. Wisbottle, a clerk in the Woods and Forests Office.

Dr. Wosky, a medical man.

MR. MINNS AND HIS COUSIN

Mr. Brogson, an elderly gentleman.

Mr. Octavius Budden, a retired corn-chandler.

Mrs. Amelia Budden, his wife.

Mr. Jones, a sharp, talkative little man.

Mr. Augustus Minns, a clerk in Somerset House; an old bachelor.

SENTIMENT

MR. THEODOSIUS BUTLER, a supposed wonderful genius.

MISS AMELIA CRUMPTON, a very tall, thin, precise maiden lady.

MISS MARIA CRUMPTON, her sister, and exact counterpart.

MR. DADSON, writing-master at the Miss Crumptons' school.

MRS. DADSON, his wife.

CORNELIUS BROOK DINGWALL, ESQ., M.P., a haughty, portentous man.

MRS. BROOK DINGWALL, his wife.

MISS LAVINIA BROOK DINGWALL, their romantic daughter.

MR. HILTON, master of the ceremonies at a ball.

MISS EMILY SMITHERS, the belle of Minerva House.

MISS CAROLINE WILSON, her bosom friend.

THE TUGGSES AT RAMSGATE

LIEUTENANT SLAUGHTER, a friend of Captain Waters.

MR. JOSEPH TUGGS, a little pursy London grocer.

MRS. TUGGS, his wife ; in charge of the cheese-department.

MISS CHARLOTTE TUGGS, their only daughter.

MR. SIMON TUGGS ("Cymon"), their only son.

CAPTAIN WALTER WATERS, a pretended military man, and a sharper.

MRS. BELINDA WATERS, his wife.

HORATIO SPARKINS

MR. JACOB BARTON, brother of Mrs. Malderton ; a grocer.

MR. FLAMWELL, a friend of Mr. Malderton's ; a little toad-eater.

MR. MALDERTON, a successful speculator.

MRS. MALDERTON, his wife; a little fat woman.

MISS MARIANNE and MISS TERESA MALDERTON, their daughters.

MR. FREDERICK and MR. THOMAS MALDERTON, their sons.

MR. HORATIO SPARKINS, a young man of dashing manners and appearance.

THE STEAM EXCURSION

MRS. BRIGGS, a widow lady; a rival of Mrs. Taunton.

MISS, MISS JULIA, and MISS KATE BRIGGS, her daughters.

MR. ALEXANDER and MR. SAMUEL BRIGGS, her sons.

MR. EDKINS, a young gentleman of the Inner Temple.

MR. HARDY, a stout, middle-aged gentleman ; a practical joker.

CAPTAIN HELVES, a military gentleman with a bass voice.

MR. PERCY NOAKES, a smart law-student.

MRS. TAUNTON, a good-looking widow of fifty.

MISS EMILY and MISS SOPHIA TAUNTON, her daughters.

THE GREAT WINGLEBURY DUEL

Miss EMILY BROWN, a young lady with more than one lover.
MR. HORACE HUNTER, rival of Mr. Trott for the hand of Miss Brown.
Miss JULIA MANNERS, a buxom and wealthy woman of forty.
JOSEPH OVERTON, ESQ., solicitor, and Mayor of Great Winglebury.
LORD PETER, a dissipated sprig of nobility.
MR. ALEXANDER TROTT, an aspirant for the hand of Miss Brown.
MRS. WILLIAMSON, landlady of the Winglebury Arms.

MRS. JOSEPH PORTER

MR. BALDERSTONE ("Uncle Tom"), a rich brother of Mrs. Gattleton.
MR. EVANS, a tall, thin, pale young gentleman.
MR. GATTLETON, a retired stockbroker, with a mania for private theatricals.
MRS. GATTLETON, his wife; a kind-hearted, good-tempered, vulgar soul.
Miss, MISS CAROLINE, and MISS LUCINA GATTLETON, their daughters.
MR. SEMPRONIUS GATTLETON, their son; stage-manager of the theatricals
MR. HARLEIGH, a singer.
MRS. JOSEPH PORTER, a sarcastic scandal-monger.
MISS EMILY PORTER, her daughter.

A PASSAGE IN THE LIFE OF MR. WATKINS TOTTLE

IKEY, the factotum of Mr. Jacobs's sponging-house.
MR. SOLOMON JACOBS, a bailiff.
MISS LILLERTON, a prim spinster of uncertain age.
MR. GABRIEL PARSONS, an elderly and rich sugar-baker.
MRS. FANNY PARSONS, his wife.
THE REV. CHARLES TIMSON, a friend of Mr. Parsons.
MR. WATKINS TOTTLE, a plump, clean, rosy bachelor of fifty.
MR. WALKER, an imprisoned debtor.

THE BLOOMSBURY CHRISTENING

MR. DANTON, an impudent young man, passing for a wit.
MR. NICODEMUS DUMPS ("Long Dumps"), an old bachelor.
MR. CHARLES KITTERBELL, a small, sharp, spare man.
MRS. JEMIMA KITTERBELL, his wife; a tall, thin young lady.
MASTER FREDERICK CHARLES WILLIAM KITTERBELL, their first baby.

THE DRUNKARD'S DEATH

TOM, one of the officers who arrest William Warden.
WARDEN, a confirmed and irreclaimable drunkard.
MARY WARDEN, his daughter.
WILLIAM WARDEN, his son.

SKETCHES BY BOZ

✳

OUR PARISH

CHAPTER I

THE BEADLE. THE PARISH ENGINE. THE SCHOOLMASTER

How much is conveyed in those two short words—"The Parish!" And with how many tales of distress and misery, of broken fortune and ruined hopes, too often of unrelieved wretchedness and successful knavery, are they associated! A poor man, with small earnings, and a large family, just manages to live on from hand to mouth, and to procure food from day to day; he has barely sufficient to satisfy the present cravings of nature, and can take no heed of the future. His taxes are in arrear, quarter-day passes by, another quarter-day arrives: he can procure no more quarter for himself, and is summoned by—the parish. His goods are distrained, his children are crying with cold and hunger, and the very bed on which his sick wife is lying, is dragged from beneath her. What can he do? To whom is he to apply for relief? To private charity? To benevolent individuals? Certainly not—there is his parish. There are the parish vestry, the parish infirmary, the parish surgeon, the parish officers, the parish beadle. Excellent institutions, and gentle, kind-hearted men. The woman dies—she is buried by the parish. The children have no protector—they are taken care of by the parish. The man first neglects, and afterwards cannot obtain, work—he is relieved by the parish; and when distress and drunkenness have done their work upon him, he is maintained, a harmless babbling idiot, in the parish asylum.

The parish beadle is one of the most, perhaps *the* most,

important member of the local administration. He is not
so well off as the churchwardens, certainly, nor is he so
learned as the vestry-clerk, nor does he order things quite
so much his own way as either of them. But his power is
very great, notwithstanding ; and the dignity of his office
is never impaired by the absence of efforts on his part to
maintain it. The beadle of our parish is a splendid fellow.
It is quite delightful to hear him, as he explains the state
of the existing poor laws to the deaf old women in the
board-room passage on business nights ; and to hear what
he said to the senior churchwarden, and what the senior
churchwarden said to him ; and what "we" (the beadle
and the other gentlemen) came to the determination of doing.
A miserable-looking woman is called into the board-room,
and represents a case of extreme destitution, affecting herself
—a widow, with six small children. "Where do you live?"
inquires one of the overseers. "I rents a two-pair back,
gentlemen, at Mrs. Brown's, Number 3, Little King William's Alley, which has lived there this fifteen year, and
knows me to be very hard-working and industrious, and
when my poor husband was alive, gentlemen, as died in the
hospital "—"Well, well," interrupts the overseer, taking
a note of the address, "I'll send Simmons, the beadle, to-
morrow morning, to ascertain whether your story is correct ;
and if so, I suppose you must have an order into the House
—Simmons, go to this woman's the first thing to-morrow
morning, will you?" Simmons bows assent, and ushers
the woman out. Her previous admiration of "the board"
(who all sit behind great books, and with their hats on)
fades into nothing before her respect for her lace-trimmed
conductor ; and her account of what has passed inside, increases—if that be possible—the marks of respect, shown
by the assembled crowd, to that solemn functionary. As
to taking out a summons, it's quite a hopeless case if Simmons attends it, on behalf of the parish. He knows all the
titles of the Lord Mayor by heart ; states the case without
a single stammer : and it is even reported that on one occasion he ventured to make a joke, which the Lord Mayor's
head footman (who happened to be present) afterwards told
an intimate friend, confidentially, was almost equal to one
of Mr. Hobler's.

See him again on Sunday in his state coat and cocked-
hat, with a large-headed staff for show in his left hand, and

a small cane for use in his right. How pompously he marshals the children into their places! and how demurely the little urchins look at him askance as he surveys them when they are all seated, with a glare of the eye peculiar to beadles! The churchwardens and overseers being duly installed in their curtained pews, he seats himself on a mahogany bracket, erected expressly for him at the top of the aisle, and divides his attention between his prayer-book and the boys. Suddenly, just at the commencement of the communion service, when the whole congregation is hushed into a profound silence, broken only by the voice of the officiating clergyman, a penny is heard to ring on the stone floor of the aisle with astounding clearness. Observe the generalship of the beadle. His involuntary look of horror is instantly changed into one of perfect indifference, as if he were the only person present who had not heard the noise. The artifice succeeds. After putting forth his right leg now and then, as a feeler, the victim who dropped the money ventures to make one or two distinct dives after it; and the beadle, gliding softly round, salutes his little round head, when it again appears above the seat, with divers double knocks, administered with the cane before noticed, to the intense delight of three young men in an adjacent pew, who cough violently at intervals until the conclusion of the sermon.

Such are a few traits of the importance and gravity of a parish beadle—a gravity which has never been disturbed in any case that has come under our observation, except when the services of that particularly useful machine, a parish fire-engine, are required : then indeed all is bustle. Two little boys run to the beadle as fast as their legs will carry them, and report from their own personal observation that some neighbouring chimney is on fire; the engine is hastily got out, and a plentiful supply of boys being obtained, and harnessed to it with ropes, away they rattle over the pavement, the beadle, running—we do not exaggerate—running at the side, until they arrive at some house, smelling strongly of soot, at the door of which the beadle knocks with considerable gravity for half-an-hour. No attention being paid to these manual applications, and the turn-cock having turned on the water, the engine turns off amidst the shouts of the boys; it pulls up once more at the workhouse, and the beadle "pulls up" the unfortunate householder next day, for the amount of his legal reward. We never saw a parish engine at a regular fire but once. It came up in gallant style—three miles and a half an hour, at least; there was a capital supply of water, and it was first on the spot. Bang went the pumps—the people cheered—the beadle perspired profusely; but it was unfortunately discovered, just as they were going to put the fire out, that nobody understood the process by which the engine was filled with water; and that eighteen boys, and a man, had exhausted themselves in pumping for twenty minutes, without producing the slightest effect!

The personages next in importance to the beadle, are the master of the workhouse and the parish schoolmaster. The vestry-clerk, as everybody knows, is a short, pudgy little man, in black, with a thick gold watch-chain of considerable length, terminating in two large seals and a key. He is an attorney, and generally in a bustle; at no time more so, than when he is hurrying to some parochial meeting, with his gloves crumpled up in one hand, and a large red book under the other arm. As to the churchwardens and overseers, we exclude them altogether, because all we know of them is, that they are usually respectable tradesmen, who wear hats with brims inclined to flatness, and who occasionally testify in gilt letters on a blue ground, in some conspicuous part of the church, to the important fact of a gallery having been enlarged and beautified, or an organ rebuilt.

The master of the workhouse is not, in our parish—nor is he usually in any other—one of that class of men the better part of whose existence has passed away, and who drag out the remainder in some inferior situation, with just enough thought of the past, to feel degraded by, and discontented with, the present. We are unable to guess precisely to our own satisfaction what station the man can have occupied before; we should think he had been an inferior sort of attorney's clerk, or else the master of a national school— whatever he was, it is clear his present position is a change for the better. His income is small certainly, as the rusty black coat and threadbare velvet collar demonstrate: but then he lives free of house-rent, has a limited allowance of coals and candles, and an almost unlimited allowance of authority in his petty kingdom. He is a tall, thin, bony man; always wears shoes and black cotton stockings with his surtout; and eyes you, as you pass his parlour-window, as if he wished you were a pauper, just to give you a speci-

The Parish Engine

men of his power. He is an admirable specimen of a small tyrant : morose, brutish, and ill-tempered ; bullying to his inferiors, cringing to his superiors, and jealous of the influence and authority of the beadle.

Our schoolmaster is just the very reverse of this amiable official. He has been one of those men one occasionally hears of, on whom misfortune seems to have set her mark ; nothing he ever did, or was concerned in, appears to have prospered. A rich old relation who had brought him up, and openly announced his intention of providing for him, left him 10,000l. in his will, and revoked the bequest in a codicil. Thus unexpectedly reduced to the necessity of providing for himself, he procured a situation in a public office. The young clerks below him, died off as if there were a plague among them ; but the old fellows over his head, for the reversion of whose places he was anxiously waiting, lived on and on, as if they were immortal. He speculated and lost. He speculated again and won—but never got his money. His talents were great ; his disposition easy, generous and liberal. His friends profited by the one, and abused the other. Loss succeeded loss ; misfortune crowded on misfortune ; each successive day brought him nearer the verge of hopeless penury, and the quondam friends who had been warmest in their professions, grew strangely cold and indifferent. He had children whom he loved, and a wife on whom he doted. The former turned their backs on him ; the latter died broken-hearted. He went with the stream —it had ever been his failing, and he had not courage sufficient to bear up against so many shocks—he had never cared for himself, and the only being who had cared for him, in his poverty and distress, was spared to him no longer. It was at this period that he applied for parochial relief. Some kind-hearted man who had known him in happier times, chanced to be churchwarden that year, and through his interest he was appointed to his present situation.

He is an old man now. Of the many who once crowded round him in all the hollow friendship of boon-companion-ship, some have died, some have fallen like himself, some have prospered—all have forgotten him. Time and misfortune have mercifully been permitted to impair his memory, and use has habituated him to his present condition. Meek, uncomplaining, and zealous in the discharge of his duties, he has been allowed to hold his situation long beyond the usual period ; and he will no doubt continue to hold it, until infirmity renders him incapable, or death releases him.   As the grey-headed old man feebly paces up and down the sunny side of the little court-yard between school hours, it would be difficult, indeed, for the most intimate of his former friends to recognise their once gay and happy associate, in the person of the Pauper Schoolmaster.

CHAPTER II

WE commenced our last chapter with the beadle of our parish, because we are deeply sensible of the importance and dignity of his office.   We will begin the present, with the clergyman.   Our curate is a young gentleman of such pre-possessing appearance, and fascinating manners, that within one month after his first appearance in the parish, half the young-lady inhabitants were melancholy with religion, and the other half desponding with love.   Never were so many young ladies seen in our parish church on Sunday before; and never had the little round angels' faces on Mr. Tom-kins's monument in the side aisle, beheld such devotion on earth as they all exhibited.   He was about five-and-twenty when he first came to astonish the parishioners.   He parted his hair on the centre of his forehead in the form of a Norman arch, wore a brilliant of the first water on the fourth finger of his left hand (which he always applied to his left cheek when he read prayers), and had a deep sepulchral voice of unusual solemnity.   Innumerable were the calls made by prudent mammas on our new curate, and innu-merable the invitations with which he was assailed, and which, to do him justice, he readily accepted.   If his manner in the pulpit had created an impression in his favour, the sensation was increased tenfold, by his appear-ance in private circles.   Pews in the immediate vicinity of the pulpit or reading-desk rose in value; sittings in the centre aisle were at a premium: an inch of room in the front row of the gallery could not be procured for love or money; and some people even went so far as to assert, that the three Miss Browns, who had an obscure family pew just behind the churchwardens', were detected, one Sunday, in the free seats by the communion-table, actually lying in wait for the curate as he passed to the vestry! He began to preach extempore sermons, and even grave papas caught the

B

infection. He got out of bed at half-past twelve o'clock one winter's night, to half-baptise a washerwoman's child in a slop-basin, and the gratitude of the parishioners knew no bounds—the very churchwardens grew generous, and insisted on the parish defraying the expense of the watch-box on wheels, which the new curate had ordered for himself, to perform the funeral service in, in wet weather. He sent three pints of gruel and a quarter of a pound of tea to a poor woman who had been brought to bed of four small children, all at once—the parish were charmed. He got up a subscription for her—the woman's fortune was made. He spoke for one hour and twenty-five minutes, at an anti-slavery meeting at the Goat and Boots—the enthusiasm was at its height. A proposal was set on foot for presenting the curate with a piece of plate, as a mark of esteem for his valuable services rendered to the parish. The list of sub-scriptions was filled up in no time ; the contest was, not who should escape the contribution, but who should be the fore-most to subscribe. A splendid silver inkstand was made, and engraved with an appropriate inscription ; the curate was invited to a public breakfast, at the before-mentioned Goat and Boots ; the inkstand was presented in a neat speech by Mr. Gubbins, the ex-churchwarden, and acknow-ledged by the curate in terms which drew tears into the eyes of all present—the very waiters were melted.

One would have supposed that, by this time, the theme of universal admiration was lifted to the very pinnacle of popularity. No such thing. The curate began to cough ; four fits of coughing one morning between the Litany and the Epistle, and five in the afternoon service. Here was a discovery—the curate was consumptive. How interestingly melancholy ! If the young ladies were energetic before, their sympathy and solicitude now knew no bounds. Such a man as the curate—such a dear—such a perfect love—to be consumptive ! It was too much. Anonymous presents of black-currant jam, and lozenges, elastic waistcoats, bosom friends, and warm stockings, poured in upon the curate until he was as completely fitted out, with winter clothing, as if he were on the verge of an expedition to the North Pole : verbal bulletins of the state of his health were circu-lated throughout the parish half-a-dozen times a day ; and the curate was in the very zenith of his popularity.

About this period a change came over the spirit of the

parish. A very quiet, respectable, dozing old gentleman, who had officiated in our chapel-of-ease for twelve years previously, died one fine morning, without having given any notice whatever of his intention. This circumstance gave rise to counter-sensation the first ; and the arrival of his successor occasioned counter-sensation the second. He was a pale, thin, cadaverous man, with large black eyes, and long straggling black hair : his dress was slovenly in the extreme, his manner ungainly, his doctrines startling; in short, he was in every respect the antipodes of the curate. Crowds of our female parishioners flocked to hear him ; at first, because he was *so* odd-looking, then because his face was *so* expressive, then because he preached *so* well ; and at last, because they really thought that, after all, there was something about him which it was quite impossible to describe. As to the curate, he was all very well ; but certainly, after all, there was no denying that—that—in short, the curate wasn't a novelty, and the other clergyman was. The inconstancy of public opinion is proverbial : the congregation migrated one by one. The curate coughed till he was black in the face—it was in vain. He respired with difficulty—it was equally ineffectual in awakening sympathy. Seats are once again to be had in any part of our parish church, and the chapel-of-ease is going to be enlarged, as it is crowded to suffocation every Sunday !

The best known and most respected among our parishioners, is an old lady, who resided in our parish long before our name was registered in the list of baptisms. Our parish is a suburban one, and the old lady lives in a neat row of houses in the most airy and pleasant part of it. The house is her own ; and it, and everything about it, except the old lady herself, who looks a little older than she did ten years ago, is in just the same state as when the old gentleman was living. The little front parlour, which is the old lady's ordinary sitting-room, is a perfect picture of quiet neatness ; the carpet is covered with brown Holland, the glass and picture-frames are carefully enveloped in yellow muslin ; the table-covers are never taken off, except when the leaves are turpentined and bees'-waxed, an operation which is regularly commenced every other morning at half-past nine o'clock— and the little nicknacks are always arranged in precisely the same manner. The greater part of these are presents from little girls whose parents live in the same row ; but some of them, such as the two old-fashioned watches (which never keep the same time, one being always a quarter of an hour too slow, and the other a quarter of an hour too fast), the little picture of the Princess Charlotte and Prince Leopold as they appeared in the Royal Box at Drury Lane Theatre, and others of the same class, have been in the old lady's possession for many years. Here the old lady sits with her spectacles on, busily engaged in needlework—near the window in summer time; and if she sees you coming up the steps, and you happen to be a favourite, she trots out to open the street-door for you before you knock, and as you must be fatigued after that hot walk, insists on your swallowing two glasses of sherry before you exert yourself by talking. If you call in the evening you will find her cheerful, but rather more serious than usual, with an open Bible on the table before her, of which "Sarah," who is just as neat and methodical as her mistress, regularly reads two or three chapters in the parlour aloud.

The old lady sees scarcely any company, except the little girls before noticed, each of whom has always a regular fixed day for a periodical tea-drinking with her, to which the child looks forward as the greatest treat of its existence. She seldom visits at a greater distance than the next door but one on either side; and when she drinks tea here, Sarah runs out first and knocks a double-knock, to prevent the possibility of her "Missis's" catching cold by having to wait at the door. She is very scrupulous in returning these little invitations, and when she asks Mr. and Mrs. So-and-so, to meet Mr. and Mrs. Somebody-else, Sarah and she dust the urn, and the best china tea-service, and the Pope Joan board; and the visitors are received in the drawing-room in great state. She has but few relations, and they are scattered about in different parts of the country, and she seldom sees them. She has a son in India, whom she always describes to you as a fine, handsome fellow—so like the profile of his poor dear father over the sideboard, but the old lady adds, with a mournful shake of the head, that he has always been one of her greatest trials; and that indeed he once almost broke her heart; but it pleased God to enable her to get the better of it, and she would prefer your never mentioning the subject to her again. She has a great number of pensioners: and on Saturday, after she comes back from market, there is a regular levee of old men and women in the passage, waiting for their weekly gratuity. Her name always heads the list of any benevolent subscriptions, and hers are always the most liberal donations to the Winter Coal and Soup Distribution Society. She subscribed twenty pounds towards the erection of an organ in our parish church, and was so overcome the first Sunday the children sang to it, that she was obliged to be carried out by the pew-opener. Her entrance into church on Sunday is always the signal for a little bustle in the side aisle, occasioned by a general rise among the poor people, who bow and curtsey until the pew-opener has ushered the old lady into her accustomed seat, dropped a respectful curtsey and shut the door: and the same ceremony is repeated on her leaving church, when she walks home with the family next door but one, and talks about the sermon all the way, invariably opening the conversation by asking the youngest boy where the text was.

Thus, with the annual variation of a trip to some quiet place on the sea-coast, passes the old lady's life. It has rolled on in the same unvarying and benevolent course for many years now, and must at no distant period be brought to its final close. She looks forward to its termination, with calmness and without apprehension. She has everything to hope and nothing to fear.

A very different personage, but one who has rendered himself very conspicuous in our parish, is one of the old lady's next-door neighbours. He is an old naval officer on half-pay, and his bluff and unceremonious behaviour disturbs the old lady's domestic economy, not a little. In the first place, he *will* smoke cigars in the front court, and when he wants something to drink with them—which is by no means an uncommon circumstance—he lifts up the old lady's knocker with his walking-stick, and demands to have a glass of table ale, handed over the rails. In addition to this cool proceeding, he is a bit of a Jack of all trades, or to use his own words, "a regular Robinson Crusoe;" and nothing delights him better than to experimentalise on the old lady's property. One morning he got up early, and planted three or four roots of full-grown marigolds in every bed of her front garden, to the inconceivable astonishment of the old lady, who actually thought when she got up and looked out of the window, that it was some strange eruption which had come out in the night. Another time he took to pieces the eight-day clock on the front landing, under pretence of

cleaning the works, which he put together again, by some
undiscovered process, in so wonderful a manner, that the
large hand has done nothing but trip up the little one ever
since. Then he took to breeding silk-worms, which he *would*
bring in two or three times a day, in little paper boxes, to
show the old lady, generally dropping a worm or two at
every visit. The consequence was, that one morning a very
stout silk-worm was discovered in the act of walking up-
stairs—probably with the view of inquiring after his friends,
for, on further inspection, it appeared that some of his
companions had already found their way to every room in
the house. The old lady went to the seaside in despair, and
during her absence he completely effaced the name from
her brass door-plate, in his attempts to polish it with aqua-
fortis.

But all this is nothing to his seditious conduct in public
life. He attends every vestry meeting that is held ; always
opposes the constituted authorities of the parish, denounces
the profligacy of the churchwardens, contests legal points
against the vestry-clerk, *will* make the tax-gatherer call for
his money till he won't call any longer, and then he sends
it : finds fault with the sermon every Sunday, says that the
organist ought to be ashamed of himself, offers to back
himself for any amount to sing the psalms better than all
the children put together, male and female ; and, in short,
conducts himself in the most turbulent and uproarious
manner. The worst of it is, that having a high regard for
the old lady, he wants to make her a convert to his views,
and therefore walks into her little parlour with his newspaper in his hand, and talks violent politics by the hour.
He is a charitable, open-hearted old fellow at bottom, after
all ; so, although he puts the old lady a little out occasionally, they agree very well in the main, and she laughs as
much at each feat of his handiwork when it is all over, as
anybody else.

CHAPTER III

THE FOUR SISTERS

THE row of houses in which the old lady and her troublesome neighbour reside, comprises, beyond all doubt, a greater number of characters within its circumscribed limits, than all the rest of the parish put together. As we cannot, consistently with our present plan, however, extend the number of our parochial sketches beyond six, it will be better, perhaps, to select the most peculiar, and to introduce them at once without further preface.

The four Miss Willises, then, settled in our parish thirteen years ago. It is a melancholy reflection that the old adage, "time and tide wait for no man," applies with equal force to the fairer portion of the creation; and willingly would we conceal the fact, that even thirteen years ago the Miss Willises were far from juvenile. Our duty as faithful parochial chroniclers, however, is paramount to every other consideration, and we are bound to state, that thirteen years since, the authorities in matrimonial cases, considered the youngest Miss Willis in a very precarious state, while the eldest sister was positively given over, as being far beyond all human hope. Well, the Miss Willises took a lease of the house; it was fresh painted and papered from top to bottom: the paint inside was all wainscoted, the marble all cleaned, the old grates taken down, and register-stoves, you could see to dress by, put up; four trees were planted in the back garden, several small baskets of gravel sprinkled over the front one, vans of elegant furniture arrived, spring blinds were fitted to the windows, carpenters who had been employed in the various preparations, alterations, and repairs, made confidential statements to the different maid-servants in the row, relative to the magnificent scale on which the Miss Willises were commencing; the maid-servants told their "Missises," the Missises told their friends, and vague rumours were circulated throughout the parish, that No. 25, in Gordon Place, had been taken by four maiden ladies of immense property.

At last, the Miss Willises moved in; and then the "calling" began. The house was the perfection of neatness—so were the four Miss Willises. Everything was formal, stiff. and cold—so were the four Miss Willises. Not a single chair of the whole set was ever seen out of its place—not a single Miss Willis of the whole four was ever seen out of hers. There they always sat, in the same places, doing precisely the same things at the same hour. The eldest Miss Willis used to knit, the second to draw, the two others to play duets on the piano. They seemed to have no separate existence, but to have made up their minds just to winter through life together. They were three long graces in drapery, with the addition, like a school-dinner, of another long grace after-wards—the three fates with another sister—the Siamese twins multiplied by two. The eldest Miss Willis grew bilious—the four Miss Willises grew bilious immediately. The eldest Miss Willis grew ill-tempered and religious—the four Miss Willises were ill-tempered and religious directly. Whatever the eldest did, the others did, and whatever anybody else did, they all disapproved of; and thus they vegetated—living in Polar harmony among themselves, and, as they sometimes went out, or saw company "in a quiet way" at home, occasionally iceing the neighbours. Three years passed over in this way, when an unlooked-for and extraordinary phe-nomenon occurred. The Miss Willises showed symptoms of summer, the frost gradually broke up; a complete thaw took place. Was it possible? one of the four Miss Willises was going to be married!

Now, where on earth the husband came from, by what feelings the poor man could have been actuated, or by what process of reasoning the four Miss Willises succeeded in per-suading themselves that it was possible for a man to marry one of them, without marrying them all, are questions too profound for us to resolve: certain it is, however, that the visits of Mr. Robinson (a gentleman in a public office, with a good salary and a little property of his own, besides) were received—that the four Miss Willises were courted in due form by the said Mr. Robinson—that the neighbours were perfectly frantic in their anxiety to discover which of the four Miss Willises was the fortunate fair, and that the diffi-culty they experienced in solving the problem was not at all lessened by the announcement of the eldest Miss Willis, —" *We* are going to marry Mr. Robinson."

It was very extraordinary. They were so completely identified, the one with the other, that the curiosity of the whole row—even of the old lady herself—was roused almost beyond endurance. The subject was discussed at every little card-table and tea-drinking. The old gentleman of silk-worm notoriety did not hesitate to express his decided opinion that Mr. Robinson was of Eastern descent, and contemplated marrying the whole family at once; and the row, generally, shook their heads with considerable gravity, and declared the business to be very mysterious. They hoped it might all end well;—it certainly had a very singular appearance, but still it would be uncharitable to express any opinion without good grounds to go upon, and certainly the Miss Willises were quite old enough to judge for themselves, and to be sure people ought to know their own business best, and so forth.

At last, one fine morning, at a quarter before eight o'clock, A.M., two glass-coaches drove up to the Miss Willises' door, at which Mr. Robinson had arrived in a cab ten minutes before, dressed in a light-blue coat and double-milled kersey pantaloons, white neckerchief, pumps, and dress-gloves. his manner denoting, as appeared from the evidence of the housemaid at No. 23, who was sweeping the door-steps at the time, a considerable degree of nervous excitement. It was also hastily reported on the same testimony, that the cook who opened the door, wore a large white bow of unusual dimensions, in a much smarter head-dress than the regulation cap to which the Miss Willises invariably restricted the somewhat excursive tastes of female servants in general.

The intelligence spread rapidly from house to house. It was quite clear that the eventful morning had at length arrived; the whole row stationed themselves behind their first and second floor blinds, and waited the result in breathless expectation.

At last the Miss Willises' door opened; the door of the first glass-coach did the same. Two gentlemen, and a pair of ladies to correspond—friends of the family, no doubt; up went the steps, bang went the door, off went the first glass-coach, and up came the second.

The street door opened again; the excitement of the whole row increased—Mr. Robinson and the eldest Miss Willis.

"I thought so," said the lady at No. 19; "I always said it was *Miss* Willis!"—"Well, I never!" ejaculated the young lady at No. 18 to the young lady at No. 17.—"Did you ever, dear!" responded the young lady at No. 17 to the young lady at No. 18. "It's too ridiculous!" exclaimed a spinster of an *un*certain age, at No. 16, joining in the conversation. But who shall portray the astonishment of Gordon Place, when Mr. Robinson handed in *all* the Miss Willises, one after the other, and then squeezed himself into an acute angle of the glass-coach, which forthwith proceeded at a brisk pace, after the other glass-coach, which other glass-coach had itself proceeded, at a brisk pace, in the direction of the parish church! Who shall depict the perplexity of the clergyman, when *all* the Miss Willises knelt down at the communion-table, and repeated the responses incidental to the marriage service in an audible voice—or who shall describe the confusion which prevailed, when—even after the difficulties thus occasioned had been adjusted—*all* the Miss Willises went into hysterics at the conclusion of the ceremony, until the sacred edifice resounded with their united wailings!

As the four sisters and Mr. Robinson continued to occupy the same house after this memorable occasion, and as the married sister, whoever she was, never appeared in public without the other three, we are not quite clear that the neighbours ever would have discovered the real Mrs. Robinson, but for a circumstance of the most gratifying description, which *will* happen occasionally in the best-regulated families. Three quarter-days elapsed, and the row, on whom a new light appeared to have been bursting for some time, began to speak with a sort of implied confidence on the subject, and to wonder how Mrs. Robinson—the youngest Miss Willis that was—got on; and servants might be seen running up the steps, about nine or ten o'clock every morning, with "Missis's compliments, and wishes to know how Mrs. Robinson finds herself this morning?" And the answer always was, "Mrs. Robinson's compliments, and she's in very good spirits, and doesn't find herself any worse." The piano was heard no longer, the knitting-needles were laid aside, drawing was neglected, and mantua-making and millinery, on the smallest scale imaginable, appeared to have become the favourite amusement of the whole family. The parlour wasn't quite as tidy as it used to be, and if you called in the morning, you would see lying on a table, with an old newspaper carelessly thrown over them, two or three particularly small caps, rather larger than if they had been made for a moderate-sized doll, with a small piece of lace, in the shape of a horse-shoe, let in behind : or perhaps a white robe, not very large in circumference, but very much out of proportion in point of length, with a little tucker round the top, and a frill round the bottom ; and once when we called, we saw a long white roller, with a kind of blue margin down each side, the probable use of which, we were at a loss to conjecture. Then we fancied that Mr. Dawson, the surgeon, &c., who displays a large lamp with a different colour in every pane of glass, at the corner of the row, began to be knocked up at night oftener than he used to be ; and once we were very much alarmed by hearing a hackney-coach stop at Mrs. Robinson's door, at half-past two o'clock in the morning, out of which there emerged a fat old woman, in a cloak and nightcap, with a bundle in one hand, and a pair of pattens in the other, who looked as if she had been suddenly knocked up out of bed for some very special purpose.

When we got up in the morning we saw that the knocker was tied up in an old white kid glove ; and we, in our innocence (we were in a state of bachelorship then), wondered what on earth it all meant, until we heard the eldest Miss Willis, *in propriâ personâ*, say, with great dignity, in answer to the next inquiry, "*My* compliments, and Mrs. Robinson's doing as well as can be expected, and the little girl thrives wonderfully." And then, in common with the rest of the row, our curiosity was satisfied, and we began to wonder it had never occurred to us what the matter was, before.

CHAPTER IV

THE ELECTION FOR BEADLE

A GREAT event has recently occurred in our parish. A contest
of paramount interest has just terminated ; a parochial convulsion has taken place. It has been succeeded by a glorious
triumph, which the country—or at least the parish—it is all
the same—will long remember. We have had an election ;
an election for beadle. The supporters of the old beadle
system have been defeated in their stronghold, and the advocates of the great new beadle principles have achieved a
proud victory.

Our parish, which, like all other parishes, is a little world
of its own, has long been divided into two parties, whose
contentions, slumbering for a while, have never failed to burst
forth with unabated vigour, on any occasion on which they
could by possibility be renewed. Watching-rates, lighting-
rates, paving-rates, sewer's-rates, church-rates, poor's-rates—all
sorts of rates, have been in their turns the subjects of a grand
struggle ; and as to questions of patronage, the asperity and
determination with which they have been contested is scarcely
credible.

The leader of the official party—the steady advocate of
the churchwardens, and the unflinching supporter of the
overseers—is an old gentleman who lives in our row. He
owns some half a dozen houses in it, and always walks on the
opposite side of the way, so that he may be able to take in
a view of the whole of his property at once. He is a tall,
thin, bony man, with an interrogative nose, and little restless
perking eyes, which appear to have been given him for the
sole purpose of peeping into other people's affairs with. He
is deeply impressed with the importance of our parish
business, and prides himself, not a little, on his style of
addressing the parishioners in vestry assembled. His views
are rather confined than extensive ; his principles more
narrow than liberal. He has been heard to declaim very

loudly in favour of the liberty of the press, and advocates the repeal of the stamp duty on newspapers, because the daily journals who now have a monopoly of the public, never give *verbatim* reports of vestry meetings. He would not appear egotistical for the world, but at the same time he must say, that there *are* speeches—that celebrated speech of his own, on the emoluments of the sexton, and the duties of the office, for instance—which might be communicated to the public, greatly to their improvement and advantage.

His great opponent in public life is Captain Purday, the old naval officer on half-pay, to whom we have already introduced our readers. The captain being a determined opponent of the constituted authorities, whoever they may chance to be, and our other friend being their steady supporter, with an equal disregard of their individual merits, it will readily be supposed that occasions for their coming into direct collision are neither few nor far between. They divided the vestry fourteen times on a motion for heating the church with warm water instead of coals: and made speeches about liberty and expenditure, and prodigality and hot water, which threw the whole parish into a state of excitement. Then the captain, when he was on the visiting committee, and his opponent overseer, brought forward certain distinct and specific charges relative to the management of the workhouse, boldly expressed his total want of confidence in the existing authorities, and moved for "a copy of the recipe by which the paupers' soup was prepared, together with any documents relating thereto." This the overseer steadily resisted; he fortified himself by precedent, appealed to the established usage, and declined to produce the papers, on the ground of the injury that would be done to the public service, if documents of a strictly private nature, passing between the master of the workhouse and the cook, were to be thus dragged to light on the motion of any individual member of the vestry. The motion was lost by a majority of two; and then the captain, who never allows himself to be defeated, moved for a committee of inquiry into the whole subject. The affair grew serious: the question was discussed at meeting after meeting, and vestry after vestry; speeches were made, attacks repudiated, personal defiances exchanged, explanations received, and the greatest excitement prevailed, until at last, just as the question was going to be finally decided, the vestry found that somehow or other, they had become entangled in a point of form, from which it was impossible to escape with propriety. So the motion was dropped, and everybody looked extremely important, and seemed quite satisfied with the meritorious nature of the whole proceeding.

This was the state of affairs in our parish a week or two since, when Simmons, the beadle, suddenly died. The lamented deceased had over-exerted himself, a day or two previously, in conveying an aged female, highly intoxicated, to the strong room of the workhouse. The excitement thus occasioned, added to a severe cold, which this indefatigable officer had caught in his capacity of director of the parish engine, by inadvertently playing over himself instead of a fire, proved too much for a constitution already enfeebled by age ; and the intelligence was conveyed to the Board one evening that Simmons had died, and left his respects.

The breath was scarcely out of the body of the deceased functionary, when the field was filled with competitors for the vacant office, each of whom rested his claims to public support, entirely on the number and extent of his family, as if the office of beadle were originally instituted as an encouragement for the propagation of the human species. " Bung for Beadle. Five small children ! "—" Hopkins for Beadle. Seven small children ! ! "—" Timkins for Beadle. Nine small children ! ! ! " Such were the placards in large black letters on a white ground, which were plentifully pasted on the walls, and posted in the windows of the principal shops. Timkins's success was considered certain : several mothers of families half promised their votes, and the nine small children would have run over the course, but for the production of another placard, announcing the appearance of a still more meritorious candidate. " Spruggins for Beadle. Ten small children (two of them twins), and a wife ! ! ! " There was no resisting this ; ten small children would have been almost irresistible in themselves, without the twins, but the touching parenthesis about that interesting production of nature, and the still more touching allusion to Mrs. Spruggins, must ensure success. Spruggins was the favourite at once, and the appearance of his lady, as she went about to solicit votes (which encouraged confident hopes of a still further addition to the house of Spruggins at no remote period), increased the general prepossession in his favour. The other candidates, Bung alone excepted, re-

The Election for Beadle

signed in despair. The day of election was fixed; and the canvass proceeded with briskness and perseverance on both sides.

The members of the vestry could not be supposed to escape the contagious excitement inseparable from the occasion. The majority of the lady inhabitants of the parish declared at once for Spruggins; and the *quondam* overseer took the same side, on the ground that men with large families always had been elected to the office, and that although he must admit that, in other respects, Spruggins was the least qualified candidate of the two, still it was an old practice, and he saw no reason why an old practice should be departed from. This was enough for the captain. He immediately sided with Bung, canvassed for him personally in all directions, wrote squibs on Spruggins, and got his butcher to skewer them up on conspicuous joints in his shop-front, frightened his neighbour, the old lady, into a palpitation of the heart, by his awful denunciations of Spruggins's party; and bounced in and out, and up and down, and backwards and forwards, until all the sober inhabitants of the parish thought it inevitable that he must die of a brain fever, long before the election began.

The day of election arrived. It was no longer an individual struggle, but a party contest between the ins and outs. The question was, whether the withering influence of the overseers, the domination of the churchwardens, and the blighting despotism of the vestry-clerk, should be allowed to render the election of beadle a form—a nullity: whether they should impose a vestry-elected beadle on the parish, to do their bidding and forward their views, or whether the parishioners, fearlessly asserting their undoubted rights, should elect an independent beadle of their own.

The nomination was fixed to take place in the vestry, but so great was the throng of anxious spectators, that it was found necessary to adjourn to the church, where the ceremony commenced with due solemnity. The appearance of the churchwardens and overseers, and the ex-churchwardens and ex-overseers, with Spruggins in the rear, excited general attention. Spruggins was a little thin man, in rusty black, with a long pale face, and a countenance expressive of care and fatigue, which might either be attributed to the extent of his family or the anxiety of his feelings. His opponent appeared in a cast-off coat of the captain's—a blue coat with bright buttons : white trousers, and that description of shoes familiarly known by the appellation of "high-lows." There was a serenity in the open countenance of Bung—a kind of moral dignity in his confident air—an "I wish you may get it" sort of expression in his eye—which infused animation into his supporters, and evidently dispirited his opponents.

The ex-churchwarden rose to propose Thomas Spruggins for beadle. He had known him long. He had had his eye upon him closely for years; he had watched him with two-fold vigilance for months. (A parishioner here suggested that this might be termed "taking a double sight," but the observation was drowned in loud cries of "Order!") He would repeat that he had had his eye upon him for years, and this he would say, that a more well-conducted, a more well-behaved, a more sober, a more quiet man, with a more well-regulated mind, he had never met with. A man with a larger family he had never known (cheers). The parish required a man who could be depended on ("Hear!" from the Spruggins side, answered by ironical cheers from the Bung party). Such a man he now proposed ("No," "Yes"). He would not allude to individuals (the ex-churchwarden continued, in the celebrated negative style adopted by great speakers). He would not advert to a gentleman who had once held a high rank in the service of his majesty; he would not say, that that gentleman was no gentleman; he would not assert, that that man was no man; he would not say, that he was a turbulent parishioner; he would not say, that he had grossly misbehaved himself, not only on this, but on all former occasions; he would not say, that he was one of those discontented and treasonable spirits, who carried confusion and disorder wherever they went; he would not say, that he harboured in his heart envy, and hatred, and malice, and all uncharitableness. No! He wished to have everything comfortable and pleasant, and therefore, he would say—nothing about him (cheers).

The captain replied in a similar parliamentary style. He would not say, he was astonished at the speech they had just heard; he would not say, he was disgusted (cheers). He would not retort the epithets which had been hurled against him (renewed cheering); he would not allude to men once in office, but now happily out of it, who had mismanaged the workhouse, ground the paupers, diluted the beer, slack-baked the bread, boned the meat, heightened the work, and lowered the soup (tremendous cheers). He would not ask what such men deserved (a voice, "Nothing a-day, and find themselves!"). He would not say, that one burst of general indignation should drive them from the parish they polluted with their presence ("Give it him!"). He would not allude to the unfortunate man who had been proposed—he would not say, as the vestry's tool, but as Beadle. He would not advert to that individual's family; he would not say, that nine children, twins, and a wife, were very bad examples for pauper imitation (loud cheers). He would not advert in detail to the qualifications of Bung. The man stood before him, and he would not say in his presence, what he might be disposed to say of him if he were absent. (Here Mr. Bung telegraphed to a friend near him, under cover of his hat, by contracting his left eye, and applying his right thumb to the tip of his nose). It had been objected to Bung that he had only five children ("Hear, hear!" from the opposition). Well; he had yet to learn that the legislature had affixed any precise amount of infantine qualification to the office of beadle; but taking it for granted that an extensive family were a great requisite, he entreated them to look to facts, and compare *data*, about which there could be no mistake. Bung was 35 years of age. Spruggins—of whom he wished to speak with all possible respect—was 50. Was it not more than possible—was it not very probable—that by the time Bung attained the latter age, he might see around him a family, even exceeding in number and extent that to which Spruggins at present laid claim? (deafening cheers and waving of handkerchiefs). The captain concluded, amidst loud applause, by calling upon the parishioners to sound the tocsin, rush to the poll, free themselves from dictation, or be slaves for ever.

On the following day the polling began, and we never have had such a bustle in our parish since we got up our famous anti-slavery petition, which was such an important one that the House of Commons ordered it to be printed, on the motion of the member for the district. The captain engaged two hackney-coaches and a cab for Bung's people—the cab for the drunken voters, and the two coaches for the old ladies, the greater portion of whom, owing to the captain's impetuosity, were driven up to the poll and home again, before they recovered from their flurry sufficiently to know, with any degree of clearness, what they had been doing.

The opposite party wholly neglected these precautions, and the consequence was, that a great many ladies who were walking leisurely up to the church—for it was a very hot day—to vote for Spruggins, were artfully decoyed into the coaches, and voted for Bung. The captain's arguments, too, had produced considerable effect : the attempted influence of the vestry produced a greater. A threat of exclusive dealing was clearly established against the vestry-clerk—a case of heartless and profligate atrocity. It appeared that the delinquent had been in the habit of purchasing six penn'orth of muffins, weekly, from an old woman who rents a small house in the parish, and resides among the original settlers ; on her last weekly visit, a message was conveyed to her through the medium of the cook, couched in mysterious terms, but indicating with sufficient clearness that the vestry-clerk's appetite for muffins, in future, depended entirely on her vote on the beadleship. This was sufficient : the stream had been turning previously, and the impulse thus administered directed its final course. The Bung party ordered one shilling's-worth of muffins weekly for the remainder of the old woman's natural life : the parishioners were loud in their exclamations ; and the fate of Spruggins was sealed.

It was in vain that the twins were exhibited in dresses of the same pattern, and night-cap to match, at the church door : the boy in Mrs. Spruggins's right arm, and the girl in her left—even Mrs. Spruggins herself failed to be an object of sympathy any longer. The majority attained by Bung on the gross poll was four hundred and twenty-eight, and the cause of the parishioners triumphed.

CHAPTER V

THE BROKER'S MAN

THE excitement of the late election has subsided, and our parish being once again restored to a state of comparative tranquillity, we are enabled to devote our attention to those parishioners who take little share in our party contests or in the turmoil and bustle of public life. And we feel sincere pleasure in acknowledging here, that in collecting materials for this task we have been greatly assisted by Mr. Bung himself, who has imposed on us a debt of obligation which we fear we can never repay. The life of this gentleman has been one of a very chequered description : he has undergone transitions—not from grave to gay, for he never was grave —not from lively to severe, for severity forms no part of his disposition ; his fluctuations have been between poverty in the extreme, and poverty modified, or, to use his own emphatic language, " between nothing to eat and just half enough." He is not, as he forcibly remarks, " one of those fortunate men who, if they were to dive under one side of a barge stark-naked, would come up on the other with a new suit of clothes on, and a ticket for soup in the waistcoat-pocket :" neither is he one of those whose spirit has been broken beyond redemption by misfortune and want. He is just one of the careless, good-for-nothing, happy fellows, who float, cork-like, on the surface, for the world to play at hockey with : knocked here, and there, and everywhere : now to the right, then to the left, again up in the air, and anon to the bottom, but always reappearing and bounding with the stream buoyantly and merrily along. Some few months before he was prevailed upon to stand a contested election for the office of beadle, necessity attached him to the service of a broker ; and on the opportunities he here acquired of ascertaining the condition of most of the poorer inhabitants of the parish, his patron, the captain, first grounded his claims to public support. Chance

threw the man in our way a short time since. We were, in
the first instance, attracted by his prepossessing impudence
at the election ; we were not surprised, on further acquaintance, to find him a shrewd knowing fellow, with no inconsiderable power of observation ; and, after conversing with
him a little, were somewhat struck (as we dare say our readers
have frequently been in other cases) with the power some
men seem to have. not only of sympathising with, but to all
appearance of understanding feelings to which they themselves are entire strangers. We had been expressing to
the new functionary our surprise that he should ever have
served in the capacity to which we have just adverted, when
we gradually led him into one or two professional anecdotes.
As we are induced to think, on reflection, that they will tell
better in nearly his own words than with any attempted
embellishments of ours, we will at once entitle them

MR. BUNG'S NARRATIVE.

"It's very true, as you say, sir," Mr. Bung commenced,
" that a broker's man's is not a life to be envied ; and in
course you know as well as I do, though you don't say it.
that people hate and scout 'em because they're the ministers
of wretchedness, like, to poor people. But what could I do.
sir ? The thing was no worse because I did it, instead of
somebody else ; and if putting me in possession of a house
would put me in possession of three and sixpence a day, and
levying a distress on another man's goods would relieve my
distress and that of my family, it can't be expected but what
I'd take the job and go through with it. I never liked it.
God knows : I always looked out for something else, and the
moment I got other work to do, I left it. If there is anything wrong in being the agent in such matters—not the
principal, mind -you—I'm sure the business, to a beginner
like I was, at all events, carries its own punishment along
with it. I wished again and again that the people would
only blow me up, or pitch into me—that I wouldn't have
minded, it's all in my way ; but it's the being shut up by
yourself in one room for five days, without so much as an
old newspaper to look at. or anything to see out o' the
winder but the roofs and chimneys at the back of the house.
or anything to listen to but the ticking, perhaps, of an old
Dutch clock, the sobbing of the missis now and then, the

low talking of friends in the next room, who speak in whispers, lest 'the man' should overhear them, or perhaps the occasional opening of the door, as a child peeps in to look at you, and then runs half-frightened away—it's all this, that makes you feel sneaking somehow, and ashamed of yourself; and then, if it's winter-time, they just give you fire enough to make you think you'd like more, and bring in your grub as if they wished it 'ud choke you—as I dare say they do, for the matter of that, most heartily. If they're very civil, they make you up a bed in the room at night, and if they don't, your master sends one in for you; but there you are, without being washed or shaved all the time, shunned by everybody, and spoken to by no one, unless some one comes in at dinner-time, and asks you whether you want any more, in a tone as much as to say, 'I hope you don't,' or, in the evening, to inquire whether you wouldn't rather have a candle, after you've been sitting in the dark half the night. When I was left in this way, I used to sit, think, think, thinking, till I felt as lonesome as a kitten in a wash-house copper with the lid on; but I believe the old brokers' men who are regularly trained to it, never think at all. I have heard some on 'em say, indeed, that they don't know how!

"I put in a good many distresses in my time (continued Mr. Bung), and in course I wasn't long in finding that some people are not as much to be pitied as others are, and that people with good incomes who get into difficulties, which they keep patching up day after day, and week after week, get so used to these sort of things in time, that at last they come scarcely to feel them at all. I remember the very first place I was put in possession of, was a gentleman's house in this parish here, that everybody would suppose couldn't help having money if he tried. I went with old Fixem, my old master, 'bout half arter eight in the morning; rang the area-bell; servant in livery opened the door: 'Governor at home?' —'Yes, he is,' says the man; 'but he's breakfasting just now.' 'Never mind,' says Fixem, 'just you tell him there's a gentleman here, as wants to speak to him partickler.' So the servant he opens his eyes, and stares about him all ways—looking for the gentleman, as it struck me, for I don't think anybody but a man as was stone-blind would mistake Fixem for one; and as for me, I was as seedy as a cheap cowcumber. Hows'ever, he turns round, and goes to the breakfast-parlour, which was a little snug sort of room at the end of the passage,

and Fixem (as we always did in that profession), without
waiting to be announced, walks in arter him, and before the
servant could get out, 'Please, sir, here's a man as wants to
speak to you,' looks in at the door as familiar and pleasant as
may be.   'Who the devil are you, and how dare you walk
into a gentleman's house without leave?' says the master, as
fierce as a bull in fits.   'My name,' says Fixem, winking to
the master to send the servant away, and putting the warrant
into his hands folded up like a note, 'My name's Smith,' says
he, 'and I called from Johnson's about that business of
Thompson's.'—'Oh,' says the other, quite down on him
directly, 'How *is* Thompson?' says he.   'Pray sit down, Mr.
Smith : John, leave the room.'   Out went the servant; and
the gentleman and Fixem looked at one another till they
couldn't look any longer, and then they varied the amusements by looking at me, who had been standing on the mat
all this time.   'Hundred and fifty pounds, I see,' said the
gentleman at last.   'Hundred and fifty pound,' said Fixem,
'besides cost of levy, sheriff's poundage, and all other incidental expenses.'—'Um,' says the gentleman, 'I shan't be
able to settle this before to-morrow afternoon.'—'Very sorry ;
but I shall be obliged to leave my man here till then,' replies
Fixem, pretending to look very miserable over it.   'That's
very unfort'nate,' says the gentleman, 'for I have got a large
party here to-night, and I'm ruined if those fellows of mine
get an inkling of the matter—just step here, Mr. Smith,' says
he, after a short pause.   So Fixem walks with him up to the
window, and after a good deal of whispering, and a little
chinking of suverins, and looking at me, he comes back and
says, 'Bung, you're a handy fellow, and very honest, I know.
This gentleman wants an assistant to clean the plate and
wait at table to-day, and if you're not particularly engaged,'
says old Fixem, grinning like mad, and shoving a couple of
suverins into my hand, 'he'll be very glad to avail himself of
your services.'   Well, I laughed : and the gentleman laughed,
and we all laughed ; and I went home and cleaned myself,
leaving Fixem there, and when I went back, Fixem went
away, and I polished up the plate, and waited at table, and
gammoned the servants, and nobody had the least idea I was
in possession, though it very nearly came out after all ; for
one of the last gentlemen who remained, came down-stairs
into the hall where I was sitting pretty late at night, and
putting half-a-crown into my hand, says, 'Here, my man,'

George Cruikshank

The Broker's Man

says he, 'run and get me a coach, will you?' I thought it was a do, to get me out of the house, and was just going to say so, sulkily enough, when the gentleman (who was up to everything) came running down-stairs, as if he was in great anxiety. 'Bung,' says he, pretending to be in a consuming passion. 'Sir,' says I. 'Why the devil an't you looking after that plate?'—'I was just going to send him for a coach for me,' says the other gentleman. 'And I was just a-going to say,' says I—'Anybody else, my dear fellow,' interrupts the master of the house, pushing me down the passage to get out of the way—'anybody else; but I have put this man in possession of all the plate and valuables, and I cannot allow him, on any consideration whatever, to leave the house. Bung, you scoundrel, go and count those forks in the break-fast-parlour instantly.' You may be sure I went laughing pretty hearty when I found it was all right. The money was paid next day, with the addition of something else for myself, and that was the best job that I (and I suspect old Fixem too) ever got in that line.

"But this is the bright side of the picture, sir, after all," resumed Mr. Bung, laying aside the knowing look, and flash air, with which he had repeated the previous anecdote— "and I'm sorry to say, it's the side one sees very, very seldom, in comparison with the dark one. The civility which money will purchase, is rarely extended to those who have none; and there's a consolation even in being able to patch up one difficulty, to make way for another, to which very poor people are strangers. I was once put into a house down George's Yard—that little dirty court at the back of the gas-works; and I never shall forget the misery of them people, dear me! It was a distress for half a year's rent—two pound ten, I think. There was only two rooms in the house, and as there was no passage, the lodgers up-stairs always went through the room of the people of the house, as they passed in and out; and every time they did so—which, on the average, was about four times every quarter of an hour— they blowed up quite frightful: for their things had been seized too, and included in the inventory. There was a little piece of enclosed dust in front of the house, with a cinder-path leading up to the door, and an open rain-water butt on one side. A dirty striped curtain, on a very slack string, hung in the window, and a little triangular bit of broken looking-glass rested on the sill inside. I suppose it

was meant for the people's use, but their appearance was so
wretched, and so miserable, that I'm certain they never
could have plucked up courage to look themselves in the
face a second time, if they survived the fright of doing so
once. There was two or three chairs that might have been
worth, in their best days, from eightpence to a shilling
a-piece; a small deal table, an old corner cupboard with
nothing in it, and one of those bedsteads which turn up half
way, and leave the bottom legs sticking out for you to knock
your head against, or hang your hat upon; no bed, no bedding. There was an old sack, by way of rug, before the fireplace, and four or five children were grovelling about, among
the sand on the floor. The execution was only put in to
get 'em out of the house, for there was nothing to take to
pay the expenses; and here I stopped for three days, though
that was a mere form too: for, in course, I knew, and we all
knew, they could never pay the money. In one of the
chairs, by the side of the place where the fire ought to have
been, was an old 'ooman—the ugliest and dirtiest I ever
see—who sat rocking herself backwards and forwards, backwards and forwards, without once stopping, except for an
instant now and then, to clasp together the withered hands
which, with these exceptions, she kept constantly rubbing
upon her knees, just raising and depressing her fingers con-
vulsively, in time to the rocking of the chair. On the other
side sat the mother with an infant in her arms, which cried
till it cried itself to sleep, and when it 'woke, cried till it
cried itself off again. The old 'ooman's voice I never heard:
she seemed completely stupefied; and as to the mother's, it
would have been better if she had been so too, for misery
had changed her to a devil. If you had heard how she
cursed the little naked children as was rolling on the floor,
and seen how savagely she struck the infant when it cried
with hunger, you'd have shuddered as much as I did. There
they remained all the time: the children ate a morsel of
bread once or twice, and I gave 'em best part of the dinners
my missis brought me, but the woman ate nothing; they
never even laid on the bedstead, nor was the room swept or
cleaned all the time. The neighbours were all too poor themselves to take any notice of 'em, but from what I could make
out from the abuse of the woman up-stairs, it seemed the
husband had been transported a few weeks before. When
the time was up, the landlord and old Fixem too, got rather

frightened about the family, and so they made a stir about it,
and had 'em taken to the workhouse. They sent the sick
couch for the old 'ooman, and Simmons took the children
away at night. The old 'ooman went into the infirmary,
and very soon died. The children are all in the house to
this day, and very comfortable they are in comparison. As
to the mother, there was no taming her at all. She had been
a quiet, hard-working woman, I believe, but her misery had
actually drove her wild ; so after she had been sent to the
house of correction half-a-dozen times. for throwing inkstands at the overseers, blaspheming the churchwardens,
and smashing everybody as come near her, she burst a
blood-vessel one mornin', and died too ; and a happy release
it was, both for herself and the old paupers, male and female.
which she used to tip over in all directions, as if they were so
many skittles, and she the ball.

 "Now this was bad enough," resumed Mr Bung, taking a
half-step towards the door, as if to intimate that he had
nearly concluded. "This was bad enough, but there was a
sort of quiet misery—if you understand what I mean by
that, sir—about a lady at one house I was put into, as
touched me a good deal more. It doesn't matter where it
was exactly : indeed, I'd rather not say, but it was the same
sort o' job. I went with Fixem in the usual way—there
was a year's rent in arrear ; a very small servant-girl opened
the door, and three or four fine-looking little children was in
the front parlour we were shown into, which was very clean,
but very scantily furnished, much like the children themselves. 'Bung,' says Fixem to me, in a low voice, when we
were left alone for a minute, ' I know something about this
here family, and my opinion is, it's no go.' 'Do you think
they can't settle ? ' says I, quite anxiously ; for I liked the
looks of them children. Fixem shook his head, and was
just about to reply, when the door opened, and in come a
lady, as white as ever I see any one in my days, except
about the eyes, which were red with crying. She walked
in, as firm as I could have done ; shut the door carefully
after her, and sat herself down with a face as composed as
if it was made of stone. 'What is the matter, gentlemen ? '
says she, in a surprisin' steady voice. '*Is* this an execution ? ' 'It is, mum,' says Fixem. The lady looked at him as
steady as ever : she didn't seem to have understood him.
'It is, mum,' says Fixem again ; ' this is my warrant of

distress, mum,' says he, handing it over as polite as if it was
a newspaper which had been bespoke arter the next gentleman.

"The lady's lip trembled as she took the printed paper.
She cast her eye over it, and old Fixem began to explain the
form, but I saw she wasn't reading it, plain enough, poor
thing. 'Oh, my God!' says she, suddenly a-bursting out
crying, letting the warrant fall, and hiding her face in her
hands. 'Oh, my God! what will become of us!' The noise
she made, brought in a young lady of about nineteen or
twenty, who, I suppose, had been a-listening at the door,
and who had got a little boy in her arms : she sat him down
in the lady's lap, without speaking, and she hugged the poor
little fellow to her bosom, and cried over him, till even old
Fixem put on his blue spectacles to hide the two tears, that
was a-trickling down, one on each side of his dirty face.
'Now, dear ma,' says the young lady, 'you know how much
you have borne. For all our sakes—for pa's sake,' says she,
'don't give way to this!'—'No, no, I won't!' says the lady,
gathering herself up, hastily, and drying her eyes, 'I am
very foolish, but I'm better now—much better.' And then
she roused herself up, went with us into every room while
we took the inventory, opened all the drawers of her own
accord, sorted the children's little clothes to make the work
easier ; and, except doing everything in a strange sort of
hurry, seemed as calm and composed as if nothing had happened. When we came down-stairs again, she hesitated a
minute or two, and at last says, 'Gentlemen,' says she, 'I
am afraid I have done wrong, and perhaps it may bring
you into trouble. I secreted just now,' she says, 'the only
trinket I have left in the world—here it is.' So she lays
down on the table a little miniature mounted in gold. 'It's
a miniature,' she says, 'of my poor dear father! I little
thought once, that I should ever thank God for depriving me
of the original, but I do, and have done for years back, most
fervently. Take it away, sir,' she says, 'it's a face that
never turned from me in sickness or distress, and I can
hardly bear to turn from it now, when, God knows, I suffer
both in no ordinary degree.' I couldn't say nothing, but I
raised my head from the inventory which I was filling up,
and looked at Fixem ; the old fellow nodded to me significantly, so I ran my pen through the '*Mini*' I had just
written, and left the miniature on the table.

" Well, sir, to make short of a long story, I was left in possession, and in possession I remained ; and though I was an ignorant man, and the master of the house a clever one, I saw what he never did, but what he would give worlds now (if he had 'em) to have seen in time. I saw, sir, that his wife was wasting away, beneath cares of which she never complained, and griefs she never told. I saw that she was dying before his eyes ; I knew that one exertion from him might have saved her, but he never made it. I don't blame him : I don't think he *could* rouse himself. She had so long anticipated all his wishes, and acted for him, that he was a lost man when left to himself. I used to think when I caught sight of her, in the clothes she used to wear, which looked shabby even upon her, and would have been scarcely decent on any one else, that if I was a gentleman it would wring my very heart to see the woman that was a smart and merry girl when I courted her, so altered through her love for me. Bitter cold and damp weather it was, yet, though her dress was thin, and her shoes none of the best, during the whole three days, from morning to night, she was out of doors running about to try and raise the money. The money *was* raised and the execution was paid out. The whole family crowded into the room where I was, when the money arrived. The father was quite happy as the inconvenience was removed—I dare say he didn't know how ; the children looked merry and cheerful again ; the eldest girl was bustling about, making preparations for the first comfortable meal they had had since the distress was put in ; and the mother looked pleased to see them all so. But if ever I saw death in a woman's face, I saw it in hers that night.

" I was right, sir," continued Mr. Bung, hurriedly passing his coat-sleeve over his face ; " the family grew more prosperous, and good fortune arrived. But it was too late. Those children are motherless now, and their father would give up all he has since gained—house, home, goods, money : all that he has, or ever can have, to restore the wife he has lost."

CHAPTER VI

THE LADIES' SOCIETIES

OUR Parish is very prolific in ladies' charitable institutions. In winter, when wet feet are common, and colds not scarce, we have the ladies' soup distribution society, the ladies' coal distribution society, and the ladies' blanket distribution society ; in summer, when stone fruits flourish and stomach aches prevail, we have the ladies' dispensary, and the ladies' sick visitation committee ; and all the year round we have the ladies' child's examination society, the ladies' bible and prayer-book circulation society, and the ladies' childbed-linen monthly loan society. The two latter are decidedly the most important ; whether they are productive of more benefit than the rest, it is not for us to say, but we can take upon ourselves to affirm, with the utmost solemnity, that they create a greater stir and more bustle, than all the others put together.

We should be disposed to affirm, on the first blush of the matter, that the bible and prayer-book society is not so popular as the childbed-linen society ; the bible and prayer-book society has, however, considerably increased in importance within the last year or two, having derived some adventitious aid from the factious opposition of the child's examination society ; which factious opposition originated in manner following : —When the young curate was popular, and all the unmarried ladies in the parish took a serious turn, the charity children all at once became objects of peculiar and especial interest. The three Miss Browns (enthusiastic admirers of the curate) taught, and exercised, and examined, and re-examined the unfortunate children, until the boys grew pale, and the girls consumptive with study and fatigue. The three Miss Browns stood it out very well, because they relieved each other ; but the children. having no relief at all, exhibited decided symptoms of weariness and care. The unthinking part of the parishioners laughed at all this, but the more reflective portion of the inhabitants abstained from expressing any opinion on the subject until that of the curate had been clearly ascertained.

The opportunity was not long wanting. The curate preached a charity sermon on behalf of the charity school, and in the charity sermon aforesaid, expatiated in glowing terms on the praiseworthy and indefatigable exertions of certain estimable individuals. Sobs were heard to issue from the three Miss Browns' pew ; the pew-opener of the division was seen to hurry down the centre aisle to the vestry door, and to return immediately, bearing a glass of water in her hand. A low moaning ensued ; two more pew-openers rushed to the spot, and the three Miss Browns, each supported by a pew-opener, were led out of the church, and led in again after the lapse of five minutes with white pocket-handkerchiefs to their eyes, as if they had been attending a funeral in the churchyard adjoining. If any doubt had for a moment existed, as to whom the allusion was intended to apply, it was at once removed. The wish to enlighten the charity children became universal, and the three Miss Browns were unanimously besought to divide the school into classes, and to assign each class to the super-intendence of two young ladies.

A little learning is a dangerous thing, but a little patron-age is more so ; the three Miss Browns appointed all the old maids, and carefully excluded the young ones. Maiden aunts triumphed, mammas were reduced to the lowest depths of despair, and there is no telling in what act of violence the general indignation against the three Miss Browns might have vented itself, had not a perfectly provi-dential occurrence changed the tide of public feeling. Mrs. Johnson Parker, the mother of seven extremely fine girls— all unmarried—hastily reported to several other mammas of several other unmarried families, that five old men, six old women, and children innumerable, in the free seats near her pew, were in the habit of coming to church every Sunday, without either bible or prayer-book. Was this to be borne in a civilised country? Could such things be tolerated in a Christian land? Never! A ladies' bible and prayer-book distribution society was instantly formed : president, Mrs. Johnson Parker ; treasurers, auditors, and secretary, the Misses Johnson Parker : subscriptions were entered into, books were bought, all the free-seat people provided there-

with, and when the first lesson was given out, on the first
Sunday succeeding these events, there was such a dropping
of books, and rustling of leaves, that it was morally impossible to hear one word of the service for five minutes
afterwards.

The three Miss Browns, and their party, saw the approaching danger, and endeavoured to avert it by ridicule and
sarcasm. Neither the old men nor the old women could
read their books, now they had got them, said the three
Miss Browns. Never mind ; they could learn, replied
Mrs. Johnson Parker. The children couldn't read either,
suggested the three Miss Browns. No matter ; they could
be taught, retorted Mrs. Johnson Parker. A balance of
parties took place. The Miss Browns publicly examined—
popular feeling inclined to the child's examination society.
The Miss Johnson Parkers publicly distributed—a reaction
took place in favour of the prayer-book distribution. A
feather would have turned the scale, and a feather did turn
it. A missionary returned from the West Indies ; he was
to be presented to the Dissenters' Missionary Society on his
marriage with a wealthy widow. Overtures were made to
the Dissenters by the Johnson Parkers. Their object was
the same, and why not have a joint meeting of the two
societies ? The proposition was accepted. The meeting
was duly heralded by public announcement, and the room
was crowded to suffocation. The Missionary appeared on
the platform ; he was hailed with enthusiasm. He repeated
a dialogue he had heard between two negroes, behind a
hedge, on the subject of distribution societies ; the approbation was tumultuous. He gave an imitation of the two
negroes in broken English ; the roof was rent with applause.
From that period we date (with one trifling exception) a
daily increase in the popularity of the distribution society,
and an increase of popularity, which the feeble and im-
potent opposition of the examination party has only tended
to augment.

Now, the great points about the childbed-linen monthly
loan society are, that it is less dependent on the fluctuations
of public opinion than either the distribution or the child's
examination ; and that, come what may, there is never any
lack of objects on which to exercise its benevolence. Our
parish is a very populous one, and, if anything, contributes,
we should be disposed to say, rather more than its due

share to the aggregate amount of births in the metropolis and its environs. The consequence is, that the monthly loan society flourishes, and invests its members with a most enviable amount of bustling patronage. The society (whose only notion of dividing time would appear to be its allotment into months) holds monthly tea-drinkings, at which the monthly report is received, a secretary elected for the month ensuing, and such of the monthly boxes as may not happen to be out on loan for the month, carefully examined.

We were never present at one of these meetings, from all of which it is scarcely necessary to say, gentlemen are carefully excluded ; but Mr. Bung has been called before the board once or twice, and we have his authority for stating that its proceedings are conducted with great order and regularity : not more than four members being allowed to speak at one time on any pretence whatever. The regular committtoo io composed exclusively of married ladies, but a vast number of young unmarried ladies of from eighteen to twenty-five years of age, respectively, are admitted as honorary members, partly because they are very useful in replenishing the boxes, and visiting the confined ; partly because it is highly desirable that they should be initiated. at an early period, into the more serious and matronly duties of after-life ; and partly because prudent mammas have not unfrequently been known to turn this circumstance to wonderfully good account in matrimonial speculations.

In addition to the loan of the monthly boxes (which are always painted blue, with the name of the society in large white letters on the lid), the society dispense occasional grants of beef-tea, and a composition of warm beer, spice, eggs, and sugar, commonly known by the name of " caudle," to its patients. And here again the services of the honorary members are called into requisition, and most cheerfully conceded. Deputations of twos or threes are sent out to visit the patients, and on these occasions there is such a tasting of caudle and beef-tea, such a stirring about of little messes in tiny saucepans on the hob, such a dressing and undressing of infants. such a tying, and folding, and pinning; such a nursing and warming of little legs and feet before the fire, such a delightful confusion of talking and cooking. bustle, importance, and officiousness, as never can be enjoyed in its full extent but on similar occasions.

In rivalry of these two institutions, and as a last expiring effort to acquire parochial popularity, the child's examination people determined, the other day, on having a grand public examination of the pupils; and the large school-room of the national seminary was, by and with the consent of the parish authorities, devoted to the purpose. Invitation circulars were forwarded to all the principal parishioners, including, of course, the heads of the other two societies, for whose especial behoof and edification the display was intended; and a large audience was confidently anticipated on the occasion. The floor was carefully scrubbed the day before, under the immediate superintendence of the three Miss Browns; forms were placed across the room for the accommodation of the visitors, specimens in writing were carefully selected, and as carefully patched and touched up, until they astonished the children who had written them, rather more than the company who read them; sums in compound addition were rehearsed and re-rehearsed until all the children had the totals by heart; and the preparations altogether were on the most laborious and most comprehensive scale. The morning arrived: the children were yellow-soaped and flannelled, and towelled, till their faces shone again; every pupil's hair was carefully combed into his or her eyes, as the case might be; the girls were adorned with snow-white tippets, and caps bound round the head by a single purple ribbon: the necks of the elder boys were fixed into collars of startling dimensions.

The doors were thrown open, and the Misses Brown and Co. were discovered in plain white muslin dresses, and caps of the same—the child's examination uniform. The room filled: the greetings of the company were loud and cordial. The distributionists trembled, for their popularity was at stake. The eldest boy fell forward, and delivered a propitiatory address from behind his collar. It was from the pen of Mr. Henry Brown; the applause was universal, and the Johnson Parkers were aghast. The examination proceeded with success, and terminated in triumph. The child's examination society gained a momentary victory, and the Johnson Parkers retreated in despair.

A secret council of the distributionists was held that night, with Mrs. Johnson Parker in the chair, to consider of the best means of recovering the ground they had lost in the favour of the parish. What could be done? Another meeting! Alas! who was to attend it? The Missionary would not do twice;

and the slaves were emancipated.   A bold step must be taken.
The parish must be astonished in some way or other ; but no
one was able to suggest what the step should be. At length,
a very old lady was heard to mumble, in indistinct tones,
" Exeter Hall."   A sudden light broke in upon the meeting.
It was unanimously resolved, that a deputation of old ladies
should wait upon a celebrated orator, imploring his assistance,
and the favour of a speech ; and the deputation should also
wait on two or three other imbecile old women, not resident
in the parish, and entreat their attendance.   The application
was successful, the meeting was held ; the orator (an Irishman)
came. He talked of green isles—other shores—vast Atlantic
—bosom of the deep—Christian charity—blood and extermi-
nation—mercy in hearts—arms in hands—altars and homes
—household gods.   He wiped his eyes, he blew his nose, and
he quoted Latin. The effect was tremendous—the Latin was
a decided hit.   Nobody know exactly what it was about, but
everybody knew it must be affecting, because even the orator
was overcome.   The popularity of the distribution society
among the ladies of our parish is unprecedented ; and the
child's examination is going fast to decay.

CHAPTER VII

OUR NEXT-DOOR NEIGHBOUR

WE are very fond of speculating as we walk through a street, on the character and pursuits of the people who inhabit it; and nothing so materially assists us in these speculations as the appearance of the house doors. The various expressions of the human countenance afford a beautiful and interesting study; but there is something in the physiognomy of street-door knockers, almost as characteristic, and nearly as infallible. Whenever we visit a man for the first time, we contemplate the features of his knocker with the greatest curiosity, for we well know, that between the man and his knocker, there will inevitably be a greater or less degree of resemblance and sympathy.

For instance, there is one description of knocker that used to be common enough, but which is fast passing away—a large round one, with the jolly face of a convivial lion smiling blandly at you, as you twist the sides of your hair into a curl or pull up your shirt-collar while you are waiting for the door to be opened; we never saw that knocker on the door of a churlish man—so far as our experience is concerned, it invariably bespoke hospitality and another bottle.

No man ever saw this knocker on the door of a small attorney or bill-broker; they always patronise the other lion; a heavy ferocious-looking fellow, with a countenance expressive of savage stupidity—a sort of grand master among the knockers, and a great favourite with the selfish and brutal.

Then there is a little pert Egyptian knocker, with a long thin face, a pinched-up nose, and a very sharp chin; he is most in vogue with your government-office people, in light drabs and starched cravats; little spare priggish men, who are perfectly satisfied with their own opinions, and consider themselves of paramount importance.

We were greatly troubled a few years ago, by the innovation of a new kind of knocker, without any face at all,

Our Next-door Neighbour

(p. 43)

composed of a wreath, depending from a hand or small truncheon. A little trouble and attention, however, enabled us to overcome this difficulty, and to reconcile the new system to our favourite theory. You will invariably find this knocker on the doors of cold and formal people, who always ask you why you *don't* come, and never say *do*.

Everybody knows the brass knocker is common to suburban villas, and extensive boarding-schools ; and having noticed this genus we have recapitulated all the most prominent and strongly-defined species.

Some phrenologists affirm, that the agitation of a man's brain by different passions, produces corresponding developments in the form of his skull. Do not let us be understood as pushing our theory to the full length of asserting, that any alteration in a man's disposition would produce a visible effect on the feature of his knocker. Our position merely is, that in such a case, the magnetism which must exist between a man and his knocker, would induce the man to remove, and seek some knocker more congenial to his altered feelings. If you ever find a man changing his habitation without any reasonable pretext, depend upon it, that, although he may not be aware of the fact himself, it is because he and his knocker are at variance. This is a new theory, but we venture to launch it, nevertheless, as being quite as ingenious and infallible as many thousands of the learned speculations which are daily broached for public good and private fortune-making.

Entertaining these feelings on the subject of knockers, it will be readily imagined with what consternation we viewed the entire removal of the knocker from the door of the next house to the one we lived in, some time ago, and the substitution of a bell. This was a calamity we had never anticipated. The bare idea of anybody being able to exist without a knocker, appeared so wild and visionary, that it had never for one instant entered our imagination.

We sauntered moodily from the spot, and bent our steps towards Eaton Square, then just building. What was our astonishment and indignation to find that bells were fast becoming the rule, and knockers the exception ! Our theory trembled beneath the shock. We hastened home ; and fancying we foresaw in the swift progress of events, its entire abolition, resolved from that day forward to vent our speculations on our next-door neighbours in person. The house adjoining ours on the left hand was uninhabited, and we had, therefore, plenty of leisure to observe our next-door neighbours on the other side.

The house without the knocker was in the occupation of a city clerk, and there was a neatly-written bill in the parlour window intimating that lodgings for a single gentleman were to be let within.

It was a neat, dull little house, on the shady side of the way, with new, narrow floorcloth in the passage, and new, narrow stair-carpets up to the first floor. The paper was new, and the paint was new, and the furniture was new; and all three, paper, paint, and furniture, bespoke the limited means of the tenant. There was a little red and black carpet in the drawing-room, with a border of flooring all the way round; a few stained chairs and a Pembroke table. A pink shell was displayed on each of the little sideboards, which, with the addition of a tea-tray and caddy, a few more shells on the mantelpiece, and three peacock's feathers tastefully arranged above them, completed the decorative furniture of the apartment.

This was the room destined for the reception of the single gentleman during the day, and a little back room on the same floor was assigned as his sleeping apartment by night.

The bill had not been long in the window, when a stout, good-humoured looking gentleman, of about five-and-thirty, appeared as a candidate for the tenancy. Terms were soon arranged, for the bill was taken down immediately after his first visit. In a day or two the single gentleman came in, and shortly afterwards his real character came out.

First of all, he displayed a most extraordinary partiality for sitting up till three or four o'clock in the morning, drinking whiskey-and-water, and smoking cigars; then he invited friends home, who used to come at ten o'clock, and begin to get happy about the small hours, when they evinced their perfect contentment by singing songs with half-a-dozen verses of two lines each, and a chorus of ten, which chorus used to be shouted forth by the whole strength of the company, in the most enthusiastic and vociferous manner, to the great annoyance of the neighbours, and the special discomfort of another single gentleman overhead.

Now, this was bad enough, occurring as it did three times a week on the average, but this was not all; for when the company *did* go away, instead of walking quietly down the street, as anybody else's company would have done, they amused themselves by making alarming and frightful noises, and counterfeiting the shrieks of females in distress ; and one night, a red-faced gentleman in a white hat knocked in the most urgent manner at the door of the powdered-headed old gentleman at No. 3, and when the powdered-headed old gentleman, who thought one of his married daughters must have been taken ill prematurely, had groped down-stairs, and after a great deal of unbolting and key-turning, opened the street door, the red-faced man in the white hat said he hoped he'd excuse his giving him so much trouble, but he'd feel obliged if he'd favour him with a glass of cold spring water, and the loan of a shilling for a cab to take him home, on which the old gentleman slammed the door and went up-stairs, and threw the contents of his water jug out of window —-very straight, only it went over the wrong man ; and the whole street was involved in confusion.

A joke's a joke ; and even practical jests are very capital in their way, if you can only get the other party to see the fun of them ; but the population of our street were so dull of apprehension, as to be quite lost to a sense of the drollery of this proceeding: and the consequence was, that our next-door neighbour was obliged to tell the single gentleman, that unless he gave up entertaining his friends at home, he really must be compelled to part with him. The single gentleman received the remonstrance with great good-humour, and promised from that time forward, to spend his evenings at a coffee-house—a determination which afforded general and unmixed satisfaction.

The next night passed off very well, everybody being delighted with the change ; but on the next, the noises were renewed with greater spirit than ever. The single gentle-man's friends being unable to see him in his own house every alternate night, had come to the determination of see-ing him home every night ; and what with the discordant greetings of the friends at parting, and the noise created by the single gentleman in his passage up-stairs, and his sub-sequent struggles to get his boots off, the evil was not to be borne. So our next-door neighbour gave the single gentle-man, who was a very good lodger in other respects, notice to quit ; and the single gentleman went away, and entertained his friends in other lodgings.

The next applicant for the vacant first floor was of a very

different character from the troublesome single gentleman who had just quitted it. He was a tall, thin young gentleman, with a profusion of brown hair, reddish whiskers, and very slightly developed moustaches. He wore a braided surtout, with frogs behind, light grey trousers, and wash-leather gloves, and had altogether rather a military appearance. So unlike the roystering single gentleman. Such insinuating manners, and such a delightful address! So seriously disposed, too! When he first came to look at the lodgings, he inquired most particularly whether he was sure to be able to get a seat in the parish church ; and when he had agreed to take them, he requested to have a list of the different local charities, as he intended to subscribe his mite to the most deserving among them.

Our next-door neighbour was now perfectly happy. He had got a lodger at last, of just his own way of thinking—a serious, well-disposed man, who abhorred gaiety, and loved retirement. He took down the bill with a light heart, and pictured in imagination a long series of quiet Sundays, on which he and his lodger would exchange mutual civilities and Sunday papers.

The serious man arrived, and his luggage was to arrive from the country next morning. He borrowed a clean shirt, and a prayer-book, from our next-door neighbour, and retired to rest at an early hour, requesting that he might be called punctually at ten o'clock next morning—not before, as he was much fatigued.

He *was* called, and did not answer: he was called again, but there was no reply. Our next-door neighbour became alarmed, and burst the door open. The serious man had left the house mysteriously ; carrying with him the shirt, the prayer-book, a teaspoon, and the bedclothes.

Whether this occurrence, coupled with the irregularities of his former lodger, gave our next-door neighbour an aversion to single gentlemen, we know not ; we only know that the next bill which made its appearance in the parlour window intimated generally, that there were furnished apartments to let on the first floor. The bill was soon removed. The new lodgers at first attracted our curiosity, and afterwards excited our interest.

They were a young lad of eighteen or nineteen, and his mother, a lady of about fifty, or it might be less. The mother wore a widow's weeds, and the boy was also clothed in deep mourning. They were poor—very poor; for their only means of support arose from the pittance the boy earned, by copying writings, and translating for booksellers.

They had removed from some country place and settled in London; partly because it afforded better chances of employment for the boy, and partly, perhaps, with the natural desire to leave a place where they had been in better circumstances, and where their poverty was known. They were proud under their reverses, and above revealing their wants and privations to strangers. How bitter those privations were, and how hard the boy worked to remove them, no one ever knew but themselves. Night after night, two, three, four hours after midnight, could we hear the occasional raking up of the scanty fire, or the hollow and half-stifled cough, which indicated his being still at work; and day after day, could we see more plainly that nature had set that unearthly light in his plaintive face, which is the beacon of her worst disease.

Actuated, we hope, by a higher feeling than mere curiosity, we contrived to establish, first an acquaintance, and then a close intimacy, with the poor strangers. Our worst fears were realised; the boy was sinking fast. Through a part of the winter, and the whole of the following spring and summer, his labours were unceasingly prolonged: and the mother attempted to procure needlework, embroidery—anything for bread.

A few shillings now and then, were all she could earn. The boy worked steadily on; dying by minutes, but never once giving utterance to complaint or murmur.

One beautiful autumn evening we went to pay our customary visit to the invalid. His little remaining strength had been decreasing rapidly for two or three days preceding, and he was lying on the sofa at the open window, gazing at the setting sun. His mother had been reading the Bible to him, for she closed the book as we entered, and advanced to meet us.

"I was telling William," she said, "that we must manage to take him into the country somewhere, so that he may get quite well. He is not ill, you know, but he is not very strong, and has exerted himself too much lately." Poor thing! The tears that streamed through her fingers, as she turned aside, as if to adjust her close widow's cap, too plainly showed how fruitless was the attempt to deceive herself.

We sat down by the head of the sofa, but said nothing, for we saw the breath of life was passing gently but rapidly from the young form before us. At every respiration, his heart beat more slowly.

The boy placed one hand in ours, grasped his mother's arm with the other, drew her hastily towards him, and fervently kissed her cheek. There was a pause. He sunk back upon his pillow, and looked long and earnestly in his mother's face.

"William, William!" murmured the mother, after a long interval, "don't look at me so—speak to me, dear!"

The boy smiled languidly, but an instant afterwards his features resolved into the same cold, solemn gaze.

"William, dear William! rouse yourself; don't look at me so, love—pray don't! Oh, my God! what shall I do!" cried the widow, clasping her hands in agony—"my dear boy! he is dying!"

The boy raised himself by a violent effort, and folded his hands together—"Mother! dear, dear mother, bury me in the open fields—anywhere but in these dreadful streets. I should like to be where you can see my grave, but not in these close crowded streets; they have killed me: kiss me again, mother; put your arm round my neck——"

He fell back, and a strange expression stole upon his features; not of pain or suffering, but an indescribable fixing of every line and muscle.

The boy was dead.

The Streets—Morning

SCENES

CHAPTER I

THE STREETS—MORNING

THE appearance presented by the streets of London an hour before sunrise, on a summer's morning, is most striking even to the few whose unfortunate pursuits of pleasure, or scarcely less unfortunate pursuits of business, cause them to be well acquainted with the scene. There is an air of cold, solitary desolation about the noiseless streets which we are accustomed to see thronged at other times by a busy, eager crowd, and over the quiet, closely-shut buildings, which throughout the day are swarming with life and bustle, that is very impressive.

The last drunken man, who shall find his way home before sunlight, has just staggered heavily along, roaring out the burden of the drinking song of the previous night: the last houseless vagrant whom penury and police have left in the streets, has coiled up his chilly limbs in some paved corner, to dream of food and warmth. The drunken, the dissipated, and the wretched have disappeared; the more sober and orderly part of the population have not yet awakened to the labours of the day, and the stillness of death is over the streets; its very hue seems to be imparted to them, cold and lifeless as they look in the grey, sombre light of daybreak. The coach-stands in the larger thoroughfares are deserted; the night-houses are closed; and the chosen promenades of profligate misery are empty.

An occasional policeman may alone be seen at the street corners, listlessly gazing on the deserted prospect before him; and now and then a rakish-looking cat runs stealthily across the road and descends his own area with as much caution and slyness—bounding first on the water-butt, then on the dust-hole, and then alighting on the flag-stones—as if he

were conscious that his character depended on his gallantry
of the preceding night escaping public observation. A
partially opened bedroom-window here and there, bespeaks
the heat of the weather, and the uneasy slumbers of its
occupant ; and the dim scanty flicker of the rushlight, through
the window-blind, denotes the chamber of watching or sickness. With these few exceptions, the streets present no
signs of life, nor the houses of habitation.

An hour wears away ; the spires of the churches and roofs
of the principal buildings are faintly tinged with the light
of the rising sun ; and the streets, by almost imperceptible
degrees, begin to resume their bustle and animation. Market-
carts roll slowly along : the sleepy waggoner impatiently
urging on his tired horses, or vainly endeavouring to awaken
the boy, who, luxuriously stretched on the top of the fruit-
baskets, forgets,in happy oblivion, his long-cherished curiosity
to behold the wonders of London.

Rough, sleepy-looking animals of strange appearance,
something between ostlers and hackney-coachmen, begin to
take down the shutters of early public-houses ; and little deal
tables, with the ordinary preparations for a street breakfast,
make their appearance at the customary stations. Numbers
of men and women (principally the latter), carrying upon
their heads heavy baskets of fruit, toil down the park side
of Piccadilly, on their way to Covent Garden, and, following
each other in rapid succession, form a long straggling line
from thence to the turn of the road at Knightsbridge.

Here and there, a bricklayer's labourer, with the day's
dinner tied up in a handkerchief, walks briskly to his work,
and occasionally a little knot of three or four schoolboys on
a stolen bathing expedition rattle merrily over the pavement,
their boisterous mirth contrasting forcibly with the demeanour of the little sweep, who, having knocked and rung
till his arm aches, and being interdicted by a merciful legislature from endangering his lungs by calling out, sits
patiently down on the door-step, until the housemaid may
happen to awake.

Covent Garden market, and the avenues leading to it, are
thronged with carts of all sorts, sizes, and descriptions, from
the heavy lumbering waggon, with its four stout horses, to
the jingling costermonger's cart, with its consumptive
donkey. The pavement is already strewed with decayed
cabbage-leaves, broken hay-bands, and all the indescribable

litter of a vegetable market ; men are shouting, carts backing, horses neighing, boys fighting, basket-women talking, piemen expatiating on the excellence of their pastry, and donkeys braying. These and a hundred other sounds form a compound discordant enough to a Londoner's ears, and remarkably disagreeable to those of country gentlemen who are sleeping at the Hummums for the first time.

Another hour passes away, and the day begins in good earnest. The servant of all work, who, under the plea of sleeping very soundly, has utterly disregarded "Missis's" ringing for half an hour previously, is warned by Master (whom Missis has sent up in his drapery to the landing-place for that purpose), that it's half-past six, whereupon she awakes all of a sudden, with well-feigned astonishment, and goes down-stairs very sulkily, wishing, while she strikes a light, that the principle of spontaneous combustion would extend itself to coals and kitchen range. When the fire is lighted, she opens the street-door to take in the milk, when, by the most singular coincidence in the world, she discovers that the servant next door has just taken in her milk too, and that Mr. Todd's young man over the way is, by an equally extraordinary chance, taking down his master's shutters. The inevitable consequence is, that she just steps, milk-jug in hand, as far as next door, just to say "good morning" to Betsy Clark, and that Mr. Todd's young man just steps over the way to say "good morning" to both of 'em ; and as the aforesaid Mr. Todd's young man is almost as good-looking and fascinating as the baker himself, the conversation quickly becomes very interesting, and probably would become more so, if Betsy Clark's Missis, who always will be a-followin' her about, didn't give an angry tap at her bedroom window, on which Mr. Todd's young man tries to whistle coolly, as he goes back to his shop much faster than he came from it ; and the two girls run back to their respective places, and shut their street-doors with surprising softness, each of them poking their heads out of the front parlour window, a minute afterwards, however, ostensibly with the view of looking at the mail which just then passes by, but really for the purpose of catching another glimpse of Mr. Todd's young man, who being fond of mails, but more of females, takes a short look at the mails, and a long look at the girls, much to the satisfaction of all parties concerned.

The mail itself goes on to the coach-office in due course,

and the passengers who are going out by the early coach,
stare with astonishment at the passengers who are coming
in by the early coach, who look blue and dismal, and are
evidently under the influence of that odd feeling produced by
travelling, which makes the events of yesterday morning
seem as if they had happened at least six months ago, and
induces people to wonder with considerable gravity whether
the friends and relations they took leave of a fortnight before,
have altered much since they have left them.   The coach-
office is all alive, and the coaches which are just going out,
are surrounded by the usual crowd of Jews and nondescripts,
who seem to consider, Heaven knows why, that it is quite
impossible any man can mount a coach without requiring at
least sixpennyworth of oranges, a penknife, a pocket-book, a
last year's annual, a pencil-case, a piece of sponge, and a
small series of caricatures.

Half an hour more, and the sun darts his bright rays
cheerfully down the still half-empty streets, and shines with
sufficient force to rouse the dismal laziness of the apprentice,
who pauses every other minute from his task of sweeping
out the shop and watering the pavement in front of it, to
tell another apprentice similarly employed, how hot it will
be to-day, or to stand with his right hand shading his eyes,
and his left resting on the broom, gazing at the " Wonder,"
or the " Tally-ho," or the " Nimrod," or some other fast coach,
till it is out of sight, when he re-enters the shop, envying
the passengers on the outside of the fast coach, and thinking
of the old red brick house " down in the country," where he
went to school : the miseries of the milk and water, and
thick bread and scrapings, fading into nothing before the
pleasant recollection of the green field the boys used to play
in, and the green pond he was caned for presuming to fall
into, and other schoolboy associations.

Cabs, with trunks and band-boxes between the drivers'
legs and outside the apron, rattle briskly up and down the
streets on their way to the coach-offices or steam-packet
wharfs ; and the cab-drivers and hackney-coachmen who are
on the stand polish up the ornamental part of their dingy
vehicles—the former wondering how people can prefer
"them wild beast cariwans of homnibuses, to a riglar cab
with a fast trotter," and the latter admiring how people can
trust their necks into one of " them crazy cabs, when they
can have a 'spectable 'ackney cotche with a pair of 'orses

George Cruikshank

A Harmonic Meeting
(*p. 56*)

as von't run away with no vun ; " a consolation unquestionably founded on fact, seeing that a hackney-coach horse never
was known to run at all. "except," as the smart cabman
in front of the rank observes, "except one, and *he* run
back'ards."

The shops are now completely opened, and apprentices and
shopmen are busily engaged in cleaning and decking the
windows for the day. The bakers' shops in town are filled
with servants and children waiting for the drawing of the
first batch of rolls—an operation which was performed a full
hour ago in the suburbs: for the early clerk population of
Somers and Camden Towns, Islington, and Pentonville, are
fast pouring into the city, or directing their steps towards
Chancery Lane and the Inns of Court. Middle-aged men,
whose salaries have by no means increased in the same
proportion as their families, plod steadily along, apparently
with no object in view but the counting-house ; knowing by
sight almost everybody they meet or overtake, for they have
seen them every morning (Sundays excepted) during the last
twenty years, but speaking to no one. If they do happen to
overtake a personal acquaintance, they just exchange a hurried salutation, and keep walking on, either by his side or in
front of him, as his rate of walking may chance to be. As
to stopping to shake hands, or to take the friend's arm, they
seem to think that as it is not included in their salary, they
have no right to do it. Small office lads in large hats, who
are made men before they are boys, hurry along in pairs,
with their first coat carefully brushed, and the white trousers
of last Sunday plentifully besmeared with dust and ink. It
evidently requires a considerable mental struggle to avoid
investing part of the day's dinner-money in the purchase of
the stale tarts so temptingly exposed in dusty tins at the
pastry-cooks' doors ; but a consciousness of their own importance and the receipt of seven shillings a week, with the
prospect of an early rise to eight, comes to their aid, and
they accordingly put their hats a little more on one side, and
look under the bonnets of all the milliners' and staymakers'
apprentices they meet—poor girls !—the hardest worked,
the worst paid, and too often, the worst used class of the
community.

Eleven o'clock, and a new set of people fill the streets.
The goods in the shop-windows are invitingly arranged ; the
shopmen in their white neckerchiefs and spruce coats, look

as if they couldn't clean a window if their lives depended on it; the carts have disappeared from Covent Garden; the waggoners have returned, and the costermongers repaired to their ordinary "beats" in the suburbs; clerks are at their offices, and gigs, cabs, omnibuses, and saddle-horses, are conveying their masters to the same destination. The streets are thronged with a vast concourse of people, gay and shabby, rich and poor, idle and industrious; and we come to the heat, bustle, and activity of NooN.

CHAPTER II

THE STREETS—NIGHT

But the streets of London, to be beheld in the very height of their glory, should be seen on a dark, dull, murky winter's night, when there is just enough damp gently stealing down to make the pavement greasy, without cleansing it of any of its impurities; and when the heavy lazy mist, which hangs over every object, makes the gas-lamps look brighter, and the brilliantly-lighted shops more splendid, from the contrast they present to the darkness around. All the people who are at home on such a night as this, seem disposed to make themselves as snug and comfortable as possible; and the passengers in the streets have excellent reason to envy the fortunate individuals who are seated by their own firesides.

In the larger and better kind of streets, dining parlour curtains are closely drawn, kitchen fires blaze brightly up, and savoury steams of hot dinners salute the nostrils of the hungry wayfarer, as he plods wearily by the area railings. In the suburbs, the muffin boy rings his way down the little street, much more slowly than he is wont to do; for Mrs. Macklin, of No. 4, has no sooner opened her little street-door, and screamed out "Muffins!" with all her might, than Mrs. Walker, at No. 5, puts her head out of the parlour-window, and screams "Muffins!" too; and Mrs. Walker has scarcely got the words out of her lips, than Mrs. Peplow, over the way, lets loose Master Peplow, who darts down the street, with a velocity which nothing but buttered muffins in perspective could possibly inspire, and drags the boy back by main force, whereupon Mrs. Macklin and Mrs. Walker, just to save the boy trouble, and to say a few neighbourly words to Mrs. Peplow at the same time, run over the way and buy their muffins at Mrs. Peplow's door, when it appears from the voluntary statement of Mrs. Walker, that her "kittle's jist a-biling, and the cups and sarsers ready laid," and that, as it was such a wretched night out o' doors, she'd made up her mind to have a nice hot comfortable cup o' tea —a determination at which, by the most singular coincidence, the other two ladies had simultaneously arrived.

After a little conversation about the wretchedness of the weather and the merits of tea, with a digression relative to the viciousness of boys as a rule, and the amiability of Master Peplow as an exception, Mrs. Walker sees her husband coming down the street; and as he must want his tea, poor man. after his dirty walk from the Docks, she instantly runs across, muffins in hand, and Mrs. Macklin does the same, and after a few words to Mrs. Walker, they all pop into their little houses, and slam their little street-doors, which are not opened again for the remainder of the evening, except to the nine o'clock " beer," who comes round . with a lantern in front of his tray, and says, as he lends Mrs. Walker " Yesterday's 'Tiser," that he's blessed if he can hardly hold the pot, much less feel the paper, for it's one of the bitterest nights he ever felt, 'cept the night when the man was frozen to death in the Brick-field.

After a little prophetic conversation with the policeman at the street-corner, touching a probable change in the weather, and the setting-in of a hard frost, the nine o'clock beer returns to his master's house, and employs himself for the remainder of the evening, in assiduously stirring the tap-room fire, and deferentially taking part in the conversation of the worthies assembled round it.

The streets in the vicinity of the Marsh Gate and Victoria Theatre present an appearance of dirt and discomfort on such a night, which the groups who lounge about them in no degree tend to diminish. Even the little block-tin temple sacred to baked potatoes, surmounted by a splendid design in variegated lamps, looks less gay than usual ; and as to the kidney-pie stand, its glory has quite departed. The candle in the transparent lamp, manufactured of oil-paper, embellished with " characters," has been blown out fifty times, so the kidney-pie merchant, tired with running backwards and forwards to the next wine-vaults, to get a light, has given up the idea of illumination in despair, and the only signs of his " whereabout," are the bright sparks, of which a long irregular train is whirled down the street every time he opens his portable oven to hand a hot kidney-pie to a customer.

Flat-fish, oyster, and fruit vendors linger hopelessly in the kennel, in vain endeavouring to attract customers; and the ragged boys who usually disport themselves about the streets, stand crouched in little knots in some projecting doorway, or under the canvas blind of a cheesemonger's, where great flaring gas-lights, unshaded by any glass, display huge piles of bright red and pale yellow cheeses, mingled with little fivepenny dabs of dingy bacon, various tubs of weekly Dorset, and cloudy rolls of "best fresh."

Here they amuse themselves with theatrical converse, arising out of their last half-price visit to the Victoria gallery, admire the terrific combat, which is nightly encored, and expatiate on the inimitable manner in which Bill Thompson can "come the double monkey," or go through the mysterious involutions of a sailor's hornpipe.

It is nearly eleven o'clock, and the cold thin rain which has been drizzling so long, is beginning to pour down in good earnest; the baked-potato man has departed—the kidney-pie man has just walked away with his warehouse on his arm—the cheesemonger has drawn in his blind, and the boys have dispersed. The constant clicking of pattens on the slippy and uneven pavement, and the rustling of umbrellas, as the wind blows against the shop-windows, bear testimony to the inclemency of the night; and the policeman, with his oilskin cape buttoned closely round him, seems as he holds his hat on his head, and turns round to avoid the gust of wind and rain which drives against him at the street-corner, to be very far from congratulating himself on the prospect before him.

The little chandler's shop with the cracked bell behind the door, whose melancholy tinkling has been regulated by the demand for quarterns of sugar and half-ounces of coffee, is shutting up. The crowds which have been passing to and fro during the whole day, are rapidly dwindling away; and the noise of shouting and quarrelling which issues from the public-houses, is almost the only sound that breaks the melancholy stillness of the night.

There was another, but it has ceased. That wretched woman with the infant in her arms, round whose meagre form the remnant of her own scanty shawl is carefully wrapped, has been attempting to sing some popular ballad, in the hope of wringing a few pence from the compassionate passer-by. A brutal laugh at her weak voice is all she has gained.

The tears fall thick and fast down her own pale face ; the child is cold and hungry, and its low half-stifled wailing adds to the misery of its wretched mother, as she moans aloud, and sinks despairingly down, on a cold damp door-step.

Singing ! How few of those who pass such a miserable creature as this, think of the anguish of heart, the sinking of soul and spirit, which the very effort of singing produces. Bitter mockery ! Disease, neglect, and starvation, faintly articulating the words of the joyish ditty, that has enlivened your hours of feasting and merriment, God knows how often ! It is no subject of jeering. The weak tremulous voice tells a fearful tale of want and famishing ; and the feeble singer of this roaring song may turn away, only to die of cold and hunger.

One o'clock ! Parties returning from the different theatres foot it through the muddy streets ; cabs, hackney-coaches, carriages, and theatre omnibuses, roll swiftly by ; watermen with dim dirty lanterns in their hands, and large brass plates upon their breasts, who have been shouting and rushing about for the last two hours, retire to their watering-houses, to solace themselves with the creature comforts of pipes and purl ; the half-price pit and box frequenters of the theatres throng to the different houses of refreshment ; and chops, kidneys, rabbits, oysters, stout, cigars, and "goes" innumerable, are served up amidst a noise and confusion of smoking, running, knife-clattering, and waiter-chattering, perfectly indescribable.

The more musical portion of the play-going community betake themselves to some harmonic meeting. As a matter of curiosity let us follow them thither for a few moments.

In a lofty room of spacious dimensions, are seated some eighty or a hundred guests knocking little pewter measures on the tables, and hammering away, with the handles of their knives, as if they were so many trunk-makers. They are applauding a glee, which has just been executed by the three "professional gentlemen" at the top of the centre table, one of whom is in the chair—the little pompous man with the bald head just emerging from the collar of his green coat. The others are seated on either side of him—the stout man with the small voice, and the thin-faced dark man in black. The little man in the chair is a most amusing personage,— *such* condescending grandeur, and *such* a voice !

Scotland Yard
(*p. 64*)

"Bass!" as the young gentleman near us with the blue stock forcibly remarks to his companion, "bass! I b'lieve you; he can go down lower than any man : so low sometimes that you can't hear him." And so he does. To hear him growling away, gradually lower and lower down, till he can't get back again, is the most delightful thing in the world, and it is quite impossible to witness unmoved the impressive solemnity with which he pours forth his soul in "My 'art's in the 'ighlands," or "The brave old Hoak." The stout man is also addicted to sentimentality, and warbles, "Fly, fly from the world, my Bessy, with me," or some such song, with lady-like sweetness, and in the most seductive tones imaginable.

"Pray give your orders, gen'l'm'n—pray give your orders," says the pale-faced man with the red head ; and demands for "goes" of gin and "goes" of brandy, and pints of stout. and cigars of peculiar mildness, are vociferously made from all parts of the room. The "professional gentlemen" are in the very height of their glory, and bestow condescending nods, or even a word or two of recognition, on the better-known frequenters of the room, in the most bland and patronising manner possible.

That little round-faced man, with the small brown surtout. white stockings and shoes, is in the comic line; the mixed air of self-denial, and mental consciousness of his own powers. with which he acknowledges the call of the chair, is particularly gratifying. "Gen'l'men,"says the little pompous man, accompanying the word with a knock of the president's hammer on the table—"Gen'l'men, allow me to claim your attention —our friend, Mr. Smuggins, will oblige."—"Bravo!" shout the company ; and Smuggins, after a considerable quantity of coughing by way of symphony, and a most facetious sniff or two, which afford general delight, sings a comic song. with a fal-de-ral—tol-de-ral chorus at the end of every verse. much longer than the verse itself. It is received with unbounded applause, and after some aspiring genius has volunteered a recitation, and failed dismally therein, the little pompous man gives another knock, and says "Gen'l'men, we will attempt a glee, if you please." This announcement calls forth tumultuous applause, and the more energetic spirits express the unqualified approbation it affords them, by knocking one or two stout glasses off their legs—a humorous device ; but one which frequently occasions some slight altercation when the form of paying the damage is proposed to be gone through by the waiter.

Scenes like these are continued until three or four o'clock in the morning ; and even when they close, fresh ones open to the inquisitive novice. But as a description of all of them, however slight, would require a volume, the contents of which, however instructive, would be by no means pleasing. we make our bow, and drop the curtain.

CHAPTER III

SHOPS AND THEIR TENANTS

WHAT inexhaustible food for speculation do the streets of London afford! We never were able to agree with Sterne in pitying the man who could travel from Dan to Beersheba, and say that all was barren; we have not the slightest commiseration for the man who can take up his hat and stick, and walk from Covent Garden to St. Paul's Churchyard, and back into the bargain, without deriving some amusement —we had almost said instruction—from his perambulation. And yet there are such beings: we meet them every day. Large black stocks and light waistcoats, jet canes and discontented countenances, are the characteristics of the race; other people brush quickly by you, steadily plodding on to business, or cheerfully running after pleasure. These men linger listlessly past, looking as happy and animated as a policeman on duty. Nothing seems to make an impression on their minds: nothing short of being knocked down by a porter, or run over by a cab, will disturb their equanimity. You will meet them on a fine day in any of the leading thoroughfares: peep through the window of a west-end cigar shop in the evening, if you can manage to get a glimpse between the blue curtains which intercept the vulgar gaze, and you see them in their only enjoyment of existence. There they are lounging about, on round tubs and pipe boxes, in all the dignity of whiskers and gilt watch-guards; whispering soft nothings to the young lady in amber, with the large ear-rings, who, as she sits behind the counter in a blaze of adoration and gas-light, is the admiration of all the female servants in the neighbourhood, and the envy of every milliner's apprentice within two miles round.

One of our principal amusements is to watch the gradual progress—the rise or fall—of particular shops. We have formed an intimate acquaintance with several, in different

D

parts of town, and are perfectly acquainted with their whole
history. We could name off-hand, twenty at least, which
we are quite sure have paid no taxes for the last six years.
They are never inhabited for more than two months consecutively, and, we verily believe, have witnessed every retail trade
in the directory.

There is one, whose history is a sample of the rest, in
whose fate we have taken especial interest, having had the
pleasure of knowing it ever since it has been a shop. It is
on the Surrey side of the water—a little distance beyond the
Marsh Gate. It was originally a substantial, good-looking
private house enough ; the landlord got into difficulties, the
house got into Chancery, the tenant went away, and the
house went to ruin. At this period our acquaintance with
it commenced ; the paint was all worn off ; the windows were
broken, the area was green with neglect and the over-
flowings of the water-butt ; the butt itself was without a
lid, and the street-door was the very picture of misery.
The chief pastime of the children in the vicinity had been
to assemble in a body on the steps, and to take it in turn
to knock loud double knocks at the door, to the great
satisfaction of the neighbours generally, and especially of
the nervous old lady next door but one. Numerous complaints were made, and several small basins of water discharged over the offenders, but without effect. In this
state of things, the marine-store dealer at the corner of the
street, in the most obliging manner took the knocker off,
and sold it: and the unfortunate house looked more wretched
than ever.

We deserted our friend for a few weeks. What was our
surprise, on our return, to find no trace of its existence ! In
its place was a handsome shop, fast approaching to a state
of completion, and on the shutters were large bills, informing
the public that it would shortly be opened with "an extensive stock of linen-drapery and haberdashery." It opened
in due course ; there was the name of the proprietor "and
Co." in gilt letters, almost too dazzling to look at. Such
ribbons and shawls ! and two such elegant young men
behind the counter, each in a clean collar and white neckcloth, like the lover in a farce. As to the proprietor, he did
nothing but walk up and down the shop, and hand seats to
the ladies, and hold important conversations with the handsomest of the young men, who was shrewdly suspected by

the neighbours to be the "Co." We saw all this with sorrow; we felt a fatal presentiment that the shop was doomed—and so it was. Its decay was slow, but sure. Tickets gradually appeared in the windows; then rolls of flannel, with labels on them, were stuck outside the door; then a bill was pasted on the street-door, intimating that the first floor was to let *un*furnished ; then one of the young men disappeared altogether, and the other took to a black neckerchief, and the proprietor took to drinking. The shop became dirty, broken panes of glass remained unmended, and the stock disappeared piecemeal. At last the company's man came to cut off the water, and then the linen-draper cut off himself, leaving the landlord his compliments and the key.

The next occupant was a fancy stationer. The shop was more modestly painted than before, still it was neat; but somehow we always thought, as we passed, that it looked like a poor and struggling concern. We wished the man well, but we trembled for his success. He was a widower evidently, and had employment elsewhere, for he passed us every morning on his road to the city. The business was carried on by his eldest daughter. Poor girl! she needed no assistance. We occasionally caught a glimpse of two or three children, in mourning like herself, as they sat in the little parlour behind the shop; and we never passed at night without seeing the eldest girl at work, either for them, or in making some elegant little trifle for sale. We often thought, as her pale face looked more sad and pensive in the dim candle-light, that if those thoughtless females who interfere with the miserable market of poor creatures such as these knew but one-half of the misery they suffer, and the bitter privations they endure, in their honourable attempts to earn a scanty subsistence, they would, perhaps, resign even opportunities for the gratification of vanity, and an immodest love of self-display, rather than drive them to a last dreadful resource, which it would shock the delicate feelings of these *charitable* ladies to hear named.

But we are forgetting the shop. Well, we continued to watch it, and every day showed too clearly the increasing poverty of its inmates. The children were clean, it is true, but their clothes were threadbare and shabby; no tenant had been procured for the upper part of the house, from the letting of which, a portion of the means of paying the rent was to have been derived, and a slow, wasting consumption prevented the eldest girl from continuing her exertions. Quarter-day arrived. The landlord had suffered from the extravagance of his last tenant, and he had no compassion for the struggles of his successor; he put in an execution. As we passed one morning, the broker's men were removing the little furniture there was in the house, and a newly-posted bill informed us it was again "To Let." What became of the last tenant we never could learn; we believe the girl is past all suffering, and beyond all sorrow. God help her! We hope she is.

We were somewhat curious to ascertain what would be the next stage—for that the place had no chance of succeeding now, was perfectly clear. The bill was soon taken down, and some alterations were being made in the interior of the shop. We were in a fever of expectation; we exhausted conjecture—we imagined all possible trades, none of which were perfectly reconcilable with our idea of the gradual decay of the tenement. It opened, and we wondered why we had not guessed at the real state of the case before. The shop—not a large one at the best of times—had been converted into two: one was a bonnet-shape maker's, the other was opened by a tobacconist, who also dealt in walking-sticks and Sunday newspapers; the two were separated by a thin partition, covered with tawdry striped paper.

The tobacconist remained in possession longer than any tenant within our recollection. He was a red-faced, impudent, good-for-nothing dog, evidently accustomed to take things as they came, and to make the best of a bad job. He sold as many cigars as he could, and smoked the rest. He occupied the shop as long as he could make peace with the landlord, and when he could no longer live in quiet, he very coolly locked the door, and bolted himself. From this period, the two little dens have undergone innumerable changes. The tobacconist was succeeded by a theatrical hair-dresser, who ornamented the window with a great variety of "characters," and terrific combats. The bonnet-shape maker gave place to a green-grocer, and the histrionic barber was succeeded, in his turn, by a tailor. So numerous have been the changes, that we have of late done little more than mark the peculiar but certain indications of a house being poorly inhabited. It has been progressing by almost imperceptible degrees. The occupiers of the shops have gradually given up room after room, until they have only reserved the little parlour for themselves. First there appeared a brass plate on the private door, with "Ladies' School" legibly engraved thereon; shortly afterwards we observed a second brass plate, then a bell, and then another bell.

When we paused in front of our old friend, and observed these signs of poverty, which are not to be mistaken, we thought as we turned away, that the house had attained its lowest pitch of degradation. We were wrong. When we last passed it, a "dairy" was established in the area, and a party of melancholy-looking fowls were amusing themselves by running in at the front door, and out at the back one.

CHAPTER IV

SCOTLAND YARD

SCOTLAND YARD is a small—a very small—tract of land, bounded on one side by the river Thames, on the other by the gardens of Northumberland House: abutting at one end on the bottom of Northumberland Street, at the other on the back of Whitehall Place. When this territory was first accidentally discovered by a country gentleman who lost his way in the Strand, some years ago, the original settlers were found to be a tailor, a publican, two eating-house keepers, and a fruit-pie maker; and it was also found to contain a race of strong and bulky men, who repaired to the wharfs in Scotland Yard regularly every morning, about five or six o'clock, to fill heavy waggons with coal, with which they proceeded to distant places up the country, and supplied the inhabitants with fuel. When they had emptied their waggons, they again returned for a fresh supply; and this trade was continued throughout the year.

As the settlers derived their subsistence from ministering to the wants of these primitive traders, the articles exposed for sale, and the places where they were sold, bore strong outward marks of being expressly adapted to their tastes and wishes. The tailor displayed in his window a Lilliputian pair of leather gaiters, and a diminutive round frock, while each doorpost was appropriately garnished with a model of a coal-sack. The two eating-house keepers exhibited joints of a magnitude, and puddings of a solidity, which coalheavers alone could appreciate; and the fruit-pie maker displayed on his well-scrubbed window-board large white compositions of flour and dripping, ornamented with pink stains, giving rich promise of the fruit within, which made their huge mouths water, as they lingered past.

But the choicest spot in all Scotland Yard was the old public-house in the corner. Here, in a dark wainscoted room of ancient appearance, cheered by the glow of a mighty fire, and decorated with an enormous clock, whereof the face was white, and the figures black, sat the lusty coal-heavers, quaffing large draughts of Barclay's best, and puffing forth volumes of smoke, which wreathed heavily above their heads, and involved the room in a thick dark cloud. From this apartment might their voices be heard on a winter's night, penetrating to the very bank of the river, as they shouted out some sturdy chorus, or roared forth the burden of a popular song; dwelling upon the last few words with a strength and length of emphasis which made the very roof tremble above them.

Here, too, would they tell old legends of what the Thames was in ancient times, when the Patent Shot Manufactory wasn't built, and Waterloo Bridge had never been thought of; and then they would shake their heads with portentous looks, to the deep edification of the rising generation of heavers, who crowded round them, and wondered where all this would end; whereat the tailor would take his pipe solemnly from his mouth, and say, how that he hoped it might end well, but he very much doubted whether it would or not, and couldn't rightly tell what to make of it—a mysterious expression of opinion, delivered with a semi-prophetic air, which never failed to elicit the fullest concurrence of the assembled company; and so they would go on drinking and wondering till ten o'clock came, and with it the tailor's wife to fetch him home, when the little party broke up, to meet again in the same room, and say and do precisely the same things, on the following evening at the same hour.

About this time the barges that came up the river began to bring vague rumours to Scotland Yard of somebody in the city having been heard to say, that the Lord Mayor had threatened in so many words to pull down the old London Bridge, and build up a new one. At first these rumours were disregarded as idle tales, wholly destitute of foundation, for nobody in Scotland Yard doubted that if the Lord Mayor contemplated any such dark design, he would just be clapped up in the Tower for a week or two, and then killed off for high treason.

By degrees, however, the reports grew stronger, and more frequent, and at last a barge, laden with numerous chaldrons of the best Wallsend, brought up the positive intelligence that several of the arches of the old bridge were stopped, and that preparations were actually in progress for constructing the new one. What an excitement was visible in the old tap-room on that memorable night! Each man looked into his neighbour's face, pale with alarm and astonishment, and read therein an echo of the sentiments which filled his own breast. The oldest heaver present proved to demonstration, that the moment the piers were removed, all the water in the Thames would run clean off, and leave a dry gully in its place. What was to become of the coal-barges—of the trade of Scotland Yard—of the very existence of its population? The tailor shook his head more sagely than usual, and grimly pointing to a knife on the table, bid them wait and see what happened. He said nothing—not he; but if the Lord Mayor didn't fall a victim to popular indignation, why he would be rather astonished; that was all.

They did wait; barge after barge arrived, and still no tidings of the assassination of the Lord Mayor. The first stone was laid: it was done by a Duke—the King's brother. Years passed away, and the bridge was opened by the King himself. In course of time the piers were removed; and when the people in Scotland Yard got up next morning in the confident expectation of being able to step over to Pedlar's Acre without wetting the soles of their shoes, they found to their unspeakable astonishment that the water was just where it used to be.

A result so different from that which they had anticipated from this first improvement, produced its full effect upon the inhabitants of Scotland Yard. One of the eating-house keepers began to court public opinion, and to look for customers among a new class of people. He covered his little dining-tables with white cloths, and got a painter's apprentice to inscribe something about hot joints from twelve to two, in one of the little panes of his shop-window. Improvement began to march with rapid strides to the very threshold of Scotland Yard. A new market sprung up at Hungerford, and the Police Commissioners established their office in Whitehall Place. The traffic in Scotland Yard increased; fresh Members were added to the House of Commons, the Metropolitan Representatives found it a near cut, and many other foot passengers followed their example.

We marked the advance of civilisation, and beheld it with a sigh. The eating-house keeper who manfully resisted the innovation of table-cloths, was losing ground every day, as his opponent gained it, and a deadly feud sprung up between them. The genteel one no longer took his evening's pint in Scotland Yard, but drank gin and water at a "parlour" in Parliament Street. The fruit-pie maker still continued to visit the old room, but he took to smoking cigars, and began to call himself a pastrycook, and to read the papers. The old heavers still assembled round the ancient fireplace, but their talk was mournful: and the loud song and the joyous shout were heard no more.

And what is Scotland Yard now? How have its old customs changed; and how has the ancient simplicity of its inhabitants faded away! The old tottering public-house is converted into a spacious and lofty "wine-vaults:" gold leaf has been used in the construction of the letters which emblazon its exterior, and the poet's art has been called into requisition, to intimate that if you drink a certain description of ale, you must hold fast by the rail. The tailor exhibits in his window the pattern of a foreign-looking brown surtout, with silk buttons, a fur collar, and fur cuffs. He wears a stripe down the outside of each leg of his trousers: and we have detected his assistants (for he has assistants now) in the act of sitting on the shop-board in the same uniform.

At the other end of the little row of houses a bootmaker has established himself in a brick box, with the additional innovation of a first floor; and here he exposes for sale, boots—real Wellington boots—an article which a few years ago, none of the original inhabitants had ever seen or heard of. It was but the other day, that a dressmaker opened another little box in the middle of the row; and when we thought that the spirit of change could produce no alteration beyond that, a jeweller appeared, and not content with exposing gilt rings and copper bracelets out of number, put up an announcement, which still sticks in his window, that "ladies' ears may be pierced within." The dressmaker employs a young lady who wears pockets in her apron; and the tailor informs the public that gentlemen may have their own materials made up.

Amidst all this change, and restlessness, and innovation, there remains but one old man, who seems to mourn the downfall of this ancient place. He holds no converse with human kind, but, seated on a wooden bench at the angle of the wall which fronts the crossing from Whitehall Place, watches in silence the gambols of his sleek and well-fed dogs.

He is the presiding genius of Scotland Yard. Years and years have rolled over his head; but in fine weather or in foul, hot or cold, wet or dry, hail, rain, or snow, he is still in his accustomed spot. Misery and want are depicted in his countenance; his form is bent by age, his head is grey with length of trial, but there he sits from day to day, brooding over the past; and thither he will continue to drag his feeble limbs, until his eyes have closed upon Scotland Yard, and upon the world together.

A few years hence, and the antiquary of another generation looking into some mouldy record of the strife and passions that agitated the world in these times, may glance his eye over the pages we have just filled: and not all his knowledge of the history of the past, not all his black-letter lore, or his skill in book-collecting, not all the dry studies of a long life, or the dusty volumes that have cost him a fortune, may help him to the whereabouts, either of Scotland Yard or of any one of the landmarks we have mentioned in describing it.

Seven Dials

CHAPTER V

SEVEN DIALS

WE have always been of opinion that if Tom King and the
Frenchman had not immortalised Seven Dials, Seven Dials
would have immortalised itself. Seven Dials! the region of
song and poetry—first effusions, and last dying speeches:
hallowed by the names of Catnach and of Pitts—names that
will entwine themselves with costermongers and barrel-
organs, when penny magazines shall have superseded penny
yards of song, and capital punishment be unknown!

Look at the construction of the place. The gordian knot
was all very well in its way : so was the maze of Hampton
Court: so is the maze at the Beulah Spa: so were the ties of
stiff white neckcloths, when the difficulty of getting one on
was only to be equalled by the apparent impossibility of ever
getting it off again. But what involutions can compare
with those of Seven Dials? Where is there such another
maze of streets, courts, lanes, and alleys? Where such a
pure mixture of Englishmen and Irishmen, as in this complicated part of London? We boldly aver that we doubt
the veracity of the legend to which we have adverted. We
can suppose a man rash enough to inquire at random—at a
house with lodgers too—for a Mr. Thompson, with all but
the certainty before his eyes of finding at least two or three
Thompsons in any house of moderate dimensions; but a
Frenchman—a Frenchman in Seven Dials! Pooh! He was
an Irishman. Tom King's education had been neglected in
his infancy, and as he couldn't understand half the man said,
he took it for granted he was talking French.

The stranger who finds himself in "The Dials" for the
first time, and stands Belzoni-like, at the entrance of seven
obscure passages, uncertain which to take, will see enough
around him to keep his curiosity and attention awake for no
inconsiderable time. From the irregular square into which
he has plunged, the streets and courts dart in all directions,

until they are lost in the unwholesome vapour which hangs over the house-tops, and renders the dirty perspective uncertain and confined; and lounging at every corner, as if they came there to take a few gasps of such fresh air as has found its way so far, but is too much exhausted already, to be enabled to force itself into the narrow alleys around, are groups of people, whose appearance and dwellings would fill any mind but a regular Londoner's with astonishment.

On one side, a little crowd has collected round a couple of ladies, who having imbibed the contents of various "three-outs" of gin and bitters in the course of the morning, have at length differed on some point of domestic arrangement, and are on the eve of settling the quarrel satisfactorily, by an appeal to blows, greatly to the interest of other ladies who live in the same house, and tenements adjoining, and who are all partisans on one side or other.

"Vy don't you pitch into her, Sarah?" exclaims one half-dressed matron by way of encouragement. "Vy don't you? if *my* 'usband had treated her with a drain last night, unbeknown to me, I'd tear her precious eyes out—a wixen!"

"What's the matter, ma'am?" inquires another old woman, who has just bustled up to the spot.

"Matter!" replies the first speaker, talking *at* the obnoxious combatant, "matter! Here's poor dear Mrs. Sulliwin, as has five blessed children of her own, can't go out a-charing for one arternoon, but what hussies must be a-comin', and 'ticing avay her oun' 'usband, as she's been married to twelve year come next Easter Monday, for I see the certificate ven I vas a-drinkin' a cup o' tea vith her, only the werry last blessed Ven'sday as ever vas sent. I 'appen'd to say promiscuously, 'Mrs. Sulliwin,' says I——"

"What do you mean by hussies?" interrupts a champion of the other party, who has evinced a strong inclination throughout to get up a branch fight on her own account ("Hooroar," ejaculates a pot-boy in parenthesis, "put the kye-bosk on her, Mary!"), "What do you mean by hussies?" reiterates the champion.

"Niver mind," replies the opposition expressively, "niver mind; *you* go home, and, ven you're quite sober, mend your stockings."

This somewhat personal allusion, not only to the lady's habits of intemperance, but also to the state of her wardrobe, rouses her utmost ire, and she accordingly complies with the

urgent request of the bystanders to "pitch in," with considerable alacrity. The scuffle became general, and terminates, in minor play-bill phraseology, with "arrival of
the policeman, interior of the station-house, and impressive
dénouement."

In addition to the numerous groups who are idling about
the gin-shops and squabbling in the centre of the road, every
post in the open space has its occupant, who leans against it
for hours, with listless perseverance. It is odd enough that
one class of men in London appear to have no enjoyment
beyond leaning against posts. We never saw a regular
bricklayer's labourer take any other recreation, fighting
excepted. Pass through St. Giles's in the evening of a
week-day, there they are in their fustian dresses, spotted
with brick-dust and whitewash, leaning against posts.
Walk through Seven Dials on Sunday morning : there they
are again, drab or light corduroy trousers, bluchor boots,
blue coats, and great yellow waistcoats, leaning against
posts. The idea of a man dressing himself in his best
clothes, to lean against a post all day!

The peculiar character of these streets, and the close
resemblance each one bears to its neighbour, by no means
tends to decrease the bewilderment in which the unexperi-
enced wayfarer through " the Dials " finds himself involved.
He traverses streets of dirty, straggling houses, with now
and then an unexpected court composed of buildings as ill-
proportioned and deformed as the half-naked children that
wallow in the kennels. Here and there, a little dark
chandler's shop, with a cracked bell hung up behind the
door to announce the entrance of a customer, or betray the
presence of some young gentleman in whom a passion for
shop tills has developed itself at an early age : others, as if
for support, against some handsome lofty building, which
usurps the place of a low dingy public-house ; long rows of
broken and patched windows expose plants that may have
flourished when " the Dials " were built, in vessels as dirty
as " the Dials " themselves ; and shops for the purchase of
rags, bones, old iron, and kitchen-stuff, vie in cleanliness
with the bird-fanciers' and rabbit-dealers', which one might
fancy so many arks, but for the irresistible conviction that
no bird in its proper senses, who was permitted to leave one
of them, would ever come back again. Brokers' shops,
which would seem to have been established by humane

individuals, as refuges for destitute bugs, interspersed with announcements of day-schools, penny theatres, petition-writers, mangles, and music for balls or routs, complete the "still life" of the subject ; and dirty men, filthy women, squalid children, fluttering shuttlecocks, noisy battledores, reeking pipes, bad fruit, more than doubtful oysters, at-tenuated cats, depressed dogs, and anatomical fowls, are its cheerful accompaniments.

If the external appearance of the houses, or a glance at their inhabitants, presents but few attractions, a closer ac-quaintance with either is little calculated to alter one's first impression. Every room has its separate tenant, and every tenant is, by the same mysterious dispensation which causes a country curate to "increase and multiply" most mar-vellously, generally the head of a numerous family.

The man in the shop, perhaps, is in the baked "jemmy" line, or the fire-wood and hearth-stone line, or any other line which requires a floating capital of eighteen-pence or thereabouts : and he and his family live in the shop, and the small back parlour behind it. Then there is an Irish labourer and *his* family in the back kitchen, and a jobbing man—carpet-beater and so forth—with *his* family in the front one. In the front one-pair, there's another man with another wife and family, and in the back one-pair, there's "a young 'oman as takes in tambour-work, and dresses quite genteel," who talks a good deal about "my friend," and can't "a-bear anything low." The second floor front, and the rest of the lodgers, are just a second edition of the people below, except a shabby-genteel man in the back attic, who has his half-pint of coffee every morning from the coffee-shop next door but one, which boasts a little front den called a coffee-room, with a fireplace, over which is an inscription, politely requesting that, "to prevent mistakes," customers will "please to pay on delivery." The shabby-genteel man is an object of some mystery, but as he leads a life of seclusion, and never was known to buy anything beyond an occasional pen, except half-pints of coffee, penny loaves, and ha'porths of ink, his fellow-lodgers very naturally suppose him to be an author ; and rumours are current in the Dials, that he writes poems for Mr. Warren.

Now anybody who passed through the Dials on a hot summer's evening, and saw the different women of the house gossiping on the steps. would be apt to think that all was harmony among them, and that a more primitive set of people than the native Diallers could not be imagined. Alas! the man in the shop ill-treats his family; the carpet-beater extends his professional pursuits to his wife; the one-pair front has an undying feud with the two-pair front, in consequence of the two-pair front persisting in dancing over his (the one-pair front's) head, when he and his family have retired for the night; the two-pair back *will* interfere with the front kitchen's children; the Irishman comes home drunk every other night, and attacks everybody; and the one-pair back screams at everything. Animosities spring up between floor and floor; the very cellar asserts his equality. Mrs. A. "smacks" Mrs. B.'s child for "making faces." Mrs. B. forthwith throws cold water over Mrs. A.'s child for "calling names." The husbands are embroiled—the quarrel becomes general—an assault is the consequence, and a police-officer the result.

CHAPTER VI

MEDITATIONS IN MONMOUTH STREET

WE have always entertained a particular attachment towards Monmouth Street, as the only true and real emporium for second-hand wearing apparel. Monmouth Street is venerable from its antiquity, and respectable from its usefulness. Holywell Street we despise; the red-headed and red-whiskered Jews who forcibly haul you into their squalid houses, and thrust you into a suit of clothes, whether you will or not, we detest.

The inhabitants of Monmouth Street are a distinct class; a peaceable and retiring race, who immure themselves for the most part in deep cellars, or small back parlours, and who seldom come forth into the world, except in the dusk and coolness of the evening, when they may be seen seated, in chairs on the pavement, smoking their pipes, or watching the gambols of their engaging children as they revel in the gutter, a happy troop of infantine scavengers. Their countenances bear a thoughtful and a dirty cast, certain indications of their love of traffic; and their habitations are distinguished by that disregard of outward appearance and neglect of personal comfort, so common among people who are constantly immersed in profound speculations, and deeply engaged in sedentary pursuits.

We have hinted at the antiquity of our favourite spot. "A Monmouth Street laced coat" was a by-word a century ago; and still we find Monmouth Street the same. Pilot great-coats with wooden buttons have usurped the place of the ponderous laced coats with full skirts; embroidered waistcoats with large flaps have yielded to double-breasted checks with roll-collars; and three-cornered hats of quaint appearance have given place to the low crowns and broad brims of the coachman school; but it is the times that have changed, not Monmouth Street. Through every alteration and every change, Monmouth Street has still remained the

Monmouth Street

burial-place of the fashions ; and such, to judge from all present appearances, it will remain until there are no more fashions to bury.

We love to walk among these extensive groves of the illustrious dead, and to indulge in the speculations to which they give rise ; now fitting a deceased coat, then a dead pair of trousers, and anon the mortal remains of a gaudy waist-coat, upon some being of our own conjuring up, and endeavouring, from the shape and fashion of the garment itself, to bring its former owner before our mind's eye. We have gone on speculating in this way, until whole rows of coats have started from their pegs, and buttoned up, of their own accord, round the waists of imaginary wearers ; lines of trousers have jumped down to meet them ; waistcoats have almost burst with anxiety to put themselves on ; and half an acre of shoes have suddenly found feet to fit them, and gone stumping down the street with a noise which has fairly awakened us from our pleasant reverie, and driven us slowly away, with a bewildered stare, an object of astonishment to the good people of Monmouth Street, and of no slight suspicion to the policemen at the opposite street corner.

We were occupied in this manner the other day, endeavouring to fit a pair of lace-up half-boots on an ideal personage, for whom, to say the truth, they were full a couple of sizes too small, when our eyes happened to alight on a few suits of clothes ranged outside a shop-window, which it immediately struck us, must at different periods have all belonged to, and been worn by, the same individual, and had now, by one of those strange conjunctions of circumstances which will occur sometimes, come to be exposed together for sale in the same shop. The idea seemed a fantastic one, and we looked at the clothes again with a firm determination not to be easily led away. No, we were right ; the more we looked, the more we were convinced of the accuracy of our previous impression. There was the man's whole life written as legibly on those clothes, as if we had his autobiography engrossed on parchment before us.

The first was a patched and much-soiled skeleton suit; one of those straight blue cloth cases in which small boys used to be confined, before belts and tunics had come in, and old notions had gone out: an ingenious contrivance for displaying the full symmetry of a boy's figure, by fastening him into a very tight jacket, with an ornamental row of buttons over each shoulder, and then buttoning his trousers over it, so as to give his legs the appearance of being hooked on, just under the armpits. This was the boy's dress. It had belonged to a town boy, we could see; there was a shortness about the legs and arms of the suit; and a bagging at the knees, peculiar to the rising youth of London streets. A small day-school he had been at, evidently. If it had been a regular boys' school they wouldn't have let him play on the floor so much, and rub his knees so white. He had an indulgent mother too, and plenty of halfpence, as the numerous smears of some sticky substance about the pockets, and just below the chin, which even the salesman's skill could not succeed in disguising, sufficiently betokened. They were decent people, but not overburdened with riches, or he would not have so far outgrown the suit when he passed into those corduroys with the round jacket; in which he went to a boys' school, however, and learnt to write—and in ink of pretty tolerable blackness, too, if the place where he used to wipe his pen might be taken as evidence.

A black suit and the jacket changed into a diminutive coat. His father had died, and the mother had got the boy a message-lad's place in some office. A long-worn suit that one; rusty and threadbare before it was laid aside, but clean and free from soil to the last. Poor woman! We could imagine her assumed cheerfulness over the scanty meal, and the refusal of her own small portion, that her hungry boy might have enough. Her constant anxiety for his welfare, her pride in his growth mingled sometimes with the thought, almost too acute to bear, that as he grew to be a man his old affection might cool, old kindnesses fade from his mind, and old promises be forgotten—the sharp pain that even then a careless word or a cold look would give her—all crowded on our thoughts as vividly as if the very scene were passing before us.

These things happen every hour, and we all know it; and yet we felt as much sorrow when we saw, or fancied we saw—it makes no difference which—the change that began to take place now, as if we had just conceived the bare possibility of such a thing for the first time. The next suit, smart but slovenly; meant to be gay, and yet not half so decent as the threadbare apparel; redolent of the idle lounge, and the blackguard companions, told us, we thought, that the widow's comfort had rapidly faded away. We could imagine that coat—imagine ! we could see it ; we *had* seen it a hundred times—sauntering in company with three or four other coats of the same cut, about some place of profligate resort at night.

We dressed, from the same shop-window in an instant, half a dozen boys of from fifteen to twenty ; and putting cigars into their mouths, and their hands into their pockets, watched them as they sauntered down the street, and lingered at the corner, with the obscene jest, and the oft-repeated oath. We never lost sight of them, till they had cocked their hats a little more on one side, and swaggered into the public-house ; and then we entered the desolate home, where the mother sat late in the night, alone ; we watched her, as she paced the room in feverish anxiety, and every now and then opened the door, looked wistfully into the dark and empty street, and again returned, to be again and again disappointed. We beheld the look of patience with which she bore the brutish threat, nay, even the drunken blow ; and we heard the agony of tears that gushed from her very heart, as she sank upon her knees in her solitary and wretched apartment.

A long period had elapsed, and a greater change had taken place, by the time of casting off the suit that hung above. It was that of a stout, broad-shouldered, sturdy-chested man; and we knew at once, as anybody would, who glanced at that broad-skirted green coat, with the large metal buttons, that its wearer seldom walked forth without a dog at his heels, and some idle ruffian, the very counterpart of him-self, at his side. The vices of the boy had grown with the man, and we fancied his home then—if such a place deserve the name.

We saw the bare and miserable room, destitute of furniture, crowded with his wife and children, pale, hungry, and emaciated ; the man cursing their lamentations, staggering to the tap-room, from whence he had just returned, followed by his wife and a sickly infant, clamouring for bread ; and heard the street-wrangle and noisy recrimination that his striking her occasioned. And then imagination led us to some metropolitan workhouse, situated in the midst of crowded streets and alleys, filled with noxious vapours, and ringing with boisterous cries, where an old and feeble woman, imploring pardon for her son, lay dying in a close dark room, with no child to clasp her hand, and no pure air from heaven to fan her brow. A stranger closed the eyes that settled into a cold unmeaning glare, and strange ears received the words that murmured from the white and half-closed lips.

A coarse round frock, with a worn cotton neckerchief, and other articles of clothing of the commonest description, completed the history. A prison, and the sentence—banishment or the gallows. What would the man have given then, to be once again the contented humble drudge of his boyish years; to have been restored to life, but for a week, a day, an hour, a minute, only for so long a time as would enable him to say one word of passionate regret to, and hear one sound of heartfelt forgiveness from, the cold and ghastly form that lay rotting in the pauper's grave! The children wild in the streets, the mother a destitute widow; both deeply tainted with the deep disgrace of the husband and father's name, and impelled by sheer necessity, down the precipice that had led him to a lingering death, possibly of many years' duration, thousands of miles away. We had no clue to the end of the tale; but it was easy to guess its termination.

We took a step or two further on, and by way of restoring the naturally cheerful tone of our thoughts, began fitting visionary feet and legs into a cellar-board full of boots and shoes, with a speed and accuracy that would have astonished the most expert artist in leather, living. There was one pair of boots in particular—a jolly, good-tempered, hearty-looking, pair of tops, that excited our warmest regard; and we had got a fine, red-faced, jovial fellow of a market-gardener into them, before we had made their acquaintance half a minute. They were just the very thing for him. There were his huge fat legs bulging over the tops, and fitting them too tight to admit of his tucking in the loops he had pulled them on by; and his knee-cords with an interval of stocking; and his blue apron tucked up round his waist; and his red neckerchief and blue coat, and a white hat stuck on one side of his head; and there he stood with a broad grin on his great red face, whistling away, as if any other idea but that of being happy and comfortable had never entered his brain.

This was the very man after our own heart; we knew all about him; we had seen him coming up to Covent Garden in his green chaise-cart, with the fat tubby little horse, half a thousand times; and even while we cast an affectionate look upon his boots, at that instant, the form of a coquettish servant-maid suddenly sprung into a pair of Denmark satin shoes that stood beside them, and we at once recognised the very girl who accepted his offer of a ride, just on this side the Hammersmith suspension-bridge, the very last Tuesday morning we rode into town from Richmond.

A very smart female, in a showy bonnet, stepped into a pair of grey cloth boots, with black fringe and binding, that were studiously pointing out their toes on the other side of the top-boots, and seemed very anxious to engage his attention, but we didn't observe that our friend the market-gardener appeared at all captivated with these blandishments; for beyond giving a knowing wink when they first began, as if to imply that he quite understood their end and object, he took no further notice of them. His indifference, however, was amply recompensed by the excessive gallantry of a very old gentleman with a silver-headed stick, who tottered into a pair of large list shoes, that were standing in one corner of the board, and indulged in a variety of gestures expressive of his admiration of the lady in the cloth boots, to the immeasurable amusement of a young fellow we put into a pair of long-quartered pumps, who we thought would have split the coat that slid down to meet him, with laughing.

We had been looking on at this little pantomime with great satisfaction for some time, when, to our unspeakable astonishment, we perceived that the whole of the characters, including a numerous *corps de ballet* of boots and shoes in the background, into which we had been hastily thrusting as many feet as we could press into the service, were arranging themselves in order for dancing; and some music striking up at the moment, to it they went without delay. It was perfectly delightful to witness the agility of the market-gardener. Out went the boots, first on one side, then on the other, then cutting, then shuffling, then setting to the Denmark satins, then advancing, then retreating, then going round, and then repeating the whole of the evolutions again, without appearing to suffer in the least from the violence of the exercise.

Nor were the Denmark satins a bit behindhand, for they jumped and bounded about in all directions; and though they were neither so regular, nor so true to the time as the cloth boots, still, as they seemed to do it from the heart, and

to enjoy it more, we candidly confess that we preferred their
style of dancing to the other.   But the old gentleman in the
list shoes was the most amusing object in the whole party ;
for, besides his grotesque attempts to appear youthful, and
amorous, which were sufficiently entertaining in themselves,
the young fellow in the pumps managed so artfully that every
time the old gentleman advanced to salute the lady in the
cloth boots, he trod with his whole weight on the old fellow's
toes, which made him roar with anguish, and rendered all
the others like to die of laughing.

We were in the full enjoyment of these festivities when
we heard a shrill, and by no means musical voice, exclaim,
"Hope you'll know me agin, imperence!" and on looking
intently forward to see from whence the sound came, we
found that it proceeded, not from the young lady in the cloth
boots, as we had at first been inclined to suppose, but from
a bulky lady of elderly appearance who was seated in a chair
at the head of the cellar-steps, apparently for the purpose of
superintending the sale of the articles arranged there.

A barrel-organ, which had been in full force close behind
us, ceased playing ; the people we had been fitting into the
shoes and boots took to flight at the interruption ; and as
we were conscious that in the depth of our meditations we
might have been rudely staring at the old lady for half an
hour without knowing it. we took to flight too. and were
soon immersed in the deepest obscurity of the adjacent
"Dials."

CHAPTER VII

HACKNEY-COACH STANDS

WE maintain that hackney-coaches, properly so called, belong solely to the metropolis. We may be told, that there are hackney-coach stands in Edinburgh ; and not to go quite so far for a contradiction to our position, we may be reminded that Liverpool, Manchester, "and other large towns" (as the Parliamentary phrase goes), have *their* hackney-coach stands. We readily concede to these places, the possession of certain vehicles, which may look almost as dirty, and even go almost as slowly, as London hackney-coaches : but that they have the slightest claim to compete with the metropolis, either in point of stands, drivers, or cattle, we indignantly deny.

Take a regular, ponderous, rickety, London hackney-coach of the old school, and let any man have the boldness to assert, if he can, that he ever beheld any object on the face of the earth which at all resembles it, unless, indeed, it were another hackney-coach of the same date. We have recently observed on certain stands, and we say it with deep regret, rather dapper green chariots, and coaches of polished yellow, with four wheels of the same colour as the coach, whereas it is perfectly notorious to every one who has studied the subject, that every wheel ought to be of a different colour, and a different size. These are innovations, and, like other mis-called improvements, awful signs of the restlessness of the public mind, and the little respect paid to our time-honoured institutions. Why should hackney-coaches be clean ? Our ancestors found them dirty, and left them so. Why should we, with a feverish wish to "keep moving," desire to roll along at the rate of six miles an hour, while they were content to rumble over the stones at four ? These are solemn considerations. Hackney-coaches are part and parcel of the law of the land ; they were settled by the Legislature ; plated and numbered by the wisdom of Parliament.

Then why have they been swamped by cabs and omni-

buses? Or why should people be allowed to ride quickly
for eightpence a mile, after Parliament had come to the
solemn decision that they should pay a shilling a mile for
riding slowly? We pause for a reply;—and, having no
chance of getting one, begin a fresh paragraph.

Our acquaintance with hackney-coach stands is of long
standing. We are a walking book of fares, feeling ourselves half bound, as it were, to be always in the right on
contested points. We know all the regular watermen
within three miles of Covent Garden by sight, and should be
almost tempted to believe that all the hackney-coach horses
in that district knew us by sight too, if one-half of them
were not blind. We take great interest in hackney-coaches,
but we seldom drive, having a knack of turning ourselves
over when we attempt to do so. We are as great friends
to horses, hackney-coach and otherwise, as the renowned
Mr. Martin, of costermonger notoriety, and yet we never ride.
We keep no horse, but a clothes-horse; enjoy no saddle so
much as a saddle of mutton; and, following our own inclinations, have never followed the hounds. Leaving these
fleeter means of getting over the ground, or of depositing
oneself upon it, to those who like them, by hackney-coach
stands we take our stand.

There is a hackney-coach stand under the very window at
which we are writing; there is only one coach on it now,
but it is a fair specimen of the class of vehicles to which we
have alluded—a great, lumbering, square concern of a dingy
yellow colour (like a bilious brunette), with very small
glasses, but very large frames; the panels are ornamented
with a faded coat of arms, in shape something like a dis-
sected bat, the axletree is red, and the majority of the
wheels are green. The box is partially covered by an old
great-coat, with a multiplicity of capes, and some extra-
ordinary-looking clothes; and the straw, with which the
canvas cushion is stuffed, is sticking up in several places,
as if in rivalry of the hay, which is peeping through the
chinks in the boot. The horses, with drooping heads, and
each with a mane and tail as scanty and straggling as those
of a worn-out rocking-horse, are standing patiently on some
damp straw, occasionally wincing, and rattling the harness;
and now and then one of them lifts his mouth to the ear of
his companion as if he were saying, in a whisper, that he
should like to assassinate the coachman. The coachman

himself is in the watering-house; and the waterman, with
his hands forced into his pockets as far as they can possibly
go, is dancing the " double shuffle," in front of the pump, to
keep his feet warm.

The servant-girl, with the pink ribbons, at No. 5, opposite, suddenly opens the street-door, and four small children
forthwith rush out, and scream "Coach!" with all their
might and main. The waterman darts from the pump,
seizes the horses by their respective bridles, and drags them,
and the coach too, round to the house, shouting all the time
for the coachman at the very top, or rather very bottom of
his voice, for it is a deep bass growl. A response is heard
from the tap-room; the coachman, in his wooden-soled
shoes, makes the street echo again as he runs across it; and
then there is such a struggling, and backing, and grating of
the kennel, to get the coach-door opposite the house-door,
that the children are in perfect ecstasies of delight. What
a commotion! The old lady, who has been stopping there
for the last month, is going back to the country. Out comes
box after box, and one side of the vehicle is filled with
luggage in no time; the children get into everybody's way,
and the youngest, who has upset himself in his attempts to
carry an umbrella, is borne off wounded and kicking. The
youngsters disappear, and a short pause ensues, during
which the old lady is, no doubt, kissing them all round in
the back parlour. She appears at last, followed by her married daughter, all the children, and both the servants, who,
with the joint assistance of the coachman and waterman,
manage to get her safely into the coach. A cloak is handed
in, and a little basket, which we could almost swear contains a small black bottle, and a paper of sandwiches. Up
go the steps, bang goes the door, " Golden Cross, Charing
Cross, Tom," says the waterman; "Good-bye, grandma,"
cry the children, off jingles the coach at the rate of three
miles an hour, and the mamma and children retire into the
house, with the exception of one little villain, who runs up
the street at the top of his speed, pursued by the servant;
not ill-pleased to have such an opportunity of displaying
her attractions. She brings him back, and, after casting
two or three gracious glances across the way, which are
either intended for us or the pot-boy (we are not quite certain
which), shuts the door, and the hackney-coach stand is again
at a standstill.

We have been frequently amused with the intense delight
with which "a servant of all work," who is sent for a coach,
deposits herself inside ; and the unspeakable gratification
which boys, who have been despatched on a similar errand,
appear to derive from mounting the box. But we never
recollect to have been more amused with a hackney-coach
party, than one we saw early the other morning in Tottenham Court Road. It was a wedding-party, and emerged from
one of the inferior streets near Fitzroy Square. There were
the bride, with a thin white dress, and a great red face ;
and the bridesmaid, a little, dumpy, good-humoured young
woman, dressed, of course, in the same appropriate costume ;
and the bridegroom and his chosen friend, in blue coats,
yellow waistcoats, white trousers, and Berlin gloves to
match. They stopped at the corner of the street, and called
a coach with an air of indescribable dignity. The moment
they were in, the bridesmaid threw a red shawl, which she
had, no doubt, brought on purpose, negligently over the
number on the door, evidently to delude pedestrians into the
belief that the hackney-coach was a private carriage ; and
away they went, perfectly satisfied that the imposition was
successful, and quite unconscious that there was a great
staring number stuck up behind, on a plate as large as a
schoolboy's slate. A shilling a mile !—the ride was worth
five, at least, to them.

What an interesting book a hackney-coach might produce,
if it could carry as much in its head as it does in its body !
The autobiography of a broken-down hackney-coach would
surely be as amusing as the autobiography of a broken-down
hackneyed dramatist ; and it might tell as much of its
travels *with* the pole, as others have of their expeditions *to*
it. How many stories might be related of the different
people it had conveyed on matters of business or profit—
pleasure or pain ! And how many melancholy tales of the
same people at different periods ! The country-girl—the
showy, over-dressed woman—the drunken prostitute ! The
raw apprentice—the dissipated spendthrift—the thief !

Talk of cabs ! Cabs are all very well in cases of expedition, when it's a matter of neck or nothing, life or death,
your temporary home or your long one. But, besides a
cab's lacking that gravity of deportment which so peculiarly
distinguishes a hackney-coach, let it never be forgotten that
a cab is a thing of yesterday, and that he never was any-

thing better. A hackney-cab has always been a hackney-cab, from his first entry into life ; whereas a hackney-coach is a remnant of past gentility, a victim to fashion, a hanger-on of an old English family, wearing their arms, and, in days of yore, escorted by men wearing their livery, stripped of his finery, and thrown upon the world, like a once-smart footman when he is no longer sufficiently juvenile for his office. progressing lower and lower in the scale of four-wheeled degradation, until at last it comes to—*a stand!*

CHAPTER VIII

DOCTORS' COMMONS

WALKING without any definite object through St. Paul's Churchyard, a little while ago, we happened to turn down a street entitled " Paul's Chain," and keeping straight forward for a few hundred yards, found ourself, as a natural consequence, in Doctors' Commons. Now Doctors' Commons being familiar by name to everybody, as the place where they grant marriage-licenses to love-sick couples, and divorces to unfaithful ones ; register the wills of people who have any property to leave, and punish hasty gentlemen who call ladies by unpleasant names, we no sooner discovered that we were really within its precincts, than we felt a laudable desire to become better acquainted therewith ; and as the first object of our curiosity was the Court, whose decrees can even unloose the bonds of matrimony, we procured a direction to it ; and bent our steps thither without delay.

Crossing a quiet and shady court-yard, paved with stone, and frowned upon by old red brick houses, on the doors of which were painted the names of sundry learned civilians, we paused before a small, green-baized, brass-headed-nailed door, which yielding to our gentle push, at once admitted us into an old quaint-looking apartment, with sunken windows, and black carved wainscoting, at the upper end of which, seated on a raised platform, of semicircular shape, were about a dozen solemn-looking gentlemen, in crimson gowns and wigs.

At a more elevated desk in the centre, sat a very fat and red-faced gentleman, in tortoise-shell spectacles, whose dignified appearance announced the judge ; and round a long green-baized table below, something like a billiard-table without the cushions and pockets, were a number of very self-important-looking personages, in stiff neckcloths, and black gowns with white fur collars, whom we at once set down as proctors. At the lower end of the billiard-table

'Coach!'
(*p. 83*)

was an individual in an arm-chair, and a wig, whom we afterwards discovered to be the registrar; and seated behind a little desk, near the door, were a respectable-looking man in black, of about twenty-stone weight or thereabouts, and a .fat-faced, smirking, civil-looking body, in a black gown, black kid gloves, knee shorts, and silks, with a shirt-frill in his bosom, curls on his head, and a silver staff in his hand, whom we had no difficulty in recognising as the officer of the Court. The latter, indeed, speedily set our mind at rest upon this point, for, advancing to our elbow, and opening a conversation forthwith, he had communicated to us, in less than five minutes, that he was the apparitor, and the other the court-keeper; that this was the Arches Court, and therefore the counsel wore red gowns, and the proctors fur collars; and that when the other Courts sat there, they didn't wear red gowns or fur collars either; with many other scraps of intelligence equally interesting. Besides these two officers, there was a little thin old man, with long grizzly hair, crouched in a remote corner, whose duty, our communicative friend informed us, was to ring a large hand-bell when the Court opened in the morning, and who, for aught his appearance betokened to the contrary, might have been similarly employed for the last two centuries at least.

The red-faced gentleman in the tortoise-shell spectacles had got all the talk to himself just then, and very well he was doing it, too, only he spoke very fast, but that was habit; and rather thick, but that was good living. So we had plenty of time to look about us. There was one individual who amused us mightily. This was one of the bewigged gentlemen in the red robes, who was straddling before the fire in the centre of the Court, in the attitude of the brazen Colossus, to the complete exclusion of everybody else. He had gathered up his robe behind, in much the same manner as a slovenly woman would her petticoats on a very dirty day, in order that he might feel the full warmth of the fire. His wig was put on all awry, with the tail straggling about his neck; his scanty grey trousers and short black gaiters, made in the worst possible style, imparted an additional inelegant appearance to his uncouth person; and his limp, badly-starched shirt-collar almost obscured his eyes. We shall never be able to claim any credit as a physiogno-mist again, for, after a careful scrutiny of this gentleman's countenance, we had come to the conclusion that it bespoke nothing but conceit and silliness, when our friend with the silver staff whispered in our ear that he was no other than a doctor of civil law, and heaven knows what besides. So of course we were mistaken, and he must be a very talented man. He conceals it so well though—perhaps with the merciful view of not astonishing ordinary people too much— that you would suppose him to be one of the stupidest dogs alive.

The gentleman in the spectacles having concluded his judgment, and a few minutes having been allowed to elapse, to afford time for the buzz in the Court to subside, the registrar called on the next cause, which was "the office of the Judge promoted by Bumple against Sludberry." A general movement was visible in the Court at this announcement, and the obliging functionary with silver staff whispered us that "there would be some fun now, for this was a brawl-ing case."

We were not rendered much the wiser by this piece of infor-mation, till we found by the opening speech of the counsel for the promoter, that, under a half-obsolete statute of one of the Edwards, the Court was empowered to visit with the penalty of excommunication, any person who should be proved guilty of the crime of "brawling," or "smiting," in any church, or vestry adjoining thereto ; and it appeared, by some eight-and-twenty affidavits, which were duly referred to, that on a certain night, at a certain vestry-meeting, in a certain parish particularly set forth, Thomas Sludberry, the party appeared against in that suit, had made use of, and applied to Michael Bumple, the promoter, the words "You be blowed ; " and that, on the said Michael Bumple and others remonstrating with the said Thomas Sludberry, on the impropriety of his conduct, the said Thomas Sludberry repeated the aforesaid expression, "You be blowed ; " and furthermore desired and requested to know, whether the said Michael Bumple "wanted anything for himself ; " adding, "that if the said Michael Bumple did want anything for himself, he, the said Thomas Sludberry, was the man to give it him ; " at the same time making use of other heinous and sinful expressions, all of which, Bumple submitted, came within the intent and meaning of the Act ; and therefore he, for the soul's health and chastening of Sludberry, prayed for sentence of excommunication against him accordingly.

Upon these facts a long argument was entered into, on both

sides, to the great edification of a number of persons interested in the parochial squabbles, who crowded the Court ; and when some very long and grave speeches had been made *pro* and *con*, the red-faced gentleman in the tortoise-shell spectacles took a review of the case, which occupied half an hour more, and then pronounced upon Sludberry the awful sentence of excommunication for a fortnight, and payment of the costs of the suit. Upon this, Sludberry, who was a little, red-faced, sly-looking, ginger-beer seller, addressed the Court, and said, if they'd be good enough to take off the costs, and excommunicate him for the term of his natural life instead, it would be much more convenient to him, for he never went to church at all. To this appeal the gentleman in the spectacles made no other reply than a look of virtuous indignation ; and Sludberry and his friends retired. As the man with the silver staff informed us that the Court was on the point of rising, we retired too—pondering, as we walked away, upon the beautiful spirit of these ancient ecclesiastical laws, the kind and neighbourly feelings they are calculated to awaken, and the strong attachment to religious institutions which they cannot fail to engender.

We were so lost in these meditations, that we had turned into the street, and run up against a door-post, before we recollected where we were walking. On looking upwards to see what house we had stumbled upon, the words "Prerogative Office," written in large characters, met our eye ; and as we were in a sight-seeing humour and the place was a public one, we walked in.

The room into which we walked was a long, busy-looking place, partitioned off, on either side, into a variety of little boxes, in which a few clerks were engaged in copying or examining deeds. Down the centre of the room were several desks nearly breast high, at each of which, three or four people were standing, poring over large volumes. As we knew that they were searching for wills, they attracted our attention at once.

It was curious to contrast the lazy indifference of the attorneys' clerks who were making a search for some legal purpose, with the air of earnestness and interest which distinguished the strangers to the place, who were looking up the will of some deceased relative ; the former pausing every now and then with an impatient yawn, or raising their heads to look at the people who passed up and down the

room ; the latter stooping over the book, and running down
column after column of names in the deepest abstraction.

There was one little dirty-faced man in a blue apron, who
after a whole morning's search, extending some fifty years
back, had just found the will to which he wished to refer,
which one of the officials was reading to him in a low hurried
voice from a thick vellum book with large clasps. It was
perfectly evident that the more the clerk read, the less the
man with the blue apron understood about the matter.
When the volume was first brought down, he took off his hat,
smoothed down his hair, smiled with great self-satisfaction,
and looked up in the reader's face with the air of a man who
had made up his mind to recollect every word he heard.
The first two or three lines were intelligible enough ; but
then the technicalities began, and the little man began to
look rather dubious. Then came a whole string of complicated trusts, and he was regularly at sea. As the reader
proceeded, it was quite apparent that it was a hopeless case,
and the little man, with his mouth open and his eyes fixed
upon his face, looked on with an expression of bewilderment
and perplexity irresistibly ludicrous.

A little further on, a hard-featured old man with a deeply-
wrinkled face, was intently perusing a lengthy will with the
aid of a pair of horn spectacles : occasionally pausing from his
task, and slily noting down some brief memorandum of the
bequests contained in it. Every wrinkle about his toothless
mouth, and sharp keen eyes, told of avarice and cunning.
His clothes were nearly threadbare, but it was easy to see
that he wore them from choice and not from necessity ; all
his looks and gestures down to the very small pinches of snuff
which he every now and then took from a little tin canister,
told of wealth, and penury, and avarice.

As he leisurely closed the register, put up his spectacles,
and folded his scraps of paper in a large leathern pocket-book,
we thought what a nice hard bargain he was driving with
some poverty-stricken legatee, who, tired of waiting year after
year, until some life-interest should fall in, was selling his
chance, just as it began to grow most valuable, for a twelfth
part of its worth. It was a good speculation—a very safe
one. The old man stowed his pocket-book carefully in the
breast of his great-coat, and hobbled away with a leer of
triumph. That will had made him ten years younger at the
lowest computation.

Having commenced our observations, we should certainly have extended them to another dozen of people at least, had not a sudden shutting up and putting away of the worm-eaten old books, warned us that the time for closing the office had arrived ; and thus deprived us of a pleasure, and spared our readers an infliction.

We naturally fell into a train of reflection as we walked homewards, upon the curious old records of likings and dislikings ; of jealousies and revenges ; of affection defying the power of death, and hatred pursued beyond the grave, which these depositories contain ; silent but striking tokens, some of them, of excellence of heart, and nobleness of soul ; melancholy examples, others, of the worst passions of human nature. How many men as they lay speechless and helpless on the bed of death, would have given worlds but for the strength and power to blot out the silent evidence of animosity and bitterness, which now stands registered against them in Doctors' Commons !

CHAPTER IX

THE wish of persons in the humbler classes of life, to ape the manners and customs of those whom fortune has placed above them, is often the subject of remark, and not unfrequently of complaint. The inclination may, and no doubt does, exist to a great extent, among the small gentility—the would-be aristocrats—of the middle classes. Tradesmen and clerks, with fashionable novel-reading families, and circulating-library-subscribing daughters, get up small assemblies in humble imitation of Almack's, and promenade the dingy "large room" of some second-rate hotel with as much complacency as the enviable few who are privileged to exhibit their magnificence in that exclusive haunt of fashion and foolery. Aspiring young ladies, who read flaming accounts of some "fancy fair in high life," suddenly grow desperately charitable; visions of admiration and matrimony float before their eyes; some wonderfully meritorious institution, which, by the strangest accident in the world, has never been heard of before, is discovered to be in a languishing condition: Thomson's great room, or Johnson's nursery-ground, is forthwith engaged, and the aforesaid young ladies, from mere charity, exhibit themselves for three days, from twelve to four, for the small charge of one shilling per head! With the exception of these classes of society, however, and a few weak and insignificant persons, we do not think the attempt at imitation to which we have alluded, prevails in any great degree. The different character of the recreations of different classes, has often afforded us amusement; and we have chosen it for the subject of our present sketch, in the hope that it may possess some amusement for our readers.

If the regular City man, who leaves Lloyd's at five o'clock, and drives home to Hackney, Clapton, Stamford Hill, or elsewhere, can be said to have any daily recreation beyond his dinner, it is his garden. He never does anything to it

George Cruikshank

London Recreations—The 'Tea-Gardens'
(*p. 96*)

with his own hands; but he takes great pride in it notwith-standing; and if you are desirous of paying your addresses to the youngest daughter, be sure to be in raptures with every flower and shrub it contains. If your poverty of expression compel you to make any distinction between the two, we would certainly recommend your bestowing more admiration on his garden than his wine. He always takes a walk round it, before he starts for town in the morning, and is particularly anxious that the fish-pond should be kept specially neat. If you call on him on Sunday in summer-time, about an hour before dinner, you will find him sitting in an arm-chair, on the lawn behind the house, with a straw hat on, reading a Sunday paper. A short distance from him you will most likely observe a handsome paroquet in a large brass-wire cage; ten to one but the two eldest girls are loitering in one of the side walks accompanied by a couple of young gentlemen, who are holding parasols over them—of course only to keep the sun off—while the younger children, with the under nursery-maid, are strolling listlessly about in the shade. Beyond these occasions, his delight in his garden appears to arise more from the consciousness of possession than actual enjoyment of it. When he drives you down to dinner on a week-day, he is rather fatigued with the occupations of the morning, and tolerably cross into the bargain; but when the cloth is removed, and he has drunk three or four glasses of his favourite port, he orders the French windows of his dining-room (which of course look into the garden) to be opened, and throwing a silk handkerchief over his head, and leaning back in his arm-chair, descants at considerable length upon its beauty, and the cost of maintaining it. This is to impress you—who are a young friend of the family—with a due sense of the excel-lence of the garden, and the wealth of its owner; and when he has exhausted the subject, he goes to sleep.

There is another and a very different class of men, whose recreation is their garden. An individual of this class resides some short distance from town—say in the Hamp-stead Road, or the Kilburn Road, or any other road where the houses are small and neat, and have little slips of back garden. He and his wife—who is as clean and compact a little body as himself—have occupied the same house ever since he retired from business twenty years ago. They have no family. They once had a son, who died at about five years old. The child's portrait hangs over the mantelpiece in the best sitting-room, and a little cart he used to draw about is carefully preserved as a relic.

In fine weather the old gentleman is almost constantly in the garden; and when it is too wet to go into it, he will look out of the window at it, by the hour together. He has always something to do there, and you will see him digging, and sweeping, and cutting, and planting, with manifest delight. In spring-time, there is no end to the sowing of seeds, and sticking little bits of wood over them, with labels, which look like epitaphs to their memory; and in the evening, when the sun has gone down, the perseverance with which he lugs a great watering-pot about is perfectly astonishing. The only other recreation he has is the newspaper, which he peruses every day, from beginning to end, generally reading the most interesting pieces of intelligence to his wife during breakfast. The old lady is very fond of flowers, as the hyacinth-glasses in the parlour-window, and geranium-pots in the little front court, testify. She takes great pride in the garden too: and when one of the four fruit-trees produces rather a larger gooseberry than usual, it is carefully preserved under a wine-glass on the sideboard, for the edification of visitors, who are duly informed that Mr. So-and-so planted the tree which produced it, with his own hands. On a summer's evening, when the large watering-pot has been filled and emptied some fourteen times, and the old couple have quite exhausted themselves by trotting about, you will see them sitting happily together in the little summer-house, enjoying the calm and peace of the twilight, and watching the shadows as they fall upon the garden, and gradually growing thicker and more sombre, obscure the tints of their gayest flowers—no bad emblem of the years that have silently rolled over their heads, deadening in their course the brightest hues of early hopes and feelings which have long since faded away. These are their only recreations, and they require no more. They have within themselves the materials of comfort and content; and the only anxiety of each is to die before the other.

This is no ideal sketch. There *used* to be many old people of this description; their numbers may have diminished, and may decrease still more. Whether the course female education has taken of late days—whether the pursuit of giddy frivolities, and empty nothings, has tended to unfit women for that quiet domestic life, in which they show far more beautifully than in the most crowded assembly, is a question we should feel little gratification in discussing : we hope not.

Let us turn now to another portion of the London population, whose recreations present about as strong a contrast as can well be conceived—we mean the Sunday pleasurers; and let us beg our readers to imagine themselves stationed by our side in some well-known rural "Tea-gardens."

The heat is intense this afternoon, and the people, of whom there are additional parties arriving every moment, look as warm as the tables which have been recently painted, and have the appearance of being red-hot. What a dust and noise! Men and women—boys and girls—sweethearts and married people—babies in arms, and children in chaises—pipes and shrimps—cigars and periwinkles—tea and tobacco. Gentlemen in alarming waistcoats, and steel watch-guards, promenading about, three abreast, with surprising dignity (or as the gentleman in the next box facetiously observes, "cutting it uncommon fat ! ")—ladies, with great, long, white pocket-handkerchiefs like small table-cloths in their hands, chasing one another on the grass in the most playful and interesting manner, with the view of attracting the attention of the aforesaid gentlemen—husbands in perspective ordering bottles of ginger-beer for the objects of their affections, with a lavish disregard of expense ; and the said objects washing down huge quantities of "shrimps" and "winkles," with an equal disregard of their own bodily health and subsequent comfort—boys, with great silk hats just balanced on the top of their heads, smoking cigars, and trying to look as if they liked them—gentlemen in pink shirts and blue waistcoats, occasionally upsetting either themselves, or somebody else, with their own canes.

Some of the finery of these people provokes a smile, but they are all clean, and happy, and disposed to be good-natured and sociable. Those two motherly-looking women in the smart pelisses, who are chatting so confidentially, inserting a "ma'am" at every fourth word, scraped an acquaintance about a quarter of an hour ago: it originated in admiration of the little boy who belongs to one of them—that diminutive specimen of mortality in the three-cornered pink satin hat with black feathers. The two men in the blue coats and drab trousers, who are walking up and down, smoking their pipes, are their husbands. The party in the

opposite box are a pretty fair specimen of the generality of
the visitors. These are the father and mother, and old
grandmother: a young man and woman, and an individual
addressed by the euphonious title of "Uncle Bill," who is
evidently the wit of the party. They have some half-dozen
children with them, but it is scarcely necessary to notice the
fact, for that is a matter of course here. Every woman in
"the gardens," who has been married for any length of time,
must have had twins on two or three occasions; it is impossible to account for the extent of juvenile population in
any other way.

Observe the inexpressible delight of the old grandmother,
at Uncle Bill's splendid joke of "tea for four: bread-and-
butter for forty;" and the loud explosion of mirth which
follows his wafering a paper "pigtail" on the waiter's collar.
The young man is evidently "keeping company" with Uncle
Bill's niece: and Uncle Bill's hints—such as "Don't forget
me at the dinner, you know," "I shall look out for the cake,
Sally," "I'll be godfather to your first—wager it's a boy,"
and so forth, are equally embarrassing to the young people,
and delightful to the elder ones. As to the old grandmother,
she is in perfect ecstasies, and does nothing but laugh herself
into fits of coughing, until they have finished the "gin-and
water warm with," of which Uncle Bill ordered "glasses
round" after tea, "just to keep the night air out, and do it
up comfortable and riglar arter sich an as-tonishing hot
day!"

It is getting dark, and the people begin to move. The
field leading to town is quite full of them; the little hand-
chaises are dragged wearily along, the children are tired, and
amuse themselves and the company generally by crying, or
resort to the much more pleasant expedient of going to sleep
—the mothers begin to wish they were at home again—
sweethearts grow more sentimental than ever, as the time
for parting arrives—the gardens look mournful enough, by
the light of the two lanterns which hang against the trees
for the convenience of smokers—and the waiters who have
been running about incessantly for the last six hours, think
they feel a little tired, as they count their glasses and their
gains.

CHAPTER X

THE RIVER

"Are you fond of the water?" is a question very frequently asked, in hot summer weather, by amphibious-looking young men. "Very," is the general reply. "An't you?"— "Hardly ever off it," is the response, accompanied by sundry adjectives, expressive of the speaker's heartfelt admiration of that element. Now, with all respect for the opinion of society in general, and cutter clubs in particular, we humbly suggest that some of the most painful reminiscences in the mind of every individual who has occasionally disported himself on the Thames, must be connected with his aquatic recreations. Who ever heard of a successful water-party?— or to put the question in a still more intelligible form, who ever saw one? We have been on water excursions out of number, but we solemnly declare that we cannot call to mind one single occasion of the kind, which was not marked by more miseries than any one would suppose could be reasonably crowded into the space of some eight or nine hours. Something has always gone wrong. Either the cork of the salad-dressing has come out, or the most anxiously expected member of the party has not come out, or the most disagreeable man in company would come out, or a child or two have fallen into the water, or the gentleman who undertook to steer has endangered everybody's life all the way, or the gentlemen who volunteered to row have been "out of practice," and performed very alarming evolutions, putting their oars down into the water and not being able to get them up again, or taking terrific pulls without putting them in at all; in either case, pitching over on the backs of their heads with startling violence, and exhibiting the soles of their pumps to the "sitters" in the boat, in a very humiliating manner.

We grant that the banks of the Thames are very beautiful at Richmond and Twickenham, and other distant havens.

often sought though seldom reached ; but from the " Red-us "
back to Blackfriars Bridge, the scene is wonderfully changed.
The Penitentiary is a noble building, no doubt, and the
sportive youths who " go in " at that particular part of the
river, on a summer's evening, may be all very well in perspective ; but when you are obliged to keep in shore coming
home, and the young ladies will colour up, and look perseveringly the other way, while the married dittoes cough
slightly, and stare very hard at the water, you feel awkward—especially if you happen to have been attempting the
most distant approach to sentimentality, for an hour or two
previously.

Although experience and suffering have produced in our
minds the result we have just stated, we are by no means
blind to a proper sense of the fun which a looker-on may
extract from the amateurs of boating. What can be more
amusing than Searle's yard on a fine Sunday morning? It's
a Richmond tide, and some dozen boats are preparing for the
reception of the parties who have engaged them. Two or
three fellows in great rough trousers and Guernsey shirts,
are getting them ready by easy stages ; now coming down
the yard with a pair of sculls and a cushion—then having
a chat with the " jack." who, like all his tribe, seems to be
wholly incapable of doing anything but lounging about—
then going back again, and returning with a rudder-line and
a stretcher—then solacing themselves with another chat—
and then wondering, with their hands in their capacious
pockets, " where them gentlemen's got to as ordered the six."
One of these, the head man, with the legs of his trousers
carefully tucked up at the bottom, to admit the water, we
presume—for it is an element in which he is infinitely more
at home than on land—is quite a character, and shares with
the defunct oyster-swallower the celebrated name of " Dando."
Watch him, as taking a few minutes' respite from his toils,
he negligently seats himself on the edge of a boat, and fans
his broad bushy chest with a cap scarcely half so furry.
Look at his magnificent, though reddish whiskers, and mark
the somewhat native humour with which he " chaffs " the
boys and 'prentices, or cunningly gammons the gen'lm'n
into the gift of a glass of gin, of which we verily believe he
swallows in one day as much as any six ordinary men, without ever being one atom the worse for it.

But the party arrives, and Dando, relieved from his state

of uncertainty, starts up into activity. They approach in full aquatic costume, with round blue jackets, striped shirts, and caps of all sizes and patterns, from the velvet skull-cap of French manufacture, to the easy head-dress familiar to the students of the old spelling-books, as having, on the authority of the portrait, formed part of the costume of the Reverend Mr. Dilworth.

This is the most amusing time to observe a regular Sunday water-party. There has evidently been up to this period no inconsiderable degree of boasting on everybody's part relative to his knowledge of navigation; the sight of the water rapidly cools their courage, and the air of self-denial with which each of them insists on somebody else's taking an oar, is perfectly delightful. At length, after a great deal of changing and fidgeting, consequent upon the election of a stroke oar; the inability of one gentleman to pull on this side, of another to pull on that, and of a third to pull at all, the boat's crew are seated. "Shove her off!" cries the coxswain, who looks as easy and comfortable as if he were steering in the Bay of Biscay. The order is obeyed; the boat is immediately turned completely round, and proceeds towards Westminster Bridge, amidst such a splashing and struggling as never was seen before, except when the Royal George went down. "Back wa'ater, sir," shouts Dando, "Back wa'ater, you sir, aft;" upon which everybody thinking he must be the individual referred to, they all back water, and back comes the boat, stern first, to the spot whence it started. "Back water, you sir, aft; pull round, you sir, for'ad, can't you?" shouts Dando, in a frenzy of excitement. "Pull round, Tom, can't you?" re-echoes one of the party. "Tom an't for'ad," replies another. "Yes, he is," cries a third; and the unfortunate young man, at the imminent risk of breaking a blood-vessel, pulls and pulls, until the head of the boat fairly lies in the direction of Vauxhall Bridge. "That's right—now pull all on you!" shouts Dando again, adding, in an under-tone, to somebody by him, "Blowed if hever I see sich a set of muffs!" and away jogs the boat in a zigzag direction, every one of the six oars dipping into the water at a different time; and the yard is once more clear, until the arrival of the next party.

A well-contested rowing-match on the Thames is a very lively and interesting scene. The water is studded with boats of all sorts, kinds, and descriptions; places in the coal-barges at the different wharfs are let to crowds of spectators, beer and tobacco flow freely about; men, women, and children wait for the start in breathless expectation; cutters of six and eight oars glide gently up and down, waiting to accompany their *protégés* during the race; bands of music add to the animation, if not to the harmony of the scene; groups of watermen are assembled at the different stairs, discussing the merits of the respective candidates; and the prize wherry, which is rowed slowly about by a pair of sculls, is an object of general interest.

Two o'clock strikes, and everybody looks anxiously in the direction of the bridge through which the candidates for the prize will come—half-past two, and the general attention which has been preserved so long begins to flag, when suddenly a gun is heard, and a noise of distant hurra'ing along each bank of the river—every head is bent forward—the noise draws nearer and nearer—the boats which have been waiting at the bridge start briskly up the river, and a well-manned galley shoots through the arch, the sitters cheering on the boats behind them, which are not yet visible.

"Here they are," is the general cry—and through darts the first boat, the men in her, stripped to the skin, and exerting every muscle to preserve the advantage they have gained—four other boats follow close astern; there are not two boats' length between them—the shouting is tremendous, and the interest intense. "Go, on Pink"—"Give it her, Red"—"Sulliwin for ever"—"Bravo! George"—"Now, Tom. now—now—now—why don't your partner stretch out?"—"Two pots to a pint on Yellow," &c., &c. Every little public-house fires its gun, and hoists its flag; and the men who win the heat, come in, amidst a splashing and shouting, and banging and confusion, which no one can imagine who has not witnessed it, and of which any description would convey a very faint idea.

One of the most amusing places we know, is the steam-wharf of the London Bridge, or St. Katharine's Dock Company, on a Saturday morning in summer, when the Gravesend and Margate steamers are usually crowded to excess; and as we have just taken a glance at the river above bridge, we hope our readers will not object to accompany us on board a Gravesend packet.

Coaches are every moment setting down at the entrance to the wharf, and the stare of bewildered astonishment with which the "fares" resign themselves and their luggage into the hands of the porters, who seize all the packages at once as a matter of course, and run away with them, heaven knows where, is laughable in the extreme. A Margate boat lies alongside the wharf, the Gravesend boat (which starts first) lies alongside that again; and as a temporary communication is formed between the two, by means of a plank and hand-rail, the natural confusion of the scene is by no means diminished.

"Gravesend?" inquires a stout father of a stout family, who follow him, under the guidance of their mother, and a servant, at the no small risk of two or three of them being left behind in the confusion. "Gravesend?"

"Pass on, if you please, sir," replies the attendant— "other boat, sir."

Hereupon the stout father, being rather mystified, and the stout mother rather distracted by maternal anxiety, the whole party deposit themselves in the Margate boat, and after having congratulated himself on having secured very comfortable seats, the stout father sallies to the chimney to look for his luggage, which he has a faint recollection of having given some man, something, to take somewhere. No luggage, however, bearing the most remote resemblance to his own, in shape or form, is to be discovered; on which the stout father calls very loudly for an officer, to whom he states the case, in the presence of another father of another family—a little thin man—who entirely concurs with him (the stout father) in thinking that it's high time something was done with these steam companies, and that as the Corporation Bill failed to do it, something else must; for really people's property is not to be sacrificed in this way; and that if the luggage isn't restored without delay, he will take care it shall be put in the papers, for the public is not to be the victim of these great monopolies. To this, the officer, in his turn, replies, that that company, ever since it has been St. Kat'rine's Dock Company, has protected life and property; that if it had been the London Bridge Wharf Company, indeed, he shouldn't have wondered, seeing that the morality of that company (they being the opposition) can't be answered for, by no one; but as it is, he's convinced there must be some mistake, and he wouldn't mind making a solemn oath afore a magistrate that the gentleman'll find his luggage afore he gets to Margate.

Here the stout father, thinking he is making a capital point, replies, that as it happens, he is not going to Margate at all, and that "Passenger to Gravesend" was on the luggage, in letters of full two inches long; on which the officer rapidly explains the mistake, and the stout mother, and the stout children, and the servant, are hurried with all possible despatch on board the Gravesend boat, which they reach just in time to discover that their luggage is there, and that their comfortable seats are not. Then the bell, which is the signal for the Gravesend boat starting, begins to ring most furiously: and people keep time to the bell, by running in and out of our boat at a double-quick pace. The bell stops; the boat starts: people who have been taking leave of their friends on board, are carried away against their will; and people who have been taking leave of their friends on shore, find that they have performed a very needless ceremony, in consequence of their not being carried away at all. The regular passengers, who have season tickets, go below to breakfast; people who have purchased morning papers, compose themselves to read them; and people who have not been down the river before, think that both the shipping and the water look a great deal better at a distance.

When we get down about as far as Blackwall, and begin to move at a quicker rate, the spirits of the passengers appear to rise in proportion. Old women who have brought large wicker hand-baskets with them, set seriously to work at the demolition of heavy sandwiches, and pass round a wine-glass, which is frequently replenished from a flat bottle like a stomach-warmer, with considerable glee: handing it first to the gentleman in the foraging-cap, who plays the harp —partly as an expression of satisfaction with his previous exertions, and partly to induce him to play "Dumbledumbdeary," for "Alick" to dance to; which being done, Alick, who is a damp earthy child in red worsted socks, takes certain small jumps upon the deck, to the unspeakable satisfaction of his family circle. Girls who have brought the first volume of some new novel in their reticule, become extremely plaintive, and expatiate to Mr. Brown, or young Mr. O'Brien, who has been looking over them, on the blueness of the sky, and brightness of the water; on which Mr.

Brown or Mr. O'Brien, as the case may be, remarks in a low voice that he has been quite insensible of late to the beauties of nature—that his whole thoughts and wishes have centred in one object alone—whereupon the young lady looks up, and failing in her attempt to appear unconscious, looks down again ; and turns over the next leaf with great difficulty, in order to afford opportunity for a lengthened pressure of the hand.

Telescopes, sandwiches, and glasses of brandy-and-water cold without, begin to be in great requisition ; and bashful men who have been looking down the hatchway at the engine, find, to their great relief, a subject on which they can converse with one another—and a copious one too—Steam.

"Wonderful thing steam, sir." "Ah ! (a deep-drawn sigh) it is indeed, sir." "Great power, sir." "Immense—immense !" "Great deal done by steam, sir." "Ah ! (another sigh at the immensity of the subject, and a knowing shake of the head) you may say that, sir." "Still in its infancy, they say, sir." Novel remarks of this kind, are generally the commencement of a conversation which is prolonged until the conclusion of the trip, and, perhaps, lays the foundation of a speaking acquaintance between half a-dozen gentlemen, who, having their families at Gravesend, take season tickets for the boat, and dine on board regularly every afternoon.

CHAPTER XI

WE never see any very large, staring, black Roman capitals, in a book, or shop-window, or placarded on a wall, without their immediately recalling to our mind an indistinct and confused recollection of the time when we were first initiated in the mysteries of the alphabet. We almost fancy we see the pin's point following the letter, to impress its form more strongly on our bewildered imagination; and wince involuntarily, as we remember the hard knuckles with which the reverend old lady who instilled into our mind the first principles of education for ninepence per week, or ten and sixpence per quarter, was wont to poke our juvenile head occasionally, by way of adjusting the confusion of ideas in which we were generally involved. The same kind of feeling pursues us in many other instances, but there is no place which recalls so strongly our recollections of childhood as Astley's. It was not a "Royal Amphitheatre" in those days, nor had Ducrow arisen to shed the light of classic taste and portable gas over the sawdust of the circus; but the whole character of the place was the same, the pieces were the same, the clown's jokes were the same, the riding-masters were equally grand, the comic performers equally witty, the tragedians equally hoarse, and the "highly-trained chargers" equally spirited. Astley's has altered for the better —we have changed for the worse. Our histrionic taste is gone, and with shame we confess, that we are far more delighted and amused with the audience, than with the pageantry we once so highly appreciated.

We like to watch a regular Astley's party in the Easter or Midsummer holidays—pa and ma, and nine or ten children, varying from five foot six to two foot eleven: from fourteen years of age to four. We had just taken our seat in one of the boxes, in the centre of the house, the other night, when the next was occupied by just such a party as we should have attempted to describe, had we depicted our *beau idéal* of a group of Astley's visitors.

First of all, there came three little boys and a little girl, who, in pursuance of pa's directions, issued in a very audible voice from the box-door, occupied the front row; then two more little girls were ushered in by a young lady, evidently the governess. Then came three more little boys, dressed like the first, in blue jackets and trousers, with lay-down shirt-collars: then a child in a braided frock, and high state of astonishment, with very large round eyes, opened to their utmost width, was lifted over the seats—a process which occasioned a considerable display of little pink legs—then came ma and pa, and then the eldest son, a boy of fourteen years old, who was evidently trying to look as if he did not belong to the family.

The first five minutes were occupied in taking the shawls off the little girls, and adjusting the bows which ornamented their hair; then it was providentially discovered that one of the little boys was seated behind a pillar and could not see, so the governess was stuck behind the pillar, and the boy lifted into her place. Then pa drilled the boys, and directed the stowing away of their pocket-handkerchiefs, and ma having first nodded and winked to the governess to pull the girls' frocks a little more off their shoulders, stood up to review the little troop—an inspection which appeared to terminate much to her own satisfaction, for she looked with a complacent air at pa, who was standing up at the further end of the seat. Pa returned the glance, and blew his nose very emphatically; and the poor governess peeped out from behind the pillar, and timidly tried to catch ma's eye, with a look expressive of her high admiration of the whole family. Then two of the little boys who had been discussing the point whether Astley's was more than twice as large as Drury Lane, agreed to refer it to "George" for his decision; at which "George," who was no other than the young gentleman before noticed, waxed indignant, and remonstrated in no very gentle terms on the gross impropriety of having his name repeated in so loud a voice at a public place, on which all the children laughed very heartily, and one of the little boys wound up by expressing his opinion, that "George began to think himself quite a man now," whereupon both pa and ma laughed too; and George (who carried a dress cane and was cultivating whiskers) muttered that

"William always was encouraged in his impertinence;" and assumed a look of profound contempt, which lasted the whole evening.

The play began, and the interest of the little boys knew no bounds. Pa was clearly interested too, although he very unsuccessfully endeavoured to look as if he wasn't. As for ma, she was perfectly overcome by the drollery of the principal comedian, and laughed till every one of the immense bows on her ample cap trembled, at which the governess peeped out from behind the pillar again, and whenever she could catch ma's eye, put her handkerchief to her mouth, and appeared, as in duty bound, to be in convulsions of laughter also. Then when the man in the splendid armour vowed to rescue the lady or perish in the attempt, the little boys applauded vehemently, especially one little fellow who was apparently on a visit to the family, and had been carrying on a child's flirtation, the whole evening, with a small coquette of twelve years old, who looked like a model of her mamma on a reduced scale; and who, in common with the other little girls (who, generally speaking, have even more coquettishness about them than much older ones), looked very properly shocked, when the knight's squire kissed the princess's confidential chambermaid.

When the scenes in the circle commenced, the children were more delighted than ever; and the wish to see what was going forward, completely conquering pa's dignity, he stood up in the box, and applauded as loudly as any of them. Between each feat of horsemanship, the governess leant across to ma, and retailed the clever remarks of the children on that which had preceded: and ma, in the openness of her heart, offered tne governess an acidulated drop, and the governess, gratified to be taken notice of, retired behind her pillar again with a brighter countenance: and the whole party seemed quite happy, except the exquisite in the back of the box, who, being too grand to take any interest in the children, and too insignificant to be taken notice of by anybody else, occupied himself, from time to time, in rubbing the place where the whiskers ought to be, and was completely alone in his glory.

We defy any one who has been to Astley's two or three times, and is consequently capable of appreciating the perseverance with which precisely the same jokes are repeated night after night, and season after season, not to be amused

with one part of the performances at least—we mean the
scenes in the circle. For ourself, we know that when the
hoop, composed of jets of gas, is let down, the curtain drawn
up for the convenience of the half-price on their ejectment
from the ring, the orange-peel cleared away, and the sawdust shaken, with mathematical precision, into a complete
circle, we feel as much enlivened as the youngest child
present; and actually join in the laugh which follows the
clown's shrill shout of "Here we are!" just for old acquaintance' sake. Nor can we quite divest ourself of our old
feeling of reverence for the riding-master, who follows the
clown with a long whip in his hand, and bows to the audience with graceful dignity. He is none of your second-rate
riding-masters in nankeen dressing-gowns, with brown frogs,
but the regular gentleman-attendant on the principal riders,
who always wears a military uniform with a table-cloth
inside the breast of the coat, in which costume he forcibly
reminds one of a fowl trussed for roasting. He is—but
why should we attempt to describe that of which no description can convey an adequate idea? Everybody knows
the man, and everybody remembers his polished boots, his
graceful demeanour, stiff, as some misjudging persons have
in their jealousy considered it, and the splendid head of
black hair, parted high on the forehead, to impart to the
countenance an appearance of deep thought and poetic
melancholy. His soft and pleasing voice, too, is in perfect
unison with his noble bearing, as he humours the clown by
indulging in a little badinage; and the striking recollection
of his own dignity, with which he exclaims, "Now, sir, if
you please, inquire for Miss Woolford, sir," can never be
forgotten. The graceful air, too, with which he introduces
Miss Woolford into the arena, and, after assisting her to
the saddle, follows her fairy courser round the circle, can
never fail to create a deep impression in the bosom of every
female servant present.

When Miss Woolford, and the horse, and the orchestra,
all stop together to take breath, he urbanely takes part in
some such dialogue as the following (commenced by the
clown): "I say, sir!"—"Well, sir?" (it's always conducted
in the politest manner).—"Did you ever happen to hear
I was in the army, sir?"—"No, sir."—"Oh, yes, sir—I can
go through my exercise, sir."—"Indeed, sir!"—"Shall I do
it now, sir?"—"If you please, sir; come, sir—make haste"

(a cut with the long whip, and "Ha' done now—I don't like it," from the clown). Here the clown throws himself on the ground, and goes through a variety of gymnastic convulsions, doubling himself up, and untying himself again, and making himself look very like a man in the most hopeless extreme of human agony, to the vociferous delight of the gallery, until he is interrupted by a second cut from the long whip, and a request to see "what Miss Woolford's stopping for?" On which, to the inexpressible mirth of the gallery, he exclaims, "Now, Miss Woolford, what can I come for to go, for to fetch, for to bring, for to carry, for to do for you, ma'am?" On the lady's announcing with a sweet smile that she wants the two flags, they are, with sundry grimaces, procured and handed up; the clown facetiously observing after the performance of the latter ceremony—"He, he, oh! I say, sir, Miss Woolford knows me; she smiled at me." Another cut from the whip, a burst from the orchestra, a start from the horse, and round goes Miss Woolford again on her graceful performance, to the delight of every member of the audience, young or old. The next pause affords an opportunity for similar witticisms, the only additional fun being that of the clown making ludicrous grimaces at the riding-master every time his back is turned; and finally quitting the circle by jumping over his head, having previously directed his attention another way.

Did any of our readers ever notice the class of people, who hang about the stage-doors of our minor theatres in the day-time? You will rarely pass one of these entrances without seeing a group of three or four men conversing on the pavement, with an indescribable public-house-parlour swagger, and a kind of conscious air, peculiar to people of this description. They always seem to think they are exhibiting; the lamps are ever before them. That young fellow in the faded brown coat, and very full light green trousers, pulls down the wristbands of his check shirt, as ostentatiously as if it were of the finest linen, and cocks the white hat of the summer-before-last as knowingly over his right eye, as if it were a purchase of yesterday. Look at the dirty white Berlin gloves, and the cheap silk handkerchief stuck in the bosom of his threadbare coat. Is it possible to see him for an instant, and not come to the conclusion that he is the walking gentleman who wears a blue surtout, clean collar, and white trousers, for half an hour, and then shrinks into his worn-out scanty clothes: who has to boast night after night of his splendid fortune, with the painful consciousness of a pound a week and his boots to find; to talk of his father's mansion in the country, with a dreary recollection of his own two-pair back, in the New Cut; and to be envied and flattered as the favoured lover of a rich heiress, remembering all the while that the ex-dancer at home is in the family way, and out of an engagement?

Next to him, perhaps, you will see a thin pale man, with a very long face, in a suit of shining black, thoughtfully knocking that part of his boot which once had a heel, with an ash stick. He is the man who does the heavy business, such as prosy fathers, virtuous servants, curates, landlords. and so forth.

By the way, talking of fathers, we should very much like to see some piece in which all the dramatis personæ were orphans. Fathers are invariably great nuisances on the stage, and always have to give the hero or heroine a long explanation of what was done before the curtain rose, usually commencing with " It is now nineteen years, my dear child, since your blessed mother (here the old villain's voice falters) confided you to my charge. You were then an infant," &c., &c. Or else they have to discover, all of a sudden, that somebody whom they have been in constant communication with, during three long acts, without the slightest suspicion, is their own child : in which case they exclaim, " Ah ! what do I see ? This bracelet ! That smile ! These documents ! Those eyes ! Can I believe my senses?—It must be !— Yes—it is, it is my child ! "—" My father ! " exclaims the child ; and they fall into each other's arms, and look over each other's shoulders, and the audience give three rounds of applause.

To return from this digression, we were about to say that these are the sort of people whom you see talking, and attitudinising, outside the stage-doors of our minor theatres. At Astley's they are always more numerous than at any other place. There is generally a groom or two, sitting on the window-sill, and two or three dirty shabby-genteel men in checked neckerchiefs, and sallow linen, lounging about, and carrying, perhaps, under one arm, a pair of stage shoes badly wrapped up in a piece of old newspaper. Some years ago we used to stand looking, open-mouthed, at these men, with a feeling of mysterious curiosity, the very recollection

of which provokes a smile at the moment we are writing.
We could not believe that the beings of light and elegance,
in milk-white tunics, salmon-coloured legs, and blue scarfs,
who flitted on sleek cream-coloured horses before our eyes
at night, with all the aid of lights, music, and artificial
flowers, could be the pale, dissipated-looking creatures we
beheld by day.

We can hardly believe it now. Of the lower class of
actors we have seen something, and it requires no great
exercise of imagination to identify the walking gentleman
with the " dirty swell," the comic singer with the public-
house chairman, or the leading tragedian with drunkenness
and distress; but these other men are mysterious beings,
never seen out of the ring, never beheld but in the costume
of gods and sylphs. With the exception of Ducrow, who
can scarcely be classed among them, who ever knew a rider
at Astley's, or saw him but on horseback? Can our friend
in the military uniform, ever appear in threadbare attire,
or descend to the comparatively un-wadded costume of
every-day life? Impossible! We cannot—we will not—
believe it.

Greenwich Fair
(p. 118)

CHAPTER XII

GREENWICH FAIR

IF the Parks be "the lungs of London," we wonder what Greenwich Fair is—a periodical breaking out, we suppose, a sort of spring-rash: a three days' fever, which cools the blood for six months afterwards, and at the expiration of which London is restored to its old habits of plodding industry, as suddenly and completely as if nothing had ever happened to disturb them.

In our earlier days, we were a constant frequenter of Greenwich Fair, for years. We have proceeded to, and returned from it, in almost every description of vehicle. We cannot conscientiously deny the charge of having once made the passage in a spring-van, accompanied by thirteen gentlemen, fourteen ladies, an unlimited number of children, and a barrel of beer; and we have a vague recollection of having, in later days, found ourself the eighth outside, on the top of a hackney-coach, at something past four o'clock in the morning, with a rather confused idea of our own name, or place of residence. We have grown older since then, and quiet, and steady: liking nothing better than to spend our Easter, and all our other holidays, in some quiet nook, with people of whom we shall never tire; but we think we still remember something of Greenwich Fair, and of those who resort to it. At all events we will try.

The road to Greenwich during the whole of Easter Monday, is in a state of perpetual bustle and noise. Cabs, hackney-coaches, "shay" carts, coal-waggons, stages, omnibuses, sociables, gigs, donkey-chaises—all crammed with people (for the question never is, what the horse can draw, but what the vehicle will hold), roll along at their utmost speed; the dust flies in clouds, ginger-beer corks go off in volleys, the balcony of every public-house is crowded with people, smoking and drinking, half the private houses are

turned into tea-shops. fiddles are in great request, every
little fruit-shop displays its stall of gilt gingerbread and
penny toys ; turnpike men are in despair ; horses won't go
on, and wheels will come off ; ladies in " carawans " scream
with fright at every fresh concussion, and their admirers
find it necessary to sit remarkably close to them, by way of
encouragement : servants-of-all-work, who are not allowed
to have followers, and have got a holiday for the day, make
the most of their time with tho faithful admirer who waits
for a stolen interview at the corner of the street every night,
when they go to fetch the beer—apprentices grow sentimental, and straw-bonnet makers kind. Everybody is
anxious to get on, and actuated by the common wish to be
at the fair. or in the park, as soon as possible.

Pedestrians linger in groups at the roadside, unable to
resist the allurements of the stout proprietress of the " Jack-
in-the-box, three shies a penny," or the more splendid offers
of the man with three thimbles and a pea on a little round
board, who astonishes the bewildered crowd with some such
address as, " Here's the sort o' game to make you laugh
seven years arter you're dead, and turn ev'ry air on your
ed grey vith delight ! Three thimbles and vun little pea—
with a vun, two, three, and a two, three, vun : catch him
who can, look on, keep your eyes open, and niver say die !
niver mind the change, and the expense : all fair and above
board : them as don't play can't vin, and luck attend the
ryal sportsman ! Bet any gen'lm'n any sum of money, from
harf-a-crown up to a suverin, as he doesn't name the thimble
as kivers the pea ! " Here some greenhorn whispers his
friend that he distinctly saw the pea roll under the middle
thimble—an impression which is immediately confirmed
by a gentleman in top-boots, who is standing by, and who,
in a low tone, regrets his own inability to bet, in consequence of having unfortunately left his purse at home, but
strongly urges the stranger not to neglect such a golden
opportunity. The "plant" is successful, the bet is made,
the stranger of course loses : and the gentleman with the
thimbles consoles him. as he pockets the money, with an
assurance that it's " all the fortin of war ! this time I vin,
next time you vin : niver mind the loss of two bob and
a bender ! Do it up in a small parcel, and break out in
a fresh place. Here's the sort o' game," &c.—and the
eloquent harangue, with such variations as the speaker's

exuberant fancy suggests, is again repeated to the gaping crowd, reinforced by the accession of several new-comers.

The chief place of resort in the daytime, after the public-houses, is the park, in which the principal amusement is to drag young ladies up the steep hill which leads to the Observatory, and then drag them down again, at the very top of their speed, greatly to the derangement of their curls and bonnet-caps, and much to the edification of lookers-on from below. "Kiss in the Ring," and "Threading my Grandmother's Needle," too, are sports which receive their full share of patronage. Love-sick swains, under the influence of gin-and-water, and the tender passion, become violently affectionate : and the fair objects of their regard enhance the value of stolen kisses, by a vast deal of struggling, and holding down of heads, and cries of " Oh! Ha' done, then, George—Oh, do tickle him for me, Mary—Well, I never !" and similar Lucretian ejaculations. Little old men and women, with a small basket under one arm, and a wine-glass, without a foot, in the other hand, tender "a drop o' the right sort" to the different groups ; and young ladies, who are persuaded to indulge in a drop of the aforesaid right sort, display a pleasing degree of reluctance to taste it, and cough afterwards with great propriety.

The old pensioners, who, for the moderate charge of a penny, exhibit the mast-house, the Thames and shipping, the place where the men used to hang in chains, and other interesting sights, through a telescope, are asked questions about objects within the range of the glass, which it would puzzle a Solomon to answer ; and requested to find out particular houses in particular streets, which it would have been a task of some difficulty for Mr. Horner (not the young gentleman who ate mince-pies with his thumb, but the man of Colosseum notoriety) to discover. Here and there, where some three or four couple are sitting on the grass together, you will see a sun-burnt woman in a red cloak " telling fortunes " and prophesying husbands, which it requires no extraordinary observation to describe, for the originals are before her. Thereupon, the lady concerned laughs and blushes, and ultimately buries her face in an imitation cambric handkerchief, and the gentleman described looks extremely foolish, and squeezes her hand, and fees the gipsy liberally ; and the gipsy goes away, perfectly satisfied herself, and leaving those behind her perfectly satisfied also : and the prophecy, like

F

many other prophecies of greater importance, fulfils itself in
time.

But it grows dark : the crowd has gradually dispersed, and
only a few stragglers are left behind. The light in the
direction of the church shows that the fair is illuminated ;
and the distant noise proves it to be filling fast. The spot,
which half an hour ago was ringing with the shouts of
boisterous mirth, is as calm and quiet as if nothing could
ever disturb its serenity ; the fine old trees, the majestic
building at their feet, with the noble river beyond, glistening
in the moonlight, appear in all their beauty, and under their
most favourable aspect ; the voices of the boys, singing their
evening hymn, are borne gently on the air ; and the humblest
mechanic who has been lingering on the grass so pleasant to
the feet that beat the same dull round from week to week
in the paved streets of London, feels proud to think as he
surveys the scene before him, that he belongs to the country
which has selected such a spot as a retreat for its oldest
and best defenders in the decline of their lives.

Five minutes' walking brings you to the fair; a scene
calculated to awaken very different feelings. The entrance is
occupied on either side by the vendors of gingerbread and
toys : the stalls are gaily lighted up, the most attractive
goods profusely disposed, and unbonneted young ladies, in
their zeal for the interest of their employers, seize you by the
coat, and use all the blandishments of " Do, dear "—" There's
a love "—" Don't be cross, now," &c., to induce you to
purchase half a pound of the real spice nuts, of which the
majority of the regular fair-goers carry a pound or two as
a present supply, tied up in a cotton pocket-handkerchief.
Occasionally you pass a deal table, on which are exposed
pen'orths of pickled salmon (fennel included), in little white
saucers : oysters, with shells as large as cheese-plates, and
divers specimens of a species of snail (*wilks*, we think they are
called), floating in a somewhat bilious-looking green liquid.
Cigars, too, are in great demand ; gentlemen must smoke, of
course, and here they are, two a penny, in a regular authentic
cigar-box, with a lighted tallow candle in the centre.

Imagine yourself in an extremely dense crowd, which swings
you to and fro, and in and out, and every way but the right
one ; add to this the screams of women, the shouts of boys,
the clanging of gongs, the firing of pistols, the ringing of
bells, the bellowings of speaking-trumpets, the squeaking of

George Cruikshank.

Private Theatres

(*p. 124*)

penny dittoes, the noise of a dozen bands, with three drums in each, all playing different tunes at the same time, the hallooing of showmen, and an occasional roar from the wild-beast shows; and you are in the very centre and heart of the fair.

This immense booth, with the large stage in front, so brightly illuminated with variegated lamps, and pots of burning fat, is "Richardson's," where you have a melo-drama (with three murders and a ghost), a pantomime, a comic song, an overture, and some incidental music, all done in five-and-twenty minutes.

The company are now promenading outside in all the dignity of wigs, spangles, red-ochre, and whitening. See with what a ferocious air the gentleman who personates the Mexican chief, paces up and down, and with what an eye of calm dignity the principal tragedian gazes on the crowd below, or converses confidentially with the harlequin! The four clowns, who are engaged in a mock broadsword combat, may be all very well for the low-minded holiday-makers; but these are the people for the reflective portion of the community. They look so noble in those Roman dresses, with their yellow legs and arms, long black curly heads, bushy eyebrows, and scowl expressive of assassination, and vengeance, and everything else that is grand and solemn. Then, the ladies—were there ever such innocent and awful-looking beings; as they walk up and down the platform in twos and threes, with their arms round each other's waists, or leaning for support on one of those majestic men! Their spangled muslin dresses and blue satin shoes and sandals (a *leetle* the worse for wear) are the admiration of all beholders; and the playful manner in which they check the advances of the clown, is perfectly enchanting.

"Just a-going to begin! Pray come for'erd, come for'erd," exclaims the man in the countryman's dress, for the seventieth time: and people force their way up the steps in crowds. The band suddenly strikes up, the harlequin and columbine set the example, reels are formed in less than no time, the Roman heroes place their arms a-kimbo, and dance with considerable agility; and the leading tragic actress, and the gentleman who enacts the "swell" in the pantomime, foot it to perfection. "All in to begin," shouts the manager, when no more people can be induced to "come for'erd," and away rush the leading members of the company to do the dreadful in the first piece.

A change of performance takes place every day during the fair, but the story of the tragedy is always pretty much the same. There is a rightful heir, who loves a young lady, and is beloved by her ; and a wrongful heir, who loves her too, and isn't beloved by her ; and the wrongful heir gets hold of the rightful heir, and throws him into a dungeon, just to kill him off when convenient, for which purpose he hires a couple of assassins—a good one and a bad one—who, the moment they are left alone, get up a little murder on their own account, the good one killing the bad one, and the bad one wounding the good one. Then the rightful heir is discovered in prison, carefully holding a long chain in his hands, and seated despondingly in a large arm-chair ; and the young lady comes in to two bars of soft music, and embraces the rightful heir ; and then the wrongful heir comes in to two bars of quick music (technically called "a hurry "), and goes on in the most shocking manner, throwing the young lady about as if she was nobody, and calling the rightful heir "Ar-recreant—ar-wretch!" in a very loud voice, which answers the double purpose of displaying his passion, and preventing the sound being deadened by the sawdust. The interest becomes intense ; the wrongful heir draws his sword, and rushes on the rightful heir ; a blue smoke is seen, a gong is heard, and a tall white figure (who has been all this time, behind the arm-chair, covered over with a table-cloth), slowly rises to the tune of " Oft in the stilly night." This is no other than the ghost of the rightful heir's father, who was killed by the wrongful heir's father, at sight of which the wrongful heir becomes apoplectic, and is literally " struck all of a heap," the stage not being large enough to admit of his falling down at full length. Then the good assassin staggers in, and says he was hired in conjunction with the bad assassin, by the wrongful heir, to kill the rightful heir ; and he's killed a good many people in his time, but he's very sorry for it, and won't do so any more—a promise which he immediately redeems, by dying off hand without any nonsense about it. Then the rightful heir throws down his chain ; and then two men, a sailor, and a young woman (the tenantry of the rightful heir) come in, and the ghost makes dumb motions to them, which they, by supernatural interference, understand—for no one else can ; and the ghost (who can't do anything without blue fire) blesses the right-ful heir and the young lady, by half suffocating them with smoke: and then a muffin-bell rings, and the curtain drops.

The exhibitions next in popularity to these itinerant theatres are the travelling menageries, or, to speak more intelligibly, the "Wild-beast shows," where a military band in beef-eater's costume, with leopard-skin caps, play incessantly; and where large highly-coloured representations of tigers tearing men's heads open, and a lion being burnt with red-hot irons to induce him to drop his victim, are hung up outside, by way of attracting visitors.

The principal officer at these places is generally a very tall, hoarse man, in a scarlet coat, with a cane in his hand, with which he occasionally raps the pictures we have just noticed, by way of illustrating his description—something in this way. "Here, here, here; the lion, the lion (tap), exactly as he is represented on the canvas outside (three taps): no waiting, remember; no deception. The fe-ro-cious lion (tap, tap) who bit off the gentleman's head last Cambervel vos a twelvemonth, and has killed on the awerage three keepers a year ever since he arrived at matoority. No extra charge on this account recollect; the price of admission is only sixpence." This address never fails to produce a considerable sensation, and sixpences flow into the treasury with wonderful rapidity.

The dwarfs are also objects of great curiosity, and as a dwarf, a giantess, a living skeleton, a wild Indian, "a young lady of singular beauty, with perfectly white hair and pink eyes," and two or three other natural curiosities, are usually exhibited together for the small charge of a penny, they attract very numerous audiences. The best thing about a dwarf is, that he has always a little box, about two feet six inches high, into which, by long practice, he can just manage to get, by doubling himself up like a boot-jack; this box is painted outside like a six-roomed house, and as the crowd see him ring a bell, or fire a pistol out of the first-floor window, they verily believe that it is his ordinary town residence, divided like other mansions into drawing-rooms, dining-parlour, and bedchambers. Shut up in this case, the unfortunate little object is brought out to delight the throng by holding a facetious dialogue with the proprietor: in the course of which, the dwarf (who is always particularly drunk) pledges himself to sing a comic song inside, and pays various compliments to the ladies, which induce them to "come for'erd" with great alacrity. As a giant is not so easily

moved, a pair of indescribables of most capacious dimensions,
and a huge shoe, are usually brought out, into which two or
three stout men get all at once, to the enthusiastic delight
of the crowd, who are quite satisfied with the solemn assurance that these habiliments form part of the giant's everyday
costume.

The grandest and most numerously-frequented booth in
the whole fair, however, is "The Crown and Anchor"—a
temporary ball-room—we forget how many hundred feet long,
the price of admission to which is one shilling. Immediately
on your right hand as you enter, after paying your money, is
a refreshment place, at which cold beef, roast and boiled,
French rolls, stout, wine, tongue, ham, even fowls, if we
recollect right, are displayed in tempting array. There is a
raised orchestra, and the place is boarded all the way down,
in patches, just wide enough for a country dance.

There is no master of the ceremonies in this artificial Eden
—all is primitive, unreserved, and unstudied. The dust is
blinding, the heat insupportable, the company somewhat noisy,
and in the highest spirits possible : the ladies, in the height
of their innocent animation, dancing in the gentlemen's hats,
and the gentlemen promenading "the gay and festive scene"
in the ladies' bonnets, or with the more expensive ornaments
of false noses, and low-crowned, tinder-box-looking hats:
playing children's drums, and accompanied by ladies on the
penny trumpet.

The noise of these various instruments, the orchestra, the
shouting, the "scratchers," and the dancing, is perfectly
bewildering. The dancing itself beggars description—every
figure lasts about an hour, and the ladies bounce up and
down the middle, with a degree of spirit which is quite indescribable. As to the gentlemen, they stamp their feet against
the ground, every time "hands four round" begins, go down
the middle and up again, with cigars in their mouths, and
silk handkerchiefs in their hands, and whirl their partners
round, nothing loth, scrambling and falling, and embracing,
and knocking up against the other couples, until they are
fairly tired out, and can move no longer. The same scene is
repeated again and again (slightly varied by an occasional
"row") until a late hour at night: and a great many clerks
and 'prentices find themselves next morning with aching
heads, empty pockets, damaged hats, and a very imperfect
recollection of how it was they did *not* get home.

CHAPTER XIII

PRIVATE THEATRES

"Richard the Third.—Duke of Glo'ster, 2*l.*; Earl of Richmond, 1*l.*; Duke of Buckingham, 15*s.*; Catesby, 12*s.*; Tressel, 10*s.* 6*d.*; Lord Stanley, 5*s*; Lord Mayor of London, 2*s.* 6*d.*"

Such are the written placards wafered up in the gentlemen's dressing-room, or the green-room (where there is any), at a private theatre; and such are the sums extracted from the shop-till, or overcharged in the office expenditure, by the donkeys who are prevailed upon to pay for permission to exhibit their lamentable ignorance and boobyism on the stage of a private theatre. This they do, in proportion to the scope afforded by the character for the display of their imbecility. For instance, the Duke of Glo'ster is well worth two pounds, because he has it all to himself; he must wear a real sword, and what is better still, he must draw it several times in the course of the piece. The soliloquies alone are well worth fifteen shillings; then there is the stabbing King Henry—decidedly cheap at three-and-sixpence, that's eighteen-and-sixpence; bullying the coffin-bearers—say eighteen-pence, though it's worth much more—that's a pound. Then the love scene with Lady Ann, and the bustle of the fourth act can't be dear at ten shillings more—that's only one pound ten, including the "off with his head!"—which is sure to bring down the applause, and it is very easy to do—"Orf with his ed" (very quick and loud;—then slow and sneeringly)—"So much for Bu-u-u-uckingham!" Lay the emphasis on the "uck;" get yourself gradually into a corner, and work with your right hand, while you're saying it, as if you were feeling your way, and it's sure to do. The tent scene is confessedly worth half-a-sovereign, and so you have the fight in, gratis, and everybody knows what an effect may be produced by a good combat. One—two—three—four—over; then, one—two—three—four—under; then thrust; then dodge and slide about; then fall down on one knee; then fight upon it, and then get up again and stagger. You may keep on doing this, as long as it seems to take —say ten minutes—and then fall down (backwards, if you can manage it without hurting yourself), and die game: nothing like it for producing an effect. They always do it at Astley's and Sadler's Wells, and if they don't know how to do this sort of thing, who in the world does? A small child, or a female in white, increases the interest of a combat materially—indeed, we are not aware that a regular legitimate terrific broadsword combat could be done without; but it would be rather difficult, and somewhat unusual, to introduce this effect in the last scene of Richard the Third, so the only thing to be done is, just to make the best of a bad bargain, and be as long as possible fighting it out.

The principal patrons of private theatres are dirty boys, low copying-clerks in attorneys' offices, capacious-headed youths from city counting-houses, Jews whose business, as lenders of fancy dresses, is a sure passport to the amateur stage, shop-boys who now and then mistake their masters' money for their own; and a choice miscellany of idle vaga-bonds. The proprietor of a private theatre may be an ex-scene-painter, a low coffee-house-keeper, a disappointed eighth-rate actor, a retired smuggler, or uncertificated bank-rupt. The theatre itself may be in Catherine Street, Strand, the purlieus of the city, the neighbourhood of Gray's Inn Lane, or the vicinity of Sadler's Wells; or it may, perhaps, form the chief nuisance of some shabby street, on the Surrey side of Waterloo Bridge.

The lady performers pay nothing for their characters, and it is needless to add, are usually selected from one class of society; the audiences are necessarily of much the same character as the performers, who receive, in return for their contributions to the management, tickets to the amount of the money they pay.

All the minor theatres in London, especially the lowest, constitute the centre of a little stage-struck neighbourhood. Each of them has an audience exclusively its own; and at any you will see dropping into the pit at half-price, or swaggering into the back of a box, if the price of admission be a reduced one, divers boys of from fifteen to twenty-one years of age, who throw back their coat and turn up their wristbands, after the portraits of Count D'Orsay, hum tunes and whistle

when the curtain is down, by way of persuading the people
near them, that they are not at all anxious to have it up
again, and speak familiarly of the inferior performers as Bill
Such-a-one, and Ned So-and-so, or tell each other how a new
piece called *The Unknown Bandit of the Invisible Cavern*, is
in rehearsal ; how Mister Palmer is to play *The Unknown
Bandit;* how Charley Scarton is to take the part of an
English sailor, and fight a broadsword combat with six
unknown bandits, at one and the same time (one theatrical
sailor is always equal to half a dozen men at least) ; how
Mister Palmer and Charley Scarton are to go through a
double hornpipe in fetters in the second act ; how the interior
of the invisible cavern is to occupy the whole extent of the
stage ; and other town-surprising theatrical announcements.
These gentlemen are the amateurs—the *Richards, Shylocks.
Beverleys,* and *Othellos*—the *Young Dorntons, Rovers, Captain
Absolutes,* and *Charles Surfaces*—of a private theatre.

See them at the neighbouring public-house or the theatrical
coffee-shop ! They are the kings of the place, supposing no
real performers to be present ; and roll about, hats on one
side, and arms a-kimbo, as if they had actually come into
possession of eighteen shillings a week, and a share of a ticket
night. If one of them does but know an Astley's supernumerary he is a happy fellow. The mingled air of envy
and admiration with which his companions will regard him,
as he converses familiarly with some mouldy-looking man in
a fancy neckerchief, whose partially corked eyebrows, and
half-rouged face, testify to the fact of his having just left
the stage or the circle, sufficiently shows in what high
admiration these public characters are held.

With the double view of guarding against the discovery
of friends or employers, and enhancing the interest of an
assumed character, by attaching a high-sounding name to its
representative, these geniuses assume fictitious names, which
are not the least amusing part of the play-bill of a private
theatre. Belville, Melville, Treville, Berkeley, Randolph,
Byron, St. Clair, and so forth, are among the humblest ; and
the less imposing titles of Jenkins, Walker, Thomson, Barker,
Solomons, &c., are completely laid aside. There is something
imposing in this, and it is an excellent apology for shabbiness
into the bargain. A shrunken, faded coat, a decayed hat,
a patched and soiled pair of trousers—nay, even a very dirty
shirt (and none of these appearances are very uncommon

among the members of the *corps dramatique*), may be worn
for the purpose of disguise, and to prevent the remotest
chance of recognition. Then it prevents any troublesome
inquiries or explanations about employment and pursuits ;
everybody is a gentleman at large, for the occasion, and there
are none of those unpleasant and unnecessary distinctions to
which even genius must occasionally succumb elsewhere. As
to the ladies (God bless them), they are quite above any
formal absurdities ; the mere circumstance of your being
behind the scenes is a sufficient introduction to their society
—for of course they know that none but strictly respectable
persons would be admitted into that close fellowship with
them, which acting engenders. They place implicit reliance
on the manager, no doubt ; and as to the manager, he is all
affability when he knows you well,—or, in other words, when
he has pocketed your money once, and entertains confident
hopes of doing so again.

A quarter before eight—there will be a full house to-
night—six parties in the boxes, already ; four little boys and
a woman in the pit ; and two fiddles and a flute in the
orchestra, who have got through five overtures since seven
o'clock (the hour fixed for the commencement of the performances), and have just begun the sixth. There will be
plenty of it, though, when it does begin, for there is enough
in the bill to last six hours at least.

That gentleman in the white hat and checked shirt, brown
coat and brass buttons, lounging behind the stage-box on the
O. P. side, is Mr. Horatio St. Julien, alias Jem Larkins. His
line is genteel comedy—his father's, coal and potato. He *does*
Alfred Highflier in the last piece, and very well he'll do it—
at the price. The party of gentlemen in the opposite box,
to whom he has just nodded, are friends and supporters of
Mr. Beverley (otherwise Loggins), the *Macbeth* of the night.
You observe their attempts to appear easy and gentlemanly,
each member of the party, with his feet cocked upon the
cushion in front of the box ! They let them do these things
here, upon the same humane principle which permits poor
people's children to knock double knocks at the door of an
empty house—because they can't do it anywhere else. The
two stout men in the centre box, with an opera-glass ostentatiously placed before them, are friends of the proprietor—
opulent country managers, as he confidentially informs every
individual among the crew behind the curtain—opulent

country managers looking out for recruits ; a representation which Mr. Nathan, the dresser, who is in the manager's interest, and has just arrived with the costumes, offers to confirm upon oath if required—corroborative evidence, how· ever, is quite unnecessary, for the gulls believe it at once.

The stout Jewess who has just entered is the mother of the pale bony little girl, with the necklace of blue glass beads, sitting by her; she is being brought up to "the profession." Pantomime is to be her line, and she is coming out to-night, in a hornpipe after the tragedy. The short thin man beside Mr. St. Julien, whose white face is so deeply seared with the small-pox, and whose dirty shirt-front is inlaid with open-work, and embossed with coral studs like ladybirds, is the low comedian and comic singer of the establishment. The remainder of the audience—a tolerably numerous one by this time—are a motley group of dupes and blackguards.

The foot-lights have just made their appearance : the wicks of the six little oil lamps round the only tier of boxes are being turned up, and the additional light thus afforded serves to show the presence of dirt, and absence of paint, which forms a prominent feature in the audience part of the house. As these preparations, however, announce the speedy commencement of the play, let us take a peep "behind," previous to the ringing-up.

The little narrow passages beneath the stage are neither especially clean nor too brilliantly lighted ; and the absence of any flooring, together with the damp mildewy smell which pervades the place, does not conduce in any great degree to their comfortable appearance. Don't fall over this plate basket—it's one of the "properties"—the caldron for the witches' cave ; and the three uncouth-looking figures, with broken clothes-props in their hands, who are drinking gin-and-water out of a pint pot, are the weird sisters. This miserable room, lighted by candles in sconces placed at lengthened intervals round the wall, is the dressing-room, common to the gentlemen performers, and the square hole in the ceiling is *the* trap-door of the stage above. You will observe that the ceiling is ornamented with the beams that support the boards, and tastefully hung with cobwebs.

The characters in the tragedy are all dressed, and their own clothes are scattered in hurried confusion over the wooden dresser which surrounds the room. That snuff-shop-looking figure, in front of the glass, is *Banquo :* and the

young lady with the liberal display of legs, who is kindly
painting his face with a hare's foot, is dressed for *Fleance*.
The large woman, who is consulting the stage directions in
Cumberland's edition of *Macbeth*, is the *Lady Macbeth* of the
night; she is always selected to play the part, because she
is tall and stout, and *looks* a little like Mrs. Siddons—at
a considerable distance. That stupid-looking milksop, with
light hair and bow legs—a kind of man whom you can
warrant town-made—is fresh caught; he plays *Malcolm* to-
night, just to accustom himself to an audience. He will get
on better by degrees; he will play *Othello* in a month, and
in a month more, will very probably be apprehended on a
charge of embezzlement. The black-eyed female with whom
he is talking so earnestly, is dressed for the "gentlewoman."
It is *her* first appearance, too—in that character. The boy
of fourteen who is having his eyebrows smeared with soap
and whitening, is *Duncan*, King of Scotland; and the two
dirty men with the corked countenances, in very old green
tunics, and dirty drab boots, are the "army."

"Look sharp below there, gents," exclaims the dresser, a
red-headed and red-whiskered Jew, calling through the trap,
"they're a-going to ring up. The flute says he'll be blowed
if he plays any more, and they're getting precious noisy in
front." A general rush immediately takes place to the half-
dozen little steep steps leading to the stage, and the heterogeneous group are soon assembled at the side scenes, in
breathless anxiety and motley confusion.

"Now," cries the manager, consulting the written list
which hangs behind the first P. S. wing, "Scene 1, open
country—lamps down—thunder and lightning—all ready.
White?" [This is addressed to one of the army.] "All
ready."—"Very well. Scene 2, front chamber. Is the front
chamber down?"—"Yes."—"Very well."—"Jones" [to the
other army who is up in the flies]. "Hallo!"—"Wind up
the open country when we ring up."—"I'll take care."—
"Scene 3, back perspective with practical bridge. Bridge
ready, White? Got the tressels there?"—"All right."

"Very well. Clear the stage," cries the manager, hastily
packing every member of the company into the little space
there is between the wings and the wall, and one wing and
another. "Places, places. Now then, Witches—Duncan—
Malcolm—bleeding officer—where's the bleeding officer?"—
"Here!" replies the officer, who has been rose-pinking for

the character. "Get ready, then ; now, White, ring the second music-bell." The actors who are to be discovered, are hastily arranged, and the actors who are not to be discovered place themselves, in their anxiety to peep at the house, just where the audience can see them. The bell rings, and the orchestra, in acknowledgment of the call, play three distinct chords. The bell rings—the tragedy (!) opens—and our description closes.

CHAPTER XIV

VAUXHALL GARDENS BY DAY

THERE was a time when if a man ventured to wonder how
Vauxhall Gardens would look by day, he was hailed with
a shout of derision at the absurdity of the idea. Vauxhall
by daylight! A porter-pot without porter, the House of
Commons without the Speaker, a gas-lamp without the gas—
pooh, nonsense, the thing was not to be thought of. It was
rumoured, too, in those times, that Vauxhall Gardens by
day were the scene of secret and hidden experiments; that
there, carvers were exercised in the mystic art of cutting
a moderate-sized ham into slices thin enough to pave the
whole of the grounds; that beneath the shade of the tall
trees, studious men were constantly engaged in chemical
experiments, with the view of discovering how much water
a bowl of negus could possibly bear; and that in some
retired nooks, appropriated to the study of ornithology,
other sage and learned men were, by a process known only
to themselves, incessantly employed in reducing fowls to
a mere combination of skin and bone. .

Vague rumours of this kind, together with many others of
a similar nature, cast over Vauxhall Gardens an air of deep
mystery; and as there is a great deal in the mysterious,
there is no doubt that to a good many people, at all events,
the pleasure they afforded was not a little enhanced by this
very circumstance.

Of this class of people we confess to having made one.
We loved to wander among these illuminated groves, thinking of the patient and laborious researches which had been
carried on there during the day, and witnessing their results
in the suppers which were served up beneath the light of
lamps and to the sound of music at night. The temples and
saloons and cosmoramas and fountains glittered and sparkled
before our eyes; the beauty of the lady singers and the
elegant deportment of the gentlemen, captivated our hearts;

a few hundred thousand of additional lamps dazzled our senses; a bowl or two of punch bewildered our brains; and we were happy.

In an evil hour, the proprietors of Vauxhall Gardens took to opening them by day. We regretted this, as rudely and harshly disturbing that veil of mystery which had hung about the property for many years, and which none but the noonday sun, and the late Mr. Simpson, had ever penetrated. We shrunk from going; at this moment we scarcely know why. Perhaps a morbid consciousness of approaching disappointment—perhaps a fatal presentiment—perhaps the weather; whatever it was, we did *not* go until the second or third announcement of a race between two balloons tempted us, and we went.

We paid our shilling at the gate, and then we saw for the first time, that the entrance, if there had been any magic about it at all, was now decidedly disenchanted, being, in fact, nothing more nor less than a combination of very roughly-painted boards and sawdust. We glanced at the orchestra and supper-room as we hurried past—we just recognised them, and that was all. We bent our steps to the firework-ground; there, at least, we should not be disappointed. We reached it, and stood rooted to the spot with mortification and astonishment. *That* the Moorish tower—that wooden shed with a door in the centre, and daubs of crimson and yellow all round, like a gigantic watchcase! *That* the place where night after night we had beheld the undaunted Mr. Blackmore make his terrific ascent, surrounded by flames of fire, and peals of artillery, and where the white garments of Madame Somebody (we forget even her name now), who nobly devoted her life to the manufacture of fireworks, had so often been seen fluttering in the wind, as she called up a red, blue, or parti-coloured light to illumine her temple! *That* the——but at this moment the bell rang; the people scampered away, pell-mell, to the spot from whence the sound proceeded; and we, from the mere force of habit, found ourself running among the first, as if for very life.

It was for the concert in the orchestra. A small party of dismal men in cocked hats were "executing" the overture to *Tancredi*, and a numerous assemblage of ladies and gentlemen, with their families, had rushed from their half-emptied stout mugs in the supper boxes, and crowded to the spot.

Intense was the low murmur of admiration when a particularly small gentleman, in a dress coat, led on a particularly tall lady in a blue sarcenet pelisse and bonnet of the same, ornamented with large white feathers, and forthwith commenced a plaintive duet.

We knew the small gentleman well; we had seen a lithographed semblance of him, on many a piece of music, with his mouth wide open as if in the act of singing; a wine-glass in his hand; and a table with two decanters and four pineapples on it in the background. The tall lady, too, we had gazed on, lost in raptures of admiration, many and many a time—how different people *do* look by daylight, and without punch, to be sure! It was a beautiful duet: first the small gentleman asked a question, and then the tall lady answered it; then the small gentleman and the tall lady sang together most melodiously; then the small gentleman went through a little piece of vehemence by himself, and got very tenor indeed, in the excitement of his feelings, to which the tall lady responded in a similar manner; then the small gentleman had a shake or two, after which the tall lady had the same, and then they both merged imperceptibly into the original air: and the band wound themselves up to a pitch of fury, and the small gentleman handed the tall lady out, and the applause was rapturous.

The comic singer, however, was the especial favourite; we really thought that a gentleman, with his dinner in a pocket-handkerchief, who stood near us, would have fainted with excess of joy. A marvellously facetious gentleman that comic singer is; his distinguishing characteristics are, a wig approaching to the flaxen, and an aged countenance, and he bears the name of one of the English counties, if we recollect right. He sang a very good song about the seven ages, the first half-hour of which afforded the assembly the purest delight; of the rest we can make no report, as we did not stay to hear any more.

We walked about, and met with a disappointment at every turn; our favourite views were mere patches of paint; the fountain that had sparkled so showily by lamp-light, presented very much the appearance of a water-pipe that had burst; all the ornaments were dingy, and all the walks gloomy. There was a spectral attempt at rope-dancing in the little open theatre. The sun shone upon the spangled dresses of the performers, and their evolutions were about as

Vauxhall Gardens by Day

inspiriting and appropriate as a country-dance in a family vault. So we retraced our steps to the firework-ground, and mingled with the little crowd of people who were contemplating Mr. Green.

Some half-dozen men were restraining the impetuosity of one of the balloons, which was completely filled, and had the car already attached ; and as rumours had gone abroad that a Lord was "going up," the crowd were more than usually anxious and talkative. There was one little man in faded black, with a dirty face and a rusty black neckerchief with a red border, tied in a narrow wisp round his neck, who entered into conversation with everybody, and had something to say upon every remark that was made within his hearing. He was standing with his arms folded, staring up at the balloon, and every now and then vented his feelings of reverence for the aëronaut, by saying, as he looked round to catch somebody's eye, "He's a rum 'un is Green, think o' this here being up'ards of his two hundredth ascent ; ecod, the man as is ekal to Green never had the toothache yet, nor won't have within this hundred year, and that's all about it. When you meets with real talent, and native, too, encourage it, that's what I say ; " and when he had delivered himself to this effect, he would fold his arms with more determination than ever, and stare at the balloon with a sort of admiring defiance of any other man alive, beyond himself and Green, that impressed the crowd with the opinion that he was an oracle.

"Ah, you're very right, sir," said another gentleman, with his wife, and children, and mother, and wife's sister, and a host of female friends, in all the gentility of white pocket-handkerchiefs, frills, and spencers, " Mr. Green is a steady hand, sir, and there's no fear about him."

"Fear ! " said the little man : " isn't it a lovely thing to see him and his wife a-going up in one balloon, and his own son and *his* wife a-jostling up against them in another, and all of them going twenty or thirty mile in three hours or so, and then coming back in pochayses ? I don't know where this here science is to stop, mind you ; that's what bothers me."

Here there was a considerable talking among the females in the spencers.

"What's the ladies a-laughing at, sir ? " inquired the little man, condescendingly.

"It's only my sister Mary," said one of the girls, "as says she hopes his lordship won't be frightened when he's in the car, and want to come out again."

"Make yourself easy about that there, my dear," replied the little man. "If he was so much as to move a inch without leave, Green would jist fetch him a crack over the head with the telescope, as would send him into the bottom of the basket in no time, and stun him till they come down again."

"Would he, though?" inquired the other man.

"Yes, would he," replied the little one, "and think nothing of it, neither, if he was the king himself. Green's presence of mind is wonderful."

Just at this moment all eyes were directed to the preparations which were being made for starting. The car was attached to the second balloon, the two were brought pretty close together, and a military band commenced playing, with a zeal and fervour which would render the most timid man in existence but too happy to accept any means of quitting that particular spot of earth on which they were stationed. Then Mr. Green, sen., and his noble companion entered one car, and Mr. Green, jun., and *his* companion the other; and then the balloons went up, and the aërial travellers stood up, and the crowd outside roared with delight, and the two gentlemen who had never ascended before, tried to wave their flags, as if they were not nervous, but held on very fast all the while; and the balloons were wafted gently away, our little friend solemnly protesting, long after they were reduced to mere specks in the air, that he could still distinguish the white hat of Mr. Green. The gardens disgorged their multitudes, boys ran up and down screaming "bal-loon;" and in all the crowded thoroughfares people rushed out of their shops into the middle of the road, and having stared up in the air at two little black objects till they almost dislocated their necks, walked slowly in again, perfectly satisfied.

The next day there was a grand account of the ascent in the morning papers, and the public were informed how it was the finest day but four in Mr. Green's remembrance; how they retained sight of the earth till they lost it behind the clouds; and how the reflection of the balloon on the undulating masses of vapour was gorgeously picturesque; together with a little science about the refraction of the sun's rays, and some mysterious hints respecting atmospheric heat and eddying currents of air.

There was also an interesting account how a man in a boat was distinctly heard by Mr. Green, jun., to exclaim, "My eye!" which Mr. Green, jun., attributed to his voice rising to the balloon, and the sound being thrown back from its surface into the car; and the whole concluded with a slight allusion to another ascent next Wednesday, all of which was very instructive and very amusing, as our readers will see if they look to the papers. If we have forgotten to mention the date, they have only to wait till next summer, and take the account of the first ascent, and it will answer the purpose equally well.

CHAPTER XV

EARLY COACHES

WE have often wondered how many months' incessant travelling in a post-chaise it would take to kill a man; and wondering by analogy, we should very much like to know how many months of constant travelling in a succession of early coaches, an unfortunate mortal could endure. Breaking a man alive upon the wheel, would be nothing to breaking his rest, his peace, his heart—everything but his fast—upon four; and the punishment of Ixion (the only practical person, by-the-bye, who has discovered the secret of the perpetual motion) would sink into utter insignificance before the one we have suggested. If we had been a powerful churchman in those good times when blood was shed as freely as water, and men were mowed down like grass, in the sacred cause of religion, we would have lain by very quietly till we got hold of some especially obstinate miscreant, who positively refused to be converted to our faith, and then we would have booked him for an inside place in a small coach, which travelled day and night: and securing the remainder of the places for stout men with a slight tendency to coughing and spitting, we would have started him forth on his last travels; leaving him mercilessly to all the tortures which the waiters. landlords, coachmen, guards, boots, chambermaids, and other familiars on his line of road, might think proper to inflict.

Who has not experienced the miseries inevitably consequent upon a summons to undertake a hasty journey? You receive an intimation from your place of business—wherever that may be, or whatever you may be—that it will be necessary to leave town without delay. You and your family are forthwith thrown into a state of tremendous excitement; an express is immediately dispatched to the washerwoman's; everybody is in a bustle; and you, yourself, with a feeling of dignity which you cannot altogether conceal, sally forth to the booking-office to secure your place. Here a painful consciousness of your own unimportance first rushes on your mind—the people are as cool and collected as if nobody were going out of town, or as if a journey of a hundred odd miles were a mere nothing. You enter a mouldy-looking room, ornamented with large posting-bills ; the greater part of the place enclosed behind a huge lumbering rough counter, and fitted up with recesses that look like the dens of the smaller animals in a travelling menagerie, without the bars. Some half-dozen people are " booking " brown-paper parcels, which one of the clerks flings into the aforesaid recesses with an air of recklessness which you, remembering the new carpet-bag you bought in the morning, feel considerably annoyed at ; porters, looking like so many Atlases, keep rushing in and out, with large packages on their shoulders ; and while you are waiting to make the necessary inquiries, you wonder what on earth the booking-office clerks can have been before they were booking-office clerks ; one of them with his pen behind his ear, and his hands behind him, is standing in front of the fire, like a full-length portrait of Napoleon ; the other with his hat half off his head, enters the passengers' names in the books with a coolness which is inexpressibly provoking; and the villain whistles—actually whistles— while a man asks him what the fare is outside, all the way to Holyhead!—in frosty weather, too ! They are clearly an isolated race, evidently possessing no sympathies or feelings in common with the rest of mankind. Your turn comes at last, and having paid the fare, you tremblingly inquire—" What time will it be necessary for me to be here in the morning? "—" Six o'clock," replies the whistler, carelessly pitching the sovereign you have just parted with, into a wooden bowl on the desk. "Rather before than arter," adds the man with the semi-roasted unmentionables, with just as much ease and complacency as if the whole world got out of bed at five. You turn into the street, ruminating as you bend your steps homewards on the extent to which men become hardened in cruelty by custom.

If there be one thing in existence more miserable than another, it most unquestionably is the being compelled to rise by candle-light. If you ever doubted the fact, you are painfully convinced of your error, on the morning of your departure. You left strict orders, overnight, to be called at half-past four, and you have done nothing all night but doze for five minutes at a time, and start up suddenly from a terrific dream of a large church-clock with the small hand running round, with astonishing rapidity, to every figure on the dial-plate. At last, completely exhausted, you fall gradually into a refreshing sleep—your thoughts grow confused—the stage-coaches, which have been "going off" before your eyes all night, become less and less distinct, until they go off altogether; one moment you are driving with all the skill and smartness of an experienced whip—the next you are exhibiting *à la* Ducrow, on the off-leader; anon you are closely muffled up, inside, and have just recognised in the person of the guard an old schoolfellow, whose funeral, even in your dream, you remember to have attended eighteen years ago. At last you fall into a state of complete oblivion, from which you are aroused, as if into a new state of existence, by a singular illusion. You are apprenticed to a trunk-maker; how, or why, or when, or wherefore, you don't take the trouble to inquire; but there you are, pasting the lining in the lid of a portmanteau. Confound that other apprentice in the back shop, how he is hammering!—rap, rap, rap—what an industrious fellow he must be! you have heard him at work for half an hour past, and he has been hammering incessantly the whole time. Rap, rap, rap, again—he's talking now—what's that he said? Five o'clock! You make a violent exertion, and start up in bed. The vision is at once dispelled; the trunk-maker's shop is your own bedroom, and the other apprentice your shivering servant, who has been vainly endeavouring to wake you for the last quarter of an hour, at the imminent risk of breaking either his own knuckles or the panels of the door.

You proceed to dress yourself, with all possible dispatch. The flaring flat candle with the long snuff gives light enough to show that the things you want are not where they ought to be, and you undergo a trifling delay in consequence of having carefully packed up one of your boots in your over-anxiety of the preceding night. You soon complete your toilet, however, for you are not particular on such an occasion, and you shaved yesterday evening; so mounting your Petersham great-coat, and green travelling shawl, and grasping your carpet-bag in your right hand, you walk lightly down-stairs, lest you should awaken any of the family, and after pausing in the common sitting-room for one moment, just to have a cup of coffee (the said common sitting-room looking remarkably comfortable, with everything out of its place, and strewed with the crumbs of last night's supper), you undo the chain and bolts of the street-door, and find yourself fairly in the street.

A thaw, by all that is miserable! The frost is completely broken up. You look down the long perspective of Oxford Street, the gas-lights mournfully reflected on the wet pavement, and can discern no speck in the road to encourage the belief that there is a cab or a coach to be had—the very coachmen have gone home in despair. The cold sleet is drizzling down with that gentle regularity, which betokens a duration of four-and-twenty hours at least; the damp hangs upon the house-tops and lamp-posts, and clings to you like an invisible cloak. The water is "coming in" in every area, the pipes have burst, the water-butts are running over; the kennels seem to be doing matches against time, pump-handles descend of their own accord, horses in market-carts fall down, and there's no one to help them up again, policemen look as if they had been carefully sprinkled with powdered glass; here and there a milk-woman trudges slowly along, with a bit of list round each foot to keep her from slipping; boys who "don't sleep in the house," and are not allowed much sleep out of it, can't wake their masters by thundering at the shop-door, and cry with the cold—the compound of ice, snow, and water on the pavement, is a couple of inches thick—nobody ventures to walk fast to keep himself warm, and nobody could succeed in keeping himself warm if he did.

It strikes a quarter past five as you trudge down Waterloo Place on your way to the Golden Cross, and you discover, for the first time, that you were called about an hour too early. You have not time to go back; there is no place open to go into, and you have, therefore, no resource but to go forward, which you do, feeling remarkably satisfied with yourself, and everything about you. You arrive at the office, and look wistfully up the yard for the Birmingham High-flier, which, for aught you can see, may have flown away altogether, for no preparations appear to be on foot for the departure of any vehicle in the shape of a coach. You wander into the booking-office, which with the gas-lights and blazing fire, looks quite comfortable by contrast—that is to say, if any place *can* look comfortable at half-past five on a winter's morning. There stands the identical book-keeper in the same position as if he had not moved since you saw him yesterday. As he informs you, that the coach

is up the yard, and will be brought round in about a quarter
of an hour, you leave your bag, and repair to "The Tap"
—not with any absurd idea of warming yourself, because you
feel such a result to be utterly hopeless, but for the purpose
of procuring some hot brandy-and-water, which you do,—
when the kettle boils! an event which occurs exactly two
minutes and a half before the time fixed for the starting of
the coach.

The first stroke of six peals from St. Martin's church
steeple just as you take the first sip of the boiling liquid.
You find yourself at the booking-office in two seconds, and
the tap-waiter finds himself much comforted by your brandy-
and-water, in about the same period. The coach is out;
the horses are in, and the guard and two or three porters
are stowing the luggage away, and running up the steps of
the booking-office, and down the steps of the booking-office,
with breathless rapidity. The place, which a few minutes
ago was so still and quiet, is now all bustle; the early
vendors of the morning papers have arrived, and you are
assailed on all sides with shouts of " Times, gen'lm'n, Times."
"Here's Chron—Chron—Chron," " Herald, ma'am," "Highly
interesting murder, gen'lm'n," "Curious case o' breach o'
promise, ladies." The inside passengers are already in their
dens, and the outsides, with the exception of yourself, are
pacing up and down the pavement to keep themselves warm;
they consist of two young men with very long hair, to which
the sleet has communicated the appearance of crystallised
rats' tails; one thin young woman cold and peevish, one old
gentleman ditto ditto, and something in a cloak and cap,
intended to represent a military officer; every member of the
party, with a large stiff shawl over his chin, looking exactly
as if he were playing a set of Pan's pipes.

"Take off the cloths, Bob," says the coachman, who now
appears for the first time, in a rough blue great-coat, of
which the buttons behind are so far apart, that you can't
see them both at the same time. " Now, gen'lm'n," cries
the guard, with the waybill in his hand. "Five minutes
behind time already!" Up jump the passengers—the two
young men smoking like lime-kilns, and the old gentleman
grumbling audibly. The thin young woman is got upon the
roof, by dint of a great deal of pulling, and pushing, and helping and trouble, and she repays it by expressing her solemn
conviction that she will never be able to get down again.

Early Coaches

"All right," sings out the guard at last, jumping up as the coach starts, and blowing his horn directly afterwards, in proof of the soundness of his wind. "Let 'em go, Harry. give 'em their heads," cried the coachman—and off we start as briskly as if the morning were "all right," as well as the coach: and looking forward as anxiously to the termination of our journey, as we fear our readers will have done, long since, to the conclusion of our paper.

CHAPTER XVI

OMNIBUSES

It is very generally allowed that public conveyances afford an extensive field for amusement and observation. Of all the public conveyances that have been constructed since the days of the Ark—we think that is the earliest on record—to the present time, commend us to an omnibus. A long stage is not to be despised, but there you have only six insides, and the chances are, that the same people go all the way with you—there is no change, no variety. Besides, after the first twelve hours or so, people get cross and sleepy, and when you have seen a man in his nightcap, you lose all respect for him; at least, that is the case with us. Then on smooth roads people frequently get prosy, and tell long stories, and even those who don't talk, may have very unpleasant predilections. We once travelled four hundred miles, inside a stage-coach, with a stout man, who had a glass of rum-and-water, warm, handed in at the window at every place where we changed horses. This was decidedly unpleasant. We have also travelled occasionally, with a small boy of a pale aspect, with light hair, and no perceptible neck, coming up to town from school under the protection of the guard, and directed to be left at the Cross Keys till called for. This is, perhaps, even worse than rum-and-water in a close atmosphere. Then there is the whole train of evils consequent on a change of the coachman; and the misery of the discovery—which the guard is sure to make the moment you begin to doze—that he wants a brown-paper parcel, which he distinctly remembers to have deposited under the seat on which you are reposing. A great deal of bustle and groping takes place, and when you are thoroughly awakened, and severely cramped, by holding your legs up by an almost supernatural exertion, while he is looking behind them, it suddenly occurs to him that he put it in the fore-boot. Bang goes the door; the parcel is immediately found; off starts the coach again; and the guard plays the key-bugle as loud as he can play it, as if in mockery of your wretchedness.

Now, you meet with none of these afflictions in an omnibus ; sameness there can never be. The passengers change as often in the course of one journey as the figures in a kaleidoscope, and though not so glittering, are far more amusing. We believe there is no instance on record, of a man's having gone to sleep in one of these vehicles. As to long stories, would any man venture to tell a long story in an omnibus? and even if he did, where would be the harm? nobody could possibly hear what he was talking about. Again ; children, though occasionally, are not often to be found in an omnibus ; and even when they are, if the vehicle be full, as is generally the case, somebody sits upon them, and we are unconscious of their presence. Yes, after mature reflection, and considerable experience, we are decidedly of opinion that of all known vehicles, from the glass-coach in which we were taken to be christened, to that sombre caravan in which we must one day make our last earthly journey, there is nothing like an omnibus.

We will back the machine in which we make our daily peregrination from the top of Oxford Street to the city, against any "buss" on the road, whether it be for the gaudiness of its exterior, the perfect simplicity of its interior, or the native coolness of its cad. This young gentleman is a singular instance of self-devotion ; his somewhat intemperate zeal on behalf of his employers is constantly getting him into trouble, and occasionally into the house of correction. He is no sooner emancipated, however, than he resumes the duties of his profession with unabated ardour. His principal distinction is his activity. His great boast is, "that he can chuck an old gen'lm'n into the buss, shut him in, and rattle off, afore he knows where it's a-going to"—a feat which he frequently performs, to the infinite amusement of every one but the old gentleman concerned, who, somehow or other, never can see the joke of the thing.

We are not aware that it has ever been precisely ascertained, how many passengers our omnibus will contain. The impression on the cad's mind evidently is, that it is amply sufficient for the accommodation of any number of persons that can be enticed into it. "Any room?" cries a very hot pedestrian. "Plenty o' room, sir," replies the conductor, gradually opening the door, and not disclosing the real state of the case until the wretched man is on the steps. "Where?" inquires the entrapped individual, with an attempt to back out again. "Either side, sir," rejoins the cad, shoving him in, and slamming the door. "All right, Bill." Retreat is impossible; the new-comer rolls about, till he falls down somewhere, and there he stops.

As we get into the city a little before ten, four or five of our party are regular passengers. We always take them up at the same places, and they generally occupy the same seats; they are always dressed in the same manner, and invariably discuss the same topics —the increasing rapidity of cabs, and the disregard of moral obligations evinced by omnibus men. There is a little testy old man, with a powdered head, who always sits on the right-hand side of the door as you enter, with his hands folded on the top of his umbrella. He is extremely impatient, and sits there for the purpose of keeping a sharp eye on the cad, with whom he generally holds a running dialogue. He is very officious in helping people in and out, and always volunteers to give the cad a poke with his umbrella, when any one wants to alight. He usually recommends ladies to have sixpence ready, to prevent delay; and if anybody puts a window down, that he can reach, he immediately puts it up again.

"Now, what are you stopping for?" says the little man every morning, the moment there is the slightest indication of "pulling up" at the corner of Regent Street, when some such dialogue as the following takes place between him and the cad:

"What are you stopping for?"

Here the cad whistles, and affects not to hear the question.

"I say [a poke], what are you stopping for?"

"For passengers, sir. Ba—nk.—Ty."

"I know you're stopping for passengers; but you've no business to do so. Why are you stopping?"

"Vy, sir, that's a difficult question. I think it is because we perfer stopping here to going on."

"Now mind," exclaims the little old man, with great vehemence, "I'll pull you up to-morrow; I've often threatened to do it; now I will."

"Thankee, sir," replies the cad, touching his hat with a mock expression of gratitude;—"werry much obliged to you indeed, sir." Here the young men in the omnibus laugh very heartily, and the old gentleman gets very red in the face, and seems highly exasperated.

The stout gentleman in the white neckcloth, at the other

end of the vehicle, looks very prophetic, and says that something must shortly be done with these fellows, or there's no
saying where all this will end ; and the shabby-genteel man
with the green bag, expresses his entire concurrence in the
opinion, as he has done regularly every morning for the last
six months.

A second omnibus now comes up, and stops immediately
behind us. Another old gentleman elevates his cane in the
air, and runs with all his might towards our omnibus; we
watch his progress with great interest ; the door is opened
to receive him, he suddenly disappears—he has been spirited
away by the opposition. Hereupon the driver of the opposition taunts our people with his having " regularly done 'em
out of that old swell," and the voice of the "old swell" is
heard, vainly protesting against this unlawful detention.
We rattle off, the other omnibus rattles after us, and every
time we stop to take up a passenger, they stop to take him
too ; sometimes we get him ; sometimes they get him :
but whoever don't get him, say they ought to have had him.
and the cads of the respective vehicles abuse one another
accordingly.

As we arrive in the vicinity of Lincoln's Inn Fields.
Bedford Row, and other legal haunts, we drop a great many
of our original passengers, and take up fresh ones, who
meet with a very sulky reception. It is rather remarkable.
that the people already in an omnibus always look at new-
comers, as if they entertained some undefined idea that they
have no business to come in at all. We are quite persuaded
the little old man has some notion of this kind, and that he
considers their entry as a sort of negative impertinence.

Conversation is now entirely dropped ; each person gazes
vacantly through the window in front of him, and everybody
thinks that his opposite neighbour is staring at him. If one
man gets out at Shoe Lane, and another at the corner of
Farringdon Street, the little old gentleman grumbles, and
suggests to the latter, that if he had got out at Shoe Lane
too, he would have saved them the delay of another stoppage :
whereupon the young men laugh again, and the old gentleman looks very solemn, and says nothing more till he gets to
the Bank, when he trots off as fast as he can, leaving us to
do the same, and to wish, as we walk away, that we could
impart to others any portion of the amusement we have
gained for ourselves.

CHAPTER XVII

THE LAST CAB-DRIVER, AND THE FIRST OMNIBUS CAD

OF all the cabriolet-drivers whom we have ever had the honour and· gratification of knowing by sight—and our acquaintance in this way has been most extensive—there is one who made an impression on our mind which can never be effaced, and who awakened in our bosom a feeling of admiration and respect, which we entertain a fatal presentiment will never be called forth again by any human being. He was a man of most simple and prepossessing appearance. He was a brown-whiskered, white-hatted, no-coated cabman ; his nose was generally red, and his bright blue eye not unfrequently stood out in bold relief against a black border of artificial workmanship ; his boots were of the Wellington form, pulled up to meet his corduroy knee-smalls, or at least to approach as near them as their dimensions would admit of ; and his neck was usually garnished with a bright yellow handkerchief. In summer he carried in his mouth a flower ; in winter, a straw—slight, but, to a contemplative mind, certain indications of a love of nature, and a taste for botany.

His cabriolet was gorgeously painted—a bright red ; and wherever we went, City or West End, Paddington or Holloway, North, East, West, or South, there was the red cab, bumping up against the posts at the street corners, and turning in and out, among hackney-coaches, and drays, and carts, and waggons, and omnibuses, and contriving by some strange means or other, to get out of places which no other vehicle but the red cab could ever by any possibility have contrived to get into at all. Our fondness for that red cab was unbounded. How we should have liked to have seen it in the circle at Astley's ! Our life upon it, that it should have performed such evolutions as would have put the whole company to shame—Indian chiefs, knights, Swiss peasants, and all.

Some people object to the exertion of getting into cabs, and others object to the difficulty of getting out of them; we think both these are objections which take their rise in perverse and ill-conditioned minds. The getting into a cab is a very pretty and graceful process, which, when well performed, is essentially melo-dramatic. First, there is the expressive pantomime of every one of the eighteen cabmen on the stand, the moment you raise your eyes from the ground. Then there is your own pantomime in reply—quite a little ballet. Four cabs immediately leave the stand, for your especial accommodation; and the evolutions of the animals who draw them are beautiful in the extreme, as they grate the wheels of the cabs against the curb-stones, and sport playfully in the kennel. You single out a particular cab, and dart swiftly towards it. One bound, and you are on the first step; turn your body lightly round to the right, and you are on the second; bend gracefully beneath the reins, working round to the left at the same time, and you are in the cab. There is no difficulty in finding a seat: the apron knocks you comfortably into it at once, and off you go.

The getting out of a cab is, perhaps, rather more complicated in its theory, and a shade more difficult in its execution. We have studied the subject a great deal, and we think the best way is, to throw yourself out, and trust to chance for alighting on your feet. If you make the driver alight first, and then throw yourself upon him, you will find that he breaks your fall materially. In the event of your contemplating an offer of eightpence, on no account make the tender, or show the money, until you are safely on the pavement. It is very bad policy attempting to save the fourpence. You are very much in the power of a cabman, and he considers it a kind of fee not to do you any wilful damage. Any instruction, however, in the art of getting out of a cab, is wholly unnecessary if you are going any distance, because the probability is that you will be shot lightly out before you have completed the third mile.

We are not aware of any instance on record in which a cab-horse has performed three consecutive miles without going down once. What of that? It is all excitement. And in these days of derangement of the nervous system and universal lassitude, people are content to pay handsomely for excitement; where can it be procured at a cheaper rate?

But to return to the red cab; it was omnipresent. You had but to walk down Holborn, or Fleet Street, or any of the principal thoroughfares in which there is a great deal of traffic, and judge for yourself. You had hardly turned into the street, when you saw a trunk or two, lying on the ground: an uprooted post, a hat-box, a portmanteau, and a carpet-bag, strewed about in a very picturesque manner: a horse in a cab standing by, looking about him with great unconcern; and a crowd, shouting and screaming with delight, cooling their flushed faces against the glass windows of a chemist's shop.—"What's the matter here, can you tell me?"—"O'ny a cab, sir."—"Anybody hurt, do you know?" —"O'ny the fare, sir. I see him a turnin' the corner, and I ses to another gen'lm'n 'That's a reg'lar little oss that, and he's a-comin' along rayther sweet, an't he?'—'He just is,' ses the other gen'lm'n, ven bump they cums agin the post, and out flies the fare like bricks." Need we say it was the red cab; or that the gentleman with the straw in his mouth, who emerged so coolly from the chemist's shop and philosophically climbing into the little dickey, started off at full gallop, was the red cab's licensed driver?

The ubiquity of this red cab, and the influence it exercised over the risible muscles of justice itself, was perfectly astonishing. You walked into the justice-room of the Mansion House; the whole court resounded with merriment. The Lord Mayor threw himself back in his chair, in a state of frantic delight at his own joke; every vein in Mr. Hobler's countenance was swollen with laughter, partly at the Lord Mayor's facetiousness, but more at his own; the constables and police-officers were (as in duty bound) in ecstasies at Mr. Hobler and the Lord Mayor combined; and the very paupers, glancing respectfully at the beadle's countenance, tried to smile, as even he relaxed. A tall, weazen-faced man, with an impediment in his speech, would be endeavouring to state a case of imposition against the red cab's driver; and the red cab's driver, and the Lord Mayor, and Mr. Hobler, would be having a little fun among themselves, to the inordinate delight of everybody but the complainant. In the end, justice would be so tickled with the red-cab-driver's native humour, that the fine would be mitigated, and he would go away full gallop, in the red cab, to impose on somebody else without loss of time.

The driver of the red cab, confident in the strength of his

own moral principles, like many other philosophers, was wont to set the feelings and opinions of society at complete defiance. Generally speaking, perhaps, he would as soon carry a fare safely to his destination, as he would upset him —sooner, perhaps, because in that case he not only got the money, but had the additional amusement of running a longer heat against some smart rival. But society made war upon him in the shape of penalties, and he must make war upon society in his own way. This was the reasoning of the red-cab-driver. So he bestowed a searching look upon the fare, as he put his hand in his waistcoat pocket, when he had gone half the mile, to get the money ready; and if he brought forth eightpence, out he went.

The last time we saw our friend was one wet evening in Tottenham Court Road, when he was engaged in a very warm and somewhat personal altercation with a loquacious little gentleman in a green coat. Poor fellow! there were great excuses to be made for him: he had not received above eighteenpence more than his fare, and consequently laboured under a great deal of very natural indignation. The dispute had attained a pretty considerable height, when at last the loquacious little gentleman, making a mental calculation of the distance, and finding that he had already paid more than he ought, avowed his unalterable determination to "pull up" the cabman in the morning.

"Now, just mark this, young man," said the little gentleman, "I'll pull you up to-morrow morning."

"No! will you though?" said our friend, with a sneer.

"I will," replied the little gentleman, "mark my words, that's all. If I live till to-morrow morning, you shall repent this."

There was a steadiness of purpose, and indignation of speech, about the little gentleman, as he took an angry pinch of snuff, after this last declaration, which made a visible impression on the mind of the red-cab-driver. He appeared to hesitate for an instant. It was only for an instant; his resolve was soon taken.

"You'll pull me up, will you?" said our friend.

"I will," rejoined the little gentleman, with even greater vehemence than before.

"Wery well," said our friend, tucking up his shirt sleeves very calmly. "There'll be three veeks for that. Wery good; that'll bring me up to the middle o' next month.

Three veeks more would carry me on to my birthday, and then I've got ten pound to draw. I may as well get board, lodgin', and washin', till then, out of the county, as pay for it myself; consequently here goes!"

So, without more ado, the red-cab-driver knocked the little gentleman down, and then called the police to take himself into custody, with all the civility in the world.

A story is nothing without the sequel; and therefore, we may state, that to our certain knowledge, the board, lodging, and washing, were all provided in due course. We happen to know the fact, for it came to our knowledge thus: We went over the House of Correction for the county of Middlesex shortly after, to witness the operation of the silent system; and looked on all the "wheels" with the greatest anxiety, in search of our long-lost friend. He was nowhere to be seen, however, and we began to think that the little gentleman in the green coat must have relented, when, as we were traversing the kitchen-garden, which lies in a sequestered part of the prison, we were startled by hearing a voice, which apparently proceeded from the wall, pouring forth its soul in the plaintive air of "All round my hat," which was then just beginning to form a recognised portion of our national music.

We started.—"What voice is that?" said we.

The Governor shook his head.

"Sad fellow," he replied, "very sad. He positively refused to work on the wheel; so, after many trials, I was compelled to order him into solitary confinement. He says he likes it very much though, and I am afraid he does, for he lies on his back on the floor, and sings comic songs all day!"

Shall we add, that our heart had not deceived us; and that the comic singer was no other than our eagerly-sought friend, the red-cab-driver?

We have never seen him since, but we have strong reason to suspect that this noble individual was a distant relative of a waterman of our acquaintance, who, on one occasion, when we were passing the coach-stand over which he presides, after standing very quietly to see a tall man struggle into a cab, ran up very briskly when it was all over (as his brethren invariably do), and, touching his hat, asked, as a matter of course, for "a copper for the waterman." Now, the fare was by no means a handsome man; and, waxing very indignant at the demand, he replied—"Money! What for? Coming up and looking at me, I suppose!"—"Vell, sir," rejoined the waterman, with a smile of immovable complacency, "*that's* worth twopence."

This identical waterman afterwards attained a very prominent station in society ; and as we know something of his life, and have often thought of telling what we *do* know, perhaps we shall never have a better opportunity than the present.

Mr. William Barker, then, for that was the gentleman's name, Mr. William Barker was born—— but why need we relate where Mr. William Barker was born, or when? Why scrutinise the entries in parochial ledgers, or seek to penetrate the Lucinian mysteries of lying-in-hospitals? Mr. William Barker *was* born, or he had never been. There is a son—there was a father. There is an effect—there was a cause. Surely this is sufficient information for the most Fatima-like curiosity ; and, if it be not, we regret our inability to supply any further evidence on the point. Can there be a more satisfactory, or more strictly parliamentary course? Impossible.

We at once avow a similar inability to record at what precise period, or by what particular process, this gentleman's patronymic, of William Barker, became corrupted into "Bill Boorker." Mr. Barker acquired a high standing, and no inconsiderable reputation, among the members of that profession to which he more peculiarly devoted his energies : and to them he was generally known, either by the familiar appellation of "Bill Boorker," or the flattering designation of "Aggerawatin Bill," the latter being a playful and expressive *sobriquet*, illustrative of Mr. Barker's great talent in "aggerawatin" and rendering wild such subjects of her Majesty as are conveyed from place to place, through the instrumentality of omnibuses. Of the early life of Mr. Barker little is known, and even that little is involved in considerable doubt and obscurity. A want of application, a restlessness of purpose, a thirsting after porter, a love of all that is roving and cadger-like in nature, shared in common with many other great geniuses, appear to have been his leading characteristics. The busy hum of a parochial free-school, and the shady repose of a county gaol, were alike inefficacious in producing the slightest alteration in Mr. Barker's disposition. His feverish attachment to change and variety nothing could repress ; his native daring no punishment could subdue.

If Mr. Barker can be fairly said to have had any weakness in his earlier years, it was an amiable one—love; love in its most comprehensive form—a love of ladies, liquids, and pocket-handkerchiefs. It was no selfish feeling; it was not confined to his own possessions, which but too many men regard with exclusive complacency. No; it was a nobler love—a general principle. It extended itself with equal force to the property of other people.

There is something very affecting in this. It is still more affecting to know, that such philanthropy is but imperfectly rewarded. Bow Street, Newgate, and Millbank, are a poor return for general benevolence, evincing itself in an irrepressible love for all created objects. Mr. Barker felt it so. After a lengthened interview with the highest legal authorities, he quitted his ungrateful country, with the consent, and at the expense, of its Government; proceeded to a distant shore; and there employed himself, like another Cincinnatus, in clearing and cultivating the soil—a peaceful pursuit, in which a term of seven years glided almost imperceptibly away.

Whether, at the expiration of the period we have just mentioned, the British Government required Mr. Barker's presence here, or did not require his residence abroad, we have no distinct means of ascertaining. We should be inclined, however, to favour the latter position, inasmuch as we do not find that he was advanced to any other public post on his return, than the post at the corner of the Haymarket, where he officiated as assistant-waterman to the hackney-coach stand. Seated, in this capacity, on a couple of tubs near the curb-stone, with a brass plate and number suspended round his neck by a massive chain, and his ankles curiously enveloped in haybands, he is supposed to have made those observations on human nature which exercised so material an influence over all his proceedings in later life.

Mr. Barker had not officiated for many months in this capacity, when the appearance of the first omnibus caused the public mind to go in a new direction, and prevented a great many hackney-coaches from going in any direction at all. The genius of Mr. Barker at once perceived the whole extent of the injury that would be eventually inflicted on cab and coach stands, and, by consequence, on watermen also, by the progress of the system of which the first omnibus was a part. He saw, too, the necessity of adopting some more profitable profession; and his active mind at once perceived how much might be done in the way of enticing the youthful and unwary, and shoving the old and helpless, into the wrong bus, and carrying them off, until, reduced to despair, they ransomed themselves by the payment of sixpence a head, or, to adopt his own figurative expression in all its native beauty, "till they was rig'larly done over, and forked out the stumpy."

An opportunity for realising his fondest anticipations soon presented itself. Rumours were rife on the hackney-coach stands, that a bus was building, to run from Lisson Grove to the Bank, down Oxford Street and Holborn; and the rapid increase of busses on the Paddington Road, encouraged the idea. Mr. Barker secretly and cautiously inquired in the proper quarters. The report was correct; the "Royal William" was to make its first journey on the following Monday. It was a crack affair altogether. An enterprising young cabman, of established reputation as a dashing whip— for he had compromised with the parents of three scrunched children, and just "worked out" his fine, for knocking down an old lady—was the driver; and the spirited proprietor, knowing Mr. Barker's qualifications, appointed him to the vacant office of cad on the very first application. The bus began to run, and Mr. Barker entered into a new suit of clothes, and on a new sphere of action.

To recapitulate all the improvements introduced by this extraordinary man, into the omnibus system—gradually, indeed, but surely—would occupy a far greater space than we are enabled to devote to this imperfect memoir. To him is universally assigned the original suggestion of the practice which afterwards became so general—of the driver of a second bus keeping constantly behind the first one, and driving the pole of his vehicle either into the door of the other, every time it was opened, or through the body of any lady or gentleman who might make an attempt to get into it; a humorous and pleasant invention, exhibiting all that origi- nality of idea, and fine bold flow of spirits, so conspicuous in every action of this great man.

Mr. Barker had opponents of course; what man in public life has not? But even his worst enemies cannot deny that he has taken more old ladies and gentlemen to Paddington who wanted to go to the Bank, and more old ladies and gentlemen to the Bank who wanted to go to Paddington,

than any six men on the road ; and however much malevolent
spirits may pretend to doubt the accuracy of the statement,
they well know it to be an established fact, that he has
forcibly conveyed a variety of ancient persons of either sex,
to both places, who had not the slightest or most distant
intention of going anywhere at all.

Mr. Barker was the identical cad who nobly distinguished
himself, some time since, by keeping a tradesman on the step
—the omnibus going at full speed all the time—till he had
thrashed him to his entire satisfaction, and finally throwing
him away, when he had quite done with him.   Mr. Barker
it *ought* to have been, who honestly indignant at being
ignominiously ejected from a house of public entertainment, kicked the landlord in the knee, and thereby caused
his death.   We say it *ought* to have been Mr. Barker, because
the action was not a common one, and could have emanated
from no ordinary mind.

It has now become matter of history ; it is recorded in
the Newgate Calendar ; and we wish we could attribute this
piece of daring heroism to Mr. Barker.   We regret being
compelled to state that it was not performed by him.   Would,
for the family credit we could add, that it was achieved by
his brother !

It was in the exercise of the nicer details of his profession,
that Mr. Barker's knowledge of human nature was beautifully displayed.   He could tell at a glance where a passenger
wanted to go to, and would shout the name of the place
accordingly, without the slightest reference to the real
destination of the vehicle.   He knew exactly the kind of
old lady that would be too much flurried by the process
of pushing in and pulling out of the caravan, to discover
where she had been put down, until too late ; had an intuitive
perception of what was passing in a passenger's mind when
he inwardly resolved to "pull that cad up to-morrow morning ;" and never failed to make himself agreeable to female
servants, whom he would place next the door, and talk to all
the way.

Human judgment is never infallible, and it would occasionally happen that Mr. Barker experimentalised with the
timidity or forbearance of the wrong person, in which case
a summons to a Police-office was, on more than one occasion,
followed by a committal to prison.   It was not in the power
of trifles such as these, however, to subdue the freedom of his

spirit. As soon as they passed away, he resumed the duties of his profession with unabated ardour.

We have spoken of Mr. Barker and of the red-cab-driver, in the past tense. Alas! Mr. Barker has again become an absentee; and the class of men to which they both belonged are fast disappearing. Improvement has peered beneath the aprons of our cabs, and penetrated to the very innermost recesses of our omnibuses. Dirt and fustian will vanish before cleanliness and livery. Slang will be forgotten when civility becomes general: and that enlightened, eloquent, sage, and profound body, the Magistracy of London, will be deprived of half their amusement, and half their occupation.

CHAPTER XVIII

A PARLIAMENTARY SKETCH

WE hope our readers will not be alarmed at this rather ominous title. We assure them that we are not about to become political, neither have we the slightest intention of being more prosy than usual—if we can help it. It has occurred to us that a slight sketch of the general aspect of "the House," and the crowds that resort to it on the night of an important debate, would be productive of some amusement : and as we have made some few calls at the aforesaid house in our time—have visited it quite often enough for our purpose, and a great deal too often for our personal peace and comfort—we have determined to attempt the description. Dismissing from our minds, therefore, all that feeling of awe, which vague ideas of breaches of privilege, Serjeant-at-Arms, heavy denunciations, and still heavier fees, are calculated to awaken, we enter at once into the building, and upon our subject.

Half-past four o'clock—and at five the mover of the Address will be "on his legs," as the newspapers announce sometimes by way of novelty, as if speakers were occasionally in the habit of standing on their heads. The members are pouring in, one after the other, in shoals. The few spectators who can obtain standing room in the passages, scrutinise them as they pass, with the utmost interest, and the man who can identify a member occasionally, becomes a person of great importance. Every now and then you hear earnest whispers of "That's Sir John Thomson." "Which? him with the gilt order round his neck?" "No, no ; that's one of the messengers—that other with the yellow gloves, is Sir John Thomson." "Here's Mr. Smith." "Lor !" "Yes, how d'ye do, sir?—(He is our new member)—How do you do, sir ? " Mr. Smith stops : turns round with an air of enchanting urbanity (for the rumour of an intended dissolution has been very extensively circulated this morning); seizes both

The Last Cab-Driver
(*p. 142*)

the hands of his gratified constituent, and, after greeting him with the most enthusiastic warmth, darts into the lobby with an extraordinary display of ardour in the public cause, leaving an immense impression in his favour on the mind of his " fellow-townsman."

The arrivals increase in number, and the heat and noise increase in very unpleasant proportion. The livery servants form a complete lane on either side of the passage, and you reduce yourself into the smallest possible space to avoid being turned out. You see that stout man with the hoarse voice, in the blue coat, queer-crowned, broad-brimmed hat, white corduroy breeches, and great boots, who has been talking incessantly for half an hour past, and whose importance has occasioned no small quantity of mirth among the strangers. That is the great conservator of the peace of Westminster. You cannot fail to have remarked the grace with which he saluted the noble Lord who passed just now, or the excessive dignity of his air, as he expostulates with the crowd. He is rather out of temper now, in consequence of the very irreverent behaviour of those two young fellows behind him, who have done nothing but laugh all the time they have been here.

"Will they divide to-night, do you think, Mr. ——?" timidly inquires a little thin man in the crowd, hoping to conciliate the man of office.

"How *can* you ask such questions, sir?" replies the functionary, in an incredibly loud key, and pettishly grasping the thick stick he carries in his right hand. "Pray do not, sir. I beg of you; pray do not, sir." The little man looks remarkably out of his element, and the uninitiated part of the throng are in positive convulsions of laughter.

Just at this moment some unfortunate individual appears, with a very smirking air, at the bottom of the long passage. He has managed to elude the vigilance of the special constable down-stairs, and is evidently congratulating himself on having made his way so far.

"Go back, sir—you must *not* come here," shouts the hoarse one, with tremendous emphasis of voice and gesture, the moment the offender catches his eye.

The stranger pauses.

"Do you hear, sir—will you go back?" continues the official dignitary, gently pushing the intruder some half-dozen yards.

"Come, don't push me," replies the stranger, turning angrily round.

"I will, sir."

"You won't, sir."

"Go out, sir."

"Take your hands off me, sir."

"Go out of the passage, sir."

"You're a Jack-in-office, sir."

"A what?" ejaculates he of the boots.

"A Jack-in-office, sir, and a very insolent fellow," reiterates the stranger, now completely in a passion.

"Pray do not force me to put you out, sir," retorts the other—"pray do not—my instructions are to keep this passage clear—it's the Speaker's orders, sir."

"D—n the Speaker, sir!" shouts the intruder.

"Here, Wilson!—Collins!" gasps the officer, actually paralysed at this insulting expression, which in his mind is all but high treason; "take this man out—take him out, I say! How dare you, sir?" and down goes the unfortunate man five stairs at a time, turning round at every stoppage, to come back again, and denouncing bitter vengeance against the commander-in-chief, and all his supernumeraries.

"Make way, gentlemen,—pray make way for the Members, I beg of you!" shouts the zealous officer, turning back, and preceding a whole string of the liberal and independent.

You see this ferocious-looking gentleman, with a complexion almost as sallow as his linen, and whose large black moustache would give him the appearance of a figure in a hairdresser's window, if his countenance possessed the thought which is communicated to those waxen caricatures of the human face divine. He is a militia-officer, and the most amusing person in the House. Can anything be more exquisitely absurd than the burlesque grandeur of his air, as he strides up to the lobby, his eyes rolling like those of a Turk's head in a cheap Dutch clock? He never appears without that bundle of dirty papers which he carries under his left arm, and which are generally supposed to be the miscellaneous estimates for 1804, or some equally important documents. He is very punctual in his attendance at the House, and his self-satisfied "He-ar-He-ar," is not unfrequently the signal for a general titter.

This is the gentleman who once actually sent a messenger up to the Strangers' gallery in the old House of Commons, to inquire the name of an individual who was using an eye-glass, in order that he might complain to the Speaker that the person in question was quizzing him! On another occasion, he is reported to have repaired to Bellamy's kitchen —a refreshment-room, where persons who are not Members are admitted on sufferance, as it were—and perceiving two or three gentlemen at supper, who he was aware were not Members, and could not, in that place, very well resent his behaviour, he indulged in the pleasantry of sitting with his booted leg on the table at which they were supping! He is generally harmless, though, and always amusing.

By dint of patience, and some little interest with our friend the constable, we have contrived to make our way to the Lobby, and you can just manage to catch an occasional glimpse of the House, as the door is opened for the admission of Members. It is tolerably full already, and little groups of Members are congregated together here, discussing the interesting topics of the day.

That smart-looking fellow in the black coat with velvet facings and cuffs, who wears his *D'Orsay* hat so rakishly, is "Honest Tom," a metropolitan representative : and the large man in the cloak with the white lining—not the man by the pillar ; the other with the light hair hanging over his coat collar behind—is his colleague. The quiet gentlemanly-looking man in the blue surtout, grey trousers, white neckerchief, and gloves, whose closely-buttoned coat displays his manly figure and broad chest to great advantage, is a very well-known character. He has fought a great many battles in his time, and conquered like the heroes of old, with no other arms than those the gods gave him. The old hard-featured man who is standing near him, is really a good specimen of a class of men now nearly extinct. He is a county Member, and has been from time whereof the memory of man is not to the contrary. Look at his loose, wide, brown coat, with capacious pockets on each side ; the knee-breeches and boots, the immensely long waistcoat, and silver watch-chain dangling below it, the wide-brimmed brown hat, and the white handkerchief tied in a great bow, with straggling ends sticking out beyond his shirt-frill. It is a costume one seldom sees nowadays, and when the few who wear it have died off, it will be quite extinct. He can tell you long stories of Fox, Pitt, Sheridan, and Canning, and how much better the House was managed in those times, when they used to get up at eight or nine o'clock, except on regular field-days, of which everybody was apprised beforehand.　He has a great contempt for all young Members of Parliament, and thinks it quite impossible that a man can say anything worth hearing, unless he has sat in the House for fifteen years at least, without saying anything at all.　He is of opinion that "that young Macaulay" was a regular impostor; he allows that Lord Stanley may do something one of these days, but "he's too young, sir—too young."　He is an excellent authority on points of precedent, and when he grows talkative, after his wine, will tell you how Sir Somebody Something, when he was whipper-in for the Government, brought four men out of their beds to vote in the majority, three of whom died on their way home again; how the House once divided on the question, that fresh candles be now brought in; how the Speaker was once upon a time left in the chair by accident, at the conclusion of business, and was obliged to sit in the House by himself for three hours, till some Member could be knocked up and brought back again, to move the adjournment; and a great many other anecdotes of a similar description.

There he stands, leaning on his stick; looking at the throng of Exquisites around him with most profound contempt; and conjuring up, before his mind's eye, the scenes he beheld in the old House, in days gone by, when his own feelings were fresher and brighter, and when, as he imagines, wit, talent, and patriotism flourished more brightly too.

You are curious to know who that young man in the rough great-coat is, who has accosted every Member who has entered the House since we have been standing here.　He is not a Member; he is only an "hereditary bondsman," or, in other words, an Irish correspondent of an Irish newspaper, who has just procured his forty-second frank from a Member whom he never saw in his life before.　There he goes again —another!　Bless the man, he has his hat and pockets full already.

We will try our fortune at the Strangers' gallery, though the nature of the debate encourages very little hope of success. What on earth are you about?　Holding up your order as if it were a talisman at whose command the wicket would fly open?　Nonsense.　Just preserve the order for an autograph, if it be worth keeping at all, and make your appearance at the door with your thumb and forefinger expressively inserted in your waistcoat-pocket.　This tall stout man in black is the door-keeper. "Any room?" "Not an inch—two or three dozen gentlemen waiting down-stairs on the chance of somebody's going out." Pull out your purse—"Are you *quite* sure there's no room?"—"I'll go and look," replies the door-keeper, with a wistful glance at your purse, "but I'm afraid there's not." He returns, and with real feeling assures you that it is morally impossible to get near the gallery. It is of no use waiting. When you are refused admission into the Strangers' gallery at the House of Commons, under such circumstances, you may return home thoroughly satisfied that the place must be remarkably full indeed [1].

Retracing our steps through the long passage, descending the stairs, and crossing Palace Yard, we halt at a small temporary door-way adjoining the King's entrance to the House of Lords. The order of the serjeant-at-arms will admit you into the Reporters' gallery, from whence you can obtain a tolerably good view of the House. Take care of the stairs, they are none of the best; through this little wicket—there. As soon as your eyes become a little used to the mist of the place, and the glare of the chandeliers below you, you will see that some unimportant personage on the Ministerial side of the House (to your right hand) is speaking, amidst a hum of voices and confusion which would rival Babel, but for the circumstance of its being all in one language.

The "hear, hear," which occasioned that laugh, proceeded from our warlike friend with the moustache; he is sitting on the back seat against the wall, behind the Member who is speaking, looking as ferocious and intellectual as usual. Take one look around you, and retire! The body of the House and the side galleries are full of Members; some, with their legs on the back of the opposite seat; some, with theirs stretched out to their utmost length on the floor; some going out, others coming in; all talking, laughing, lounging, coughing, oh-ing, questioning, or groaning; presenting a conglomeration of noise and confusion, to be met with in no other place in existence, not even excepting Smithfield on a market-day, or a cock-pit in its glory.

But let us not omit to notice Bellamy's kitchen, or, in other words, the refreshment-room, common to both Houses

---

[1] This paper was written before the practice of exhibiting Members of Parliament, like other curiosities, for the small charge of half-a-crown, was abolished.

of Parliament, where Ministerialists and Oppositionists, Whigs
and Tories, Radicals, Peers, and Destructives, strangers from
the gallery, and the more favoured strangers from below the
bar, are alike at liberty to resort ; where divers honourable
members prove their perfect independence by remaining
during the whole of a heavy debate, solacing themselves
with the creature comforts ; and whence they are summoned
by whippers-in, when the House is on the point of dividing ;
either to give their " conscientious votes " on questions of
which they are conscientiously innocent of knowing anything
whatever, or to find a vent for the playful exuberance of
their wine-inspired fancies, in boisterous shouts of "Divide,"
occasionally varied with a little howling, barking, crowing,
or other ebullitions of senatorial pleasantry.

When you have ascended the narrow staircase which, in
the present temporary House of Commons, leads to the place
we are describing, you will probably observe a couple of
rooms on your right hand, with tables spread for dining.
Neither of these is the kitchen, although they are both
devoted to the same purpose ; the kitchen is further on
to our left, up these half-dozen stairs. Before we ascend
the staircase, however, we must request you to pause in
front of this little bar-place with the sash-windows ; and
beg your particular attention to the steady honest-looking
old fellow in black, who is its sole occupant. Nicholas
(we do not mind mentioning the old fellow's name, for if
Nicholas be not a public man, who is?—and public men's
names are public property)—Nicholas is the butler of
Bellamy's, and has held the same place, dressed exactly
in the same manner, and said precisely the same things,
ever since the oldest of its present visitors can remember.
An excellent servant Nicholas is—an unrivalled compounder
of salad-dressing—an admirable preparer of soda-water and
lemon—a special mixer of cold grog and punch—and, above
all, an unequalled judge of cheese. If the old man have
such a thing as vanity in his composition, this is certainly
his pride ; and if it be possible to imagine that anything in
this world could disturb his impenetrable calmness, we
should say it would be the doubting his judgment on this
important point.

We needn't tell you all this, however, for if you have an
atom of observation, one glance at his sleek, knowing-looking
head and face—his prim white neckerchief, with the wooden

tie into which it has been regularly folded for twenty years past, merging by imperceptible degrees into a small-plaited shirt-frill—and his comfortable-looking form encased in a well-brushed suit of black—would give you a better idea of his real character than a column of our poor description could convey.

Nicholas is rather out of his element now ; he cannot see the kitchen as he used to in the old House ; there, one window of his glass-case opened into the room, and then, for the edification and behoof of more juvenile questioners, he would stand for an hour together, answering deferential questions about Sheridan, and Perceval, and Castlereagh, and Heaven knows who beside, with manifest delight, always inserting a " Mister " before every commoner's name.

Nicholas, like all men of his age and standing, has a great idea of the degeneracy of the times. He seldom expresses any political opinions, but we managed to ascertain, just before the passing of the Reform Bill, that Nicholas was a thorough Reformer. What was our astonishment to discover shortly after the meeting of the first reformed Parliament, that he was a most inveterate and decided Tory ! It was very odd: some men change their opinions from necessity, others from expediency, others from inspiration ; but that Nicholas should undergo any change in any respect, was an event we had never contemplated, and should have considered impossible. His strong opinion against the clause which empowered the metropolitan districts to return Members to Parliament, too, was perfectly unaccountable.

We discovered the secret at last ; the metropolitan Members always dined at home. The rascals ! As for giving additional Members to Ireland, it was even worse—decidedly unconstitutional. Why, sir, an Irish Member would go up there, and eat more dinner than three English Members put together. He took no wine ; drank table-beer by the half-gallon ; and went home to Manchester Buildings, or Millbank Street, for his whiskey-and-water. And what was the consequence? Why, the concern lost—actually lost, sir—by his patronage. A queer old fellow is Nicholas, and as completely a part of the building as the house itself. We wonder he ever left the old place, and fully expected to see in the papers, the morning after the fire, a pathetic account of an old gentleman in black, of decent appearance, who was seen at one of the upper windows when the flames were at their height,

and declared his resolute intention of falling with the floor.
He must have been got out by force. However, he was got
out—here he is again, looking as he always does, as if he
had been in a bandbox ever since the last session.   There
he is, at his old post every night, just as we have described
him : and, as characters are scarce, and faithful servants
scarcer, long may he be there, say we !

Now, when you have taken your seat in the kitchen, and
duly noticed the large fire and roasting-jack at one end of
the room—the little table for washing glasses and draining
jugs at the other—the clock over the window opposite
St. Margaret's Church—the deal tables and wax candles—
the damask table-cloths and bare floor—the plate and china
on the tables, and the gridiron on the fire ; and a few other
anomalies peculiar to the place—we will point out to your
notice two or three of the people present, whose station or
absurdities render them the most worthy of remark.

It is half-past twelve o'clock, and as the division is not
expected for an hour or two, a few Members are lounging
away the time here in preference to standing at the bar of
the House, or sleeping in one of the side galleries.   That
singularly awkward and ungainly-looking man, in the
brownish-white hat, with the straggling black trousers which
reach about half-way down the legs of his boots, who is leaning
against the meat-screen, apparently deluding himself into the
belief that he is thinking about something, is a splendid
sample of a Member of the House of Commons concentrating
in his own person the wisdom of a constituency.   Observe
the wig, of a dark hue but indescribable colour, for if it be
naturally brown, it has acquired a black tint by long service,
and if it be naturally black, the same cause has imparted to
it a tinge of rusty brown ; and remark how very materially
the great blinker-like spectacles assist the expression of that
most intelligent face.   Seriously speaking, did you ever see
a countenance so expressive of the most hopeless extreme of
heavy dulness, or behold a form so strangely put together ?
He is no great speaker : but when he *does* address the House,
the effect is absolutely irresistible.

The small gentleman with the sharp nose, who has just
saluted him, is a Member of Parliament, an ex-Alderman,
and a sort of amateur fireman.   He, and the celebrated
fireman's dog, were observed to be remarkably active at the
conflagration of the two Houses of Parliament—they both

Public Dinners

(p. 167)

[*Dickens and Cruikshank (with beard) are seen behind the leading stewards, who may be intended for Chapman and Hall*]

ran up and down, and in and out, getting under people's feet, and into everybody's way, fully impressed with the belief that they were doing a great deal of good, and barking tremendously. The dog went quietly back to his kennel with the engine, but the gentleman kept up such an incessant noise for some weeks after the occurrence, that he became a positive nuisance. As no more parliamentary fires have occurred, however, and as he has consequently had no more opportunities of writing to the newspapers to relate how, by way of preserving pictures he cut them out of their frames, and performed other great national services, he has gradually relapsed into his old state of calmness.

That female in black—not the one whom the Lord's-Day-Bill Baronet has just chucked under the chin ; the shorter of the two—is "Jane : " the Hebe of Bellamy's. Jane is as great a character as Nicholas, in her way. Her leading features are a thorough contempt for the great majority of her visitors ; her predominant quality, love of admiration, as you cannot fail to observe, if you mark the glee with which she listens to something the young Member near her mutters somewhat unintelligibly in her ear (for his speech is rather thick from some cause or other), and how playfully she digs the handle of a fork into the arm with which he detains her, by way of reply.

Jane is no bad hand at repartees, and showers them about, with a degree of liberality and total absence of reserve or constraint, which occasionally excites no small amazement in the minds of strangers. She cuts jokes with Nicholas, too, but looks up to him with a great deal of respect ; the immovable stolidity with which Nicholas receives the aforesaid jokes, and looks on, at certain pastoral friskings and rompings (Jane's only recreations, and they are very innocent too) which occasionally take place in the passage. is not the least amusing part of his character.

The two persons who are seated at the table in the corner, at the farther end of the room, have been constant guests here, for many years past ; and one of them has feasted within these walls many a time, with the most brilliant characters of a brilliant period. He has gone up to the other House since then ; the greater part of his boon companions have shared Yorick's fate, and his visits to Bellamy's are comparatively few.

If he really be eating his supper now, at what hour can he

possibly have dined! A second solid mass of rump-steak has disappeared, and he eat the first in four minutes and three quarters, by the clock over the window. Was there ever such a personification of Falstaff! Mark the air with which he gloats over that Stilton, as he removes the napkin which has been placed beneath his chin to catch the superfluous gravy of the steak, and with what gusto he imbibes the porter which has been fetched, expressly for him, in the pewter pot. Listen to the hoarse sound of that voice, kept down as it is by layers of solids, and deep draughts of rich wine, and tell us if you ever saw such a perfect picture of a regular *gourmand;* and whether he is not exactly the man whom you would pitch upon as having been the partner of Sheridan's parliamentary carouses, the volunteer driver of the hackney-coach that took him home, and the involuntary upsetter of the whole party?

What an amusing contrast between his voice and appearance, and that of the spare, squeaking old man, who sits at the same table, and who, elevating a little cracked bantam sort of voice to its highest pitch, invokes damnation upon his own eyes or somebody else's at the commencement of every sentence he utters. "The Captain," as they call him, is a very old frequenter of Bellamy's; much addicted to stopping "after the House is up" (an inexpiable crime in Jane's eyes), and a complete walking reservoir of spirits and water.

The old Peer—or rather, the old man—for his peerage is of comparatively recent date—has a huge tumbler of hot punch brought him; and the other damns and drinks, and drinks and damns, and smokes. Members arrive every moment in a great bustle to report that "The Chancellor of the Exchequer's up," and to get glasses of brandy-and-water to sustain them during the division; people who have ordered supper, countermand it, and prepare to go down-stairs, when suddenly a bell is heard to ring with tremendous violence, and a cry of "Di-vi-sion!" is heard in the passage. This is enough; away rush the members pell-mell. The room is cleared in an instant; the noise rapidly dies away; you hear the creaking of the last boot on the last stair, and are left alone with the leviathan of rump-steaks.

CHAPTER XIX

ALL public dinners in London, from the Lord Mayor's annual
banquet at Guildhall, to the Chimney-sweepers' anniversary
at White Conduit House; from the Goldsmiths' to the
Butchers', from the Sheriffs' to the Licensed Victuallers'; are
amusing scenes. Of all entertainments of this description,
however, we think the annual dinner of some public charity
is the most amusing. At a Company's dinner, the people are
nearly all alike—regular old stagers, who make it a matter of
business, and a thing not to be laughed at. At a political
dinner, everybody is disagreeable, and inclined to speechify—
much the same thing, by-the-bye; but at a charity dinner
you see people of all sorts, kinds, and descriptions. The
wine may not be remarkably special, to be sure, and we
have heard some hard-hearted monsters grumble at the
collection; but we really think the amusement to be derived
from the occasion, sufficient to counterbalance even these
disadvantages.

Let us suppose you are induced to attend a dinner of this
description—"Indigent Orphans' Friends' Benevolent Institution," we think it is. The name of the charity is a line or
two longer, but never mind the rest. You have a distinct
recollection, however, that you purchased a ticket at the
solicitation of some charitable friend : and you deposit yourself in a hackney-coach, the driver of which—no doubt that
you may do the thing in style—turns a deaf ear to your
earnest entreaties to be set down at the corner of Great
Queen Street, and persists in carrying you to the very door
of the Freemasons', round which a crowd of people are
assembled to witness the entrance of the indigent orphans'
friends. You hear great speculations as you pay the fare,
on the possibility of your being the noble Lord who is
announced to fill the chair on the occasion, and are highly

gratified to hear it eventually decided that you are only a "wocalist."

The first thing that strikes you, on your entrance, is the astonishing importance of the committee. You observe a door on the first landing, carefully guarded by two waiters, in and out of which stout gentlemen with very red faces keep running, with a degree of speed highly unbecoming the gravity of persons of their years and corpulency. You pause, quite alarmed at the bustle, and thinking, in your innocence, that two or three people must have been carried out of the dining-room in fits, at least. You are immediately undeceived by the waiter—"Up-stairs, if you please, sir; this is the committee-room." Up-stairs you go, accordingly; wondering, as you mount, what the duties of the committee can be, and whether they ever do anything beyond confusing each other, and running over the waiters.

Having deposited your hat and cloak, and received a re-markably small scrap of pasteboard in exchange (which, as a matter of course, you lose, before you require it again), you enter the hall, down which there are three long tables for the less distinguished guests, with a cross table on a raised platform at the upper end for the reception of the very particular friends of the indigent orphans. Being fortunate enough to find a plate without anybody's card in it, you wisely seat yourself at once, and have a little leisure to look about you. Waiters, with wine-baskets in their hands, are placing decanters of sherry down the tables, at very respect-able distances; melancholy-looking salt-cellars, and decayed vinegar-cruets, which might have belonged to the parents of the indigent orphans in their time, are scattered at distant intervals on the cloth; and the knives and forks look as if they had done duty at every public dinner in London since the accession of George the First. The musicians are scraping and grating and screwing tremendously—playing no notes but notes of preparation; and several gentlemen are gliding along the sides of the tables, looking into plate after plate with frantic eagerness, the expression of their countenances growing more and more dismal as they meet with everybody's card but their own.

You turn round to take a look at the table behind you, and—not being in the habit of attending public dinners—are somewhat struck by the appearance of the party on which your eyes rest. One of its principal members appears to be a little man, with a long and rather inflamed face, and grey hair brushed bolt upright in front ; he wears a wisp of black silk round his neck, without any stiffener, as an apology for a neckerchief, and is addressed by his companions by the familiar appellation of "Fitz," or some such monosyllable. Near him is a stout man in a white neckerchief and buff waistcoat, with shining dark hair, cut very short in front, and a great round healthy-looking face, on which he studiously preserves a half sentimental simper. Next him, again, is a large-headed man, with black hair and bushy whiskers ; and opposite them are two or three others, one of whom is a little round-faced person in a dress-stock and blue under-waistcoat. There is something peculiar in their air and manner, though you could hardly describe what it is ; you cannot divest yourself of the idea that they have come for some other purpose than mere eating and drinking. You have no time to debate the matter, however, for the waiters (who have been arranged in lines down the room, placing the dishes on table) retire to the lower end ; the dark man in the blue coat and bright buttons, who has the direction of the music, looks up to the gallery, and calls out "band" in a very loud voice ; out burst the orchestra, up rise the visitors, in march fourteen stewards, each with a long wand in his hand, like the evil genius in a pantomime ; then the chairman, then the titled visitors ; they all make their way up the room, as fast as they can, bowing, and smiling, and smirking, and looking remarkably amiable. The applause ceases, grace is said, the clatter of plates and dishes begins ; and every one appears highly gratified, either with the presence of the distinguished visitors, or the commencement of the anxiously-expected dinner.

As to the dinner itself—the mere dinner—it goes off much the same everywhere. Tureens of soup are emptied with awful rapidity—waiters take plates of turbot away, to get lobster-sauce, and bring back plates of lobster-sauce without turbot ; people who can carve poultry, are great fools if they own it, and people who can't have no wish to learn. The knives and forks form a pleasing accompaniment to Auber's music, and Auber's music would form a pleasing accompaniment to the dinner, if you could hear anything besides the cymbals. The substantials disappear—moulds of jelly vanish like lightning—hearty eaters wipe their foreheads, and appear rather overcome by their recent exertions—people who have looked very cross hitherto, become remarkably bland, and ask you to take wine in the most friendly manner possible—old gentlemen direct your attention to the ladies' gallery, and take great pains to impress you with the fact that the charity is always peculiarly favoured in this respect—every one appears disposed to become talkative—and the hum of conversation is loud and general.

"Pray, silence, gentlemen, if you please, for *Non nobis!*" shouts the toast-master with stentorian lungs—a toast-master's shirt-front, waistcoat, and neckerchief, by-the-bye, always exhibit three distinct shades of cloudy-white.—"Pray, silence, gentlemen, for *Non nobis!*" The singers, whom you discover to be no other than the very party that excited your curiosity at first, after "pitching" their voices immediately begin *tootoo*ing most dismally, on which the regular old stagers burst into occasional cries of—"Sh—Sh—waiters!—Silence, waiters—stand still, waiters—keep back, waiters," and other exorcisms, delivered in a tone of indignant remonstrance. The grace is soon concluded, and the company resume their seats. The uninitiated portion of the guests applaud *Non nobis* as vehemently as if it were a capital comic song, greatly to the scandal and indignation of the regular diners, who immediately attempt to quell this sacrilegious approbation, by cries of "Hush, hush!" whereupon the others, mistaking these sounds for hisses, applaud more tumultuously than before, and, by way of placing their approval beyond the possibility of doubt, shout "*Encore!*" most vociferously.

The moment the noise ceases, up starts the toast-master: —"Gentlemen, charge your glasses, if you please!" Decanters having been handed about, and glasses filled, the toast-master proceeds, in a regular ascending scale:—"Gentlemen—*air*—you—all charged? Pray—silence—gentlemen—for—the cha—i—r!" The chairman rises, and after stating that he feels it quite unnecessary to preface the toast he is about to propose, with any observations whatever, wanders into a maze of sentences, and flounders about in the most extraordinary manner, presenting a lamentable spectacle of mystified humanity, until he arrives at the words, "constitutional sovereign of these realms," at which elderly gentlemen exclaim "Bravo!" and hammer the table tremendously with their knife-handles. "Under any circumstances, it would give him the greatest pride, it would give him the greatest pleasure—he might almost say, it would afford him satisfaction [cheers] to propose that toast.   What must be his feelings, then, when he has the gratification of announcing, that he has received her Majesty's commands to apply to the Treasurer of her Majesty's Household, for her Majesty's annual donation of 25*l.* in aid of the funds of this charity ! " This announcement (which has been regularly made by every chairman, since the first foundation of the charity, forty-two years ago) calls forth the most vociferous applause ; the toast is drunk with a great deal of cheering and knocking ; and " God save the Queen " is sung by the " professional gentlemen ; " the unprofessional gentlemen joining in the chorus. and giving the national anthem an effect which the newspapers, with great justice, describe as " perfectly electrical."

The other " loyal and patriotic " toasts having been drunk with all due enthusiasm, a comic song having been well sung by the gentleman with the small neckerchief, and a sentimental one by the second of the party, we come to the most important toast of the evening—" Prosperity to the charity." Here again we are compelled to adopt newspaper phraseology, and to express our regret at being " precluded from giving even the substance of the noble lord's observations."   Suffice it to say, that the speech, which is somewhat of the longest, is rapturously received ; and the toast having been drunk, the stewards (looking more important than ever) leave the room, and presently return, heading a procession of indigent orphans, boys and girls, who walk round the room, curtseying, and bowing, and treading on each other's heels, and looking very much as if they would like a glass of wine apiece, to the high gratification of the company generally, and especially of the lady patronesses in the gallery.   *Exeunt* children, and re-enter stewards, each with a blue plate in his hand.   The band plays a lively air ; the majority of the company put their hands into their pockets and look rather serious ; and the noise of sovereigns, rattling on crockery, is heard from all parts of the room.

After a short interval, occupied in singing and toasting, the secretary puts on his spectacles, and proceeds to read the report and list of subscriptions, the latter being listened to with great attention.   " Mr. Smith, one guinea — Mr. Tompkins, one guinea—Mr. Wilson, one guinea—Mr. Hickson, one guinea—Mr. Nixon, one guinea—Mr. Charles Nixon, one guinea—[hear, hear !]—Mr. James Nixon, one guinea —Mr. Thomas Nixon, one pound one [tremendous applause].

H

Lord Fitz Binkle, the chairman of the day, in addition to an
annual donation of fifteen pounds—thirty guineas [prolonged
knocking: several gentlemen knock the stems off their wine-
glasses, in the vehemence of their approbation]. Lady Fitz
Binkle, in addition to an annual donation of ten pound—
twenty pound " [protracted knocking and shouts of "Bravo!"].
The list being at length concluded, the chairman rises, and
proposes the health of the secretary, than whom he knows
no more zealous or estimable individual. The secretary, in
returning thanks, observes that *he* knows no more excellent
individual than the chairman—except the senior officer of the
charity, whose health *he* begs to propose. The senior officer,
in returning thanks, observes that *he* knows no more worthy
man than the secretary—except Mr. Walker, the auditor,
whose health *he* begs to propose. Mr. Walker, in returning thanks, discovers some other estimable individual, to
whom alone the senior officer is inferior—and so they go on
toasting and lauding and thanking : the only other toast of
importance being "The Lady Patronesses now present ! " on
which all the gentlemen turn their faces towards the ladies'
gallery, shouting tremendously ; and little priggish men,
who have imbibed more wine than usual, kiss their hands
and exhibit distressing contortions of visage.

We have protracted our dinner to so great a length, that
we have hardly time to add one word by way of grace. We
can only entreat our readers not to imagine, because we have
attempted to extract some amusement from a charity dinner,
that we are at all disposed to underrate, either the excellence
of the benevolent institutions with which London abounds,
or the estimable motives of those who support them.

The First of May

(*p. 175*)

CHAPTER XX

THE FIRST OF MAY

" Now ladies, up in the sky-parlour : only once a year, if you please !"
                    YOUNG LADY WITH BRASS LADLE.
              "Sweep—sweep—sw-e-ep ! "
                    ILLEGAL WATCHWORD.

THE first of May! There is a merry freshness in the sound, calling to our minds a thousand thoughts of all that is pleasant in nature and beautiful in her most delightful form. What man is there, over whose mind a bright spring morning does not exercise a magic influence—carrying him back to the days of his childish sports, and conjuring up before him the old green field with its gently-waving trees, where the birds sang as he has never heard them since—where the butterfly fluttered far more gaily than he ever sees him now, in all his ramblings—where the sky seemed bluer, and the sun shone more brightly—where the air blew more freshly over greener grass, and sweeter-smelling flowers—where everything wore a richer and more brilliant hue than it is ever dressed in now ! Such are the deep feelings of child-hood, and such are the impressions which every lovely object stamps upon its heart ! The hardy traveller wanders through the maze of thick and pathless woods, where the sun's rays never shone, and heaven's pure air never played ; he stands on the brink of the roaring waterfall, and, giddy and bewildered, watches the foaming mass as it leaps from stone to stone, and from crag to crag ; he lingers in the fertile plains of a land of perpetual sunshine, and revels in the luxury of their balmy breath. But what are the deep forests, or the thundering waters, or the richest landscapes that bounteous nature ever spread, to charm the eyes, and captivate the senses of man, compared with the recollection of the old scenes of his early youth ? Magic scenes indeed ; for the fancies of childhood dressed them in colours brighter than the rainbow, and almost as fleeting !

In former times, spring brought with it not only such associations as these, connected with the past, but sports and games for the present—merry dances round rustic pillars, adorned with emblems of the season, and reared in honour of its coming. Where are they now? Pillars we have, but they are no longer rustic ones; and as to dancers, they are used to rooms, and lights, and would not show well in the open air. Think of the immorality, too! What would your sabbath enthusiasts say, to an aristocratic ring encircling the Duke of York's column in Carlton Terrace—a grand *poussette* of the middle classes, round Alderman Waithman's monument in Fleet Street,—or a general hands-four-round of ten-pound householders, at the foot of the Obelisk in St. George's Fields? Alas! romance can make no head against the riot act; and pastoral simplicity is not understood by the police.

Well; many years ago we began to be a steady and matter-of-fact sort of people, and dancing in spring being beneath our dignity, we gave it up, and in course of time it descended to the sweeps—a fall certainly, because, though sweeps are very good fellows in their way, and moreover very useful in a civilised community, they are not exactly the sort of people to give the tone to the little elegances of society. The sweeps, however, got the dancing to themselves, and they kept it up, and handed it down. This was a severe blow to the romance of spring-time, but it did not entirely destroy it either; for a portion of it descended to the sweeps with the dancing, and rendered them objects of great interest. A mystery hung over the sweeps in those days. Legends were in existence of wealthy gentlemen who had lost children, and who, after many years of sorrow and suffering, had found them in the character of sweeps. Stories were related of a young boy who, having been stolen from his parents in his infancy, and devoted to the occupation of chimney-sweeping, was sent, in the course of his professional career, to sweep the chimney of his mother's bedroom; and how, being hot and tired when he came out of the chimney, he got into the bed he had so often slept in as an infant, and was discovered and recognised therein by his mother, who once every year of her life, thereafter, requested the pleasure of the company of every London sweep, at half-past one o'clock, to roast beef, plum-pudding, porter, and sixpence.

Such stories as these, and there were many such, threw an air of mystery round the sweeps, and produced for them some of those good effects which animals derive from the doctrine of the transmigration of souls. No one (except the masters) thought of ill-treating a sweep, because no one knew who he might be, or what nobleman's or gentleman's son he might turn out. Chimney-sweeping was, by many believers in the marvellous, considered as a sort of probationary term, at an earlier or later period of which, divers young noblemen were to come into possession of their rank and titles : and the profession was held by them in great respect accordingly.

We remember, in our young days, a little sweep about our own age, with curly hair and white teeth, whom we devoutly and sincerely believed to be the lost son and heir of some illustrious personage—an impression which was resolved into an unchangeable conviction on our infant mind, by the subject of our speculations informing us, one day, in reply to our question, propounded a few moments before his ascent to the summit of the kitchen chimney, "that he believed he'd been born in the vurkis, but he'd never know'd his father." We felt certain, from that time forth, that he would one day be owned by a lord ; and we never heard the church-bells ring, or saw a flag hoisted in the neighbourhood, without thinking that the happy event had at last occurred, and that his long-lost parent had arrived in a coach-and-six, to take him home to Grosvenor Square. He never came, however ; and, at the present moment, the young gentleman in question is settled down as a master sweep in the neighbourhood of Battle Bridge, his distinguishing characteristics being a decided antipathy to washing himself, and the possession of a pair of legs very inadequate to the support of his unwieldy and corpulent body.

The romance of spring having gone out before our time, we were fain to console ourselves as we best could with the uncertainty that enveloped the birth and parentage of its attendant dancers, the sweeps ; and we *did* console ourselves with it, for many years. But even this wretched source of comfort received a shock from which it has never recovered— a shock which has been in reality its death-blow. We could not disguise from ourselves the fact that whole families of sweeps were regularly born of sweeps, in the rural districts of Somers Town and Camden Town—that the eldest son succeeded to the father's business, that the other branches assisted him therein, and commenced on their own account ; that their children again, were educated to the profession ;

and that about their identity there could be no mistake whatever. We could not be blind, we say, to this melancholy truth, but we could not bring ourselves to admit it, nevertheless, and we lived on for some years in a state of voluntary ignorance. We were roused from our pleasant slumber by certain dark insinuations thrown out by a friend of ours, to the effect that children in the lower ranks of life were beginning to *choose* chimney-sweeping as their particular walk; that applications had been made by various boys to the constituted authorities, to allow them to pursue the object of their ambition with the full concurrence and sanction of the law; that the affair, in short, was becoming one of mere legal contract. We turned a deaf ear to these rumours at first, but slowly and surely they stole upon us. Month after month, week after week, nay, day after day, at last, did we meet with accounts of similar applications. The veil was removed, all mystery was at an end, and chimney-sweeping had become a favourite and chosen pursuit. There is no longer any occasion to steal boys; for boys flock in crowds to bind themselves. The romance of the trade has fled, and the chimney-sweeper of the present day is no more like unto him of thirty years ago, than is a Fleet Street pickpocket to a Spanish brigand, or Paul Pry to Caleb Williams.

This gradual decay and disuse of the practice of leading noble youths into captivity, and compelling them to ascend chimneys, was a severe blow, if we may so speak, to the romance of chimney-sweeping, and to the romance of spring at the same time. But even this was not all, for some few years ago the dancing on May-day began to decline; small sweeps were observed to congregate in twos or threes, unsupported by a "green," with no "My Lord" to act as master of the ceremonies, and no "My Lady" to preside over the exchequer. Even in companies where there was a "green" it was an absolute nothing—a mere sprout—and the instrumental accompaniments rarely extended beyond the shovels and a set of Pan-pipes, better known to the many, as a "mouth-organ."

These were signs of the times, portentous omens of a coming change; and what was the result which they shadowed forth? Why, the master sweeps, influenced by a restless spirit of innovation, actually interposed their authority, in opposition to the dancing, and substituted a dinner—an anniversary dinner at White Conduit House— where clean faces appeared in lieu of black ones smeared with rose pink; and knee cords and tops superseded nankeen drawers and rosetted shoes.

Gentlemen who were in the habit of riding shy horses; and steady-going people who have no vagrancy in their souls, lauded this alteration to the skies, and the conduct of the master sweeps was described as beyond the reach of praise. But how stands the real fact? Let any man deny, if he can, that when the cloth had been removed, fresh pots and pipes laid upon the table, and the customary loyal and patriotic toasts proposed, the celebrated Mr. Sluffen, of Adam-and-Eve Court, whose authority not the most malignant of our opponents can call in question, expressed himself in a manner following: "That now he'd cotcht the cheerman's hi, he vished he might be jolly vell blessed, if he worn't a goin' to have his innings, vich ho vould say these here obserwashuns— that how some mischeevus coves as know'd nuffin about the consarn, had tried to sit people agin the mas'r swips, and take the shine out o' their bis'nes, and the bread out o' the traps o' their preshus kids, by a makin' o' this here remark, as chimblies could be as vell svept by 'sheenery as by boys; and that the makin' use o' boys for that there purpuss vos barbareous; vereas, he 'ad been a chummy—he begged the cheerman's parding for usin' such a wulgar hexpression— more nor thirty year—he might say he'd been born in a chimbley—and he know'd uncommon vell as 'sheenery vos vus nor o' no use; and as to kerhewelty to the boys. everybody in the chimbley line know'd as vell as he did. that they liked the climbin' better nor nuffin as vos." From this day, we date the total fall of the last lingering remnant of May-day dancing, among the *elite* of the profession: and from this period we commence a new era in that portion of our spring associations which relates to the 1st of May.

We are aware that the unthinking part of the population will meet us here, with the assertion that dancing on May-day still continues—that "greens" are annually seen to roll along the streets—that youths in the garb of clowns precede them, giving vent to the ebullitions of their sportive fancies; and that lords and ladies follow in their wake.

Granted. We are ready to acknowledge that in outward show, these processions have greatly improved: we do not deny the introduction of solos on the drum; we will even go

so far as to admit an occasional fantasia on the triangle, but
here our admissions end. We positively deny that the sweeps
have art or part in these proceedings. We distinctly charge
the dustmen with throwing what they ought to clear away,
into the eyes of the public. We accuse scavengers, brick-
makers, and gentlemen who devote their energies to the
costermongering line, with obtaining money once a year,
under false pretences. We cling with peculiar fondness to
the custom of days gone by, and have shut out conviction as
long as we could, but it has forced itself upon us ; and we
now proclaim to a deluded public, that the May-day dancers
are *not* sweeps. The size of them, alone, is sufficient to
repudiate the idea. It is a notorious fact that the widely-
spread taste for register-stoves has materially increased the
demand for small boys ; whereas the men who, under a
fictitious character, dance about the streets on the first of
May nowadays, would be a tight fit in a kitchen flue, to say
nothing of the parlour. This is strong presumptive evidence,
but we have positive proof—the evidence of our own senses.
And here is our testimony.

Upon the morning of the second of the merry month of
May, in the year of our Lord one thousand eight hundred
and thirty-six, we went out for a stroll, with a kind of forlorn hope of seeing something or other which might induce
us to believe that it was really spring, and not Christmas.
After wandering as far as Copenhagen House, without meeting anything calculated to dispel our impression that there
was a mistake in the almanacks, we turned back down
Maiden Lane, with the intention of passing through the
extensive colony lying between it and Battle Bridge, which
is inhabited by proprietors of donkey-carts, boilers of horse-
flesh, makers of tiles, and sifters of cinders ; through which
colony we should have passed, without stoppage or interruption, if a little crowd gathered round a shed had not
attracted our attention, and induced us to pause.

When we say a "shed," we do not mean the conservatory
sort of building which, according to the old song, Love
tenanted when he was a young man, but a wooden house
with windows stuffed with rags and paper, and a small yard
at the side, with one dust-cart, two baskets, a few shovels,
and little heaps of cinders, and fragments of china and tiles,
scattered about it. Before this inviting spot we paused : an
the longer we looked, the more we wondered what exciting

circumstance it could be, that induced the foremost members
of the crowd to flatten their noses against the parlour
window, in the vain hope of catching a glimpse of what was
going on inside. After staring vacantly about us for some
minutes, we appealed, touching the cause of this assemblage,
to a gentleman in a suit of tarpaulin, who was smoking his
pipe on our right hand ; but as the only answer we obtained
was a playful inquiry whether our mother had disposed of
her mangle, we determined to await the issue in silence.

Judge of our virtuous indignation, when the street-door
of the shed opened, and a party emerged therefrom, clad
in the costume and emulating the appearance, of May-day
sweeps !

The first person who appeared was "my lord," habited in
a blue coat and bright buttons, with gilt paper tacked over
the seams, yellow knee-breeches, pink cotton stockings, and
shoes ; a cocked hat, ornamented with shreds of various-
coloured paper, on his head, a *bouquet* the size of a prize
cauliflower in his button-hole, a long Belcher handkerchief
in his right hand, and a thin cane in his left. A murmur of
applause ran through the crowd (which was chiefly composed
of his lordship's personal friends), when this graceful figure
made his appearance, which swelled into a burst of applause
as his fair partner in the dance bounded forth to join him.
Her ladyship was attired in pink crape over bed-furniture,
with a low body and short sleeves. The symmetry of her
ankles was partially concealed by a very perceptible pair
of frilled trousers ; and the inconvenience which might have
resulted from the circumstance of her white satin shoes being
a few sizes too large, was obviated by their being firmly
attached to her legs with strong tape sandals.

Her head was ornamented with a profusion of artificial
flowers ; and in her hand she bore a large brass ladle, wherein
to receive what she figuratively denominated "the tin." The
other characters were a young gentleman in girl's clothes and
a widow's cap ; two clowns who walked upon their hands in
the mud, to the immeasurable delight of all the spectators ;
a man with a drum ; another man with a flageolet ; a dirty
woman in a large shawl, with a box under her arm for the
money,—and last, though not least, the "green," animated
by no less a personage than our identical friend in the
tarpaulin suit.

The man hammered away at the drum, the flageolet

squeaked, the shovels rattled, the "green" rolled about, pitching first on one side and then on the other; my lady threw her right foot over her left ankle, and her left foot over her right ankle, alternately; my lord ran a few paces forward, and butted at the "green," and then a few paces backward upon the toes of the crowd, and then went to the right, and then to the left, and then dodged my lady round the "green;" and finally drew her arm through his, and called upon the boys to shout, which they did lustily—for this was the dancing.

We passed the same group, accidentally, in the evening. We never saw a "green" so drunk, a lord so quarrelsome (no: not even in the house of peers after dinner), a pair of clowns so melancholy, a lady so muddy, or a party so miserable.

How has May-day decayed!

CHAPTER XXI

BROKERS' AND MARINE-STORE SHOPS

WHEN we affirm that brokers' shops are strange places, and that if an authentic history of their contents could be procured, it would furnish many a page of amusement, and many a melancholy tale, it is necessary to explain the class of shops to which we allude. Perhaps when we make use of the term "Brokers' Shop," the minds of our readers will at once picture large, handsome warehouses, exhibiting a long perspective of French-polished dining-tables, rosewood chiffoniers, and mahogany wash-hand-stands, with an occasional vista of a four-post bedstead and hangings, and an appropriate foreground of dining-room chairs. Perhaps they will imagine that we mean an humble class of second-hand furniture repositories. Their imagination will then naturally lead them to that street at the back of Long Acre, which is composed almost entirely of brokers' shops; where you walk through groves of deceitful, showy-looking furniture, and where the prospect is occasionally enlivened by a bright red, blue, and yellow hearth-rug, embellished with the pleasing device of a mail-coach at full speed, or a strange animal, supposed to have been originally intended for a dog, with a mass of worsted-work in his mouth, which conjecture has likened to a basket of flowers.

This, by-the-bye, is a tempting article to young wives in the humbler ranks of life, who have a first-floor front to furnish—they are lost in admiration, and hardly know which to admire most. The dog is very beautiful, but they have a dog already on the best tea-tray, and two more on the mantel-piece. Then, there is something so genteel about that mail-coach; and the passengers outside (who are all hat) give it such an air of reality!

The goods here are adapted to the taste, or rather to the means, of cheap purchasers. There are some of the most beautiful *looking* Pembroke tables that were ever beheld:

the wood as green as the trees in the Park, and the leaves almost as certain to fall off in the course of a year.   There is also a most extensive assortment of tent and turn-up bedsteads, made of stained wood, and innumerable specimens of that base imposition on society—a sofa bedstead.

A turn-up bedstead is a blunt, honest piece of furniture ; it may be slightly disguised with a sham drawer ; and some- times a mad attempt is even made to pass it off for a book- case ; ornament it as you will, however, the turn-up bedstead seems to defy disguise, and to insist on having it distinctly understood that he is a turn-up bedstead, and nothing else— that he is indispensably necessary, and that being so useful, he disdains to be ornamental.

How different is the demeanour of a sofa bedstead ! Ashamed of its real use, it strives to appear an article of luxury and gentility—an attempt in which it miserably fails. It has neither the respectability of a sofa, nor the virtues of a bed ; every man who keeps a sofa bedstead in his house, becomes a party to a wilful and designing fraud—we question whether you could insult him more, than by insinuating that you entertain the least suspicion of its real use.

To return from this digression, we beg to say, that neither of these classes of brokers' shops forms the subject of this sketch.   The shops to which we advert, are immeasurably inferior to those on whose outward appearance we have slightly touched.   Our readers must often have observed in some by-street, in a poor neighbourhood, a small dirty shop, exposing for sale the most extraordinary and confused jumble of old, worn-out, wretched articles, that can well be imagined. Our wonder at their ever having been bought, is only to be equalled by our astonishment at the idea of their ever being sold again.   On a board, at the side of the door, are placed about twenty books—all odd volumes ; and as many wine- glasses—all different patterns ; several locks, an old earthen- ware pan, full of rusty keys ; two or three gaudy chimney- ornaments—cracked, of course ; the remains of a lustre, without any drops ; a round frame like a capital O, which has once held a mirror ; a flute, complete with the exception of the middle joint ; a pair of curling-irons ; and a tinder-box. In front of the shop window are ranged some half-dozen high-backed chairs, with spinal complaints and wasted legs ; a corner cupboard ; two or three very dark mahogany tables with flaps like mathematical problems ; some pickle-jars, some surgeons' ditto, with gilt labels and without stoppers; an unframed portrait of some lady who flourished about the beginning of the thirteenth century, by an artist who never flourished at all; an incalculable host of miscellanies of every description, including bottles and cabinets, rags and bones, fenders and street-door knockers, fire-irons, wearing apparel and bedding, a hall-lamp, and a room-door. Imagine, in addition to this incongruous mass, a black doll in a white frock, with two faces—one looking up the street, and the other looking down, swinging over the door; a board with the squeezed-up inscription "Dealer in marine stores," in lanky white letters, whose height is strangely out of proportion to their width; and you have before you precisely the kind of shop to which we wish to direct your attention.

Although the same heterogeneous mixture of things will be found at all these places, it is curious to observe how truly and accurately some of the minor articles which are exposed for sale—articles of wearing apparel, for instance— mark the character of the neighbourhood. Take Drury Lane and Covent Garden for example.

This is essentially a theatrical neighbourhood. There is not a potboy in the vicinity who is not, to a greater or less extent, a dramatic character. The errand-boys and chandler's-shop-keepers' sons are all stage-struck: they "gets up" plays in back kitchens hired for the purpose, and will stand before a shop-window for hours, contemplating a great staring portrait of Mr. Somebody or other, of the Royal Coburg Theatre, "as he appeared in the character of Tongo the Denounced." The consequence is, that there is not a marine-store shop in the neighbourhood, which does not exhibit for sale some faded articles of dramatic finery, such as three or four pairs of soiled buff boots with turn-over red tops, heretofore worn by a "fourth robber," or "fifth mob;" a pair of rusty broadswords, a few gauntlets, and certain resplendent ornaments, which, if they were yellow instead of white, might be taken for insurance plates of the Sun Fire Office. There are several of these shops in the narrow streets and dirty courts, of which there are so many near the national theatres, and they all have tempting goods of this description, with the addition, perhaps, of a lady's pink dress covered with spangles; white wreaths, stage shoes, and a tiara like a tin lamp reflector. They have been purchased of some wretched supernumeraries, or sixth-rate

actors, and are now offered for the benefit of the rising
generation, who, on condition of making certain weekly payments, amounting in the whole to about ten times their
value, may avail themselves of such desirable bargains.

Let us take a very different quarter, and apply it to the
same test. Look at a marine-store dealer's, in that reservoir
of dirt, drunkenness, and drabs: thieves, oysters, baked
potatoes, and pickled salmon—Ratcliff Highway. Here,
the wearing apparel is all nautical. Rough blue jackets,
with mother-of-pearl buttons, oil-skin hats, coarse checked
shirts, and large canvas trousers that look as if they were
made for a pair of bodies instead of a pair of legs, are the
staple commodities. Then, there are large bunches of cotton
pocket-handkerchiefs, in colour and pattern unlike any one
ever saw before, with the exception of those on the backs of
the three young ladies without bonnets who passed just now.
The furniture is much the same as elsewhere, with the
addition of one or two models of ships, and some old prints
of naval engagements in still older frames. In the window
are a few compasses, a small tray containing silver watches
in clumsy thick cases; and tobacco-boxes, the lid of each
ornamented with a ship, or an anchor, or some such trophy.
A sailor generally pawns or sells all he has before he has
been long ashore, and if he does not, some favoured companion kindly saves him the trouble. In either case, it is
an even chance that he afterwards unconsciously repur-
chases the same things at a higher price than he gave for
them at first.

Again: pay a visit with a similar object, to a part of
London, as unlike both of these as they are to each other.
Cross over to the Surrey side, and look at such shops of this
description as are to be found near the King's Bench prison,
and in "the Rules." How different, and how strikingly
illustrative of the decay of some of the unfortunate residents
in this part of the metropolis! Imprisonment and neglect
have done their work. There is contamination in the
profligate denizens of a debtor's prison; old friends have
fallen off; the recollection of former prosperity has passed
away; and with it all thoughts for the past, all care for the
future. First, watches and rings, then cloaks, coats, and all
the more expensive articles of dress, have found their way to
the pawnbroker's. That miserable resource has failed at last,
and the sale of some trifling article at one of these shops

has been the only mode left of raising a shilling or two, to meet the urgent demands of the moment. Dressing-cases and writing-desks, too old to pawn but too good to keep ; guns, fishing-rods, musical instruments, all in the same condition ; have first been sold, and the sacrifice has been but slightly felt. But hunger must be allayed, and what has already become a habit is easily resorted to, when an emergency arises. Light articles of clothing, first of the ruined man, then of his wife, at last of their children, even of the youngest, have been parted with, piecemeal. There they are, thrown carelessly together until a purchaser presents himself, old, and patched and repaired, it is true ; but the make and materials tell of better days ; and the older they are, the greater the misery and destitution of those whom they once adorned.

CHAPTER XXII.

GIN-SHOPS

IT is a remarkable circumstance, that different trades appear to partake of the disease to which elephants and dogs are especially liable, and to run stark, staring, raving mad, periodically. The great distinction between the animals and the trades is, that the former run mad with a certain degree of propriety—they are very regular in their irregularities. We know the period at which the emergency will arise, and provide against it accordingly. If an elephant run mad, we are all ready for him—kill or cure—pills or bullets, calomel in conserve of roses, or lead in a musket-barrel. If a dog happen to look unpleasantly warm in the summer months, and to trot about the shady side of the streets with a quarter of a yard of tongue hanging out of his mouth, a thick leather muzzle, which has been previously prepared in compliance with the thoughtful injunctions of the Legislature, is instantly clapped over his head, by way of making him cooler, and he either looks remarkably unhappy for the next six weeks, or becomes legally insane, and goes mad, as it were, by Act of Parliament. But these trades are as eccentric as comets; nay, worse, for no one can calculate on the recurrence of the strange appearances which betoken the disease. Moreover, the contagion is general, and the quickness with which it diffuses itself, almost incredible.

We will cite two or three cases in illustration of our meaning. Six or eight years ago, the epidemic began to display itself among the linen-drapers and haberdashers. The primary symptoms were an inordinate love of plate-glass, and a passion for gas-lights and gilding. The disease gradually progressed, and at last attained a fearful height. Quiet dusty old shops in different parts of town, were pulled down; spacious premises with stuccoed fronts and gold letters, were erected instead; floors were covered with

Turkey carpets; roofs supported by massive pillars; doors knocked into windows, a dozen squares of glass into one; one shopman into a dozen; and there is no knowing what would have been done, if it had not been fortunately discovered, just in time, that the Commissioners of Bankruptcy were as competent to decide such cases as the Commissioners of Lunacy, and that a little confinement and gentle examination did wonders. The disease abated. It died away. A year or two of comparative tranquillity ensued. Suddenly it burst out again amongst the chemists; the symptoms were the same, with the addition of a strong desire to stick the royal arms over the shop-door, and a great rage for mahogany, varnish, and expensive floor-cloth. Then the hosiers were infected, and began to pull down their shop-fronts with frantic recklessness. The mania again died away, and the public began to congratulate themselves on its entire disappearance, when it burst forth with ten-fold violence among the publicans, and keepers of "wine vaults." From that moment it has spread among them with unprecedented rapidity, exhibiting a concatenation of all the previous symptoms; onward it has rushed to every part of town, knocking down all the old public-houses, and depositing splendid mansions, stone balustrades, rosewood fittings, immense lamps, and illuminated clocks, at the corner of every street.

The extensive scale on which these places are established, and the ostentatious manner in which the business of even the smallest among them is divided into branches, is amusing. A handsome plate of ground glass in one door directs you "To the Counting-house;" another to the "Bottle Department;" a third to the "Wholesale Department;" a fourth to "The Wine Promenade;" and so forth, until we are in daily expectation of meeting with a "Brandy Bell," or a "Whiskey Entrance." Then, ingenuity is exhausted in devising attractive titles for the different descriptions of gin; and the dram-drinking portion of the community as they gaze upon the gigantic black and white announcements, which are only to be equalled in size by the figures beneath them, are left in a state of pleasing hesitation between "The Cream of the Valley," "The Out and Out," "The No Mistake," "The Good for Mixing," "The Real Knock-me-down," "The celebrated Butter Gin," "The regular Flare-up," and a dozen other, equally inviting and wholesome *liqueurs*.

Although places of this description are to be met with in
every second street, they are invariably numerous and splendid in precise proportion to the dirt and poverty of the
surrounding neighbourhood.   The gin-shops in and near
Drury Lane, Holborn, St. Giles's, Covent Garden, and Clare
Market, are the handsomest in London.   There is more of
filth and squalid misery near those great thoroughfares than
in any part of this mighty city.

We will endeavour to sketch the bar of a large gin-shop,
and its ordinary customers, for the edification of such of our
readers as may not have had opportunities of observing such
scenes ; and on the chance of finding one well suited to our
purpose, we will make for Drury Lane, through the narrow
streets and dirty courts which divide it from Oxford Street,
and that classical spot adjoining the brewery at the bottom
of Tottenham Court Road, best known to the initiated as the
"Rookery."

The filthy and miserable appearance of this part of London
can hardly be imagined by those (and there are many such)
who have not witnessed it.   Wretched houses with broken
windows patched with rags and paper : every room let out
to a different family, and in many instances to two or even
three—fruit and "sweet-stuff" manufacturers in the cellars,
barbers and red-herring vendors in the front parlours, cob-
blers in the back ; a bird-fancier in the first floor, three
families on the second, starvation in the attics, Irishmen in
the passage, a "musician" in the front kitchen, and a char-
woman and five hungry children in the back one—filth
everywhere—a gutter before the houses and a drain behind
—clothes drying and slops emptying, from the windows ;
girls of fourteen or fifteen, with matted hair, walking about
barefoot, and in white great-coats, almost their only covering ;
boys of all ages, in coats of all sizes and no coats at all ;
men and women, in every variety of scanty and dirty apparel, lounging, scolding, drinking, smoking, squabbling,
fighting, and swearing.

You turn the corner.   What a change !   All is light and
brilliancy.   The hum of many voices issues from that splendid
gin-shop which forms the commencement of the two streets
opposite ; and the gay building with the fantastically ornamented parapet, the illuminated clock, the plate-glass windows
surrounded by stucco rosettes, and its profusion of gas-lights
in richly-gilt burners, is perfectly dazzling when contrasted

The Gin Shop

with the darkness and dirt we have just left. The interior is even gayer than the exterior. A bar of French-polished mahogany, elegantly carved, extends the whole width of the place ; and there are two side-aisles of great casks, painted green and gold, enclosed within a light brass rail, and bearing such inscriptions as " Old Tom, 549 ; " " Young Tom, 360 ; " "Samson, 1421 "—the figures agreeing, we presume, with " gallons," understand. Beyond the bar is a lofty and spacious saloon, full of the same enticing vessels, with a gallery running round it, equally well furnished. On the counter, in addition to the usual spirit apparatus, are two or three little baskets of cakes and biscuits, which are carefully secured at the top with wicker-work, to prevent their contents being unlawfully abstracted. Behind it are two showily-dressed damsels with large necklaces, dispensing the spirits and " compounds." They are assisted by the ostensible proprietor of the concern, a stout coarse fellow in a fur cap, put on very much on one side to give him a knowing air, and to display his sandy whiskers to the best advantage.

The two old washerwomen, who are seated on the little bench to the left of the bar, are rather overcome by the head-dresses and haughty demeanour of the young ladies who officiate. They receive their half-quartern of gin and pepper-mint, with considerable deference, prefacing a request for " one of them soft biscuits," with a " Jist be good enough, ma'am." They are quite astonished at the impudent air of the young fellow in a brown coat and bright buttons, who, ushering in his two companions, and walking up to the bar in as careless a manner as if he had been used to green and gold ornaments all his life, winks at one of the young ladies with singular coolness, and calls for a "kervorten and a three-out-glass," just as if the place were his own. "Gin for you, sir ? " says the young lady when she has drawn it : carefully looking every way but the right one, to show that the wink had no effect upon her. "For me, Mary, my dear," replies the gentleman in brown. "My name an't Mary as it happens," says the young girl, rather relaxing as she delivers the change. "Well, if it an't, it ought to be," responds the irresistible one ; " all the Marys as ever I see, was handsome gals." Here the young lady, not precisely remembering how blushes are managed in such cases, abruptly ends the flirtation by addressing the female in the faded feathers who has just entered, and who, after stating explicitly, to prevent any subsequent misunderstanding, that "this gentleman pays," calls for "a glass of port wine and a bit of sugar."

Those two old men who came in "just to have a drain," finished their third quartern a few seconds ago ; they have made themselves crying drunk ; and the fat comfortable-looking elderly women, who had "a glass of rum-srub" each, having chimed in with their complaints on the hardness of the times, one of the women has agreed to stand a glass round, jocularly observing that "grief never mended no broken bones, and as good people's wery scarce, what I says is, make the most on 'em, and that's all about it ! " a sentiment which appears to afford unlimited satisfaction to those who have nothing to pay.

It is growing late, and the throng of men, women, and children, who have been constantly going in and out, dwindles down to two or three occasional stragglers—cold, wretched-looking creatures, in the last stage of emaciation and disease. The knot of Irish labourers at the lower end of the place, who have been alternately shaking hands with, and threatening the life of each other, for the last hour, become furious in their disputes, and finding it impossible to silence one man, who is particularly anxious to adjust the difference, they resort to the expedient of knocking him down and jumping on him afterwards. The man in the fur cap, and the potboy rush out ; a scene of riot and confusion ensues ; half the Irishmen get shut out, and the other half get shut in ; the potboy is knocked among the tubs in no time ; the landlord hits everybody, and everybody hits the landlord ; the barmaids scream ; the police come in ; the rest is a confused mixture of arms, legs, staves, torn coats, shouting, and struggling. Some of the party are borne off to the station-house, and the remainder slink home to beat their wives for complaining, and kick the children for daring to be hungry.

We have sketched this subject very slightly, not only because our limits compel us to do so, but because, if it were pursued farther, it would be painful and repulsive. Well-disposed gentlemen, and charitable ladies, would alike turn with coldness and disgust from a description of the drunken besotted men, and wretched broken-down miserable women, who form no inconsiderable portion of the frequenters of these haunts ; forgetting, in the pleasant consciousness of their own rectitude, the poverty of the one, and the temptation of the other. Gin-drinking is a great vice in England, but wretchedness and dirt are a greater; and until you improve the homes of the poor, or persuade a half-famished wretch not to seek relief in the temporary oblivion of his own misery, with the pittance which, divided among his family, would furnish a morsel of bread for each, gin-shops will increase in number and splendour. If Temperance Societies would suggest an antidote against hunger, filth, and foul air, or could establish dispensaries for the gratuitous distribution of bottles of Lethe-water, gin-palaces would be numbered among the things that were.

CHAPTER XXIII

THE PAWNBROKER'S SHOP

OF the numerous receptacles for misery and distress with which the streets of London unhappily abound, there are, perhaps, none which present such striking scenes as the pawnbrokers' shops. The very nature and description of these places occasions their being but little known, except to the unfortunate beings whose profligacy or misfortune drives them to seek the temporary relief they offer. The subject may appear, at first sight, to be anything but an inviting one, but we venture on it nevertheless, in the hope that, as far as the limits of our present paper are concerned, it will present nothing to disgust even the most fastidious reader.

There are some pawnbrokers' shops of a very superior description. There are grades in pawning as in everything else, and distinctions must be observed even in poverty. The aristocratic Spanish cloak and the plebeian calico shirt, the silver fork and the flat iron, the muslin cravat and the Belcher neckerchief, would but ill assort together ; so the better sort of pawnbroker calls himself a silversmith, and decorates his shop with handsome trinkets and expensive jewellery, while the more humble money-lender boldly advertises his calling. and invites observation. It is with pawnbrokers' shops of the latter class, that we have to do. We have selected one for our purpose, and will endeavour to describe it.

The pawnbroker's shop is situated near Drury Lane, at the corner of a court, which affords a side entrance for the accommodation of such customers as may be desirous of avoiding the observation of the passers-by, or the chance of recognition in the public street. It is a low, dirty-looking, dusty shop, the door of which stands always doubtfully a little way open : half inviting, half repelling the hesitating visitor, who, if he be as yet uninitiated, examines one of the old garnet brooches in the window for a minute or two with affected eagerness, as if he contemplated making a purchase ;

and then looking cautiously round to ascertain that no one watches him, hastily slinks in: the door closing of itself after him, to just its former width. The shop front and the window-frames bear evident marks of having been once painted; but what the colour was originally, or at what date it was probably laid on, are at this remote period questions which may be asked, but cannot be answered. Tradition states that the transparency in the front door, which displays at night three red balls on a blue ground, once bore also, inscribed in graceful waves, the words "Money advanced on plate, jewels, wearing apparel, and every description of property," but a few illegible hieroglyphics are all that now remain to attest the fact. The plate and jewels would seem to have disappeared, together with the announcement, for the articles of stock, which are displayed in some profusion in the window, do not include any very valuable luxuries of either kind. A few old china cups; some modern vases, adorned with paltry paintings of three Spanish cavaliers playing three Spanish guitars; or a party of boors carousing: each boor with one leg painfully elevated in the air, by way of expressing his perfect freedom and gaiety; several sets of chessmen, two or three flutes, a few fiddles, a round-eyed portrait staring in astonishment from a very dark ground; some gaudily-bound prayer-books and testaments, two rows of silver watches quite as clumsy and almost as large as Ferguson's first; numerous old-fashioned table and tea spoons, displayed, fan-like, in half-dozens; strings of coral with great broad gilt snaps; cards of rings and brooches, fastened and labelled separately, like the insects in the British Museum; cheap silver penholders and snuff-boxes, with a masonic star, complete the jewellery department; while five or six beds in smeary clouded ticks, strings of blankets and sheets, silk and cotton handkerchiefs, and wearing apparel of every description, form the more useful, though even less ornamental, part, of the articles exposed for sale. An extensive collection of planes, chisels, saws, and other carpenters' tools, which have been pledged, and never redeemed, form the foreground of the picture; while the large frames full of ticketed bundles, which are dimly seen through the dirty casement up-stairs— the squalid neighbourhood—the adjoining houses, straggling, shrunken, and rotten, with one or two filthy, unwholesome-looking heads, thrust out of every window, and old red pans and stunted plants exposed on the tottering parapets, to the

manifest hazard of the heads of the passers-by—the noisy
men loitering under the archway at the corner of the court,
or about the gin-shop next door—and their wives patiently
standing on the curbstone, with large baskets of cheap
vegetables slung round them for sale, are its immediate
auxiliaries.

If the outside of the pawnbroker's shop be calculated to
attract the attention, or excite the interest, of the speculative
pedestrian, its interior cannot fail to produce the same effect
in an increased degree. The front door, which we have
before noticed, opens into the common shop, which is the
resort of all those customers whose habitual acquaintance
with such scenes renders them indifferent to the observation
of their companions in poverty. The side door opens into
a small passage from which some half-dozen doors (which
may be secured on the inside by bolts) open into a corresponding number of little dens, or closets, which face the
counter. Here, the more timid or respectable portion of the
crowd shroud themselves from the notice of the remainder,
and patiently wait until the gentleman behind the counter,
with the curly black hair, diamond ring, and double silver
watch-guard, shall feel disposed to favour them with his
notice—a consummation which depends considerably on the
temper of the aforesaid gentleman for the time being.

At the present moment, this elegantly-attired individual
is in the act of entering the duplicate he has just made out,
in a thick book: a process from which he is diverted occasionally, by a conversation he is carrying on with another
young man similarly employed at a little distance from him,
whose allusions to "that last bottle of soda-water last night,"
and "how regularly round my hat he felt himself when the
young 'ooman gave 'em in charge," would appear to refer to
the consequences of some stolen joviality of the preceding
evening. The customers generally, however, seem unable
to participate in the amusement derivable from this source,
for an old sallow-looking woman, who has been leaning with
both arms on the counter with a small bundle before her,
for half an hour previously, suddenly interrupts the conversation by addressing the jewelled shopman—" Now, Mr.
Henry, do make haste, there's a good soul, for my two
grandchildren's locked up at home, and I'm afeer'd of the
fire." The shopman slightly raises his head with an air
of deep abstraction, and resumes his entry with as much

deliberation as if he were engraving. " You're in a hurry, Mrs. Tatham, this ev'nin', an't you ? " is the only notice he deigns to take, after the lapse of five minutes or so. " Yes, I am indeed, Mr. Henry ; now, do serve me next, there's a good creetur. I wouldn't worry you, only it's all along o' them botherin' children." " What have you got here ? " inquires the shopman, unpinning the bundle—" old concern, I suppose—pair o' stays and a petticut. You must look up somethin' else, old 'ooman ; I can't lend you anything more upon them ; they're completely worn out by this time, if it's only by putting in, and taking out again, three times a week." " Oh ! you're a rum un, you are," replies the old woman, laughing extremely, as in duty bound ; " I wish I'd got the gift of the gab like you ; see if I'd be up the spout so often then ! No, no ; it an't the petticut ; it's a child's frock and a beautiful silk ankecher, as belongs to my husband. He gave four shillin' for it, the werry same blessed day as he broke his arm."—" What do you want upon these ? " inquires Mr. Henry, slightly glancing at the articles, which in all probability are old acquaintances. " What do you want upon these ?—" Eighteenpence."—" Lend you ninepence."— " Oh, make it a shillin' ; there's a dear—do now ? "—" Not another farden."—" Well, I suppose I must take it." The duplicate is made out, one ticket pinned on the parcel, the other given to the old woman ; the parcel is flung carelessly down into a corner, and some other customer prefers his claim to be served without further delay.

The choice falls on an unshaven, dirty, sottish-looking fellow, whose tarnished paper-cap, stuck negligently over one eye, communicates an additionally repulsive expression to his very uninviting countenance. He was enjoying a little relaxation from his sedentary pursuits a quarter of an hour ago, in kicking his wife up the court. He has come to redeem some tools:—probably to complete a job with, on account of which he has already received some money, if his inflamed countenance and drunken stagger may be taken as evidence of the fact. Having waited some little time, he makes his presence known by venting his ill-humour on a ragged urchin, who, being unable to bring his face on a level with the counter by any other process, has employed himself in climbing up, and then hooking himself on with his elbows —an uneasy perch, from which he has fallen at intervals, generally alighting on the toes of the person in his immediate

vicinity.   In the present case, the unfortunate little wretch
has received a cuff which sends him reeling to the door ; and
the donor of the blow is immediately the object of general
indignation.

"What do you strike the boy for, you brute ? " exclaims
a slipshod woman, with two flat irons in a little basket.
" Do you think he's your wife, you willin ? "   " Go and hang
yourself ! " replies the gentleman addressed, with a drunken
look of savage stupidity, aiming at the same time a blow at
the woman which fortunately misses its object.   " Go and
hang yourself ; and wait till I come and cut you down."—
" Cut you down," rejoins the woman, " I wish I had the
cutting of you up, you wagabond ! (loud.)   Oh ! you precious
wagabond ! (rather louder.)   Where's your wife, you willin ?
(louder still ; women of this class are always sympathetic,
and work themselves into a tremendous passion on the
shortest notice.)   Your poor dear wife as you uses worser
nor a dog—strike a woman—you a man ! (very shrill ;)
I wish I had you—I'd murder you, I would, if I died for it ! "
—" Now be civil," retorts the man fiercely.   " Be civil, you
wiper ! " ejaculates the woman contemptuously.   " An't it
shocking ? " she continues, turning round, and appealing to
an old woman who is peeping out of one of the little closets
we have before described, and who has not the slightest
objection to join in the attack, possessing, as she does, the
comfortable conviction that she is bolted in.   " An't it shocking, ma'am ? (Dreadful ! says the old woman in a parenthesis, not exactly knowing what the question refers to.)
He's got a wife, ma'am, as takes in mangling, and is as
'dustrious and hard-working a young 'ooman as can be,
(very fast) as lives in the back parlour of our 'ous, which my
husband and me lives in the front one (with great rapidity)
—and we hears him a beaten' on her sometimes when he
comes home drunk, the whole night through, and not only
a beaten' her, but beaten' his own child too, to make her
more miserable—ugh, you beast ! and she, poor creater,
won't swear the peace agin him, nor do nothin', because she
likes the wretch arter all—worse luck ! "   Here, as the
woman has completely run herself out of breath, the pawnbroker himself, who has just appeared behind the counter in
a gay dressing-gown, embraces the favourable opportunity
of putting in a word :—" Now I won't have none of this
sort of thing on my premises ! " he interposes with an air of

The Pawnbroker's Shop
(*p. 190*)

authority. "Mrs. Mackin, keep yourself to yourself, or you don't get fourpence for a flat iron here; and Jinkins, you leave your ticket here till you're sober, and send your wife for them two planes, for I won't have you in my shop at no price; so make yourself scarce, before I make you scarcer."

This eloquent address produces anything but the effect desired; the women rail in concert; the man hits about him in all directions, and is in the act of establishing an indisputable claim to gratuitous lodgings for the night, when the entrance of his wife, a wretched worn-out woman, apparently in the last stage of consumption, whose face bears evident marks of recent ill-usage, and whose strength seems hardly equal to the burden—light enough, God knows!—of the thin, sickly child she carries in her arms, turns his cowardly rage in a safer direction. "Come home, dear," cries the miserable creature, in an imploring tone; "do come home, there's a good fellow, and go to bed."— "Go home yourself," rejoins the furious ruffian. "Do come home quietly," repeats the wife, bursting into tears. "Go home yourself," retorts the husband again, enforcing his argument by a blow which sends the poor creature flying out of the shop. Her "natural protector" follows her up the court, alternately venting his rage in accelerating her progress, and in knocking the little scanty blue bonnet of the unfortunate child over its still more scanty and faded-looking face.

In the last box, which is situated in the darkest and most obscure corner of the shop, considerably removed from either of the gas-lights, are a young delicate girl of about twenty, and an elderly female, evidently her mother from the resemblance between them, who stand at some distance back, as if to avoid the observation even of the shopman. It is not their first visit to a pawnbroker's shop, for they answer without a moment's hesitation the usual questions, put in a rather respectful manner, and in a much lower tone than usual, of "What name shall I say?—Your own property, of course?—Where do you live?—Housekeeper or lodger?" They bargain, too, for a higher loan than the shopman is at first inclined to offer, which a perfect stranger would be little disposed to do; and the elder female urges her daughter on, in scarcely audible whispers, to exert her utmost powers of persuasion to obtain an advance of the sum, and expatiate

I

on the value of the articles they have brought to raise a present supply upon. They are a small gold chain and a "Forget-me-not" ring: the girl's property, for they are both too small for the mother; given her in better times; prized, perhaps, once, for the giver's sake, but parted with now without a struggle; for want has hardened the mother, and her example has hardened the girl, and the prospect of receiving money, coupled with a recollection of the misery they have both endured from the want of it—the coldness of old friends—the stern refusal of some, and the still more galling compassion of others—appears to have obliterated the consciousness of self-humiliation, which the idea of their present situation would once have aroused.

In the next box is a young female, whose attire, miserably poor but extremely gaudy, wretchedly cold but extravagantly fine, too plainly bespeaks her station. The rich satin gown with its faded trimmings, the worn-out thin shoes, and pink silk stockings, the summer bonnet in winter, and the sunken face, where a daub of rouge only serves as an index to the ravages of squandered health never to be regained, and lost happiness never to be restored, and where the practised smile is a wretched mockery of the misery of the heart, cannot be mistaken. There is something in the glimpse she has just caught of her young neighbour, and in the sight of the little trinkets she has offered in pawn, that seems to have awakened in this woman's mind some slumbering recollection, and to have changed, for an instant, her whole demeanour. Her first hasty impulse was to bend forward as if to scan more minutely the appearance of her half-concealed companions; her next, on seeing them involuntarily shrink from her, to retreat to the back of the box, cover her face with her hands, and burst into tears.

There are strange chords in the human heart, which will lie dormant through years of depravity and wickedness, but which will vibrate at last to some slight circumstance apparently trivial in itself, but connected by some undefined and indistinct association with past days that can never be recalled, and with bitter recollections from which the most degraded creature in existence cannot escape.

There has been another spectator, in the person of a woman in the common shop; the lowest of the low; dirty, unbonneted, flaunting, and slovenly. Her curiosity was at first attracted by the little she could see of the group; then her attention. The half-intoxicated leer changed to an expression of something like interest, and a feeling similar to that we have described, appeared for a moment, and only a moment, to extend itself even to her bosom.

Who shall say how soon these women may change places? The last has but two more stages—the hospital and the grave. How many females situated as her two companions are, and as she may have been once, have terminated the same wretched course, in the same wretched manner! One is already tracing her footsteps with frightful rapidity. How soon may the other follow her example! How many have done the same!

CHAPTER XXIV

CRIMINAL COURTS

WE shall never forget the mingled feelings of awe and respect with which we used to gaze on the exterior of Newgate in our schoolboy days. How dreadful its rough heavy walls, and low massive doors, appeared to us—the latter looking as if they were made for the express purpose of letting people in, and never letting them out again. Then the fetters over the debtors' door, which we used to think were a *bonâ fide* set of irons, just hung up there for convenience sake, ready to be taken down at a moment's notice, and riveted on the limbs of some refractory felon! We were never tired of wondering how the hackney-coachmen on the opposite stand could cut jokes in the presence of such horrors, and drink pots of half-and-half so near the last drop.

Often have we strayed here, in sessions time, to catch a glimpse of the whipping-place, and that dark building on one side of the yard, in which is kept the gibbet with all its dreadful apparatus, and on the door of which we half expected to see a brass plate, with the inscription "Mr. Ketch;" for we never imagined that the distinguished functionary could by possibility live anywhere else! The days of these childish dreams have passed away, and with them many other boyish ideas of a gayer nature. But we still retain so much of our original feeling, that to this hour we never pass the building without something like a shudder.

What London pedestrian is there who has not, at some time or other, cast a hurried glance through the wicket at which prisoners are admitted into this gloomy mansion, and surveyed the few objects he could discern, with an indescribable feeling of curiosity? The thick door, plated with iron and mounted with spikes, just low enough to enable you to see, leaning over them, an ill-looking fellow in a broad-brimmed hat, Belcher handkerchief and top-boots: with a brown coat, something between a great-coat and a "sporting" jacket, on his back, and an immense key in his left hand. Perhaps you are lucky enough to pass, just as the gate is being opened ; then, you see on the other side of the lodge, another gate, the image of its predecessor, and two or three more turnkeys, who look like multiplications of the first one, seated round a fire which just lights up the whitewashed apartment sufficiently to enable you to catch a hasty glimpse of these different objects. We have a great respect for Mrs. Fry, but she certainly ought to have written more romances than Mrs. Radcliffe.

We were walking leisurely down the Old Bailey, some time ago, when, as we passed this identical gate, it was opened by the officiating turnkey. We turned quickly round, as a matter of course, and saw two persons descending the steps. We could not help stopping and observing them.

They were an elderly woman, of decent appearance, though evidently poor, and a boy of about fourteen or fifteen. The woman was crying bitterly ; she carried a small bundle in her hand, and the boy followed at a short distance behind her. Their little history was obvious. The boy was her son, to whose early comfort she had perhaps sacrificed her own—for whose sake she had borne misery without repining, and poverty without a murmur—looking steadily forward to the time when he who had so long witnessed her struggles for himself might be enabled to make some exertions for their joint support. He had formed dissolute connexions ; idleness had led to crime ; and he had been committed to take his trial for some petty theft. He had been long in prison, and, after receiving some trifling additional punishment, had been ordered to be discharged that morning. It was his first offence, and his poor old mother, still hoping to reclaim him, had been waiting at the gate to implore him to return home.

We cannot forget the boy ; he descended the steps with a dogged look, shaking his head with an air of bravado and obstinate determination. They walked a few paces, and paused. The woman put her hand upon his shoulder in an agony of entreaty, and the boy sullenly raised his head as if in refusal. It was a brilliant morning, and every object looked fresh and happy in the broad, gay sunlight ; he gazed round him for a few moments, bewildered with the brightness of the scene, for it was long since he had beheld anything save the gloomy walls of a prison. Perhaps the wretchedness of his mother made some impression on the boy's heart; perhaps some undefined recollection of the time when he was a happy child, and she his only friend and best companion, crowded on him—he burst into tears; and covering his face with one hand, and hurriedly placing the other in his mother's, walked away with her.

Curiosity has occasionally led us into both Courts at the Old Bailey. Nothing is so likely to strike the person who enters them for the first time, as the calm indifference with which the proceedings are conducted; every trial seems a mere matter of business. There is a great deal of form, but no compassion; considerable interest, but no sympathy. Take the Old Court for example. There sit the Judges, with whose great dignity everybody is acquainted, and of whom therefore we need say no more. Then, there is the Lord Mayor in the centre, looking as cool as a Lord Mayor *can* look, with an immense *bouquet* before him, and habited in all the splendour of his office. Then, there are the Sheriffs. who are almost as dignified as the Lord Mayor himself; and the Barristers, who are quite dignified enough in their own opinion; and the spectators, who having paid for their admission, look upon the whole scene as if it were got up especially for their amusement. Look upon the whole group in the body of the Court—some wholly engrossed in the morning papers, others carelessly conversing in low whispers, and others, again, quietly dozing away an hour—and you can scarcely believe that the result of the trial is a matter of life or death to one wretched being present. But turn your eyes to the dock; watch the prisoner attentively for a few moments; and the fact is before you, in all its painful reality. Mark how restlessly he has been engaged for the last ten minutes, in forming all sorts of fantastic figures with the herbs which are strewed upon the ledge before him; observe the ashy paleness of his face when a particular witness appears, and how he changes his position and wipes his clammy forehead and feverish hands, when the case for the prosecution is closed, as if it were a relief to him to feel that the jury knew the worst.

The defence is concluded; the judge proceeds to sum up the evidence; and the prisoner watches the countenances of the jury, as a dying man, clinging to life to the very last, vainly looks in the face of his physician for a slight ray of hope. They turn round to consult; you can almost hear the man's heart beat, as he bites the stalk of rosemary, with a desperate effort to appear composed. They resume their places—a dead silence prevails as the foreman delivers in the verdict—" Guilty! " A shriek bursts from a female in the gallery; the prisoner casts one look at the quarter from whence the noise proceeded; and is immediately hurried from the dock by the gaoler. The clerk directs one of the officers of the Court to "take the woman out," and fresh business is proceeded with, as if nothing had occurred.

No imaginary contrast to a case like this, could be as complete as that which is constantly presented in the New Court, the gravity of which is frequently disturbed in no small degree, by the cunning and pertinacity of juvenile offenders. A boy of thirteen is tried, say for picking the pocket of some subject of her Majesty, and the offence is about as clearly proved as an offence can be. He is called upon for his defence, and contents himself with a little declamation about the jurymen and his country—asserts that all the witnesses have committed perjury, and hints that the police force generally have entered into a conspiracy "again " him. However probable this statement may be, it fails to convince the Court, and some such scene as the following then takes place:

Court: Have you any witnesses to speak to your character, boy?

Boy: Yes, my Lord; fifteen gen'lm'n is a vaten outside, and vos a vaten all day yesterday, vich they told me the night afore my trial vos a comin' on.

Court: Inquire for these witnesses.

Here, a stout beadle runs out, and vociferates for the witnesses at the very top of his voice; for you hear his cry grow fainter and fainter as he descends the steps into the court-yard below. After an absence of five minutes, he returns, very warm and hoarse, and informs the Court of what it knew perfectly well before—namely, that there are no such witnesses in attendance. Hereupon, the boy sets up a most awful howling; screws the lower part of the palms of his hands into the corners of his eyes; and endeavours to look the picture of injured innocence. The jury at once find him "guilty," and his endeavours to squeeze out a tear or two are redoubled. The governor of the gaol then states, in reply to an inquiry from the bench, that the prisoner has been under his care twice before. This the urchin resolutely denies in some such terms as—"S'elp me, gen'lm'n, I never vos in trouble afore—indeed, my Lord, I never vos. It's all a howen to my having a twin brother, vich has wrongfully got into trouble, and vich is so exactly like me, that no vun ever knows the difference atween us."

This representation, like the defence, fails in producing the desired effect, and the boy is sentenced, perhaps, to seven years' transportation. Finding it impossible to excite compassion, he gives vent to his feelings in an imprecation bearing reference to the eyes of "old big vig!" and as he declines to take the trouble of walking from the dock, is forthwith carried out, congratulating himself on having succeeded in giving everybody as much trouble as possible.

CHAPTER XXV

A VISIT TO NEWGATE

" The force of habit " is a trite phrase in everybody's mouth ; and it is not a little remarkable that those who use it most as applied to others, unconsciously afford in their own persons singular examples of the power which habit and custom exercise over the minds of men, and of the little reflection they are apt to bestow on subjects with which every day's experience has rendered them familiar. If Bedlam could be suddenly removed like another Aladdin's palace, and set down on the space now occupied by Newgate, scarcely one man out of a hundred, whose road to business every morning lies through Newgate Street, or the Old Bailey, would pass the building without bestowing a hasty glance on its small, grated windows, and a transient thought upon the condition of the unhappy beings immured in its dismal cells ; and yet these same men, day by day, and hour by hour, pass and repass this gloomy depository of the guilt and misery of London, in one perpetual stream of life and bustle, utterly unmindful of the throng of wretched creatures pent up within it—nay, not even knowing, or if they do, not heeding, the fact, that as they pass one particular angle of the massive wall with a light laugh or a merry whistle, they stand within one yard of a fellow-creature, bound and helpless, whose hours are numbered, from whom the last feeble ray of hope has fled for ever, and whose miserable career will shortly terminate in a violent and shameful death. Contact with death, even in its least terrible shape, is solemn and appalling. How much more awful is it to reflect on this near vicinity to the dying—to men in full health and vigour, in the flower of youth or the prime of life, with all their faculties and perceptions as acute and perfect as your own ; but dying, nevertheless—dying as surely—with the hand of death imprinted upon them as indelibly—as if mortal disease had wasted their frames to shadows, and corruption had already begun !

It was with some such thoughts as these that we determined, not many weeks since, to visit the interior of Newgate—in an amateur capacity, of course; and, having carried our intention into effect, we proceed to lay its results before our readers, in the hope—founded more upon the nature of the subject, than on any presumptuous confidence in our own descriptive powers—that this paper may not be found wholly devoid of interest. We have only to premise, that we do not intend to fatigue the reader with any statistical accounts of the prison; they will be found at length in numerous reports of numerous committees, and a variety of authorities of equal weight. We took no notes, made no memoranda, measured none of the yards, ascertained the exact number of inches in no particular room : are unable even to report of how many apartments the gaol is composed.

We saw the prison, and saw the prisoners; and what we did see, and what we thought, we will tell at once in our own way.

Having delivered our credentials to the servant who answered our knock at the door of the governor's house, we were ushered into the "office;" a little room, on the right-hand side as you enter, with two windows looking into the Old Bailey: fitted up like an ordinary attorney's office, or merchant's counting-house, with the usual fixtures—a wainscoted partition, a shelf or two, a desk, a couple of stools, a pair of clerks, an almanack, a cloak, and a few maps. After a little delay, occasioned by sending into the interior of the prison for the officer whose duty it was to conduct us, that functionary arrived; a respectable-looking man of about two or three and fifty, in a broad-brimmed hat, and full suit of black, who, but for his keys, would have looked quite as much like a clergyman as a turnkey. We were disappointed; he had not even top-boots on. Following our conductor by a door opposite to that at which we had entered, we arrived at a small room, without any other furniture than a little desk, with a book for visitors' autographs, and a shelf, on which were a few boxes for papers, and casts of the heads and faces of the two notorious murderers, Bishop and Williams; the former, in particular, exhibiting a style of head and set of features, which might have afforded sufficient moral grounds for his instant execution at any time, even had there been no other evidence against him. Leaving this room also, by an opposite door, we found ourself in the lodge which opens on the Old Bailey ; one side of which is plentifully garnished with a choice collection of heavy sets of irons, including those worn by the redoubtable Jack Sheppard—genuine ; and those *said* to have been graced by the sturdy limbs of the no less celebrated Dick Turpin— doubtful. From this lodge, a heavy oaken gate, bound with iron, studded with nails of the same material, and guarded by another turnkey, opens on a few steps, if we remember right, which terminate in a narrow and dismal stone passage, running parallel with the Old Bailey, and leading to the different yards, through a number of tortuous and intricate windings, guarded in their turn by huge gates and gratings, whose appearance is sufficient to dispel at once the slightest hope of escape that any new-comer may have entertained ; and the very recollection of which, on eventually traversing the place again, involves one in a maze of confusion.

It is necessary to explain here, that the buildings in the prison, or in other words the different wards—form a square, of which the four sides abut respectively on the Old Bailey, the old College of Physicians (now forming a part of New-gate Market), the Sessions House, and Newgate Street. The intermediate space is divided into several paved yards, in which the prisoners take such air and exercise as can be had in such a place. These yards, with the exception of that in which prisoners under sentence of death are confined (of which we shall presently give a more detailed description), run parallel with Newgate Street, and consequently from the Old Bailey, as it were, to Newgate Market. The women's side is in the right wing of the prison nearest the Sessions House. As we were introduced into this part of the building first, we will adopt the same order, and introduce our readers to it also.

Turning to the right, then, down the passage to which we just now adverted, omitting any mention of intervening gates—for if we noticed every gate that was unlocked for us to pass through, and locked again as soon as we had passed, we should require a gate at every comma—we came to a door composed of thick bars of wood, through which were discernible, passing to and fro in a narrow yard, some twenty women : the majority of whom, however, as soon as they were aware of the presence of strangers, retreated to their wards. One side of this yard is railed off at a considerable distance, and formed into a kind of iron cage, about five feet ten inches in height, roofed at the top, and defended in front by iron bars, from which the friends of the female prisoners communicate with them. In one corner of this singular-looking den, was a yellow, haggard, decrepit old woman, in a tattered gown that had once been black, and the remains of an old straw bonnet, with faded ribbon of the same hue, in earnest conversation with a young girl—a prisoner, of course—of about two-and-twenty. It is impossible to imagine a more poverty-stricken object, or a creature so borne down in soul and body, by excess of misery and destitution, as the old woman. The girl was a good-looking robust female, with a profusion of hair streaming about in the wind—for she had no bonnet on—and a man's silk pocket-handkerchief loosely thrown over a most ample pair of shoulders. The old woman was talking in that low, stifled tone of voice which tells so forcibly of mental anguish; and every now and then burst into an irrepressible sharp, abrupt cry of grief, the most distressing sound that ears can hear. The girl was perfectly unmoved. Hardened beyond all hope of redemption, she listened doggedly to her mother's entreaties, whatever they were: and, beyond inquiring after "Jem," and eagerly catching at the few halfpence her miserable parent had brought her, took no more apparent interest in the conversation than the most unconcerned spectators. Heaven knows there were enough of them, in the persons of the other prisoners in the yard, who were no more concerned by what was passing before their eyes, and within their hearing, than if they were blind and deaf. Why should they be? Inside the prison, and out, such scenes were too familiar to them, to excite even a passing thought, unless of ridicule or contempt for feelings which they had long since forgotten.

A little farther on, a squalid-looking woman in a slovenly, thick-bordered cap, with her arms muffled in a large red shawl, the fringed ends of which straggled nearly to the bottom of a dirty white apron, was communicating some instructions to *her* visitor—her daughter evidently. The girl was thinly clad, and shaking with the cold. Some ordinary word of recognition passed between her and her mother when she appeared at the grating, but neither hope, condolence, regret, nor affection was expressed on either side. The mother whispered her instructions, and the girl received them with her pinched-up half-starved features twisted into an expression of careful cunning. It was some scheme for the woman's defence that she was disclosing, perhaps; and a sullen smile came over the girl's face for an instant, as if she were pleased: not so much at the probability of her mother's liberation, as at the chance of her "getting off" in spite of her prosecutors. The dialogue was soon concluded; and with the same careless indifference with which they had approached each other, the mother turned towards the inner end of the yard, and the girl to the gate at which she had entered.

The girl belonged to a class—unhappily but too extensive—the very existence of which snould make men's hearts bleed. Barely past her childhood, it required but a glance to discover that she was one of those children, born and bred in neglect and vice, who have never known what childhood is: who have never been taught to love and court a parent's smile, or to dread a parent's frown. The thousand nameless endearments of childhood, its gaiety and its innocence, are alike unknown to them. They have entered at once upon the stern realities and miseries of life, and to their better nature it is almost hopeless to appeal in after-times, by any of the references which will awaken, if it be only for a moment, some good feeling in ordinary bosoms, however corrupt they may have become. Talk to *them* of parental solicitude, the happy days of childhood, and the merry games of infancy! Tell them of hunger and the streets, beggary and stripes, the gin-shop, the station-house, and the pawnbroker's, and they will understand you.

Two or three women were standing at different parts of the grating, conversing with their friends, but a very large proportion of the prisoners appeared to have no friends at all, beyond such of their old companions as might happen to be within the walls. So, passing hastily down the yard, and pausing only for an instant to notice the little incidents we have just recorded, we were conducted up a clean and well-lighted flight of stone stairs to one of the wards. There are several in this part of the building, but a description of one is a description of the whole.

It was a spacious, bare, whitewashed apartment, lighted, of course, by windows looking into the interior of the prison, but far more light and airy than one could reasonably expect to find in such a situation. There was a large fire with a deal table before it, round which ten or a dozen women were seated on wooden forms at dinner. Along both sides of the room ran a shelf; below it, at regular intervals, a row of large hooks were fixed in the wall, on each of which was hung the sleeping mat of a prisoner: her rug and blanket being folded up, and placed on the shelf above. At night, these mats are placed on the floor, each beneath the hook on which it hangs during the day; and the ward is thus made to answer the purposes both of a day-room and sleeping apartment. Over the fireplace was a large sheet of pasteboard, on which were displayed a variety of texts from Scripture, which were also scattered about the room in scraps about the size and shape of the copy-slips which are used in schools. On the table was a sufficient provision of a kind of stewed beef and brown bread, in pewter dishes, which are kept perfectly bright, and displayed on shelves in great order and regularity when they are not in use.

The women rose hastily, on our entrance, and retired in a hurried manner to either side of the fireplace. They were all cleanly—many of them decently—attired, and there was nothing peculiar, either in their appearance or demeanour. One or two resumed the needlework which they had probably laid aside at the commencement of their meal; others gazed at the visitors with listless curiosity; and a few retired behind their companions to the very end of the room, as if desirous to avoid even the casual observation of the strangers. Some old Irish women, both in this and other wards, to whom the thing was no novelty, appeared perfectly indifferent to our presence, and remained standing close to the seats from which they had just risen; but the general feeling among the females seemed to be one of uneasiness during the period of our stay among them: which was very brief. Not a word was uttered during the time of our remaining, unless, indeed, by the wardswoman in reply to some question which we put to the turnkey who accompanied us. In every ward on the female side, a wardswoman is appointed to preserve order, and a similar regulation is adopted among the males. The wardsmen and wardswomen are all prisoners, selected for good conduct. They alone are allowed the privilege of sleeping on bedsteads; a small stump bedstead being placed in every ward for that purpose. On both sides of the gaol is a small receiving-room, to which prisoners are conducted on their first reception, and whence they cannot be removed until they have been examined by the surgeon of the prison [1].

Retracing our steps to the dismal passage in which we found ourselves at first (and which, by-the-bye, contains three or four dark cells for the accommodation of refractory prisoners), we were led through a narrow yard to the "school" —a portion of the prison set apart for boys under fourteen years of age. In a tolerable-sized room, in which were writing-materials and some copy-books, was the schoolmaster, with a couple of his pupils; the remainder having been fetched from an adjoining apartment, the whole were drawn up in line for our inspection. There were fourteen of them in all, some with shoes, some without; some in pinafores without jackets, others in jackets without pinafores, and one in scarce anything at all. The whole number, without an exception we believe, had been committed for trial on charges of pocket-picking; and fourteen such terrible little faces we never beheld.—There was not one redeeming feature among them—not a glance of honesty—not a wink expressive of anything but the gallows and the hulks, in the whole collection. As to anything like shame or contrition, that was entirely out of the question. They were evidently quite gratified at being thought worth the trouble of looking at; their idea appeared to be, that we had come to see Newgate as a grand affair, and that they were an indispensable part of the show; and every boy as he "fell in" to the line, actually seemed as pleased and important as if he had done something excessively meritorious in getting there at all. We never looked upon a more disagreeable sight, because we never saw fourteen such hopeless creatures of neglect, before.

On either side of the school-yard is a yard for men, in one of which—that towards Newgate Street—prisoners of the more respectable class are confined. Of the other, we have little description to offer, as the different wards necessarily partake of the same character. They are provided, like the wards on the women's side, with mats and rugs, which are

---

[1] The regulations of the prison relative to the confinement of prisoners during the day, their sleeping at night, their taking their meals, and other matters of gaol economy, have been all altered—greatly for the better—since this sketch was first published. Even the construction of the prison itself has been changed.

disposed of in the same manner during the day; the only very striking difference between their appearance and that of tho wards inhabited by the females, is the utter absence of any employm nt Huddled together on two opposite forms, by the fireside, sit twenty men perhaps; here, a boy in livery; there, a man in a rough great-coat and top-boots; farther on, a desperate-looking fellow in his shirt-sleeves, with an old Scotch cap upon his shaggy head; near him again, a tall ruffian, in a smock-frock; next to him, a miserable being of distressed appearance, with his head resting on his hand;— all alike in one respect, all idle and listless. When they do leave the fire, sauntering moodily about, lounging in the window, or leaning against the wall, vacantly swinging their bodies to and fro. With the exception of a man reading an old newspaper, in two or three instances, this was the case in every ward we entered.

The only communication these men have with their friends, is through two close iron gratings, with an intermediate space of about a yard in width between the two, so that nothing can be handed across, nor can the prisoner have any communication by touch with the person who visits him. The married men have a separate grating, at which to see their wives, but its construction is the same.

The prison chapel is situated at the back of the governor's house: the latter having no windows looking into the interior of the prison. Whether the associations connected with the place—the knowledge that here a portion of the burial service is, on some dreadful occasions, performed over the quick and not upon the dead—cast over it a still more gloomy and sombre air than art has imparted to it, we know not, but its appearance is very striking. There is something in a silent and deserted place of worship, solemn and impressive at any time; and the very dissimilarity of this one from any we have been accustomed to, only enhances the impression. The meanness of its appointments—the bare and scanty pulpit, with the paltry painted pillars on either side—the women's gallery with its great heavy curtain—the men's with its unpainted benches and dingy front—the tottering little table at the altar, with the commandments on the wall above it, scarcely legible through lack of paint, and dust and damp— so unlike the velvet and gilding, the marble and wood, of a modern church—are strange and striking. There is one object, too, which rivets the attention and fascinates the gaze, and from which we may turn horror-stricken in vain, for the recollection of it will haunt us, waking and sleeping, for a long time afterwards. Immediately below the reading-desk, on the floor of the chapel, and forming the most conspicuous object in its little area, is *the condemned pew*; a huge black pen, in which the wretched people, who are singled out for death, are placed on the Sunday preceding their execution, in sight of all their fellow-prisoners, from many of whom they may have been separated but a week before, to hear prayers for their own souls, to join in the responses of their own burial service, and to listen to an address, warning their recent companions to take example by their fate, and urging themselves, while there is yet time—nearly four-and-twenty hours—to "turn, and flee from the wrath to come!" Imagine what have been the feelings of the men whom that fearful pew has enclosed, and of whom, between the gallows and the knife, no mortal remnant may now remain! Think of the hopeless clinging to life to the last, and the wild despair, far exceeding in anguish the felon's death itself, by which they have heard the certainty of their speedy transmission to another world, with all their crimes upon their heads, rung into their ears by the officiating clergyman!

At one time—and at no distant period either—the coffins of the men about to be executed, were placed in that pew, upon the seat by their side, during the whole service. It may seem incredible, but it is true. Let us hope that the increased spirit of civilisation and humanity which abolished this frightful and degrading custom, may extend itself to other usages equally barbarous; usages which have not even the plea of utility in their defence, as every year's experience has shown them to be more and more inefficacious.

Leaving the chapel, descending to the passage so frequently alluded to, and crossing the yard before noticed as being allotted to prisoners of a more respectable description than the generality of men confined here, the visitor arrives at a thick iron gate of great size and strength. Having been admitted through it by the turnkey on duty, he turns sharp round to the left, and pauses before another gate; and, having passed this last barrier, he stands in the most terrible part of this gloomy building—the condemned ward.

The press-yard, well known by name to newspaper readers, from its frequent mention in accounts of executions, is at the corner of the building, and next to the ordinary's house, in Newgate Street: running from Newgate Street, towards the centre of the prison, parallel with Newgate Market. It is a long, narrow court, of which a portion of the wall in Newgate Street forms one end, and the gate the other. At the upper end, on the left hand—that is, adjoining the wall in Newgate Street—is a cistern of water, and at the bottom a double grating (of which the gate itself forms a part) similar to that before described. Through these grates the prisoners are allowed to see their friends ; a turnkey always remaining in the vacant space between, during the whole interview. Immediately on the right as you enter, is a building containing the press-room, day-room, and cells ; the yard is on every side surrounded by lofty walls guarded by *chevaux de frise*; and the whole is under the constant inspection of vigilant and experienced turnkeys.

In the first apartment into which we were conducted— which was at the top of a staircase, and immediately over the press-room—were five-and-twenty or thirty prisoners, all under sentence of death, awaiting the result of the recorder's report—men of all ages and appearances, from a hardened old offender with swarthy face and grizzly beard of three days' growth, to a handsome boy, not fourteen years old, and of singularly youthful appearance even for that age, who had been condemned for burglary. There was nothing remarkable in the appearance of these prisoners. One or two decently-dressed men were brooding with a dejected air over the fire ; several little groups of two or three had been engaged in conversation at the upper end of the room, or in the windows ; and the remainder were crowded round a young man seated at a table, who appeared to be engaged in teaching the younger ones to write. The room was large, airy, and clean. There was very little anxiety or mental suffering depicted in the countenance of any of the men ;—they had all been sentenced to death, it is true, and the recorder's report had not yet been made ; but we question whether there was a man among them, notwithstanding, who did not *know* that although he had undergone the ceremony, it never was intended that his life should be sacrificed. On the table lay a Testament, but there were no tokens of its having been in recent use.

In the press-room below were three men, the nature of whose offence rendered it necessary to separate them even from their companions in guilt. It is a long, sombre room, with two windows sunk into the stone wall, and here the wretched men are pinioned on the morning of their execution, before moving towards the scaffold. The fate of one of these prisoners was uncertain; some mitigatory circumstances having come to light since his trial, which had been humanely represented in the proper quarter. The other two had nothing to expect from the mercy of the crown; their doom was sealed; no plea could be urged in extenuation of their crime, and they well knew that for them there was no hope in this world. "The two short ones," the turnkey whispered, "were dead men."

The man to whom we have alluded as entertaining some hopes of escape, was lounging, at the greatest distance he could place between himself and his companions, in the window nearest to the door. He was probably aware of our approach, and had assumed an air of courageous indifference; his face was purposely averted towards the window, and he stirred not an inch while we were present. The other two men were at the upper end of the room. One of them, who was imperfectly seen in the dim light, had his back towards us, and was stooping over the fire, with his right arm on the mantel-piece, and his head sunk upon it. The other was leaning on the sill of the farthest window. The light fell full upon him, and communicated to his pale, haggard face, and disordered hair, an appearance which, at that distance, was ghastly. His cheek rested upon his hand; and, with his face a little raised, and his eyes wildly staring before him, he seemed to be unconsciously intent on counting the chinks in the opposite wall. We passed this room again afterwards. The first man was pacing up and down the court with a firm military step—he had been a soldier in the foot-guards—and a cloth cap jauntily thrown on one side of his head. He bowed respectfully to our conductor, and the salute was returned. The other two still remained in the positions we have described, and were as motionless as statues [1].

A few paces up the yard, and forming a continuation of the building, in which are the two rooms we have just quitted, lie the condemned cells. The entrance is by a narrow and obscure staircase leading to a dark passage, in which a char-

---

[1] These two men were executed shortly afterwards. The other was respited during his Majesty's pleasure.

coal stove casts a lurid tint over the objects in its immediate vicinity, and diffuses something like warmth around. From the left-hand side of this passage, the massive door of every cell on the story opens; and from it alone can they be approached. There are three of these passages, and three of these ranges of cells, one above the other; but in size, furniture and appearance, they are all precisely alike. Prior to the recorder's report being made, all the prisoners under sentence of death are removed from the day-room at five o'clock in the afternoon, and locked up in these cells, where they are allowed a candle until ten o'clock; and here they remain until seven next morning. When the warrant for a prisoner's execution arrives, he is removed to the cells and confined in one of them until he leaves it for the scaffold. He is at liberty to walk in the yard; but, both in his walks and in his cell, he is constantly attended by a turnkey who never leaves him on any pretence.

We entered the first cell. It was a stone dungeon, eight feet long by six wide, with a bench at the upper end, under which were a common rug, a bible, and prayer-book. An iron candlestick was fixed into the wall at the side; and a small high window in the back admitted as much air and light as could struggle in between a double row of heavy, crossed iron bars. It contained no other furniture of any description.

Conceive the situation of a man, spending his last night on earth in this cell. Buoyed up with some vague and undefined hope of reprieve, he knew not why—indulging in some wild and visionary idea of escaping, he knew not how—hour after hour of the three preceding days allowed him for preparation, has fled with a speed which no man living would deem possible, for none but this dying man can know. He has wearied his friends with entreaties, exhausted the attendants with importunities, neglected in his feverish restlessness the timely warnings of his spiritual consoler; and, now that the illusion is at last dispelled, now that eternity is before him and guilt behind, now that his fears of death amount almost to madness, and an overwhelming sense of his helpless, hopeless state rushes upon him, he is lost and stupefied, and has neither thoughts to turn to, nor power to call upon, the Almighty Being, from whom alone he can seek mercy and forgiveness, and before whom his repentance can alone avail.

Hours have glided by, and still he sits upon the same stone bench with folded arms, heedless alike of the fast decreasing time before him, and the urgent entreaties of the good man at his side. The feeble light is wasting gradually, and the deathlike stillness of the street without, broken only by the rumbling of some passing vehicle which echoes mournfully through the empty yards, warns him that the night is waning fast away. The deep bell of St. Paul's strikes—one! He heard it; it has roused him. Seven hours left! He paces the narrow limits of his cell with rapid strides, cold drops of terror starting on his forehead, and every muscle of his frame quivering with agony. Seven hours! He suffers himself to be led to his seat, mechanically takes the bible which is placed in his hand, and tries to read and listen. No: his thoughts will wander. The book is torn and soiled by use—and like the book he read his lessons in, at school, just forty years ago! He has never bestowed a thought upon it, perhaps, since he left it as a child: and yet the place, the time, the room—nay, the very boys he played with, crowd as vividly before him as if they were scenes of yesterday; and some forgotten phrase, some childish word, rings in his ears like the echo of one uttered but a minute since. The voice of the clergyman recalls him to himself. He is reading from the sacred book its solemn promises of pardon for repentance, and its awful denunciation of obdurate men. He falls upon his knees and clasps his hands to pray. Hush! what sound was that? He starts upon his feet. It cannot be two yet. Hark! Two quarters have struck;—the third—the fourth. It is! Six hours left. Tell him not of repentance! Six hours' repentance for eight times six years of guilt and sin! He buries his face in his hands, and throws himself on the bench.

Worn with watching and excitement, he sleeps, and the same unsettled state of mind pursues him in his dreams. An insupportable load is taken from his breast; he is walking with his wife in a pleasant field, with the bright sky above them, and a fresh and boundless prospect on every side—how different from the stone walls of Newgate! She is looking —not as she did when he saw her for the last time in that dreadful place, but as she used when he loved her—long, long ago, before misery and ill-treatment had altered her looks, and vice had changed his nature, and she is leaning upon his arm, and looking up into his face with tenderness and affection—and he does *not* strike her now, nor rudely shake her from him. And oh! how glad he is to tell her all he had forgotten in that last hurried interview, and to fall on his knees before her and fervently beseech her pardon for all the unkindness and cruelty that wasted her form and broke her heart! The scene suddenly changes. He is on his trial again : there are the judge and jury, and prosecutors, and witnesses, just as they were before. How full the court is—what a sea of heads—with a gallows, too, and a scaffold —and how all those people stare at *him!* Verdict, "Guilty." No matter ; he will escape.

The night is dark and cold, the gates have been left open, and in an instant he is in the street, flying from the scene of his imprisonment like the wind. The streets are cleared, the open fields are gained and the broad wide country lies before him. Onward he dashes in the midst of darkness, over hedge and ditch, through mud and pool, bounding from spot to spot with a speed and lightness, astonishing even to himself. At length he pauses ; he must be safe from pursuit now ; he will stretch himself on that bank and sleep till sunrise.

A period of unconsciousness succeeds. He wakes, cold and wretched. The dull grey light of morning is stealing into the cell, and falls upon the form of the attendant turnkey. Confused by his dreams, he starts from his uneasy bed in momentary uncertainty. It is but momentary. Every object in the narrow cell is too frightfully real to admit of doubt or mistake. He is the condemned felon again, guilty and despairing ; and in two hours more will be dead.

CHARACTERS

CHAPTER I

THOUGHTS ABOUT PEOPLE

It is strange with how little notice, good, bad, or indifferent, a man may live and die in London. He awakens no sympathy in the breast of any single person; his existence is a matter of interest to no one save himself; he cannot be said to be forgotten when he dies, for no one remembered him when he was alive. There is a numerous class of people in this great metropolis who seem not to possess a single friend, and whom nobody appears to care for. Urged by imperative necessity in the first instance, they have resorted to London in search of employment, and the means of subsistence. It is hard, we know, to break the ties which bind us to our homes and friends, and harder still to efface the thousand recollections of happy days and old times, which have been slumbering in our bosoms for years, and only rush upon the mind, to bring before it associations connected with the friends we have left, the scenes we have beheld too probably for the last time, and the hopes we once cherished, but may entertain no more. These men, however, happily for themselves, have long forgotten such thoughts. Old country friends have died or emigrated; former correspondents have become lost, like themselves, in the crowd and turmoil of some busy city; and they have gradually settled down into mere passive creatures of habit and endurance.

We were seated in the enclosure of St. James's Park the other day, when our attention was attracted by a man whom we immediately put down in our own mind as one of this class. He was a tall, thin, pale person, in a black coat, scanty grey trousers, little pinched-up gaiters, and brown beaver gloves. He had an umbrella in his hand—not for use, for the day was fine—but, evidently, because he always carried one to the office in the morning. He walked up and down.

before the little patch of grass on which the chairs are placed
for hire, not as if he were doing it for pleasure or recreation,
but as if it were a matter of compulsion, just as he would
walk to the office every morning from the back settlements
of Islington. It was Monday; he had escaped for four-and-
twenty hours from the thraldom of the desk; and was
walking here for exercise and amusement—perhaps for the
first time in his life. We were inclined to think he had
never had a holiday before, and that he did not know what
to do with himself. Children were playing on the grass;
groups of people were loitering about, chatting and laughing;
but the man walked steadily up and down, unheeding and
unheeded, his spare pale face looking as if it were incapable
of bearing the expression of curiosity or interest.

There was something in the man's manner and appearance
which told us, we fancied, his whole life, or rather his whole
day, for a man of this sort has no variety of days. We thought
we almost saw the dingy little back office into which he walks
every morning, hanging his hat on the same peg, and placing
his legs beneath the same desk: first, taking off that black
coat which lasts the year through, and putting on the one
which did duty last year, and which he keeps in his desk to
save the other. There he sits till five o'clock, working on, all
day, as regularly as the dial over the mantel-piece, whose
loud ticking is as monotonous as his whole existence: only
raising his head when some one enters the counting-house, or
when, in the midst of some difficult calculation, he looks up
to the ceiling as if there were inspiration in the dusty skylight with a green knot in the centre of every pane of glass.
About five, or half-past, he slowly dismounts from his accustomed stool, and again changing his coat, proceeds to his
usual dining-place, somewhere near Bucklersbury. The
waiter recites the bill of fare in a rather confidential manner
—for he is a regular customer—and after inquiring "What's
in the best cut?" and "What was up last?" he orders
a small plate of roast beef, with greens, and half-à-pint of
porter. He has a small plate to-day, because greens are
a penny more than potatoes, and he had "two breads" yesterday, with the additional enormity of "a cheese" the day
before. This important point settled, he hangs up his hat—
he took it off the moment he sat down—and bespeaks the
paper after the next gentleman. If he can get it while he
is at dinner, he eats with much greater zest; balancing it

The Poor Clerk

against the water-bottle, and eating a bit of beef, and reading a line or two, alternately. Exactly at five minutes before the hour is up, he produces a shilling, pays the reckoning, carefully deposits the change in his waistcoat-pocket (first deducting a penny for the waiter), and returns to the office, from which, if it is not foreign post night, he again sallies forth in about half an hour. He then walks home, at his usual pace, to his little back room at Islington, where he has his tea; perhaps solacing himself during the meal with the conversation of his landlady's little boy, whom he occasionally rewards with a penny, for solving problems in simple addition. Sometimes, there is a letter or two to take up to his employer's, in Russell Square; and then, the wealthy man of business, hearing his voice, calls out from the dining-parlour,—"Come in, Mr. Smith:" and Mr. Smith, putting his hat at the feet of one of the hall chairs, walks timidly in, and being condescendingly desired to sit down, carefully tucks his legs under his chair, and sits at a considerable distance from the table while he drinks the glass of sherry which is poured out for him by the eldest boy, and after drinking which, he backs and slides out of the room, in a state of nervous agitation from which he does not perfectly recover, until he finds himself once more in the Islington Road. Poor, harmless creatures such men are; contented but not happy; broken-spirited and humbled, they may feel no pain, but they never know pleasure.

Compare these men with another class of beings who, like them, have neither friend nor companion, but whose position in society is the result of their own choice. These are generally old fellows with white heads and red faces, addicted to port wine and Hessian boots, who from some cause, real or imaginary—generally the former, the excellent reason being that they are rich, and their relations poor—grow suspicious of everybody, and do the misanthropical in chambers, taking great delight in thinking themselves unhappy, and making everybody they come near, miserable. You may see such men as these anywhere; you will know them at coffee-houses by their discontented exclamations and the luxury of their dinners; at theatres, by their always sitting in the same place and looking with a jaundiced eye on all the young people near them; at church, by the pomposity with which they enter, and the loud tone in which they repeat the responses; at parties, by their getting cross at whist and hating music. An old fellow of this kind will have his chambers splendidly furnished, and collect books, plate, and pictures about him in profusion ; not so much for his own gratification, as to be superior to those who have the desire, but not the means, to compete with him. He belongs to two or three clubs, and is envied, and flattered, and hated by the members of them all. Sometimes he will be appealed to by a poor relation—a married nephew perhaps—for some little assistance : and then he will declaim with honest indig- nation on the improvidence of young married people, the worthlessness of a wife, the insolence of having a family, the atrocity of getting into debt with a hundred and twenty-five pounds a year, and other unpardonable crimes ; winding up his exhortations with a complacent review of his own con- duct, and a delicate allusion to parochial relief. He dies, some day after dinner, of apoplexy, having bequeathed his property to a Public Society, and the Institution erects a tablet to his memory, expressive of their admiration of his Christian conduct in this world, and their comfortable conviction of his happiness in the next.

But, next to our very particular friends, hackney-coachmen, cabmen and cads, whom we admire in proportion to the extent of their cool impudence and perfect self-possession, there is no class of people who amuse us more than London apprentices. They are no longer an organised body, bound down by solemn compact to terrify his Majesty's subjects whenever it pleases them to take offence in their heads and staves in their hands. They are only bound, now, by inden- tures, and, as to their valour, it is easily restrained by the wholesome dread of the New Police, and a perspective view of a damp station-house, terminating in a police-office and a reprimand. They are still, however, a peculiar class, and not the less pleasant for being inoffensive. Can any one fail to have noticed them in the streets on Sunday ? And were there ever such harmless efforts at the grand and magnificent as the young fellows display ! We walked down the Strand, a Sunday or two ago, behind a little group ; and they furnished food for our amusement the whole way. They had come out of some part of the city ; it was between three and four o'clock in the afternoon ; and they were on their way to the Park. There were four of them, all arm-in-arm, with white kid gloves like so many bridegrooms, light trousers of unprecedented patterns, and coats for which the

English language has yet no name—a kind of cross between a great-coat and a surtout, with the collar of the one, the skirts of the other, and pockets peculiar to themselves.

Each of the gentlemen carried a thick stick, with a large tassel at the top, which he occasionally twirled gracefully round ; and the whole four, by way of looking easy and unconcerned, were walking with a paralytic swagger irresistibly ludicrous. One of the party had a watch about the size and shape of a reasonable Ribstone pippin, jammed into his waistcoat-pocket, which he carefully compared with the clocks at St. Clement's and the New Church, the illuminated clock at Exeter 'Change, the clock of St. Martin's Church, and the clock of the Horse Guards. When they at last arrived in St. James's Park, the member of the party who had the best-made boots on, hired a second chair expressly for his feet, and flung himself on this two-pennyworth of sylvan luxury with an air which levelled all distinctions between Brookes's and Snooks's, Crockford's and Bagnigge Wells.

We may smile at such people, but they can never excite our anger. They are usually on the best terms with themselves, and it follows almost as a matter of course, in good humour with every one about them. Besides, they are always the faint reflection of higher lights ; and, if they do display a little occasional foolery in their own proper persons, it is surely more tolerable than precocious puppyism in the Quadrant, whiskered dandyism in Regent Street and Pall Mall, or gallantry in its dotage anywhere.

CHAPTER II

A CHRISTMAS DINNER

CHRISTMAS time! That man must be a misanthrope indeed, in whose breast something like a jovial feeling is not roused —in whose mind some pleasant associations are not awakened —by the recurrence of Christmas. There are people who will tell you that Christmas is not to them what it used to be; that each succeeding Christmas has found some cherished hope, or happy prospect, of the year before, dimmed or passed away; that the present only serves to remind them of reduced circumstances and straitened incomes—of the feasts they once bestowed on hollow friends, and of the cold looks that meet them now, in adversity and misfortune. Never heed such dismal reminiscences. There are few men who have lived long enough in the world, who cannot call up such thoughts any day in the year. Then do not select the merriest of the three hundred and sixty-five, for your doleful recollections, but draw your chair nearer the blazing fire— fill the glass and send round the song—and if your room be smaller than it was a dozen years ago, or if your glass be filled with reeking punch, instead of sparkling wine, put a good face on the matter, and empty it off-hand, and fill another, and troll off the old ditty you used to sing, and thank God it's no worse. Look on the merry faces of your children (if you have any) as they sit round the fire. One little seat may be empty; one slight form that gladdened the father's heart, and roused the mother's pride to look upon, may not be there. Dwell not upon the past; think not that one short year ago, the fair child now resolving into dust, sat before you, with the bloom of health upon its cheek, and the gaiety of infancy in its joyous eye. Reflect upon your present blessings—of which every man has many —not on your past misfortunes, of which all men have some. Fill your glass again, with a merry face and contented heart. Our life on it, but your Christmas shall be merry, and your new year a happy one!

Who can be insensible to the outpourings of good feeling, and the honest interchange of affectionate attachment, which abound at this season of the year? A Christmas family-party! We know nothing in nature more delightful! There seems a magic in the very name of Christmas. Petty jealousies and discords are forgotten; social feelings are awakened, in bosoms to which they have long been strangers; father and son, or brother and sister, who have met and passed with averted gaze, or a look of cold recognition, for months before, proffer and return the cordial embrace, and bury their past animosities in their present happiness. Kindly hearts that have yearned towards each other, but have been withheld by false notions of pride and self-dignity, are again reunited, and all is kindness and benevolence! Would that Christmas lasted the whole year through (as it ought), and that the prejudices and passions which deform our better nature, were never called into action among those to whom they should ever be strangers!

The Christmas family-party that we mean, is not a mere assemblage of relations, got up at a week or two's notice, originating this year, having no family precedent in the last, and not likely to be repeated in the next. No. It is an annual gathering of all the accessible members of the family, young or old, rich or poor; and all the children look forward to it, for two months beforehand, in a fever of anticipation. Formerly, it was held at grandpapa's; but grandpapa getting old, and grandmamma getting old too, and rather infirm, they have given up house-keeping, and domesticated themselves with uncle George; so the party always takes place at uncle George's house, but grandmamma sends in most of the good things, and grandpapa always *will* toddle down, all the way to Newgate Market, to buy the turkey, which he engages a porter to bring home behind him in triumph, always insisting on the man's being rewarded with a glass of spirits, over and above his hire, to drink "a merry Christmas and a happy new year" to aunt George. As to grandmamma, she is very secret and mysterious for two or three days beforehand, but not sufficiently so to prevent rumours getting afloat that she has purchased a beautiful new cap with pink ribbons for each of the servants, together with sundry books, and pen-knives, and pencil-cases, for the younger branches; to say nothing of divers secret additions to the order originally given by aunt George at the pastrycook's, such as another dozen of mince-pies for the dinner, and a large plum-cake for the children.

On Christmas Eve, grandmamma is always in excellent spirits, and after employing all the children, during the day, in stoning the plums, and all that, insists, regularly every year, on uncle George coming down into the kitchen, taking off his coat, and stirring the pudding for half an hour or so, which uncle George good-humouredly does, to the vociferous delight of the children and servants. The evening concludes with a glorious game of blind-man's-buff, in an early stage of which grandpapa takes great care to be caught, in order that he may have an opportunity of displaying his dexterity.

On the following morning, the old couple, with as many of the children as the pew will hold, go to church in great state : leaving aunt George at home dusting decanters and filling casters, and uncle George carrying bottles into the dining-parlour, and calling for corkscrews, and getting into everybody's way.

When the church-party return to lunch, grandpapa produces a small sprig of mistletoe from his pocket, and tempts the boys to kiss their little cousins under it—a proceeding which affords both the boys and the old gentleman unlimited satisfaction, but which rather outrages grandmamma's ideas of decorum, until grandpapa says that when he was just thirteen years and three months old, *he* kissed grandmamma under a mistletoe too, on which the children clap their hands, and laugh very heartily, as do aunt George and uncle George ; and grandmamma looks pleased, and says, with a benevolent smile, that grandpapa was an impudent young dog, on which the children laugh very heartily again, and grandpapa more heartily than any of them.

But all these diversions are nothing to the subsequent excitement when grandmamma in a high cap, and slate-coloured silk gown ; and grandpapa with a beautifully plaited shirt-frill, and white neckerchief ; seat themselves on one side of the drawing-room fire, with uncle George's children and little cousins innumerable, seated in the front, waiting the arrival of the expected visitors. Suddenly a hackney-coach is heard to stop, and uncle George, who has been looking out of the window, exclaims, " Here's Jane ! " on which the children rush to the door, and helter-skelter downstairs ; and uncle Robert and aunt Jane, and the dear little baby, and the nurse, and the whole party, are ushered up·

stairs amidst tumultuous shouts of "Oh, my!" from the children, and frequently repeated warnings not to hurt baby from the nurse. And grandpapa takes the child, and grandmamma kisses her daughter, and the confusion of this first entry has scarcely subsided, when some other aunts and uncles with more cousins arrive, and the grown-up cousins flirt with each other, and so do the little cousins too, for that matter, and nothing is to be heard but a confused din of talking, laughing, and merriment.

A hesitating double knock at the street-door, heard during a momentary pause in the conversation, excites a general inquiry of "Who's that?" and two or three children, who have been standing at the window, announce in a low voice, that it's "poor aunt Margaret." Upon which, aunt George leaves the room to welcome the new-comer; and grandmamma draws herself up, rather stiff and stately; for Margaret married a poor man without her consent, and poverty not being a sufficiently weighty punishment for her offence, has been discarded by her friends, and debarred the society of her dearest relatives. But Christmas has come round, and the unkind feelings that have struggled against better dispositions during the year, have melted away before its genial influence, like half-formed ice beneath the morning sun. It is not difficult in a moment of angry feeling for a parent to denounce a disobedient child; but to banish her at a period of general good-will and hilarity, from the hearth round which she has sat on so many anniversaries of the same day, expanding by slow degrees from infancy to girlhood, and then bursting, almost imperceptibly, into a woman, is widely different. The air of conscious rectitude, and cold forgiveness, which the old lady has assumed, sits ill upon her; and when the poor girl is led in by her sister, pale in looks and broken in hope—not from poverty, for that she could bear, but from the consciousness of undeserved neglect, and unmerited unkindness—it is easy to see how much of it is assumed. A momentary pause succeeds; the girl breaks suddenly from her sister and throws herself, sobbing, on her mother's neck. The father steps hastily forward, and takes her husband's hand. Friends crowd round to offer their hearty congratulations, and happiness and harmony again prevail.

As to the dinner, it's perfectly delightful—nothing goes wrong, and everybody is in the very best of spirits, and

K

disposed to please and be pleased. Grandpapa relates a
circumstantial account of the purchase of the turkey, with a
slight digression relative to the purchase of previous turkeys,
on former Christmas-days, which grandmamma corroborates
in the minutest particular. Uncle George tells stories, and
carves poultry, and takes wine, and jokes with the children
at the side-table, and winks at the cousins that are making
love, or being made love to, and exhilarates everybody with
his good humour and hospitality; and when, at last, a stout
servant staggers in with a gigantic pudding, with a sprig of
holly in the top, there is such a laughing, and shouting, and
clapping of little chubby hands, and kicking up of fat dumpy
legs, as can only be equalled by the applause with which the
astonishing feat of pouring lighted brandy into mince-pies
is received by the younger visitors. Then the dessert!—and
the wine!—and the fun! Such beautiful speeches, and *such*
songs, from aunt Margaret's husband, who turns out to be
such a nice man, and *so* attentive to grandmamma! Even
grandpapa not only sings his annual song with unprecedented
vigour, but on being honoured with an unanimous *encore*,
according to annual custom, actually comes out with a new
one which nobody but grandmamma ever heard before; and
a young scape-grace of a cousin, who has been in some disgrace with the old people, for certain heinous sins of omission
and commission—neglecting to call, and persisting in drinking
Burton Ale—astonishes everybody into convulsions of laughter
by volunteering the most extraordinary comic songs that ever
were heard. And thus the evening passes, in a strain of
rational good-will and cheerfulness, doing more to awaken
the sympathies of every member of the party in behalf of his
neighbour, and to perpetuate their good feeling during the
ensuing year, than half the homilies that have ever been
written, by half the Divines that have ever lived.

Samuel Wilkins and the Evanses
(*p. 230*)

CHAPTER III

THE NEW YEAR

NEXT to Christmas-day, the most pleasant annual epoch in existence is the advent of the New Year. There are a lachrymose set of people who usher in the New Year with watching and fasting, as if they were bound to attend as chief mourners at the obsequies of the old one. Now, we cannot but think it a great deal more complimentary, both to the old year that has rolled away, and to the New Year that is just beginning to dawn upon us, to see the old fellow out, and the new one in, with gaiety and glee.

There must have been some few occurrences in the past year to which we can look back, with a smile of cheerful recollection, if not with a feeling of heartfelt thankfulness. And we are bound by every rule of justice and equity to give the New Year credit for being a good one, until he proves himself unworthy the confidence we repose in him.

This is our view of the matter; and entertaining it, notwithstanding our respect for the old year, one of the few remaining moments of whose existence passes away with every word we write, here we are, seated by our fireside on this last night of the old year, one thousand eight hundred and thirty-six, penning this article with as jovial a face as if nothing extraordinary had happened, or was about to happen, to disturb our good humour.

Hackney-coaches and carriages keep rattling up the street and down the street in rapid succession, conveying, doubtless, smartly-dressed coachfuls to crowded parties; loud and repeated double knocks at the house with green blinds, opposite, announce to the whole neighbourhood that there's one large party in the street at all events; and we saw through the window, and through the fog too, till it grew so thick that we rung for candles, and drew our curtains, pastrycooks' men with green boxes on their heads, and rout-furniture-warehouse-carts, with cane seats and French lamps, hurrying to the numerous houses where an annual festival is held in honour of the occasion.

We can fancy one of these parties, we think, as well as if we were duly dress-coated and pumped, and had just been announced at the drawing-room door.

Take the house with the green blinds for instance. We know it is a quadrille party, because we saw some men taking up the front drawing-room carpet while we sat at breakfast this morning, and if further evidence be required, and we must tell the truth, we just now saw one of the young ladies "doing" another of the young ladies' hair, near one of the bedroom windows, in an unusual style of splendour, which nothing else but a quadrille party could possibly justify.

The master of the house with the green blinds is in a public office; we know the fact by the cut of his coat, the tie of his neckcloth, and the self-satisfaction of his gait—the very green blinds themselves have a Somerset House air about them.

Hark!—a cab! That's a junior clerk in the same office; a tidy sort of young man, with a tendency to cold and corns, who comes in a pair of boots with black cloth fronts, and brings his shoes in his coat-pocket, which shoes he is at this very moment putting on in the hall. Now he is announced by the man in the passage to another man in a blue coat, who is a disguised messenger from the office.

The man on the first landing precedes him to the drawing-room door. "Mr. Tupple!" shouts the messenger. "How *are* you, Tupple?" says the master of the house, advancing from the fire, before which he has been talking politics and airing himself. "My dear, this is Mr. Tupple (a courteous salute from the lady of the house); Tupple, my eldest daughter; Julia, my dear, Mr. Tupple; Tupple, my other daughters; my son, sir;" Tupple rubs his hands very hard, and smiles as if it were all capital fun, and keeps constantly bowing and turning himself round, till the whole family have been introduced, when he glides into a chair at the corner of the sofa, and opens a miscellaneous conversation with the young ladies upon the weather, and the theatres, and the old year, and the last new murder, and the balloon, and the ladies' sleeves, and the festivities of the season, and a great many other topics of small talk.

More double knocks! what an extensive party! what an incessant hum of conversation and general sipping of coffee!

We see Tupple now, in our mind's eye, in the height of his glory. He has just handed that stout old lady's cup to the servant; and now he dives among the crowd of young men by the door, to intercept the other servant, and secure the muffin-plate for the old lady's daughter, before he leaves the room ; and now, as he passes the sofa on his way back, he bestows a glance of recognition and patronage upon the young ladies, as condescending and familiar as if he had known them from infancy.

Charming person Mr. Tupple—perfect ladies' man—such a delightful companion, too! Laugh!—nobody ever understood papa's jokes half so well as Mr. Tupple, who laughs himself into convulsions at every fresh burst of facetiousness. Most delightful partner! talks through the whole set! and although he does seem at first rather gay and frivolous, so romantic and with so *much* feeling ! Quite a love. No great favourite with the young men, certainly, who sneer at, and affect to despise him ; but everybody knows that's only envy, and they needn't give themselves the trouble to depreciate his merits at any rate, for Ma says he shall be asked to every future dinner-party, if it's only to talk to people between the courses, and distract their attention when there's any unexpected delay in the kitchen.

At supper, Mr. Tupple shows to still greater advantage than he has done throughout the evening, and when Pa requests every one to fill their glasses for the purpose of drinking happiness throughout the year, Mr. Tupple is *so* droll: insisting on all the young ladies having their glasses filled, notwithstanding their repeated assurances that they never can, by any possibility, think of emptying them: and subsequently begging permission to say a few words on the sentiment which has just been uttered by Pa—when he makes one of the most brilliant and poetical speeches that can possibly be imagined, about the old year and the new one. After the toast has been drunk, and when the ladies have retired, Mr. Tupple requests that every gentleman will do him the favour of filling his glass, for he has a toast to propose : on which all the gentlemen cry " Hear ! hear ! " and pass the decanters accordingly : and Mr. Tupple being informed by the master of the house that they are all charged, and waiting for his toast, rises, and begs to remind the gentlemen present, how much they have been delighted by the dazzling array of elegance and beauty which the drawing-room has

exhibited that night, and how their senses have been charmed,
and their hearts captivated, by the bewitching concentration
of female loveliness which that very room has so recently
displayed. (Loud cries of "Hear!") Much as he (Tupple)
would be disposed to deplore the absence of the ladies, on
other grounds, he cannot but derive some consolation from
the reflection that the very circumstance of their not being
present, enables him to propose a toast, which he would have
otherwise been prevented from giving—that toast he begs
to say is—"The Ladies!" (Great applause.) The Ladies!
among whom the fascinating daughters of their excellent host
are alike conspicuous for their beauty, their accomplishments,
and their elegance. He begs them to drain a bumper to
"The Ladies, and a happy new year to them!" (Prolonged
approbation ; above which the noise of the ladies dancing
the Spanish dance among themselves, overhead, is distinctly
audible.)

The applause consequent on this toast has scarcely subsided,
when a young gentleman in a pink under-waistcoat, sitting
towards the bottom of the table, is observed to grow very
restless and fidgety, and to evince strong indications of some
latent desire to give vent to his feelings in a speech, which
the wary Tupple at once perceiving, determines to forestall
by speaking himself. He, therefore, rises again, with an air
of solemn importance, and trusts he may be permitted to
propose another toast (unqualified approbation, and Mr.
Tupple proceeds.) He is sure they must all be deeply impressed with the hospitality—he may say the splendour—
with which they have been that night received by their
worthy host and hostess. (Unbounded applause.) Although
this is the first occasion on which he has had the pleasure
and delight of sitting at that board, he has known his friend
Dobble long and intimately ; he has been connected with
him in business—he wishes everybody present knew Dobble
as well as he does. (A cough from the host.) He (Tupple)
can lay his hand upon his (Tupple's) heart, and declare his
confident belief that a better man, a better husband, a better
father, a better brother, a better son, a better relation in any
relation of life, than Dobble, never existed. (Loud cries of
"Hear!") They have seen him to-night in the peaceful
bosom of his family ; they should see him in the morning,
in the trying duties of his office. Calm in the perusal of the
morning papers, uncompromising in the signature of his

name, dignified in his replies to the inquiries of stranger applicants, deferential in his behaviour to his superiors, majestic in his deportment to the messengers. (Cheers.) When he bears this merited testimony to the excellent qualities of his friend Dobble, what can he say in approaching such a subject as Mrs. Dobble? Is it requisite for him to expatiate on the qualities of that amiable woman? No; he will spare his friend Dobble's feelings; he will spare the feelings of his friend—if he will allow him to have the honour of calling him so—Mr. Dobble, junior. (Here Mr. Dobble, junior, who has been previously distending his mouth to a considerable width, by thrusting a particularly fine orange into that feature, suspends operations, and assumes a proper appearance of intense melancholy.) He will simply say—and he is quite certain it is a sentiment in which all who hear him will readily concur—that his friend Dobble is as superior to any man he ever knew, as Mrs. Dobble is far beyond any woman he ever saw (except her daughters); and he will conclude by proposing their worthy "Host and Hostess, and may they live to enjoy many more new years!"

The toast is drunk with acclamation; Dobble returns thanks, and the whole party rejoin the ladies in the drawing-room. Young men who were too bashful to dance before supper, find tongues and partners; the musicians exhibit unequivocal symptoms of having drunk the new year in, while the company were out; and dancing is kept up until far in the first morning of the new year.

We have scarcely written the last word of the previous sentence, when the first stroke of twelve peals from the neighbouring churches. There certainly—we must confess it now—is something awful in the sound. Strictly speaking, it may not be more impressive now than at any other time; for the hours steal as swiftly on at other periods, and their flight is little heeded. But we measure man's life by years, and it is a solemn knell that warns us we have passed another of the landmarks which stand between us and the grave. Disguise it as we may, the reflection will force itself on our minds, that when the next bell announces the arrival of a new year, we may be insensible alike of the timely warning we have so often neglected, and of all the warm feelings that glow within us now.

CHAPTER IV

MR. SAMUEL WILKINS was a carpenter, a journeyman carpenter of small dimensions, decidedly below the middle size—bordering, perhaps, upon the dwarfish. His face was round and shining, and his hair carefully twisted into the outer corner of each eye, till it formed a variety of that description of semi-curls, usually known as "aggerawators." His earnings were all-sufficient for his wants, varying from eighteen shillings to one pound five, weekly—his manner undeniable—his sabbath waistcoats dazzling. No wonder that, with these qualifications, Samuel Wilkins found favour in the eyes of the other sex: many women have been captivated by far less substantial qualifications. But Samuel was proof against their blandishments, until at length his eyes rested on those of a Being for whom, from that time forth, he felt fate had destined him. He came, and conquered—proposed, and was accepted—loved, and was beloved. Mr. Wilkins "kept company" with Jemima Evans.

Miss Evans (or Ivins, to adopt the pronunciation most in vogue with her circle of acquaintance) had adopted in early life the useful pursuit of shoe-binding, to which she had afterwards superadded the occupation of a straw-bonnet maker. Herself, her maternal parent, and two sisters, formed an harmonious quartett in the most secluded portion of Camden Town; and here it was that Mr. Wilkins presented himself, one Monday afternoon, in his best attire, with his face more shining and his waistcoat more bright than either had ever appeared before. The family were just going to tea, and were *so* glad to see him. It was quite a little feast; two ounces of seven-and-sixpenny green, and a quarter of a pound of the best fresh; and Mr. Wilkins had brought a pint of shrimps, neatly folded up in a clean belcher, to give a zest to the meal, and propitiate Mrs. Ivins. Jemima was " cleaning herself " up-stairs; so Mr. Samuel Wilkins sat down and talked domestic economy with Mrs. Ivins, whilst the two youngest Miss Ivinses poked bits of lighted brown paper between the bars under the kettle, to make the water boil for tea.

"I wos a-thinking," said Mr. Samuel Wilkins, during a pause in the conversation—"I wos a-thinking of taking J'mima to the Eagle to-night."—"O my!" exclaimed Mrs. Ivins. "Lor! how nice!" said the youngest Miss Ivins. "Well, I declare!" added the youngest Miss Ivins but one. "Tell J'mima to put on her white muslin, Tilly," screamed Mrs. Ivins, with motherly anxiety; and down came J'mima herself soon afterwards in a white muslin gown carefully hooked and eyed, a little red shawl, plentifully pinned, a white straw bonnet trimmed with red ribbons, a small neck-lace, a large pair of bracelets, Denmark satin shoes, and open-worked stockings; white cotton gloves on her fingers, and a cambric pocket-handkerchief, carefully folded up, in her hand—all quite genteel and ladylike. And away went Miss J'mima Ivins and Mr. Samuel Wilkins, and a dress-cane with a gilt knob at the top, to the admiration and envy of the street in general, and to the high gratification of Mrs. Ivins, and the two youngest Miss Ivinses in particular. They had no sooner turned into the Pancras Road, than who should Miss J'mima Ivins stumble upon, by the most for-tunate accident in the world, but a young lady as she knew, with *her* young man!—And it is so strange how things do turn out sometimes—they were actually going to the Eagle too. So Mr. Samuel Wilkins was introduced to Miss J'mima Ivins's friend's young man, and they all walked on together, talking, and laughing, and joking away like anything; and when they got as far as Pentonville, Miss Ivins's friend's young man *would* have the ladies go into the Crown to taste some shrub, which, after a great blushing and giggling, and hiding of faces in elaborate pocket-handkerchiefs, they con-sented to do. Having tasted it once, they were easily pre-vailed upon to taste it again; and they sat out in the garden tasting shrub, and looking at the Busses alternately, till it was just the proper time to go to the Eagle; and then they resumed their journey, and walked very fast, for fear they should lose the beginning of the concert in the Rotunda.

"How ev'nly!" said Miss J'mima Ivins, and Miss J'mima Ivins's friend, both at once, when they had passed the gate and were fairly inside the gardens. There were the walks, beautifully gravelled and planted—and the refreshment-boxes, painted and ornamented like so many snuff-boxes—and the variegated lamps shedding their rich light upon the company's heads—and the place for dancing ready chalked for the company's feet—and a Moorish band playing at one end of the gardens—and an opposition military band playing away at the other. Then, the waiters were rushing to and fro with glasses of negus, and glasses of brandy-and-water, and bottles of ale, and bottles of stout; and ginger-beer was going off in one place, and practical jokes were going on in another; and people were crowding to the door of the Rotunda; and in short the whole scene was, as Miss J'mima Ivins, inspired by the novelty, or the shrub, or both, observed —"one of dazzling excitement." As to the concert-room, never was anything half so splendid. There was an orchestra for the singers, all paint, gilding, and plate-glass; and such an organ! Miss J'mima Ivins's friend's young man whispered it had cost "four hundred pound," which Mr. Samuel Wilkins said was "not dear neither;" an opinion in which the ladies perfectly coincided. The audience were seated on elevated benches round the room, and crowded into every part of it; and everybody was eating and drinking as comfortably as possible. Just before the concert commenced, Mr. Samuel Wilkins ordered two glasses of rum-and-water "warm with—" and two slices of lemon, for himself and the other young man, together with "a pint o' sherry wine for the ladies, and some sweet carraway-seed biscuits;" and they would have been quite comfortable and happy, only a strange gentleman with large whiskers *would* stare at Miss J'mima Ivins, and another gentleman in a plaid waistcoat *would* wink at Miss J'mima Ivins's friend; on which Miss J'mima Ivins's friend's young man exhibited symptoms of boiling over, and began to mutter about "people's imperence," and "swells out o' luck;" and to intimate, in oblique terms, a vague intention of knocking somebody's head off; which he was only prevented from announcing more emphatically, by both Miss J'mima Ivins and her friend threatening to faint away on the spot if he said another word.

The concert commenced—overture on the organ. "How solemn!" exclaimed Miss J'mima Ivins, glancing, perhaps unconsciously, at the gentleman with the whiskers. Mr. Samuel Wilkins, who had been muttering apart for some time past, as if he were holding a confidential conversation with the gilt knob of the dress-cane, breathed hard—breathing vengeance, perhaps,—but said nothing. "The soldier tired," Miss Somebody in white satin. "Ancore!" cried Miss J'mima Ivins's friend. "Ancore!" shouted the gentleman in the plaid waistcoat immediately, hammering the table with a stout-bottle. Miss J'mima Ivins's friend's young man eyed the man behind the waistcoat from head to foot, and cast a look of interrogative contempt towards Mr. Samuel Wilkins. Comic song, accompanied on the organ. Miss J'mima Ivins was convulsed with laughter—so was the man with the whiskers. Everything the ladies did, the plaid waistcoat and whiskers did, by way of expressing unity of sentiment and congeniality of soul; and Miss J'mima Ivins, and Miss J'mima Ivins's friend, grew lively and talkative, as Mr. Samuel Wilkins, and Miss J'mima Ivins's friend's young man, grew morose and surly in inverse proportion.

Now, if the matter had ended here, the little party might soon have recovered their former equanimity; but Mr. Samuel Wilkins and his friend began to throw looks of defiance upon the waistcoat and whiskers. And the waistcoat and whiskers, by way of intimating the slight degree in which they were affected by the looks aforesaid, bestowed glances of increased admiration upon Miss J'mima Ivins and friend. The concert and vaudeville concluded, they promenaded the gardens. The waistcoat and whiskers did the same; and made divers remarks complimentary to the ankles of Miss J'mima Ivins and friend, in an audible tone. At length, not satisfied with these numerous atrocities, they actually came up and asked Miss J'mima Ivins, and Miss J'mima Ivins's friend, to dance, without taking no more notice of Mr. Samuel Wilkins, and Miss J'mima Ivins's friend's young man, than if they was nobody!

"What do you mean by that, scoundrel!" exclaimed Mr. Samuel Wilkins, grasping the gilt-knobbed dress-cane firmly in his right hand. "What's the matter with *you*, you little humbug?" replied the whiskers. "How dare you insult me and my friend?" inquired the friend's young man. "You and your friend be hanged!" responded the waistcoat. "Take that," exclaimed Mr. Samuel Wilkins. The ferrule of the gilt-knobbed dress-cane was visible for an instant, and then the light of the variegated lamps shone brightly upon it as it whirled into the air, cane and all. "Give it him," said the waistcoat. "Horficer!" screamed the ladies. Miss J'mima Ivins's beau, and the friend's young man, lay gasping on the gravel, and the waistcoat and whiskers were seen no more.

Miss J'mima Ivins and friend being conscious that the affray was in no slight degree attributable to themselves, of course went into hysterics forthwith; declared themselves the most injured of women; exclaimed, in incoherent ravings, that they had been suspected—wrongfully suspected —oh! that they should ever have lived to see the day—and so forth; suffered a relapse every time they opened their eyes and saw their unfortunate little admirers; and were carried to their respective abodes in a hackney-coach, and a state of insensibility, compounded of shrub, sherry, and excitement.

CHAPTER V

THE PARLOUR ORATOR

WE had been lounging one evening, down Oxford Street, Holborn, Cheapside, Coleman Street, Finsbury Square, and so on, with the intention of returning westward, by Pentonville and the New Road, when we began to feel rather thirsty, and disposed to rest for five or ten minutes. So we turned back towards an old, quiet, decent public-house, which we remembered to have passed but a moment before (it was not far from the City Road), for the purpose of solacing ourself with a glass of ale. The house was none of your stuccoed, French-polished, illuminated palaces, but a modest public-house of the old school, with a little old bar, and a little old landlord, who, with a wife and daughter of the same pattern, was comfortably seated in the bar aforesaid— a snug little room with a cheerful fire, protected by a large screen : from behind which the young lady emerged on our representing our inclination for a glass of ale.

"Won't you walk into the parlour, sir?" said the young lady, in seductive tones.

"You had better walk into the parlour, sir," said the little old landlord, throwing his chair back, and looking round one side of the screen to survey our appearance.

"You had much better step into the parlour, sir," said the little old lady, popping out her head on the other side of the screen.

We cast a slight glance around, as if to express our ignorance of the locality so much recommended. The little old landlord observed it ; bustled out of the small door of the small bar ; and forthwith ushered us into the parlour itself.

It was an ancient, dark-looking room, with oaken wainscoting, a sanded floor, and a high mantelpiece. The walls were ornamented with three or four old coloured prints in black frames, each print representing a naval engagement, with a couple of men-of-war banging away at each other

most vigorously, while another vessel or two were blowing up
in the distance, and the foreground presented a miscellaneous
collection of broken masts and blue legs sticking up out of
the water. Depending from the ceiling in the centre of the
room, were a gas-light and bell-pull ; on each side were three
or four long narrow tables, behind which was a thickly-
planted row of those slippery, shiny-looking wooden chairs,
peculiar to hostelries of this description. The monotonous
appearance of the sanded boards was relieved by an occasional
spittoon ; and a triangular pile of those useful articles
adorned the two upper corners of the apartment.

At the furthest table, nearest the fire, with his face towards
the door at the bottom of the room, sat a stoutish man of
about forty, whose short, stiff, black hair curled closely
round a broad high forehead, and a face to which something
besides water and exercise had communicated a rather
inflamed appearance. He was smoking a cigar, with his
eyes fixed on the ceiling, and had that confident oracular
air which marked him as the leading politician, general
authority, and universal anecdote-relater, of the place. He
had evidently just delivered himself of something very
weighty ; for the remainder of the company were puffing
at their respective pipes and cigars in a kind of solemn
abstraction, as if quite overwhelmed with the magnitude of
the subject recently under discussion.

On his right hand sat an elderly gentleman with a white
head, and broad-brimmed brown hat ; on his left, a sharp-
nosed, light-haired man in a brown surtout reaching nearly
to his heels, who took a whiff at his pipe, and an admiring
glance at the red-faced man, alternately.

"Very extraordinary !" said the light-haired man after
a pause of five minutes. A murmur of assent ran through
the company.

"Not at all extraordinary—not at all," said the red-faced
man, awakening suddenly from his reverie, and turning
upon the light-haired man the moment he had spoken.

"Why should it be extraordinary?—why is it extraordinary?—prove it to be extraordinary !"

"Oh, if you come to that— " said the light-haired man,
meekly.

"Come to that !" ejaculated the man with the red face ;
"but we *must* come to that. We stand, in these times,
upon a calm elevation of intellectual attainment, and not in

the dark recess of mental deprivation. Proof is what I require—proof, and not assertions, in these stirring times. Every gen'lem'n that knows me, knows what was the nature and effect of my observations, when it was in the contemplation of the Old Street Suburban Representative Discovery Society, to recommend a candidate for that place in Cornwall there—I forget the name of it. 'Mr. Snobee,' said Mr. Wilson, 'is a fit and proper person to represent the borough in Parliament.' 'Prove it,' says I. 'He is a friend to Reform,' says Mr. Wilson. 'Prove it,' says I. 'The abolitionist of the national debt, the unflinching opponent of pensions, the uncompromising advocate of the negro, the reducer of sinecures and the duration of Parliaments; the extender of nothing but the suffrages of the people,' says Mr. Wilson. 'Prove it,' says I. 'His acts prove it,' says he. 'Prove them,' says I.

"And he could not prove them," said the red faced man, looking round triumphantly; "and the borough didn't have him; and if you carried this principle to the full extent, you'd have no debt, no pensions, no sinecures, no negroes, no nothing. And then, standing upon an elevation of intellectual attainment, and having reached the summit of popular prosperity, you might bid defiance to the nations of the earth, and erect yourselves in the proud confidence of wisdom and superiority. This is my argument—this always has been my argument—and if I was a Member of the House of Commons to-morrow, I'd make 'em shake in their shoes with it." And the red-faced man, having struck the table very hard with his clenched fist, to add weight to the declaration, smoked away like a brewery.

"Well!" said the sharp-nosed man, in a very slow and soft voice, addressing the company in general, "I always do say, that of all the gentlemen I have the pleasure of meeting in this room, there is not one whose conversation I like to hear so much as Mr. Rogers's, or who is such improving company."

"Improving company!" said Mr. Rogers, for that, it seemed, was the name of the red-faced man. "You may say I am improving company, for I've improved you all to some purpose; though as to my conversation being as my friend Mr. Ellis here describes it, that is not for me to say anything about. You, gentlemen, are the best judges on that point; but this I will say, when I came into this parish, and first used this room, ten years ago, I don't believe there was one man in it, who knew he was a slave—and now you all know it, and writhe under it. Inscribe that upon my tomb, and I am satisfied."

"Why, as to inscribing it on your tomb," said a little greengrocer with a chubby face, "of course you can have anything chalked up, as you likes to pay for, so far as it relates to yourself and your affairs; but when you come to talk about slaves, and that there abuse, you'd better keep it in the family, 'cos I for one don't like to be called them names, night after night."

"You *are* a slave," said the red-faced man, "and the most pitiable of all slaves."

"Werry hard if I am," interrupted the greengrocer, "for I got no good out of the twenty million that was paid for 'mancipation, anyhow."

"A willing slave," ejaculated the red-faced man, getting more red with eloquence and contradiction—"resigning the dearest birthright of your children—neglecting the sacred call of Liberty—who, standing imploringly before you, appeals to the warmest feelings of your heart, and points to your helpless infants, but in vain."

"Prove it," said the greengrocer.

"Prove it!" sneered the man with the red face. "What! bending beneath the yoke of an insolent and factious oligarchy; bowed down by the domination of cruel laws; groaning beneath tyranny and oppression on every hand, at every side, and in every corner. Prove it!—" The red-faced man abruptly broke off, sneered melo-dramatically, and buried his countenance and his indignation together, in a quart pot.

"Ah, to be sure, Mr. Rogers," said a stout broker in a large waistcoat, who had kept his eyes fixed on this luminary all the time he was speaking. "Ah, to be sure," said the broker with a sigh, "that's the point."

"Of course, of course," said divers members of the company, who understood almost as much about the matter as the broker himself.

"You had better let him alone, Tommy," said the broker, by way of advice to the little greengrocer; "he can tell what's o'clock by an eight-day, without looking at the minute hand, he can. Try it on, on some other suit; it won't do with him, Tommy."

A Pickpocket in Custody
(*p. 241*)

"What is a man?" continued the red-faced specimen of the species, jerking his hat indignantly from its peg on the wall. "What is an Englishman? Is he to be trampled upon by every oppressor? Is he to be knocked down at everybody's bidding? What's freedom? Not a standing army. What's a standing army? Not freedom. What's general happiness? Not universal misery. Liberty ain't the window-tax, is it? The Lords ain't the Commons, are they?" And the red-faced man, gradually bursting into a radiating sentence, in which such adjectives as "dastardly," "oppressive," "violent," and "sanguinary," formed the most conspicuous words, knocked his hat indignantly over his eyes, left the room, and slammed the door after him.

"Wonderful man!" said he of the sharp nose.

"Splendid speaker!" added the broker.

"Great power!" said everybody but the greengrocer. And as they said it, the whole party shook their heads mysteriously, and one by one retired, leaving us alone in the old parlour.

If we had followed the established precedent in all such instances, we should have fallen into a fit of musing, without delay. The ancient appearance of the room—the old panelling of the wall—the chimney blackened with smoke and age—would have carried us back a hundred years at least, and we should have gone dreaming on, until the pewter-pot on the table, or the little beer-chiller on the fire, had started into life, and addressed to us a long story of days gone by. But, by some means or other, we were not in a romantic humour; and although we tried very hard to invest the furniture with vitality, it remained perfectly unmoved, obstinate, and sullen. Being thus reduced to the unpleasant necessity of musing about ordinary matters, our thoughts reverted to the red-faced man, and his oratorical display.

A numerous race are these red-faced men; there is not a parlour, or club-room, or benefit society, or humble party of any kind, without its red-faced man. Weak-pated dolts they are, and a great deal of mischief they do to their cause, however good. So, just to hold a pattern one up, to know the others by, we took his likeness at once, and put him in here. And that is the reason why we have written this paper.

CHAPTER VI

THE HOSPITAL PATIENT

In our rambles through the streets of London after evening has set in, we often pause beneath the windows of some public hospital, and picture to ourself the gloomy and mournful scenes that are passing within. The sudden moving of a taper as its feeble ray shoots from window to window, until its light gradually disappears, as if it were carried farther back into the room to the bedside of some suffering patient, is enough to awaken a whole crowd of reflections; the mere glimmering of the low-burning lamps, which, when all other habitations are wrapped in darkness and slumber, denote the chamber where so many forms are writhing with pain, or wasting with disease, is sufficient to check the most boisterous merriment.

Who can tell the anguish of those weary hours, when the only sound the sick man hears is the disjointed wanderings of some feverish slumberer near him, the low moan of pain, or perhaps the muttered, long-forgotten prayer of a dying man? Who, but they who have felt it, can imagine the sense of loneliness and desolation which must be the portion of those who in the hour of dangerous illness are left to be tended by strangers; for what hands, be they ever so gentle, can wipe the clammy brow, or smooth the restless bed, like those of mother, wife, or child?

Impressed with these thoughts, we have turned away through the nearly-deserted streets; and the sight of the few miserable creatures still hovering about them has not tended to lessen the pain which such meditations awaken. The hospital is a refuge and resting-place for hundreds, who but for such institutions must die in the streets and door-ways; but what can be the feelings of some outcasts when they are stretched on the bed of sickness with scarcely a hope of recovery? The wretched woman who lingers about the pavement, hours after midnight, and the miserable shadow

of a man—the ghastly remnant that want and drunkenness
have left—which crouches beneath a window-ledge, to sleep
where there is some shelter from the rain, have little to bind
them to life, but what have they to look back upon, in
death? What are the unwonted comforts of a roof and
a bed to them, when the recollections of a whole life of
debasement stalk before them; when repentance seems a
mockery, and sorrow comes too late?

About a twelvemonth ago, as we were strolling through
Covent Garden (we had been thinking about these things
over-night), we were attracted by the very prepossessing
appearance of a pickpocket, who having declined to take the
trouble of walking to the Police Office, on the ground that
he hadn't the slightest wish to go there at all, was being
conveyed thither in a wheelbarrow, to the huge delight of
a crowd.

Somehow, we never can resist joining a crowd, so we
turned back with the mob, and entered the office, in company with our friend the pickpocket, a couple of policemen,
and as many dirty-faced spectators as could squeeze their
way in.

There was a powerful, ill-looking young fellow at the bar,
who was undergoing an examination, on the very common
charge of having, on the previous night, ill-treated a woman,
with whom he lived in some court hard by. Several witnesses bore testimony to acts of the grossest brutality; and
a certificate was read from the house-surgeon of a neighbouring hospital, describing the nature of the injuries the woman
had received, and intimating that her recovery was extremely
doubtful.

Some question appeared to have been raised about the
identity of the prisoner; for when it was agreed that the
two magistrates should visit the hospital at eight o'clock
that evening, to take her deposition, it was settled that the
man should be taken there also. He turned pale at this,
and we saw him clench the bar very hard when the order
was given. He was removed directly afterwards, and he
spoke not a word.

We felt an irrepressible curiosity to witness this interview, although it is hard to tell why, at this instant, for
we knew it must be a painful one. It was no very difficult
matter for us to gain permission, and we obtained it.

The prisoner, and the officer who had him in custody,

were already at the hospital when we reached it, and waiting
the arrival of the magistrates in a small room below stairs.
The man was handcuffed, and his hat was pulled forward
over his eyes. It was easy to see, though, by the whiteness
of his countenance, and the constant twitching of the muscles
of his face, that he dreaded what was to come. After a short
interval, the magistrates and clerk were bowed in by the
house-surgeon and a couple of young men who smelt very
strong of tobacco-smoke—they were introduced as "dressers"
—and after one magistrate had complained bitterly of the
cold, and the other of the absence of any news in the
evening paper, it was announced that the patient was prepared; and we were conducted to the "casualty ward" in
which she was lying.

The dim light which burnt in the spacious room, increased rather than diminished the ghastly appearance of
the hapless creatures in the beds, which were ranged in two
long rows on either side. In one bed lay a child enveloped
in bandages, with its body half-consumed by fire; in another,
a female, rendered hideous by some dreadful accident, was
wildly beating her clenched fists on the coverlet, in pain;
on a third, there lay stretched a young girl, apparently in
the heavy stupor often the immediate precursor of death:
her face was stained with blood, and her breast and arms
were bound up in folds of linen. Two or three of the beds
were empty, and their recent occupants were sitting beside
them, but with faces so wan, and eyes so bright and glassy,
that it was fearful to meet their gaze. On every face was
stamped the expression of anguish and suffering.

The object of the visit was lying at the upper end of the
room. She was a fine young woman of about two or three
and twenty. Her long black hair, which had been hastily
cut from near the wounds on her head, streamed over the
pillow in jagged and matted locks. Her face bore deep
marks of the ill-usage she had received; her hand was
pressed upon her side, as if her chief pain were there; her
breathing was short and heavy; and it was plain to see that
she was dying fast. She murmured a few words in reply to
the magistrate's inquiry whether she was in great pain;
and, having been raised on the pillow by the nurse, looked
vacantly upon the strange countenances that surrounded her
bed. The magistrate nodded to the officer, to bring the
man forward. He did so, and stationed him at the bedside.

Mr. John Dounce at the Oyster-Shop
(p. 247)

The girl looked on with a wild and troubled expression of face ; but her sight was dim, and she did not know him.

"Take off his hat," said the magistrate. The officer did as he was desired, and the man's features were disclosed.

The girl started up, with an energy quite preternatural ; the fire gleamed in her heavy eyes, and the blood rushed to her pale and sunken cheeks. It was a convulsive effort. She fell back upon her pillow, and covering her scarred and bruised face with her hands, burst into tears. The man cast an anxious look towards her, but otherwise appeared wholly unmoved. After a brief pause the nature of the errand was explained, and the oath tendered.

"Oh, no, gentlemen," said the girl, raising herself once more, and folding her hands together ; "no, gentlemen, for God's sake ! I did it myself—it was nobody's fault—it was an accident. He didn't hurt me ; he wouldn't for all the world. Jack, dear Jack, you know you wouldn't !"

Her sight was fast failing her, and her hand groped over the bedclothes in search of his. Brute as the man was, he was not prepared for this. He turned his face from the bed, and sobbed. The girl's colour changed, and her breathing grew more difficult. She was evidently dying.

"We respect the feelings which prompt you to this," said the gentleman who had spoken first, "but let me warn you not to persist in what you know to be untrue, until it is too late. It cannot save him."

"Jack," murmured the girl, laying her hand upon his arm, "they shall not persuade me to swear your life away. He didn't do it, gentlemen. He never hurt me." She grasped his arm tightly, and added, in a broken whisper, "I hope God Almighty will forgive me all the wrong I have done, and the life I have led. God bless you, Jack. Some kind gentleman take my love to my poor old father. Five years ago, he said he wished I had died a child. Oh, I wish I had ! I wish I had !"

The nurse bent over the girl for a few seconds, and then drew the sheet over her face. It covered a corpse.

CHAPTER VII

THE MISPLACED ATTACHMENT OF MR. JOHN DOUNCE

If we had to make a classification of society, there are a particular kind of men whom we should immediately set down under the head of "Old Boys;" and a column of most extensive dimensions the old boys would require. To what precise causes the rapid advance of old-boy population is to be traced, we are unable to determine. It would be an interesting and curious speculation, but, as we have not sufficient space to devote to it here, we simply state the fact that the numbers of the old boys have been gradually augmenting within the last few years, and that they are at this moment alarmingly on the increase.

Upon a general review of the subject, and without considering it minutely in detail, we should be disposed to subdivide the old boys into two distinct classes—the gay old boys, and the steady old boys. The gay old boys are paunchy old men in the disguise of young ones, who frequent the Quadrant and Regent Street in the day-time: the theatres (especially theatres under lady management) at night; and who assume all the foppishness and levity of boys, without the excuse of youth or inexperience. The steady old boys are certain stout old gentlemen of clean appearance, who are always to be seen in the same taverns, at the same hours every evening, smoking and drinking in the same company.

There was once a fine collection of old boys to be seen round the circular table at Offley's every night, between the hours of half-past eight and half-past eleven. We have lost sight of them for some time. There were, and may be still, for aught we know, two splendid specimens in full blossom at the Rainbow Tavern in Fleet Street, who always used to sit in the box nearest the fire-place, and smoked long cherry-stick pipes which went under the table, with the bowls resting on the floor. Grand old boys they were—fat, red-faced, white-headed old fellows—always there—one on one side the table, and the other opposite—puffing and drinking away in great state. Everybody knew them, and it was supposed by some people that they were both immortal.

Mr. John Dounce was an old boy of the latter class (we don't mean immortal, but steady), a retired glove and braces maker, a widower, resident with three daughters—all grown up, and all unmarried—in Cursitor Street, Chancery Lane. He was a short, round, large-faced, tubbish sort of man, with a broad-brimmed hat, and a square coat; and had that grave, but confident, kind of roll, peculiar to old boys in general. Regular as clockwork—breakfast at nine—dress and tittivate a little—down to the Sir Somebody's Head— a glass of ale and the paper—come back again, and take daughters out for a walk—dinner at three—glass of grog and pipe—nap—tea—little walk—Sir Somebody's Head again—capital house—delightful evenings. There were Mr. Harris, the law-stationer, and Mr. Jennings, the robe-maker (two jolly young fellows like himself), and Jones, the barrister's clerk—rum fellow that Jones—capital company— full of anecdote!—and there they sat every night till just ten minutes before twelve, drinking their brandy-and-water, and smoking their pipes, and telling stories, and enjoying themselves with a kind of solemn joviality particularly edifying.

Sometimes Jones would propose a half-price visit to Drury Lane or Covent Garden, to see two acts of a five-act play, and a new farce, perhaps, or a ballet, on which occasions the whole four of them went together: none of your hurrying and nonsense, but having their brandy-and-water first, com-fortably, and ordering a steak and some oysters for their supper against they came back, and then walking coolly into the pit, when the "rush" had gone in, as all sensible people do, and did when Mr. Dounce was a young man, except when the celebrated Master Betty was at the height of his popu-larity, and then, sir,—then—Mr. Dounce perfectly well remembered getting a holiday from business; and going to the pit doors at eleven o'clock in the forenoon, and waiting there till six in the afternoon, with some sandwiches in a pocket-handkerchief and some wine in a phial; and fainting after all, with the heat and fatigue, before the play began; in which situation he was lifted out of the pit, into one of the dress boxes, sir, by five of the finest women of that day, sir, who compassionated his situation and administered restoratives, and sent a black servant, six foot high, in blue and silver livery, next morning with their compliments, and to know how he found himself, sir, by G—! Between the acts Mr. Dounce, and Mr. Harris, and Mr. Jennings, used to stand up, and look round the house, and Jones—knowing fellow that Jones—knew everybody—pointed out the fashionable and celebrated Lady So-and-So in the boxes, at the mention of whose name Mr. Dounce, after brushing up his hair, and adjusting his neckerchief, would inspect the aforesaid Lady So-and-So through an immense glass, and remark, either that she was a "fine woman—very fine woman, indeed," or that "there might be a little more of her,— eh, Jones?" just as the case might happen to be. When the dancing began, John Dounce and the other old boys were particularly anxious to see what was going forward on the stage, and Jones—wicked dog that Jones—whispered little critical remarks into the ears of John Dounce, which John Dounce retailed to Mr. Harris, and Mr. Harris to Mr. Jennings; and then they all four laughed until the tears ran down out of their eyes.

When the curtain fell, they walked back together, two and two, to the steaks and oysters; and when they came to the second glass of brandy-and-water, Jones—hoaxing scamp, that Jones—used to recount how he had observed a lady in white feathers, in one of the pit boxes, gazing intently on Mr. Dounce all the evening, and how he had caught Mr. Dounce, whenever he thought no one was looking at him, bestowing ardent looks of intense devotion on the lady in return; on which Mr. Harris and Mr. Jennings used to laugh very heartily, and John Dounce more heartily than either of them, acknowledging, however, that the time *had* been when he *might* have done such things; upon which Mr. Jones used to poke him in the ribs, and tell him he had been a sad dog in his time, which John Dounce with chuckles confessed. And after Mr. Harris and Mr. Jennings had preferred their claims to the character of having been sad dogs too, they separated harmoniously, and trotted home.

The decrees of Fate, and the means by which they are brought about, are mysterious and inscrutable. John Dounce had led this life for twenty years and upwards, without wish for change, or care for variety, when his whole social system was suddenly upset, and turned completely topsy-turvy—not by an earthquake, or some other dreadful convulsion of nature, as the reader would be inclined to suppose, but by the simple agency of an oyster ; and thus it happened.

Mr. John Dounce was returning one night from the Sir Somebody's Head, to his residence in Cursitor Street—not tipsy, but rather excited, for it was Mr. Jennings's birthday, and they had had a brace of partridges for supper, and a brace of extra glasses afterwards, and Jones had been more than ordinarily amusing—when his eyes rested on a newly-opened oyster-shop, on a magnificent scale, with natives laid, one deep, in circular marble basins in the windows, together with little round barrels of oysters directed to Lords and Baronets, and Colonels and Captains, in every part of the habitable globe.

Behind the natives were the barrels, and behind the barrels was a young lady of about five-and-twenty, all in blue, and all alone—splendid creature, charming face and lovely figure ! It is difficult to say whether Mr. John Dounce's red countenance, illuminated as it was by the flickering gas-light in the window before which he paused, excited the lady's risibility, or whether a natural exuberance of animal spirits proved too much for that staidness of demeanour which the forms of society rather dictatorially prescribe.   But certain it is, that the lady smiled ; then put her finger upon her lip, with a striking recollection of what was due to herself ; and finally retired, in oyster-like bashfulness, to the very back of the counter.   The sad-dog sort of feeling came strongly upon John Dounce : he lingered—the lady in blue made no sign. He coughed—still she came not.   He entered the shop.

"Can you open me an oyster, my dear ? " said Mr. John Dounce.

"Dare say I can, sir," replied the lady in blue, with playfulness.   And Mr. John Dounce eat one oyster, and then looked at the young lady, and then eat another, and then squeezed the young lady's hand as she was opening the third, and so forth, until he had devoured a dozen of those at eightpence in less than no time.

"Can you open me half-a-dozen more, my dear ? " inquired Mr. John Dounce.

"I'll see what I can do for you, sir," replied the young lady in blue, even more bewitchingly than before ; and Mr. John Dounce eat half-a-dozen more of those at eightpence.

"You couldn't manage to get me a glass of brandy-and-water, my dear, I suppose?" said Mr. John Dounce, when he had finished the oysters: in a tone which clearly implied his supposition that she could.

"I'll see, sir," said the young lady: and away she ran out of the shop, and down the street, her long auburn ringlets shaking in the wind in the most enchanting manner; and back she came again, tripping over the coal-cellar lids like a whipping-top, with a tumbler of brandy-and-water, which Mr. John Dounce insisted on her taking a share of, as it was regular ladies' grog—hot, strong, sweet, and plenty of it.

So the young lady sat down with Mr. John Dounce, in a little red box with a green curtain, and took a small sip of the brandy-and-water, and a small look at Mr. John Dounce, and then turned her head away, and went through various other serio-pantomimic fascinations, which forcibly reminded Mr. John Dounce of the first time he courted his first wife, and which made him feel more affectionate than ever; in pursuance of which affection, and actuated by which feeling, Mr. John Dounce sounded the young lady on her matrimonial engagements, when the young lady denied having formed any such engagements at all—she couldn't abear the men, they were such deceivers; thereupon Mr. John Dounce inquired whether this sweeping condemnation was meant to include other than very young men; on which the young lady blushed deeply—at least she turned away her head, and said Mr. John Dounce had made her blush, so of course she *did* blush— and Mr. John Dounce was a long time drinking the brandy-and-water; and, at last, John Dounce went home to bed, and dreamed of his first wife, and his second wife, and the young lady, and partridges, and oysters, and brandy-and-water, and disinterested attachments.

The next morning, John Dounce was rather feverish with the extra brandy-and-water of the previous night; and, partly in the hope of cooling himself with an oyster, and partly with the view of ascertaining whether he owed the young lady anything or not, went back to the oyster-shop. If the young lady had appeared beautiful by night, she was perfectly irresistible by day; and, from this time forward, a change came over the spirit of John Dounce's dream. He bought shirt-pins; wore a ring on his third finger; read poetry; bribed a cheap miniature-painter to perpetrate a faint resemblance to a youthful face, with a curtain over his head, six large books in the background, and an open country in the distance (this he called his portrait); "went on" altogether in such an uproarious manner, that the three Miss Dounces went off on small pensions, he having made the tenement in Cursitor Street too warm to contain them; and in short, comported and demeaned himself in every respect like an unmitigated old Saracen, as he was.

As to his ancient friends, the other old boys, at the Sir Somebody's Head, he dropped off from them by gradual degrees; for even when he did go there, Jones—vulgar fellow, that Jones—persisted in asking "when it was to be?" and "whether he was to have any gloves?" together with other inquiries of an equally offensive nature: at which not only Harris laughed, but Jennings also; so he cut the two altogether, and attached himself solely to the blue young lady at the smart oyster-shop.

Now comes the moral of the story—for it has a moral after all. The last mentioned young lady, having derived sufficient profit and emolument from John Dounce's attachment, not only refused, when matters came to a crisis, to take him for better for worse, but expressly declared, to use her own forcible words, that she "wouldn't have him at no price;" and John Dounce, having lost his old friends, alienated his relations, and rendered himself ridiculous to everybody, made offers successively to a schoolmistress, a landlady, a feminine tobacconist, and a housekeeper; and, being directly rejected by each and every of them, was accepted by his cook, with whom he now lives, a henpecked husband, a melancholy monument of antiquated misery, and a living warning to all uxorious old boys.

CHAPTER VIII

THE MISTAKEN MILLINER.   A TALE OF AMBITION

Miss Amelia Martin was pale, tallish, thin, and two-and-thirty—what ill-natured people would call plain, and police reports interesting. She was a milliner and dressmaker, living on her business and not above it. If you had been a young lady in service, and had wanted Miss Martin, as a great many young ladies in service did, you would just have stepped up, in the evening, to number forty-seven, Drummond Street, George Street, Euston Square, and after casting your eye on a brass door-plate, one foot ten by one and a half, ornamented with a great brass knob at each of the four corners, and bearing the inscription " Miss Martin ; millinery and dressmaking, in all its branches ; " you'd just have knocked two loud knocks at the street-door ; and down would have come Miss Martin herself, in a merino gown of the newest fashion, black velvet bracelets on the genteelest principle, and other little elegancies of the most approved description.

If Miss Martin knew the young lady who called, or if the young lady who called had been recommended by any other young lady whom Miss Martin knew, Miss Martin would forthwith show her up-stairs into the two-pair front, and chat she would—*so* kind, and *so* comfortable—it really wasn't like a matter of business, she was so friendly ; and then Miss Martin, after contemplating the figure and general appearance of the young lady in service with great apparent admiration, would say how well she would look, to be sure, in a low dress with short sleeves ; made very full in the skirts, with four tucks in the bottom ; to which the young lady in service would reply in terms expressive of her entire concurrence in the notion, and of the virtuous indignation with which she reflected on the tyranny of " Missis," who wouldn't allow a young girl to wear a short sleeve of an arternoon—

no, nor nothing smart, not even a pair of ear-rings ; let alone hiding people's heads of hair under them frightful caps. At the termination of this complaint, Miss Amelia Martin would distantly suggest certain dark suspicions that some people were jealous on account of their own daughters, and were obliged to keep their servants' charms under, for fear they should get married first, which was no uncommon circumstance—leastways she had known two or three young ladies in service, who had married a great deal better than their missises, and *they* were not very good-looking either ; and then the young lady would inform Miss Martin, in confidence, that how one of their young ladies was engaged to a young man and was a-going to be married, and Missis was so proud about it there was no bearing of her ; but how she needn't hold her head quite so high neither, for, after all, he was only a clerk.   And, after expressing due contempt for clerks in general, and the engaged clerk in particular, and the highest opinion possible of themselves and each other, Miss Martin and the young lady in service would bid each other good night, in a friendly but perfectly genteel manner : and the one went back to her " place," and the other to her room on the second-floor front.

There is no saying how long Miss Amelia Martin might have continued this course of life ; how extensive a connection she might have established among young ladies in service ; or what amount her demands upon their quarterly receipts might have ultimately attained, had not an unforeseen train of circumstances directed her thoughts to a sphere of action very different from dressmaking or millinery.

A friend of Miss Martin's who had long been keeping company with an ornamental painter and decorator's journeyman, at last consented (on being at last asked to do so) to name the day which would make the aforesaid journeyman a happy husband.   It was a Monday that was appointed for the celebration of the nuptials, and Miss Amelia Martin was invited, among others, to honour the wedding-dinner with her presence.   It was a charming party ; Somers Town the locality, and a front parlour the apartment.   The ornamental painter and decorator's journeyman had taken the house—no lodgings nor vulgarity of that kind, but a house—four beautiful rooms, and a delightful little washhouse at the end of the passage—which was the most convenient thing in the world, for the bridesmaids could sit in the front parlour and receive the company, and then run into the little washhouse and see how the pudding and boiled pork were getting on in the copper, and then pop back into the parlour again, as snug and comfortable as possible. And such a parlour as it was! Beautiful Kidderminster carpet—six bran-new cane-bottomed stained chairs—three wine-glasses and a tumbler on each sideboard—farmer's girl and farmer's boy on the mantel-piece : girl tumbling over a stile, and boy spitting himself on the handle of a pitchfork—long white dimity curtains in the window—and, in short, everything on the most genteel scale imaginable.

Then, the dinner. There was baked leg of mutton at the top, boiled leg of mutton at the bottom, pair of fowls and leg of pork in the middle ; porter-pots at the corners ; pepper, mustard, and vinegar in the centre ; vegetables on the floor : and plum-pudding and apple-pie and tartlets without number : to say nothing of cheese, and celery, and water-cresses, and all that sort of thing. As to the company ! Miss Amelia Martin herself declared, on a subsequent occasion, that, much as she had heard of the ornamental painter's journeyman's connexion, she never could have supposed it was half so genteel. There was his father, such a funny old gentleman—and his mother, such a dear old lady —and his sister, such a charming girl—and his brother, such a manly-looking young man—with such a eye! But even all these were as nothing when compared with his musical friends, Mr. and Mrs. Jennings Rodolph, from White Conduit, with whom the ornamental painter's journeyman had been fortunate enough to contract an intimacy while engaged in decorating the concert-room of that noble institution. To hear them sing separately was divine, but when they went through the tragic duet of "Red Ruffian, retire!" it was, as Miss Martin afterwards remarked, "thrilling." And why (as Mr. Jennings Rodolph observed) why were they not engaged at one of the patent theatres? If he was to be told that their voices were not powerful enough to fill the House, his only reply was, that he would back himself for any amount to fill Russell Square—a statement in which the company, after hearing the duet, expressed their full belief ; so they all said it was shameful treatment ; and both Mr. and Mrs. Jennings Rodolph said it was shameful too ; and Mr. Jennings Rodolph looked very serious, and said he knew who his malignant opponents were, but they had better take care how far they went, for if they irritated him too much he had not quite made up his mind whether he wouldn't bring the subject before Parliament; and they all agreed that it "'ud serve 'em quite right, and it was very proper that such people should be made an example of." So Mr. Jennings Rodolph said he'd think of it.

When the conversation resumed its former tone, Mr. Jennings Rodolph claimed his right to call upon a lady, and the right being conceded, trusted Miss Martin would favour the company—a proposal which met with unanimous approbation, whereupon Miss Martin, after sundry hesitatings and coughings, with a preparatory choke or two, and an introductory declaration that she was frightened to death to attempt it before such great judges of the art, commenced a species of treble chirruping containing frequent allusions to some young gentleman of the name of Hen-e-ry, with an occasional reference to madness and broken hearts. Mr. Jennings Rodolph frequently interrupted the progress of the song, by ejaculating "Beautiful!"—"Charming!"— "Brilliant!"—"Oh! splendid," &c.; and at its close the admiration of himself, and his lady, knew no bounds.

"Did you ever hear so sweet a voice, my dear?" inquired Mr. Jennings Rodolph of Mrs. Jennings Rodolph.

"Never; indeed I never did, love," replied Mrs. Jennings Rodolph.

"Don't you think Miss Martin, with a little cultivation, would be very like Signora Marra Boni, my dear?" asked Mr. Jennings Rodolph.

"Just exactly the very thing that struck me, my love," answered Mrs. Jennings Rodolph.

And thus the time passed away; Mr. Jennings Rodolph played tunes on a walking-stick, and then went behind the parlour-door and gave his celebrated imitations of actors, edge-tools, and animals; Miss Martin sang several other songs with increased admiration every time; and even the funny old gentleman began singing. His song had properly seven verses, but as he couldn't recollect more than the first one, he sung that over seven times, apparently very much to his own personal gratification. And then all the company sang the national anthem with national independence—each for himself, without reference to the other—and finally separated: all declaring that they never had spent so pleasant an evening: and Miss Martin inwardly resolving to adopt the advice of Mr. Jennings Rodolph, and to "come out" without delay.

Now, "coming out," either in acting, or singing, or society, or facetiousness, or anything else, is all very well, and re markably pleasant to the individual principally concerned, if he or she can but manage to come out with a burst, and being out to keep out, and not go in again; but it does unfortunately happen that both consummations are extremely difficult to accomplish, and that the difficulties of getting out at all in the first instance, and if you surmount them, of keeping out in the second, are pretty much on a par, and no slight ones either—and so Miss Amelia Martin shortly discovered. It is a singular fact (there being ladies in the case) that Miss Amelia Martin's principal foible was vanity, and the leading characteristic of Mrs. Jennings Rodolph an attachment to dress. Dismal wailings were heard to issue from the second-floor front of number forty-seven, Drummond Street, George Street, Euston Square; it was Miss Martin practising. Half-suppressed murmurs disturbed the calm dignity of the White Conduit orchestra at the commencement of the season. It was the appearance of Mrs. Jennings Rodolph in full dress, that occasioned them. Miss Martin studied incessantly—the practising was the consequence. Mrs. Jennings Rodolph taught gratuitously now and then—the dresses were the result.

Weeks passed away; the White Conduit season had begun, and progressed, and was more than half over. The dressmaking business had fallen off, from neglect; and its profits had dwindled away almost imperceptibly. A benefit-night approached; Mr. Jennings Rodolph yielded to the earnest solicitations of Miss Amelia Martin, and introduced her personally to the "comic gentleman" whose benefit it was. The comic gentleman was all smiles and blandness—he had composed a duet expressly for the occasion, and Miss Martin should sing it with him. The night arrived; there was an immense room—ninety-seven sixpenn'orths of gin-and-water, thirty-two small glasses of brandy-and-water, five-and-twenty bottled ales, and forty-one neguses; and the ornamental painter's journeyman, with his wife and a select circle of acquaintance, were seated at one of the side-tables near the orchestra. The concert began. Song—sentimental —by a light-haired young gentleman in a blue coat, and bright basket buttons—[applause]. Another song, doubtful, by another gentleman in another blue coat and more bright basket buttons—[increased applause]. Duet, Mr. Jennings Rodolph, and Mrs. Jennings Rodolph, "Red Ruffian, retire!"—[great applause]. Solo, Miss Julia Montague (positively on this occasion only)—"I am a Friar"—[enthusiasm]. Original duet, comic—Mr. H. Taplin (the comic gentleman) and Miss Martin—"The Time of Day." "Brayvo!—Brayvo!" cried the ornamental painter's journeyman's party, as Miss Martin was gracefully led in by the comic gentleman. "Go to work, Harry," cried the comic gentleman's personal friends. "Tap—tap—tap," went the leader's bow on the music-desk. The symphony began, and was soon afterwards followed by a faint kind of ventriloquial chirping, proceeding apparently from the deepest recesses of the interior of Miss Amelia Martin. "Sing out"—shouted one gentleman in a white great-coat. "Don't be afraid to put the steam on, old gal," exclaimed another. "S—s—s—s—s—s—s"—went the five-and-twenty bottled ales. "Shame, shame!" remonstrated the ornamental painter's journeyman's party—"S—s—s—s" went the bottled ales again, accompanied by all the gins, and a majority of the brandies.

"Turn them geese out," cried the ornamental painter's journeyman's party, with great indignation.

"Sing out," whispered Mr. Jennings Rodolph.

"So I do," responded Miss Amelia Martin.

"Sing louder," said Mrs. Jennings Rodolph.

"I can't," replied Miss Amelia Martin.

"Off, off, off," cried the rest of the audience.

"Bray-vo!" shouted the painter's party. It wouldn't do —Miss Amelia Martin left the orchestra, with much less ceremony than she had entered it; and, as she couldn't sing out, never came out. The general good humour was not restored until Mr. Jennings Rodolph had become purple in the face, by imitating divers quadrupeds for half an hour, without being able to render himself audible; and, to this day, neither has Miss Amelia Martin's good humour been restored, nor the dresses made for and presented to Mrs. Jennings Rod lph, nor the vocal abilities which Mr. Jennings Rodolph once staked his professional reputation that Miss Martin possessed.

CHAPTER IX

THE DANCING ACADEMY

OF all the dancing academies that ever were established, there never was one more popular in its immediate vicinity than Signor Billsmethi's, of the "King's Theatre." It was not in Spring Gardens, or Newman Street, or Berners Street, or Gower Street, or Charlotte Street, or Percy Street, or any other of the numerous streets which have been devoted time out of mind to professional people, dispensaries, and boarding-houses; it was not in the West End at all—it rather approximated to the eastern portion of London, being situated in the populous and improving neighbourhood of Gray's Inn Lane. It was not a dear dancing academy—four-and-sixpence a quarter is decidedly cheap upon the whole. It was *very* select, the number of pupils being strictly limited to seventy-five, and a quarter's payment in advance being rigidly exacted. There was public tuition and private tuition—an assembly-room and a parlour. Signor Billsmethi's family were always thrown in with the parlour, and included in parlour price; that is to say, a private pupil had Signor Billsmethi's parlour to dance *in*, and Signor Billsmethi's family to dance *with*; and when he had been sufficiently broken in in the parlour, he began to run in couples in the assembly-room.

Such was the dancing academy of Signor Billsmethi, when Mr. Augustus Cooper, of Fetter Lane, first saw an unstamped advertisement walking leisurely down Holborn Hill, announcing to the world that Signor Billsmethi, of the King's Theatre, intended opening for the season with a Grand Ball.

Now, Mr. Augustus Cooper was in the oil and colour line—just of age, with a little money, a little business, and a little mother, who, having managed her husband and *his* business in his lifetime, took to managing her son and *his* business after his decease; and so, somehow or other, he

Signor
Bill Smith's
Grand
Ball
will take place
on
the first of March
take notice

George Cruikshank

The Dancing Academy
(p. 259)

had been cooped up in the little back parlour behind the shop on week-days, and in a little deal box without a lid (called by courtesy a pew) at Bethel Chapel, on Sundays, and had seen no more of the world than if he had been an infant all his days; whereas Young White, at the gas-fitter's over the way, three years younger than him, had been flaring away like winkin'—going to the theatre—supping at harmonic meetings—eating oysters by the barrel—drinking stout by the gallon—even stopping out all night, and coming home as cool in the morning as if nothing had happened. So Mr. Augustus Cooper made up his mind that he would not stand it any longer, and had that very morning expressed to his mother a firm determination to be "blowed," in the event of his not being instantly provided with a street-door key. And he was walking down Holborn Hill, thinking about all these things, and wondering how he could manage to get introduced into genteel society for the first time, when his eyes rested on Signor Billsmethi's announcement, which it immediately struck him was just the very thing he wanted; for he should not only be able to select a genteel circle of acquaintance at once, out of the five-and-seventy pupils at four-and-sixpence a quarter, but should qualify himself at the same time to go through a hornpipe in private society, with perfect ease to himself and great delight to his friends. So he stopped the unstamped advertisement—an animated sandwich, composed of a boy between two boards—and having procured a very small card with the Signor's address indented thereon, walked straight at once to the Signor's house—and very fast he walked too, for fear the list should be filled up, and the five-and-seventy completed, before he got there. The Signor was at home, and, what was still more gratifying, he was an Englishman! Such a nice man—and so polite! The list was not full, but it was a most extraordinary circumstance that there was only just one vacancy, and even that one would have been filled up, that very morning, only Signor Billsmethi was dissatisfied with the reference, and, being very much afraid that the lady wasn't select, wouldn't take her.

"And very much delighted I am, Mr. Cooper," said Signor Billsmethi, "that I did *not* take her. I assure you, Mr. Cooper—I don't say it to flatter you, for I know you're above it—that I consider myself extremely fortunate in having a gentleman of your manners and appearance, sir."

"I am very glad of it too, sir," said Augustus Cooper.

"And I hope we shall be better acquainted, sir," said Signor Billsmethi.

"And I'm sure I hope we shall too, sir," responded Augustus Cooper. Just then, the door opened, and in came a young lady, with her hair curled in a crop all over her head, and her shoes tied in sandals all over her ankles.

"Don't run away, my dear," said Signor Billsmethi; for the young lady didn't know Mr. Cooper was there when she ran in, and was going to run out again in her modesty, all in confusion-like. "Don't run away, my dear," said Signor Billsmethi, "this is Mr. Cooper—Mr. Cooper, of Fetter Lane. Mr. Cooper, my daughter, sir—Miss Billsmethi, sir, who I hope will have the pleasure of dancing many a quadrille, minuet, gavotte, country-dance, fandango, double-hornpipe, and farinagholkajingo with you, sir. She dances them all, sir; and so shall you, sir, before you're a quarter older, sir."

And Signor Billsmethi slapped Mr. Augustus Cooper on the back, as if he had known him a dozen years,—so friendly;—and Mr. Cooper bowed to the young lady, and the young lady curtseyed to him, and Signor Billsmethi said they were as handsome a pair as ever he'd wish to see; upon which the young lady exclaimed, "Lor, pa!" and blushed as red as Mr. Cooper himself—you might have thought they were both standing under a red lamp at a chemist's shop; and before Mr. Cooper went away it was settled that he should join the family circle that very night —taking them just as they were—no ceremony nor nonsense of that kind—and learn his positions in order that he might lose no time, and be able to come out at the forthcoming ball.

Well; Mr. Augustus Cooper went away to one of the cheap shoemakers' shops in Holborn, where gentlemen's dress-pumps are seven-and-sixpence, and men's strong walking just nothing at all, and bought a pair of the regular seven-and-sixpenny, long-quartered, town-mades, in which he astonished himself quite as much as his mother, and sallied forth to Signor Billsmethi's. There were four other private pupils in the parlour: two ladies and two gentlemen. Such nice people! Not a bit of pride about them. One of the ladies in particular, who was in training for a Columbine, was remarkably affable; and she and Miss Billsmethi took such an interest in Mr. Augustus Cooper, and joked, and smiled, and looked so bewitching, that he got quite at home, and learnt his steps in no time. After the practising was over, Signor Billsmethi, and Miss Billsmethi, and Master Billsmethi, and a young lady, and the two ladies, and the two gentlemen, danced a quadrille—none of your slipping and sliding about, but regular warm work, flying into corners, and diving among chairs, and shooting out at the door,—something like dancing! Signor Billsmethi in particular, notwithstanding his having a little fiddle to play all the time, was out on the landing every figure, and Master Billsmethi, when everybody else was breathless, danced a hornpipe, with a cane in his hand, and a cheese-plate on his head, to the unqualified admiration of the whole company. Then, Signor Billsmethi insisted, as they were so happy, that they should all stay to supper, and proposed sending Master Billsmethi for the beer and spirits, where-upon the two gentlemen swore, "strike 'em wulgar if they'd stand that ; " and were just going to quarrel who should pay for it, when Mr. Augustus Cooper said he would, if they'd have the kindness to allow him—and they *had* the kindness to allow him ; and Master Billsmethi brought the beer in a can, and, the rum in a quart pot. They had a regular night of it ; and Miss Billsmethi squeezed Mr. Augustus Cooper's hand under the table ; and Mr. Augustus Cooper returned the squeeze, and returned home too, at something to six o'clock in the morning, when he was put to bed by main force by the apprentice, after repeatedly expressing an un-controllable desire to pitch his revered parent out of the second-floor window, and to throttle the apprentice with his own neck-handkerchief.

Weeks had worn on, and the seven-and-sixpenny town-mades had nearly worn-out, when the night arrived for the grand dress-ball at which the whole of the five-and-seventy pupils were to meet together, for the first time that season, and to take out some portion of their respective four-and-sixpences in lamp-oil and fiddlers. Mr. Augustus Cooper had ordered a new coat for the occasion—a two-pound-tenner from Turnstile. It was his first appearance in public ; and, after a grand Sicilian shawl-dance by fourteen young ladies in character, he was to open the quadrille department with Miss Billsmethi herself, with whom he had become quite intimate since his first introduction. It *was* a night ! Everything was admirably arranged. The sandwich-boy took the hats and bonnets at the street-door; there was a turn-up bedstead in the back-parlour, on which Miss Billsmethi made tea and coffee for such of the gentlemen as chose to pay for it, and such of the ladies as the gentlemen treated; red port-wine negus and lemonade were handed round at eighteen-pence a head; and in pursuance of a previous engagement with the public-house at the corner of the street, an extra potboy was laid on for the occasion. In short, nothing could exceed the arrangements, except the company. Such ladies! Such pink silk stockings! Such artificial flowers! Such a number of cabs! No sooner had one cab set down a couple of ladies, than another cab drove up and set down another couple of ladies, and they all knew: not only one another, but the majority of the gentlemen into the bargain, which made it all as pleasant and lively as could be. Signor Billsmethi, in black tights, with a large blue bow in his buttonhole, introduced the ladies to such of the gentlemen as were strangers: and the ladies talked away—and laughed they did—it was delightful to see them.

As to the shawl-dance, it was the most exciting thing that ever was beheld; there was such a whisking, and rustling, and fanning, and getting ladies into a tangle with artificial flowers, and then disentangling them again! And as to Mr. Augustus Cooper's share in the quadrille, he got through it admirably. He was missing from his partner, now and then, certainly, and discovered on such occasions to be either dancing with laudable perseverance in another set, or sliding about in perspective, without any definite object; but, generally speaking, they managed to shove him through the figure, until he turned up in the right place. Be this as it may, when he had finished, a great many ladies and gentlemen came up and complimented him very much, and said they had never seen a beginner do anything like it before; and Mr. Augustus Cooper was perfectly satisfied with himself, and everybody else into the bargain; and "stood" considerable quantities of spirits-and-water, negus, and compounds, for the use and behoof of two or three dozen very particular friends, selected from the select circle of five-and-seventy pupils.

Now, whether it was the strength of the compounds, or the beauty of the ladies, or what not, it did so happen that Mr. Augustus Cooper encouraged, rather than repelled, the

very flattering attentions of a young lady in brown gauze
over white calico who had appeared particularly struck with
him from the first; and when the encouragements had been
prolonged for some time, Miss Billsmethi betrayed her spite
and jealousy thereat by calling the young lady in brown
gauze a "creeter," which induced the young lady in brown
gauze to retort, in certain sentences containing a taunt
founded on the payment of four-and-sixpence a quarter,
which reference Mr. Augustus Cooper, being then and there
in a state of considerable bewilderment, expressed his entire
concurrence in. Miss Billsmethi, thus renounced, forthwith
began screaming in the loudest key of her voice, at the rate
of fourteen screams a minute; and being unsuccessful, in an
onslaught on the eyes and face, first of the lady in gauze
and then of Mr. Augustus Cooper, called distractedly on the
other three and-seventy pupils to furnish her with oxalic
acid for her own private drinking; and, the call not being
honoured, made another rush at Mr. Cooper, and then had
her stay-lace cut, and was carried off to bed. Mr. Augustus
Cooper, not being remarkable for quickness of apprehension,
was at a loss to understand what all this meant, until Signor
Billsmethi explained it in a most satisfactory manner, by
stating to the pupils, that Mr. Augustus Cooper had made
and confirmed divers promises of marriage to his daughter
on divers occasions, and had now basely deserted her; on
which the indignation of the pupils became universal; and
as several chivalrous gentlemen inquired rather pressingly
of Mr. Augustus Cooper, whether he required anything for
his own use, or, in other words, whether he "wanted anything for himself," he deemed it prudent to make a pre-
cipitate retreat. And the upshot of the matter was, that
a lawyer's letter came next day, and an action was commenced next week; and that Mr. Augustus Cooper, after
walking twice to the Serpentine for the purpose of drowning
himself, and coming twice back without doing it, made
a confidante of his mother, who compromised the matter
with twenty pounds from the till: which made twenty
pounds four shillings and sixpence paid to Signor Billsmethi,
exclusive of treats and pumps. And Mr. Augustus Cooper
went back and lived with his mother, and there he lives to
this day; and as he has lost his ambition for society, and
never goes into the world, he will never see this account of
himself, and will never be any the wiser.

CHAPTER X

SHABBY-GENTEEL PEOPLE

THERE are certain descriptions of people who, oddly enough, appear to appertain exclusively to the metropolis. You meet them, every day, in the streets of London, but no one ever encounters them elsewhere; they seem indigenous to the soil, and to belong as exclusively to London as its own smoke, or the dingy bricks and mortar. We could illustrate the remark by a variety of examples, but, in our present sketch, we will only advert to one class as a specimen—that class which is so aptly and expressively designated as "shabby-genteel."

Now, shabby people, God knows, may be found anywhere, and genteel people are not articles of greater scarcity out of London than in it; but this compound of the two—this shabby-gentility—is as purely local as the statue at Charing Cross, or the pump at Aldgate. It is worthy of remark, too, that only men are shabby-genteel; a woman is always either dirty and slovenly in the extreme, or neat and respectable, however poverty-stricken in appearance. A very poor man, "who has seen better days," as the phrase goes, is a strange compound of dirty-slovenliness and wretched attempts at faded smartness.

We will endeavour to explain our conception of the term which forms the title of this paper. If you meet a man, lounging up Drury Lane, or leaning with his back against a post in Long Acre, with his hands in the pockets of a pair of drab trousers plentifully besprinkled with grease-spots: the trousers made very full over the boots, and ornamented with two cords down the outside of each leg—wearing, also, what has been a brown coat with bright buttons, and a hat very much pinched up at the side, cocked over his right eye—don't pity him. He is not shabby-genteel. The "harmonic meetings" at some fourth-rate public-house, or the purlieus of a private theatre, are his chosen haunts; he entertains a rooted antipathy to any kind of work, and is on familiar terms with several pantomime men at the large houses. But, if you see hurrying along a by-street, keeping as close as he can to the area-railings, a man of about forty or fifty, clad in an old rusty suit of threadbare black cloth which shines with constant wear as if it had been bees-waxed—the trousers tightly strapped down, partly for the look of the thing and partly to keep his old shoes from slipping off at the heels,—if you observe, too, that his yellowish-white neckerchief is carefully pinned up, to conceal the tattered garment underneath, and that his hands are encased in the remains of an old pair of beaver gloves, you may set him down as a shabby-genteel man. A glance at that depressed face, and timorous air of conscious poverty, will make your heart ache—always supposing that you are neither a philosopher nor a political economist.

We were once haunted by a shabby-genteel man; he was bodily present to our senses all day, and he was in our mind's eye all night. The man of whom Sir Walter Scott speaks in his Demonology, did not suffer half the persecution from his imaginary gentleman-usher in black velvet, that we sustained from our friend in quondam black cloth. He first attracted our notice, by sitting opposite to us in the reading-room at the British Museum; and what made the man more remark-able was, that he always had before him a couple of shabby-genteel books—two old dog's-eared folios, in mouldy worm-eaten covers, which had once been smart. He was in his chair every morning, just as the clock struck ten; he was always the last to leave the room in the afternoon; and when he did, he quitted it with the air of a man who knew not where else to go for warmth and quiet. There he used to sit all day, as close to the table as possible, in order to conceal the lack of buttons on his coat: with his old hat carefully deposited at his feet, where he evidently flattered himself it escaped observation.

About two o'clock, you would see him munching a French roll or a penny loaf; not taking it boldly out of his pocket at once, like a man who knew he was only making a lunch; but breaking off little bits in his pocket, and eating them by stealth. He knew too well it was his dinner.

When we first saw this poor object, we thought it quite impossible that his attire could ever become worse. We even went so far as to speculate on the possibility of his shortly appearing in a decent second-hand suit. We knew nothing about the matter; he grew more and more shabby-genteel every day. The buttons dropped off his waistcoat one by one; then, he buttoned his coat; and when one side of the coat was reduced to the same condition as the waist-coat, he buttoned it over on the other side. He looked somewhat better at the beginning of the week than at the conclusion, because the neckerchief, though yellow, was not quite so dingy; and, in the midst of all this wretchedness, he never appeared without gloves and straps. He remained in this state for a week or two. At length, one of the buttons on the back of the coat fell off, and then the man himself disappeared, and we thought he was dead.

We were sitting at the same table about a week after his disappearance, and as our eyes rested on his vacant chair, we insensibly fell into a train of meditation on the subject of his retirement from public life. We were wondering whether he had hung himself, or thrown himself off a bridge —whether he really was dead or had only been arrested— when our conjectures were suddenly set at rest by the entry of the man himself. He had undergone some strange meta-morphosis, and walked up the centre of the room with an air which showed he was fully conscious of the improvement in his appearance. It was very odd. His clothes were a fine, deep, glossy black; and yet they looked like the same suit; nay, there were the very darns with which old acquain-tance had made us familiar. The hat, too—nobody could mistake the shape of that hat, with its high crown gradually increasing in circumference towards the top. Long service had imparted to it a reddish-brown tint; but now it was as black as the coat. The truth flashed suddenly upon us— they had been "revived." It is a deceitful liquid that black and blue reviver; we have watched its effects on many a shabby-genteel man. It betrays its victims into a tem-porary assumption of importance: possibly into the purchase of a new pair of gloves, or a cheap stock, or some other trifling article of dress. It elevates their spirits for a week, only to depress them, if possible, below their original level. It was so in this case; the transient dignity of the unhappy man decreased, in exact proportion as the "reviver" wore off. The knees of the unmentionables, and the elbows of the coat, and the seams generally, soon began to get alarmingly white. The hat was once more deposited under the table, and its owner crept into his seat as quietly as ever.

There was a week of incessant small rain and mist. At its expiration the "reviver" had entirely vanished, and the shabby-genteel man never afterwards attempted to effect any improvement in his outward appearance.

It would be difficult to name any particular part of town as the principal resort of shabby-genteel men. We have met a great many persons of this description in the neighbourhood of the Inns of Court. They may be met with in Holborn between eight and ten any morning; and whoever has the curiosity to enter the Insolvent Debtors' Court will observe, both among spectators and practitioners, a great variety of them. We never went on 'Change, by any chance, without seeing some shabby-genteel men, and we have often wondered what earthly business they can have there. They will sit there, for hours, leaning on great, dropsical, mildewed umbrellas, or eating Abernethy biscuits. Nobody speaks to them, nor they to any one. On consideration, we remember to have occasionally seen two shabby-genteel men conversing together on 'Change, but our experience assures us that this is an uncommon circumstance, occasioned by the offer of a pinch of snuff, or some such civility.

It would be a task of equal difficulty, either to assign any particular spot for the residence of these beings, or to endeavour to enumerate their general occupations. We were never engaged in business with more than one shabby-genteel man; and he was a drunken engraver, and lived in a damp back-parlour in a new row of houses at Camden Town, half street, half brick-field, somewhere near the canal. A shabby-genteel man may have no occupation, or he may be a corn agent, or a coal agent, or a wine merchant, or a collector of debts, or a broker's assistant, or a broken-down attorney. He may be a clerk of the lowest description, or a contributor to the press of the same grade. Whether our readers have noticed these men, in their walks, as often as we have, we know not; this we know—that the miserably poor man (no matter whether he owes his distresses to his own conduct, or that of others) who feels his poverty and vainly strives to conceal it, is one of the most pitiable objects in human nature. Such objects, with few exceptions, are shabby-genteel people.

CHAPTER XI

MAKING A NIGHT OF IT

DAMON and Pythias were undoubtedly very good fellows in their way: the former for his extreme readiness to put in special bail for a friend: and the latter for a certain trump-like punctuality in turning up just in the very nick of time, scarcely less remarkable. Many points in their character have, however, grown obsolete. Damons are rather hard to find, in these days of imprisonment for debt (except the sham ones, and they cost half-a-crown); and, as to the Pythiases, the few that have existed in these degenerate times, have had an unfortunate knack of making themselves scarce, at the very moment when their appearance would have been strictly classical. If the actions of these heroes, however, can find no parallel in modern times. their friendship can. We have Damon and Pythias on the one hand. We have Potter and Smithers on the other; and, lest the two last-mentioned names should never have reached the ears of our unenlightened readers, we can do no better than make them acquainted with the owners thereof.

Mr. Thomas Potter, then, was a clerk in the city, and Mr. Robert Smithers was a ditto in the same; their incomes were limited, but their friendship was unbounded. They lived in the same street, walked into town every morning at the same hour, dined at the same slap-bang every day, and revelled in each other's company every night. They were knit together by the closest ties of intimacy and friendship, or, as Mr. Thomas Potter touchingly observed, they were "thick-and-thin pals, and nothing but it." There was a spice of romance in Mr. Smithers's disposition, a ray of poetry, a gleam of misery, a sort of consciousness of he didn't exactly know what, coming across him he didn't precisely know why—which stood out in fine relief against the off-hand, dashing, amateur-pickpocket-sort-of-manner, which distinguished Mr. Potter in an eminent degree.

The peculiarity of their respective dispositions extended itself to their individual costume. Mr. Smithers generally appeared in public in a surtout and shoes, with a narrow black neckerchief and a brown hat, very much turned up at the sides—peculiarities which Mr. Potter wholly eschewed, for it was his ambition to do something in the celebrated "kiddy" or stage-coach way, and he had even gone so far as to invest capital in the purchase of a rough blue coat with wooden buttons, made upon the fireman's principle, in which, with the addition of a low-crowned, flower-pot-saucer-shaped hat, he had created no inconsiderable sensation at the Albion in Little Russell Street, and divers other places of public and fashionable resort.

Mr. Potter and Mr. Smithers had mutually agreed that, on the receipt of their quarter's salary, they would jointly and in company "spend the evening"—an evident misnomer—the spending applying, as everybody knows, not to the evening itself but to all the money the individual may chance to be possessed of, on the occasion to which reference is made ; and they had likewise agreed that, on the evening aforesaid, they would "make a night of it"—an expressive term, implying the borrowing of several hours from to-morrow morning, adding them to the night before, and manufacturing a com-pound night of the whole.

The quarter-day arrived at last—we say at last, because quarter-days are as eccentric as comets: moving wonderfully quick when you have a good deal to pay, and marvellously slow when you have a little to receive. Mr. Thomas Potter and Mr. Robert Smithers met by appointment to begin the evening with a dinner ; and a nice, snug, comfortable dinner they had, consisting of a little procession of four chops and four kidneys, following each other, supported on either side by a pot of the real draught stout, and attended by divers cushions of bread and wedges of cheese.

When the cloth was removed, Mr. Thomas Potter ordered the waiter to bring in two goes of his best Scotch whiskey, with warm water and sugar, and a couple of his "very mildest" Havannahs, which the waiter did. Mr. Thomas Potter mixed his grog, and lighted his cigar ; Mr. Robert Smithers did the same ; and then Mr. Thomas Potter jocularly proposed as the first toast, "the abolition of all offices whatever" (not sinecures, but counting-houses), which was immediately drunk by Mr. Robert Smithers, with

enthusiastic applause. So they went on, talking politics,
puffing cigars, and sipping whiskey-and-water, until the
"goes"—most appropriately so called—were both gone, which
Mr. Robert Smithers perceiving, immediately ordered in two
more goes of the best Scotch whiskey, and two more of the
very mildest Havannahs ; and the goes kept coming in, and
the mild Havannahs kept going out, until, what with the
drinking, and lighting, and puffing, and the stale ashes on
the table, and the tallow-grease on the cigars, Mr. Robert
Smithers began to doubt the mildness of the Havannahs,
and to feel very much as if he had been sitting in a hackney-
coach with his back to the horses.

As to Mr. Thomas Potter, he *would* keep laughing out
loud, and volunteering inarticulate declarations that he was
"all right ; " in proof of which he feebly bespoke the evening
paper after the next gentleman, but finding it a matter of
some difficulty to discover any news in its columns, or to
ascertain distinctly whether it had any columns at all, walked
slowly out to look for the moon, and, after coming back
quite pale with looking up at the sky so long, and attempting
to express mirth at Mr. Robert Smithers having fallen asleep,
by various galvanic chuckles, laid his head on his arm, and
went to sleep also.   When he awoke again, Mr. Robert
Smithers awoke too, and they both very gravely agreed that
it was extremely unwise to eat so many pickled walnuts with
the chops, as it was a notorious fact that they always made
people queer and sleepy ; indeed, if it had not been for the
whiskey and cigars, there was no knowing what harm they
mightn't have done 'em. So they took some coffee, and after
paying the bill,—twelve and twopence the dinner, and the
odd tenpence for the waiter—thirteen shillings in all—
started out on their expedition to manufacture a night.

It was just half-past eight, so they thought they couldn't
do better than go at half-price to the slips at the City
Theatre, which they did accordingly. Mr. Robert Smithers,
who had become extremely poetical after the settlement of the
bill, enlivening the walk by informing Mr. Thomas Potter in
confidence that he felt an inward presentiment of approaching
dissolution, and subsequently embellishing the theatre by
falling asleep, with his head and both arms gracefully drooping over the front of the boxes.

Such was the quiet demeanour of the unassuming Smithers,
and such were the happy effects of Scotch whiskey and

Havannahs on that interesting person! But Mr. Thomas Potter, whose great aim it was to be considered as a "knowing card," a "fast-goer," and so forth, conducted himself in a very different manner, and commenced going very fast indeed —rather too fast at last, for the patience of the audience to keep pace with him. On his first entry, he contented himself by earnestly calling upon the gentlemen. in the gallery to "flare up," accompanying the demand with another request, expressive of his wish that they would instantaneously "form a union," both which requisitions were responded to, in the manner most in vogue on such occasions.

"Give that dog a bone!" cried one gentleman in his shirt-sleeves.

"Where have you been a-having half a pint of intermediate beer?" cried a second. "Tailor!" screamed a third. "Barber's clerk!" shouted a fourth. "Throw him o—ver!" roared a fifth; while numerous voices concurred in desiring Mr. Thomas Potter to "go home to his mother!" All these taunts Mr. Thomas Potter received with supreme contempt, cocking the low-crowned hat a little more on one side, whenever any reference was made to his personal appearance, and, standing up with his arms a-kimbo, expressing defiance melodramatically.

The overture—to which these various sounds had been an *ad libitum* accompaniment—concluded, the second piece began, and Mr. Thomas Potter, emboldened by impunity, proceeded to behave in a most unprecedented and outrageous manner. First of all, he imitated the shake of the principal female singer; then, groaned at the blue fire; then, affected to be frightened into convulsions of terror at the appearance of the ghost; and, lastly, not only made a running commentary, in an audible voice, upon the dialogue on the stage, but actually awoke Mr. Robert Smithers, who, hearing his companion making a noise, and having a very indistinct notion where he was, or what was required of him, immediately, by way of imitating a good example, set up the most unearthly, unremitting, and appalling howling that ever audience heard. It was too much. "Turn them out!" was the general cry. A noise, as of shuffling of feet, and men being knocked up with violence against wainscoting, was heard: a hurried dialogue of "Come out!"—"I won't!"— "You shall!"—"I shan't!"—"Give me your card, Sir!" —"You're a scoundrel, Sir!" and so forth, succeeded.

A round of applause betokened the approbation of the audience, and Mr. Robert Smithers and Mr. Thomas Potter found themselves shot with astonishing swiftness into the road, without having had the trouble of once putting foot to ground during the whole progress of their rapid descent.

Mr. Robert Smithers, being constitutionally one of the slow-goers, and having had quite enough of fast-going, in the course of his recent expulsion, to last until the quarter-day then next ensuing at the very least, had no sooner emerged with his companion from the precincts of Milton Street, than he proceeded to indulge in circuitous references to the beauties of sleep, mingled with distant allusions to the propriety of returning to Islington, and testing the influence of their patent Bramahs over the street-door locks to which they respectively belonged. Mr. Thomas Potter, however, was valorous and peremptory. They had come out to make a night of it: and a night must be made. So Mr. Robert Smithers, who was three parts dull, and the other dismal, despairingly assented; and they went into a wine-vaults, to get materials for assisting them in making a night; where they found a good many young ladies, and various old gentlemen, and a plentiful sprinkling of hackney-coachmen and cab-drivers, all drinking and talking together; and Mr. Thomas Potter and Mr. Robert Smithers drank small glasses of brandy, and large glasses of soda, until they began to have a very confused idea, either of things in general, or of anything in particular; and when they had done treating themselves they began to treat everybody else; and the rest of the entertainment was a confused mixture of heads and heels, black eyes and blue uniforms, mud and gas-lights, thick doors, and stone paving.

Then, as standard novelists expressively inform us—"all was a blank!" and in the morning the blank was filled up with the words "STATION-HOUSE," and the station-house was filled up with Mr. Thomas Potter, Mr. Robert Smithers, and the major part of their wine-vault companions of the preceding night, with a comparatively small portion of clothing of any kind. And it was disclosed at the Police Office, to the indignation of the Bench, and the astonishment of the spectators, how one Robert Smithers, aided and abetted by one Thomas Potter, had knocked down and beaten, in divers streets, at different times, five men, four boys, and three women; how the said Thomas Potter had feloniously obtained possession of five door-knockers, two bell-handles, and a bonnet; how Robert Smithers, his friend, had sworn at least forty pounds' worth of oaths, at the rate of five shillings apiece; terrified whole streets full of her Majesty's subjects with awful shrieks and alarms of fire; destroyed the uniforms of five policemen; and committed various other atrocities, too numerous to recapitulate. And the magistrate, after an appropriate reprimand, fined Mr. Thomas Potter and Mr. Robert Smithers five shillings each, for being what the law vulgarly terms drunk; and thirty-four pounds for seventeen assaults at forty shillings a-head, with liberty to speak to the prosecutors.

The prosecutors *were* spoken to, and Messrs. Potter and Smithers lived on credit, for a quarter, as best they might; and, although the prosecutors expressed their readiness to be assaulted twice a week, on the same terms, they have never since been detected in "making a night of it."

CHAPTER XII

THE PRISONERS' VAN

WE were passing the corner of Bow Street, on our return from a lounging excursion the other afternoon, when a crowd, assembled round the door of the Police Office, attracted our attention. We turned up the street accordingly. There were thirty or forty people, standing on the pavement and half across the road ; and a few stragglers were patiently stationed on the opposite side of the way—all evidently waiting in expectation of some arrival. We waited too, a few minutes, but nothing occurred ; so we turned round to an unshorn, sallow-looking cobbler, who was standing next us with his hands under the bib of his apron, and put the usual question of "What's the matter?" The cobbler eyed us from head to foot, with superlative contempt, and laconically replied "Nuffin."

Now, we were perfectly aware that if two men stop in the street to look at any given object, or even to gaze in the air, two hundred men will be assembled in no time ; but as we knew very well that no crowd of people could by possibility remain in a street for five minutes without getting up a little amusement among themselves, unless they had some absorbing object in view, the natural inquiry next in order was, "What are all these people waiting here for?"—"Her Majesty's carriage," replied the cobbler. This was still more extraordinary. We could not imagine what earthly business her Majesty's carriage could have at the Public Office, Bow Street. We were beginning to ruminate on the possible causes of such an uncommon appearance, when a general exclamation from all the boys in the crowd of "Here's the wan!" caused us to raise our heads, and look up the street.

The covered vehicle, in which prisoners are conveyed from the police offices to the different prisons, was coming along at full speed. It then occurred to us, for the first time, that her Majesty's carriage was merely another name for the prisoners' van, conferred upon it, not only by reason of the superior gentility of the term, but because the aforesaid van is maintained at her Majesty's expense: having been originally started for the exclusive accommodation of ladies and gentlemen under the necessity of visiting the various houses of call known by the general denomination of "Her Majesty's Gaols."

The van drew up at the office-door, and the people thronged round the steps, just leaving a little alley for the prisoners to pass through. Our friend the cobbler, and the other stragglers, crossed over, and we followed their example. The driver, and another man who had been seated by his side in front of the vehicle, dismounted, and were admitted into the office. The office-door was closed after them, and the crowd were on the tiptoe of expectation.

After a few minutes' delay, the door again opened, and the two first prisoners appeared. They were a couple of girls, of whom the elder could not be more than sixteen, and the younger of whom had certainly not attained her fourteenth year. That they were sisters was evident from the resemblance which still subsisted between them, though two additional years of depravity had fixed their brand upon the elder girl's features, as legibly as if a red-hot iron had seared them. They were both gaudily dressed, the younger one especially; and, although there was a strong similarity between them in both respects, which was rendered the more obvious by their being handcuffed together, it is impossible to conceive a greater contrast than the demeanour of the two presented. The younger girl was weeping bitterly—not for display, or in the hope of producing effect, but for very shame; her face was buried in her handkerchief: and her whole manner was but too expressive of bitter and unavailing sorrow.

"How long are you for, Emily?" screamed a red-faced woman in the crowd. "Six weeks and labour," replied the elder girl with a flaunting laugh; "and that's better than the stone jug anyhow; the mill's a deal better than the Sessions, and here's Bella a-going too for the first time. Hold up your head, you chicken," she continued, boisterously tearing the other girl's handkerchief away; "Hold up your head, and show 'em your face. I an't jealous, but I'm blessed if I an't game!"—"That's right, old gal," exclaimed a man in a paper cap, who, in common with the greater part of the crowd, had been inexpressibly delighted with this little incident.—"Right!" replied the girl; "ah, to be sure; what's the odds, eh?"—"Come! In with you," interrupted the driver. "Don't you be in a hurry, coachman," replied the girl, "and recollect I want to be set down in Cold Bath Fields—large house with a high garden-wall in front; you can't mistake it. Hallo! Bella, where are you going to—you'll pull my precious arm off!" This was addressed to the younger girl, who, in her anxiety to hide herself in the caravan, had ascended the steps first, and forgotten the strain upon the handcuff. "Come down, and let's show you the way." And after jerking the miserable girl down with a force which made her stagger on the pavement, she got into the vehicle, and was followed by her wretched companion.

These two girls had been thrown upon London streets, their vices and debauchery, by a sordid and rapacious mother. What the younger girl was then, the elder had been once; and what the elder then was, the younger must soon become. A melancholy prospect, but how surely to be realised; a tragic drama, but how often acted! Turn to the prisons and police offices of London—nay, look into the very streets themselves. These things pass before our eyes, day after day, and hour after hour—they have become such matters of course, that they are utterly disregarded. The progress of these girls in crime will be as rapid as the flight of a pestilence, resembling it too in its baneful influence and wide-spreading infection. Step by step, how many wretched females, within the sphere of every man's observation, have become involved in a career of vice, frightful to contemplate; hopeless at its commencement, loathsome and repulsive in its course; friendless, forlorn, and unpitied, at its miserable conclusion!

There were other prisoners—boys of ten, as hardened in vice as men of fifty—a houseless vagrant, going joyfully to prison as a place of food and shelter, handcuffed to a man whose prospects were ruined, character lost, and family rendered destitute, by his first offence. Our curiosity, however, was satisfied. The first group had left an impression on our mind we would gladly have avoided, and would willingly have effaced.

The crowd dispersed; the vehicle rolled away with its load of guilt and misfortune; and we saw no more of the Prisoners' Van.

TALES

CHAPTER I

THE BOARDING-HOUSE. CHAPTER I

MRS. TIBBS was, beyond all dispute, the most tidy, fidgety, thrifty little personage that ever inhaled the smoke of London; and the house of Mrs. Tibbs was, decidedly, the neatest in all Great Coram Street. The area and the area-steps, and the street-door and the street-door steps, and the brass handle, and the door-plate, and the knocker, and the fan-light, were all as clean and bright, as indefatigable white-washing, and hearth-stoning, and scrubbing and rubbing, could make them. The wonder was, that the brass door-plate, with the interesting inscription "MRS. TIBBS," had never caught fire from constant friction, so perseveringly was it polished. There were meat-safe-looking blinds in the parlour-windows, blue and gold curtains in the drawing-room, and spring-roller blinds, as Mrs. Tibbs was wont in the pride of her heart to boast, "all the way up." The bell-lamp in the passage looked as clear as a soap-bubble; you could see yourself in all the tables, and French-polish your-self on any one of the chairs. The banisters were bees-waxed; and the very stair-wires made your eyes wink, they were so glittering.

Mrs. Tibbs was somewhat short of stature, and Mr. Tibbs was by no means a large man. He had, moreover, very short legs, but, by way of indemnification, his face was peculiarly long. He was to his wife what the o is in 90—he was of some importance *with* her—he was nothing without her. Mrs. Tibbs was always talking. Mr. Tibbs rarely spoke; but, if it were at any time possible to put in a word, when he should have said nothing at all, he had that talent. Mrs. Tibbs detested long stories, and Mr. Tibbs had one, the conclusion of which had never been heard by his most intimate friends. It always began, "I recollect when I was in the volunteer corps, in eighteen hundred and six,"—but, as he spoke very slowly and softly, and his better half very quickly and loudly, he rarely got beyond the introductory sentence. He was a melancholy specimen of the story-teller. He was the wandering Jew of Joe Millerism.

Mr. Tibbs enjoyed a small independence from the pension-list—about 43*l.* 15*s.* 10*d.* a year. His father, mother, and five interesting scions from the same stock, drew a like sum from the revenue of a grateful country, though for what particular service was never known. But, as this said independence was not quite sufficient to furnish two people with *all* the luxuries of this life, it had occurred to the busy little spouse of Tibbs, that the best thing she could do with a legacy of 700*l.*, would be to take and furnish a tolerable house—somewhere in that partially-explored tract of country which lies between the British Museum, and a remote village called Somers Town—for the reception of boarders. Great Coram Street was the spot pitched upon. The house had been furnished accordingly; two female servants and a boy engaged; and an advertisement inserted in the morning papers, informing the public that "Six individuals would meet with all the comforts of a cheerful musical home in a select private family, residing within ten minutes' walk of"—everywhere. Answers out of number were received, with all sorts of initials; all the letters of the alphabet seemed to be seized with a sudden wish to go out boarding and lodging; voluminous was the correspondence between Mrs. Tibbs and the applicants; and most profound was the secrecy observed. "E." didn't like this; "I." couldn't think of putting up with that; "I. O. U." didn't think the terms would suit him; and "G. R." had never slept in a French bed. The result, however, was that three gentlemen became inmates of Mrs. Tibbs's house, on terms which were "agreeable to all parties." In went the advertisement again, and a lady with her two daughters proposed to increase—not their families, but Mrs. Tibbs's.

"Charming woman, that Mrs. Maplesone!" said Mrs. Tibbs, as she and her spouse were sitting by the fire after breakfast; the gentlemen having gone out on their several avocations. "Charming woman, indeed!" repeated little Mrs. Tibbs, more by way of soliloquy than anything else,. for she never thought of consulting her husband. "And the two daughters are delightful. We must have some fish to-day; they'll join us at dinner for the first time."

Mr. Tibbs placed the poker at right angles with the fire shovel, and essayed to speak, but recollected he had nothing to say.

"The young ladies," continued Mrs. T., "have kindly volunteered to bring their own piano."

Tibbs thought of the volunteer story, but did not venture it. A bright thought struck him—

"It's very likely——" said he.

"Pray don't lean your head against the paper," interrupted Mrs. Tibbs; "and don't put your feet on the steel fender; that's worse."

Tibbs took his head from the paper, and his feet from the fonder, and proceeded. "It's very likely one of the young ladies may set her cap at young Mr. Simpson, and you know a marriage—— "

"A what!" shrieked Mrs. Tibbs. Tibbs modestly repeated his former suggestion.

"I beg you won't mention such a thing," said Mrs. T. "A marriage, indeed!—to rob me of my boarders—no, not for the world."

Tibbs thought in his own mind that the event was by no means unlikely, but, as he never argued with his wife, he put a stop to the dialogue, by observing it was "time to go to business." He always went out at ten o'clock in the morning, and returned at five in the afternoon, with an exceedingly dirty face, and smelling mouldy. Nobody knew what he was, or where he went; but Mrs. Tibbs used to say with an air of great importance, that he was engaged in the City.

The Miss Maplesones and their accomplished parent arrived in the course of the afternoon in a hackney-coach, and accompanied by a most astonishing number of packages. Trunks, bonnet-boxes, muff-boxes and parasols, guitar-cases, and parcels of all imaginable shapes, done up in brown paper, and fastened with pins, filled the passage. Then, there was such a running up and down with the luggage, such scampering for warm water for the ladies to wash in, and such a bustle, and confusion, and heating of servants, and curling-irons, as had never been known in Great Coram Street before. Little Mrs. Tibbs was quite in her element, bustling about, talking incessantly, and distributing towels and soap, like a head nurse in a hospital. The house was not restored to its usual state of quiet repose, until the ladies were safely shut up in their respective bedrooms, engaged in the important occupation of dressing for dinner.

"Are these gals 'andsome?" inquired Mr. Simpson of Mr. Septimus Hicks, another of the boarders, as they were amusing themselves in the drawing-room, before dinner, by lolling on sofas, and contemplating their pumps.

"Don't know," replied Mr. Septimus Hicks, who was a tallish, white-faced young man, with spectacles, and a black ribbon round his neck instead of a neckerchief—a most interesting person; a poetical walker of the hospitals, and a "very talented young man." He was fond of "lugging" into conversation all sorts of quotations from Don Juan, without fettering himself by the propriety of their application; in which particular he was remarkably independent. The other, Mr. Simpson, was one of those young men, who are in society what walking gentlemen are on the stage, only infinitely worse skilled in his vocation than the most indifferent artist. He was as empty-headed as the great bell of St. Paul's; always dressed according to the caricatures published in the monthly fashions; and spelt Character with a K.

"I saw a devilish number of parcels in the passage when I came home," simpered Mr. Simpson.

"Materials for the toilet, no doubt," rejoined the Don Juan reader.

> ———— "Much linen, lace, and several pair
> Of stockings, slippers, brushes, combs, complete;
> With other articles of ladies fair,
> To keep them beautiful, or leave them neat."

"Is that from Milton?" inquired Mr. Simpson.

"No—from Byron," returned Mr. Hicks, with a look of contempt. He was quite sure of his author, because he had never read any other. "Hush! Here come the gals," and they both commenced talking in a very loud key.

"Mrs. Maplesone and the Miss Maplesones, Mr. Hicks. Mr. Hicks—Mrs. Maplesone and the Miss Maplesones," said Mrs. Tibbs, with a very red face, for she had been superintending the cooking operations below stairs, and looked like a wax doll on a sunny day. "Mr. Simpson, I beg your pardon—Mr. Simpson—Mrs. Maplesone and the Miss Maplesones"—and *vice versâ*. The gentlemen immediately began to slide about with much politeness, and to look as if they wished their arms had been legs, so little did they know what to do with them. The ladies smiled, curtseyed, and glided into chairs, and dived for dropped pocket-handkerchiefs : the gentlemen leant against two of the curtain-pegs ; Mrs. Tibbs went through an admirable bit of serious pantomime with a servant who had come up to ask some question about the fish-sauce ; and then the two young ladies looked at each other ; and everybody else appeared to discover something very attractive in the pattern of the fender.

"Julia, my love," said Mrs. Maplesone to her youngest daughter, in a tone loud enough for the remainder of the company to hear—"Julia."

"Yes, Ma."

"Don't stoop."—This was said for the purpose of directing general attention to Miss Julia's figure, which was undeniable. Everybody looked at her, accordingly, and there was another pause.

"We had the most uncivil hackney-coachman to-day, you can imagine," said Mrs. Maplesone to Mrs. Tibbs, in a confidential tone.

"Dear me !" replied the hostess, with an air of great commiseration. She couldn't say more, for the servant again appeared at the door, and commenced telegraphing most earnestly to her "Missis."

"I think hackney-coachmen generally *are* uncivil," said Mr. Hicks, in his most insinuating tone.

"Positively I think they are," replied Mrs. Maplesone, as if the idea had never struck her before.

"And cabmen, too," said Mr. Simpson. This remark was a failure, for no one intimated, by word or sign, the slightest knowledge of the manners and customs of cabmen.

"Robinson, what *do* you want ?" said Mrs. Tibbs to the servant, who, by way of making her presence known to her mistress, had been giving sundry hems and sniffs outside the door during the preceding five minutes.

"Please, ma'am, master wants his clean things," replied the servant, taken off her guard. The two young men turned their faces to the window, and "went off" like a couple of bottles of ginger-beer ; the ladies put their handkerchiefs to their mouths ; and little Mrs. Tibbs bustled out of the room to give Tibbs his clean linen,—and the servant warning.

M

Mr. Calton, the remaining boarder, shortly afterwards made his appearance, and proved a surprising promoter of the conversation. Mr. Calton was a superannuated beau— an old boy. He used to say of himself that although his features were not regularly handsome, they were striking. They certainly were. It was impossible to look at his face without being reminded of a chubby street-door knocker, half-lion half-monkey; and the comparison might be extended to his whole character and conversation. He had stood still, while everything else had been moving. He never originated a conversation, or started an idea; but if any commonplace topic were broached, or, to pursue the comparison, if anybody *lifted him up*, he would hammer away with surprising rapidity. He had the tic-douloureux occasionally, and then he might be said to be muffled, because he did not make quite as much noise as at other times, when he would go on prosing, rat-tat-tat the same thing over and over again. He had never been married; but he was still on the look-out for a wife with money. He had a life interest worth about 300*l.* a year—he was exceedingly vain, and inordinately selfish. He had acquired the reputation of being the very pink of politeness, and he walked round the park, and up Regent Street, every day.

This respectable personage had made up his mind to render himself exceedingly agreeable to Mrs. Maplesone— indeed, the desire of being as amiable as possible extended itself to the whole party; Mrs. Tibbs having considered it an admirable little bit of management to represent to the gentlemen that she had *some* reason to believe the ladies were fortunes, and to hint to the ladies, that all the gentlemen were "eligible." A little flirtation, she thought, might keep her house full, without leading to any other result.

Mrs. Maplesone was an enterprising widow of about fifty: shrewd, scheming, and good-looking. She was amiably anxious on behalf of her daughters; in proof whereof she used to remark, that she would have no objection to marry again, if it would benefit her dear girls—she could have no other motive. The "dear girls" themselves were not at all insensible to the merits of "a good establishment." One of them was twenty-five; the other, three years younger. They had been at different watering-places, for four seasons; they had gambled at libraries, read books in balconies, sold at fancy fairs, danced at assemblies, talked sentiment—in short, they had done all that industrious girls could do—but, as yet, to no purpose.

"What a magnificent dresser Mr. Simpson is!" whispered Matilda Maplesone to her sister Julia.

"Splendid!" returned the youngest. The magnificent individual alluded to wore a maroon-coloured dress-coat, with a velvet collar and cuffs of the same tint—very like that which usually invests the form of the distinguished unknown who condescends to play the "swell" in the pantomime at "Richardson's Show."

"What whiskers!" said Miss Julia.

"Charming!" responded her sister; "and what hair!" His hair was like a wig, and distinguished by that insinuating wave which graces the shining locks of those *chef-d'œuvres* of art surmounting the waxen images in Bartellot's window in Regent Street; his whiskers meeting beneath his chin, seemed strings wherewith to tie it on, ere science had rendered them unnecessary by her patent invisible springs.

"Dinner's on the table, ma'am, if you please," said the boy, who now appeared for the first time, in a revived black coat of his master's.

"Oh! Mr. Calton, will you lead Mrs. Maplesone?—Thank you." Mr. Simpson offered his arm to Miss Julia; Mr. Septimus Hicks escorted the lovely Matilda; and the procession proceeded to the dining-room. Mr. Tibbs was introduced, and Mr. Tibbs bobbed up and down to the three ladies like a figure in a Dutch clock, with a powerful spring in the middle of his body, and then dived rapidly into his seat at the bottom of the table, delighted to screen himself behind a soup-tureen, which he could just see over, and that was all. The boarders were seated, a lady and gentleman alternately, like the layers of bread and meat in a plate of sandwiches; and then Mrs. Tibbs directed James to take off the covers. Salmon, lobster-sauce, giblet-soup, and the usual accompaniments were *dis*-covered: potatoes like petrifactions, and bits of toasted bread, the shape and size of blank dice.

"Soup for Mrs. Maplesone, my dear," said the bustling Mrs. Tibbs. She always called her husband "my dear" before company. Tibbs, who had been eating his bread, and calculating how long it would be before he should get any fish, helped the soup in a hurry, made a small island on the table-cloth, and put his glass upon it to hide it from his wife.

"Miss Julia, shall I assist you to some fish?"

"If you please—very little—oh! plenty, thank you" (a bit about the size of a walnut put upon the plate).

"Julia is a *very* little eater," said Mrs. Maplesone to Mr. Calton.

The knocker gave a single rap. He was busy eating the fish with his eyes: so he only ejaculated, "Ah!"

"My dear," said Mrs. Tibbs to her spouse after every one else had been helped, "what do *you* take?" The inquiry was accompanied with a look intimating that he mustn't say fish, because there was not much left. Tibbs thought the frown referred to the island on the table-cloth; he therefore coolly replied, "Why—I'll take a little—fish, I think."

"Did you say fish, my dear?" (another frown).

"Yes, dear," replied the villain, with an expression of acute hunger depicted in his countenance. The tears almost started to Mrs. Tibbs's eyes, as she helped her "wretch of a husband," as she inwardly called him, to the last eatable bit of salmon on the dish.

"James, take this to your master, and take away your master's knife." This was deliberate revenge, as Tibbs never could eat fish without one. He was, however, constrained to chase small particles of salmon round and round his plate with a piece of bread and a fork, the number of successful attempts being about one in seventeen.

"Take away, James," said Mrs. Tibbs, as Tibbs swallowed the fourth mouthful—and away went the plates like lightning.

"I'll take a bit of bread, James," said the poor "master of the house," more hungry than ever.

"Never mind your master now, James," said Mrs. Tibbs, "see about the meat." This was conveyed in the tone in which ladies usually give admonitions to servants in company, that is to say, a low one; but which, like a stage whisper, from its peculiar emphasis, is most distinctly heard by every-body present.

A pause ensued, before the table was replenished—a sort of parenthesis in which Mr. Simpson, Mr. Calton, and Mr. Hicks, produced respectively a bottle of sauterne, bucellas, and sherry, and took wine with everybody—except Tibbs. No one ever thought of him.

Between the fish and an intimated sirloin, there was a prolonged interval.

Here was an opportunity for Mr. Hicks. He could not resist the singularly appropriate quotation—

> "But beef is rare within these oxless isles ;
> Goats' flesh there is, no doubt, and kid, and mutton,
> And when a holiday upon them smiles,
> A joint upon their barbarous spits they put on."

"Very ungentlemanly behaviour," thought little Mrs. Tibbs, "to talk in that way."

"Ah," said Mr. Calton, filling his glass. "Tom Moore is my poet."

"And mine," said Mrs. Maplesone.

"And mine," said Miss Julia.

"And mine," added Mr. Simpson.

"Look at his compositions," resumed the knocker.

"To be sure," said Simpson, with confidence

"Look at Don Juan," replied Mr. Septimus Hicks.

"Julia's letter," suggested Miss Matilda.

"Can anything be grander than the Fire Worshippers?" inquired Miss Julia.

"To be sure," said Simpson.

"Or Paradise and the Peri," said the old beau.

"Yes ; or Paradise and the Peer," repeated Simpson, who thought he was getting through it capitally.

"It's all very well," replied Mr. Septimus Hicks, who, as we have before hinted, never had read anything but Don Juan. "Where will you find anything finer than the description of the siege, at the commencement of the seventh canto?"

"Talking of a siege," said Tibbs, with a mouthful of bread—"when I was in the volunteer corps, in eighteen hundred and six, our commanding officer was Sir Charles Rampart ; and one day, when we were exercising on the ground on which the London University now stands, he says, says he, Tibbs (calling me from the ranks), Tibbs—— "

"Tell your master, James," interrupted Mrs. Tibbs, in an awfully distinct tone, "tell your master if he *won't* carve those fowls, to send them to me." The discomfited volunteer instantly set to work, and carved the fowls almost as expeditiously as his wife operated on the haunch of mutton. Whether he ever finished the story is not known ; but, if he did, nobody heard it.

As the ice was now broken, and the new inmates more at home, every member of the company felt more at ease. Tibbs himself most certainly did, because he went to sleep immediately after dinner. Mr. Hicks and the ladies discoursed most eloquently about poetry, and the theatres, and Lord Chesterfield's Letters; and Mr. Calton followed up what everybody said, with continuous double knocks. Mrs. Tibbs highly approved of every observation that fell from Mrs. Maplesone; and as Mr. Simpson sat with a smile upon his face and said "Yes," or "Certainly," at intervals of about four minutes each, he received full credit for understanding what was going forward. The gentlemen rejoined the ladies in the drawing-room very shortly after they had left the dining-parlour. Mrs. Maplesone and Mr. Calton played cribbage, and the "young people" amused themselves with music and conversation. The Miss Maplesones sang the most fascinating duets, and accompanied themselves on guitars, ornamented with bits of ethereal blue ribbon. Mr. Simpson put on a pink waistcoat, and said he was in raptures; and Mr. Hicks felt in the seventh heaven of poetry or the seventh canto of Don Juan—it was the same thing to him. Mrs. Tibbs was quite charmed with the new-comers; and Mr. Tibbs spent the evening in his usual way—he went to sleep, and woke up, and went to sleep again, and woke at supper-time.

*   *   *   *   *   *

We are not about to adopt the licence of novel-writers, and to let "years roll on;" but we will take the liberty of requesting the reader to suppose that six months have elapsed, since the dinner we have described, and that Mrs. Tibbs's boarders have, during that period, sang, and danced, and gone to theatres and exhibitions, together, as ladies and gentlemen, wherever they board, often do. And we will beg them, the period we have mentioned having elapsed, to imagine farther that Mr. Septimus Hicks received, in his own bedroom (a front attic), at an early hour one morning, a note from Mr. Calton, requesting the favour of seeing him, as soon as convenient to himself, in his (Calton's) dressing-room on the second-floor back.

"Tell Mr. Calton I'll come down directly," said Mr. Septimus to the boy. "Stop—is Mr. Calton unwell?" inquired this excited walker of hospitals, as he put on a bed-furniture-looking dressing-gown.

"Not as I knows on, sir," replied the boy. "Please, sir, he looked rather rum, as it might be."

"Ah, that's no proof of his being ill," returned Hicks, unconsciously. "Very well: I'll be down directly." Downstairs ran the boy with the message, and down went the excited Hicks himself, almost as soon as the message was delivered. "Tap, tap." "Come in."—Door opens, and discovers Mr. Calton sitting in an easy chair. Mutual shakes of the hand exchanged, and Mr. Septimus Hicks motioned to a seat. A short pause. Mr. Hicks coughed, and Mr. Calton took a pinch of snuff. It was one of those interviews where neither party knows what to say. Mr. Septimus Hicks broke silence.

"I received a note— " he said, very tremulously, in a voice like a Punch with a cold.

"Yes," returned the other, "you did."

"Exactly."

"Yes."

Now, although this dialogue must have been satisfactory, both gentlemen felt there was something more important to be said; therefore they did as most men in such a situation would have done—they looked at the table with a determined aspect. The conversation had been opened, however, and Mr. Calton had made up his mind to continue it with a regular double knock. He always spoke very pompously.

"Hicks," said he, "I have sent for you, in consequence of certain arrangements which are pending in this house, connected with a marriage."

"With a marriage!" gasped Hicks, compared with whose expression of countenance, Hamlet's, when he sees his father's ghost, is pleasing and composed.

"With a marriage," returned the knocker. "I have sent for you to prove the great confidence I can repose in you."

"And will you betray me?" eagerly inquired Hicks, who in his alarm had even forgotten to quote.

"*I* betray *you!* Won't *you* betray *me?*"

"Never: no one shall know, to my dying day, that you had a hand in the business," responded the agitated Hicks, with an inflamed countenance, and his hair standing on end as if he were on the stool of an electrifying machine in full operation.

"People must know that, some time or other—within a

year, I imagine," said Mr. Calton, with an air of great self complacency. "We *may* have a family."

"*We!*—That won't affect you, surely?"

"The devil it won't!"

"No! how can it?" said the bewildered Hicks. Calton was too much inwrapped in the contemplation of his happiness to see the equivoque between Hicks and himself; and threw himself back in his chair. "Oh, Matilda!" sighed the antique beau, in a lack-a-daisical voice, and applying his right hand a little to the left of the fourth button of his waistcoat, counting from the bottom. "Oh, Matilda!"

"What Matilda?" inquired Hicks, starting up.

"Matilda Maplesone," responded the other, doing the same.

"I marry her to-morrow morning," said Hicks.

"It's false," rejoined his companion: "I marry her!"

"You marry her?"

"I marry her!"

"You marry Matilda Maplesone?"

"Matilda Maplesone."

"*Miss* Maplesone marry *you?*"

"Miss Maplesone! No: Mrs. Maplesone."

"Good Heaven!" said Hicks, falling into his chair: "You marry the mother, and I the daughter!"

"Most extraordinary circumstance!" replied Mr. Calton, "and rather inconvenient too; for the fact is, that owing to Matilda's wishing to keep her intention secret from her daughters until the ceremony had taken place, she doesn't like applying to any of her friends to give her away. I entertain an objection to making the affair known to my acquaintance just now; and the consequence is, that I sent to you to know whether you'd oblige me by acting as father."

"I should have been most happy, I assure you," said Hicks, in a tone of condolence; "but, you see, I shall be acting as bridegroom. One character is frequently a consequence of the other; but it is not usual to act in both at the same time. There's Simpson—I have no doubt he'll do it for you."

"I don't like to ask him," replied Calton, "he's such a donkey."

Mr. Septimus Hicks looked up at the ceiling, and down at the floor; at last an idea struck him. "Let the man of the house, Tibbs, be the father," he suggested; and then he quoted, as peculiarly applicable to Tibbs and the pair—

> "Oh Powers of Heaven! what dark eyes meets she there?
> 'Tis—'tis her father's—fixed upon the pair."

"The idea has struck me already," said Mr. Calton: "but, you see, Matilda, for what reason I know not, is very anxious that Mrs. Tibbs should know nothing about it, till it's all over. It's a natural delicacy, after all, you know."

"He's the best-natured little man in existence, if you manage him properly," said Mr. Septimus Hicks. "Tell him not to mention it to his wife, and assure him she won't mind it, and he'll do it directly. My marriage is to be a secret one, on account of the mother and *my* father; therefore he must be enjoined to secrecy."

A small double knock, like a presumptuous single one, was that instant heard at the street-door. It was Tibbs; it could be no one else; for no one else occupied five minutes in rubbing his shoes. He had been out to pay the baker's bill.

"Mr. Tibbs," called Mr. Calton in a very bland tone, looking over the banisters.

"Sir!" replied he of the dirty face.

"Will you have the kindness to step up-stairs for a moment?"

"Certainly, sir," said Tibbs, delighted to be taken notice of. The bedroom door was carefully closed, and Tibbs, having put his hat on the floor (as most timid men do), and been accommodated with a seat, looked as astounded as if he were suddenly summoned before the familiars of the Inquisition.

"A rather unpleasant occurrence, Mr. Tibbs," said Calton, in a very portentous manner, "obliges me to consult you, and to beg you will not communicate what I am about to say, to your wife."

Tibbs acquiesced, wondering in his own mind what the deuce the other could have done, and imagining that at least he must have broken the best decanters.

Mr. Calton resumed; "I am placed, Mr. Tibbs, in rather an unpleasant situation."

Tibbs looked at Mr. Septimus Hicks, as if he thought Mr. H.'s being in the immediate vicinity of his fellow-boarder might constitute the unpleasantness of his situation; but as he did not exactly know what to say, he merely ejaculated the monosyllable "Lor!"

"Now," continued the knocker, "let me beg you will exhibit no manifestations of surprise, which may be overheard by the domestics, when I tell you—command your feelings of astonishment—that two inmates of this house intend to be married to-morrow morning." And he drew back his chair several feet, to perceive the effect of the unlooked-for announcement.

If Tibbs had rushed from the room, staggered down-stairs, and fainted in the passage—if he had instantaneously jumped out of the window into the mews behind the house, in an agony of surprise—his behaviour would have been much less inexplicable to Mr. Calton than it was, when he put his hands into his inexpressible-pockets, and said with a half-chuckle, "Just so."

"You are not surprised, Mr. Tibbs?" inquired Mr. Calton.

"Bless you, no, sir," returned Tibbs; "after all, it's very natural. When two young people get together, you know——"

"Certainly, certainly," said Calton, with an indescribable air of self-satisfaction.

"You don't think it's at all an out-of-the-way affair then?" asked Mr. Septimus Hicks, who had watched the countenance of Tibbs in mute astonishment.

"No, sir," replied Tibbs; "I was just the same at his age." He actually smiled when he said this.

"How devilish well I must carry my years!" thought the delighted old beau, knowing he was at least ten years older than Tibbs at that moment.

"Well, then, to come to the point at once," he continued, "I have to ask you whether you will object to act as father on the occasion?"

"Certainly not," replied Tibbs; still without evincing an atom of surprise.

"You will not?"

"Decidedly not," reiterated Tibbs, still as calm as a pot of porter with the head off.

Mr. Calton seized the hand of the petticoat-governed little man, and vowed eternal friendship from that hour. Hicks, who was all admiration and surprise, did the same.

"Now, confess," asked Mr. Calton of Tibbs, as he picked up his hat, "were you not a little surprised?"

"I b'lieve you!" replied that illustrious person, holding up one hand; "I b'lieve you! When I first heard of it."

The Boarding-House (I)

"So sudden," said Septimus Hicks.

"So strange to ask *me*, you know," said Tibbs.

"So odd altogether!" said the superannuated love-maker; and then all three laughed.

"I say," said Tibbs, shutting the door which he had previously opened, and giving full vent to a hitherto corked-up giggle, "what bothers me is, what *will* his father say?"

Mr. Septimus Hicks looked at Mr. Calton.

"Yes; but the best of it is," said the latter, giggling in his turn, "I haven't got a father—he! he! he!"

"*You* haven't got a father. No; but *he* has," said Tibbs.

"*Who* has?" inquired Septimus Hicks.

"Why, *him*."

"Him, who? Do you know my secret? Do you mean me?"

"You! No; you know who I mean," returned Tibbs with a knowing wink.

"For Heaven's sake, whom *do* you mean?" inquired Mr. Calton, who, like Septimus Hicks, was all but out of his senses at the strange confusion.

"Why, Mr. Simpson, of course," replied Tibbs; "who else could I mean?"

"I see it all," said the Byron-quoter; "Simpson marries Julia Maplesone to-morrow morning!"

"Undoubtedly," replied Tibbs, thoroughly satisfied, "of course he does."

It would require the pencil of Hogarth to illustrate—our feeble pen is inadequate to describe—the expression which the countenances of Mr. Calton and Mr. Septimus Hicks respectively assumed, at this unexpected announcement. Equally impossible is it to describe, although perhaps it is easier for our lady readers to imagine, what arts the three ladies could have used, so completely to entangle their separate partners. Whatever they were, however, they were successful. The mother was perfectly aware of the intended marriage of both daughters; and the young ladies were equally acquainted with the intention of their estimable parent. They agreed, however, that it would have a much better appearance if each feigned ignorance of the other's engagement; and it was equally desirable that all the marriages should take place on the same day, to prevent the discovery of one clandestine alliance, operating prejudicially on the others. Hence, the mystification of Mr. Calton and Mr. Septimus Hicks, and the pre-engagement of the unwary Tibbs.

On the following morning, Mr. Septimus Hicks was united to Miss Matilda Maplesone. Mr. Simpson also entered into a "holy alliance" with Miss Julia; Tibbs acting as father, "his first appearance in that character." Mr. Calton, not being quite so eager as the two young men, was rather struck by the double discovery; and as he had found some difficulty in getting any one to give the lady away, it occurred to him that the best mode of obviating the inconvenience would be not to take her at all. The lady, however, "appealed," as her counsel said on the trial of the cause, *Maplesone* v. *Calton*, for a breach of promise, "with a broken heart, to the outraged laws of her country." She recovered damages to the amount of 1,000*l*. which the unfortunate knocker was compelled to pay. Mr. Septimus Hicks having walked the hospitals, took it into his head to walk off altogether. His injured wife is at present residing with her mother at Boulogne. Mr. Simpson, having the misfortune to lose his wife six weeks after marriage (by her eloping with an officer during his temporary sojourn in the Fleet Prison, in consequence of his inability to discharge her little mantuamaker's bill), and being disinherited by his father, who died soon afterwards, was fortunate enough to obtain a permanent engagement at a fashionable haircutter's; hairdressing being a science to which he had frequently directed his attention. In this situation he had necessarily many opportunities of making himself acquainted with the habits, and style of thinking, of the exclusive portion of the nobility of this kingdom. To this fortunate circumstance are we indebted for the production of those brilliant efforts of genius, his fashionable novels, which so long as good taste, unsullied by exaggeration, cant, and quackery, continues to exist, cannot fail to instruct and amuse the thinking portion of the community.

It only remains to add, that this complication of disorders completely deprived poor Mrs. Tibbs of all her inmates, except the one whom she could have best spared—her husband. That wretched little man returned home, on the day of the wedding, in a state of partial intoxication; and, under the influence of wine, excitement, and despair, actually dared to brave the anger of his wife. Since that ill-fated hour he has constantly taken his meals in the kitchen, to which apartment, it is understood, his witticisms will be in future confined : a turn-up bedstead having been conveyed there by Mrs. Tibbs's order for his exclusive accommodation. It is possible that he will be enabled to finish, in that seclusion, his story of the volunteers.

The advertisement has again appeared in the morning papers. Results must be reserved for another chapter.

CHAPTER THE SECOND

"WELL!" said little Mrs. Tibbs to herself, as she sat in the front parlour of the Coram Street mansion one morning, mending a piece of stair-carpet off the first landing ;— "Things have not turned out so badly, either, and if I only get a favourable answer to the advertisement, we shall be full again."

Mrs. Tibbs resumed her occupation of making worsted lattice-work in the carpet, anxiously listening to the two-penny postman, who was hammering his way down the street, at the rate of a penny a knock. The house was as quiet as possible. There was only one low sound to be heard—it was the unhappy Tibbs cleaning the gentlemen's boots in the back kitchen, and accompanying himself with a buzzing noise, in wretched mockery of humming a tune.

The postman drew near the house. He paused—so did Mrs. Tibbs. A knock—a bustle—a letter—post-paid.

"T. I. presents compt. to I. T. and T. I. begs To say that i see the advertisement And she will Do Herself the pleasure of calling On you at 12 o'clock to-morrow morning.

"T. I. as To apologise to I. T. for the shortness Of the notice But i hope it will not unconvenience you.

"I remain yours Truly

"Wednesday evening.

Little Mrs. Tibbs perused the document, over and over again ; and the more she read it, the more was she confused by the mixture of the first and third person ; the substitution of the "i" for the "T. I. "; and the transition from the "I. T." to the "you." The writing looked like a skein of thread in a tangle, and the note was ingeniously folded into a perfect square, with the direction squeezed up into the right-hand corner, as if it were ashamed of itself. The back of the epistle was pleasingly ornamented with a large red wafer, which, with the addition of divers ink-stains, bore a marvellous resemblance to a black beetle trodden upon. One thing, however, was perfectly clear to the perplexed Mrs. Tibbs. Somebody was to call at twelve. The drawing-room was forthwith dusted for the third time that morning ; three or four chairs were pulled out of their places, and a corresponding number of books carefully upset, in order that there might be a due absence of formality. Down went the piece of stair-carpet before noticed, and up ran Mrs. Tibbs " to make herself tidy."

The clock of New Saint Pancras Church struck twelve, and the Foundling, with laudable politeness, did the same ten minutes afterwards. Saint something else struck the quarter, and then there arrived a single lady with a double knock, in a pelisse the colour of the interior of a damson pie ; a bonnet of the same, with a regular conservatory of artificial flowers; a white veil, and a green parasol, with a cobweb border.

The visitor (who was very fat and red-faced) was shown into the drawing-room ; Mrs. Tibbs presented herself, and the negotiation commenced.

"I called in consequence of an advertisement," said the stranger, in a voice as if she had been playing a set of Pan's pipes for a fortnight without leaving off.

"Yes!" said Mrs. Tibbs, rubbing her hands very slowly, and looking the applicant full in the face—two things she always did on such occasions.

"Money isn't no object whatever to me," said the lady, "so much as living in a state of retirement and obtrusion."

Mrs. Tibbs, as a matter of course, acquiesced in such an exceedingly natural desire.

"I am constantly attended by a medical man," resumed the pelisse wearer ; "I have been a shocking unitarian for some time—I, indeed, have had very little peace since the death of Mr. Bloss."

Mrs. Tibbs looked at the relict of the departed Bloss, and thought he must have had very little peace in his time. Of course she could not say so ; so she looked very sympathising.

"I shall be a good deal of trouble to you," said Mrs. Bloss ; "but for that trouble I am willing to pay. I am going through a course of treatment which renders attention necessary. I have one mutton-chop in bed at half-past eight, and another at ten, every morning."

Mrs. Tibbs, as in duty bound, expressed the pity she felt for anybody placed in such a distressing situation; and the carnivorous Mrs. Bloss proceeded to arrange the various preliminaries with wonderful despatch. "Now mind," said that lady, after terms were arranged; "I am to have the second-floor front, for my bedroom?"

"Yes, ma'am."

"And you'll find room for my little servant Agnes?"

"Oh! certainly."

"And I can have one of the cellars in the area for my bottled porter."

"With the greatest pleasure;—James shall get it ready for you by Saturday."

"And I'll join the company at the breakfast-table on Sunday morning," said Mrs. Bloss, "I shall get up on purpose."

"Very well," returned Mrs. Tibbs, in her most amiable tone; for satisfactory references had "been given and required," and it was quite certain that the new-comer had plenty of money. "It's rather singular," continued Mrs. Tibbs, with what was meant for a most bewitching smile, "that we have a gentleman now with us, who is in a very delicate state of health—a Mr. Gobler.—His apartment is the back drawing-room."

"The next room?" inquired Mrs. Bloss.

"The next room," repeated the hostess.

"How very promiscuous!" ejaculated the widow.

"He hardly ever gets up," said Mrs. Tibbs in a whisper.

"Lor!" cried Mrs. Bloss, in an equally low tone.

"And when he is up," said Mrs. Tibbs, "we never can persuade him to go to bed again."

"Dear me!" said the astonished Mrs. Bloss, drawing her chair nearer Mrs. Tibbs. "What is his complaint?"

"Why, the fact is," replied Mrs. Tibbs, with a most communicative air, "he has no stomach whatever."

"No what?" inquired Mrs. Bloss, with a look of the most indescribable alarm.

"No stomach," repeated Mrs. Tibbs, with a shake of the head.

"Lord bless us! what an extraordinary case!" gasped Mrs. Bloss, as if she understood the communication in its

literal sense, and was astonished at a gentleman without a
stomach finding it necessary to board anywhere.

"When I say he has no stomach," explained the chatty
little Mrs. Tibbs, "I mean that his digestion is so much
impaired, and his interior so deranged, that his stomach is
not of the least use to him ;—in fact, it's an inconvenience."

"Never heard such a case in my life!" exclaimed Mrs.
Bloss. "Why, he's worse than I am."

"Oh, yes!" replied Mrs. Tibbs ;—"certainly." She said
this with great confidence, for the damson pelisse suggested
that Mrs. Bloss, at all events, was not suffering under Mr.
Gobler's complaint.

"You have quite incited my curiosity," said Mrs. Bloss,
as she rose to depart. "How I long to see him!"

"He generally comes down once a week," replied Mrs.
Tibbs ; "I dare say you'll see him on Sunday." With this
consolatory promise Mrs. Bloss was obliged to be contented.
She accordingly walked slowly down the stairs, detailing
her complaints all the way; and Mrs. Tibbs followed her,
uttering an exclamation of compassion at every step. James
(who looked very gritty, for he was cleaning the knives) fell
up the kitchen-stairs, and opened the street-door ; and, after
mutual farewells, Mrs. Bloss slowly departed, down the shady
side of the street.

It is almost superfluous to say, that the lady whom we
have just shown out at the street-door (and whom the two
female servants are now inspecting from the second-floor
windows) was exceedingly vulgar, ignorant, and selfish. Her
deceased better-half had been an eminent cork-cutter, in
which capacity he had amassed a decent fortune. He had
no relative but his nephew, and no friend but his cook. The
former had the insolence one morning to ask for the loan of
fifteen pounds ; and, by way of retaliation, he married the
latter next day ; he made a will immediately afterwards,
containing a burst of honest indignation against his nephew
(who supported himself and two sisters on 100*l.* a year),
and a bequest of his whole property to his wife. He felt ill
after breakfast, and died after dinner. There is a mantel-
piece-looking tablet in a civic parish church, setting forth
his virtues, and deploring his loss. He never dishonoured a
bill, or gave away a halfpenny.

The relict and sole executrix of this noble-minded man
was an odd mixture of shrewdness and simplicity, liberality

and meanness. Bred up as she had been, she knew no mode of living so agreeable as a boarding-house; and having nothing to do, and nothing to wish for, she naturally imagined she must be very ill—an impression which was most assiduously promoted by her medical attendant, Dr. Wosky, and her handmaid Agnes: both of whom, doubtless for good reasons, encouraged all her extravagant notions.

Since the catastrophe recorded in the last chapter, Mrs. Tibbs had been very shy of young-lady boarders. Her present inmates were all lords of the creation, and she availed herself of the opportunity of their assemblage at the dinner-table, to announce the expected arrival of Mrs. Bloss. The gentlemen received the communication with stoical indifference, and Mrs. Tibbs devoted all her energies to prepare for the reception of the valetudinarian. The second-floor front was scrubbed, and washed, and flannelled, till the wet went through to the drawing-room ceiling. Clean white counterpanes, and curtains, and napkins, water-bottles as clear as crystal, blue jugs, and mahogany furniture, added to the splendour, and increased the comfort, of the apartment. The warming-pan was in constant requisition, and a fire lighted in the room every day. The chattels of Mrs. Bloss were forwarded by instalments. First, there came a large hamper of Guinness's stout, and an umbrella; then, a train of trunks; then, a pair of clogs and a bandbox; then, an easy chair with an air-cushion; then, a variety of suspicious-looking packages; and—"though last not least"—Mrs. Bloss and Agnes: the latter in a cherry-coloured merino dress, open-work stockings, and shoes with sandals: like a disguised Columbine.

The installation of the Duke of Wellington as Chancellor of the University of Oxford was nothing, in point of bustle and turmoil, to the installation of Mrs. Bloss in her new quarters. True, there was no bright doctor of civil law to deliver a classical address on the occasion; but there were several other old women present, who spoke quite as much to the purpose, and understood themselves equally well. The chop-eater was so fatigued with the process of removal that she declined leaving her room until the following morning; so a mutton-chop, pickle, a pill, a pint bottle of stout, and other medicines, were carried up-stairs for her consumption.

"Why, what *do* you think, ma'am?" inquired the inquisitive Agnes of her mistress, after they had been in the house some three hours; "what *do* you think, ma'am? the lady of the house is married."

"Married!" said Mrs. Bloss, taking the pill and a draught of Guinness—"married! Unpossible!"

"She is indeed, ma'am," returned the Columbine; "and her husband, ma'am, lives—he—he—he—lives in the kitchen, ma'am."

"In the kitchen!"

"Yes, ma'am: and he—he—he—the housemaid says, he never goes into the parlour except on Sundays: and that Mrs. Tibbs makes him clean the gentlemen's boots; and that he cleans the windows, too, sometimes; and that one morning early, when he was in the front balcony cleaning the drawing-room windows, he called out to a gentleman on the opposite side of the way, who used to live here—'Ah! Mr. Calton, sir, how are you?'" Here the attendant laughed till Mrs. Bloss was in serious apprehension of her chuckling herself into a fit.

"Well, I never!" said Mrs. Bloss.

"Yes. And please, ma'am, the servants gives him gin-and-water sometimes; and then he cries, and says he hates his wife and the boarders, and wants to tickle them."

"Tickle the boarders!" exclaimed Mrs. Bloss, seriously alarmed.

"No, ma'am, not the boarders, the servants."

"Oh, is that all!" said Mrs. Bloss, quite satisfied.

"He wanted to kiss me as I came up the kitchen-stairs, just now," said Agnes, indignantly; "but I gave it him—a little wretch!"

This intelligence was but too true. A long course of snubbing and neglect; his days spent in the kitchen, and his nights in the turn-up bedstead, had completely broken the little spirit that the unfortunate volunteer had ever possessed. He had no one to whom he could detail his injuries but the servants, and they were almost of necessity his chosen confidants. It is no less strange than true, however, that the little weaknesses which he had incurred, most probably during his military career, seemed to increase as his comforts diminished. He was actually a sort of journeyman Giovanni of the basement story.

The next morning, being Sunday, breakfast was laid in the front parlour at ten o'clock. Nine was the usual time, but the family always breakfasted an hour later on sabbath. Tibbs enrobed himself in his Sunday costume—a black coat, and exceedingly short, thin trousers ; with a very large white waistcoat, white stockings and cravat, and Blucher boots— and mounted to the parlour aforesaid. Nobody had come down, and he amused himself by drinking the contents of the milkpot with a teaspoon.

A pair of slippers were heard descending the stairs. Tibbs flew to a chair ; and a stern-looking man, of about fifty, with very little hair on his head, and a Sunday paper in his hand, entered the room.

"Good morning, Mr. Evenson," said Tibbs, very humbly, with something between a nod and a bow.

"How do you do, Mr. Tibbs?" replied he of the slippers, as he sat himself down, and began to read his paper without saying another word.

"Is Mr. Wisbottle in town to-day, do you know, sir?" inquired Tibbs, just for the sake of saying something.

"I should think he was," replied the stern gentleman. "He was whistling 'The Light Guitar,' in the next room to mine, at five o'clock this morning."

"He's very fond of whistling," said Tibbs, with a slight smirk.

"Yes—I ain't," was the laconic reply.

Mr. John Evenson was in the receipt of an independent income, arising chiefly from various houses he owned in the different suburbs. He was very morose and discontented. He was a thorough radical, and used to attend a great variety of public meetings, for the express purpose of finding fault with everything that was proposed. Mr. Wisbottle, on the other hand, was a high Tory. He was a clerk in the Woods and Forests Office, which he considered rather an aristocratic employment ; he knew the peerage by heart, and could tell you, off-hand, where any illustrious personage lived. He had a good set of teeth, and a capital tailor. Mr. Evenson looked on all these qualifications with profound contempt ; and the consequence was that the two were always disputing, much to the edification of the rest of the house. It should be added, that, in addition to his partiality for whistling, Mr. Wisbottle had a great idea of his singing powers. There were two other boarders, besides the gentleman in the back drawing-room —Mr. Alfred Tomkins and Mr. Frederick O'Bleary. Mr. Tomkins was a clerk in a wine-house ; he was a connoisseur

in paintings, and had a wonderful eye for the picturesque.
Mr. O'Bleary was an Irishman, recently imported; he was in
a perfectly wild state; and had come over to England to
be an apothecary, a clerk in a government office, an actor,
a reporter, or anything else that turned up—he was not
particular. He was on familiar terms with two small Irish
members, and got franks for everybody in the house. He
felt convinced that his intrinsic merits must procure him a
high destiny. He wore shepherd's-plaid inexpressibles, and
used to look under all the ladies' bonnets as he walked along
the streets. His manners and appearance reminded one of
Orson.

"Here comes Mr. Wisbottle," said Tibbs; and Mr. Wisbottle forthwith appeared in blue slippers, and a shawl
dressing-gown, whistling "*Di piacer.*"

"Good morning, sir," said Tibbs again. It was almost
the only thing he ever said to anybody.

"How are you, Tibbs?" condescendingly replied the
amateur; and he walked to the window, and whistled louder
than ever.

"Pretty air, that!" said Evenson, with a snarl, and without taking his eyes off the paper.

"Glad you like it," replied Wisbottle, highly gratified.

"Don't you think it would sound better, if you whistled
it a little louder?" inquired the mastiff.

"No; I don't think it would," rejoined the unconscious
Wisbottle.

"I'll tell you what, Wisbottle," said Evenson, who had
been bottling up his anger for some hours—"the next time
you feel disposed to whistle 'The Light Guitar' at five
o'clock in the morning, I'll trouble you to whistle it with
your head out o' window. If you don't, I'll learn the
triangle—I will, by—— "

The entrance of Mrs. Tibbs (with the keys in a little basket)
interrupted the threat, and prevented its conclusion.

Mrs. Tibbs apologised for being down rather late; the
bell was rung; James brought up the urn, and received an
unlimited order for dry toast and bacon. Tibbs sat down at
the bottom of the table, and began eating water-cresses like
a Nebuchadnezzar. Mr. O'Bleary appeared, and Mr. Alfred
Tomkins. The compliments of the morning were exchanged,
and the tea was made.

"God bless me!" exclaimed Tomkins, who had been

looking out at the window. "Here—Wisbottle—pray come here—make haste."

Mr. Wisbottle started from the table, and every one looked up.

"Do you see," said the connoisseur, placing Wisbottle in the right position—"a little more this way : there—do you see how splendidly the light falls upon the left side of that broken chimney-pot at No. 48?"

"Dear me! I see," replied Wisbottle, in a tone of admiration.

"I never saw an object stand out so beautifully against the clear sky in my life," ejaculated Alfred. Everybody (except John Evenson) echoed the sentiment; for Mr. Tomkins had a great character for finding out beauties which no one else could discover—he certainly deserved it.

"I have frequently observed a chimney-pot in College Green, Dublin, which has a much better effect," said the patriotic O'Bleary, who never allowed Ireland to be outdone on any point.

The assertion was received with obvious incredulity, for Mr. Tomkins declared that no other chimney-pot in the United Kingdom, broken or unbroken, could be so beautiful as the one at No. 48.

The room-door was suddenly thrown open, and Agnes appeared, leading in Mrs. Bloss, who was dressed in a geranium-coloured muslin gown, and displayed a gold watch of huge dimensions; a chain to match; and a splendid assortment of rings, with enormous stones. A general rush was made for a chair, and a regular introduction took place. Mr. John Evenson made a slight inclination of the head; Mr. Frederick O'Bleary, Mr. Alfred Tomkins, and Mr. Wisbottle, bowed like the mandarins in a grocer's shop; Tibbs rubbed hands, and went round in circles. He was observed to close one eye, and to assume a clock-work sort of expression with the other; this has been considered as a wink, and it has been reported that Agnes was its object. We repel the calumny, and challenge contradiction.

Mrs. Tibbs inquired after Mrs. Bloss's health in a low tone. Mrs. Bloss, with a supreme contempt for the memory of Lindley Murray, answered the various questions in a most satisfactory manner; and a pause ensued, during which the eatables disappeared with awful rapidity.

"You must have been very much pleased with the appearance of the ladies going to the Drawing-room the other day, Mr. O'Bleary?" said Mrs. Tibbs, hoping to start a topic.

"Yes," replied Orson, with a mouthful of toast.

"Never saw anything like it before, I suppose?" suggested Wisbottle.

"No — except the Lord Lieutenant's levees," replied O'Bleary.

"Are they at all equal to our drawing-rooms?"

"Oh, infinitely superior!"

"Gad! I don't know," said the aristocratic Wisbottle, "the Dowager Marchioness of Publiccash was most magnificently dressed, and so was the Baron Slappenbachenhausen."

"What was he presented on?" inquired Evenson.

"On his arrival in England."

"I thought so," growled the radical; "you never hear of these fellows being presented on their going away again. They know better than that."

"Unless somebody pervades them with an apintment," said Mrs. Bloss, joining in the conversation in a faint voice.

"Well," said Wisbottle, evading the point, "it's a splendid sight."

"And did it never occur to you," inquired the radical, who never would be quiet; "did it never occur to you, that you pay for these precious ornaments of society?"

"It certainly *has* occurred to me," said Wisbottle, who thought this answer was a poser; "it *has* occurred to me, and I am willing to pay for them."

"Well, and it has occurred to me too," replied John Evenson, "and I ain't willing to pay for 'em. Then why should I?—I say, why should I?" continued the politician, laying down the paper, and knocking his knuckles on the table. "There are two great principles—demand——"

"A cup of tea if you please, dear," interrupted Tibbs.

"And supply——"

"May I trouble you to hand this tea to Mr. Tibbs?" said Mrs. Tibbs, interrupting the argument, and unconsciously illustrating it.

The thread of the orator's discourse was broken. He drank his tea and resumed the paper.

"If it's very fine," said Mr. Alfred Tomkins, addressing the company in general, "I shall ride down to Richmond to-day, and come back by the steamer. There are some splendid effects of light and shade on the Thames; the contrast between the blueness of the sky and the yellow water is frequently exceedingly beautiful." Mr. Wisbottle hummed, "Flow on, thou shining river."

"We have some splendid steam-vessels in Ireland," said O'Bleary.

"Certainly," said Mrs. Bloss, delighted to find a subject broached in which she could take part.

"The accommodations are extraordinary," said O'Bleary.

"Extraordinary indeed," returned Mrs. Bloss. "When Mr. Bloss was alive, he was promiscuously obligated to go to Ireland on business. I went with him, and raly the manner in which the ladies and gentlemen were accommodated with berths, is not creditable."

Tibbs, who had been listening to the dialogue, looked aghast, and evinced a strong inclination to ask a question, but was checked by a look from his wife. Mr. Wisbottle laughed, and said Tomkins had made a pun; and Tomkins laughed too, and said he had not.

The remainder of the meal passed off as breakfasts usually do. Conversation flagged, and people played with their tea-spoons. The gentlemen looked out at the window; walked about the room; and, when they got near the door, dropped off one by one. Tibbs retired to the back parlour by his wife's orders, to check the greengrocer's weekly account; and ultimately Mrs. Tibbs and Mrs. Bloss were left alone together.

"Oh dear!" said the latter, "I feel alarmingly faint; it's very singular." (It certainly was, for she had eaten four pounds of solids that morning.) "By-the-bye," said Mrs. Bloss, "I have not seen Mr. What's-his-name yet."

"Mr. Gobler?" suggested Mrs. Tibbs.

"Yes."

"Oh!" said Mrs. Tibbs, "he is a most mysterious person. He has his meals regularly sent up-stairs, and sometimes don't leave his room for weeks together."

"I haven't seen or heard nothing of him," repeated Mrs. Bloss.

"I dare say you'll hear him to-night," replied Mrs. Tibbs; "he generally groans a good deal on Sunday evenings."

"I never felt such an interest in any one in my life," ejaculated Mrs. Bloss. A little double-knock interrupted the conversation; Dr. Wosky was announced, and duly shown in. He was a little man with a red face.—dressed of course in black, with a stiff white neckerchief. He had a very good practice, and plenty of money, which he had amassed by invariably humouring the worst fancies of all the females of all the families he had ever been introduced into. Mrs. Tibbs offered to retire, but was entreated to stay.

"Well, my dear ma'am, and how are we?" inquired Wosky, in a soothing tone.

"Very ill, doctor—very ill," said Mrs. Bloss, in a whisper.

"Ah! we must take care of ourselves;—we must, indeed," said the obsequious Wosky, as he felt the pulse of his interesting patient.

"How is your appetite?"

Mrs. Bloss shook her head.

"Our friend requires great care," said Wosky, appealing to Mrs. Tibbs, who of course assented. "I hope, however, with the blessing of Providence, that we shall be enabled to make her quite stout again." Mrs. Tibbs wondered in her own mind what the patient would be when she was made quite stout.

"We must take stimulants," said the cunning Wosky— "plenty of nourishment, and above all, we must keep our nerves quiet; we positively must not give way to our sensibilities. We must take all we can get," concluded the doctor, as he pocketed his fee, "and we must keep quiet."

"Dear man!" exclaimed Mrs. Bloss, as the doctor stepped into his carriage.

"Charming creature indeed—quite a lady's man!" said Mrs. Tibbs, and Dr. Wosky rattled away to make fresh gulls of delicate females, and pocket fresh fees.

As we had occasion, in a former paper, to describe a dinner at Mrs. Tibbs's; and as one meal went off very like another on all ordinary occasions; we will not fatigue our readers by entering into any other detailed account of the domestic economy of the establishment. We will therefore proceed to events, merely premising that the mysterious tenant of the back drawing-room was a lazy, selfish hypochondriac; always complaining and never ill. As his character in many respects closely assimilated to that of Mrs. Bloss, a very warm friendship soon sprung up between them. He was tall, thin, and pale; he always fancied he had a severe pain somewhere or other, and his face invariably wore a pinched, screwed-up expression; he looked, indeed, like a man who had got his feet in a tub of exceedingly hot water, against his will.

The Boarding-House (II)
(*p. 310*)

For two or three months after Mrs. Bloss's first appearance in Coram Street, John Evenson was observed to become, every day, more sarcastic and more ill-natured; and there was a degree of additional importance in his manner, which clearly showed that he fancied he had discovered something, which he only wanted a proper opportunity of divulging. He found it at last.

One evening, the different inmates of the house were assembled in the drawing-room engaged in their ordinary occupations. Mr. Gobler and Mrs. Bloss were sitting at a small card-table near the centre window, playing cribbage; Mr. Wisbottle was describing semicircles on the music-stool, turning over the leaves of a book on the piano, and humming most melodiously; Alfred Tomkins was sitting at the round table, with his elbows duly squared, making a pencil sketch of a head considerably larger than his own; O'Bleary was reading Horace, and trying to look as if he understood it; and John Evenson had drawn his chair close to Mrs. Tibbs's work-table, and was talking to her very earnestly in a low tone.

"I can assure you, Mrs. Tibbs," said the radical, laying his forefinger on the muslin she was at work on; "I can assure you, Mrs. Tibbs, that nothing but the interest I take in your welfare would induce me to make this communication. I repeat, I fear Wisbottle is endeavouring to gain the affections of that young woman, Agnes, and that he is in the habit of meeting her in the store-room on the first floor, over the leads. From my bedroom I distinctly heard voices there, last night. I opened my door immediately, and crept very softly on to the landing; there I saw Mr. Tibbs, who, it seems, had been disturbed also.—Bless me, Mrs. Tibbs, you change colour!"

"No, no—it's nothing," returned Mrs. T. in a hurried manner; "it's only the heat of the room."

"A flush!" ejaculated Mrs. Bloss from the card-table; "that's good for four."

"If I thought it was Mr. Wisbottle," said Mrs. Tibbs, after a pause, "he should leave this house instantly."

"Go!" said Mrs. Bloss again.

"And if I thought," continued the hostess with a most threatening air, "if I thought he was assisted by Mr. Tibbs—"

"One for his nob!" said Gobler.

"Oh," said Evenson, in a most soothing tone—he liked

to make mischief—"I should hope Mr. Tibbs was not in any way implicated. He always appeared to me very harmless."

"I have generally found him so," sobbed poor little Mrs. Tibbs; crying like a watering-pot.

"Hush! hush! pray—Mrs. Tibbs—consider—we shall be observed—pray, don't!" said John Evenson, fearing his whole plan would be interrupted. "We will set the matter at rest with the utmost care, and I shall be most happy to assist you in doing so."

Mrs. Tibbs murmured her thanks.

"When you think every one has retired to rest to-night," said Evenson very pompously, "if you'll meet me without a light, just outside my bedroom door, by the staircase window, I think we can ascertain who the parties really are, and you will afterwards be enabled to proceed as you think proper."

Mrs. Tibbs was easily persuaded; her curiosity was excited, her jealousy was roused, and the arrangement was forthwith made. She resumed her work, and John Evenson walked up and down the room with his hands in his pockets, looking as if nothing had happened. The game of cribbage was over, and conversation began again.

"Well, Mr. O'Bleary," said the humming-top, turning round on his pivot, and facing the company, "what did you think of Vauxhall the other night?"

"Oh, it's very fair," replied Orson, who had been enthusiastically delighted with the whole exhibition.

"Never saw anything like that Captain Ross's set-out —eh?"

"No," returned the patriot, with his usual reservation— "except in Dublin."

"I saw the Count de Canky and Captain Fitzthompson in the Gardens," said Wisbottle; "they appeared much delighted."

"Then it *must* be beautiful," snarled Evenson.

"I think the white bears is partickerlerly well done," suggested Mrs. Bloss. "In their shaggy white coats, they look just like Polar bears—don't you think they do, Mr. Evenson?"

"I think they look a great deal more like omnibus cads on all fours," replied the discontented one.

"Upon the whole, I should have liked our evening very

well," gasped Gobler ; "only I caught a desperate cold which increased my pain dreadfully ! I was obliged to have several shower-baths before I could leave my room."

"Capital things those shower-baths!" ejaculated Wisbottle.

"Excellent!" said Tomkins.

"Delightful!" chimed in O'Bleary. (He had once seen one, outside a tinman's.)

"Disgusting machines!" rejoined Evenson, who extended his dislike to almost every created object, masculine, feminine, or neuter.

"Disgusting, Mr. Evenson!" said Gobler, in a tone of strong indignation.—"Disgusting! Look at their utility— consider how many lives they have saved by promoting perspiration."

"Promoting perspiration, indeed," growled John Evenson, stopping short in his walk across the large squares in the pattern of the carpet "I was ass enough to be persuaded some time ago to have one in my bedroom. 'Gad, I was in it once, and it effectually cured *me*, for the mere sight of it threw me into a profuse perspiration for six months afterwards."

A titter followed this announcement, and before it had subsided James brought up "the tray," containing the remains of a leg of lamb which had made its *début* at dinner ; bread ; cheese ; an atom of butter in a forest of parsley ; one pickled walnut and the third of another ; and so forth. The boy disappeared, and returned again with another tray, containing glasses and jugs of hot and cold water. The gentlemen brought in their spirit-bottles ; the housemaid placed divers plated bedroom candlesticks under the card-table ; and the servants retired for the night.

Chairs were drawn round the table, and the conversation proceeded in the customary manner. John Evenson, who never ate supper, lolled on the sofa, and amused himself by contradicting everybody. O'Bleary ate as much as he could conveniently carry, and Mrs. Tibbs felt a due degree of indignation thereat ; Mr. Gobler and Mrs. Bloss conversed most affectionately on the subject of pill-taking, and other innocent amusements ; and Tomkins and Wisbottle "got into an argument ;" that is to say, they both talked very loudly and vehemently, each flattering himself that he had got some advantage about something, and neither of them having more than a very indistinct idea of what they were talking about. An hour or two passed away ; and the boarders and the brass candlesticks retired in pairs to their respective bedrooms. John Evenson pulled off his boots, locked his door, and determined to sit up until Mr. Gobler had retired. He always sat in the drawing-room an hour after everybody else had left it, taking medicine, and groaning.

Great Coram Street was hushed into a state of profound repose: it was nearly two o'clock. A hackney-coach now and then rumbled slowly by; and occasionally some stray lawyer's clerk, on his way home to Somers Town, struck his iron heel on the top of the coal-cellar with a noise resembling the click of a smoke-jack. A low, monotonous, gushing sound was heard, which added considerably to the romantic dreariness of the scene. It was the water "coming in" at number eleven.

"He must be asleep by this time," said John Evenson to himself, after waiting with exemplary patience for nearly an hour after Mr. Gobler had left the drawing-room. He listened for a few moments; the house was perfectly quiet; he extinguished his rushlight, and opened his bedroom door. The staircase was so dark that it was impossible to see anything.

"S—s—s!" whispered the mischief-maker, making a noise like the first indication a catherine-wheel gives of the probability of its going off.

"Hush!" whispered somebody else.

"Is that you, Mrs. Tibbs?"

"Yes, sir."

"Where?"

"Here;" and the misty outline of Mrs. Tibbs appeared at the staircase window, like the ghost of Queen Anne in the tent scene in Richard.

"This way, Mrs. Tibbs," whispered the delighted busybody: "give me your hand—there! Whoever these people are, they are in the store-room now, for I have been looking down from my window, and I could see that they accidentally upset their candlestick, and are now in darkness. You have no shoes on, have you?"

"No," said little Mrs. Tibbs, who could hardly speak for trembling.

"Well; I have taken my boots off, so we can go down, close to the store-room door, and listen over the banisters;" and down-stairs they both crept accordingly, every board creaking like a patent mangle on a Saturday afternoon.

"It's Wisbottle and somebody, I'll swear," exclaimed the

Mr. Minns and His Cousin
(*p. 314*)

radical in an energetic whisper, when they had listened for a few moments.

"Hush—pray let's hear what they say!" exclaimed Mrs. Tibbs, the gratification of whose curiosity was now paramount to every other consideration.

"Ah! if I could but believe you," said a female voice coquettishly, "I'd be bound to settle my missis for life."

"What does she say?" inquired Mr. Evenson, who was not quite so well situated as his companion.

"She says she'll settle her missis's life," replied Mrs. Tibbs. "The wretch! they're plotting murder."

"I know you want money," continued the voice, which belonged to Agnes; "and if you'd secure me the five hundred pound, I warrant she should take fire soon enough."

"What's that?" inquired Evenson again. He could just hear enough to want to hear more.

"I think she says she'll set the house on fire," replied the affrighted Mrs. Tibbs. "But, thank God, I'm insured in the Phœnix!"

"The moment I have secured your mistress, my dear," said a man's voice in a strong Irish brogue, "you may depend on having the money."

"Bless my soul, it's Mr. O'Bleary!" exclaimed Mrs. Tibbs, in a parenthesis.

"The villain!" said the indignant Mr. Evenson.

"The first thing to be done," continued the Hibernian, "is to poison Mr. Gobler's mind."

"Oh, certainly," returned Agnes.

"What's that?" inquired Evenson again, in an agony of curiosity and a whisper.

"He says she's to mind and poison Mr. Gobler," replied Mrs. Tibbs, aghast at this sacrifice of human life.

"And in regard of Mrs. Tibbs," continued O'Bleary.— Mrs. Tibbs shuddered.

"Hush!" exclaimed Agnes, in a tone of the greatest alarm, just as Mrs. Tibbs was on the extreme verge of a fainting fit. "Hush!"

"Hush!" exclaimed Evenson, at the same moment, to Mrs. Tibbs.

"There's somebody coming up-stairs," said Agnes to O'Bleary.

"There's somebody coming down-stairs," whispered Evenson to Mrs. Tibbs.

"Go into the parlour, sir," said Agnes to her companion. "You will get there before whoever it is gets to the top of the kitchen stairs."

"The drawing-room, Mrs. Tibbs!" whispered the astonished Evenson to his equally astonished companion; and for the drawing-room they both made, plainly hearing the rustling of two persons, one coming down-stairs, and one coming up.

"What can it be?" exclaimed Mrs. Tibbs. "It's like a dream. I wouldn't be found in this situation for the world!"

"Nor I," returned Evenson, who could never bear a joke at his own expense. "Hush! here they are at the door."

"What fun!" whispered one of the new-comers.—It was Wisbottle.

"Glorious!" replied his companion, in an equally low tone.—This was Alfred Tomkins. "Who would have thought it?"

"I told you so," said Wisbottle, in a most knowing whisper. "Lord bless you, he has paid her most extraordinary attention for the last two months. I saw 'em when I was sitting at the piano to-night."

"Well, do you know I didn't notice it?" interrupted Tomkins.

"Not notice it!" continued Wisbottle. "Bless you; I saw him whispering to her, and she crying; and then I'll swear I heard him say something about to-night when we were all in bed."

"They're talking of *us!*" exclaimed the agonised Mrs. Tibbs, as the painful suspicion, and a sense of their situation, flashed upon her mind.

"I know it—I know it," replied Evenson, with a melancholy consciousness that there was no mode of escape.

"What's to be done? we cannot both stop here!" ejaculated Mrs. Tibbs, in a state of partial derangement.

"I'll get up the chimney," replied Evenson, who really meant what he said.

"You can't," said Mrs. Tibbs, in despair. "You can't—it's a register stove."

"Hush!" repeated John Evenson.

"Hush—hush!" cried somebody down-stairs.

"What a d—d hushing!" said Alfred Tomkins, who began to get rather bewildered.

"There they are!" exclaimed the sapient Wisbottle, as a rustling noise was heard in the store-room.

"Hark!" whispered both the young men.

"Hark!" repeated Mrs. Tibbs and Evenson.

"Let me alone, sir," said a female voice in the store-room.

"Oh, Hagnes!" cried another voice, which clearly belonged to Tibbs, for nobody else ever owned one like it. "Oh, Hagnes—lovely creature!"

"Be quiet, sir!" (A bounce.)

"Hag——"

"Be quiet, sir—I am ashamed of you. Think of your wife, Mr. Tibbs. Be quiet, sir!"

"My wife!" exclaimed the valorous Tibbs, who was clearly under the influence of gin-and-water, and a misplaced attachment; "I ate her! Oh, Hagnes! when I was in the volunteer corps, in eighteen hundred and——"

"I declare I'll scream. Be quiet, sir, will you?" (Another bounce and a scuffle.)

"What's that?" exclaimed Tibbs, with a start.

"What's what?" said Agnes, stopping short.

"Why, that!"

"Ah! you have done it nicely now, sir," sobbed the frightened Agnes, as a tapping was heard at Mrs. Tibbs's bedroom door, which would have beaten any dozen woodpeckers hollow.

"Mrs. Tibbs! Mrs. Tibbs!" called out Mrs. Bloss. "Mrs. Tibbs, pray get up." (Here the imitation of a woodpecker was resumed with tenfold violence.)

"Oh, dear—dear!" exclaimed the wretched partner of the depraved Tibbs. "She's knocking at my door. We must be discovered! What will they think?"

"Mrs. Tibbs! Mrs. Tibbs!" screamed the woodpecker again.

"What's the matter!" shouted Gobler, bursting out of the back drawing-room, like the dragon at Astley's.

"Oh, Mr. Gobler!" cried Mrs. Bloss, with a proper approximation to hysterics; "I think the house is on fire, or else there's thieves in it. I have heard the most dreadful noises!"

"The devil you have!" shouted Gobler again, bouncing back into his den, in happy imitation of the aforesaid dragon, and returning immediately with a lighted candle. "Why, what's this? Wisbottle! Tomkins! O'Bleary! Agnes! What the deuce! all up and dressed?"

"Astonishing!" said Mrs. Bloss, who had run down-stairs, and taken Mr. Gobler's arm.

"Call Mrs. Tibbs directly, somebody," said Gobler, turning into the front drawing-room.—"What! Mrs. Tibbs and Mr. Evenson!!"

"Mrs. Tibbs and Mr. Evenson!" repeated everybody, as that unhappy pair were discovered: Mrs. Tibbs seated in an arm-chair by the fireplace, and Mr. Evenson standing by her side.

We must leave the scene that ensued to the reader's imagination. We could tell how Mrs. Tibbs forthwith fainted away, and how it required the united strength of Mr. Wisbottle and Mr. Alfred Tomkins to hold her in her chair; how Mr. Evenson explained, and how his explanation was evidently disbelieved; how Agnes repelled the accusations of Mrs. Tibbs by proving that she was negotiating with Mr. O'Bleary to influence her mistress's affections in his behalf; and how Mr. Gobler threw a damp counterpane on the hopes of Mr. O'Bleary by avowing that he (Gobler) had already proposed to, and been accepted by, Mrs. Bloss; how Agnes was discharged from that lady's service; how Mr. O'Bleary discharged himself from Mrs. Tibbs's house, without going through the form of previously discharging his bill; and how that disappointed young gentleman rails against England and the English, and vows there is no virtue or fine feeling extant, "except in Ireland." We repeat that we *could* tell all this, but we love to exercise our self-denial, and we therefore prefer leaving it to be imagined.

The lady whom we have hitherto described as Mrs. Bloss, is no more. Mrs. Gobler exists: Mrs. Bloss has left us for ever. In a secluded retreat in Newington Butts, far, far removed from the noisy strife of that great boarding-house, the world, the enviable Gobler and his pleasing wife revel in retirement: happy in their complaints, their table, and their medicine; wafted through life by the grateful prayers of all the purveyors of animal food within three miles round.

We would willingly stop here, but we have a painful duty imposed upon us, which we must discharge. Mr. and Mrs. Tibbs have separated by mutual consent, Mrs. Tibbs receiving one moiety of 43*l*. 15*s*. 10*d*., which we before stated to be the amount of her husband's annual income, and Mr. Tibbs the other. He is spending the evening of his days in retirement; and he is spending also, annually, that small but honourable independence. He resides among the original settlers at Walworth ; and it has been stated, on unquestionable authority, that the conclusion of the volunteer story has been heard in a small tavern in that respectable neighbourhood.

The unfortunate Mrs. Tibbs has determined to dispose of the whole of her furniture by public auction, and to retire from a residence in which she has suffered so much. Mr. Robins has been applied to, to conduct the sale, and the transcendent abilities of the literary gentlemen connected with his establishment are now devoted to the task of drawing up the preliminary advertisement. It is to contain, among a variety of brilliant matter, seventy-eight words in large capitals, and six original quotations in inverted commas.

CHAPTER II

MR. MINNS AND HIS COUSIN

Mr. Augustus Minns was a bachelor, of about forty as he said—of about eight-and-forty as his friends said. He was always exceedingly clean, precise, and tidy; perhaps somewhat priggish, and the most retiring man in the world. He usually wore a brown frock-coat without a wrinkle, light inexplicables without a spot, a neat neckerchief with a remarkably neat tie, and boots without a fault; moreover, he always carried a brown silk umbrella with an ivory handle. He was a clerk in Somerset House, or, as he said himself, he held "a responsible situation under Government." He had a good and increasing salary, in addition to some 10,000*l.* of his own (invested in the funds), and he occupied a first floor in Tavistock Street, Covent Garden, where he had resided for twenty years, having been in the habit of quarrelling with his landlord the whole time: regularly giving notice of his intention to quit on the first day of every quarter, and as regularly countermanding it on the second. There were two classes of created objects which he held in the deepest and most unmingled horror; these were dogs, and children. He was not unamiable, but he could, at any time, have viewed the execution of a dog, or the assassination of an infant, with the liveliest satisfaction. Their habits were at variance with his love of order; and his love of order was as powerful as his love of life. Mr. Augustus Minns had no relations in or near London, with the exception of his cousin, Mr. Octavius Budden, to whose son, whom he had never seen (for he disliked the father), he had consented to become godfather by proxy. Mr. Budden having realised a moderate fortune by exercising the trade or calling of a corn-chandler, and having a great predilection for the country, had purchased a cottage in the vicinity of Stamford Hill, whither he retired with the wife of his bosom, and his only son, Master Alexander Augustus Budden. One evening, as Mr. and Mrs. B. were admiring their son, discussing his various merits, talking over his education, and disputing whether the classics should be made an essential part thereof, the lady pressed so strongly upon her husband the propriety of cultivating the friendship of Mr. Minns in behalf of their son, that Mr. Budden at last made up his mind, that it should not be his fault if he and his cousin were not in future more intimate.

"I'll break the ice, my love," said Mr. Budden, stirring up the sugar at the bottom of his glass of brandy-and-water, and casting a sidelong look at his spouse to see the effect of the announcement of his determination, "by asking Minns down to dine with us on Sunday."

"Then pray, Budden, write to your cousin at once," replied Mrs. Budden. "Who knows, if we could only get him down here, but he might take a fancy to our Alexander, and leave him his property?—Alick, my dear, take your legs off the rail of the chair!"

"Very true," said Mr. Budden, musing, "very true indeed, my love!"

On the following morning, as Mr. Minns was sitting at his breakfast-table, alternately biting his dry toast and casting a look upon the columns of his morning paper, which he always read from the title to the printer's name, he heard a loud knock at the street-door; which was shortly afterwards followed by the entrance of his servant, who put into his hands a particularly small card, on which was engraven in immense letters, "Mr. Octavius Budden, Amelia Cottage (Mrs. B.'s name was Amelia), Poplar Walk, Stamford Hill."

"Budden!" ejaculated Minns, "what can bring that vulgar man here!—say I'm asleep—say I'm out, and shall never be home again—anything to keep him down-stairs."

"But please, sir, the gentleman's coming up," replied the servant, and the fact was made evident by an appalling creaking of boots on the staircase accompanied by a pattering noise; the cause of which Minns could not, for the life of him, divine.

"Hem—show the gentleman in," said the unfortunate bachelor. Exit servant, and enter Octavius preceded by a large white dog, dressed in a suit of fleecy hosiery, with pink eyes, large ears, and no perceptible tail.

The cause of the pattering on the stairs was but too plain. Mr. Augustus Minns staggered beneath the shock of the dog's appearance.

"My dear fellow, how are you?" said Budden, as he entered.

He always spoke at the top of his voice, and always said the same thing half-a-dozen times.

"How are you, my hearty?"

"How do you do, Mr. Budden?—pray take a chair!" politely stammered the discomfited Minns.

"Thank you—thank you—well—how are you, eh?"

"Uncommonly well, thank you," said Minns, casting a diabolical look at the dog, who, with his hind legs on the floor, and his fore paws resting on the table, was dragging a bit of bread and butter out of a plate, preparatory to devouring it, with the buttered side next the carpet.

"Ah, you rogue!" said Budden to his dog; "you see, Minns, he's like me, always at home, eh, my boy?—Egad, I'm precious hot and hungry! I've walked all the way from Stamford Hill this morning."

"Have you breakfasted?" inquired Minns.

"Oh, no!—came to breakfast with you; so ring the bell, my dear fellow, will you? and let's have another cup and saucer, and the cold ham.—Make myself at home, you see!" continued Budden, dusting his boots with a table-napkin. "Ha!—ha!—ha!—'pon my life, I'm hungry."

Minns rang the bell, and tried to smile.

"I decidedly never was so hot in my life," continued Octavius, wiping his forehead; "well, but how are you, Minns? 'Pon my soul, you wear capitally!"

"D'ye think so?" said Minns; and he tried another smile.

"'Pon my life, I do!"

"Mrs. B. and—what's his name—quite well?"

"Alick—my son, you mean; never better—never better. But at such a place as we've got at Poplar Walk, you know, he couldn't be ill if he tried. When I first saw it, by Jove! it looked so knowing, with the front garden, and the green railings, and the brass knocker, and all that—I really thought it was a cut above me."

"Don't you think you'd like the ham better," interrupted Minns, "if you cut it the other way?" He saw, with feelings which it is impossible to describe, that his visitor was cutting, or rather maiming, the ham, in utter violation of all established rules.

"No, thank ye," returned Budden, with the most barbarous indifference to crime, "I prefer it this way, it eats short.

But I say, Minns, when will you come down and see us?
You will be delighted with the place; I know you will.
Amelia and I were talking about you the other night, and
Amelia said—another lump of sugar, please; thank ye—she
said, don't you think you could contrive, my dear, to say to
Mr. Minns, in a friendly way—come down, sir—damn the
dog! he's spoiling your curtains, Minns—ha!—ha!—ha!"
Minns leaped from his seat as though he had received the
discharge from a galvanic battery.

"Come out, sir!—go out, hoo!" cried poor Augustus,
keeping, nevertheless, at a very respectful distance from the
dog; having read of a case of hydrophobia in the paper of
that morning. By dint of great exertion, much shouting,
and a marvellous deal of poking under the tables with
a stick and umbrella, the dog was at last dislodged, and
placed on the landing outside the door, where he immediately
commenced a most appalling howling; at the same time
vehemently scratching the paint off the two nicely-varnished
bottom panels, until they resembled the interior of a back-
gammon-board.

"A good dog for the country that!" coolly observed
Budden to the distracted Minns, "but he's not much used to
confinement. But now, Minns, when will you come down?
I'll take no denial, positively. Let's see, to-day's Thursday.
—Will you come on Sunday? We dine at five, don't say
no—do."

After a great deal of pressing, Mr. Augustus Minns, driven
to despair, accepted the invitation, and promised to be at
Poplar Walk on the ensuing Sunday, at a quarter before five
to the minute.

" Now mind the direction," said Budden: "the coach goes
from the Flower Pot, in Bishopsgate Street, every half-hour.
When the coach stops at the Swan, you'll see, immediately
opposite you, a white house."

"Which is your house—I understand," said Minns,
wishing to cut short the visit, and the story, at the same
time.

"No, no, that's not mine; that's Grogus's, the great iron-
monger's. I was going to say—you turn down by the side of
the white house till you can't go another step further—mind
that!—and then you turn to your right, by some stables—
well; close to you, you'll see a wall with 'Beware of the
Dog' written on it in large letters—(Minns shuddered)—go

along by the side of that wall for about a quarter of a mile —and anybody will show you which is my place."

"Very well—thank ye—good-bye."

"Be punctual."

"Certainly : good morning."

"I say, Minns, you've got a card."

"Yes, I have ; thank ye." And Mr. Octavius Budden departed, leaving his cousin looking forward to his visit on the following Sunday, with the feelings of a penniless poet to the weekly visit of his Scotch landlady.

Sunday arrived ; the sky was bright and clear ; crowds of people were hurrying along the streets, intent on their different schemes of pleasure for the day ; everything and everybody looked cheerful and happy except Mr. Augustus Minns.

The day was fine, but the heat was considerable ; when Mr. Minns had fagged up the shady side of Fleet Street, Cheapside, and Threadneedle Street, he had become pretty warm, tolerably dusty, and it was getting late into the bargain. By the most extraordinary good fortune, however, a coach was waiting at the Flower Pot, into which Mr. Augustus Minns got, on the solemn assurance of the cad that the vehicle would start in three minutes—that being the very utmost extremity of time it was allowed to wait by Act of Parliament. A quarter of an hour elapsed, and there were no signs of moving. Minns looked at his watch for the sixth time.

"Coachman, are you going or not?" bawled Mr. Minns, with his head and half his body out of the coach window.

"Di—rectly, sir," said the coachman, with his hands in his pockets, looking as much unlike a man in a hurry as possible.

"Bill, take them cloths off." Five minutes more elapsed : at the end of which time the coachman mounted the box, from whence he looked down the street, and up the street, and hailed all the pedestrians for another five minutes.

"Coachman! if you don't go this moment, I shall get out," said Mr. Minns, rendered desperate by the lateness of the hour, and the impossibility of being in Poplar Walk at the appointed time.

"Going this minute, sir," was the reply ;—and, accordingly, the machine trundled on for a couple of hundred yards, and then stopped again. Minns doubled himself up in a corner of the coach, and abandoned himself to his fate, as a child, a mother, a bandbox and a parasol, became his fellow-passengers.

The child was an affectionate and an amiable infant; the little dear mistook Minns for his other parent, and screamed to embrace him.

"Be quiet, dear," said the mamma, restraining the impetuosity of the darling, whose little fat legs were kicking, and stamping, and twining themselves into the most complicated forms, in an ecstasy of impatience. "Be quiet, dear, that's not your papa."

"Thank Heaven I am not!" thought Minns, as the first gleam of pleasure he had experienced that morning shone like a meteor through his wretchedness.

Playfulness was agreeably mingled with affection in the disposition of the boy. When satisfied that Mr. Minns was not his parent, he endeavoured to attract his notice by scraping his drab trousers with his dirty shoes, poking his chest with his mamma's parasol, and other nameless endearments peculiar to infancy, with which he beguiled the tediousness of the ride, apparently very much to his own satisfaction.

When the unfortunate gentleman arrived at the Swan, he found to his great dismay, that it was a quarter past five. The white house, the stables, the "Beware of the Dog,"— every landmark was passed, with a rapidity not unusual to a gentleman of a certain age when too late for dinner. After the lapse of a few minutes, Mr. Minns found himself opposite a yellow brick house with a green door, brass knocker, and door-plate, green window-frames and ditto railings, with "a garden" in front, that is to say, a small loose bit of gravelled ground, with one round and two scalene triangular beds, containing a fir-tree, twenty or thirty bulbs, and an unlimited number of marigolds. The taste of Mr. and Mrs. Budden was further displayed by the appearance of a Cupid on each side of the door, perched upon a heap of large chalk flints, variegated with pink conch-shells. His knock at the door was answered by a stumpy boy, in drab livery, cotton stockings and high-lows, who, after hanging his hat on one of the dozen brass pegs which ornamented the passage, denominated by courtesy "The Hall," ushered him into a front drawing-room commanding a very extensive view of the backs of the neighbouring houses. The usual ceremony of introduction, and so forth, over, Mr. Minns took his seat : not a little agitated at finding that he was the last comer, and, somehow or other, the Lion of about a dozen people, sitting together in a small drawing-room, getting rid of that most tedious of all time, the time preceding dinner.

"Well, Brogson," said Budden, addressing an elderly gentleman in a black coat, drab knee-breeches, and long gaiters, who, under pretence of inspecting the prints in an Annual, had been engaged in satisfying himself on the subject of Mr. Minns's general appearance, by looking at him over the tops of the leaves—"Well, Brogson, what do Ministers mean to do ? Will they go out, or what ? "

" Oh—why—really, you know, I'm the last person in the world to ask for news. Your cousin, from his situation, is the most likely person to answer the question."

Mr. Minns assured the last speaker, that although he was in Somerset House, he possessed no official communication relative to the projects of his Majesty's Ministers. But his remark was evidently received incredulously ; and no further conjectures being hazarded on the subject, a long pause ensued, during which the company occupied themselves in coughing and blowing their noses, until the entrance of Mrs. Budden caused a general rise.

The ceremony of introduction being over, dinner was announced, and down-stairs the party proceeded accordingly —Mr. Minns escorting Mrs. Budden as far as the drawing-room door, but being prevented, by the narrowness of the staircase, from extending his gallantry any farther. The dinner passed off as such dinners usually do. Ever and anon, amidst the clatter of knives and forks, and the hum of conversation, Mr. B.'s voice might be heard, asking a friend to take wine, and assuring him he was glad to see him ; and a great deal of by-play took place between Mrs. B. and the servants, respecting the removal of the dishes, during which her countenance assumed all the variations of a weather-glass, from "stormy" to "set fair."

Upon the dessert and wine being placed on the table, the servant, in compliance with a significant look from Mrs. B., brought down "Master Alexander," habited in a sky-blue suit with silver buttons ; and possessing hair of nearly the same colour as the metal. After sundry praises from his mother, and various admonitions as to his behaviour from his father, he was introduced to his godfather.

"Well, my little fellow—you are a fine boy, ain't you?" said Mr. Minns, as happy as a tomtit on birdlime.

"Yes."

"How old are you?"

"Eight, next We'nsday. How old are *you*?"

"Alexander," interrupted his mother, "how dare you ask Mr. Minns how old he is!"

"He asked me how old *I* was," said the precocious child, to whom Minns had from that moment internally resolved that he never would bequeath one shilling. As soon as the titter occasioned by the observation had subsided, a little smirking man with red whiskers, sitting at the bottom of the table, who during the whole of dinner had been endeavouring to obtain a listener to some stories about Sheridan, called out, with a very patronising air, "Alick, what part of speech is *be*?"

"A verb."

"That's a good boy," said Mrs. Budden, with all a mother's pride. "Now, you know what a verb is?"

"A verb is a word which signifies to be, to do, or to suffer; as, I am—I rule—I am ruled. Give me an apple, Ma."

"I'll give you an apple," replied the man with the red whiskers, who was an established friend of the family, or in other words was always invited by Mrs. Budden, whether Mr. Budden liked it or not, "if you'll tell me what is the meaning of *be*."

"Be?" said the prodigy, after a little hesitation—"an insect that gathers honey."

"No, dear," frowned Mrs. Budden; "B double E is the substantive."

"I don't think he knows much yet about *common* substantives," said the smirking gentleman, who thought this an admirable opportunity for letting off a joke. "It's clear he's not very well acquainted with *proper names*. He! he! he!"

"Gentlemen," called out Mr. Budden, from the end of the table, in a stentorian voice, and with a very important air, "will you have the goodness to charge your glasses? I have a toast to propose."

"Hear! hear!" cried the gentlemen, passing the decanters. After they had made the round of the table, Mr. Budden proceeded—"Gentlemen; there is an individual present——"

"Hear! hear!" said the little man with red whiskers.

" *Pray* be quiet, Jones," remonstrated Budden.

" I say, gentlemen, there is an individual present," resumed
the host, " in whose society I am sure we must take great
delight—and—and—the conversation of that individual must
have afforded to every one present, the utmost pleasure."
[" Thank Heaven, he does not mean me ! " thought Minns,
conscious that his diffidence and exclusiveness had prevented
his saying above a dozen words since he entered the house.]
" Gentlemen, I am but a humble individual myself, and I
perhaps ought to apologise for allowing any individual feelings of friendship and affection for the person I allude to,
to induce me to venture to rise, to propose the health of
that person—a person that, I am sure—that is to say, a
person whose virtues must endear him to those who know
him—and those who have not the pleasure of knowing him,
cannot dislike him."

" Hear ! hear ! " said the company, in a tone of encouragement and approval.

" Gentlemen," continued Budden, " my cousin is a man
who—who is a relation of my own." (Hear ! hear !) Minns
groaned audibly. " Who I am most happy to see here, and
who, if he were not here, would certainly have deprived us
of the great pleasure we all feel in seeing him. (Loud cries
of hear !) Gentlemen, I feel that I have already trespassed
on your attention for too long a time. With every feeling
—of—with every sentiment of—of — "

" Gratification "—suggested the friend of the family.

" —Of gratification, I beg to propose the health of Mr.
Minns."

" Standing, gentlemen ! " shouted the indefatigable little
man with the whiskers—" and with the honours. Take your
time from me, if you please. Hip ! hip ! hip !—Za !—Hip !
hip ! hip !—Za !—Hip ! hip !—Za—a—a ! "

All eyes were now fixed on the subject of the toast, who
by gulping down port wine at the imminent hazard of suffocation, endeavoured to conceal his confusion. After as long
a pause as decency would admit, he rose, but, as the
newspapers sometimes say in their reports, " we regret that
we are quite unable to give even the substance of the honourable gentleman's observations." The words " present company
—honour—present occasion," and " great happiness "—heard
occasionally, and repeated at intervals, with a countenance
expressive of the utmost confusion and misery, convinced the

company that he was making an excellent speech; and, accordingly, on his resuming his seat, they cried "Bravo!" and manifested tumultuous applause. Jones, who had been long watching his opportunity, then darted up.

"Budden," said he, "will you allow *me* to propose a toast?"

"Certainly," replied Budden, adding in an under-tone to Minns right across the table, "Devilish sharp fellow that: you'll be very much pleased with his speech. He talks equally well on any subject." Minns bowed, and Mr. Jones proceeded:

"It has on several occasions, in various instances, under many circumstances, and in different companies, fallen to my lot to propose a toast to those by whom, at the time, I have had the honour to be surrounded. I have sometimes, I will cheerfully own—for why should I deny it?—felt the over-whelming nature of the task I have undertaken, and my own utter incapability to do justice to the subject. If such have been my feelings, however, on former occasions, what must they be now—now—under the extraordinary circumstances in which I am placed. (Hear! hear!) To describe my feelings accurately, would be impossible; but I cannot give you a better idea of them, gentlemen, than by referring to a circumstance which happens, oddly enough, to occur to my mind at the moment. On one occasion, when that truly great and illustrious man, Sheridan, was—— "

Now, there is no knowing what new villainy in the form of a joke would have been heaped on the grave of that very ill-used man, Mr. Sheridan, if the boy in drab had not at that moment entered the room in a breathless state, to report that, as it was a very wet night, the nine o'clock stage had come round, to know whether there was anybody going to town, as, in that case, he (the nine o'clock) had room for one inside.

Mr. Minns started up; and, despite countless exclamations of surprise and entreaties to stay, persisted in his determination to accept the vacant place. But the brown silk umbrella was nowhere to be found; and as the coachman couldn't wait, he drove back to the Swan, leaving word for Mr. Minns to "run round" and catch him. However, as it did not occur to Mr. Minns for some ten minutes or so, that he had left the brown silk umbrella with the ivory handle in the other coach, coming down; and, moreover, as he was by no means remarkable for speed, it is no matter of surprise that when he accomplished the feat of "running round" to the Swan, the coach—the last coach—had gone without him.

It was somewhere about three o'clock in the morning, when Mr. Augustus Minns knocked feebly at the street-door of his lodgings in Tavistock Street, cold, wet, cross, and miserable. He made his will next morning, and his professional man informs us, in that strict confidence in which we inform the public, that neither the name of Mr. Octavius Budden, nor of Mrs. Amelia Budden, nor of Master Alexander Augustus Budden, appears therein.

CHAPTER III

THE Miss Crumptons, or to quote the authority of the inscription on the garden-gate of Minerva House, Hammersmith, "The Misses Crumpton," were two unusually tall, particularly thin, and exceedingly skinny personages: very upright, and very yellow. Miss Amelia Crumpton owned to thirty-eight, and Miss Maria Crumpton admitted she was forty; an admission which was rendered perfectly unnecessary by the self-evident fact of her being at least fifty. They dressed in the most interesting manner—like twins! and looked as happy and comfortable as a couple of marigolds run to seed. They were very precise, had the strictest possible ideas of propriety, wore false hair, and always smelt very strongly of lavender.

Minerva House, conducted under the auspices of the two sisters, was a "finishing establishment for young ladies," where some twenty girls of the ages of from thirteen to nineteen inclusive, acquired a smattering of everything, and a knowledge of nothing; instruction in French and Italian, dancing lessons twice a week; and other necessaries of life. The house was a white one, a little removed from the roadside, with close palings in front. The bedroom windows were always left partly open, to afford a bird's-eye view of numerous little bedsteads with very white dimity furniture, and thereby impress the passer-by with a due sense of the luxuries of the establishment; and there was a front parlour hung round with highly varnished maps which nobody ever looked at, and filled with books which no one ever read, appropriated exclusively to the reception of parents, who, whenever they called, could not fail to be struck with the very deep appearance of the place.

"Amelia, my dear," said Miss Maria Crumpton, entering the school-room one morning, with her false hair in papers:

as she occasionally did, in order to impress the young ladies
with a conviction of its reality. "Amelia, my dear, here is
a most gratifying note I have just received. You needn't
mind reading it aloud."

Miss Amelia, thus advised, proceeded to read the following
note with an air of great triumph:

"Cornelius Brook Dingwall, Esq., M.P., presents his compliments to Miss Crumpton, and will feel much obliged by
Miss Crumpton's calling on him, if she conveniently can, to-
morrow morning at one o'clock, as Cornelius Brook Dingwall,
Esq., M.P., is anxious to see Miss Crumpton on the subject
of placing Miss Brook Dingwall under her charge.

"Adelphi.

"Monday morning."

"A Member of Parliament's daughter!" ejaculated Amelia,
in an ecstatic tone.

"A Member of Parliament's daughter!" repeated Miss
Maria, with a smile of delight, which, of course, elicited a
concurrent titter of pleasure from all the young ladies.

"It's exceedingly delightful!" said Miss Amelia; whereupon all the young ladies murmured their admiration again.
Courtiers are but school-boys, and court-ladies school-girls.

So important an announcement at once superseded the
business of the day. A holiday was declared, in commemora-
tion of the great event; the Miss Crumptons retired to their
private apartment to talk it over; the smaller girls discussed
the probable manners and customs of the daughter of a
Member of Parliament; and the young ladies verging on
eighteen wondered whether she was engaged, whether she
was pretty, whether she wore much bustle, and many other
whethers of equal importance.

The two Miss Crumptons proceeded to the Adelphi at the
appointed time next day, dressed, of course, in their best
style, and looking as amiable as they possibly could—which,
by-the-bye, is not saying much for them. Having sent in
their cards, through the medium of a red-hot looking footman
in bright livery, they were ushered into the august presence
of the profound Dingwall.

Cornelius Brook Dingwall, Esq., M.P., was very haughty,
solemn, and portentous. He had, naturally, a somewhat
spasmodic expression of countenance, which was not rendered

the less remarkable by his wearing an extremely stiff cravat. He was wonderfully proud of the M.P. attached to his name, and never lost an opportunity of reminding people of his dignity. He had a great idea of his own abilities, which must have been a great comfort to him, as no one else had; and in diplomacy, on a small scale, in his own family arrangements, he considered himself unrivalled. He was a county magistrate, and discharged the duties of his station with all due justice and impartiality; frequently committing poachers, and occasionally committing himself. Miss Brook Dingwall was one of that numerous class of young ladies who, like adverbs, may be known by their answering to a commonplace question, and doing nothing else.

On the present occasion, this talented individual was seated in a small library at a table covered with papers, doing nothing, but trying to look busy, playing at shop. Acts of Parliament, and letters directed to "Cornelius Brook Dingwall, Esq., M.P.," were ostentatiously scattered over the table; at a little distance from which, Mrs. Brook Dingwall was seated at work. One of those public nuisances, a spoilt child, was playing about the room, dressed after the most approved fashion—in a blue tunic with a black belt a quarter of a yard wide, fastened with an immense buckle—looking like a robber in a melodrama, seen through a diminishing glass.

After a little pleasantry from the sweet child, who amused himself by running away with Miss Maria Crumpton's chair as fast as it was placed for her, the visitors were seated, and Cornelius Brook Dingwall, Esq., opened the conversation.

He had sent for Miss Crumpton, he said, in consequence of the high character he had received of her establishment from his friend, Sir Alfred Muggs.

Miss Crumpton murmured her acknowledgments to him (Muggs), and Cornelius proceeded.

"One of my principal reasons, Miss Crumpton, for parting with my daughter, is, that she has lately acquired some sentimental ideas, which it is most desirable to eradicate from her young mind." (Here the little innocent before noticed, fell out of an arm-chair with an awful crash.)

"Naughty boy!" said his mamma, who appeared more surprised at his taking the liberty of falling down, than at anything else; "I'll ring the bell for James to take him away."

"Pray don't check him, my love," said the diplomatist, as soon as he could make himself heard amidst the unearthly howling consequent upon the threat and the tumble. "It all arises from his great flow of spirits." This last explanation was addressed to Miss Crumpton.

"Certainly, sir," replied the antique Maria: not exactly seeing, however, the connexion between a flow of animal spirits and a fall from an arm-chair.

Silence was restored, and the M.P. resumed: "Now, I know nothing so likely to effect this object, Miss Crumpton, as her mixing constantly in the society of girls of her own age; and, as I know that in your establishment she will meet such as are not likely to contaminate her young mind, I propose to send her to you."

The youngest Miss Crumpton expressed the acknowledgments of the establishment generally. Maria was rendered speechless by bodily pain. The dear little fellow, having recovered his animal spirits, was standing upon her most tender foot, by way of getting his face (which looked like a capital O in a red-lettered play-bill) on a level with the writing-table.

"Of course, Lavinia will be a parlour boarder," continued the enviable father; "and on one point I wish my directions to be strictly observed. The fact is, that some ridiculous love affair, with a person much her inferior in life, has been the cause of her present state of mind. Knowing that of course, under your care, she can have no opportunity of meeting this person, I do not object to—indeed, I should rather prefer—her mixing with such society as you see yourself."

This important statement was again interrupted by the high-spirited little creature, in the excess of his joyousness breaking a pane of glass, and nearly precipitating himself into an adjacent area. James was rung for; considerable confusion and screaming succeeded; two little blue legs were seen to kick violently in the air as the man left the room, and the child was gone.

"Mr. Brook Dingwall would like Miss Brook Dingwall to learn everything," said Mrs. Brook Dingwall, who hardly ever said anything at all.

"Certainly," said both the Miss Crumptons together.

"And as I trust the plan I have devised will be effectual in weaning my daughter from this absurd idea, Miss Crumpton," continued the legislator, " I hope you will have the goodness to comply, in all respects, with any request I may forward to you."

The promise was of course made ; and after a lengthened discussion, conducted on behalf of the Dingwalls with the most becoming diplomatic gravity, and on that of the Crumptons with profound respect, it was finally arranged that Miss Lavinia should be forwarded to Hammersmith on the next day but one, on which occasion the half-yearly ball given at the establishment was to take place. It might divert the dear girl's mind. This, by the way, was another bit of diplomacy.

Miss Lavinia was introduced to her future governess, and both the Miss Crumptons pronounced her " a most charming girl ; " an opinion which, by a singular coincidence, they always entertained of any new pupil.

Courtesies were exchanged, acknowledgments expressed, condescension exhibited, and the interview terminated.

Preparations, to make use of theatrical phraseology, " on a scale of magnitude never before attempted," were incessantly made at Minerva House to give every effect to the forth-coming ball. The largest room in the house was pleasingly ornamented with blue calico roses, plaid tulips, and other equally natural-looking artificial flowers, the work of the young ladies themselves. The carpet was taken up, the folding-doors were taken down, the furniture was taken out, and rout-seats were taken in. The linen-drapers of Hammer-smith were astounded at the sudden demand for blue sarsenet ribbon, and long white gloves. Dozens of geraniums were purchased for bouquets, and a harp and two violins were bespoke from town, in addition to the grand piano already on the premises. The young ladies who were selected to show off on the occasion, and do credit to the establish-ment, practised incessantly, much to their own satisfaction, and greatly to the annoyance of the lame old gentleman over the way ; and a constant correspondence was kept up between the Misses Crumpton and the Hammersmith pastrycook.

The evening came ; and then there was such a lacing of stays, and tying of sandals, and dressing of hair, as never can take place with a proper degree of bustle out of a boarding-school. The smaller girls managed to be in every-body's way, and were pushed about accordingly ; and the elder ones dressed. and tied, and flattered, and envied one another, as earnestly and sincerely as if they had actually *come out.*

"How do I look, dear?" inquired Miss Emily Smithers, the belle of the house, of Miss Caroline Wilson, who was her bosom friend, because she was the ugliest girl in Hammersmith, or out of it.

"Oh! charming, dear. How do I?"

"Delightful! you never looked so handsome," returned the belle, adjusting her own dress, and not bestowing a glance on her poor companion.

"I hope young Hilton will come early," said another young lady to Miss somebody else, in a fever of expectation.

"I'm sure he'd be highly flattered if he knew it," returned the other, who was practising *l'été.*

"Oh! he's so handsome," said the first.

"Such a charming person!" added a second.

"Such a *distingué* air!" said a third.

"Oh, what *do* you think?" said another girl, running into the room; "Miss Crumpton says her cousin's coming."

"What! Theodosius Butler?" said everybody in raptures.

"Is *he* handsome?" inquired a novice.

"No, not particularly handsome," was the general reply; "but, oh, so clever!"

Mr. Theodosius Butler was one of those immortal geniuses who are to be met with in almost every circle. They have, usually, very deep, monotonous voices. They always persuade themselves that they are wonderful persons, and that they ought to be very miserable, though they don't precisely know why. They are very conceited, and usually possess half an idea; but, with enthusiastic young ladies, and silly young gentlemen, they are very wonderful persons. The individual in question, Mr. Theodosius, had written a pamphlet containing some very weighty considerations on the expediency of doing something or other; and as every sentence contained a good many words of four syllables, his admirers took it for granted that he meant a good deal.

"Perhaps that's he," exclaimed several young ladies, as the first pull of the evening threatened destruction to the bell of the gate.

An awful pause ensued. Some boxes arrived and a young lady—Miss Brook Dingwall, in full ball costume, with an immense gold chain round her neck, and her dress looped up

Theodosius Introduced to the New Pupil
(*p. 330*)

with a single rose; an ivory fan in her hand, and a most interesting expression of despair in her face.

The Miss Crumptons inquired after the family, with the most excruciating anxiety, and Miss Brook Dingwall was formally introduced to her future companions. The Miss Crumptons conversed with the young ladies in the most mellifluous tones, in order that Miss Brook Dingwall might be properly impressed with their amiable treatment.

Another pull at the bell. Mr. Dadson the writing-master, and his wife. The wife in green silk, with shoes and cap-trimmings to correspond : the writing-master in a white waistcoat, black knee-shorts, and ditto silk stockings, displaying a leg large enough for two writing-masters. The young ladies whispered one another, and the writing-master and his wife flattered the Miss Crumptons, who were dressed in amber, with long sashes, like dolls.

Repeated pulls at the bell, and arrivals too numerous to particularise : papas and mammas, and aunts and uncles, the owners and guardians of the different pupils ; the singing-master, Signor Lobskini, in a black wig ; the piano-forte player and the violins ; the harp, in a state of intoxication ; and some twenty young men, who stood near the door, and talked to one another, occasionally bursting into a giggle. A general hum of conversation. Coffee handed round, and plentifully partaken of by fat mammas, who looked like the stout people who come on in pantomimes for the sole purpose of being knocked down.

The popular Mr. Hilton was the next arrival; and he having, at the request of the Miss Crumptons, undertaken the office of Master of the Ceremonies, the quadrilles commenced with considerable spirit. The young men by the door gradually advanced into the middle of the room, and in time became sufficiently at ease to consent to be introduced to partners. The writing-master danced every set, springing about with the most fearful agility, and his wife played a rubber in the back-parlour—a little room with five book-shelves, dignified by the name of the study. Setting her down to whist was a half-yearly piece of generalship on the part of the Miss Crumptons ; it was necessary to hide her somewhere, on account of her being a fright.

The interesting Lavinia Brook Dingwall was the only girl present who appeared to take no interest in the proceedings of the evening. In vain was she solicited to dance ; in vain was the universal homage paid to her as the daughter of a member of parliament. She was equally unmoved by the splendid tenor of the inimitable Lobskini, and the brilliant execution of Miss Lætitia Parsons, whose performance of "The Recollections of Ireland" was universally declared to be almost equal to that of Moscheles himself. Not even the announcement of the arrival of Mr. Theodosius Butler could induce her to leave the corner of the back drawing-room in which she was seated.

" Now, Theodosius," said Miss Maria Crumpton, after that enlightened pamphleteer had nearly run the gauntlet of the whole company, "I must introduce you to our new pupil."

Theodosius looked as if he cared for nothing earthly.

"She's the daughter of a member of parliament," said Maria.—Theodosius started.

"And her name is——?" he inquired.

"Miss Brook Dingwall."

"Great Heaven!" poetically exclaimed Theodosius, in a low tone.

Miss Crumpton commenced the introduction in due form. Miss Brook Dingwall languidly raised her head.

"Edward!" she exclaimed, with a half-shriek, on seeing the well-known nankeen legs.

Fortunately, as Miss Maria Crumpton possessed no remarkable share of penetration, and as it was one of the diplomatic arrangements that no attention was to be paid to Miss Lavinia's incoherent exclamations, she was perfectly unconscious of the mutual agitation of the parties; and therefore, seeing that the offer of his hand for the next quadrille was accepted, she left him by the side of Miss Brook Dingwall.

"Oh, Edward!" exclaimed that most romantic of all romantic young ladies, as the light of science seated himself beside her, "Oh, Edward, is it you?"

Mr. Theodosius assured the dear creature, in the most impassioned manner, that he was not conscious of being anybody but himself.

"Then why—why—this disguise? Oh! Edward M'Neville Walter, what have I not suffered on your account?"

"Lavinia, hear me," replied the hero, in his most poetic strain. "Do not condemn me unheard. If anything that emanates from the soul of such a wretch as I, can occupy a place in your recollection—if any being, so vile, deserve your notice—you may remember that I once published a pamphlet (and paid for its publication) entitled 'Considerations on the Policy of Removing the Duty on Bees'-wax.'"

"I do—I do!" sobbed Lavinia.

"That," continued the lover, "was a subject to which your father was devoted, heart and soul."

"He was— he was!" reiterated the sentimentalist.

"I knew it," continued Theodosius, tragically; "I knew it—I forwarded him a copy. He wished to know me. Could I disclose my real name? Never! No, I assumed that name which you have so often pronounced in tones of endearment. As M'Neville Walter, I devoted myself to the stirring cause; as M'Neville Walter, I gained your heart; in the same character I was ejected from your house by your father's domestics; and in no character at all have I since been enabled to see you. We now meet again, and I proudly own that I am—Theodosius Butler."

The young lady appeared perfectly satisfied with this argumentative address, and bestowed a look of the most ardent affection on the immortal advocate of bees'-wax.

"May I hope," said he, "that the promise your father's violent behaviour interrupted, may be renewed?"

"Let us join this set," replied Lavinia, coquettishly—for girls of nineteen *can* coquette.

"No," ejaculated he of the nankeens; "I stir not from this spot, writhing under this torture of suspense. May I— may I—hope?"

"You may."

"The promise is renewed?"

"It is."

"I have your permission?"

"You have."

"To the fullest extent?"

"You know it," returned the blushing Lavinia. The contortions of the interesting Butler's visage expressed his raptures.

We could dilate upon the occurrences that ensued. How Mr. Theodosius and Miss Lavinia danced, and talked, and sighed for the remainder of the evening—how the Miss Crumptons were delighted thereat. How the writing-master continued to frisk about with one-horse power, and how his wife, from some unaccountable freak, left the whist-table in the little back-parlour, and persisted in displaying her green head-dress in the most conspicuous part of the drawing-room. How the supper consisted of small triangular sandwiches in trays, and a tart here and there by way of variety; and how the visitors consumed warm water disguised with lemon, and dotted with nutmeg, under the denomination of negus. These, and other matters of as much interest, however, we pass over, for the purpose of describing a scene of even more importance.

A fortnight after the date of the ball, Cornelius Brook Dingwall, Esq., M.P., was seated at the same library-table, and in the same room, as we have before described. He was alone, and his face bore an expression of deep thought and solemn gravity—he was drawing up "A Bill for the better observance of Easter Monday."

The footman tapped at the door—the legislator started from his reverie, and "Miss Crumpton" was announced. Permission was given for Miss Crumpton to enter the *sanctum*; Maria came sliding in, and having taken her seat with a due portion of affectation, the footman retired, and the governess was left alone with the M.P. Oh! how she longed for the presence of a third party! Even the facetious young gentleman would have been a relief.

Miss Crumpton began the duet. She hoped Mrs. Brook Dingwall and the handsome little boy were in good health.

They were. Mrs. Brook Dingwall and little Frederick were at Brighton.

"Much obliged to you, Miss Crumpton," said Cornelius, in his most dignified manner, "for your attention in calling this morning. I should have driven down to Hammersmith, to see Lavinia, but your account was so very satisfactory, and my duties in the House occupy me so much, that I determined to postpone it for a week. How has she gone on?"

"Very well indeed, sir," returned Maria, dreading to inform the father that she had gone off.

"Ah, I thought the plan on which I proceeded would be a match for her."

Here was a favourable opportunity to say that somebody else had been a match for her. But the unfortunate governess was unequal to the task.

"You have persevered strictly in the line of conduct I prescribed, Miss Crumpton?"

"Strictly, sir."

"You tell me in your note that her spirits gradually improved."

"Very much indeed, sir."

"To be sure. I was convinced they would."

"But I fear, sir," said Miss Crumpton, with visible emotion, "I fear the plan has not succeeded quite so well as we could have wished."

"No!" exclaimed the prophet. "Bless me! Miss Crumpton, you look alarmed. What has happened?"

"Miss Brook Dingwall, sir——"

"Yes, ma'am?"

"Has gone, sir"—said Maria, exhibiting a strong inclination to faint.

"Gone!"

"Eloped, sir."

"Eloped!—Who with—when—where—how?" almost shrieked the agitated diplomatist.

The natural yellow of the unfortunate Maria's face changed to all the hues of the rainbow, as she laid a small packet on the Member's table.

He hurriedly opened it. A letter from his daughter, and another from Theodosius. He glanced over their contents— "Ere this reaches you, far distant—appeal to feelings—love to distraction—bees'-wax—slavery," &c., &c. He dashed his hand to his forehead, and paced the room with fearfully long strides, to the great alarm of the precise Maria.

"Now mind; from this time forward," said Mr. Brook Dingwall, suddenly stopping at the table, and beating time upon it with his hand; "from this time forward, I never will, under any circumstances whatever, permit a man who writes pamphlets to enter any other room of this house but the kitchen.—I'll allow my daughter and her husband one hundred and fifty pounds a year, and never see their faces again: and, damme! ma'am, I'll bring in a bill for the abolition of finishing-schools."

Some time has elapsed since this passionate declaration. Mr. and Mrs. Butler are at present rusticating in a small cottage at Ball's Pond, pleasantly situated in the immediate vicinity of a brick-field. They have no family. Mr. Theodosius looks very important, and writes incessantly ; but, in consequence of a gross combination on the part of publishers, none of his productions appear in print. His young wife begins to think that ideal misery is preferable to real un-

happiness ; and that a marriage contracted in haste, and re-
pented at leisure, is the cause of more substantial wretchedness than she ever anticipated.

On cool reflection, Cornelius Brook Dingwall, Esq., M.P.,
was reluctantly compelled to admit that the untoward result
of his admirable arrangements was attributable, not to the
Miss Crumptons, but his own diplomacy. He however consoles himself, like some other small diplomatists, by satisfactorily proving that if his plans did not succeed, they ought
to have done so.   Minerva House is *in statu quo*, and "The
Misses Crumpton " remain in the peaceable and undisturbed
enjoyment of all the advantages resulting from their
Finishing-School.

CHAPTER IV

THE TUGGSES AT RAMSGATE

ONCE upon a time there dwelt, in a narrow street on the Surrey side of the water, within three minutes' walk of old London Bridge, Mr. Joseph Tuggs—a little dark-faced man, with shiny hair, twinkling eyes, short legs, and a body of very considerable thickness, measuring from the centre button of his waistcoat in front, to the ornamental buttons of his coat behind. The figure of the amiable Mrs. Tuggs, if not perfectly symmetrical, was decidedly comfortable; and the form of her only daughter, the accomplished Miss Charlotte Tuggs, was fast ripening into that state of luxuriant plumpness which had enchanted the eyes, and captivated the heart, of Mr. Joseph Tuggs in his earlier days. Mr. Simon Tuggs, his only son, and Miss Charlotte Tuggs's only brother, was as differently formed in body, as he was differently constituted in mind, from the remainder of his family. There was that elongation in his thoughtful face, and that tendency to weakness in his interesting legs, which tell so forcibly of a great mind and romantic disposition. The slightest traits of character in such a being, possess no mean interest to speculative minds. He usually appeared in public, in capacious shoes with black cotton stockings; and was observed to be particularly attached to a black glazed stock, without tie or ornament of any description.

There is perhaps no profession, however useful; no pursuit, however meritorious; which can escape the petty attacks of vulgar minds. Mr. Joseph Tuggs was a grocer. It might be supposed that a grocer was beyond the breath of calumny; but no—the neighbours stigmatised him as a chandler; and the poisonous voice of envy distinctly asserted that he dispensed tea and coffee by the quartern, retailed sugar by the ounce, cheese by the slice, tobacco by the screw, and butter by the pat. These taunts, however, were lost upon the Tuggses. Mr. Tuggs attended to the grocery

department; Mrs. Tuggs to the cheesemongery; and Miss
Tuggs to her education. Mr. Simon Tuggs kept his father's
books, and his own counsel.

One fine spring afternoon, the latter gentleman was seated
on a tub of weekly Dorset, behind the little red desk with a
wooden rail, which ornamented a corner of the counter;
when a stranger dismounted from a cab, and hastily entered
the shop. He was habited in black cloth, and bore with him
a green umbrella and a blue bag.

"Mr. Tuggs?" said the stranger, inquiringly.

"*My* name is Tuggs," replied Mr. Simon.

"It's the other Mr. Tuggs," said the stranger, looking
towards the glass door which led into the parlour behind
the shop, and on the inside of which, the round face of
Mr. Tuggs, senior, was distinctly visible, peeping over the
curtain.

Mr. Simon gracefully waved his pen, as if in intimation of
his wish that his father would advance. Mr. Joseph Tuggs,
with considerable celerity, removed his face from the curtain
and placed it before the stranger.

"I come from the Temple," said the man with the bag.

"From the Temple!" said Mrs. Tuggs, flinging open the
door of the little parlour and disclosing Miss Tuggs in
perspective.

"From the Temple!" said Miss Tuggs and Mr. Simon
Tuggs at the same moment.

"From the Temple!" said Mr. Joseph Tuggs, turning as
pale as a Dutch cheese.

"From the Temple," repeated the man with the bag;
"from Mr. Cower's, the solicitor's. Mr. Tuggs, I congratulate you, sir. Ladies, I wish you joy of your prosperity!
We have been successful." And the man with the bag
leisurely divested himself of his umbrella and glove, as a
preliminary to shaking hands with Mr. Joseph Tuggs.

Now the words "we have been successful," had no sooner
issued from the mouth of the man with the bag, than Mr.
Simon Tuggs rose from the tub of weekly Dorset, opened
his eyes very wide, gasped for breath, made figures of eight
in the air with his pen, and finally fell into the arms of his
anxious mother, and fainted away without the slightest
ostensible cause or pretence.

"Water!" screamed Mrs. Tuggs.

"Look up, my son," exclaimed Mr. Tuggs.

"Simon! dear Simon!" shrieked Miss Tuggs.

"I'm better now," said Mr. Simon Tuggs. "What! successful!" And then, as corroborative evidence of his being better, he fainted away again, and was borne into the little parlour by the united efforts of the remainder of the family, and the man with the bag.

To a casual spectator, or to any one unacquainted with the position of the family, this fainting would have been unaccountable. To those who understood the mission of the man with the bag, and were moreover acquainted with the excitability of the nerves of Mr. Simon Tuggs, it was quite comprehensible. A long-pending law-suit respecting the validity of a will, had been unexpectedly decided; and Mr. Joseph Tuggs was the possessor of twenty thousand pounds.

A prolonged consultation took place, that night, in the little parlour—a consultation that was to settle the future destinies of the Tuggses. The shop was shut up, at an unusually early hour; and many were the unavailing kicks bestowed upon the closed door by applicants for quarterns of sugar, or half-quarterns of bread, or penn'orths of pepper, which were to have been "left till Saturday," but which fortune had decreed were to be left alone altogether.

"We must certainly give up business," said Miss Tuggs.

"Oh, decidedly," said Mrs. Tuggs.

"Simon shall go to the bar," said Mr. Joseph Tuggs.

"And I shall always sign myself 'Cymon' in future," said his son.

"And I shall call myself Charlotta," said Miss Tuggs.

"And you must always call me 'Ma,' and father 'Pa,'" said Mrs. Tuggs.

"Yes, and Pa must leave off all his vulgar habits," interposed Miss Tuggs.

"I'll take care of all that," responded Mr. Joseph Tuggs, complacently. He was, at that very moment, eating pickled salmon with a pocket-knife.

"We must leave town immediately," said Mr. Cymon Tuggs.

Everybody concurred that this was an indispensable preliminary to being genteel. The question then arose, Where should they go?

"Gravesend?" mildly suggested Mr. Joseph Tuggs. The idea was unanimously scouted. Gravesend was *low*.

" Margate ? " insinuated Mrs. Tuggs. Worse and worse—nobody there, but tradespeople.

" Brighton ? "   Mr. Cymon Tuggs opposed an insurmount-able objection.   All the coaches had been upset, in turn, within the last three weeks ; each coach had averaged two passengers killed, and six wounded ; and, in every case, the newspapers had distinctly understood that " no blame what-ever was attributable to the coachman."

" Ramsgate ? " ejaculated Mr. Cymon, thoughtfully.   To be sure ; how stupid they must have been, not to have thought of that before !   Ramsgate was just the place of all others.

Two months after this conversation, the City of London Ramsgate steamer was running gaily down the river.   Her flag was flying, her band was playing, her passengers were conversing ; everything about her seemed gay and lively.—No wonder—the Tuggses were on board.

" Charming, ain't it ? " said Mr. Joseph Tuggs, in a bottle-green great-coat, with a velvet collar of the same ; and a blue travelling-cap with a gold band.

" Soul-inspiring," replied Mr. Cymon Tuggs—he was entered at the bar.   " Soul-inspiring ! "

" Delightful morning, sir ! " said a stoutish, military-look-ing gentleman in a blue surtout buttoned up to his chin, and white trousers chained down to the soles of his boots.

Mr. Cymon Tuggs took upon himself the responsibility of answering the observation.   " Heavenly ! " he replied.

" You are an enthusiastic admirer of the beauties of Nature, sir ? " said the military gentleman.

" I am, sir," replied Mr. Cymon Tuggs.

" Travelled much, sir ? " inquired the military gentleman.

" Not much," replied Mr. Cymon Tuggs.

" You've been on the continent, of course ? " inquired the military gentleman.

" Not exactly," replied Mr. Cymon Tuggs—in a qualified tone, as if he wished it to be implied that he had gone half-way and come back again.

" You of course intend your son to make the grand tour, sir ? " said the military gentleman, addressing Mr. Joseph Tuggs.

As Mr. Joseph Tuggs did not precisely understand what the grand tour was, or how such an article was manufac-tured, he replied, " Of course."   Just as he said the word, there came tripping up, from her seat at the stern of the vessel, a young lady in a puce-coloured silk cloak, and boots of the same ; with long black ringlets, large black eyes, brief petticoats, and unexceptionable ankles.

"Walter, my dear," said the young lady to the military gentleman.

"Yes, Belinda, my love," responded the military gentleman to the black-eyed young lady.

"What have you left me alone so long for?" said the young lady. "I have been stared out of countenance by those rude young men."

"What! stared at?" exclaimed the military gentleman, with an emphasis which made Mr. Cymon Tuggs withdraw his eyes from the young lady's face with inconceivable rapidity. "Which young men—where?" and the military gentleman clenched his fist, and glared fearfully on the cigar-smokers around.

"Be calm, Walter, I entreat," said the young lady.

"I won't," said the military gentleman.

"Do, sir," interposed Mr. Cymon Tuggs. "They ain't worth your notice."

"No—no—they are not, indeed," urged the young lady.

"I *will* be calm," said the military gentleman. "You speak truly, sir. I thank you for a timely remonstrance, which may have spared me the guilt of manslaughter." Calming his wrath, the military gentleman wrung Mr. Cymon Tuggs by the hand.

"My sister, sir!" said Mr. Cymon Tuggs ; seeing that the military gentleman was casting an admiring look towards Miss Charlotta.

"My wife, ma'am—Mrs. Captain Waters," said the military gentleman, presenting the black-eyed young lady.

"My mother, ma'am—Mrs. Tuggs," said Mr. Cymon. The military gentleman and his wife murmured enchanting courtesies ; and the Tuggses looked as unembarrassed as they could.

"Walter, my dear," said the black-eyed young lady, after they had sat chatting with the Tuggses some half-hour.

"Yes, my love," said the military gentleman.

"Don't you think this gentleman (with an inclination of the head towards Mr. Cymon Tuggs) is very much like the Marquis Carriwini?"

"Lord bless me, very!" said the military gentleman.

"It struck me the moment I saw him," said the young lady, gazing intently, and with a melancholy air, on the scarlet countenance of Mr. Cymon Tuggs. Mr. Cymon Tuggs looked at everybody; and finding that everybody was looking at him, appeared to feel some temporary difficulty in disposing of his eyesight.

"So exactly the air of the marquis," said the military gentleman.

"Quite extraordinary!" sighed the military gentleman's lady.

"You don't know the marquis, sir?" inquired the military gentleman.

Mr. Cymon Tuggs stammered a negative.

"If you did," continued Captain Walter Waters, "you would feel how much reason you have to be proud of the resemblance—a most elegant man, with a most prepossessing appearance."

"He is—he is indeed!" exclaimed Belinda Waters energetically. As her eye caught that of Mr. Cymon Tuggs, she withdrew it from his features in bashful confusion.

All this was highly gratifying to the feelings of the Tuggses; and when, in the course of farther conversation, it was discovered that Miss Charlotta Tuggs was the *facsimile* of a titled relative of Mrs. Belinda Waters, and that Mrs. Tuggs herself was the very picture of the Dowager Duchess of Dobbleton, their delight in the acquisition of so genteel and friendly an acquaintance knew no bounds. Even the dignity of Captain Walter Waters relaxed to that degree, that he suffered himself to be prevailed upon by Mr. Joseph Tuggs to partake of cold pigeon-pie and sherry, on deck; and a most delightful conversation, aided by these agreeable stimulants, was prolonged until they ran alongside Ramsgate Pier.

"Good by'e, dear!" said Mrs. Captain Waters to Miss Charlotta Tuggs, just before the bustle of landing commenced; "we shall see you on the sands in the morning; and, as we are sure to have found lodgings before then, I hope we shall be inseparables for many weeks to come."

"Oh! I hope so," said Miss Charlotta Tuggs, emphatically.

"Tickets, ladies and gen'lm'n," said the man on the paddle-box.

"Want a porter, sir?" inquired a dozen men in smock-frocks.

"Now, my dear!" said Captain Waters.

"Good by'e!" said Mrs. Captain Waters—"good by'e, Mr. Cymon!" and with a pressure of the hand which threw the amiable young man's nerves into a state of considerable derangement, Mrs. Captain Waters disappeared among the crowd. A pair of puce-coloured boots were seen ascending the steps, a white handkerchief fluttered, a black eye gleamed. The Waterses were gone, and Mr. Cymon Tuggs was alone in a heartless world.

Silently and abstractedly did that too sensitive youth follow his revered parents, and a train of smock-frocks and wheelbarrows, along the pier, until the bustle of the scene around recalled him to himself. The sun was shining brightly; the sea, dancing to its own music, rolled merrily in; crowds of people promenaded to and fro; young ladies tittered; old ladies talked; nursemaids displayed their charms to the greatest possible advantage; and their little charges ran up and down, and to and fro, and in and out, under the feet, and between the legs, of the assembled concourse, in the most playful and exhilarating manner. There were old gentlemen, trying to make out objects through long telescopes; and young ones, making objects of themselves in open shirt-collars; ladies, carrying about portable chairs, and portable chairs carrying about invalids; parties, waiting on the pier for parties who had come by the steamboat; and nothing was to be heard but talking, laughing, welcoming, and merriment.

"Fly, sir?" exclaimed a chorus of fourteen men and six boys, the moment Mr. Joseph Tuggs, at the head of his little party, set foot in the street.

"Here's the gen'lm'n at last!" said one, touching his hat with mock politeness. "Werry glad to see you, sir,—been a-waitin' for you these six weeks. Jump in, if you please, sir!"

"Nice light fly and a fast trotter, sir," said another: "fourteen mile a hour, and surroundin' objects rendered inwisible by ex-treme welocity!"

"Large fly for your luggage, sir," cried a third. "Werry large fly here, sir—reg'lar bluebottle!"

"Here's your fly, sir!" shouted another aspiring charioteer, mounting the box, and inducing an old grey horse to indulge in some imperfect reminiscences of a canter. "Look at him, sir!—temper of a lamb and haction of a steam-ingein!"

Resisting even the temptation of securing the services of so valuable a quadruped as the last named, Mr. Joseph Tuggs beckoned to the proprietor of a dingy conveyance of a greenish hue, lined with faded striped calico ; and, the luggage and the family having been deposited therein, the animal in the shafts, after describing circles in the road for a quarter of an hour, at last consented to depart in quest of lodgings.

"How many beds have you got ?" screamed Mrs. Tuggs out of the fly, to the woman who opened the door of the first house which displayed a bill intimating that apartments were to be let within.

"How many did you want, ma'am ?" was, of course, the reply.

"Three."

"Will you step in, ma'am ?" Down got Mrs. Tuggs. The family were delighted. Splendid view of the sea from the front windows—charming! A short pause. Back came Mrs. Tuggs again.—One parlour and a mattress.

"Why the devil didn't they say so at first ?" inquired Mr. Joseph Tuggs, rather pettishly.

"Don't know," said Mrs. Tuggs.

"Wretches !" exclaimed the nervous Cymon. Another bill —another stoppage. Same question—same answer—similar result.

"What do they mean by this ?" inquired Mr. Joseph Tuggs, thoroughly out of temper.

"Don't know," said the placid Mrs. Tuggs.

"Orvis the vay here, sir," said the driver, by way of accounting for the circumstance in a satisfactory manner ; and off they went again, to make fresh inquiries, and encounter fresh disappointments.

It had grown dusk when the "fly"—the rate of whose progress greatly belied its name—after climbing up four or five perpendicular hills, stopped before the door of a dusty house, with a bay window, from which you could obtain a beautiful glimpse of the sea—if you thrust half of your body out of it, at the imminent peril of falling into the area. Mrs. Tuggs alighted. One ground-floor sitting-room, and three cells with beds in them up-stairs. A double house. Family on the opposite side. Five children milk-and-watering in the parlour, and one little boy, expelled for bad behaviour, screaming on his back in the passage.

"What's the terms?" said Mrs. Tuggs. The mistress of the house was considering the expediency of putting on an extra guinea; so she coughed slightly, and affected not to hear the question.

"What's the terms?" said Mrs. Tuggs, in a louder key.

"Five guineas a week, ma'am, *with* attendance," replied the lodging-house keeper. (Attendance means the privilege of ringing the bell as often as you like, for your own amusement.)

"Rather dear," said Mrs. Tuggs.

"Oh dear, no, ma'am!" replied the mistress of the house, with a benign smile of pity at the ignorance of manners and customs which the observation betrayed, "Very cheap!"

Such an authority was indisputable. Mrs. Tuggs paid a week's rent in advance, and took the lodgings for a month. In an hour's time, the family were seated at tea in their new abode.

"Capital srimps!" said Mr. Joseph Tuggs.

Mr. Cymon eyed his father with a rebellious scowl, as he emphatically said "*Shrimps.*"

"Well then, shrimps," said Mr. Joseph Tuggs. "Srimps or shrimps, don't much matter."

There was pity, blended with malignity, in Mr. Cymon's eye, as he replied, "Don't matter, father! What would Captain Waters say, if he heard such vulgarity?"

"Or what would dear Mrs. Captain Waters say," added Charlotta, "if she saw mother—ma, I mean—eating them whole, heads and all!"

"It won't bear thinking of!" ejaculated Mr. Cymon, with a shudder. "How different," he thought, "from the Dowager Duchess of Dobbleton!"

"Very pretty woman, Mrs. Captain Waters, is she not, Cymon?" inquired Miss Charlotta.

A glow of nervous excitement passed over the countenance of Mr. Cymon Tuggs, as he replied, "An angel of beauty!"

"Hallo!" said Mr. Joseph Tuggs. "Hallo, Cymon, my boy, take care. Married lady, you know;" and he winked one of his twinkling eyes knowingly.

"Why," exclaimed Cymon, starting up with an ebullition of fury, as unexpected as alarming, "why am I to be reminded of that blight of my happiness, and ruin of my

hopes?   Why am I to be taunted with the miseries which
are heaped upon my head?   Is it not enough to—to—to—"
and the orator paused ; but whether for want of words, or
lack of breath, was never distinctly ascertained.

There was an impressive solemnity in the tone of this
address, and in the air with which the romantic Cymon,
at its conclusion, rang the bell, and demanded a flat candlestick, which effectually forbade a reply.   He stalked dra-
matically to bed, and the Tuggses went to bed too, half an
hour afterwards, in a state of considerable mystification and
perplexity.

If the pier had presented a scene of life and bustle to the
Tuggses on their first landing at Ramsgate, it was far sur-
passed by the appearance of the sands on the morning after
their arrival.   It was a fine, bright, clear day, with a light
breeze from the sea.   There were the same ladies and gentlemen, the same children, the same nursemaids, the same
telescopes, the same portable chairs.   The ladies were employed in needlework, or watch-guard making, or knitting,
or reading novels ; the gentlemen were reading newspapers
and magazines ; the children were digging holes in the
sand with wooden spades, and collecting water therein ; the
nursemaids, with their youngest charges in their arms, were
running in after the waves, and then running back with the
waves after them ; and, now and then, a little sailing-boat
either departed with a gay and talkative cargo of passengers,
or returned with a very silent and particularly uncomfortable-
looking one.

"Well, I never!" exclaimed Mrs. Tuggs, as she and Mr.
Joseph Tuggs, and Miss Charlotta Tuggs, and Mr. Cymon
Tuggs, with their eight feet in a corresponding number of
yellow shoes, seated themselves on four rush-bottomed chairs,
which, being placed in a soft part of the sand, forthwith
sunk down some two feet and a half—"Well, I never!"

Mr. Cymon, by an exertion of great personal strength,
uprooted the chairs, and removed them further back.

"Why, I'm blessed if there ain't some ladies a-going in!"
exclaimed Mr. Joseph Tuggs, with intense astonishment.

"Lor, pa!" exclaimed Miss Charlotta.

"There *is*, my dear," said Mr. Joseph Tuggs.   And, sure
enough, four young ladies, each furnished with a towel,
tripped up the steps of a bathing-machine.   In went the
horse, floundering about in the water ; round turned the

The Tuggses at Ramsgate

(p. 354)

machine; down sat the driver; and presently out burst the young ladies aforesaid, with four distinct splashes.

"Well, that's sing'ler, too!" ejaculated Mr. Joseph Tuggs, after an awkward pause. Mr. Cymon coughed slightly.

"Why, here's some gentlemen a-going in on this side!" exclaimed Mrs. Tuggs, in a tone of horror.

Three machines—three horses—three flounderings—three turnings round—three splashes—three gentlemen, disporting themselves in the water like so many dolphins.

"Well, *that's* sing'ler!" said Mr. Joseph Tuggs again. Miss Charlotta coughed this time, and another pause ensued. It was agreeably broken.

"How d'ye do, dear?" We have been looking for you all the morning," said a voice to Miss Charlotta Tuggs. Mrs. Captain Waters was the owner of it.

"How d'ye do?" said Captain Walter Waters, all suavity; and a most cordial interchange of greetings ensued.

"Belinda, my love," said Captain Walter Waters, applying his glass to his eye, and looking in the direction of the sea.

"Yes, my dear," replied Mrs. Captain Waters.

"There's Harry Thompson!"

"Where?" said Belinda, applying her glass to her eye.

"Bathing."

"Lor, so it is! He don't see us, does he?"

"No, I don't think he does," replied the captain. "Bless my soul, how very singular!"

"What?" inquired Belinda.

"There's Mary Golding, too."

"Lor!—where?" (Up went the glass again.)

"There!" said the captain, pointing to one of the young ladies before noticed, who, in her bathing costume, looked as if she was enveloped in a patent Mackintosh, of scanty dimensions.

"So it is, I declare!" exclaimed Mrs. Captain Waters. "How very curious we should see them both!"

"Very," said the captain, with perfect coolness.

"It's the reg'lar thing here, you see," whispered Mr. Cymon Tuggs to his father.

"I see it is," whispered Mr. Joseph Tuggs in reply. "Queer, though—ain't it?" Mr. Cymon Tuggs nodded assent.

"What do you think of doing with yourself this morning?" inquired the captain. "Shall we lunch at Pegwell?"

"I should like that very much indeed," interposed Mrs. Tuggs. She had never heard of Pegwell; but the word "lunch" had reached her ears, and it sounded very agreeably.

"How shall we go?" inquired the captain; "it's too warm to walk."

"A shay?" suggested Mr. Joseph Tuggs.

"Chaise," whispered Mr. Cymon.

"I should think one would be enough," said Mr. Joseph Tuggs aloud, quite unconscious of the meaning of the correction. "However, two shays if you like."

"I should like a donkey so much," said Belinda.

"Oh, so should I!" echoed Charlotta Tuggs.

"Well, we can have a fly," suggested the captain, "and you can have a couple of donkeys."

A fresh difficulty arose. Mrs. Captain Waters declared it would be decidedly improper for two ladies to ride alone. The remedy was obvious. Perhaps young Mr. Tuggs would be gallant enough to accompany them.

Mr. Cymon Tuggs blushed, smiled, looked vacant, and faintly protested that he was no horseman. The objection was at once overruled. A fly was speedily found; and three donkeys—which the proprietor declared on his solemn asseveration to be "three parts blood, and the other corn" —were engaged in the service.

"Kim up!" shouted one of the two boys who followed behind, to propel the donkeys, when Belinda Waters and Charlotta Tuggs had been hoisted, and pushed, and pulled, into their respective saddles.

"Hi—hi—hi!" groaned the other boy behind Mr. Cymon Tuggs. Away went the donkey, with the stirrups jingling against the heels of Cymon's boots, and Cymon's boots nearly scraping the ground.

"Way—way! Wo—o—o—o—!" cried Mr. Cymon Tuggs as well as he could, in the midst of the jolting.

"Don't make it gallop!" screamed Mrs. Captain Waters, behind.

"My donkey will go into the public-house!" shrieked Miss Tuggs in the rear.

"Hi—hi—hi!" groaned both the boys together; and on went the donkeys as if nothing would ever stop them.

Everything has an end, however; even the galloping of donkeys will cease in time. The animal which Mr. Cymon

Tuggs bestrode, feeling sundry uncomfortable tugs at the bit, the intent of which he could by no means divine, abruptly sidled against a brick wall, and expressed his uneasiness by grinding Mr. Cymon Tuggs's leg on the rough surface. Mrs. Captain Waters's donkey, apparently under the influence of some playfulness of spirit, rushed suddenly, head first, into a hedge, and declined to come out again : and the quadruped on which Miss Tuggs was mounted, expressed his delight at this humorous proceeding by firmly planting his fore-feet against the ground, and kicking up his hind-legs in a very agile, but somewhat alarming manner.

This abrupt termination to the rapidity of the ride naturally occasioned some confusion. Both the ladies indulged in vehement screaming for several minutes ; and Mr. Cymon Tuggs, besides sustaining intense bodily pain, had the additional mental anguish of witnessing their distressing situation, without having the power to rescue them, by reason of his leg being firmly screwed in between the animal and the wall. The efforts of the boys, however, assisted by the ingenious expedient of twisting the tail of the most rebellious donkey, restored order in a much shorter time than could have reasonably been expected, and the little party jogged slowly on together.

"Now let 'em walk," said Mr. Cymon Tuggs. " It's cruel to overdrive 'em."

"Werry well, sir," replied the boy, with a grin at his companion, as if he understood Mr. Cymon to mean that the cruelty applied less to the animals than to their riders.

"What a lovely day, dear ! " said Charlotta.

"Charming ; enchanting, dear ! " responded Mrs. Captain Waters. "What a beautiful prospect, Mr. Tuggs ! "

Cymon looked full in Belinda's face, as he responded— "Beautiful, indeed ! " The lady cast down her eyes, and suffered the animal she was riding to fall a little back. Cymon Tuggs instinctively did the same.

There was a brief silence, broken only by a sigh from Mr. Cymon Tuggs.

"Mr. Cymon," said the lady suddenly, in a low tone, "Mr. Cymon—I am another's."

Mr. Cymon expressed his perfect concurrence in a statement which it was impossible to controvert.

" If I had not been—— " resumed Belinda ; and there she stopped.

"What—what?" said Mr. Cymon earnestly. "Do not torture me. What would you say?"

"If I had not been"—continued Mrs. Captain Waters— "if, in earlier life, it had been my fate to have known, and been beloved by, a noble youth—a kindred soul—a congenial spirit—one capable of feeling and appreciating the sentiments which——"

"Heavens! what do I hear?" exclaimed Mr. Cymon Tuggs. "Is it possible! can I believe my—Come up!" (This last unsentimental parenthesis was addressed to the donkey, who, with his head between his fore-legs, appeared to be examining the state of his shoes with great anxiety.)

"Hi—hi—hi," said the boys behind. "Come up," expostulated Cymon Tuggs again. "Hi—hi—hi," repeated the boys. And whether it was that the animal felt indignant at the tone of Mr. Tuggs's command, or felt alarmed by the noise of the deputy proprietor's boots running behind him; or whether he burned with a noble emulation to outstrip the other donkeys; certain it is that he no sooner heard the second series of "hi—hi's," than he started away, with a celerity of pace which jerked Mr. Cymon's hat off instantaneously, and carried him to the Pegwell Bay hotel in no time, where he deposited his rider without giving him the trouble of dismounting, by sagaciously pitching him over his head into the very doorway of the tavern.

Great was the confusion of Mr. Cymon Tuggs, when he was put right end uppermost by two waiters; considerable was the alarm of Mrs. Tuggs in behalf of her son; agonizing were the apprehensions of Mrs. Captain Waters on his account. It was speedily discovered, however, that he had not sustained much more injury than the donkey—he was grazed, and the animal was grazing—and then it *was* a delightful party to be sure! Mr. and Mrs. Tuggs, and the captain, had ordered lunch in the little garden behind:— small saucers of large shrimps, dabs of butter, crusty loaves, and bottled ale. The sky was without a cloud; there were flower-pots and turf before them; the sea, from the foot of the cliff, stretching away as far as the eye could discern anything at all; vessels in the distance with sails as white, and as small, as nicely-got-up cambric handkerchiefs. The shrimps were delightful, the ale better, and the captain even more pleasant than either. Mrs. Captain Waters was in *such* spirits after lunch!—chasing, first the captain across the turf, and among the flower-pots; and then Mr. Cymon Tuggs; and then Miss Tuggs; and laughing, too, quite boisterously. But as the captain said, it didn't matter; who knew what they were, there? For all the people of the house knew, they might be common people. To which Mr. Joseph Tuggs responded, "To be sure." And then they went down the steep wooden steps a little further on, which led to the bottom of the cliff; and looked at the crabs, and the seaweed, and the eels, till it was more than fully time to go back to Ramsgate again. Finally, Mr. Cymon Tuggs ascended the steps last, and Mrs. Captain Waters last but one; and Mr. Cymon Tuggs discovered that the foot and ankle of Mrs. Captain Waters were even more unexceptionable than he had at first supposed.

Taking a donkey towards his ordinary place of residence is a very different thing, and a feat much more easily to be accomplished, than taking him from it. It requires a great deal of foresight and presence of mind in the one case, to anticipate the numerous flights of his discursive imagination; whereas, in the other, all you have to do is to hold on, and place a blind confidence in the animal. Mr. Cymon Tuggs adopted the latter expedient on his return; and his nerves were so little discomposed by the journey, that he distinctly understood they were all to meet again at the library in the evening.

The library was crowded. There were the same ladies, and the same gentlemen, who had been on the sands in the morning, and on the pier the day before. There were young ladies, in maroon-coloured gowns and black velvet bracelets, dispensing fancy articles in the shop, and presiding over games of chance in the concert-room. There were marriageable daughters, and marriage-making mammas, gaming and promenading, and turning over music, and flirting. There were some male beaux doing the sentimental in whispers, and others doing the ferocious in moustache. There were Mrs. Tuggs in amber, Miss Tuggs in sky-blue, Mrs. Captain Waters in pink. There was Captain Waters in a braided surtout; there was Mr. Cymon Tuggs in pumps and a gilt waistcoat; there was Mr. Joseph Tuggs in a blue coat and a shirt-frill.

"Numbers three, eight, and eleven!" cried one of the young ladies in the maroon-coloured gowns.

" Numbers three, eight, and eleven ! " echoed another young lady in the same uniform.

" Number three's gone," said the first young lady.   " Numbers eight and eleven ! "

"Numbers eight and eleven!" echoed the second young lady.

"Number eight's gone, Mary Ann," said the first young lady.

" Number eleven ! " screamed the second.

"The numbers are all taken now, ladies, if you please," said the first.   The representatives of numbers three, eight, and eleven, and the rest of the numbers, crowded round the table.

"Will you throw, ma'am ? " said the presiding goddess, handing the dice-box to the eldest daughter of a stout lady, with four girls.

There was a profound silence among the lookers-on.

"Throw, Jane, my dear," said the stout lady.   An interesting display of bashfulness—a little blushing in a cambric handkerchief—a whispering to a younger sister.

" Amelia, my dear, throw for your sister," said the stout lady ; and then she turned to a walking advertisement of Rowlands' Macassar Oil, who stood next her, and said, "Jane is so *very* modest and retiring ; but I can't be angry with her for it.   An artless and unsophisticated girl is *so* truly amiable, that I often wish Amelia was more like her sister ! "

The gentleman with the whiskers whispered his admiring approval.

" Now, my dear ! " said the stout lady.   Miss Amelia threw —eight for her sister, ten for herself.

" Nice figure, Amelia," whispered the stout lady to a thin youth beside her.

" Beautiful ! "

"And *such* a spirit !   I am like you in that respect.   I can *not* help admiring that life and vivacity.   Ah ! (a sigh) I wish I could make poor Jane a little more like my dear Amelia ! "

The young gentleman cordially acquiesced in the sentiment ; both he, and the individual first addressed, were perfectly contented.

"Who's this ? " inquired Mr. Cymon Tuggs of Mrs. Captain Waters, as a short female, in a blue velvet hat and feathers, was led into the orchestra, by a fat man in black tights and cloudy Berlins.

"Mrs. Tippin, of the London theatres," replied Belinda, referring to the programme of the concert.

The talented Tippin having condescendingly acknowledged the clapping of hands and shouts of "bravo!" which greeted her appearance, proceeded to sing the popular cavatina of "Bid me discourse," accompanied on the piano by Mr. Tippin; after which, Mr. Tippin sang a comic song, accompanied on the piano by Mrs. Tippin: the applause consequent upon which, was only to be exceeded by the enthusiastic approbation bestowed upon an air with variations on the guitar, by Miss Tippin, accompanied on the chin by Master Tippin.

Thus passed the evening; thus passed the days and evenings of the Tuggses, and the Waterses, for six weeks. Sands in the morning—donkeys at noon—pier in the afternoon—library at night—and the same people everywhere.

On that very night six weeks, the moon was shining brightly over the calm sea, which dashed against the feet of the tall gaunt cliffs, with just enough noise to lull the old fish to sleep, without disturbing the young ones, when two figures were discernible—or would have been, if anybody had looked for them—seated on one of the wooden benches which are stationed near the verge of the western cliff. The moon had climbed higher into the heavens, by two hours' journeying, since those figures first sat down—and yet they had moved not. The crowd of loungers had thinned and dispersed; the noise of itinerant musicians had died away; light after light had appeared in the windows of the different houses in the distance; blockade-man after blockade-man had passed the spot, wending his way towards his solitary post; and yet those figures had remained stationary. Some portions of the two forms were in deep shadow, but the light of the moon fell strongly on a puce-coloured boot and a glazed stock. Mr. Cymon Tuggs and Mrs. Captain Waters were seated on that bench. They spoke not, but were silently gazing on the sea.

"Walter will return to-morrow," said Mrs. Captain Waters, mournfully breaking silence.

Mr. Cymon Tuggs sighed like a gust of wind through a forest of gooseberry bushes, as he replied, "Alas! he will."

"Oh, Cymon!" resumed Belinda, "the chaste delight, the calm happiness, of this one week of Platonic love, is too much for me!"

Cymon was about to suggest that it was too little for him, but he stopped himself, and murmured unintelligibly.

"And to think that even this gleam of happiness, innocent as it is," exclaimed Belinda, "is now to be lost for ever!"

"Oh, do not say for ever, Belinda," exclaimed the excitable Cymon, as two strongly-defined tears chased each other down his pale face—it was so long that there was plenty of room for a chase. "Do not say for ever!"

"I must," replied Belinda.

"Why?" urged Cymon, "oh why? Such Platonic acquaintance as ours is so harmless, that even your husband can never object to it."

"My husband!" exclaimed Belinda. "You little know him. Jealous and revengeful; ferocious in his revenge—a maniac in his jealousy! Would you be assassinated before my eyes?" Mr. Cymon Tuggs, in a voice broken by emotion, expressed his disinclination to undergo the process of assassination before the eyes of anybody.

"Then leave me," said Mrs. Captain Waters. "Leave me, this night, for ever. It is late: let us return."

Mr. Cymon Tuggs sadly offered the lady his arm, and escorted her to her lodgings. He paused at the door—he felt a Platonic pressure of his hand. "Good night," he said, hesitating.

"Good night," sobbed the lady. Mr. Cymon Tuggs paused again.

"Won't you walk in, sir?" said the servant. Mr. Tuggs hesitated.. Oh, that hesitation! He *did* walk in.

"Good night!" said Mr. Cymon Tuggs again, when he reached the drawing-room.

"Good night!" replied Belinda; "and, if at any period of my life, I—Hush!" The lady paused and stared, with a steady gaze of horror, on the ashy countenance of Mr. Cymon Tuggs. There was a double knock at the street-door.

"It is my husband!" said Belinda, as the captain's voice was heard below.

"And my family!" added Cymon Tuggs, as the voices of his relatives floated up the staircase.

"The curtain! The curtain!" gasped Mrs. Captain Waters, pointing to the window, before which some chintz hangings were closely drawn.

"But I have done nothing wrong," said the hesitating Cymon.

"The curtain!" reiterated the frantic lady: "you will be murdered." This last appeal to his feelings was irresistible. The dismayed Cymon concealed himself behind the curtain with pantomimic suddenness.

Enter the captain, Joseph Tuggs, Mrs. Tuggs, and Charlotta.

"My dear," said the captain, "Lieutenant Slaughter." Two iron-shod boots and one gruff voice was heard by Mr. Cymon to advance, and acknowledge the honour of the introduction. The sabre of the lieutenant rattled heavily upon the floor, as he seated himself at the table. Mr. Cymon's fears almost overcame his reason.

"The brandy, my dear!" said the captain. Here was a situation! They were going to make a night of it! And Mr. Cymon Tuggs was pent up behind the curtain and afraid to breathe!

"Slaughter," said the captain, "a cigar?"

Now, Mr. Cymon Tuggs never could smoke without feeling it indispensably necessary to retire immediately, and never could smell smoke without a strong disposition to cough. The cigars were introduced: the captain was a professed smoker; so was the lieutenant; so was Joseph Tuggs. The apartment was small, the door was closed, the smoke powerful: it hung in heavy wreaths over the room, and at length found its way behind the curtain. Cymon Tuggs held his nose, his mouth, his breath. It was all of no use—out came the cough.

"Bless my soul!" said the captain, "I beg your pardon, Miss Tuggs. You dislike smoking?"

"Oh, no; I don't indeed," said Charlotta.

"It makes you cough."

"Oh dear no."

"You coughed just now."

"Me, Captain Waters! Lor! how can you say so?"

"Somebody coughed," said the captain.

"I certainly thought so," said Slaughter. No; everybody denied it.

"Fancy," said the captain.

"Must be," echoed Slaughter.

Cigars resumed—more smoke—another cough—smothered, but violent.

"Damned odd!" said the captain, staring about him.

"Sing'ler!" ejaculated the unconscious Mr. Joseph Tuggs.

Lieutenant Slaughter looked first at one person mysteriously, then at another: then laid down his cigar, then
approached the window on tiptoe, and pointed with his
right thumb over his shoulder, in the direction of the
curtain.

"Slaughter!" ejaculated the captain, rising from table,
"what do you mean?"

The lieutenant, in reply, drew back the curtain and discovered Mr. Cymon Tuggs behind it: pallid with apprehension, and blue with wanting to cough.

"Aha!" exclaimed the captain, furiously. "What do I
see? Slaughter, your sabre!"

"Cymon!" screamed the Tuggses.

"Mercy!" said Belinda.

"Platonic!" gasped Cymon.

"Your sabre!" roared the captain: "Slaughter—unhand
me—the villain's life!"

"Murder!" screamed the Tuggses.

"Hold him fast, sir!" faintly articulated Cymon.

"Water!" exclaimed Joseph Tuggs—and Mr. Cymon
Tuggs and all the ladies forthwith fainted away, and formed
a tableau.

Most willingly would we conceal the disastrous termination
of the six weeks' acquaintance. A troublesome form, and an
arbitrary custom, however, prescribe that a story should have
a conclusion, in addition to a commencement; we have therefore no alternative. Lieutenant Slaughter brought a message
—the captain brought an action. Mr. Joseph Tuggs interposed—the lieutenant negotiated. When Mr. Cymon Tuggs
recovered from the nervous disorder into which misplaced
affection, and exciting circumstances, had plunged him, he
found that his family had lost their pleasant acquaintance;
that his father was minus fifteen hundred pounds; and the
captain plus the precise sum. The money was paid to hush
the matter up, but it got abroad notwithstanding; and
there are not wanting some who affirm that three designing
impostors never found more easy dupes, than did Captain
Waters, Mrs. Waters, and Lieutenant Slaughter, in the
Tuggses at Ramsgate.

CHAPTER V

HORATIO SPARKINS

"INDEED, my love, he paid Teresa very great attention on the last assembly night," said Mrs. Malderton, addressing her spouse, who, after the fatigues of the day in the City, was sitting with a silk handkerchief over his head, and his feet on the fender, drinking his port;—"very great attention; and I say again, every possible encouragement ought to be given him. He positively must be asked down here to dine."

"Who must?" inquired Mr. Malderton.

"Why, you know whom I mean, my dear—the young man with the black whiskers and the white cravat, who has just come out at our assembly, and whom all the girls are talking about. Young—— dear me! what's his name?—Marianne, what *is* his name?" continued Mrs. Malderton, addressing her youngest daughter, who was engaged in netting a purse, and looking sentimental.

"Mr. Horatio Sparkins, ma," replied Miss Marianne, with a sigh.

"Oh! yes. to be sure—Horatio Sparkins," said Mrs. Malderton. "Decidedly the most gentleman-like young man I ever saw. I am sure in the beautifully-made coat he wore the other night, he looked like—like—— "

"Like Prince Leopold. ma—so noble. so full of sentiment!" suggested Marianne, in a tone of enthusiastic admiration.

"You should recollect, my dear," resumed Mrs. Malderton, "that Teresa is now eight-and-twenty; and that it really is very important that something should be done."

Miss Teresa Malderton was a very little girl, rather fat, with vermilion cheeks, but good-humoured, and still disengaged, although, to do her justice, the misfortune arose from no lack of perseverance on her part. In vain had she flirted for ten years; in vain had Mr. and Mrs. Malderton assiduously kept up an extensive acquaintance among the young eligible bachelors of Camberwell, and even of Wandsworth and Brixton; to say nothing of those who "dropped in" from town. Miss Malderton was as well known as the lion on the top of Northumberland House, and had an equal chance of "going off."

"I am quite sure you'd like him," continued Mrs. Malderton, "he is so gentlemanly!"

"So clever!" said Miss Marianne.

"And has such a flow of language!" added Miss Teresa.

"He has a great respect for you, my dear," said Mrs. Malderton to her husband. Mr. Malderton coughed, and looked at the fire.

"Yes, I'm sure he's very much attached to pa's society," said Miss Marianne.

"No doubt of it," echoed Miss Teresa.

"Indeed, he said as much to me in confidence," observed Mrs. Malderton.

"Well, well," returned Mr. Malderton, somewhat flattered; "if I see him at the assembly to-morrow, perhaps I'll ask him down. I hope he knows we live at Oak Lodge, Camberwell, my dear?"

"Of course—and that you keep a one-horse carriage."

"I'll see about it," said Mr. Malderton, composing himself for a nap; "I'll see about it."

Mr. Malderton was a man whose whole scope of ideas was limited to Lloyd's, the Exchange, the India House, and the Bank. A few successful speculations had raised him from a situation of obscurity and comparative poverty, to a state of affluence. As frequently happens in such cases, the ideas of himself and his family became elevated to an extraordinary pitch as their means increased; they affected fashion, taste, and many other fooleries, in imitation of their betters, and had a very decided and becoming horror of anything which could, by possibility, be considered *low*. He was hospitable from ostentation, illiberal from ignorance, and prejudiced from conceit. Egotism and the love of display induced him to keep an excellent table: convenience, and a love of good things of this life, ensured him plenty of guests. He liked to have clever men, or what he considered such, at his table, because it was a great thing to talk about; but he never could endure what he called "sharp fellows." Probably he cherished this feeling out of compliment to his two sons, who gave their respected parent no uneasiness in that particular.

The family were ambitious of forming acquaintances and connexions in some sphere of society superior to that in which they themselves moved ; and one of the necessary consequences of this desire, added to their utter ignorance of the world beyond their own small circle, was, that any one who could lay claim to an acquaintance with people of rank and title, had a sure passport to the table at Oak Lodge, Camberwell.

The appearance of Mr. Horatio Sparkins at the assembly had excited no small degree of surprise and curiosity among its regular frequenters. Who could he be? He was evidently reserved, and apparently melancholy. Was he a clergyman?—He danced too well. A barrister?—He said he was not called. He used very fine words, and talked a great deal. Could he be a distinguished foreigner, come to England for the purpose of describing the country, its manners and customs; and frequenting public balls and public dinners, with the view of becoming acquainted with high life, polished etiquette, and English refinement?—No, he had not a foreign accent. Was he a surgeon, a contributor to the magazines, a writer of fashionable novels, or an artist?—No; to each and all of these surmises, there existed some valid objection.—"Then," said everybody, "he must be *somebody*."—"I should think he must be," reasoned Mr. Malderton, within himself, "because he perceives our superiority, and pays us so much attention."

The night succeeding the conversation we have just recorded, was "assembly night." The double-fly was ordered to be at the door of Oak Lodge at nine o'clock precisely. The Miss Maldertons were dressed in sky-blue satin trimmed with artificial flowers; and Mrs. M. (who was a little fat woman), in ditto ditto, looked like her eldest daughter multiplied by two. Mr. Frederick Malderton, the eldest son, in full-dress costume, was the very *beau idéal* of a smart waiter; and Mr. Thomas Malderton, the youngest, with his white dress-stock, blue coat, bright buttons, and red watch-ribbon, strongly resembled the portrait of that interesting but rash young gentleman, George Barnwell. Every member of the party had made up his or her mind to cultivate the acquaintance of Mr. Horatio Sparkins. Miss Teresa, of course, was to be as amiable and interesting as ladies of eight-and-twenty on the look-out for a husband, usually are. Mrs. Malderton would be all smiles and graces. Miss

Marianne would request the favour of some verses for her album. Mr. Malderton would patronise the great unknown by asking him to dinner. Tom intended to ascertain the extent of his information on the interesting topics of snuff and cigars. Even Mr. Frederick Malderton himself, the family authority on all points of taste, dress, and fashionable arrangement; who had lodgings of his own in town; who had a free admission to Covent Garden theatre; who always dressed according to the fashions of the months; who went up the water twice a week in the season; and who actually had an intimate friend who once knew a gentleman who formerly lived in the Albany,—even he had determined that Mr. Horatio Sparkins must be a devilish good fellow, and that he would do him the honour of challenging him to a game at billiards.

The first object that met the anxious eyes of the expectant family on their entrance into the ball-room, was the interesting Horatio, with his hair brushed off his forehead, and his eyes fixed on the ceiling, reclining in a contemplative attitude on one of the seats.

"There he is, my dear," whispered Mrs. Malderton to Mr. Malderton.

"How like Lord Byron!" murmured Miss Teresa.

"Or Montgomery!" whispered Miss Marianne.

"Or the portraits of Captain Cook!" suggested Tom.

"Tom—don't be an ass!" said his father, who checked him on all occasions, probably with a view to prevent his becoming "sharp"—which was very unnecessary.

The elegant Sparkins attitudinised with admirable effect, until the family had crossed the room. He then started up, with the most natural appearance of surprise and delight; accosted Mrs. Malderton with the utmost cordiality; saluted the young ladies in the most enchanting manner; bowed to, and shook hands with, Mr. Malderton, with a degree of respect amounting almost to veneration; and returned the greetings of the two young men in a half-gratified, half-patronising manner, which fully convinced them that he must be an important, and, at the same time, condescending personage.

"Miss Malderton," said Horatio, after the ordinary salutations, and bowing very low, "may I be permitted to presume to hope that you will allow me to have the pleasure—— "

"I don't *think* I am engaged," said Miss Teresa, with

a dreadful affectation of indifference—"but, really—so many——"

Horatio looked handsomely miserable.

"I shall be most happy," simpered the interesting Teresa, at last. Horatio's countenance brightened up, like an old hat in a shower of rain.

"A very genteel young man, certainly!" said the gratified Mr. Malderton, as the obsequious Sparkins and his partner joined the quadrille which was just forming.

"He has a remarkably good address," said Mr. Frederick.

"Yes, he is a prime fellow," interposed Tom, who always managed to put his foot in it—"he talks just like an auctioneer."

"Tom!" said his father solemnly, "I think I desired you, before, not to be a fool." Tom looked as happy as a cock on a drizzly morning.

"How delightful!" said the interesting Horatio to his partner, as they promenaded the room at the conclusion of the set—"how delightful, how refreshing it is, to retire from the cloudy storms, the vicissitudes, and the troubles of life, even if it be but for a few short fleeting moments: and to spend those moments, fading and evanescent though they be, in the delightful, the blessed society of one individual—whose frowns would be death, whose coldness would be madness, whose falsehood would be ruin, whose constancy would be bliss; the possession of whose affection would be the brightest and best reward that Heaven could bestow on man!"

"What feeling! what sentiment!" thought Miss Teresa, as she leaned more heavily on her companion's arm.

"But enough—enough!" resumed the elegant Sparkins, with a theatrical air. "What have I said? what have I—I—to do with sentiments like these? Miss Malderton"—here he stopped short—"may I hope to be permitted to offer the humble tribute of——"

"Really, Mr. Sparkins," returned the enraptured Teresa, blushing in the sweetest confusion, "I must refer you to papa. I never can, without his consent, venture to——"

"Surely he cannot object——"

"Oh, yes. Indeed, indeed, you know him not!" interrupted Miss Teresa, well knowing there was nothing to fear, but wishing to make the interview resemble a scene in some romantic novel.

"He cannot object to my offering you a glass of negus," returned the adorable Sparkins, with some surprise.

"Is that all?" thought the disappointed Teresa. "What a fuss about nothing!"

"It will give me the greatest pleasure, sir, to see you to dinner at Oak Lodge, Camberwell, on Sunday next at five o'clock, if you have no better engagement," said Mr. Malderton, at the conclusion of the evening, as he and his sons were standing in conversation with Mr. Horatio Sparkins.

Horatio bowed his acknowledgments, and accepted the flattering invitation.

"I must confess," continued the father, offering his snuff-box to his new acquaintance, "that I don't enjoy these assemblies half so much as the comfort—I had almost said the luxury—of Oak Lodge. They have no great charms for an elderly man."

"And after all, sir, what is man?" said the metaphysical Sparkins. "I say, what is man?"

"Ah! very true," said Mr. Malderton; "very true."

"We know that we live and breathe," continued Horatio; "that we have wants and wishes, desires and appetites——"

"Certainly," said Mr. Frederick Malderton, looking profound.

"I say, we know that we exist," repeated Horatio, raising his voice, "but there we stop; there, is an end to our knowledge; there, is the summit of our attainments; there, is the termination of our ends. What more do we know?"

"Nothing," replied Mr. Frederick—than whom no one was more capable of answering for himself in that particular. Tom was about to hazard something, but, fortunately for his reputation, he caught his father's angry eye, and slunk off like a puppy convicted of petty larceny.

"Upon my word," said Mr. Malderton the elder, as they were returning home in the fly, "that Mr. Sparkins is a wonderful young man. Such surprising knowledge! such extraordinary information! and such a splendid mode of expressing himself!"

"I think he must be somebody in disguise," said Miss Marianne. "How charmingly romantic!"

"He talks very loud and nicely," timidly observed Tom, "but I don't exactly understand what he means."

"I almost begin to despair of *your* understanding any-

Horatio Sparkins
(*p. 369*)

thing, Tom," said his father, who, of course, had been much enlightened by Mr. Horatio Sparkins's conversation.

"It strikes me, Tom," said Miss Teresa, "that you have made yourself very ridiculous this evening."

"No doubt of it," cried everybody—and the unfortunate Tom reduced himself into the least possible space. That night, Mr. and Mrs. Malderton had a long conversation respecting their daughter's prospects and future arrangements. Miss Teresa went to bed, considering whether, in the event of her marrying a title, she could conscientiously encourage the visits of her present associates; and dreamed, all night, of disguised noblemen, large routs, ostrich plumes, bridal favours, and Horatio Sparkins.

Various surmises were hazarded on the Sunday morning, as to the mode of conveyance which the anxiously-expected Horatio would adopt. Did he keep a gig?—was it possible he could come on horseback?—or would he patronize the stage? These, and other various conjectures of equal importance, engrossed the attention of Mrs. Malderton and her daughters during the whole morning after church.

"Upon my word, my dear, it's a most annoying thing that that vulgar brother of yours should have invited himself to dine here to-day," said Mr. Malderton to his wife. "On account of Mr. Sparkins's coming down, I purposely abstained from asking any one but Flamwell. And then to think of your brother—a tradesman—it's insufferable! I declare I wouldn't have him mention his shop, before our new guest —no, not for a thousand pounds! I wouldn't care if he had the good sense to conceal the disgrace he is to the family; but he's so fond of his horrible business, that he *will* let people know what he is."

Mr. Jacob Barton, the individual alluded to, was a large grocer; so vulgar, and so lost to all sense of feeling, that he actually never scrupled to avow that he wasn't above his business: "he'd made his money by it, and he didn't care who know'd it."

"Ah! Flamwell, my dear fellow, how d'ye do?" said Mr. Malderton, as a little spoffish man, with green spectacles, entered the room. "You got my note?"

"Yes, I did; and here I am in consequence."

"You don't happen to know this Mr. Sparkins by name? You know everybody!"

Mr. Flamwell was one of those gentlemen of remarkably

extensive information whom one occasionally meets in society.
who pretend to know everybody but in reality know nobody.
At Malderton's, where any stories about great people were
received with a greedy ear, he was an especial favourite;
and, knowing the kind of people he had to deal with,
he carried his passion of claiming acquaintance with everybody, to the most immoderate length. He had rather a
singular way of telling his greatest lies in a parenthesis,
and with an air of self-denial, as if he feared being thought
egotistical.

"Why, no, I don't know him by that name," returned
Flamwell, in a low tone, and with an air of immense importance. "I have no doubt I know him, though. Is
he tall?"

"Middle-sized," said Miss Teresa.

"With black hair?" inquired Flamwell, hazarding a bold
guess.

"Yes," returned Miss Teresa, eagerly.

"Rather a snub nose?"

"No," said the disappointed Teresa, "he has a Roman nose."

"I said a Roman nose, didn't I?" inquired Flamwell.
"He's an elegant young man?"

"Oh, certainly."

"With remarkably prepossessing manners?"

"Oh, yes!" said all the family together. "You must
know him."

"Yes, I thought you knew him, if he was anybody,"
triumphantly exclaimed Mr. Malderton. "Who d'ye think
he is?"

"Why, from your description," said Flamwell, ruminating,
and sinking his voice almost to a whisper, "he bears a strong
resemblance to the Honourable Augustus Fitz-Edward Fitz-
John Fitz-Osborne. He's a very talented young man, and
rather eccentric. It's extremely probable he may have changed
his name for some temporary purpose."

Teresa's heart beat high. Could he be the Honourable
Augustus Fitz-Edward Fitz-John Fitz-Osborne! What a
name to be elegantly engraved upon two glazed cards, tied
together with a piece of white satin ribbon! "The Honourable Mrs. Augustus Fitz-Edward Fitz-John Fitz-Osborne!"
The thought was transport.

"It's five minutes to five," said Mr. Malderton, looking at
his watch: "I hope he's not going to disappoint us."

"There he is!" exclaimed Miss Teresa, as a loud double-knock was heard at the door. Everybody endeavoured to look—as people when they particularly expect a visitor always do—as if they were perfectly unsuspicious of the approach of anybody.

The room-door opened—"Mr. Barton!" said the servant.

"Confound the man!" murmured Malderton. "Ah! my dear sir, how d'ye do! Any news?"

"Why no," returned the grocer, in his usual bluff manner. "No, none partickler. None that I am much aware of. How d'ye do, gals and boys? Mr. Flamwell, sir—glad to see you."

"Here's Mr. Sparkins!" said Tom, who had been looking out at the window, "on *such* a black horse!" There was Horatio, sure enough, on a large black horse, curvetting and prancing along, like an Astley's supernumerary. After a great deal of reining in, and pulling up, with the accompaniments of snorting, rearing, and kicking, the animal consented to stop at about a hundred yards from the gate, where Mr. Sparkins dismounted, and confided him to the care of Mr. Malderton's groom. The ceremony of introduction was gone through, in all due form. Mr. Flamwell looked from behind his green spectacles at Horatio with an air of mysterious importance; and the gallant Horatio looked unutterable things at Teresa.

"Is he the Honourable Mr. Augustus What's-his-name?" whispered Mrs. Malderton to Flamwell, as he was escorting her to the dining-room.

"Why, no—at least not exactly," returned that great authority—"not exactly."

"Who *is* he then?"

"Hush!" said Flamwell, nodding his head with a grave air, importing that he knew very well; but was prevented, by some grave reasons of state, from disclosing the important secret. It might be one of the ministers making himself acquainted with the views of the people.

"Mr. Sparkins," said the delighted Mrs. Malderton, "pray divide the ladies. John, put a chair for the gentleman between Miss Teresa and Miss Marianne." This was addressed to a man who, on ordinary occasions, acted as half-groom, half-gardener; but who, as it was important to make an impression on Mr. Sparkins. had been forced into

P

a white neckerchief and shoes, and touched up, and brushed, to look like a second footman.

The dinner was excellent; Horatio was most attentive to Miss Teresa, and every one felt in high spirits, except Mr. Malderton, who, knowing the propensity of his brother-in-law, Mr. Barton, endured that sort of agony which the newspapers inform us is experienced by the surrounding neighbourhood when a pot-boy hangs himself in a hay-loft, and which is "much easier to be imagined than described."

"Have you seen your friend, Sir Thomas Noland, lately, Flamwell?" inquired Mr. Malderton, casting a sidelong look at Horatio, to see what effect the mention of so great a man had upon him.

"Why, no—not very lately. I saw Lord Gubbleton the day before yesterday."

"Ah! I hope his lordship is very well?" said Malderton, in a tone of the greatest interest. It is scarcely necessary to say that, until that moment, he had been quite innocent of the existence of such a person.

"Why, yes; he was very well—very well indeed. He's a devilish good fellow. I met him in the City, and had a long chat with him. Indeed, I'm rather intimate with him. I couldn't stop to talk to him as long as I could wish, though, because I was on my way to a banker's, a very rich man, and a member of Parliament, with whom I am also rather, indeed I may say very, intimate."

"I know whom you mean," returned the host, consequentially—in reality knowing as much about the matter as Flamwell himself. "He has a capital business."

This was touching on a dangerous topic.

"Talking of business," interposed Mr. Barton, from the centre of the table. "A gentleman whom you knew very well, Malderton, before you made that first lucky spec of yours, called at our shop the other day, and —— "

"Barton, may I trouble you for a potato?" interrupted the wretched master of the house, hoping to nip the story in the bud.

"Certainly," returned the grocer, quite insensible of his brother-in-law's object — "and he said in a very plain manner —— "

"*Floury*, if you please," interrupted Malderton again; dreading the termination of the anecdote, and fearing a repetition of the word "shop."

"He said, says he," continued the culprit, after dispatching the potato; "says he, how goes on your business? So I said, jokingly—you know my way—says I, I'm never above my business, and I hope my business will never be above me. Ha, ha!"

"Mr. Sparkins," said the host, vainly endeavouring to conceal his dismay, "a glass of wine?"

"With the utmost pleasure, sir."

"Happy to see you."

"Thank you."

"We were talking the other evening," resumed the host, addressing Horatio, partly with the view of displaying the conversational powers of his new acquaintance, and partly in the hope of drowning the grocer's stories—"we were talking the other night about the nature of man. Your argument struck me very forcibly."

"And me," said Mr. Frederick. Horatio made a graceful inclination of the head.

"Pray, what is your opinion of woman, Mr. Sparkins?" inquired Mrs. Malderton. The young ladies simpered.

"Man," replied Horatio, "man, whether he ranged the bright, gay, flowery plains of a second Eden, or the more sterile, barren, and I may say, commonplace regions, to which we are compelled to accustom ourselves, in times such as these; man, under any circumstances, or in any place— whether he were bending beneath the withering blasts of the frigid zone, or scorching under the rays of a vertical sun— man, without woman, would be—alone."

"I am very happy to find you entertain such honourable opinions, Mr. Sparkins," said Mrs. Malderton.

"And I," added Miss Teresa. Horatio looked his delight, and the young lady blushed.

"Now, it's my opinion——" said Mr. Barton.

"I know what you're going to say," interposed Malderton, determined not to give his relation another opportunity, "and I don't agree with you."

"What!" inquired the astonished grocer.

"I am sorry to differ from you, Barton," said the host, in as positive a manner as if he really were contradicting a position which the other had laid down, "but I cannot give my assent to what I consider a very monstrous proposition."

"But I meant to say——"

"You never can convince me," said Malderton, with an air of obstinate determination. "Never."

"And I," said Mr. Frederick, following up his father's attack, "cannot entirely agree in Mr. Sparkins's argument."

"What!" said Horatio, who became more metaphysical, and more argumentative, as he saw the female part of the family listening in wondering delight—"what! Is effect the consequence of cause? Is cause the precursor of effect?"

"That's the point," said Flamwell.

"To be sure," said Mr. Malderton.

"Because, if effect is the consequence of cause, and if cause does precede effect, I apprehend you are wrong," added Horatio.

"Decidedly," said the toad-eating Flamwell.

"At least, I apprehend that to be the just and logical deduction?" said Sparkins, in a tone of interrogation.

"No doubt of it," chimed in Flamwell again. "It settles the point."

"Well, perhaps it does," said Mr. Frederick; "I didn't see it before."

"I don't exactly see it now," thought the grocer; "but I suppose it's all right."

"How wonderfully clever he is!" whispered Mrs. Malderton to her daughters, as they retired to the drawing-room.

"Oh, he's quite a love!" said both the young ladies together; "he talks like an oracle. He must have seen a great deal of life."

The gentlemen being left to themselves, a pause ensued, during which everybody looked very grave, as if they were quite overcome by the profound nature of the previous discussion. Flamwell, who had made up his mind to find out who and what Mr. Horatio Sparkins really was, first broke silence.

"Excuse me, sir," said that distinguished personage, "I presume you have studied for the bar? I thought of entering once, myself—indeed, I'm rather intimate with some of the highest ornaments of that distinguished profession."

"N—no!" said Horatio, with a little hesitation; "not exactly."

"But you have been much among the silk gowns, or I mistake?" inquired Flamwell, deferentially.

"Nearly all my life," returned Sparkins.

The question was thus pretty well settled in the mind of

Mr. Flamwell. He was a young gentleman "about to be called."

"I shouldn't like to be a barrister," said Tom, speaking for the first time, and looking round the table to find somebody who would notice the remark.

No one made any reply.

"I shouldn't like to wear a wig," said Tom, hazarding another observation.

"Tom, I beg you will not make yourself ridiculous," said his father. "Pray listen, and improve yourself by the conversation you hear, and don't be constantly making these absurd remarks."

"Very well, father," replied the unfortunate Tom, who had not spoken a word since he had asked for another slice of beef at a quarter-past five o'clock P.M., and it was then eight.

"Well, Tom," observed his good-natured uncle, "never mind! *I* think with you. *I* shouldn't like to wear a wig. I'd rather wear an apron."

Mr. Malderton coughed violently. Mr. Barton resumed— "For if a man's above his business——"

The cough returned with tenfold violence, and did not cease until the unfortunate cause of it, in his alarm, had quite forgotten what he intended to say.

"Mr. Sparkins," said Flamwell, returning to the charge, "do you happen to know Mr. Delafontaine, of Bedford Square?"

"I have exchanged cards with him; since which, indeed, I have had an opportunity of serving him considerably," replied Horatio, slightly colouring; no doubt, at having been betrayed into making the acknowledgment.

"You are very lucky, if you have had an opportunity of obliging that great man," observed Flamwell, with an air of profound respect.

"I don't know who he is," he whispered to Mr. Malderton, confidentially, as they followed Horatio up to the drawing-room. "It's quite clear, however, that he belongs to the law, and that he is somebody of great importance, and very highly connected."

"No doubt, no doubt," returned his companion.

The remainder of the evening passed away most delightfully. Mr. Malderton, relieved from his apprehensions by the circumstance of Mr. Barton's falling into a profound sleep, was

as affable and gracious as possible. Miss Teresa played the
"Fall of Paris," as Mr. Sparkins declared, in a most masterly
manner, and both of them, assisted by Mr. Frederick, tried
over glees and trios without number ; they having made the
pleasing discovery that their voices harmonised beautifully.
To be sure, they all sang the first part ; and Horatio, in
addition to the slight drawback of having no ear, was perfectly
innocent of knowing a note of music ; still, they passed the
time very agreeably, and it was past twelve o'clock before
Mr. Sparkins ordered the mourning-coach-looking steed to be
brought out—an order which was only complied with on the
distinct understanding that he was to repeat his visit on
the following Sunday.

"But perhaps Mr. Sparkins will form one of our party
to-morrow evening?" suggested Mrs. M.   "Mr. Malderton
intends taking the girls to see the pantomime."   Mr. Sparkins
bowed, and promised to join the party in box 48, in the
course of the evening.

"We will not tax you for the morning," said Miss Teresa,
bewitchingly ; "for ma is going to take us to all sorts of
places, shopping.   I know that gentlemen have a great horror
of that employment."   Mr. Sparkins bowed again, and
declared that he should be delighted, but business of importance occupied him in the morning.   Flamwell looked at
Malderton significantly.—"It's term time !" he whispered.

At twelve o'clock on the following morning, the "fly" was
at the door of Oak Lodge, to convey Mrs. Malderton and
her daughters on their expedition for the day.   They were
to dine and dress for the play at a friend's house.   First,
driving thither with their band-boxes, they departed on their
first errand to make some purchases at Messrs. Jones, Spruggins, and Smith's, of Tottenham Court Road; after which, they
were to go to Redmayne's in Bond Street ; thence, to innumerable places that no one ever heard of.   The young ladies
beguiled the tediousness of the ride by eulogising Mr. Horatio
Sparkins, scolding their mamma for taking them so far to
save a shilling, and wondering whether they should ever reach
their destination.   At length, the vehicle stopped before a
dirty-looking ticketed linen-draper's shop, with goods of all
kinds, and labels of all sorts and sizes, in the window.   There
were dropsical figures of seven with a little three-farthings in
the corner, "perfectly invisible to the naked eye;" three
hundred and fifty thousand ladies' boas, *from* one shilling

and a penny halfpenny; real French kid shoes, at two and ninepence per pair; green parasols, at an equally cheap rate; and "every description of goods," as the proprietors said—and they must know best—"fifty per cent. under cost price."

"Lor! ma, what a place you have brought us to!" said Miss Teresa; "what *would* Mr. Sparkins say if he could see us!"

"Ah! what, indeed!" said Miss Marianne, horrified at the idea.

"Pray be seated, ladies. What is the first article?" inquired the obsequious master of the ceremonies of the establishment, who, in his large white neckcloth and formal tie, looked like a bad "portrait of a gentleman" in the Somerset House exhibition.

"I want to see some silks," answered Mrs. Malderton.

"Directly, ma'am.—Mr. Smith! Where *is* Mr. Smith?"

"Here, sir," cried a voice at the back of the shop.

"Pray make haste, Mr. Smith," said the M.C. "You never are to be found when you're wanted, sir."

Mr. Smith, thus enjoined to use all possible dispatch, leaped over the counter with great agility, and placed himself before the newly-arrived customers. Mrs. Malderton uttered a faint scream; Miss Teresa, who had been stooping down to talk to her sister, raised her head, and beheld—Horatio Sparkins!

"We will draw a veil," as novel-writers say, over the scene that ensued. The mysterious, philosophical, romantic, metaphysical Sparkins—he who, to the interesting Teresa, seemed like the embodied idea of the young dukes and poetical exquisites in blue silk dressing-gowns, and ditto ditto slippers, of whom she had read and dreamed, but had never expected to behold, was suddenly converted into Mr. Samuel Smith, the assistant at a "cheap shop;" the junior partner in a slippery firm of some three weeks' existence. The dignified evanishment of the hero of Oak Lodge, on this unexpected recognition, could only be equalled by that of a furtive dog with a considerable kettle at his tail. All the hopes of the Maldertons were destined at once to melt away, like the lemon ices at a Company's dinner; Almack's was still to them as distant as the North Pole; and Miss Teresa had as much chance of a husband as Captain Ross had of the north-west passage.

Years have elapsed since the occurrence of this dreadful morning. The daisies have thrice bloomed on Camberwell

Green ; the sparrows have thrice repeated their vernal chirps in Camberwell Grove ; but the Miss Maldertons are still un-mated. Miss Teresa's case is more desperate than ever ; but Flamwell is yet in the zenith of his reputation ; and the family have the same predilection for aristocratic personages, with an increased aversion to anything *low*.

CHAPTER VI

THE BLACK VEIL

ONE winter's evening, towards the close of the year 1800, or within a year or two of that time, a young medical practitioner, recently established in business, was seated by a cheerful fire in his little parlour, listening to the wind which was beating the rain in pattering drops against the window, or rumbling dismally in the chimney. The night was wet and cold; he had been walking through mud and water the whole day, and was now comfortably reposing in his dressing-gown and slippers, more than half asleep and less than half awake, revolving a thousand matters in his wandering imagination. First, he thought how hard the wind was blowing, and how the cold, sharp rain would be at that moment beating in his face, if he were not comfortably housed at home. Then, his mind reverted to his annual Christmas visit to his native place and dearest friends; he thought how glad they would all be to see him, and how happy it would make Rose if he could only tell her that he had found a patient at last, and hoped to have more, and to come down again, in a few months' time, and marry her, and take her home to gladden his lonely fireside, and stimulate him to fresh exertions. Then, he began to wonder when his first patient would appear, or whether he was destined, by a special dispensation of Providence, never to have any patients at all; and then, he thought about Rose again, and dropped to sleep and dreamed about her, till the tones of her sweet merry voice sounded in his ears, and her soft tiny hand rested on his shoulder.

There *was* a hand upon his shoulder, but it was neither soft nor tiny; its owner being a corpulent round-headed boy, who, in consideration of the sum of one shilling per week and his food, was let out by the parish to carry medicine and messages. As there was no demand for the medicine, however, and no necessity for the messages, he usually occupied his unemployed hours—averaging fourteen a day—in abstracting peppermint drops, taking animal nourishment, and going to sleep.

"A lady, sir—a lady!" whispered the boy, rousing his master with a shake.

"What lady?" cried our friend, starting up, not quite certain that his dream was an illusion, and half expecting that it might be Rose herself.—"What lady? Where?"

"*There*, sir!" replied the boy, pointing to the glass door leading into the surgery, with an expression of alarm which the very unusual apparition of a customer might have tended to excite.

The surgeon looked towards the door, and started himself, for an instant, on beholding the appearance of his unlooked-for visitor.

It was a singularly tall woman, dressed in deep mourning, and standing so close to the door that her face almost touched the glass. The upper part of her figure was carefully muffled in a black shawl, as if for the purpose of concealment; and her face was shrouded by a thick black veil. She stood perfectly erect, her figure was drawn up to its full height, and though the surgeon *felt* that the eyes beneath the veil were fixed on him, she stood perfectly motionless, and evinced, by no gesture whatever, the slightest consciousness of his having turned towards her.

"Do you wish to consult me?" he inquired, with some hesitation, holding open the door. It opened inwards, and therefore the action did not alter the position of the figure, which still remained motionless on the same spot.

She slightly inclined her head, in token of acquiescence.

"Pray walk in," said the surgeon.

The figure moved a step forward; and then, turning its head in the direction of the boy—to his infinite horror—appeared to hesitate.

"Leave the room, Tom," said the young man, addressing the boy, whose large round eyes had been extended to their utmost width during this brief interview. "Draw the curtain, and shut the door."

The boy drew a green curtain across the glass part of the door, retired into the surgery, closed the door after him, and immediately applied one of his large eyes to the keyhole on the other side.

The surgeon drew a chair to the fire, and motioned the

visitor to a seat. The mysterious figure slowly moved towards it. As the blaze shone upon the black dress, the surgeon observed that the bottom of it was saturated with mud and rain.

"You are very wet," he said.

"I am," said the stranger, in a low deep voice.

"And you are ill?" added the surgeon, compassionately, for the tone was that of a person in pain.

"I am," was the reply—"very ill; not bodily, but mentally. It is not for myself, or on my own behalf," continued the stranger, "that I come to you. If I laboured under bodily disease, I should not be out, alone, at such an hour, or on such a night as this; and if I were afflicted with it, twenty-four hours hence, God knows how gladly I would lie down and pray to die. It is for another that I beseech your aid, sir. I may be mad to ask it for him—I think I am; but, night after night, through the long dreary hours of watching and weeping, the thought has been ever present to my mind; and though even *I* see the hopelessness of human assistance availing him, the bare thought of laying him in his grave without it makes my blood run cold!" And a shudder, such as the surgeon well knew art could not produce, trembled through the speaker's frame.

There was a desperate earnestness in this woman's manner, that went to the young man's heart. He was young in his profession, and had not yet witnessed enough of the miseries which are daily presented before the eyes of its members, to have grown comparatively callous to human suffering.

"If," he said, rising hastily, "the person of whom you speak, be in so hopeless a condition as you describe, not a moment is to be lost. I will go with you instantly. Why did you not obtain medical advice before?"

"Because it would have been useless before—because it is useless even now," replied the woman, clasping her hands passionately.

The surgeon gazed, for a moment, on the black veil, as if to ascertain the expression of the features beneath it; its thickness, however, rendered such a result impossible.

"You *are* ill," he said, gently, "although you do not know it. The fever which has enabled you to bear, without feeling it, the fatigue you have evidently undergone, is burning within you now. Put that to your lips," he continued, pouring out a glass of water—"compose yourself for a few moments, and then tell me, as calmly as you can, what the disease of the patient is, and how long he has been ill. When I know what it is necessary I should know, to render my visit serviceable to him, I am ready to accompany you."

The stranger lifted the glass of water to her mouth, without raising the veil; put it down again untasted; and burst into tears.

"I know," she said, sobbing aloud, "that what I say to you now, seems like the ravings of fever. I have been told so before, less kindly than by you. I am not a young woman; and they do say, that as life steals on towards its final close, the last short remnant, worthless as it may seem to all beside, is dearer to its possessor than all the years that have gone before, connected though they be with the recollection of old friends long since dead, and young ones—children perhaps—who have fallen off from, and forgotten one as completely as if they had died too. My natural term of life cannot be many years longer, and should be dear on that account; but I would lay it down without a sigh—with cheerfulness—with joy—if what I tell you now were only false or imaginary. To-morrow morning he of whom I speak will be, I *know*, though I would fain think otherwise, beyond the reach of human aid; and yet, to-night, though he is in deadly peril, you must not see, and could not serve, him."

"I am unwilling to increase your distress," said the surgeon, after a short pause, "by making any comment on what you have just said, or appearing desirous to investigate a subject you are so anxious to conceal; but there is an inconsistency in your statement which I cannot reconcile with probability. This person is dying to-night, and I cannot see him when my assistance might possibly avail; you apprehend it will be useless to-morrow, and yet you would have me see him then! If he be, indeed, as dear to you as your words and manner would imply, why not try to save his life before delay and the progress of his disease render it impracticable?"

"God help me!" exclaimed the woman, weeping bitterly, "how can I hope strangers will believe what appears incredible, even to myself? You will *not* see him then, sir?" she added, rising suddenly.

"I did not say that I declined to see him," replied the surgeon; "but I warn you, that if you persist in this extraordinary procrastination, and the individual dies, a fearful responsibility rests with you."

"The responsibility will rest heavily somewhere," replied the stranger bitterly. "Whatever responsibility rests with me, I am content to bear, and ready to answer."

"As I incur none," continued the surgeon, "by acceding to your request, I will see him in the morning, if you leave me the address. At what hour can he be seen?"

"*Nine,*" replied the stranger.

"You must excuse me pressing these inquiries," said the surgeon. "But is he in your charge now?"

"He is not," was the rejoinder.

"Then, if I gave you instructions for his treatment through the night, you could not assist him?"

The woman wept bitterly, as she replied, "I could not."

Finding that there was but little prospect of obtaining more information by prolonging the interview; and anxious to spare the woman's feelings, which, subdued at first by a violent effort, were now irrepressible and most painful to witness; the surgeon repeated his promise of calling in the morning at the appointed hour. His visitor, after giving him a direction to an obscure part of Walworth, left the house in the same mysterious manner in which she had entered it.

It will be readily believed that so extraordinary a visit produced a considerable impression on the mind of the young surgeon; and that he speculated a great deal and to very little purpose on the possible circumstances of the case. In common with the generality of people, he had often heard and read of singular instances, in which a presentiment of death, at a particular day, or even minute, had been entertained and realised. At one moment he was inclined to think that the present might be such a case; but then it occurred to him that all the anecdotes of the kind he had ever heard, were of persons who had been troubled with a foreboding of their own death. This woman, however, spoke of another person —a man; and it was impossible to suppose that a mere dream or delusion of fancy would induce her to speak of his approaching dissolution with such terrible certainty as she had spoken. It could not be that the man was to be murdered in the morning, and that the woman, originally a consenting party, and bound to secrecy by an oath, had relented, and, though unable to prevent the commission of some outrage on the victim, had determined to prevent his death if possible, by the timely interposition of medical aid? The idea of such things happening within two miles of the metropolis appeared too wild and preposterous to be entertained beyond the instant. Then, his original impression that the woman's intellects were disordered, recurred; and, as it was the only mode of solving the difficulty with any degree of satisfaction, he obstinately made up his mind to believe that she was mad. Certain misgivings upon this point, however, stole upon his thoughts at the time, and presented themselves again and again through the long dull course of a sleepless night; during which, in spite of all his efforts to the contrary, he was unable to banish the black veil from his disturbed imagination.

The back part of Walworth, at its greatest distance from town, is a straggling miserable place enough, even in these days; but, five-and-thirty years ago, the greater portion of it was little better than a dreary waste, inhabited by a few scattered people of questionable character, whose poverty prevented their living in any better neighbourhood, or whose pursuits and mode of life rendered its solitude desirable. Very many of the houses which have since sprung up on all sides, were not built until some years afterwards; and the great majority even of those which were sprinkled about, at irregular intervals, were of the rudest and most miserable description.

The appearance of the place through which he walked in the morning, was not calculated to raise the spirits of the young surgeon, or to dispel any feeling of anxiety or depression which the singular kind of visit he was about to make, had awakened. Striking off from the high road, his way lay across a marshy common, through irregular lanes, with here and there a ruinous and dismantled cottage fast falling to pieces with decay and neglect. A stunted tree, or pool of stagnant water, roused into a sluggish action by the heavy rain of the preceding night, skirted the path occasionally; and, now and then, a miserable patch of garden-ground, with a few old boards knocked together for a summer-house, and old palings imperfectly mended with stakes pilfered from the neighbouring hedges, bore testimony, at once to the poverty of the inhabitants, and the little scruple they entertained in appropriating the property of other people to their own use. Occasionally, a filthy-looking woman would make her appearance from the door of a dirty house, to empty the contents of some cooking utensil into the gutter in front, or to scream

Steam Excursion (I)
(*p. 398*)

after a little slip-shod girl, who had contrived to stagger a few yards from the door under the weight of a sallow infant almost as big as herself; but scarcely anything was stirring around; and so much of the prospect as could be faintly traced through the cold damp mist which hung heavily over it, presented a lonely and dreary appearance perfectly in keeping with the objects we have described.

After plodding wearily through the mud and mire; making many inquiries for the place to which he had been directed; and receiving as many contradictory and unsatisfactory replies in return; the young man at length arrived before the house which had been pointed out to him as the object of his destination. It was a small low building, one story above the ground, with even a more desolate and unpromising exterior than any he had yet passed. An old yellow curtain was closely drawn across the window up-stairs, and the parlour shutters were closed, but not fastened. The house was detached from any other, and, as it stood at an angle of a narrow lane, there was no other habitation in sight.

When we say that the surgeon hesitated, and walked a few paces beyond the house, before he could prevail upon himself to lift the knocker, we say nothing that need raise a smile upon the face of the boldest reader. The police of London were a very different body in that day; the isolated position of the suburbs, when the rage for building and the progress of improvement had not yet begun to connect them with the main body of the city and its environs, rendered many of them (and this in particular) a place of resort for the worst and most depraved characters. Even the streets in the gayest parts of London were imperfectly lighted at that time; and such places as these were left entirely to the mercy of the moon and stars. The chances of detecting desperate characters, or of tracing them to their haunts, were thus rendered very few, and their offences naturally increased in boldness, as the consciousness of comparative security became the more impressed upon them by daily experience. Added to these considerations, it must be remembered that the young man had spent some time in the public hospitals of the metropolis, and, although neither Burke nor Bishop had then gained a horrible notoriety, his own observation might have suggested to him how easily the atrocities to which the former has since given his name, might be committed. Be this as it may, whatever reflection made him hesitate, he *did* hesitate:

but, being a young man of strong mind and great personal courage, it was only for an instant ;—he stepped briskly back and knocked gently at the door.

A low whispering was audible, immediately afterwards, as if some person at the end of the passage were conversing stealthily with another on the landing above. It was suc-ceeded by the noise of a pair of heavy boots upon the bare floor. The door-chain was softly unfastened; the door opened; and a tall, ill-favoured man, with black hair, and a face, as the surgeon often declared afterwards, as pale and haggard as the countenance of any dead man he ever saw, presented himself.

"Walk in, sir," he said in a low tone.

The surgeon did so, and the man having secured the door again, by the chain, led the way to a small back parlour at the extremity of the passage.

"Am I in time ?"

"Too soon !" replied the man. The surgeon turned hastily round, with a gesture of astonishment not unmixed with alarm, which he found it impossible to repress.

"If you'll step in here, sir," said the man, who had evi-dently noticed the action—"if you'll step in here, sir, you won't be detained five minutes, I assure you."

The surgeon at once walked into the room. The man closed the door, and left him alone.

It was a little cold room, with no other furniture than two deal chairs, and a table of the same material. A handful of fire, unguarded by any fender, was burning in the grate, which brought out the damp if it served no more comfortable purpose, for the unwholesome moisture was stealing down the walls, in long slug-like tracks. The window, which was broken and patched in many places, looked into a small enclosed piece of ground, almost covered with water. Not a sound was to be heard, either within the house or without. The young surgeon sat down by the fireplace, to await the result of his first professional visit.

He had not remained in this position many minutes, when the noise of some approaching vehicle struck his ear. It stopped; the street-door was opened; a low talking succeeded, accompanied with a shuffling noise of footsteps, along the passage and on the stairs, as if two or three men were engaged in carrying some heavy body to the room above. The creak-ing of the stairs, a few seconds afterwards, announced that the new-comers having completed their task, whatever it was, were leaving the house. The door was again closed, and the former silence was restored.

Another five minutes had elapsed, and the surgeon had resolved to explore the house, in search of some one to whom he might make his errand known, when the room-door opened, and his last night's visitor, dressed in exactly the same manner, with the veil lowered as before, motioned him to advance. The singular height of her form, coupled with the circumstance of her not speaking, caused the idea to pass across his brain for an instant, that it might be a man disguised in woman's attire. The hysteric sobs which issued from beneath the veil, and the convulsive attitude of grief of the whole figure, however, at once exposed the absurdity of the suspicion; and he hastily followed.

The woman led the way up-stairs to the front room, and paused at the door, to let him enter first. It was scantily furnished with an old deal box, a few chairs, and a tent bedstead, without hangings or cross-rails, which was covered with a patchwork counterpane. The dim light admitted through the curtain which he had noticed from the outside, rendered the objects in the room so indistinct, and communicated to all of them so uniform a hue, that he did not, at first, perceive the object on which his eye at once rested when the woman rushed frantically past him, and flung herself on her knees by the bedside.

Stretched upon the bed, closely enveloped in a linen wrapper, and covered with blankets, lay a human form, stiff and motionless. The head and face, which were those of a man, were uncovered, save by a bandage which passed over the head and under the chin. The eyes were closed. The left arm lay heavily across the bed, and the woman held the passive hand.

The surgeon gently pushed the woman aside, and took the hand in his.

"My God!" he exclaimed, letting it fall involuntarily—"the man is dead!"

The woman started to her feet and beat her hands together. "Oh! don't say so, sir," she exclaimed, with a burst of passion, amounting almost to frenzy. "Oh! don't say so, sir! I can't bear it! Men have been brought to life, before, when unskilful people have given them up for lost; and men have died, who might have been restored, if proper means had been resorted to. Don't let him lie here, sir, without one effort to save him! This very moment life may be passing away. Do try, sir,—do, for Heaven's sake!"—And while speaking, she hurriedly chafed, first the forehead, and then the breast, of the senseless form before her; and then, wildly beat the cold hands, which, when she ceased to hold them, fell listlessly and heavily back on the coverlet.

"It is of no use, my good woman," said the surgeon, soothingly, as he withdrew his hand from the man's breast. "Stay—undraw that curtain!"

"Why?" said the woman, starting up.

"Undraw that curtain!" repeated the surgeon in an agitated tone.

"*I* darkened the room on purpose," said the woman, throwing herself before him as he rose to undraw it.— "Oh! sir, have pity on me! If it can be of no use, and he is really dead, do not expose that form to other eyes than mine!"

"This man died no natural or easy death," said the surgeon. "I *must* see the body!" With a motion so sudden, that the woman hardly knew that he had slipped from beside her, he tore open the curtain, admitted the full light of day, and returned to the bedside.

"There has been violence here," he said, pointing towards the body, and gazing intently on the face, from which the black veil was now, for the first time, removed. In the excitement of a minute before, the female had thrown off the bonnet and veil, and now stood with her eyes fixed upon him. Her features were those of a woman about fifty, who had once been handsome. Sorrow and weeping had left traces upon them which not time itself would ever have produced without their aid; her face was deadly pale; and there was a nervous contortion of the lip, and an unnatural fire in her eye, which showed too plainly that her bodily and mental powers had nearly sunk beneath an accumulation of misery.

"There has been violence here," said the surgeon, preserving his searching glance.

"There has!" replied the woman.

"This man has been murdered."

"That I call God to witness he has," said the woman, passionately; "pitilessly, inhumanly murdered!"

"By whom?" said the surgeon, seizing the woman by the arm.

"Look at the butchers' marks, and then ask me!" she replied.

The surgeon turned his face towards the bed, and bent over the body which now lay full in the light of the window. The throat was swollen, and a livid mark encircled it. The truth flashed suddenly upon him.

"This is one of the men who were hanged this morning!" he exclaimed, turning away with a shudder.

"It is," replied the woman, with a cold, unmeaning stare.

"Who was he?" inquired the surgeon.

"*My son*," rejoined the woman; and fell senseless at his feet.

It was true. A companion, equally guilty with himself, had been acquitted for want of evidence; and this man had been left for death, and executed. To recount the circumstances of the case, at this distant period, must be unnecessary, and might give pain to some persons still alive. The history was an every-day one. The mother was a widow without friends or money, and had denied herself necessaries to bestow them on her orphan boy. That boy, unmindful of her prayers, and forgetful of the sufferings she had endured for him—incessant anxiety of mind, and voluntary starvation of body—had plunged into a career of dissipation and crime. And this was the result; his own death by the hangman's hands, and his mother's shame, and incurable insanity.

For many years after this occurrence, and when profitable and arduous avocations would have led many men to forget that such a miserable being existed, the young surgeon was a daily visitor at the side of the harmless mad woman; not only soothing her by his presence and kindness, but alleviating the rigour of her condition by pecuniary donations for her comfort and support, bestowed with no sparing hand. In the transient gleam of recollection and consciousness which preceded her death, a prayer for his welfare and protection, as fervent as mortal ever breathed, rose from the lips of this poor friendless creature. That prayer flew to Heaven, and was heard. The blessings he was instrumental in conferring, have been repaid to him a thousand-fold; but, amid all the honours of rank and station which have since been heaped upon him, and which he has so well earned, he can have no reminiscence more gratifying to his heart than that connected with The Black Veil.

CHAPTER VII

Mr. Percy Noakes was a law student, inhabiting a set of chambers on the fourth floor, in one of those houses in Gray's Inn Square which command an extensive view of the gardens, and their usual adjuncts—flaunting nursery-maids, and town-made children, with parenthetical legs. Mr. Percy Noakes was what is generally termed—"a devilish good fellow." He had a large circle of acquaintance, and seldom dined at his own expense. He used to talk politics to papas, flatter the vanity of mammas, do the amiable to their daughters, make pleasure engagements with their sons, and romp with the younger branches. Like those paragons of perfection, advertising footmen out of place, he was always "willing to make himself generally useful." If any old lady, whose son was in India, gave a ball, Mr. Percy Noakes was master of the ceremonies; if any young lady made a stolen match, Mr. Percy Noakes gave her away; if a juvenile wife presented her husband with a blooming cherub, Mr. Percy Noakes was either godfather, or deputy-godfather; and if any member of a friend's family died, Mr. Percy Noakes was invariably to be seen in the second mourning coach, with a white handkerchief to his eyes, sobbing—to use his own appropriate and expressive description—"like winkin'!"

It may readily be imagined that these numerous avocations were rather calculated to interfere with Mr. Percy Noakes's professional studies. Mr. Percy Noakes was perfectly aware of the fact, and had, therefore, after mature reflection, made up his mind not to study at all—a laudable determination, to which he adhered in the most praiseworthy manner. His sitting-room presented a strange chaos of dress-gloves, boxing-gloves, caricatures, albums, invitation-cards, foils, cricket-bats, cardboard drawings, paste, gum, and fifty other miscellaneous articles, heaped together in the strangest confusion. He was always making something for somebody, or planning some party of pleasure, which was his great *forte*. He invariably spoke with astonishing rapidity; was smart, spoffish, and eight-and-twenty.

"Splendid idea, 'pon my life!" soliloquised Mr. Percy Noakes, over his morning's coffee, as his mind reverted to a suggestion which had been thrown out on the previous night, by a lady at whose house he had spent the evening. " Glorious idea!—Mrs. Stubbs."

"Yes, sir," replied a dirty old woman with an inflamed countenance, emerging from the bedroom with a barrel of dirt and cinders.—This was the laundress. "Did you call, sir?"

"Oh! Mrs. Stubbs, I'm going out. If that tailor should call again, you'd better say—you'd better say I'm out of town, and shan't be back for a fortnight; and if that boot-maker should come, tell him I've lost his address, or I'd have sent him that little amount. Mind he writes it down; and if Mr. Hardy should call—you know Mr. Hardy?"

"The funny gentleman, sir?"

"Ah! the funny gentleman. If Mr. Hardy should call, say I've gone to Mrs. Taunton's about that water-party."

"Yes, sir."

"And if any fellow calls, and says he's come about a steamer, tell him to be here at five o'clock this afternoon, Mrs. Stubbs."

"Very well, sir."

Mr. Percy Noakes brushed his hat, whisked the crumbs off his inexplicables with a silk handkerchief, gave the ends of his hair a persuasive roll round his forefinger, and sallied forth for Mrs. Taunton's domicile in Great Marlborough Street, where she and her daughters occupied the upper part of a house. She was a good-looking widow of fifty, with the form of a giantess and the mind of a child. The pursuit of pleasure, and some means of killing time, were the sole end of her existence. She doted on her daughters, who were as frivolous as herself.

A general exclamation of satisfaction hailed the arrival of Mr. Percy Noakes, who went through the ordinary salutations, and threw himself into an easy chair near the ladies' work-table, with the ease of a regularly established friend of the family. Mrs. Taunton was busily engaged in planting immense bright bows on every part of a smart cap on which it was possible to stick one; Miss Emily Taunton was making a watch-guard; Miss Sophia was at the piano, practising a new song—poetry by the young officer, or the police-officer, or the custom-house officer, or some other interesting amateur.

"You good creature!" said Mrs. Taunton, addressing the gallant Percy. "You really are a good soul! You've come about the water-party, I know."

"I should rather suspect I had," replied Mr. Noakes, triumphantly. "Now, come here, girls, and I'll tell you all about it." Miss Emily and Miss Sophia advanced to the table.

"Now," continued Mr. Percy Noakes, "it seems to me that the best way will be, to have a committee of ten, to make all the arrangements, and manage the whole set-out. Then, I propose that the expenses shall be paid by these ten fellows jointly."

"Excellent, indeed!" said Mrs. Taunton, who highly approved of this part of the arrangements.

"Then, my plan is, that each of these ten fellows shall have the power of asking five people. There must be a meeting of the committee, at my chambers, to make all the arrangements, and these people shall be then named; every member of the committee shall have the power of black-balling any one who is proposed; and one black ball shall exclude that person. This will ensure our having a pleasant party, you know."

"What a manager you are!" interrupted Mrs. Taunton again.

"Charming!" said the lovely Emily.

"I never did!" ejaculated Sophia.

"Yes, I think it'll do," replied Mr. Percy Noakes, who was now quite in his element. "I think it'll do. Then you know we shall go down to the Nore, and back, and have a regular capital cold dinner laid out in the cabin before we start, so that everything may be ready without any confusion; and we shall have the lunch laid out, on deck, in those little tea-garden-looking concerns by the paddle-boxes —I don't know what you call 'em. Then, we shall hire a steamer expressly for our party, and a band, and have the deck chalked, and we shall be able to dance quadrilles all day; and then, whoever we know that's musical, you know,

why they'll make themselves useful and agreeable ; and—
and—upon the whole, I really hope we shall have a glorious
day, you know ! "

The announcement of these arrangements was received
with the utmost enthusiasm. Mrs. Taunton, Emily, and
Sophia, were loud in their praises.

" Well, but tell me, Percy," said Mrs. Taunton, " who are
the ten gentlemen to be ? "

" Oh ! I know plenty of fellows who'll be delighted with
the scheme," replied Mr. Percy Noakes ; " of course we shall
have—— "

" Mr. Hardy !" interrupted the servant, announcing a
visitor. Miss Sophia and Miss Emily hastily assumed the
most interesting attitudes that could be adopted on so short
a notice.

" How are you ? " said a stout gentleman of about forty,
pausing at the door in the attitude of an awkward harlequin.
This was Mr. Hardy, whom we have before described, on
the authority of Mrs. Stubbs, as " the funny gentleman."
He was an Astley-Cooperish Joe Miller—a practical joker,
immensely popular with married ladies, and a general
favourite with young men. He was always engaged in
some pleasure excursion or other, and delighted in getting
somebody into a scrape on such occasions. He could sing
comic songs, imitate hackney-coachmen and fowls, play airs
on his chin, and execute concertos on the Jews'-harp. He
always eat and drank most immoderately, and was the
bosom friend of Mr. Percy Noakes. He had a red face,
a somewhat husky voice, and a tremendous laugh.

" How *are* you ? " said this worthy, laughing, as if it were
the finest joke in the world to make a morning call, and
shaking hands with the ladies with as much vehemence as
if their arms had been so many pump-handles.

" You're just the very man I wanted," said Mr. Percy
Noakes, who proceeded to explain the cause of his being in
requisition.

" Ha ! ha ! ha !" shouted Hardy, after hearing the statement, and receiving a detailed account of the proposed
excursion. " Oh, capital ! glorious ! What a day it will
be ! what fun !—But, I say, when are you going to begin
making the arrangements ? "

" No time like the present—at once, if you please."

" Oh, charming !" cried the ladies. " Pray, do !"

Writing materials were laid before Mr. Percy Noakes, and the names of the different members of the committee were agreed on, after as much discussion between him and Mr. Hardy as if the fate of nations had depended on their appointment. It was then agreed that a meeting should take place at Mr. Percy Noakes's chambers on the ensuing Wednesday evening at eight o'clock, and the visitors departed.

Wednesday evening arrived ; eight o'clock came, and eight members of the committee were punctual in their attendance. Mr. Loggins, the solicitor, of Boswell Court, sent an excuse. and Mr. Samuel Briggs, the ditto of Furnival's Inn, sent his brother: much to his (the brother's) satisfaction, and greatly to the discomfiture of Mr. Percy Noakes. Between the Briggses and the Tauntons there existed a degree of implacable hatred, quite unprecedented. The animosity between the Montagues and Capulets, was nothing to that which prevailed between these two illustrious houses. Mrs. Briggs was a widow, with three daughters and two sons ; Mr. Samuel, the eldest, was an attorney, and Mr. Alexander, the youngest, was under articles to his brother. They resided in Portland Street, Oxford Street, and moved in the same orbit as the Tauntons—hence their mutual dislike. If the Miss Briggses appeared in smart bonnets, the Miss Tauntons eclipsed them with smarter. If Mrs. Taunton appeared in a cap of all the hues of the rainbow, Mrs. Briggs forthwith mounted a toque, with all the patterns of the kaleidoscope. If Miss Sophia Taunton learnt a new song, two of the Miss Briggses came out with a new duet. The Tauntons had once gained a temporary triumph with the assistance of a harp, but the Briggses brought three guitars into the field, and effectually routed the enemy. There was no end to the rivalry between them.

Now, as Mr. Samuel Briggs was a mere machine, a sort of self-acting legal walking-stick ; and as the party was known to have originated, however remotely, with Mrs. Taunton, the female branches of the Briggs family had arranged that Mr. Alexander should attend, instead of his brother ; and as the said Mr. Alexander was deservedly celebrated for possessing all the pertinacity of a bankruptcy-court attorney, combined with the obstinacy of that useful animal which browses on the thistle, he required but little tuition. He was especially enjoined to make himself as disagreeable as possible; and, above all, to black-ball the Tauntons at every hazard.

The proceedings of the evening were opened by Mr. Percy Noakes. After successfully urging on the gentlemen present the propriety of their mixing some brandy-and-water, he briefly stated the object of the meeting, and concluded by observing that the first step must be the selection of a chairman, necessarily possessing some arbitrary—he trusted not unconstitutional—powers, to whom the personal direction of the whole of the arrangements (subject to the approval of the committee) should be confided. A pale young gentleman, in a green stock and spectacles of the same, a member of the honourable society of the Inner Temple, immediately rose for the purpose of proposing Mr. Percy Noakes. He had known him long, and this he would say, that a more honourable, a more excellent, or a better-hearted fellow, never existed.—(Hear, hear!) The young gentleman, who was a member of a debating society, took this opportunity of entering into an examination of the state of the English law, from the days of William the Conqueror down to the present period; he briefly adverted to the code established by the ancient Druids; slightly glanced at the principles laid down by the Athenian law-givers; and concluded with a most glowing eulogium on pic-nics and constitutional rights.

Mr. Alexander Briggs opposed the motion. He had the highest esteem for Mr. Percy Noakes as an individual, but he did consider that he ought not to be entrusted with these immense powers—(oh, oh!)—He believed that in the proposed capacity Mr. Percy Noakes would not act fairly, impartially, or honourably; but he begged it to be distinctly understood, that he said this without the slightest personal disrespect. Mr. Hardy defended his honourable friend, in a voice rendered partially unintelligible by emotion and brandy-and-water. The proposition was put to the vote, and there appearing to be only one dissentient voice, Mr. Percy Noakes was declared duly elected, and took the chair accordingly.

The business of the meeting now proceeded with rapidity. The chairman delivered in his estimate of the probable expense of the excursion, and every one present subscribed his portion thereof. The question was put that "The Endeavour" be hired for the occasion; Mr. Alexander Briggs moved as an amendment, that the word "Fly" be substituted

for the word "Endeavour;" but after some debate consented
to withdraw his opposition. The important ceremony of
balloting then commenced. A tea-caddy was placed on a
table in a dark corner of the apartment, and every one was
provided with two backgammon men, one black and one
white.

The chairman with great solemnity then read the following
list of the guests whom he proposed to introduce:—Mrs.
Taunton and two daughters, Mr. Wizzle, Mr. Simson. The
names were respectively balloted for, and Mrs. Taunton and
her daughters were declared to be black-balled. Mr. Percy
Noakes and Mr. Hardy exchanged glances.

"Is your list prepared, Mr. Briggs?" inquired the chairman.

"It is," replied Alexander, delivering in the following:—
"Mrs. Briggs and three daughters, Mr. Samuel Briggs." The
previous ceremony was repeated, and Mrs. Briggs and three
daughters were declared to be black-balled. Mr. Alexander
Briggs looked rather foolish, and the remainder of the company appeared somewhat overawed by the mysterious nature
of the proceedings.

The balloting proceeded; but one little circumstance
which Mr. Percy Noakes had not originally foreseen, prevented
the system from working quite as well as he had anticipated.
Everybody was black-balled. Mr. Alexander Briggs, by way
of retaliation, exercised his power of exclusion in every
instance, and the result was, that after three hours had
been consumed in hard balloting, the names of only three
gentlemen were found to have been agreed to. In this
dilemma what was to be done? either the whole plan must
fall to the ground, or a compromise must be effected. The
latter alternative was preferable; and Mr. Percy Noakes
therefore proposed that the form of balloting should be dispensed with, and that every gentleman should merely be
required to state whom he intended to bring. The proposal
was acceded to; the Tauntons and the Briggses were rein-
stated; and the party was formed.

The next Wednesday was fixed for the eventful day, and
it was unanimously resolved that every member of the committee should wear a piece of blue sarsenet ribbon round his
left arm. It appeared from the statement of Mr. Percy
Noakes, that the boat belonged to the General Steam Navigation Company, and was then lying off the Custom-house;

and, as he proposed that the dinner and wines should be provided by an eminent city purveyor, it was arranged that Mr. Percy Noakes should be on board by seven o'clock to superintend the arrangements, and that the remaining members of the committee, together with the company generally, should be expected to join her by nine o'clock. More brandy-and-water was dispatched; several speeches were made by the different law students present; thanks were voted to the chairman; and the meeting separated.

The weather had been beautiful up to this period, and beautiful it continued to be. Sunday passed over, and Mr. Percy Noakes became unusually fidgety—rushing constantly to and from the Steam Packet Wharf, to the astonishment of the clerks, and the great emolument of the Holborn cabmen. Tuesday arrived, and the anxiety of Mr. Percy Noakes knew no bounds. He was every instant running to the window, to look out for clouds; and Mr. Hardy astonished the whole square by practising a new comic song for the occasion, in the chairman's chambers.

Uneasy were the slumbers of Mr. Percy Noakes that night; he tossed and tumbled about, and had confused dreams of steamers starting off, and gigantic clocks with the hands pointing to a quarter-past nine, and the ugly face of Mr. Alexander Briggs looking over the boat's side, and grinning, as if in derision of his fruitless attempts to move. He made a violent effort to get on board, and awoke. The bright sun was shining cheerfully into the bedroom, and Mr. Percy Noakes started up for his watch, in the dreadful expectation of finding his worst dreams realised.

It was just five o'clock. He calculated the time—he should be a good half-hour dressing himself; and as it was a lovely morning, and the tide would be then running down, he would walk leisurely to Strand Lane, and have a boat to the Custom House.

He dressed himself, took a hasty apology for a breakfast, and sallied forth. The streets looked as lonely and deserted as if they had been crowded, overnight, for the last time. Here and there, an early apprentice, with quenched-looking sleepy eyes, was taking down the shutters of a shop; and a policeman or milkwoman might occasionally be seen pacing slowly along; but the servants had not yet begun to clean the doors, or light the kitchen fires, and London looked the picture of desolation. At the corner of a by-street, near

Temple Bar, was stationed a "street-breakfast." The coffee was boiling over a charcoal fire, and large slices of bread and butter were piled one upon the other, like deals in a timber-yard. The company were seated on a form, which, with a view both to security and comfort, was placed against a neighbouring wall. Two young men, whose uproarious mirth and disordered dress bespoke the conviviality of the preceding evening, were treating three "ladies" and an Irish labourer. A little sweep was standing at a short distance, casting a longing eye at the tempting delicacies; and a policeman was watching the group from the opposite side of the street. The wan looks and gaudy finery of the thinly-clad women contrasted as strangely with the gay sunlight, as did their forced merriment with the boisterous hilarity of the two young men, who, now and then, varied their amusements by "bonneting" the proprietor of this itinerant coffee-house.

Mr. Percy Noakes walked briskly by, and when he turned down Strand Lane, and caught a glimpse of the glistening water, he thought he had never felt so important or so happy in his life.

"Boat, sir?" cried one of the three watermen who were mopping out their boats, and all whistling. "Boat, sir?"

"No," replied Mr. Percy Noakes, rather sharply; for the inquiry was not made in a manner at all suitable to his dignity.

"Would you prefer a wessel, sir?" inquired another, to the infinite delight of the "Jack-in-the-water."

Mr. Percy Noakes replied with a look of supreme contempt.

"Did you want to be put on board a steamer, sir?" inquired an old fireman-waterman, very confidentially. He was dressed in a faded red suit, just the colour of the cover of a very old Court-guide.

"Yes, make haste—the Endeavour—off the Custom House."

"Endeavour!" cried the man who had convulsed the "Jack" before. "Vy, I see the Endeavour go up half an hour ago."

"So did I," said another; "and I should think she'd gone down by this time, for she's a precious sight too full of ladies and gen'lemen."

Mr. Percy Noakes affected to disregard these representations, and stepped into the boat, which the old man, by dint of scrambling, and shoving, and grating, had brought up to the causeway. "Shove her off!" cried Mr. Percy Noakes, and away the boat glided down the river; Mr. Percy Noakes seated on the recently mopped seat, and the watermen at the stairs offering to bet him any reasonable sum that he'd never reach the "Custum 'us."

"Here she is, by Jove!" said the delighted Percy, as they ran alongside the Endeavour.

"Hold hard!" cried the steward over the side, and Mr. Percy Noakes jumped on board.

"Hope you will find everything as you wished, sir. She looks uncommon well this morning."

"She does, indeed," replied the manager, in a state of ecstasy which it is impossible to describe. The deck was scrubbed, and the seats were scrubbed, and there was a bench for the band, and a place for dancing, and a pile of camp-stools, and an awning; and then Mr. Percy Noakes bustled down below, and there were the pastrycook's men, and the steward's wife, laying out the dinner on two tables the whole length of the cabin; and then Mr. Percy Noakes took off his coat and rushed backwards and forwards, doing nothing, but quite convinced he was assisting everybody; and the steward's wife laughed till she cried, and Mr. Percy Noakes panted with the violence of his exertions. And then the bell at London Bridge wharf rang; and a Margate boat was just starting; and a Gravesend boat was just starting; and people shouted, and porters ran down the steps with luggage that would crush any men but porters; and sloping boards, with bits of wood nailed on them, were placed between the outside boat and the inside boat; and the passengers ran along them, and looked like so many fowls coming out of an area; and then the bell ceased, and the boards were taken away, and the boats started, and the whole scene was one of the most delightful bustle and confusion.

The time wore on; half-past eight o'clock arrived; the pastrycook's men went ashore; the dinner was completely laid out; and Mr. Percy Noakes locked the principal cabin, and put the key in his pocket, in order that it might be suddenly disclosed, in all its magnificence, to the eyes of the astonished company. The band came on board, and so did the wine.

Ten minutes to nine and the committee embarked in a

body. There was Mr. Hardy, in a blue jacket and waistcoat, white trousers, silk stockings, and pumps—in full aquatic costume, with a straw hat on his head, and an immense telescope under his arm ; and there was the young gentleman with the green spectacles, in nankeen inexplicables, with a ditto waistcoat and bright buttons, like the pictures of Paul —not the saint, but he of Virginia notoriety. The remainder of the committee, dressed in white hats, light jackets, waist-coats, and trousers, looked something between waiters and West India planters.

Nine o'clock struck, and the company arrived in shoals. Mr. Samuel Briggs, Mrs. Briggs, and the Misses Briggs, made their appearance in a smart private wherry. The three guitars, in their respective dark green cases, were carefully stowed away in the bottom of the boat, accompanied by two immense portfolios of music, which it would take at least a week's incessant playing to get through. The Tauntons arrived at the same moment with more music, and a lion— a gentleman with a bass voice and an incipient red moustache. The colours of the Taunton party were pink ; those of the Briggses a light blue. The Tauntons had artificial flowers in their bonnets ; here the Briggses gained a decided advan-tage—they wore feathers.

"How d'ye do, dear?" said the Misses Briggs to the Misses Taunton. (The word "dear" among girls is frequently synonymous with "wretch.")

" Quite well, thank you, dear," replied the Misses Taunton to the Misses Briggs ; and then there was such a kissing, and congratulating, and shaking of hands, as might have induced one to suppose that the two families were the best friends in the world, instead of each wishing the other over-board, as they most sincerely did.

Mr. Percy Noakes received the visitors, and bowed to the strange gentleman, as if he should like to know who he was. This was just what Mrs. Taunton wanted. Here was an opportunity to astonish the Briggses.

"Oh! I beg your pardon," said the general of the Taunton party, with a careless air.—"Captain Helves—Mr. Percy Noakes—Mrs. Briggs—Captain Helves."

Mr. Percy Noakes bowed very low ; the gallant captain did the same with all due ferocity, and the Briggses were clearly overcome.

"Our friend, Mr. Wizzle, being unfortunately prevented

Steam Excursion (II)
(*p. 401*)

from coming," resumed Mrs. Taunton, "I did myself the pleasure of bringing the captain, whose musical talents I knew would be a great acquisition."

"In the name of the committee I have to thank you for doing so, and to offer you welcome, sir," replied Percy. (Here the scraping was renewed.) "But pray be seated— won't you walk aft? Captain, will you conduct Miss Taunton?—Miss Briggs, will you allow me?"

"Where could they have picked up that military man?" inquired Mrs. Briggs of Miss Kate Briggs, as they followed the little party.

"I can't imagine," replied Miss Kate, bursting with vexation; for the very fierce air with which the gallant captain regarded the company, had impressed her with a high sense of his importance.

Boat after boat came alongside, and guest after guest arrived. The invites had been excellently arranged: Mr. Percy Noakes having considered it as important that the number of young men should exactly tally with that of the young ladies, as that the quantity of knives on board should be in precise proportion to the forks.

"Now, is every one on board?" inquired Mr. Percy Noakes. The committee (who, with their bits of blue ribbon, looked as if they were all going to be bled) bustled about to ascertain the fact, and reported that they might safely start.

"Go on!" cried the master of the boat from the top of one of the paddle-boxes.

"Go on!" echoed the boy, who was stationed over the hatchway to pass the directions down to the engineer; and away went the vessel with that agreeable noise which is peculiar to steamers, and which is composed of a mixture of creaking, gushing, clanging, and snorting.

"Hoi—oi—oi—oi—oi—oi—o—i—i—i!" shouted half-a-dozen voices from a boat, a quarter of a mile astern.

"Ease her!" cried the captain: "do these people belong to us, sir?"

"Noakes," exclaimed Hardy, who had been looking at every object, far and near, through the large telescope, "it's the Fleetwoods and the Wakefields—and two children with them, by Jove!"

"What a shame to bring children!" said everybody; "how very inconsiderate!"

"I say, it would be a good joke to pretend not to see 'em, wouldn't it?" suggested Hardy, to the immense delight of the company generally. A council of war was hastily held, and it was resolved that the new-comers should be taken on board, on Mr. Hardy solemnly pledging himself to tease the children during the whole of the day.

"Stop her!" cried the captain.

"Stop her!" repeated the boy; whizz went the steam, and all the young ladies, as in duty bound, screamed in concert. They were only appeased by the assurance of the martial Helves, that the escape of steam consequent on stopping a vessel was seldom attended with any great loss of human life.

Two men ran to the side; and after some shouting, and swearing, and angling for the wherry with a boat-hook, Mr. Fleetwood, and Mrs. Fleetwood, and Master Fleetwood, and Mr. Wakefield, and Mrs. Wakefield, and Miss Wakefield, were safely deposited on the deck. The girl was about six years old, the boy about four; the former was dressed in a white frock with a pink sash and dog's-eared-looking little spencer: a straw bonnet and green veil, six inches by three and a half; the latter was attired for the occasion in a nankeen frock, between the bottom of which, and the top of his plaid socks, a considerable portion of two small mottled legs was discernible. He had a light blue cap with a gold band and tassel on his head, and a damp piece of gingerbread in his hand, with which he had slightly embossed his countenance.

The boat once more started off; the band played "Off she goes;" the major part of the company conversed cheerfully in groups; and the old gentlemen walked up and down the deck in pairs, as perseveringly and gravely as if they were doing a match against time for an immense stake. They ran briskly down the Pool; the gentlemen pointed out the Docks, the Thames Police Office, and other elegant public edifices; and the young ladies exhibited a proper display of horror at the appearance of the coal-whippers and ballast-heavers. Mr. Hardy told stories to the married ladies, at which they laughed very much in their pocket-handkerchiefs, and hit him on the knuckles with their fans, declaring him to be "a naughty man—a shocking creature"—and so forth; and Captain Helves gave slight descriptions of battles and duels, with a most bloodthirsty air, which made him the admiration of the women, and the envy of the men. Quadrilling commenced; Captain Helves danced one set with Miss Emily Taunton, and another set with Miss Sophia Taunton. Mrs. Taunton was in ecstasies. The victory appeared to be complete; but alas! the inconstancy of man! Having performed this necessary duty, he attached himself solely to Miss Julia Briggs, with whom he danced no less than three sets consecutively, and from whose side he evinced no intention of stirring for the remainder of the day.

Mr. Hardy, having played one or two very brilliant fantasias on the Jews'-harp, and having frequently repeated the exquisitely amusing joke of slily chalking a large cross on the back of some member of the committee, Mr. Percy Noakes expressed his hope that some of their musical friends would oblige the company by a display of their abilities.

"Perhaps," he said in a very insinuating manner, "Captain Helves will oblige us?" Mrs. Taunton's countenance lighted up, for the captain only sang duets, and couldn't sing them with anybody but one of her daughters.

"Really," said that warlike individual, "I should be very happy, but——"

"Oh! pray do," cried all the young ladies.

"Miss Emily, have you any objection to join in a duet?"

"Oh! not the slightest," returned the young lady, in a tone which clearly showed she had the greatest possible objection.

"Shall I accompany you, dear?" inquired one of the Miss Briggses, with the bland intention of spoiling the effect.

"Very much obliged to you, Miss Briggs," sharply retorted Mrs. Taunton, who saw through the manœuvre; "my daughters always sing without accompaniments."

"And without voices," tittered Mrs. Briggs, in a low tone.

"Perhaps," said Mrs. Taunton, reddening, for she guessed the tenor of the observation, though she had not heard it clearly—"Perhaps it would be as well for some people, if their voices were not quite so audible as they are to other people."

"And, perhaps, if gentlemen who are kidnapped to pay attention to some persons' daughters, had not sufficient discernment to pay attention to other persons' daughters," returned Mrs. Briggs, "some persons would not be so ready to display that ill-temper which, thank God, distinguishes them from other persons."

"Persons!" ejaculated Mrs. Taunton.

"Persons," replied Mrs. Briggs.

"Insolence!"

"Creature!"

"Hush! hush!" interrupted Mr. Percy Noakes, who was one of the very few by whom this dialogue had been overheard. "Hush!—pray, silence for the duet."

After a great deal of preparatory crowing and humming, the captain began the following duet from the opera of "Paul and Virginia," in that grunting tone in which a man gets down, Heaven knows where, without the remotest chance of ever getting up again. This, in private circles, is frequently designated "a bass voice."

> "See (sung the captain) from o—ce—an ri—sing
> Bright flames the or—b of d—ay.
> From yon gro—ove, the varied so—ongs—"

Here, the singer was interrupted by varied cries of the most dreadful description, proceeding from some grove in the immediate vicinity of the starboard paddle-box.

"My child!" screamed Mrs. Fleetwood. "My child! it is his voice—I know it."

Mr. Fleetwood, accompanied by several gentlemen, here rushed to the quarter from whence the noise proceeded, and an exclamation of horror burst from the company; the general impression being, that the little innocent had either got his head in the water, or his legs in the machinery.

"What is the matter?" shouted the agonised father, as he returned with the child in his arms.

"Oh! oh! oh!" screamed the small sufferer again.

"What is the matter, dear?" inquired the father once more—hastily stripping off the nankeen frock, for the purpose of ascertaining whether the child had one bone which was not smashed to pieces.

"Oh! oh!—I'm so frightened!"

"What at, dear?—what at?" said the mother, soothing the sweet infant.

"Oh! he's been making such dreadful faces at me," cried the boy, relapsing into convulsions at the bare recollection.

"He!—who?" cried everybody, crowding round him.

"Oh!—him!" replied the child, pointing at Hardy, who affected to be the most concerned of the whole group.

The real state of the case at once flashed upon the minds

of all present, with the exception of the Fleetwoods and the Wakefields. The facetious Hardy, in fulfilment of his promise, had watched the child to a remote part of the vessel, and, suddenly appearing before him with the most awful contortions of visage, had produced his paroxysm of terror.   Of course, he now observed that it was hardly necessary for him to deny the accusation ; and the unfortunate little victim was accordingly led below, after receiving sundry thumps on the head from both his parents, for having the wickedness to tell a story.

This little interruption having been adjusted, the captain resumed, and Miss Emily chimed in, in due course.   The duet was loudly applauded, and, certainly, the perfect independence of the parties deserved great commendation.   Miss Emily sang her part, without the slightest reference to the captain ; and the captain sang so loud, that he had not the slightest idea what was being done by his partner.   After having gone through the last few eighteen or nineteen bars by himself, therefore, he acknowledged the plaudits of the circle with that air of self-denial which men usually assume when they think they have done something to astonish the company.

"Now," said Mr. Percy Noakes, who had just ascended from the fore-cabin, where he had been busily engaged in decanting the wine, "if the Misses Briggs will oblige us with something before dinner, I am sure we shall be very much delighted."

One of those hums of admiration followed the suggestion, which one frequently hears in society, when nobody has the most distant notion what he is expressing his approval of. The three Misses Briggs looked modestly at their mamma, and the mamma looked approvingly at her daughters, and Mrs. Taunton looked scornfully at all of them.   The Misses Briggs asked for their guitars, and several gentlemen seriously damaged the cases in their anxiety to present them.   Then there was a very interesting production of three little keys for the aforesaid cases, and a melodramatic expression of horror at finding a string broken ; and a vast deal of screwing and tightening, and winding and turning, during which Mrs. Briggs expatiated to those near her on the immense difficulty of playing a guitar, and hinted at the wondrous proficiency of her daughters in that mystic art.   Mrs. Taunton whispered to a neighbour that it was "quite sickening !" and the Misses Taunton looked as if they knew how to play, but disdained to do it.

At length, the Misses Briggs began in real earnest. It was a new Spanish composition, for three voices and three guitars. The effect was electrical. All eyes were turned upon the captain, who was reported to have once passed through Spain with his regiment, and who must be well acquainted with the national music. He was in raptures. This was sufficient; the trio was encored; the applause was universal; and never had the Tauntons suffered such a complete defeat.

"Bravo! bravo!" ejaculated the captain;—"bravo!"

"Pretty? isn't it, sir?" inquired Mr. Samuel Briggs, with the air of a self-satisfied showman. By-the-bye, these were the first words he had been heard to utter since he left Boswell Court the evening before.

"De—lightful!" returned the captain, with a flourish and a military cough;—"de—lightful!"

"Sweet instrument!" said an old gentleman with a bald head, who had been trying all the morning to look through a telescope, inside the glass of which Mr. Hardy had fixed a large black wafer.

"Did you ever hear a Portuguese tambourine?" inquired that jocular individual.

"Did *you* ever hear a tom-tom, sir?" sternly inquired the captain, who lost no opportunity of showing off his travels, real or pretended.

"A what?" asked Hardy, rather taken aback.

"A tom-tom."

"Never!"

"Nor a gum-gum?"

"Never!"

"What *is* a gum-gum?" eagerly inquired several young ladies.

"When I was in the East Indies," replied the captain—(here was a discovery—he had been in the East Indies!)—"when I was in the East Indies, I was once stopping a few thousand miles up the country, on a visit at the house of a very particular friend of mine, Ram Chowdar Doss Azuph Al Bowlar—a devilish pleasant fellow. As we were enjoying our hookahs, one evening, in the cool verandah in front of his villa, we were rather surprised by the sudden appearance of thirty-four of his Kit-ma-gars (for he had rather a large establishment there), accompanied by an equal number of Con-su-mars, approaching the house with a threatening aspect, and beating a tom-tom. The Ram started up——"

"Who?" inquired the bald gentleman, intensely inte-rested.

"The Ram—Ram Chowdar——"

"Oh!" said the old gentleman, "I beg your pardon; pray go on."

"—Started up and drew a pistol. 'Helves,' said he, 'my boy,'—he always called me, my boy—'Helves,' said he, 'do you hear that tom-tom?' 'I do,' said I. His countenance, which before was pale, assumed a most frightful appearance; his whole visage was distorted, and his frame shaken by violent emotions. 'Do you see that gum-gum?' said he. 'No,' said I, staring about me. 'You don't?' said he. 'No, I'll be damned if I do,' said I; 'and what's more, I don't know what a gum-gum is,' said I. I really thought the Ram would have dropped. He drew me aside, and with an expression of agony I shall never forget, said in a low whisper——"

"Dinner's on the table, ladies," interrupted the steward's wife.

"Will you allow me?" said the captain, immediately suiting the action to the word, and escorting Miss Julia Briggs to the cabin, with as much ease as if he had finished the story.

"What an extraordinary circumstance!" ejaculated the same old gentleman, preserving his listening attitude.

"What a traveller!" said the young ladies.

"What a singular name!" exclaimed the gentlemen, rather confused by the coolness of the whole affair.

"I wish he had finished the story," said an old lady. "I wonder what a gum-gum really is?"

"By Jove!" exclaimed Hardy, who until now had been lost in utter amazement, "I don't know what it may be in India, but in England I think a gum-gum has very much the same meaning as a hum-bug."

"How illiberal! how envious!" cried everybody, as they made for the cabin, fully impressed with a belief in the captain's amazing adventures. Helves was the sole lion for the remainder of the day—impudence and the marvellous are pretty sure passports to any society.

The party had by this time reached their destination, and

put about on their return home. The wind, which had
been with them the whole day, was now directly in their
teeth ; the weather had become gradually more and more
overcast ; and the sky, water, and shore, were all of that
dull, heavy, uniform lead-colour, which house-painters daub
in the first instance over a street-door which is gradually
approaching a state of convalescence. It had been "spitting"
with rain for the last half-hour, and now began to pour in
good earnest. The wind was freshening very fast, and the
waterman at the wheel had unequivocally expressed his
opinion that there would shortly be a squall. A slight
emotion on the part of the vessel, now and then, seemed to
suggest the possibility of its pitching to a very uncomfortable extent in the event of its blowing harder ; and every
timber began to creak, as if the boat were an overladen
clothes-basket. Sea-sickness, however, is like a belief in
ghosts—every one entertains some misgivings on the subject, but few will acknowledge any. The majority of the
company, therefore, endeavoured to look peculiarly happy,
feeling all the while especially miserable.

"Don't it rain?" inquired the old gentleman before
noticed, when, by dint of squeezing and jamming, they
were all seated at table.

"I think it does—a little," replied Mr. Percy Noakes, who
could hardly hear himself speak, in consequence of the
pattering on the deck.

"Don't it blow?" inquired some one else.

"No, I don't think it does," responded Hardy, sincerely
wishing that he could persuade himself that it did not ;
for he sat near the door, and was almost blown off his seat.

"It'll soon clear up," said Mr. Percy Noakes, in a cheerful
tone.

"Oh, certainly!" ejaculated the committee generally.

"No doubt of it!" said the remainder of the company,
whose attention was now pretty well engrossed by the serious
business of eating, carving, taking wine, and so forth.

The throbbing motion of the engine was but too perceptible. There was a large, substantial, cold boiled leg of
mutton, at the bottom of the table, shaking like blanc-
mange ; a previously hearty sirloin of beef looked as if it
had been suddenly seized with the palsy ; and some tongues,
which were placed on dishes rather too large for them, went
through the most surprising evolutions ; darting from side

to side, and from end to end, like a fly in an inverted wine-glass. Then, the sweets shook and trembled, till it was quite impossible to help them, and people gave up the attempt in despair; and the pigeon-pies looked as if the birds, whose legs were stuck outside, were trying to get them in. The table vibrated and started like a feverish pulse, and the very legs were convulsed—everything was shaking and jarring. The beams in the roof of the cabin seemed as if they were put there for the sole purpose of giving people headaches, and several elderly gentlemen became ill-tempered in consequence. As fast as the steward put the fire-irons up, they *would* fall down again; and the more the ladies and gentlemen tried to sit comfortably on their seats, the more the seats seemed to slide away from the ladies and gentlemen. Several ominous demands were made for small glasses of brandy; the countenances of the company gradually underwent most extraordinary changes; one gentleman was observed suddenly to rush from table without the slightest ostensible reason, and dart up the steps with incredible swiftness: thereby greatly damaging both himself and the steward, who happened to be coming down at the same moment.

The cloth was removed; the dessert was laid on the table; and the glasses were filled. The motion of the boat increased; several members of the party began to feel rather vague and misty, and looked as if they had only just got up. The young gentleman with the spectacles, who had been in a fluctuating state for some time—at one moment bright, and at another dismal, like a revolving light on the sea-coast—rashly announced his wish to propose a toast. After several ineffectual attempts to preserve his perpendicular, the young gentleman, having managed to hook himself to the centre leg of the table with his left hand, proceeded as follows:

"Ladies and gentlemen. A gentleman is among us—I may say a stranger—(here some painful thought seemed to strike the orator; he paused, and looked extremely odd)—whose talents, whose travels, whose cheerfulness—— "

"I beg your pardon, Edkins," hastily interrupted Mr. Percy Noakes,—" Hardy, what's the matter?"

"Nothing," replied the "funny gentleman," who had just life enough left to utter two consecutive syllables.

"Will you have some brandy?"

" No ! " replied Hardy in a tone of great indignation, and looking as comfortable as Temple Bar in a Scotch mist; " what should I want brandy for ? "

" Will you go on deck ? "

" No, I will *not*." This was said with a most determined air, and in a voice which might have been taken for an imitation of anything; it was quite as much like a guinea-pig as a bassoon.

"I beg your pardon, Edkins," said the courteous Percy ; " I thought our friend was ill. Pray go on."

A pause.

" Pray go on."

" Mr. Edkins *is* gone," cried somebody.

"I beg your pardon, sir," said the steward, running up to Mr. Percy Noakes, " I beg your pardon, sir, but the gentle-man as just went on deck—him with the green spectacles—is uncommon bad, to be sure ; and the young man as played the wiolin says, that unless he has some brandy he can't answer for the consequences. He says he has a wife and two children, whose werry subsistence depends on his break-ing a wessel, and he expects to do so every moment. The flageolet's been werry ill, but he's better, only he's in a dreadful prusperation."

All disguise was now useless ; the company staggered on deck ; the gentlemen tried to see nothing but the clouds ; and the ladies, muffled up in such shawls and cloaks as they had brought with them, lay about on the seats, and under the seats, in the most wretched condition. Never was such a blowing, and raining, and pitching, and tossing, endured by any pleasure party before. Several remonstrances were sent down below, on the subject of Master Fleetwood, but they were totally unheeded in consequence of the indisposition of his natural protectors. That interesting child screamed at the top of his voice, until he had no voice left to scream with ; and then Miss Wakefield began, and screamed for the remainder of the passage.

Mr. Hardy was observed, some hours afterwards, in an attitude which induced his friends to suppose that he was busily engaged in contemplating the beauties of the deep ; they only regretted that his taste for the picturesque should lead him to remain so long in a position, very injurious at all times, but especially so to an individual labouring under a tendency of blood to the head.

The party arrived off the Custom House at about two o'clock on the Thursday morning, dispirited and worn out. The Tauntons were too ill to quarrel with the Briggses, and the Briggses were too wretched to annoy the Tauntons. One of the guitar-cases was lost on its passage to a hackney-coach, and Mrs. Briggs has not scrupled to state that the Tauntons bribed a porter to throw it down an area.   Mr. Alexander Briggs opposes vote by ballot—he says from personal experience of its inefficacy; and Mr. Samuel Briggs, whenever he is asked to express his sentiments on the point, says he has no opinion on that or any other subject.

Mr. Edkins—the young gentleman in the green spectacles —makes a speech on every occasion on which a speech can possibly be made : the eloquence of which can only be equalled by its length.   In the event of his not being previously appointed to a judgeship, it is probable that he will practice as a barrister in the New Central Criminal Court.

Captain Helves continued his attention to Miss Julia Briggs, whom he might possibly have espoused, if it had not unfortunately happened that Mr. Samuel arrested him, in the way of business, pursuant to instructions received from Messrs. Scroggins and Payne, whose town-debts the gallant captain had condescended to collect, but whose accounts, with the indiscretion sometimes peculiar to military minds, he had omitted to keep with that dull accuracy which custom has rendered necessary.   Mrs. Taunton complains that she has been much deceived in him.   He introduced himself to the family on board a Gravesend steam-packet, and certainly, therefore, ought to have proved respectable.

Mr. Percy Noakes is as light-hearted and careless as ever.

CHAPTER VIII

THE GREAT WINGLEBURY DUEL

THE little town of Great Winglebury is exactly forty-two miles and three-quarters from Hyde Park corner. It has a long, straggling, quiet High Street, with a great black and white clock at a small red Town Hall, half-way up—a market-place—a cage—an assembly-room—a church—a bridge—a chapel—a theatre—a library—an inn—a pump—and a Post Office. Tradition tells of a "Little Winglebury," down some cross-road about two miles off; and, as a square mass of dirty paper, supposed to have been originally intended for a letter, with certain tremulous characters inscribed thereon, in which a lively imagination might trace a remote resemblance to the word "Little," was once stuck up to be owned in the sunny window of the Great Winglebury Post Office, from which it only disappeared when it fell to pieces with dust and extreme old age, there would appear to be some foundation for the legend. Common belief is inclined to bestow the name upon a little hole at the end of a muddy lane about a couple of miles long, colonised by one wheel-wright, four paupers, and a beer-shop; but even this authority, slight as it is, must be regarded with extreme suspicion, inasmuch as the inhabitants of the hole aforesaid concur in opining that it never had any name at all, from the earliest ages down to the present day.

The Winglebury Arms, in the centre of the High Street, opposite the small building with the big clock, is the principal inn of Great Winglebury;—the commercial-inn, posting-house, and excise-office; the "Blue" house at every election, and the Judges' house at every assizes. It is the head-quarters of the Gentlemen's Whist Club of Winglebury Blues (so called in opposition to the Gentlemen's Whist Club of Winglebury Buffs, held at the other house, a little further down): and whenever a juggler, or wax-work man, or concert-giver, takes Great Winglebury in his circuit, it is immediately placarded all over the town that Mr. So-and-so, "trusting

to that liberal support which the inhabitants of Great
Winglebury have long been so liberal in bestowing, has at a
great expense engaged the elegant and commodious assembly-
rooms, attached to the Winglebury Arms." The house is a
large one, with a red brick and stone front; a pretty spacious
hall, ornamented with evergreen plants, terminates in a
perspective view of the bar, and a glass case, in which are
displayed a choice variety of delicacies ready for dressing, to
catch the eye of a new-comer the moment he enters, and
excite his appetite to the highest possible pitch. Opposite
doors lead to the "coffee" and "commercial" rooms; and a
great wide, rambling staircase,—three stairs and a landing
—four stairs and another landing—one step and another
landing—half-a-dozen stairs and another landing—and so on
—conducts to galleries of bedrooms, and labyrinths of sitting-
rooms, denominated "private," where you may enjoy yourself,
as privately as you can in any place where some bewildered
being walks into your room every five minutes, by mistake,
and then walks out again, to open all the doors along the
gallery until he finds his own.

Such is the Winglebury Arms, at this day, and such was
the Winglebury Arms some time since—no matter when—
two or three minutes before the arrival of the London stage.
Four horses with cloths on—change for a coach—were standing quietly at the corner of the yard, surrounded by a listless
group of post-boys in shiny hats and smock-frocks, engaged
in discussing the merits of the cattle; half a dozen ragged
boys were standing a little apart, listening with evident
interest to the conversation of these worthies; and a few
loungers were collected round the horse-trough, awaiting the
arrival of the coach.

The day was hot and sunny, the town in the zenith of its
dulness, and with the exception of these few idlers, not a
living creature was to be seen. Suddenly, the loud notes of
a key-bugle broke the monotonous stillness of the street;
in came the coach, rattling over the uneven paving with a
noise startling enough to stop even the large-faced clock
itself. Down got the outsides, up went the windows in all
directions, out came the waiters, up started the ostlers, and
the loungers, and the post-boys, and the ragged boys, as
if they were electrified—unstrapping, and unchaining, and
unbuckling, and dragging willing horses out, and forcing
reluctant horses in, and making a most exhilarating bustle.

"Lady inside, here!" said the guard. "Please to alight, ma'am," said the waiter. "Private sitting-room?" interrogated the lady. "Certainly, ma'am," responded the chambermaid. "Nothing but these 'ere trunks, ma'am?" inquired the guard. "Nothing more," replied the lady. Up got the outsides again, and the guard, and the coachman; off came the cloths, with a jerk; "All right," was the cry; and away they went. The loungers lingered a minute or two in the road, watching the coach until it turned the corner, and then loitered away one by one. The street was clear again, and the town, by contrast, quieter than ever.

"Lady in number twenty-five," screamed the landlady.— "Thomas!"

"Yes, ma'am."

"Letter just been left for the gentleman in number nineteen. Boots at the Lion left it. No answer."

"Letter for you, sir," said Thomas, depositing the letter on number nineteen's table.

"For me?" said number nineteen, turning from the window, out of which he had been surveying the scene just described.

"Yes, sir,"—(waiters always speak in hints, and never utter complete sentences,)—"yes, sir,—Boots at the Lion, sir,—Bar, sir,—Missis said number nineteen, sir—Alexander Trott, Esq., sir?—Your card at the bar, sir, I think, sir?"

"My name *is* Trott," replied number nineteen, breaking the seal. "You may go, waiter." The waiter pulled down the window-blind, and then pulled it up again—for a regular waiter must do something before he leaves the room—adjusted the glasses on the sideboard, brushed a place that was *not* dusty, rubbed his hands very hard, walked stealthily to the door, and evaporated.

There was, evidently, something in the contents of the letter, of a nature, if not wholly unexpected, certainly extremely disagreeable. Mr. Alexander Trott laid it down, and took it up again, and walked about the room on particular squares of the carpet, and even attempted, though unsuccessfully, to whistle an air. It wouldn't do. He threw himself into a chair, and read the following epistle aloud:—

> "*Blue Lion and Stomach-warmer,*
> *Great Winglebury.*
> *Wednesday Morning.*

"Sir. Immediately on discovering your intentions, I left our counting-house, and followed you. I know the purport of your journey;—that journey shall never be completed.

"I have no friend here, just now, on whose secrecy I can rely. This shall be no obstacle to my revenge. Neither shall Emily Brown be exposed to the mercenary solicitations of a scoundrel, odious in her eyes, and contemptible in everybody else's: nor will I tamely submit to the clandestine attacks of a base umbrella-maker.

"Sir. From Great Winglebury church, a footpath leads through four meadows to a retired spot known to the townspeople as Stiffun's Acre." [Mr. Trott shuddered.] "I shall be waiting there alone, at twenty minutes before six o'clock to-morrow morning. Should I be disappointed in seeing you there, I will do myself the pleasure of calling with a horsewhip.

"Horace Hunter.

"PS. There is a gunsmith's in the High Street; and they won't sell gunpowder after dark—you understand me.

"PPS. You had better not order your breakfast in the morning until you have met me. It may be an unnecessary expense."

"Desperate-minded villain! I knew how it would be!" ejaculated the terrified Trott. "I always told father, that once start me on this expedition, and Hunter would pursue me like the Wandering Jew. It's bad enough as it is, to marry with the old people's commands, and without the girl's consent; but what will Emily think of me, if I go down there breathless with running away from this infernal salamander? What *shall* I do? What *can* I do? If I go back to the city, I'm disgraced for ever—lose the girl—and, what's more, lose the money too. Even if I did go on to the Browns' by the coach, Hunter would be after me in a post-chaise; and if I go to this place, this Stiffun's Acre (another shudder), I'm as good as dead. I've seen him hit the man at the Pall-mall shooting-gallery, in the second button-hole of the waistcoat, five times out of every six, and when he didn't hit him there, he hit him in the head." With this consolatory reminiscence Mr. Alexander Trott again ejaculated, "What shall I do?"

Long and weary were his reflections, as, burying his face in his hand, he sat, ruminating on the best course to be pursued. His mental direction-post pointed to London. He thought of the "governor's" anger, and the loss of the fortune which the paternal Brown had promised the paternal Trott his daughter should contribute to the coffers of his son. Then the words "To Brown's" were legibly inscribed on the said direction-post, but Horace Hunter's denunciation rung in his ears;—last of all it bore, in red letters, the words, "To Stiffun's Acre;" and then Mr. Alexander Trott decided on adopting a plan which he presently matured.

First and foremost, he dispatched the under-boots to the Blue Lion and Stomach-warmer, with a gentlemanly note to Mr. Horace Hunter, intimating that he thirsted for his destruction and would do himself the pleasure of slaughtering him next morning, without fail. He then wrote another letter, and requested the attendance of the other boots—for they kept a pair. A modest knock at the room-door was heard. "Come in," said Mr. Trott. A man thrust in a red head with one eye in it, and being again desired to "come in," brought in the body and the legs to which the head belonged, and a fur cap which belonged to the head.

"You are the upper-boots, I think?" inquired Mr. Trott.

"Yes, I am the upper-boots," replied a voice from inside a velveteen case, with mother-of-pearl buttons—"that is, I'm the boots as b'longs to the house; the other man's my man, as goes errands and does odd jobs. Top-boots and half-boots, I calls us."

"You're from London?" inquired Mr. Trott.

"Driv a cab once," was the laconic reply.

"Why don't you drive it now?" asked Mr. Trott.

"Over-driv the cab, and driv over a 'ooman," replied the top-boots, with brevity.

"Do you know the mayor's house?" inquired Mr. Trott.

"Rather," replied the boots, significantly, as if he had some good reason to remember it.

"Do you think you could manage to leave a letter there?" interrogated Trott.

"Shouldn't wonder," responded boots.

"But this letter," said Trott, holding a deformed note with a paralytic direction in one hand, and five shillings in the other—"this letter is anonymous."

"A—what?" interrupted the boots.

"Anonymous—he's not to know who it comes from."

"Oh! I see," responded the reg'lar, with a knowing wink,

Under Restraint
(*p. 416*)

but without evincing the slightest disinclination to undertake the charge—"I see—bit o' Sving, eh?" and his one eye wandered round the room, as if in quest of a dark lantern and phosphorus-box. "But, I say!" he continued, recalling the eye from its search, and bringing it to bear on Mr. Trott. "I say, he's a lawyer, our mayor, and insured in the County. If you've a spite agen him, you'd better not burn his house down—blessed if I don't think it would be the greatest favour you could do him." And he chuckled inwardly.

If Mr. Alexander Trott had been in any other situation, his first act would have been to kick the man down-stairs by deputy; or, in other words, to ring the bell, and desire the landlord to take his boots off. He contented himself, however, with doubling the fee and explaining that the letter merely related to a breach of the peace. The top-boots retired, solemnly pledged to secrecy; and Mr. Alexander Trott sat down to a fried sole, maintenon outlet. Madeira, and sundries, with greater composure than he had experienced since the receipt of Horace Hunter's letter of defiance.

The lady who alighted from the London coach had no sooner been installed in number twenty-five, and made some alteration in her travelling-dress, than she indited a note to Joseph Overton, esquire, solicitor, and mayor of Great Winglebury, requesting his immediate attendance on private business of paramount importance—a summons which that worthy functionary lost no time in obeying; for after sundry openings of his eyes, divers ejaculations of "Bless me!" and other manifestations of surprise, he took his broad-brimmed hat from its accustomed peg in his little front office, and walked briskly down the High Street to the Winglebury Arms; through the hall and up the staircase of which establishment he was ushered by the landlady, and a crowd of officious waiters, to the door of number twenty-five.

"Show the gentleman in," said the stranger lady, in reply to the foremost waiter's announcement. The gentleman was shown in accordingly.

The lady rose from the sofa; the mayor advanced a step from the door; and there they both paused, for a minute or two, looking at one another as if by mutual consent. The mayor saw before him a buxom richly-dressed female of about forty; the lady looked upon a sleek man, about ten years older, in drab shorts and continuations, black coat, neckcloth, and gloves.

"Miss Julia Manners!" exclaimed the mayor at length, "you astonish me."

"That's very unfair of you, Overton," replied Miss Julia, "for I have known you long enough not to be surprised at anything you do, and you might extend equal courtesy to me."

"But to run away—actually run away—with a young man!" remonstrated the mayor.

"You wouldn't have me actually run away with an old one, I presume?" was the cool rejoinder.

"And then to ask me—me—of all people in the world —a man of my age and appearance—mayor of the town— to promote such a scheme!" pettishly ejaculated Joseph Overton; throwing himself into an arm-chair, and producing Miss Julia's letter from his pocket, as if to corroborate the assertion that he *had* been asked.

"Now, Overton," replied the lady, "I want your assistance in this matter, and I must have it. In the lifetime of that poor old dear, Mr. Cornberry, who—who——"

"Who was to have married you, and didn't, because he died first; and who left you his property unencumbered with the addition of himself," suggested the mayor.

"Well," replied Miss Julia, reddening slightly, "in the lifetime of the poor old dear, the property had the encumbrance of your management; and all I will say of that, is, that I only wonder *it* didn't die of consumption instead of its master. You helped yourself then :—help me now."

Mr. Joseph Overton was a man of the world, and an attorney; and as certain indistinct recollections of an odd thousand pounds or two, appropriated by mistake, passed across his mind, he hemmed deprecatingly, smiled blandly, remained silent for a few seconds; and finally inquired, " What do you wish me to do?"

"I'll tell you," replied Miss Julia—"I'll tell you in three words. Dear Lord Peter——"

"That's the young man, I suppose——" interrupted the mayor.

"That's the young Nobleman," replied the lady, with a great stress on the last word. "Dear Lord Peter is considerably afraid of the resentment of his family ; and we have therefore thought it better to make the match a stolen one. He left town, to avoid suspicion, on a visit to his friend, the Honourable Augustus Flair, whose seat, as you

know, is about thirty miles from this, accompanied only by
his favourite tiger. We arranged that I should come here
alone in the London coach; and that he, leaving his tiger
and cab behind him, should come on, and arrive here as
soon as possible this afternoon."

"Very well," observed Joseph Overton, "and then he can
order the chaise, and you can go on to Gretna Green together,
without requiring the presence or interference of a third
party, can't you?"

"No," replied Miss Julia. "We have every reason to
believe—dear Lord Peter not being considered very prudent
or sagacious by his friends, and they having discovered his
attachment to me—that, immediately on his absence being
observed, pursuit will be made in this direction:—to elude
which, and to prevent our being traced, I wish it to be
understood in this house, that dear Lord Peter is slightly
deranged, though perfectly harmless; and that I am, unknown
to him, awaiting his arrival to convey him in a post-chaise to
a private asylum—at Berwick, say. If I don't show myself
much, I dare say I can manage to pass for his mother."

The thought occurred to the mayor's mind that the
lady might show herself a good deal without fear of de-
tection; seeing that she was about double the age of her
intended husband. He said nothing, however, and the lady
proceeded.

"With the whole of this arrangement dear Lord Peter
is acquainted; and all I want you to do is, to make the
delusion more complete by giving it the sanction of your
influence in this place, and assigning this as a reason to the
people of the house for my taking the young gentleman
away. As it would not be consistent with the story that
I should see him until after he has entered the chaise,
I also wish you to communicate with him, and inform him
that it is all going on well."

"Has he arrived?" inquired Overton.

"I don't know," replied the lady.

"Then how am I to know!" inquired the mayor. "Of
course he will not give his own name at the bar."

"I begged him, immediately on his arrival, to write you
a note," replied Miss Manners; "and to prevent the possibility of our project being discovered through its means,
I desired him to write anonymously, and in mysterious
terms, to acquaint you with the number of his room."

"Bless me!" exclaimed the mayor, rising from his seat, and searching his pockets—"most extraordinary circumstance —he *has* arrived—mysterious note left at my house in a most mysterious manner, just before yours—didn't know what to make of it before, and certainly shouldn't have attended to it.—Oh! here it is." And Joseph Overton pulled out of an inner coat-pocket the identical letter penned by Alexander Trott. "Is this his lordship's hand?"

"Oh yes," replied Julia; "good, punctual creature! I have not seen it more than once or twice, but I know he writes very badly and very large. These dear, wild young noblemen. you know, Overton ——"

"Aye, aye, I see," replied the mayor.—"Horses and dogs, play and wine—grooms, actresses, and cigars—the stable, the green-room, the saloon, and the tavern; and the legislative assembly at last."

"Here's what he says," pursued the mayor; "'Sir,—A young gentleman in number nineteen at the Winglebury Arms, is bent on committing a rash act to-morrow morning at an early hour.' (That's good—he means marrying.) 'If you have any regard for the peace of this town, or the preservation of one—it may be two—human lives'—What the deuce does he mean by that?"

"That he's so anxious for the ceremony, he will expire if it's put off, and that I may possibly do the same," replied the lady with great complacency.

"Oh! I see—not much fear of that;—well—'two human lives, you will cause him to be removed to-night.' (He wants to start at once.) 'Fear not to do this on your responsibility: for to-morrow the absolute necessity of the proceeding will be but too apparent. Remember: number nineteen. The name is Trott. No delay; for life and death depend upon your promptitude.' Passionate language, certainly. Shall I see him?"

"Do," replied Miss Julia; "and entreat him to act his part well. I am half afraid of him. Tell him to be cautious."

"I will," said the mayor.

"Settle all the arrangements."

"I will," said the mayor again.

"And say I think the chaise had better be ordered for one o'clock."

"Very well," said the mayor once more; and, ruminating

on the absurdity of the situation in which fate and old acquaintance had placed him, he desired a waiter to herald his approach to the temporary representative of number nineteen.

The announcement, "Gentleman to speak with you, sir," induced Mr. Trott to pause half-way in the glass of port, the contents of which he was in the act of imbibing at the moment; to rise from his chair; and retreat a few paces towards the window, as if to secure a retreat, in the event of the visitor assuming the form and appearance of Horace Hunter. One glance at Joseph Overton, however, quieted his apprehensions. He courteously motioned the stranger to a seat. The waiter, after a little jingling with the decanter and glasses, consented to leave the room ; and Joseph Overton, placing the broad-brimmed hat on the chair next him, and bending his body gently forward, opened the business by saying in a very low and cautious tone,

"My lord——"

"Eh ?" said Mr. Alexander Trott, in a loud key, with the vacant and mystified stare of a chilly somnambulist.

"Hush—hush !" said the cautious attorney: " to be sure —quite right—no titles here—my name is Overton, sir."

"Overton ?"

"Yes: the mayor of this place—you sent me a letter with anonymous information, this afternoon."

"I, sir ?" exclaimed Trott with ill-dissembled surprise; for, coward as he was, he would willingly have repudiated the authorship of the letter in question. "I, sir ?"

"Yes, you, sir; did you not ?" responded Overton, annoyed with what he supposed to be an extreme degree of unnecessary suspicion. "Either this letter is yours, or it is not. If it be, we can converse securely upon the subject at once. If it be not, of course I have no more to say."

"Stay, stay," said Trott, "it *is* mine ; I *did* write it. What could I do, sir ? I had no friend here."

"To be sure, to be sure," said the mayor, encouragingly, "you could not have managed it better. Well, sir ; it will be necessary for you to leave here to-night in a post-chaise and four. And the harder the boys drive, the better. You are not safe from pursuit."

"Bless me !" exclaimed Trott, in an agony of apprehension, "can such things happen in a country like this? Such unrelenting and cold-blooded hostility !" He wiped off the concentrated essence of cowardice that was oozing fast down his forehead, and looked aghast at Joseph Overton.

"It certainly is a very hard case," replied the mayor with a smile, ' that, in a free country, people can't marry whom they like vithout being hunted down as if they were criminals. _Iowever, in the present instance the lady is willing, you know, and that's the main point, after all."

"Lady willing," repeated Trott, mechanically. "How do you know the lady's willing?"

"Come, that's a good one," said the mayor, benevolently tapping Mr. Trott on the arm with his broad-brimmed hat; "I have known her, well, for a long time; and if anybody could entertain the remotest doubt on the subject, I assure you I have none, nor need you have."

"Dear me!" said Mr. Trott, ruminating. "This is *very* extraordinary!"

"Well, Lord Peter," said the mayor, rising.

"Lord Peter?" repeated Mr. Trott.

"Oh—ah, I forgot. Mr. Trott, then—Trott—very good, ha! ha!—Well, sir, the chaise shall be ready at half-past twelve."

"And what is to become of me until then?" inquired Mr. Trott, anxiously. "Wouldn't it save appearances, if I were placed under some restraint?"

"Ah!" replied Overton, "very good thought—capital idea indeed. I'll send somebody up directly. And if you make a little resistance when we put you in the chaise it wouldn't be amiss—look as if you didn't want to be taken away, you know."

"To be sure," said Trott—"to be sure."

"Well, my lord," said Overton, in a low tone, "until then, I wish your lordship a good evening."

"Lord—lordship?" ejaculated Trott again, falling back a step or two, and gazing, in unutterable wonder, on the countenance of the mayor.

"Ha-ha! I see, my lord—practising the madman?—very good indeed—very vacant look—capital, my lord, capital—good evening, Mr.—Trott—ha! ha! ha!"

"That mayor's decidedly drunk," soliloquised Mr. Trott, throwing himself back in his chair, in an attitude of reflection.

"He is a much cleverer fellow than I thought him, that young nobleman—he carries it off uncommonly well," thought

Overton, as he went his way to the bar, there to complete his arrangements. This was soon done. Every word of the story was implicitly believed, and the one-eyed boots was immediately instructed to repair to number nineteen, to act as custodian of the person of the supposed lunatic until half-past twelve o'clock. In pursuance of this direction, that somewhat eccentric gentleman armed himself with a walking-stick of gigantic dimensions, and repaired, with his usual equanimity of manner, to Mr. Trott's apartment, which he entered without any ceremony, and mounted guard in, by quietly depositing himself on a chair near the door, where he proceeded to beguile the time by whistling a popular air with great apparent satisfaction.

"What do you want here, you scoundrel?" exclaimed Mr. Alexander Trott, with a proper appearance of indignation at his detention.

The boots beat time with his head, as he looked gently round at Mr. Trott with a smile of pity, and whistled an *adagio* movement.

"Do you attend in this room by Mr. Overton's desire?" inquired Trott, rather astonished at the man's demeanour.

"Keep yourself to yourself, young feller," calmly responded the boots, "and don't say nothin' to nobody." And he whistled again.

"Now, mind!" ejaculated Mr. Trott, anxious to keep up the farce of wishing with great earnestness to fight a duel if they'd let him. "I protest against being kept here. I deny that I have any intention of fighting with anybody. But as it's useless contending with superior numbers, I shall sit quietly down."

"You'd better," observed the placid boots, shaking the large stick expressively.

"Under protest, however," added Alexander Trott, seating himself with indignation in his face, but great content in his heart. "Under protest."

"Oh, certainly!" responded the boots; "anything you please. If you're happy, I'm transported; only don't talk too much—it'll make you worse."

"Make me worse?" exclaimed Trott, in unfeigned astonishment: "the man's drunk!"

"You'd better be quiet, young feller," remarked the boots, going through a threatening piece of pantomime with the stick.

"Or mad!" said Mr. Trott, rather alarmed. "Leave the room, sir, and tell them to send somebody else."

"Won't do!" replied the boots.

"Leave the room!" shouted Trott, ringing the bell violently: for he began to be alarmed on a new score.

"Leave that 'ere bell alone, you wretched loo-nattic!" said the boots, suddenly forcing the unfortunate Trott back into his chair, and brandishing the stick aloft. "Be quiet, you miserable object, and don't let everybody know there's a madman in the house."

"He *is* a madman! He *is* a madman!" exclaimed the terrified Mr. Trott, gazing on the one eye of the red-headed boots with a look of abject horror.

"Madmam!" replied the boots, "dam'me, I think he *is* a madman with a vengeance! Listen to me, you unfort'nate. Ah! would you?" [a slight tap on the head with the large stick, as Mr. Trott made another move towards the bell-handle] "I caught you there! did I?"

"Spare my life!" exclaimed Trott, raising his hands imploringly.

"I don't want your life," replied the boots, disdainfully, "though I think it 'ud be a charity if somebody took it."

"No, no, it wouldn't," interrupted poor Mr. Trott, hurriedly; "no, no, it wouldn't! I—I—'d rather keep it!"

"O werry well," said the boots: "that's a mere matter of taste—ev'ry one to his liking. Hows'ever, all I've got to say is this here: You sit quietly down in that chair, and I'll sit hoppersite you here, and if you keep quiet and don't stir, I won't damage you; but if you move hand or foot till half-past twelve o'clock, I shall alter the expression of your countenance so completely, that the next time you look in the glass you'll ask vether you're gone out of town, and ven you're likely to come back again. So sit down."

"I will—I will," responded the victim of mistakes; and down sat Mr. Trott and down sat the boots too, exactly opposite him, with the stick ready for immediate action in case of emergency.

Long and dreary were the hours that followed. The bell of Great Winglebury church had just struck ten, and two hours and a half would probably elapse before succour arrived.

For half an hour, the noise occasioned by shutting up the shops in the street beneath, betokened something like life in the town, and rendered Mr. Trott's situation a little less insupportable; but when even these ceased, and nothing was heard beyond the occasional rattling of a post-chaise as it drove up the yard to change horses, and then drove away again, or the clattering of horses' hoofs in the stables behind, it became almost unbearable. The boots occasionally moved an inch or two, to knock superfluous bits of wax off the candles, which were burning low, but instantaneously resumed his former position; and as he remembered to have heard, somewhere or other, that the human eye had an unfailing effect in controlling mad people, he kept his solitary organ of vision constantly fixed on Mr. Alexander Trott. That unfortunate individual stared at his companion in his turn, until his features grew more and more indistinct—his hair gradually less red—and the room more misty and obscure. Mr. Alexander Trott fell into a sound sleep, from which he was awakened by a rumbling in the street, and a cry of "Chaise-and-four for number twenty-five!" A bustle on the stairs succeeded; the room-door was hastily thrown open; and Mr. Joseph Overton entered, followed by four stout waiters, and Mrs. Williamson, the stout landlady of the Winglebury Arms.

"Mr. Overton!" exclaimed Mr. Alexander Trott, jumping up in a frenzy. "Look at this man, sir; consider the situation in which I have been placed for three hours past—the person you sent to guard me, sir, was a madman—a madman—a raging, ravaging, furious madman."

"Bravo!" whispered Overton.

"Poor dear!" said the compassionate Mrs. Williamson, "mad people always thinks other people's mad."

"Poor dear!" ejaculated Mr. Alexander Trott. "What the devil do you mean by poor dear! Are you the landlady of this house?"

"Yes, yes," replied the stout old lady, "don't exert yourself, there's a dear! Consider your health, now; do."

"Exert myself!" shouted Mr. Alexander Trott; "it's a mercy, ma'am, that I have any breath to exert myself with! I might have been assassinated three hours ago by that one-eyed monster with the oakum head. How dare you have a madman, ma'am—how dare you have a madman, to assault and terrify the visitors to your house?"

"I'll never have another," said Mrs. Williamson, casting a look of reproach at the mayor.

"Capital, capital," whispered Overton again, as he en-veloped Mr. Alexander Trott in a thick travelling-cloak.

"Capital, sir!" exclaimed Trott, aloud; "it's horrible. The very recollection makes me shudder. I'd rather fight four duels in three hours, if I survived the first three, than I'd sit for that time face to face with a madman."

"Keep it up, my lord, as you go down-stairs," whispered Overton, "your bill is paid, and your portmanteau in the chaise." And then he added aloud, "Now, waiters, the gentleman's ready."

At this signal, the waiters crowded round Mr. Alexander Trott. One took one arm; another, the other; a third, walked before with a candle; the fourth, behind with another candle; the boots and Mrs. Williamson brought up the rear; and down-stairs they went: Mr. Alexander Trott expressing alternately at the very top of his voice either his feigned reluctance to go, or his unfeigned indignation at being shut up with a madman.

Mr. Overton was waiting at the chaise-door, the boys were ready mounted, and a few ostlers and stable nondescripts were standing round to witness the departure of "the mad gentle-man." Mr. Alexander Trott's foot was on the step, when he observed (which the dim light had prevented his doing before) a figure seated in the chaise, closely muffled up in a cloak like his own.

"Who's that?" he inquired of Overton, in a whisper.

"Hush, hush," replied the mayor: "the other party of course."

"The other party!" exclaimed Trott, with an effort to retreat.

"Yes, yes; you'll soon find that out, before you go far. I should think—but make a noise, you'll excite suspicion if you whisper to me so much."

"I won't go in this chaise!" shouted Mr. Alexander Trott, all his original fears recurring with tenfold violence. "I shall be assassinated—I shall be—— "

"Bravo, bravo," whispered Overton. "I'll push you in."

"But I won't go," exclaimed Mr. Trott. "Help here, help! They're carrying me away against my will. This is a plot to murder me."

"Poor dear!" said Mrs. Williamson again.

"Now, boys, put 'em along," cried the mayor, pushing Trott in and slamming the door. "Off with you, as quick as you can, and stop for nothing till you come to the next stage—all right ! "

"Horses are paid, Tom," screamed Mrs. Williamson ; and away went the chaise, at the rate of fourteen miles an hour, with Mr. Alexander Trott and Miss Julia Manners carefully shut up in the inside.

Mr. Alexander Trott remained coiled up in one corner of the chaise, and his mysterious companion in the other, for the first two or three miles ; Mr. Trott edging more and more into his corner, as he felt his companion gradually edging more and more from hers ; and vainly endeavouring in the darkness to catch a glimpse of the furious face of the supposed Horace Hunter.

"We may speak now," said his fellow-traveller, at length ; "the post-boys can neither see nor hear us."

"That's not Hunter's voice ! "—thought Alexander, aston-Ished.

"Dear Lord Peter ! " said Miss Julia, most winningly : putting her arm on Mr. Trott's shoulder. "Dear Lord Peter. Not a word ? "

"Why, it's a woman ! " exclaimed Mr. Trott, in a low tone of excessive wonder.

"Ah ! Whose voice is that ? " said Julia ; "tis not Lord Peter's."

"No,—it's mine," replied Mr. Trott.

"Yours ! " ejaculated Miss Julia Manners ; "a strange man ! Gracious heaven ! How came you here ! "

"Whoever you are, you might have known that I came against my will, ma'am," replied Alexander, "for I made noise enough when I got in."

"Do you come from Lord Peter ? " inquired Miss Manners.

"Confound Lord Peter," replied Trott pettishly. "I don't know any Lord Peter. I never heard of him before to-night, when I've been Lord Peter'd by one and Lord Peter'd by another, till I verily believe I'm mad, or dreaming—— "

"Whither are we going ? " inquired the lady tragically.

"How should I know, ma'am ? " replied Trott with singular coolness ; for the events of the evening had completely hardened him.

"Stop ! stop ! " cried the lady, letting down the front glasses of the chaise.

"Stay, my dear ma'am ! " said Mr. Trott, pulling the

glasses up again with one hand, and gently squeezing Miss Julia's waist with the other. "There is some mistake here; give me till the end of this stage to explain my share of it. We must go so far; you cannot be set down here alone, at this hour of the night."

The lady consented; the mistake was mutually explained. Mr. Trott was a young man, had highly promising whiskers, an undeniable tailor, and an insinuating address—he wanted nothing but valour, and who wants that with three thousand a year? The lady had this, and more; she wanted a young husband, and the only course open to Mr. Trott to retrieve his disgrace was a rich wife. So they came to the conclusion that it would be a pity to have all this trouble and expense for nothing; and that as they were so far on the road already, they had better go to Gretna Green, and marry each other; and they did so. And the very next preceding entry in the Blacksmith's book, was an entry of the marriage of Emily Brown with Horace Hunter. Mr. Hunter took his wife home, and begged pardon, and *was* pardoned; and Mr. Trott took *his* wife home, begged pardon too, and was pardoned also. And Lord Peter, who had been detained beyond his time by drinking champagne and riding a steeple-chase, went back to the Honourable Augustus Flair's, and drank more champagne, and rode another steeple-chase, and was thrown and killed. And Horace Hunter took great credit to himself for practising on the cowardice of Alexander Trott; and all these circumstances were discovered in time, and carefully noted down; and if you ever stop a week at the Winglebury Arms, they will give you just this account of The Great Winglebury Duel.

CHAPTER IX

MRS. JOSEPH PORTER

Most extensive were the preparations at Rose Villa, Clapham Rise, in the occupation of Mr. Gattleton (a stock-broker in especially comfortable circumstances), and great was the anxiety of Mr. Gattleton's interesting family, as the day fixed for the representation of the Private Play which had been "many months in preparation," approached. The whole family was infected with the mania for Private Theatricals; the house, usually so clean and tidy, was, to use Mr. Gattleton's expressive description, "regularly turned out o' windows;" the large dining-room, dismantled of its furniture and ornaments, presented a strange jumble of flats, flies, wings, lamps, bridges, clouds, thunder and lightning, festoons and flowers, daggers and foil, and various other messes in theatrical slang included under the comprehensive name of "properties." The bedrooms were crowded with scenery, the kitchen was occupied by carpenters. Rehearsals took place every other night in the drawing-room, and every sofa in the house was more or less damaged by the perseverance and spirit with which Mr. Sempronius Gattleton, and Miss Lucina, rehearsed the smothering scene in "Othello"—it having been determined that that tragedy should form the first portion of the evening's entertainments.

"When we're a *leetle* more perfect, I think it will go admirably," said Mr. Sempronius, addressing his *corps dramatique*, at the conclusion of the hundred and fiftieth rehearsal. In consideration of his sustaining the trifling inconvenience of bearing all the expenses of the play, Mr. Sempronius had been, in the most handsome manner, unanimously elected stage-manager. "Evans," continued Mr. Gattleton the younger, addressing a tall, thin, pale young gentleman, with extensive whiskers—"Evans, you play *Roderigo* beautifully."

"Beautifully," echoed the three Miss Gattletons; for Mr. Evans was pronounced by all his lady friends to be "quite

R

a dear." He looked so interesting, and had such lovely whiskers: to say nothing of his talent for writing verses in albums and playing the flute! *Roderigo* simpered and bowed.

"But I think," added the manager, "you are hardly perfect in the—fall—in the fencing-scene, where you are—you understand?"

"It's very difficult," said Mr. Evans, thoughtfully; "I've fallen about a good deal in our counting-house lately, for practice, only I find it hurts one so. Being obliged to fall backward you see, it bruises one's head a good deal."

"But you must take care you don't knock a wing down," said Mr. Gattleton, the elder, who had been appointed prompter, and who took as much interest in the play as the youngest of the company. "The stage is very narrow, you know."

"Oh! don't be afraid," said Mr. Evans, with a very self-satisfied air: "I shall fall with my head 'off,' and then I can't do any harm."

"But, egad," said the manager, rubbing his hands, "we shall make a decided hit in 'Masaniello.' Harleigh sings that music admirably."

Everybody echoed the sentiment. Mr. Harleigh smiled, and looked foolish—not an unusual thing with him—hummed "Behold how brightly breaks the morning," and blushed as red as the fisherman's nightcap he was trying on.

"Let's see," resumed the manager, telling the number on his fingers, "we shall have three dancing female peasants, besides *Fenella*, and four fishermen. Then, there's our man Tom; he can have a pair of ducks of mine, and a check shirt of Bob's, and a red nightcap, and he'll do for another—that's five. In the choruses, of course, we can sing at the sides; and in the market-scene we can walk about in cloaks and things. When the revolt takes place, Tom must keep rushing in on one side and out on the other, with a pickaxe, as fast as he can. The effect will be electrical; it will look exactly as if there were an immense number of 'em. And in the eruption-scene we must burn the red fire, and upset the tea-trays, and make all sorts of noises—and it's sure to do."

"Sure! sure!" cried all the performers *unâ voce*—and away hurried Mr. Sempronius Gattleton to wash the burnt cork off his face, and superintend the "setting up" of some of the amateur-painted, but never-sufficiently-to-be-admired, scenery.

Mrs. Gattleton was a kind, good-tempered, vulgar soul, exceedingly fond of her husband and children, and entertaining only three dislikes. In the first place, she had a natural antipathy to anybody else's unmarried daughters; in the second, she was in bodily fear of anything in the shape of ridicule; lastly—almost a necessary consequence of this feeling—she regarded, with feelings of the utmost horror, one Mrs. Joseph Porter, over the way. However, the good folks of Clapham and its vicinity stood very much in awe of scandal and sarcasm; and thus Mrs. Joseph Porter was courted, and flattered, and caressed, and invited, for much the same reason that induces a poor author, without a farthing in his pocket, to behave with extraordinary civility to a two-penny postman.

"Never mind, ma," said Miss Emma Porter, in colloquy with her respected relative, and trying to look unconcerned; "if they had invited me, you know that neither you nor pa would have allowed me to take part in such an exhibition."

"Just what I should have thought from your high sense of propriety," returned the mother. "I am glad to see, Emma, you know how to designate the proceeding." Miss P., by-the-bye, had only the week before made "an exhibition" of herself for four days, behind a counter at a fancy fair, to all and every of her Majesty's liege subjects who were disposed to pay a shilling each for the privilege of seeing some four dozen girls flirting with strangers, and playing at shop.

"There!" said Mrs. Porter, looking out of window; "there are two rounds of beef and a ham going in—clearly for sandwiches; and Thomas, the pastry-cook, says, there have been twelve dozen tarts ordered, besides blanc-mange and jellies. Upon my word! think of the Miss Gattletons in fancy dresses, too!"

"Oh, it's too ridiculous!" said Miss Porter, hysterically.

"I'll manage to put them a little out of conceit with the business, however," said Mrs. Porter; and out she went on her charitable errand.

"Well, my dear Mrs. Gattleton," said Mrs. Joseph Porter, after they had been closeted for some time, and when, by dint of indefatigable pumping, she had managed to extract all the news about the play, "well, my dear, people may say what they please; indeed we know they will, for some folks

are *so* ill-natured. Ah, my dear Miss Lucina, how d'ye do?
I was just telling your mamma that I have heard it said,
that——"

"What?"

"Mrs. Porter is alluding to the play, my dear," said Mrs.
Gattleton; "she was, I am sorry to say, just informing me
that——"

"Oh, now pray don't mention it," interrupted Mrs. Porter;
"it's most absurd—quite as absurd as young What's-his-
name saying he wondered how Miss Caroline, with such a
foot and ankle, could have the vanity to play *Fenella*."

"Highly impertinent, whoever said it," said Mrs. Gattleton,
bridling up.

"Certainly, my dear," chimed in the delighted Mrs.
Porter; "most undoubtedly! Because, as I said, if Miss
Caroline *does* play *Fenella*, it doesn't follow, as a matter of
course, that she should think she has a pretty foot;—and
then—such puppies as these young men are—he had the
impudence to say, that——"

How far the amiable Mrs. Porter might have succeeded
in her pleasant purpose, it is impossible to say, had not the
entrance of Mr. Thomas Balderstone, Mrs. Gattleton's brother,
familiarly called in the family "Uncle Tom," changed the
course of conversation, and suggested to her mind an excellent
plan of operation on the evening of the play.

Uncle Tom was very rich, and exceedingly fond of his
nephews and nieces: as a matter of course, therefore, he was
an object of great importance in his own family. He was
one of the best-hearted men in existence: always in a good
temper, and always talking. It was his boast that he wore
top-boots on all occasions, and had never worn a black silk
neckerchief; and it was his pride that he remembered all the
principal plays of Shakspeare from beginning to end—and
so he did. The result of this parrot-like accomplishment
was, that he was not only perpetually quoting himself, but
that he could never sit by, and hear a misquotation from the
"Swan of Avon" without setting the unfortunate delinquent
right. He was also something of a wag; never missed an
opportunity of saying what he considered a good thing, and
invariably laughed until he cried at anything that appeared
to him mirth-moving or ridiculous.

"Well, girls!" said Uncle Tom, after the preparatory ceremony of kissing and how-d'ye-do-ing had been gone through

Mr. Sempronius Gattleton as Othello

—" how d'ye get on? Know your parts, eh?—Lucina, my dear, act ii., scene 1—place, left—cue—' Unknown fate,'—What's next, eh?—Go on—'The Heavens——'"

"Oh, yes," said Miss Lucina, "I recollect—

> 'The heavens forbid
> But that our loves and comforts should increase
> Even as our days do grow!'"

"Make a pause here and there," said the old gentleman, who was a great critic. "'But that our loves and comforts should increase'—emphasis on the last syllable, 'crease,'—loud 'even,'—one, two, three, four; then loud again, 'as our days do grow;' emphasis on *days*. That's the way, my dear; trust to your uncle for emphasis. Ah! Sem, my boy, how are you?"

"Very well, thankee, uncle," returned Mr. Sempronius, who had just appeared, looking something like a ringdove with a small circle round each eye: the result of his constant corking. "Of course we see you on Thursday."

"Of course, of course, my dear boy."

"What a pity it is your nephew didn't think of making you prompter, Mr. Balderstone!" whispered Mrs. Joseph Porter; "you would have been invaluable."

"Well, I flatter myself, I *should* have been tolerably up to the thing," responded Uncle Tom.

"I must bespeak sitting next you on the night," resumed Mrs. Porter; "and then, if our dear young friends here should be at all wrong, you will be able to enlighten me. I shall be so interested."

"I am sure I shall be most happy to give you any assistance in my power."

"Mind, it's a bargain."

"Certainly."

"I don't know how it is," said Mrs. Gattleton to her daughters, as they were sitting round the fire in the evening, looking over their parts, "but I really very much wish Mrs. Joseph Porter wasn't coming on Thursday. I am sure she's scheming something."

"She can't make *us* ridiculous, however," observed Mr. Sempronius Gattleton, haughtily.

The long-looked-for Thursday arrived in due course, and brought with it, as Mr. Gattleton, senior, philosophically observed, "no disappointments, to speak of." True, it was yet a matter of doubt whether *Cassio* would be enabled to get into the dress which had been sent for him from the masquerade warehouse. It was equally uncertain whether the principal female singer would be sufficiently recovered from the influenza to make her appearance; Mr. Harleigh, the *Masaniello* of the night, was hoarse, and rather unwell, in consequence of the great quantity of lemon and sugar-candy he had eaten to improve his voice; and two flutes and a violoncello had pleaded severe colds. What of that? the audience were all coming. Everybody knew his part; the dresses were covered with tinsel and spangles; the white plumes looked beautiful; Mr. Evans had practised falling until he was bruised from head to foot and quite perfect; *Iago* was sure that, in the stabbing-scene, he should make "a decided hit." A self-taught deaf gentleman, who had kindly offered to bring his flute, would be a most valuable addition to the orchestra; Miss Jenkins's talent for the piano was too well known to be doubted for an instant; Mr. Cape had practised the violin accompaniment with her frequently; and Mr. Brown, who had kindly undertaken, at a few hours' notice, to bring his violoncello, would, no doubt, manage extremely well.

Seven o'clock came, and so did the audience; all the rank and fashion of Clapham and its vicinity was fast filling the theatre. There were the Smiths, the Gubbinses, the Nixons, the Dixons, the Hicksons, people with all sorts of names, two aldermen, a sheriff in perspective, Sir Thomas Glumper (who had been knighted in the last reign for carrying up an address on somebody's escaping from nothing); and last, not least, there were Mrs. Joseph Porter and Uncle Tom, seated in the centre of the third row from the stage; Mrs. P. amusing Uncle Tom with all sorts of stories, and Uncle Tom amusing every one else by laughing most immoderately.

Ting, ting, ting! went the prompter's bell at eight o'clock precisely, and dash went the orchestra into the overture to "The Men of Prometheus." The pianoforte player hammered away with laudable perseverance; and the violoncello, which struck in at intervals, "sounded very well, considering." The unfortunate individual, however, who had undertaken to play the flute accompaniment "at sight," found, from fatal experience, the perfect truth of the old adage, "out of sight, out of mind;" for being very near-sighted, and being placed at a considerable distance from his music-book, all he had an opportunity of doing was to play a bar now and then in the wrong place, and put the other performers out. It is, however, but justice to Mr. Brown to say that he did this to admiration. The overture, in fact, was not unlike a race between the different instruments ; the piano came in first by several bars, and the violoncello next, quite distancing the poor flute ; for the deaf gentleman *too-too'd* away, quite unconscious that he was at all wrong, until apprised, by the applause of the audience, that the overture was concluded. A considerable bustle and shuffling of feet was then heard upon the stage, accompanied by whispers of "Here's a pretty go !—what's to be done?" &c. The audience applauded again, by way of raising the spirits of the performers; and then Mr. Sempronius desired the prompter, in a very audible voice, to "clear the stage, and ring up."

Ting, ting, ting ! went the bell again. Everybody sat down ; the curtain shook ; rose sufficiently high to display several pair of yellow boots paddling about; and there remained.

Ting, ting, ting ! went the bell again. The curtain was violently convulsed, but rose no higher; the audience tittered; Mrs. Porter looked at Uncle Tom ; Uncle Tom looked at everybody, rubbing his hands, and laughing with perfect rapture. After as much ringing with the little bell as a muffin-boy would make in going down a tolerably long street, and a vast deal of whispering, hammering, and calling for nails and cord, the curtain at length rose, and discovered Mr. Sempronius Gattleton *solus*, and decked for *Othello*. After three distinct rounds of applause, during which Mr. Sempronius applied his right hand to his left breast, and bowed in the most approved manner, the manager advanced and said :

"Ladies and Gentlemen—I assure you it is with sincere regret, that I regret to be compelled to inform you, that *Iago* who was to have played Mr. Wilson—I beg your pardon, Ladies and Gentlemen, but I am naturally somewhat agitated (applause)—I mean, Mr. Wilson, who was to have played *Iago*, is—that is, has been—or, in other words, Ladies and Gentlemen, the fact is, that I have just received a note, in which I am informed that *Iago* is unavoidably detained at the Post Office this evening. Under these circumstances, I trust—a—a—amateur performance—a—another gentleman undertaken to read the part—request indulgence for a short

time—courtesy and kindness of a British audience." Over-
whelming applause. Exit Mr. Sempronius Gattleton, and
curtain falls.

The audience were, of course, exceedingly good-humoured ;
the whole business was a joke ; and accordingly they waited
for an hour with the utmost patience, being enlivened by
an interlude of rout-cakes and lemonade. It appeared by
Mr. Sempronius's subsequent explanation, that the delay
would not have been so great, had it not so happened that
when the substitute *Iago* had finished dressing, and just as
the play was on the point of commencing, the original *Iago*
unexpectedly arrived. The former was therefore compelled
to undress, and the latter to dress for his part ; which, as
he found some difficulty in getting into his clothes, occupied
no inconsiderable time. At last, the tragedy began in real
earnest. It went off well enough, until the third scene of
the first act, in which *Othello* addresses the Senate : the only
remarkable circumstance being, that as *Iago* could not get
on any of the stage boots, in consequence of his feet being
violently swelled with the heat and excitement, he was under
the necessity of playing the part in a pair of Wellingtons,
which contrasted rather oddly with his richly embroidered
pantaloons. When *Othello* started with his address to the
Senate (whose dignity was represented by the *Duke*, a
carpenter, two men engaged on the recommendation of the
gardener, and a boy), Mrs. Porter found the opportunity she
so anxiously sought.

Mr. Sempronius proceeded :

> " 'Most potent, grave, and reverend signiors,
> My very noble and approv'd good masters,
> That I have ta'en away this old man's daughter,
> It is most true ;—rude am I in my speech——' "

" Is that right ? " whispered Mrs. Porter to Uncle Tom.
" No."
" Tell him so, then."
" I will. Sem ! " called out Uncle Tom, "that's wrong,
my boy."
" What's wrong, uncle ? " demanded *Othello*, quite forgetting
the dignity of his situation.
" You've left out something. 'True I have married—— ' "
" Oh, ah ! " said Mr. Sempronius, endeavouring to hide his
confusion as much and as ineffectually as the audience

attempted to conceal their half-suppressed tittering, by coughing with extraordinary violence—

> ———"'true I have married her ;—
> The very head and front of my offending
> Hath this extent ; no more.'

(*Aside*) Why don't you prompt, father ? "

"Because I've mislaid my spectacles," said poor Mr. Gattleton, almost dead with the heat and bustle.

"There, now it's 'rude am I,'" said Uncle Tom.

"Yes, I know it is," returned the unfortunate manager, proceeding with his part.

It would be useless and tiresome to quote the number of instances in which Uncle Tom, now completely in his element, and instigated by the mischievous Mrs. Porter, corrected the mistakes of the performers ; suffice it to say that, having mounted his hobby, nothing could induce him to dismount ; so, during the whole remainder of the play, he performed a kind of running accompaniment, by muttering everybody's part as it was being delivered, in an under-tone. The audience were highly amused, Mrs. Porter delighted, the performers embarrassed ; Uncle Tom never was better pleased in all his life ; and Uncle Tom's nephews and nieces had never, although the declared heirs to his large property, so heartily wished him gathered to his fathers as on that memorable occasion.

Several other minor causes, too, united to damp the ardour of the *dramatis personæ*. None of the performers could walk in their tights, or move their arms in their jackets ; the pantaloons were too small, the boots too large, and the swords of all shapes and sizes. Mr. Evans, naturally too tall for the scenery, wore a black velvet hat with immense white plumes, the glory of which was lost in "the flies ; " and the only other inconvenience of which was, that when it was off his head he could not put it on, and when it was on he could not take it off. Notwithstanding all his practice, too, he fell with his head and shoulders as neatly through one of the side scenes, as a harlequin would jump through a panel in a Christmas pantomime. The pianoforte player, overpowered by the extreme heat of the room, fainted away at the commencement of the entertainment, leaving the music of "Masaniello" to the flute and violoncello. The orchestra complained that Mr. Harleigh put them out, and Mr. Harleigh declared that the orchestra prevented his singing a note. The fishermen, who were hired for the occasion, revolted to the very life, positively refusing to play without an increased allowance of spirits ; and, their demand being complied with, getting drunk in the eruption-scene as naturally as possible. The red fire, which was burnt at the conclusion of the second act, not only nearly suffocated the audience, but nearly set the house on fire into the bargain ; and, as it was, the remainder of the piece was acted in a thick fog.

In short, the whole affair was, as Mrs. Joseph Porter triumphantly told everybody, "a complete failure." The audience went home at four o'clock in the morning, exhausted with laughter, suffering from severe headaches, and smelling terribly of brimstone and gunpowder. The Messrs. Gattleton, senior and junior, retired to rest, with the vague idea of emigrating to Swan River early in the ensuing week.

Rose Villa has once again resumed its wonted appearance ; the dining-room furniture has been replaced ; the tables are as nicely polished as formerly ; the horsehair chairs are ranged against the wall, as regularly as ever ; Venetian blinds have been fitted to every window in the house to intercept the prying gaze of Mrs. Joseph Porter. The subject of theatricals is never mentioned in the Gattleton family, unless, indeed, by Uncle Tom, who cannot refrain from sometimes expressing his surprise and regret at finding that his nephews and nieces appear to have lost the relish they once possessed for the beauties of Shakspeare, and quotations from the works of that immortal bard.

CHAPTER X

A PASSAGE IN THE LIFE OF MR. WATKINS TOTTLE

CHAPTER THE FIRST

MATRIMONY is proverbially a serious undertaking. Like an overweening predilection for brandy-and-water, it is a misfortune into which a man easily falls, and from which he finds it remarkably difficult to extricate himself. It is of no use telling a man who is timorous on these points, that it is but one plunge, and all is over. They say the same thing at the Old Bailey, and the unfortunate victims derive as much comfort from the assurance in the one case as in the other.

Mr. Watkins Tottle was a rather uncommon compound of strong uxorious inclinations, and an unparalleled degree of anti-connubial timidity. He was about fifty years of age; stood four feet six inches and three-quarters in his socks—for he never stood in stockings at all—plump, clean, and rosy. He looked something like a vignette to one of Richardson's novels, and had a clean-cravatish formality of manner, and kitchen-pokerness of carriage, which Sir Charles Grandison himself might have envied. He lived on an annuity, which was well adapted to the individual who received it, in one respect—it was rather small. He received it in periodical payments on every alternate Monday; but he ran himself out, about a day after the expiration of the first week, as regularly as an eight-day clock; and then, to make the comparison complete, his landlady wound him up, and he went on with a regular tick.

Mr. Watkins Tottle had long lived in a state of single blessedness, as bachelors say, or single cursedness, as spinsters think; but the idea of matrimony had never ceased to haunt him. Wrapt in profound reveries on this never-failing theme, fancy transformed his small parlour in Cecil Street, Strand, into a neat house in the suburbs; the half-hundredweight of coals under the kitchen-stairs suddenly sprang up into three

tons of the best Walls-end ; his small French bedstead was
converted into a regular matrimonial four-poster ; and in the
empty chair on the opposite side of the fireplace, imagination seated a beautiful young lady, with a very little independence or will of her own, and a very large independence
under a will of her father's.

"Who's there ? " inquired Mr. Watkins Tottle, as a gentle
tap at his room-door disturbed these meditations one
evening.

"Tottle, my dear fellow, how *do* you do ? " said a short
elderly gentleman with a gruffish voice, bursting into the
room, and replying to the question by asking another.

"Told you I should drop in some evening," said the short
gentleman, as he delivered his hat into Tottle's hand, after a
little struggling and dodging.

"Delighted to see you, I'm sure," said Mr. Watkins Tottle,
wishing internally that his visitor had "dropped in" to the
Thames at the bottom of the street, instead of dropping into
his parlour.   The fortnight was nearly up, and Watkins was
hard up.

"How is Mrs. Gabriel Parsons ? " inquired Tottle.

"Quite well, thank you," replied Mr. Gabriel Parsons, for
that was the name the short gentleman revelled in.   Here
there was a pause ; the short gentleman looked at the left hob
of the fireplace ; Mr. Watkins Tottle stared vacancy out of
countenance.

"Quite well," repeated the short gentleman, when five
minutes had expired.   "I may say remarkably well."   And
he rubbed the palms of his hands as hard as if he were going
to strike a light by friction.

"What will you take ? " inquired Tottle, with the desperate
suddenness of a man who knew that unless the visitor took
his leave, he stood very little chance of taking anything else.

"Oh, I don't know—have you any whiskey ? "

"Why," replied Tottle, very slowly, for all this was gaining
time, "I *had* some capital, and remarkably strong whiskey
last week ; but it's all gone—and therefore its strength——"

"Is much beyond proof ; or, in other words, impossible to
be proved," said the short gentleman ; and he laughed very
heartily, and seemed quite glad the whiskey had been drunk.
Mr. Tottle smiled—but it was the smile of despair.   When
Mr. Gabriel Parsons had done laughing, he delicately insinuated that, in the absence of whiskey, he would not be

averse to brandy. And Mr. Watkins Tottle, lighting a flat candle very ostentatiously; and displaying an immense key, which belonged to the street-door, but which, for the sake of appearances, occasionally did duty in an imaginary wine-cellar; left the room to entreat his landlady to charge their glasses, and charge them in the bill. The application was successful; the spirits were speedily called—not from the vasty deep, but the adjacent wine-vaults. The two short gentlemen mixed their grog; and then sat cosily down before the fire—a pair of shorts airing themselves.

"Tottle," said Mr. Gabriel Parsons, "you know my way—off-hand, open, say what I mean, mean what I say, hate reserve, and can't bear affectation. One is a bad domino which only hides what good people have about 'em, without making the bad look better; and the other is much about the same thing as pinking a white cotton stocking to make it look like a silk one. Now listen to what I'm going to say."

Here, the little gentleman paused, and took a long pull at his brandy-and-water. Mr. Watkins Tottle took a sip of his, stirred the fire, and assumed an air of profound attention.

"It's of no use humming and ha'ing about the matter," resumed the short gentleman.—"You want to get married."

"Why," replied Mr. Watkins Tottle evasively; for he trembled violently, and felt a sudden tingling throughout his whole frame; "why—I should certainly—at least, I *think* I should like——"

"Won't do," said the short gentleman.—"Plain and free—or there's an end of the matter. Do you want money?"

"You know I do."

"You admire the sex?"

"I do."

"And you'd like to be married?"

"Certainly."

"Then you shall be. There's an end of that." Thus saying, Mr. Gabriel Parsons took a pinch of snuff, and mixed another glass.

"Let me entreat you to be more explanatory," said Tottle. "Really, as the party principally interested, I cannot consent to be disposed of in this way."

"I'll tell you," replied Mr. Gabriel Parsons, warming with the subject, and the brandy-and-water—"I know a lady—she's stopping with my wife now—who is just the thing for you. Well educated; talks French; plays the piano; knows a good deal about flowers, and shells, and all that sort of thing; and has five hundred a year, with an uncontrolled power of disposing of it, by her last will and testament."

"I'll pay my addresses to her," said Mr. Watkins Tottle. "She isn't *very* young—is she?"

"Not very; just the thing for you. I've said that already."

"What coloured hair has the lady?" inquired Mr. Watkins Tottle.

"Egad, I hardly recollect," replied Gabriel, with coolness. "Perhaps I ought to have observed at first, she wears a front."

"A what?" ejaculated Tottle.

"One of those things with curls, along here," said Parsons, drawing a straight line across his forehead, just over his eyes, in illustration of his meaning. "I know the front's black; I can't speak quite positively about her own hair; because, unless one walks behind her, and catches a glimpse of it under her bonnet, one seldom sees it; but I should say that it was *rather* lighter than the front—a shade of a greyish tinge, perhaps."

Mr. Watkins Tottle looked as if he had certain misgivings of mind. Mr. Gabriel Parsons perceived it, and thought it would be safe to begin the next attack without delay.

"Now, were you ever in love, Tottle?" he inquired.

Mr. Watkins Tottle blushed up to the eyes, and down to the chin, and exhibited a most extensive combination of colours as he confessed the soft impeachment.

"I suppose you popped the question more than once when you were a young—I beg your pardon—a younger—man?" said Parsons.

"Never in my life!" replied his friend, apparently indignant at being suspected of such an act. "Never! The fact is that I entertain, as you know, peculiar opinions on these subjects. I am not afraid of ladies, young or old— far from it; but I think that, in compliance with the custom of the present day, they allow too much freedom of speech and manner to marriageable men. Now, the fact is that anything like this easy freedom I never could acquire; and as I am always afraid of going too far, I am generally, I dare say, considered formal and cold."

"I shouldn't wonder if you were," replied Parsons, gravely; "I shouldn't wonder. However, you'll be all right in this case; for the strictness and delicacy of this lady's ideas greatly exceed your own. Lord bless you, why when she came to our house, there was an old portrait of some man or other, with two large black staring eyes, hanging up in her bedroom ; she positively refused to go to bed there, till it was taken down, considering it decidedly wrong."

"I think so, too," said Mr. Watkins Tottle; "certainly."

"And then, the other night—I never laughed so much in my life"—resumed Mr. Gabriel Parsons; "I had driven home in an easterly wind, and caught a devil of a face-ache. Well; as Fanny—that's Mrs. Parsons, you know—and this friend of hers, and I, and Frank Ross, were playing a rubber. I said, jokingly, that when I went to bed I should wrap my head in Fanny's flannel petticoat. She instantly threw up her cards. and left the room."

"Quite right!" said Mr. Watkins Tottle; "she could not possibly have behaved in a more dignified manner. What did you do?"

"Do?—Frank took dummy; and I won sixpence."

"But didn't you apologise for hurting her feelings?"

"Devil a bit. Next morning at breakfast, we talked it over. She contended that any reference to a flannel petti-coat was improper;—men ought not to be supposed to know that such things were. I pleaded my coverture; being a married man."

"And what did the lady say to that?" inquired Tottle, deeply interested.

"Changed her ground, and said that Frank being a single man, its impropriety was obvious."

"Noble-minded creature!" exclaimed the enraptured Tottle.

"Oh! both Fanny and I said, at once, that she was regu-larly cut out for you."

A gleam of placid satisfaction shone on the circular face of Mr. Watkins Tottle, as he heard the prophecy.

"There's one thing I can't understand," said Mr. Gabriel Parsons, as he rose to depart; "I cannot, for the life and soul of me, imagine how the deuce you'll ever contrive to come together. The lady would certainly go into convul-sions if the subject were mentioned." Mr. Gabriel Parsons sat down again, and laughed until he was weak. Tottle owed him money, so he had a perfect right to laugh at Tottle's expense.

Mr. Watkins Tottle feared, in his own mind, that this was another characteristic which he had in common with this modern Lucretia. He, however, accepted the invitation to dine with the Parsonses on the next day but one, with great firmness: and looked forward to the introduction, when again left alone, with tolerable composure.

The sun that rose on the next day but one, had never beheld a sprucer personage on the outside of the Norwood stage, than Mr. Watkins Tottle; and when the coach drew up before a cardboard-looking house with disguised chimneys, and a lawn like a large sheet of green letter-paper, he certainly had never lighted to his place of destination a gentleman who felt more uncomfortable.

The coach stopped, and Mr. Watkins Tottle jumped—we beg his pardon—alighted, with great dignity. "All right!" said he, and away went the coach up the hill with that beautiful equanimity of pace for which "short" stages are generally remarkable.

Mr. Watkins Tottle gave a faltering jerk to the handle of the garden-gate bell. He essayed a more energetic tug, and his previous nervousness was not at all diminished by hearing the bell ringing like a fire alarum.

"Is Mr. Parsons at home?" inquired Tottle of the man who opened the gate. He could hardly hear himself speak, for the bell had not yet done tolling.

"Here I am," shouted a voice on the lawn,—and there was Mr. Gabriel Parsons in a flannel jacket, running backwards and forwards, from a wicket to two hats piled on each other, and from the two hats to the wicket, in the most violent manner, while another gentleman with his coat off was getting down the area of the house, after a ball. When the gentleman without the coat had found it—which he did in less than ten minutes—he ran back to the hats, and Gabriel Parsons pulled up. Then the gentleman without the coat called out "play," very loudly, and bowled. Then Mr. Gabriel Parsons knocked the ball several yards, and took another run. Then the other gentleman aimed at the wicket, and didn't hit it; and Mr. Gabriel Parsons, having finished running on his own account, laid down the bat and ran after the ball, which went into a neighbouring field. They called this cricket.

"Tottle, will you 'go in'?" inquired Mr. Gabriel Parsons, as he approached him, wiping the perspiration off his face.

Mr. Watkins Tottle declined the offer, the bare idea of accepting which made him even warmer than his friend.

"Then we'll go into the house, as it's past four, and I shall have to wash my hands before dinner," said Mr. Gabriel Parsons. "Here, I hate ceremony, you know! Timson, that's Tottle—Tottle, that's Timson; bred for the church, which I fear will never be bread for him;" and he chuckled at the old joke. Mr. Timson bowed carelessly. Mr. Watkins Tottle bowed stiffly. Mr. Gabriel Parsons led the way to the house. He was a rich sugar-baker, who mistook rudeness for honesty, and abrupt bluntness for an open and candid manner; many besides Gabriel mistake bluntness for sincerity.

Mrs. Gabriel Parsons received the visitors most graciously on the steps, and preceded them to the drawing-room. On the sofa, was seated a lady of very prim appearance, and remarkably inanimate. She was one of those persons at whose age it is impossible to make any reasonable guess; her features might have been remarkably pretty when she was younger, and they might always have presented the same appearance. Her complexion—with a slight trace of powder here and there—was as clear as that of a well-made wax doll, and her face as expressive. She was handsomely dressed, and was winding up a gold watch.

"Miss Lillerton, my dear, this is our friend Mr. Watkins Tottle; a very old acquaintance I assure you," said Mrs. Parsons, presenting the Strephon of Cecil Street, Strand. The lady rose, and made a deep curtsey; Mr. Watkins Tottle made a bow.

"Splendid, majestic creature!" thought Tottle.

Mr. Timson advanced, and Mr. Watkins Tottle began to hate him. Men generally discover a rival, instinctively, and Mr. Watkins Tottle felt that his hate was deserved.

"May I beg," said the reverend gentleman,—"May I beg to call upon you, Miss Lillerton, for some trifling donation to my soup, coals, and blanket distribution society?"

"Put my name down for two sovereigns, if you please," responded Miss Lillerton.

"You are truly charitable, madam," said the Reverend Mr. Timson, "and we know that charity will cover a multitude of sins. Let me beg you to understand that I do not say this from the supposition that you have many sins which require palliation; believe me when I say that I never yet met any one who had fewer to atone for, than Miss Lillerton."

Something like a bad imitation of animation lighted up the lady's face as she acknowledged the compliment. Watkins Tottle incurred the sin of wishing that the ashes of the Reverend Charles Timson were quietly deposited in the churchyard of his curacy, wherever it might be.

"I'll tell you what," interrupted Parsons, who had just appeared with clean hands and a black coat, "it's my private opinion, Timson, that your 'distribution society' is rather a humbug."

"You are so severe," replied Timson, with a Christian smile: he disliked Parsons, but liked his dinners.

"So positively unjust!" said Miss Lillerton.

"Certainly," observed Tottle. The lady looked up; her eyes met those of Mr. Watkins Tottle. She withdrew them in a sweet confusion, and Mr. Watkins Tottle did the same —the confusion was mutual.

"Why," urged Mr. Parsons, pursuing his objections, "what on earth is the use of giving a man coals who has nothing to cook, or giving him blankets when he hasn't a bed, or giving him soup when he requires substantial food? —'like sending them ruffles when wanting a shirt.' Why not give 'em a trifle of money, as I do, when I think they deserve it, and let them purchase what they think best? Why?—because your subscribers wouldn't see their names flourishing in print on the church-door—that's the reason."

"Really, Mr. Parsons, I hope you don't mean to insinuate that I wish to see *my* name in print, on the church-door," interrupted Miss Lillerton.

"I hope not," said Mr. Watkins Tottle, putting in another word, and getting another glance.

"Certainly not," replied Parsons. "I dare say you wouldn't mind seeing it in writing, though, in the church register—eh?"

"Register! What register?" inquired the lady, gravely.

"Why, the register of marriages, to be sure," replied Parsons, chuckling at the sally, and glancing at Tottle. Mr. Watkins Tottle thought he should have fainted for shame, and it is quite impossible to imagine what effect the joke would have had upon the lady, if dinner had not been, at that moment, announced. Mr. Watkins Tottle, with an unprecedented effort of gallantry, offered the tip of his little finger; Miss Lillerton accepted it gracefully, with maiden modesty: and they proceeded in due state to the dinner-table, where they were soon deposited side by side. The room was very snug, the dinner very good, and the little party in spirits. The conversation became pretty general, and when Mr. Watkins Tottle had extracted one or two cold observations from his neighbour, and had taken wine with her, he began to acquire confidence rapidly. The cloth was removed; Mrs. Gabriel Parsons drank four glasses of port on the plea of being a nurse just then; and Miss Lillerton took about the same number of sips, on the plea of not wanting any at all. At length, the ladies retired, to the great gratification of Mr. Gabriel Parsons, who had been coughing and frowning at his wife, for half-an-hour previously—signals which Mrs. Parsons never happened to observe, until she had been pressed to take her ordinary quantum, which, to avoid giving trouble, she generally did at once.

"What do you think of her?" inquired Mr. Gabriel Parsons of Mr. Watkins Tottle, in an under-tone.

"I dote on her with enthusiasm already!" replied Mr. Watkins Tottle.

"Gentleman, pray let us drink 'the ladies,'" said the Reverend Mr. Timson.

"The ladies!" said Mr. Watkins Tottle, emptying his glass. In the fulness of his confidence, he felt as if he could make love to a dozen ladies, off-hand.

"Ah!" said Mr. Gabriel Parsons, "I remember when I was a young man—fill your glass, Timson."

"I have this moment emptied it."

"Then fill again."

"I will," said Timson, suiting the action to the word.

"I remember," resumed Mr. Gabriel Parsons, "when I was a younger man, with what a strange compound of feelings I used to drink that toast, and how I used to think every woman was an angel."

"Was that before you were married?" mildly inquired Mr. Watkins Tottle.

"Oh! certainly," replied Mr. Gabriel Parsons. "I have never thought so since; and a precious milksop I must have been, ever to have thought so at all. But, you know, I married Fanny under the oddest and most ridiculous circumstances possible."

"What were they, if one may inquire?" asked Timson, who had heard the story, on an average, twice a week for the last six months. Mr. Watkins Tottle listened attentively, in the hope of picking up some suggestion that might be useful to him in his new undertaking.

"I spent my wedding-night in a back-kitchen chimney," said Parsons, by way of a beginning.

"In a back-kitchen chimney!" ejaculated Watkins Tottle. "How dreadful!"

"Yes, it wasn't very pleasant," replied the small host. "The fact is, Fanny's father and mother liked me well enough as an individual, but had a decided objection to my becoming a husband. You see, I hadn't any money in those days, and they had; and so they wanted Fanny to pick up somebody else. However, we managed to discover the state of each other's affections somehow. I used to meet her at some mutual friends' parties; at first we danced together, and talked, and flirted, and all that sort of thing; then I used to like nothing so well as sitting by her side— we didn't talk so much then, but I remember I used to have a great notion of looking at her out of the extreme corner of my left eye—and then I got very miserable and sentimental, and began to write verses, and use Macassar oil. At last I couldn't bear it any longer, and after I had walked up and down the sunny side of Oxford Street in tight boots for a week—and a devilish hot summer it was too—in the hope of meeting her, I sat down and wrote a letter, and begged her to manage to see me clandestinely, for I wanted to hear her decision from her own mouth. I said I had discovered, to my perfect satisfaction, that I couldn't live without her, and that if she didn't have me, I had made up my mind to take prussic acid, or take to drinking, or emigrate, so as to take myself off in some way or other. Well, I borrowed a pound, and bribed the housemaid to give her the note, which she did."

"And what was the reply?" inquired Timson, who had found, before, that to encourage the repetition of old stories is to get a general invitation.

"Oh, the usual one! Fanny expressed herself very miserable; hinted at the possibility of an early grave; said that nothing should induce her to swerve from the duty she owed her parents; implored me to forget her, and find out somebody more deserving, and all that sort of thing. She said she could, on no account, think of meeting me unknown to her pa and ma; and entreated me, as she should be in

The Courtship of Mr. Parsons

a particular part of Kensington Gardens at eleven o'clock next morning, not to attempt to meet her there."

"You didn't go, of course?" said Watkins Tottle.

"Didn't I?—Of course I did. There she was, with the identical housemaid in perspective, in order that there might be no interruption. We walked about for a couple of hours; made ourselves delightfully miserable; and were regularly engaged. Then, we began to 'correspond'—that is to say, we used to exchange about four letters a day; what we used to say in 'em I can't imagine. And I used to have an interview, in the kitchen, or the cellar, or some such place, every evening. Well, things went on in this way for some time; and we got fonder of each other every day. At last, as our love was raised to such a pitch, and as my salary had been raised too, shortly before, we determined on a secret marriage. Fanny arranged to sleep at a friend's on the previous night; we were to be married early in the morning; and then we were to return to her home and be pathetic. She was to fall at the old gentleman's feet, and bathe his boots with her tears; and I was to hug the old lady and call her 'mother,' and use my pocket-handkerchief as much as possible. Married we were, the next morning; two girls—friends of Fanny's—acting as bridesmaids; and a man, who was hired for five shillings and a pint of porter, officiating as father. Now, the old lady unfortunately put off her return from Ramsgate, where she had been paying a visit, until the next morning; and as we placed great reliance on her, we agreed to postpone our confession for four-and-twenty hours. My newly-made wife returned home, and I spent my wedding-day in strolling about Hampstead Heath, and execrating my father-in-law. Of course, I went to comfort my dear little wife at night, as much as I could, with the assurance that our troubles would soon be over. I opened the garden-gate, of which I had a key, and was shown by the servant to our old place of meeting—a back kitchen, with a stone-floor and a dresser: upon which, in the absence of chairs, we used to sit and make love."

"Make love upon a kitchen-dresser!" interrupted Mr. Watkins Tottle, whose ideas of decorum were greatly outraged.

"Ah! On a kitchen-dresser!" replied Parsons. "And let me tell you, old fellow, that, if you were really over head-and-ears in love, and had no other place to make

love in, you'd be devilish glad to avail yourself of such an
opportunity. However, let me see ;—where was I ? "

" On the dresser," suggested Timson.

" Oh—ah ! Well, here I found poor Fanny, quite disconsolate and uncomfortable. The old boy had been very cross
all day, which made her feel still more lonely ; and she was
quite out of spirits. So I put a good face on the matter,
and laughed it off, and said we should enjoy the pleasures of
a matrimonial life more by contrast ; and, at length, poor
Fanny brightened up a little. I stopped there till about
eleven o'clock, and, just as I was taking my leave for the
fourteenth time, the girl came running down the stairs,
without her shoes, in a great fright, to tell us that the old
villain—Heaven forgive me for calling him so, for he is
dead and gone now !—prompted I suppose by the prince of
darkness, was coming down, to draw his own beer for supper
—a thing he had not done before, for six months, to my
certain knowledge ; for the cask stood in that very back
kitchen. If he discovered me there, explanation would have
been out of the question ; for he was so outrageously violent,
when at all excited, that he never would have listened to
me. There was only one thing to be done. The chimney
was a very wide one ; it had been originally built for an
oven ; went up perpendicularly for a few feet, and then
shot backward and formed a sort of small cavern. My
hopes and fortune—the means of our joint existence almost
—were at stake. I scrambled in like a squirrel ; coiled
myself up in this recess ; and, as Fanny and the girl replaced the deal chimney-board, I could see the light of the
candle which my unconscious father-in-law carried in his
hand. I heard him draw the beer ; and I never heard beer
run so slowly. He was just leaving the kitchen, and I was
preparing to descend, when down came the infernal chimney-board with a tremendous crash. He stopped and put
down the candle and the jug of beer on the dresser ; he was
a nervous old fellow, and any unexpected noise annoyed
him. He coolly observed that the fireplace was never used,
and sending the frightened servant into the next kitchen for
a hammer and nails, actually nailed up the board, and locked
the door on the outside. So there was I, on my wedding-
night, in the light kerseymere trousers, fancy waistcoat, and
blue coat, that I had been married in in the morning, in a
back-kitchen chimney, the bottom of which was nailed up,

and the top of which had been formerly raised some fifteen feet, to prevent the smoke from annoying the neighbours. And there," added Mr. Gabriel Parsons, as he passed the bottle, "there I remained till half-past seven the next morning, when the housemaid's sweetheart, who was a carpenter, unshelled me. The old dog had nailed me up so securely, that, to this very hour, I firmly believe that no one but a carpenter could ever have got me out."

"And what did Mrs. Parsons's father say, when he found you were married?" inquired Watkins Tottle, who, although he never saw a joke, was not satisfied until he heard a story to the very end.

"Why, the affair of the chimney so tickled his fancy, that he pardoned us off-hand, and allowed us something to live on till he went the way of all flesh. I spent the next night in his second-floor front, much more comfortably than I had spent the preceding one; for, as you will probably guess—— "

"Please, sir, missis has made tea," said a middle-aged female servant, bobbing into the room.

"That's the very housemaid that figures in my story," said Mr. Gabriel Parsons. "She went into Fanny's service when we were first married, and has been with us ever since; but I don't think she has felt one atom of respect for me since the morning she saw me released, when she went into violent hysterics, to which she has been subject ever since. Now, shall we join the ladies?"

"If you please," said Mr. Watkins Tottle.

"By all means," added the obsequious Mr. Timson; and the trio made for the drawing-room accordingly.

Tea being concluded, and the toast and cups having been duly handed, and occasionally upset, by Mr. Watkins Tottle. a rubber was proposed. They cut for partners—Mr. and Mrs. Parsons; and Mr. Watkins Tottle and Miss Lillerton. Mr. Timson having conscientious scruples on the subject of card-playing, drank brandy-and-water, and kept up a running spar with Mr. Watkins Tottle. The evening went off well; Mr. Watkins Tottle was in high spirits, having some reason to be gratified with his reception by Miss Lillerton; and before he left, a small party was made up to visit the Beulah Spa on the following Saturday.

"It's all right, I think," said Mr. Gabriel Parsons to Mr. Watkins Tottle as he opened the garden gate for him.

"I hope so," he replied, squeezing his friend's hand.

"You'll be down by the first coach on Saturday," said Mr. Gabriel Parsons.

"Certainly," replied Mr. Watkins Tottle. "Undoubtedly."

But fortune had decreed that Mr. Watkins Tottle should not be down by the first coach on Saturday. His adventures on that day, however, and the success of his wooing, are subjects for another chapter.

CHAPTER THE SECOND

"THE first coach has not come in yet, has it, Tom?" inquired Mr. Gabriel Parsons, as he very complacently paced up and down the fourteen feet of gravel which bordered the "lawn," on the Saturday morning which had been fixed upon for the Beulah Spa jaunt.

"No, sir; I haven't seen it," replied a gardener in a blue apron, who let himself out to do the ornamental for half-a-crown a day and his "keep."

"Time Tottle was down," said Mr. Gabriel Parsons, ruminating—"Oh, here he is, no doubt," added Gabriel, as a cab drove rapidly up the hill; and he buttoned his dressing-gown, and opened the gate to receive the expected visitor. The cab stopped, and out jumped a man in a coarse Petersham great coat, whity-brown neckerchief, faded black suit, gamboge-coloured top-boots, and one of those large-crowned hats, formerly seldom met with, but now very generally patronised by gentlemen and costermongers.

"Mr. Parsons?" said the man, looking at the superscription of a note he held in his hand, and addressing Gabriel with an inquiring air.

" *My* name is Parsons," responded the sugar-baker.

" I've brought this here note," replied the individual in the painted tops, in a hoarse whisper: "I've brought this here note from a gen'lm'n as come to our house this mornin'."

"I expected the gentleman at my house," said Parsons, as he broke the seal, which bore the impression of her Majesty's profile as it is seen on a sixpence.

" I've no doubt the gen'lm'n would ha' been here," replied the stranger, "if he hadn't happened to call at our house first; but we never trusts no gen'lm'n furder nor we can see him—no mistake about that there"—added the unknown, with a facetious grin; "beg your pardon, sir, no offence meant, only—once in, and I wish you may—catch the idea, sir?"

Mr. Gabriel Parsons was not remarkable for catching anything suddenly, but a cold. He therefore only bestowed a glance of profound astonishment on his mysterious companion, and proceeded to unfold the note of which he had been the bearer. Once opened and the idea was caught with very little difficulty. Mr. Watkins Tottle had been suddenly arrested for 33*l*. 10*s*. 4*d*., and dated his communication from a lock-up house in the vicinity of Chancery Lane.

"Unfortunate affair this!" said Parsons, refolding the note.

"Oh! nothin' ven you're used to it," coolly observed the man in the Petersham.

"Tom!" exclaimed Parsons, after a few minutes' consideration, "just put the horse in, will you?—Tell the gentleman that I shall be there almost as soon as you are," he continued, addressing the sheriff-officer's Mercury.

"Werry well," replied that important functionary; adding, in a confidential manner, "I'd adwise the gen'lm'n's friends to settle. You see it's a mere trifle; and, unless the gen'lm'n means to go up afore the court, it's hardly worth while waiting for detainers, you know. Our governor's wide awake, he is. I'll never say nothin' agin him, nor no man; but he knows what's o'clock, he does, uncommon." Having delivered this eloquent, and, to Parsons, particularly intelligible harangue, the meaning of which was eked out by divers nods and winks, the gentleman in the boots reseated himself in the cab, which went rapidly off, and was soon out of sight. Mr. Gabriel Parsons continued to pace up and down the pathway for some minutes, apparently absorbed in deep meditation. The result of his cogitations seemed to be perfectly satisfactory to himself, for he ran briskly into the house; said that business had suddenly summoned him to town; that he had desired the messenger to inform Mr. Watkins Tottle of the fact; and that they would return together to dinner. He then hastily equipped himself for a drive, and mounting his gig, was soon on his way to the establishment of Mr. Solomon Jacobs, situate (as Mr. Watkins Tottle had informed him), in Cursitor Street, Chancery Lane.

When a man is in a violent hurry to get on, and has

a specific object in view, the attainment of which depends on
the completion of his journey, the difficulties which interpose
themselves in his way appear not only to be innumerable,
but to have been called into existence especially for the
occasion.   The remark is by no means a new one, and Mr.
Gabriel Parsons had practical and painful experience of its
justice in the course of his drive.   There are three classes of
animated objects which prevent your driving with any degree
of comfort or celerity through streets which are but little
frequented—they are pigs, children, and old women.   On
the occasion we are describing, the pigs were luxuriating on
cabbage-stalks, and the shuttlecocks fluttered from the little
deal battledores, and the children played in the road; and
women, with a basket in one hand, and the street-door key
in the other, *would* cross just before the horse's head, until
Mr. Gabriel Parsons was perfectly savage with vexation, and
quite hoarse with hoi-ing and imprecating.   Then, when he
got into Fleet Street, there was "a stoppage," in which people
in vehicles have the satisfaction of remaining stationary for
half an hour, and envying the slowest pedestrians; and where
policemen rush about, and seize hold of horses' bridles, and
back them into shop-windows, by way of clearing the road
and preventing confusion.   At length Mr. Gabriel Parsons
turned into Chancery Lane, and having inquired for, and
been directed to Cursitor Street (for it was a locality of
which he was quite ignorant), he soon found himself opposite
the house of Mr. Solomon Jacobs.   Confiding his horse
and gig to the care of one of the fourteen boys who had
followed him from the other side of Blackfriars Bridge on
the chance of his requiring their services, Mr. Gabriel Parsons
crossed the road and knocked at an inner door, the upper
part of which was of glass, grated like the windows of this
inviting mansion with iron bars—painted white to look
comfortable.

The knock was answered by a sallow-faced, red-haired, sulky
boy, who, after surveying Mr. Gabriel Parsons through the
glass, applied a large key to an immense wooden excrescence,
which was in reality a lock, but which, taken in conjunction
with the iron nails with which the panels were studded,
gave the door the appearance of being subject to warts.

"I want to see Mr. Watkins Tottle," said Parsons.

"It's the gentleman that come in this morning, Jem,"
screamed a voice from the top of the kitchen-stairs, which

belonged to a dirty woman who had just brought her chin to a level with the passage-floor. "The gentleman's in the coffee-room."

"Up-stairs, sir," said the boy, just opening the door wide enough to let Parsons in without squeezing him, and double-locking it the moment he had made his way through the aperture—"First floor—door on the left."

Mr. Gabriel Parsons thus instructed, ascended the uncarpeted and ill-lighted staircase, and after giving several subdued taps at the before-mentioned "door on the left," which were rendered inaudible by the hum of voices within the room, and the hissing noise attendant on some frying operations which were carrying on below stairs, turned the handle, and entered the apartment. Being informed that the unfortunate object of his visit had just gone up-stairs to write a letter, he had leisure to sit down and observe the scene before him.

The room—which was a small, confined den—was partitioned off into boxes, like the common-room of some inferior eating-house. The dirty floor had evidently been as long a stranger to the scrubbing-brush as to carpet or floor-cloth: and the ceiling was completely blackened by the flare of the oil-lamp by which the room was lighted at night. The grey ashes on the edges of the tables, and the cigar ends which were plentifully scattered about the dusty grate, fully accounted for the intolerable smell of tobacco which pervaded the place; and the empty glasses and half-saturated slices of lemon on the tables, together with the porter pots beneath them, bore testimony to the frequent libations in which the individuals who honoured Mr. Solomon Jacobs by a temporary residence in his house indulged. Over the mantel-shelf was a paltry looking-glass, extending about half the width of the chimney-piece; but by way of counterpoise, the ashes were confined by a rusty fender about twice as long as the hearth.

From this cheerful room itself, the attention of Mr. Gabriel Parsons was naturally directed to its inmates. In one of the boxes two men were playing at cribbage with a very dirty pack of cards, some with blue, some with green, and some with red backs—selections from decayed packs. The cribbage-board had been long ago formed on the table by some ingenious visitor with the assistance of a pocket-knife and a two-pronged fork, with which the necessary number of holes had been made in the table at proper distances for the reception of the wooden pegs. In another box a stout, hearty-looking man, of about forty, was eating some dinner which his wife—an equally comfortable-looking personage—had brought him in a basket: and in a third, a genteel-looking young man was talking earnestly, and in a low tone, to a young female, whose face was concealed by a thick veil, but whom Mr. Gabriel Parsons immediately set down in his own mind as the debtor's wife. A young fellow of vulgar manners, dressed in the very extreme of the prevailing fashion, was pacing up and down the room, with a lighted cigar in his mouth and his hands in his pockets, ever and anon puffing forth volumes of smoke, and occasionally applying, with much apparent relish, to a pint pot, the contents of which were "chilling" on the hob.

"Fourpence more, by gum!" exclaimed one of the cribbage-players, lighting a pipe, and addressing his adversary at the close of the game; "one 'ud think you'd got luck in a pepper-cruet, and shook it out when you wanted it."

"Well, that a'n't a bad un," replied the other, who was a horse-dealer from Islington.

"No; I'm blessed if it is," interposed the jolly-looking fellow, who, having finished his dinner, was drinking out of the same glass as his wife, in truly conjugal harmony, some hot gin-and-water. The faithful partner of his cares had brought a plentiful supply of the anti-temperance fluid in a large flat stone bottle, which looked like a half-gallon jar that had been successfully tapped for the dropsy. "You're a rum chap, you are, Mr. Walker—will you dip your beak into this, sir?"

"Thank'ee, sir," replied Mr. Walker, leaving his box, and advancing to the other to accept the proffered glass. "Here's your health, sir, and your good 'ooman's here. Gentlemen all—yours, and better luck still. Well, Mr. Willis," continued the facetious prisoner, addressing the young man with the cigar, "you seem rather down to-day—floored, as one may say. What's the matter, sir? Never say die, you know."

"Oh! I'm all right," replied the smoker. "I shall be bailed out to-morrow."

"Shall you, though?" inquired the other. "Damme, I wish I could say the same. I am as regularly over head and ears as the Royal George, and stand about as much chance of being *bailed out*. Ha! ha! ha!"

"Why," said the young man, stopping short, and speaking

The Lock-Up House

in a very loud key, "look at me. What d'ye think I've stopped here two days for?"

"'Cause you couldn't get out, I suppose," interrupted Mr. Walker, winking to the company. "Not that you're exactly obliged to stop here, only you can't help it. No compulsion, you know, only you must—eh?"

"A'n't he a rum un?" inquired the delighted individual, who had offered the gin-and-water, of his wife.

"Oh, he just is!" replied the lady, who was quite overcome by these flashes of imagination.

"Why, my case," frowned the victim, throwing the end of his cigar into the fire, and illustrating his argument by knocking the bottom of the pot on the table, at intervals,— "my case is a very singular one. My father's a man of large property, and I am his son."

"That's a very strange circumstance!" interrupted the jocose Mr. Walker, en passant.

"—I am his son, and have received a liberal education. I don't owe no man nothing—not the value of a farthing, but I was induced, you see, to put my name to some bills for a friend—bills to a large amount, I may say a very large amount, for which I didn't receive no consideration. What's the consequence?"

"Why, I suppose the bills went out, and you came in. The acceptances weren't taken up, and you were, eh?" inquired Walker.

"To be sure," replied the liberally educated young gentleman. "To be sure; and so here I am, locked up for a matter of twelve hundred pound."

"Why don't you ask your old governor to stump up?" inquired Walker, with a somewhat sceptical air.

"Oh! bless you, he'd never do it," replied the other, in a tone of expostulation—"Never!"

"Well, it is very odd to—be—sure," interposed the owner of the flat bottle, mixing another glass, "but I've been in difficulties, as one may say, now for thirty year. I went to pieces when I was in a milk-walk, thirty year ago; arterwards, when I was a fruiterer, and kept a spring wan; and arter that again in the coal and 'tatur line—but all that time I never see a youngish chap come into a place of this kind, who wasn't going out again directly, and who hadn't been arrested on bills which he'd given a friend and for which he'd received nothing whatsomever—not a fraction."

"Oh! it's always the cry," said Walker. "I can't see the use on it; that's what makes me so wild. Why, I should have a much better opinion of an individual, if he'd say at once in an honourable and gentlemanly manner as he'd done everybody he possibly could."

"Aye, to be sure," interposed the horse-dealer, with whose notions of bargain and sale the axiom perfectly coincided, "so should I."

The young gentlemen, who had given rise to these observations, was on the point of offering a rather angry reply to these sneers, but the rising of the young man before noticed, and of the female who had been sitting by him, to leave the room, interrupted the conversation. She had been weeping bitterly, and the noxious atmosphere of the room acting upon her excited feelings and delicate frame, rendered the support of her companion necessary as they quitted it together.

There was an air of superiority about them both, and something in their appearance so unusual in such a place, that a respectful silence was observed until the *whirr—r— bang* of the spring door announced that they were out of hearing. It was broken by the wife of the ex-fruiterer.

"Poor creetur!" said she, quenching a sigh in a rivulet of gin-and-water. "She's very young."

"She's a nice-looking 'ooman too," added the horse-dealer.

"What's he in for, Ikey?" inquired Walker, of an individual who was spreading a cloth with numerous blotches of mustard upon it, on one of the tables, and whom Mr. Gabriel Parsons had no difficulty in recognising as the man who had called upon him in the morning.

"Vy," responded the factotum, "it's one of the rummiest rigs you ever heard on. He come in here last Vensday, which by-the-bye he's a-going over the water to-night—hows'ever that's neither here nor there. You see I've been a-going back'ards and for'ards about his business, and ha' managed to pick up some of his story from the servants and them; and so far as I can make it out, it seems to be summat to this here effect —— "

"Cut it short, old fellow," interrupted Walker, who knew from former experience that he of the top-boots was neither very concise nor intelligible in his narratives.

"Let me alone," replied Ikey, "and I'll ha' vound up, and made my lucky in five seconds. This here young gen'lm'n's father—so I'm told, mind ye—and the father o' the young voman, have always been on very bad, out-and-out, rig'lar knock-me-down sort o' terms; but somehow or another, ven he vos a-wisitin' at some gentlefolk's house, as he knowed at college, he came into contract with the young lady. He seed her several times, and then he up and said he'd keep company vith her, if so be as she vos agreeable. Vell, she vos as sweet upon him as he vos upon her, and so I s'pose they made it all right; for they got married 'bout six months arterwards, unbeknown, mind ye, to the two fathers—leastways so I'm told. When they heard on it—my eyes, there vos such a combustion! Starvation vos the very least that vos to be done to 'em. The young gen'lm'n's father cut him off vith a bob, 'cos he'd cut himself off vith a wife; and the young lady's father he behaved even worser and more unnat'ral, for he not only blow'd her up dreadful, and swore he'd never see her again, but he employed a chap as I knows—and as you knows, Mr. Valker, a precious sight too well—to go about and buy up the bills and them things on which the young husband, thinking his governor 'ud come round agin, had raised the vind just to blow himself on vith for a time; besides vich, he made all the interest he could to set other people agin him. Consequence vos, that he paid as long as he could : but things he never expected to have to meet till he'd had time to turn himself round, come fast upon him, and he vos nabbed. He vos brought here, as I said afore, last Vensday, and I think there's about—ah, half-a-dozen detainers agin him down-stairs now. I have been," added Ikey, "in the purfession these fifteen year, and I never met vith such windictive-ness afore!"

"Poor creeturs!" exclaimed the coal-dealer's wife once more: again resorting to the same excellent prescription for nipping a sigh in the bud. "Ah! when they've seen as much trouble as I and my old man here have, they'll be as comfortable under it as we are."

"The young lady's a pretty creature," said Walker, "only she's a little too delicate for my taste—there ain't enough of her. As to the young cove, he may be very respectable and what not, but he's too down in the mouth for me—he ain't game."

"Game!" exclaimed Ikey, who had been altering the position of a green-handled knife and fork at least a dozen times, in order that he might remain in the room under the pretext of having something to do. "He's game enough ven

there's anything to be fierce about; but who could be game
as you call it, Mr. Walker, with a pale young creetur like
that, hanging about him?—It's enough to drive any man's
heart into his boots to see 'em together—and no mistake at
all about it. I never shall forget her first comin' here; he
wrote to her on the Thursday to come—I know he did, 'cos
I took the letter. Uncommon fidgety he vos all day to be
sure, and in the evening he goes down into the office, and
he says to Jacobs, says he, 'Sir, can I have the loan of a
private room for a few minutes this evening, without in-
curring any additional expense—just to see my wife in?'
says he. Jacobs looked as much as to say—'Strike me
bountiful if you ain't one of the modest sort!' but as the
gen'lm'n who had been in the back parlour had just gone out,
and had paid for it for that day, he says—werry grave—'Sir,'
says he, 'it's agin our rules to let private rooms to our lodgers
on gratis terms, but,' says he, 'for a gentleman, I don't mind
breaking through them for once.' So then he turns round
to me, and says, 'Ikey, put two mould candles in the back
parlour, and charge 'em to this gen'lm'n's account, vich I did.
Vell, by-and-bye a hackney-coach comes up to the door, and
there, sure enough, vos the young lady, wrapped up in a
hopera-cloak, as it might be, and all alone. I opened the
gate that night, so I went up ven the coach come, and he
vos a-waitin' at the parlour door—and wasn't he a-trembling,
neither? The poor creetur see him, and could hardly walk
to meet him. 'Oh, Harry!' she says, 'that it should have
come to this; and all for my sake,' says she, putting her
hand upon his shoulder. So he puts his arm round her
pretty little waist, and leading her gently a little way into
the room, so that he might be able to shut the door, he says,
so kind and soft-like—'Why, Kate,' says he——"

"Here's the gentleman you want," said Ikey, abruptly
breaking off in his story, and introducing Mr. Gabriel
Parsons to the crest-fallen Watkins Tottle, who at that
moment entered the room. Watkins advanced with a
wooden expression of passive endurance, and accepted the
hand which Mr. Gabriel Parsons held out.

"I want to speak to you," said Gabriel, with a look
strongly expressive of his dislike of the company.

"This way," replied the imprisoned one, leading the way
to the front drawing-room, where rich debtors did the
luxurious at the rate of a couple of guineas a day.

"Well, here I am," said Mr. Watkins, as he sat down on the sofa ; and placing the palms of his hands on his knees, anxiously glanced at his friend's countenance.

"Yes ; and here you're likely to be," said Gabriel, coolly, as he rattled the money in his unmentionable pockets, and looked out of the window.

"What's the amount with the costs ? " inquired Parsons, after an awkward pause.

"37l. 3s. 10d."

"Have you any money? "

"Nine and sixpence halfpenny."

Mr. Gabriel Parsons walked up and down the room for a few seconds, before he could make up his mind to disclose the plan he had formed; he was accustomed to drive hard bargains, but was always most anxious to conceal his avarice. At length he stopped short, and said, "Tottle, you owe me fifty pounds."

"I do."

"And from all I see, I infer that you are likely to owe it to me."

"I fear I am."

"Though you have every disposition to pay me if you could? "

"Certainly."

"Then," said Mr. Gabriel Parsons, "listen: here's my proposition. You know my way of old. Accept it—yes or no—I will or I won't. I'll pay the debt and costs, and I'll lend you 10l. more (which, added to your annuity, will enable you to carry on the war well) if you'll give me your note of hand to pay me one hundred and fifty pounds within six months after you are married to Miss Lillerton."

"My dear—— "

"Stop a minute—on one condition ; and that is, that you propose to Miss Lillerton at once."

"At once ! My dear Parsons, consider."

"It's for you to consider, not me. She knows you well from reputation, though she did not know you personally until lately. Notwithstanding all her maiden modesty, I think she'd be devilish glad to get married out of hand with as little delay as possible. My wife has sounded her on the subject, and she has confessed."

"What—what ? " eagerly interrupted the enamoured Watkins.

"Why," replied Parsons, "to say exactly what she has confessed, would be rather difficult, because they only spoke in hints, and so forth; but my wife, who is no bad judge in these cases, declared to me that what she had confessed was as good as to say that she was not insensible of your merits —in fact, that no other man should have her."

Mr. Watkins Tottle rose hastily from his seat, and rang the bell.

"What's that for?" inquired Parsons.

"I want to send the man for the bill stamp," replied Mr. Watkins Tottle.

"Then you've made up your mind?"

"I have,"—and they shook hands most cordially. The note of hand was given—the debt and costs were paid—Ikey was satisfied for his trouble, and the two friends soon found themselves on that side of Mr. Solomon Jacobs's establishment, on which most of his visitors were very happy when they found themselves once again—to wit, the *out*side.

"Now," said Mr. Gabriel Parsons, as they drove to Norwood together—"you shall have an opportunity to make the disclosure to-night, and mind you speak out, Tottle."

"I will—I will!" replied Watkins, valorously.

"How I should like to see you together," ejaculated Mr. Gabriel Parsons.—"What fun!" and he laughed so long and so loudly, that he disconcerted Mr. Watkins Tottle, and frightened the horse.

"There's Fanny and your intended walking about on the lawn," said Gabriel, as they approached the house. "Mind your eye, Tottle."

"Never fear," replied Watkins, resolutely, as he made his way to the spot where the ladies were walking.

"Here's Mr. Tottle, my dear," said Mrs. Parsons, addressing Miss Lillerton. The lady turned quickly round, and acknowledged his courteous salute with the same sort of confusion that Watkins had noticed on their first interview, but with something like a slight expression of disappointment or carelessness.

"Did you see how glad she was to see you?" whispered Parsons to his friend.

"Why I really thought she looked as if she would rather have seen somebody else," replied Tottle.

"Pooh, nonsense!" whispered Parsons again—"it's always the way with the women, young or old. They never show

how delighted they are to see those whose presence makes their hearts beat. It's the way with the whole sex, and no man should have lived to your time of life without knowing it. Fanny confessed it to me, when we were first married, over and over again—see what it is to have a wife."

"Certainly," whispered Tottle, whose courage was vanishing fast.

"Well, now, you'd better begin to pave the way," said Parsons, who, having invested some money in the speculation, assumed the office of director.

"Yes, yes, I will—presently," replied Tottle, greatly flurried.

"Say something to her, man," urged Parsons again. "Confound it! pay her a compliment, can't you?"

"No! not till after dinner," replied the bashful Tottle, anxious to postpone the evil moment.

"Well, gentlemen," said Mrs. Parsons, "you are really very polite; you stay away the whole morning, after promising to take us out, and when you do come home, you stand whispering together and take no notice of us."

"We were talking of the *business*, my dear, which detained us this morning," replied Parsons, looking significantly at Tottle.

"Dear me! how very quickly the morning has gone," said Miss Lillerton, referring to the gold watch, which was wound up on state occasions, whether it required it or not.

"*I* think it has passed very slowly," mildly suggested Tottle.

("That's right—bravo!") whispered Parsons.

"Indeed!" said Miss Lillerton, with an air of majestic surprise.

"I can only impute it to my unavoidable absence from your society, madam," said Watkins, "and that of Mrs. Parsons."

During this short dialogue the ladies had been leading the way to the house.

"What the deuce did you stick Fanny into that last compliment for?" inquired Parsons, as they followed together; "it quite spoilt the effect."

"Oh! it really would have been too broad without," replied Watkins Tottle, "much too broad!"

"He's mad!" Parsons whispered his wife, as they entered the drawing-room, "mad from modesty."

"Dear me!" ejaculated the lady, "I never heard of such a thing."

"You'll find we have quite a family dinner, Mr. Tottle," said Mrs. Parsons, when they sat down to table: "Miss Lillerton is one of us, and, of course, we make no stranger of you."

Mr. Watkins Tottle expressed a hope that the Parsons family never would make a stranger of him; and wished internally that his bashfulness would allow him to feel a little less like a stranger himself.

"Take off the covers, Martha," said Mrs. Parsons, directing the shifting of the scenery with great anxiety. The order was obeyed, and a pair of boiled fowls, with tongue and et ceteras, were displayed at the top, and a fillet of veal at the bottom. On one side of the table two green sauce-tureens, with ladles of the same, were setting to each other in a green dish; and on the other was a curried rabbit, in a brown suit, turned up with lemon.

"Miss Lillerton, my dear," said Mrs. Parsons, "shall I assist you?"

"Thank you, no; I think I'll trouble Mr. Tottle."

Watkins started—trembled—helped the rabbit—and broke a tumbler. The countenance of the lady of the house, which had been all smiles previously, underwent an awful change.

"Extremely sorry," stammered Watkins, assisting himself to currie and parsley and butter, in the extremity of his confusion.

"Not the least consequence," replied Mrs. Parsons, in a tone which implied that it was of the greatest consequence possible,—directing aside the researches of the boy, who was groping under the table for the bits of broken glass.

"I presume," said Miss Lillerton, "that Mr. Tottle is aware of the interest which bachelors usually pay in such cases; a dozen glasses for one is the lowest penalty."

Mr. Gabriel Parsons gave his friend an admonitory tread on the toe. Here was a clear hint that the sooner he ceased to be a bachelor and emancipated himself from such penalties, the better. Mr. Watkins Tottle viewed the observation in the same light, and challenged Mrs. Parsons to take wine, with a degree of presence of mind which, under all the circumstances, was really extraordinary.

"Miss Lillerton," said Gabriel, "may I have the pleasure?"

Mr. Watkins Tottle and Miss Lillerton
(*p.* 460)

"I shall be most happy."

"Tottle, will you assist Miss Lillerton, and pass the decanter. Thank you." (The usual pantomimic ceremony of nodding and sipping gone through)—

"Tottle, were you ever in Suffolk?" inquired the master of the house, who was burning to tell one of his seven stock stories.

"No," responded Watkins, adding, by way of a saving clause, "but I've been in Devonshire."

"Ah!" replied Gabriel, "it was in Suffolk that a rather singular circumstance happened to me many years ago. Did you ever happen to hear me mention it?"

Mr. Watkins Tottle *had* happened to hear his friend mention it some four hundred times. Of course he expressed great curiosity, and evinced the utmost impatience to hear the story again. Mr. Gabriel Parsons forthwith attempted to proceed, in spite of the interruptions to which, as our readers must frequently have observed, the master of the house is often exposed in such cases. We will attempt to give them an idea of our meaning.

"When I was in Suffolk——" said Mr. Gabriel Parsons.

"Take off the fowls first, Martha," said Mrs. Parsons. "I beg your pardon, my dear."

"When I was in Suffolk," resumed Mr. Parsons, with an impatient glance at his wife, who pretended not to observe it, "which is now some years ago, business led me to the town of Bury St. Edmund's. I had to stop at the principal places in my way, and therefore, for the sake of convenience, I travelled in a gig. I left Sudbury one dark night—it was winter time—about nine o'clock; the rain poured in torrents, the wind howled among the trees that skirted the roadside, and I was obliged to proceed at a foot-pace, for I could hardly see my hand before me, it was so dark——"

"John," interrupted Mrs. Parsons, in a low, hollow voice, "don't spill that gravy."

"Fanny," said Parsons impatiently, "I wish you'd defer these domestic reproofs to some more suitable time. Really, my dear, these constant interruptions are very annoying."

"My dear, I didn't interrupt you," said Mrs. Parsons.

"But, my dear, you *did* interrupt me," remonstrated Mr. Parsons.

"How very absurd you are, my love! I must give directions to the servants; I am quite sure that if I sat here and allowed John to spill the gravy over the new carpet, you'd be the first to find fault when you saw the stain to-morrow morning."

"Well," continued Gabriel, with a resigned air, as if he knew there was no getting over the point about the carpet, "I was just saying, it was so dark that I could hardly see my hand before me. The road was very lonely, and I assure you, Tottle (this was a device to arrest the wandering attention of that individual, which was distracted by a confidential communication between Mrs. Parsons and Martha, accompanied by the delivery of a large bunch of keys), I assure you, Tottle, I became somehow impressed with a sense of the loneliness of my situation——"

"Pie to your master," interrupted Mrs. Parsons, again directing the servant.

"Now, pray, my dear," remonstrated Parsons once more, very pettishly. Mrs. P. turned up her hands and eyebrows, and appealed in dumb show to Miss Lillerton. "As I turned a corner of the road," resumed Gabriel, "the horse stopped short, and reared tremendously. · I pulled up, jumped out, ran to his head, and found a man lying on his back in the middle of the road, with his eyes fixed on the sky. I thought he was dead; but no, he was alive, and there appeared to be nothing the matter with him. He jumped up, and putting his hand to his chest, and fixing upon me the most earnest gaze you can imagine, exclaimed——"

"Pudding here," said Mrs. Parsons.

"Oh! it's no use," exclaimed the host, now rendered desperate. "Here, Tottle; a glass of wine. It's useless to attempt relating anything when Mrs. Parsons is present."

This attack was received in the usual way. Mrs. Parsons talked *to* Miss Lillerton and *at* her better half; expatiated on the impatience of men generally; hinted that her husband was peculiarly vicious in this respect, and wound up by insinuating that she must be one of the best tempers that ever existed, or she never could put up with it. Really what she had to endure sometimes, was more than any one who saw her in every-day life could by possibility suppose. —The story was now a painful subject, and therefore Mr. Parsons declined to enter into any details, and contented himself by stating that the man was a maniac, who had escaped from a neighbouring mad-house.

The cloth was removed; the ladies soon afterwards retired, and Miss Lillerton played the piano in the drawing-room overhead, very loudly, for the edification of the visitor. Mr. Watkins Tottle and Mr. Gabriel Parsons sat chatting comfortably enough, until the conclusion of the second bottle, when the latter, in proposing an adjournment to the drawing-room, informed Watkins that he had concerted a plan with his wife for leaving him and Miss Lillerton alone, soon after tea.

"I say," said Tottle, as they went up-stairs, "don't you think it would be better if we put it off till—till—to-morrow?"

"Don't *you* think it would have been much better if I had left you in that wretched hole I found you in this morning?" retorted Parsons bluntly.

"Well—well—I only made a suggestion," said poor Watkins Tottle, with a deep sigh.

Tea was soon concluded, and Miss Lillerton, drawing a small work-table on one side of the fire, and placing a little wooden frame upon it, something like a miniature clay-mill without the horse, was soon busily engaged in making a watch-guard with brown silk.

"God bless me!" exclaimed Parsons, starting up with well-feigned surprise, "I've forgotten those confounded letters. Tottle, I know you'll excuse me."

If Tottle had been a free agent, he would have allowed no one to leave the room on any pretence, except himself. As it was, however, he was obliged to look cheerful when Parsons quitted the apartment.

He had scarcely left, when Martha put her head into the room, with—"Please, ma'am, you're wanted."

Mrs. Parsons left the room, shut the door carefully after her, and Mr. Watkins Tottle was left alone with Miss Lillerton.

For the first five minutes there was a dead silence.—Mr. Watkins Tottle was thinking how he should begin, and Miss Lillerton appeared to be thinking of nothing. The fire was burning low; Mr. Watkins Tottle stirred it, and put some coals on.

"Hem!" coughed Miss Lillerton; Mr. Watkins Tottle thought the fair creature had spoken. "I beg your pardon," said he.

"Eh?"

"I thought you spoke."

"No."

"Oh!"

"There are some books on the sofa, Mr. Tottle, if you would like to look at them," said Miss Lillerton, after the lapse of another five minutes.

"No, thank you," returned Watkins; and then he added, with a courage which was perfectly astonishing, even to himself, "Madam, that is Miss Lillerton, I wish to speak to you."

"To me!" said Miss Lillerton, letting the silk drop from her hands, and sliding her chair back a few paces.—"Speak —to me!"

"To you, madam—and on the subject of the state of your affections." The lady hastily rose and would have left the room; but Mr. Watkins Tottle gently detained her by the hand, and holding it as far from him as the joint length of their arms would permit, he thus proceeded: "Pray do not misunderstand me, or suppose that I am led to address you, after so short an acquaintance, by any feeling of my own merits—for merits I have none which could give me a claim to your hand. I hope you will acquit me of any presumption when I explain that I have been acquainted, through Mrs. Parsons, with the state—that is, that Mrs. Parsons has told me—at least, not Mrs. Parsons, but——" here Watkins began to wander, but Miss Lillerton relieved him.

"Am I to understand, Mr. Tottle, that Mrs. Parsons has acquainted you with my feeling—my affection—I mean my respect, for an individual of the opposite sex?"

"She has."

"Then, what?" inquired Miss Lillerton, averting her face, with a girlish air, "what could induce *you* to seek such an interview as this? What can your object be? How can I promote your happiness, Mr. Tottle?"

Here was the time for a flourish—"By allowing me," replied Watkins, falling bump on his knees, and breaking two brace-buttons and a waistcoat-string, in the act—"By allowing me to be your slave, your servant—in short, by unreservedly making me the confidant of your heart's feelings —may I say for the promotion of your own happiness—may I say, in order that you may become the wife of a kind and affectionate husband?"

"Disinterested creature!" exclaimed Miss Lillerton, hiding her face in a white pocket-handkerchief with an eyelet-hole border.

Mr. Watkins Tottle thought that if the lady knew all, she might possibly alter her opinion on this last point. He raised the tip of her middle finger ceremoniously to his lips, and got off his knees as gracefully as he could. "My information was correct?" he tremulously inquired, when he was once more on his feet.

"It was." Watkins elevated his hands, and looked up to the ornament in the centre of the ceiling, which had been made for a lamp, by way of expressing his rapture.

"Our situation, Mr. Tottle," resumed the lady, glancing at him through one of the eyelet-holes, " is a most peculiar and delicate one."

"It is," said Mr. Tottle.

"Our acquaintance has been of *so* short duration," said Miss Lillerton.

"Only a week," assented Watkins Tottle.

"Oh! more than that," exclaimed the lady, in a tone of surprise.

"Indeed!" said Tottle.

"More than a month—more than two months!" said Miss Lillerton.

"Rather odd, this," thought Watkins.

"Oh!" he said, recollecting Parsons's assurance that she had known him from report, "I understand. But, my dear madam, pray consider. The longer this acquaintance has existed, the less reason is there for delay now. Why not at once fix a period for gratifying the hopes of your devoted admirer?"

"It has been represented to me again and again that this is the course I ought to pursue," replied Miss Lillerton, "but pardon my feelings of delicacy, Mr. Tottle—pray excuse this embarrassment—I have peculiar ideas on such subjects, and I am quite sure that I never could summon up fortitude enough to name the day to my future husband."

"Then allow *me* to name it," said Tottle eagerly.

"I should like to fix it myself," replied Miss Lillerton, bashfully, "but I cannot do so without at once resorting to a third party."

"A third party!" thought Watkins Tottle; "who the deuce is that to be, I wonder!"

"Mr. Tottle," continued Miss Lillerton, "you have made me a most disinterested and kind offer—that offer I accept. Will you at once be the bearer of a note from me to—to Mr. Timson?"

"Mr. Timson!" said Watkins.

"After what has passed between us," responded Miss Lillerton, still averting her head, "you must understand whom I mean; Mr. Timson, the—the—clergyman."

"Mr. Timson, the clergyman!" ejaculated Watkins Tottle, in a state of inexpressible beatitude, and positive wonder at his own success. "Angel! Certainly—this moment!"

"I'll prepare it immediately," said Miss Lillerton, making for the door; "the events of this day have flurried me so much, Mr. Tottle, that I shall not leave my room again this evening; I will send you the note by the servant."

"Stay,—stay," cried Watkins Tottle, still keeping a most respectful distance from the lady; "when shall we meet again?"

"Oh! Mr. Tottle," replied Miss Lillerton, coquettishly, "when *we* are married, I can never see you too often, nor thank you too much;" and she left the room.

Mr. Watkins Tottle flung himself into an arm-chair, and indulged in the most delicious reveries of future bliss, in which the idea of "Five hundred pounds per annum, with an uncontrolled power of disposing of it by her last will and testament," was somehow or other the foremost. He had gone through the interview so well, and it had terminated so admirably, that he almost began to wish he had expressly stipulated for the settlement of the annual five hundred on himself.

"May I come in?" said Mr. Gabriel Parsons, peeping in at the door.

"You may," replied Watkins.

"Well, have you done it?" anxiously inquired Gabriel.

"Have I done it!" said Watkins Tottle. "Hush—I'm going to the clergyman."

"No!" said Parsons. "How well you have managed it!"

"Where does Timson live?" inquired Watkins.

"At his uncle's," replied Gabriel, "just round the lane. He's waiting for a living, and has been assisting his uncle here for the last two or three months. But how well you have done it—I didn't think you could have carried it off so!"

Mr. Watkins Tottle was proceeding to demonstrate that the Richardsonian principle was the best on which love could possibly be made, when he was interrupted by the entrance of Martha, with a little pink note folded like a fancy cocked-hat.

"Miss Lillerton's compliments," said Martha, as she delivered it into Tottle's hands, and vanished.

"Do you observe the delicacy?" said Tottle, appealing to Mr. Gabriel Parsons. "*Compliments*, not *love*, by the servant, eh?"

Mr. Gabriel Parsons didn't exactly know what reply to make, so he poked the forefinger of his right hand between the third and fourth ribs of Mr. Watkins Tottle.

"Come," said Watkins, when the explosion of mirth, consequent on this practical jest, had subsided, "we'll be off at once—let's lose no time."

"Capital!" echoed Gabriel Parsons; and in five minutes they were at the garden-gate of the villa tenanted by the uncle of Mr. Timson.

"Is Mr. Charles Timson at home?" inquired Mr. Watkins Tottle of Mr. Charles Timson's uncle's man.

"Mr. Charles *is* at home," replied the man, stammering; "but he desired me to say he couldn't be interrupted, sir, by any of the parishioners."

"*I* am not a parishioner," replied Watkins.

"Is Mr. Charles writing a sermon, Tom?" inquired Parsons, thrusting himself forward.

"No, Mr. Parsons, sir; he's not exactly writing a sermon, but he is practising the violoncello in his own bedroom, and gave strict orders not to be disturbed."

"Say I'm here," replied Gabriel, leading the way across the garden; "Mr. Parsons and Mr. Tottle, on private and particular business."

They were shown into the parlour, and the servant departed to deliver his message. The distant groaning of the violoncello ceased; footsteps were heard on the stairs; and Mr. Timson presented himself, and shook hands with Parsons with the utmost cordiality.

"How do you do, sir?" said Watkins Tottle, with great solemnity.

"How do *you* do, sir?" replied Timson, with as much coldness as if it were a matter of perfect indifference to him how he did, as it very likely was.

"I beg to deliver this note to you," said Watkins Tottle, producing the cocked-hat.

"From Miss Lillerton!" said Timson, suddenly changing colour. "Pray sit down."

Mr. Watkins Tottle sat down; and while Timson perused the note, fixed his eyes on an oyster-sauce-coloured portrait of the Archbishop of Canterbury, which hung over the fireplace.

Mr. Timson rose from his seat when he had concluded the note, and looked dubiously at Parsons. "May I ask," he inquired, appealing to Watkins Tottle, "whether our friend here is acquainted with the object of your visit?"

"Our friend is in *my* confidence," replied Watkins, with considerable importance.

"Then, sir," said Timson, seizing both Tottle's hands, "allow me in his presence to thank you most unfeignedly and cordially, for the noble part you have acted in this affair."

"He thinks I recommended him," thought Tottle. "Confound these fellows! they never think of anything but their fees."

"I deeply regret having misunderstood your intentions, my dear sir," continued Timson. "Disinterested and manly, indeed! There are very few men who would have acted as you have done."

Mr. Watkins Tottle could not help thinking that this last remark was anything but complimentary. He therefore inquired, rather hastily, "When is it to be?"

"On Thursday," replied Timson,—"on Thursday morning at half-past eight."

"Uncommonly early," observed Watkins Tottle, with an air of triumphant self-denial. "I shall hardly be able to get down here by that hour." (This was intended for a joke.)

"Never mind, my dear fellow," replied Timson, all suavity, shaking hands with Tottle again most heartily, "so long as we see you to breakfast, you know——"

"Eh!" said Parsons, with one of the most extraordinary expressions of countenance that ever appeared in a human face.

"What!" ejaculated Watkins Tottle, at the same moment.

"I say that so long as we see you to breakfast," replied Timson, "we will excuse your being absent from the ceremony, though of course your presence at it would give us the utmost pleasure."

Mr. Watkins Tottle staggered against the wall, and fixed his eyes on Timson with appalling perseverance.

"Timson," said Parsons, hurriedly brushing his hat with his left arm, "when you say 'us,' whom do you mean?"

Mr. Timson looked foolish in his turn, when he replied, "Why—Mrs. Timson that will be this day week: Miss Lillerton that is——"

"Now don't stare at that idiot in the corner," angrily exclaimed Parsons, as the extraordinary convulsions of Watkins Tottle's countenance excited the wondering gaze of Timson,—"but have the goodness to tell me in three words the contents of that note."

"This note," replied Timson, "is from Miss Lillerton, to whom I have been for the last five weeks regularly engaged. Her singular scruples and strange feeling on some points have hitherto prevented my bringing the engagement to that termination which I so anxiously desire. She informs me here, that she sounded Mrs. Parsons with the view of making her her confidante and go-between, that Mrs. Parsons Informed this elderly gentleman, Mr. Tottle, of the circumstance, and that he, in the most kind and delicate terms, offered to assist us in any way, and even undertook to convey this note, which contains the promise I have long sought in vain—an act of kindness for which I can never be sufficiently grateful."

"Good night, Timson," said Parsons, hurrying off, and carrying the bewildered Tottle with him.

"Won't you stay— and have something?" said Timson.

"No, thank ye." replied Parsons; "I've had quite enough;" and away he went, followed by Watkins Tottle in a state of stupefaction.

Mr. Gabriel Parsons whistled until they had walked some quarter of a mile past his own gate, when he suddenly stopped. and said—

"You are a clever fellow, Tottle, ain't you?"

"I don't know," said the unfortunate Watkins.

"I suppose you'll say this is Fanny's fault, won't you?" inquired Gabriel.

"I don't know anything about it," replied the bewildered Tottle.

"Well," said Parsons, turning on his heel to go home, "the next time you make an offer, you had better speak plainly, and don't throw a chance away. And the next time you're locked up in a spunging-house, just wait there till I come and take you out, there's a good fellow,'

How, ·or at what hour, Mr. Watkins Tottle returned to Cecil Street is unknown. His boots were seen outside his bedroom-door next morning; but we have the authority of his landlady for stating that he neither emerged therefrom nor accepted sustenance for four-and-twenty hours. At the expiration of that period, and when a council of war was being held in the kitchen on the propriety of summoning the parochial beadle to break his door open, he rang his bell, and demanded a cup of milk-and-water. The next morning he went through the formalities of eating and drinking as usual, but a week afterwards he was seized with a relapse, while perusing the list of marriages in a morning paper, from which he never perfectly recovered.

A few weeks after the last-named occurrence, the body of a gentleman unknown was found in the Regent's canal. In the trousers-pockets were four shillings and threepence half-penny; a matrimonial advertisement from a lady, which appeared to have been cut out of a Sunday paper; a tooth-pick, and a card-case, which it is confidently believed would have led to the identification of the unfortunate gentleman, but for the circumstance of there being none but blank cards in it. Mr. Watkins Tottle absented himself from his lodgings shortly before. A bill, which has not been taken up, was presented next morning ; and a bill, which has not been taken down, was soon afterwards affixed in his parlour-window.

CHAPTER XI

THE BLOOMSBURY CHRISTENING

Mr. Nicodemus Dumps, or, as his acquaintance called him, "long Dumps," was a bachelor, six feet high, and fifty years old : cross, cadaverous, odd, and ill-natured. He was never happy but when he was miserable ; and always miserable when he had the best reason to be happy. The only real comfort of his existence was to make everybody about him wretched—then he might be truly said to enjoy life. He was afflicted with a situation in the Bank worth five hundred a year, and he rented a "first-floor furnished," at Pentonville, which he originally took because it commanded a dismal prospect of an adjacent churchyard. He was familiar with the face of every tombstone, and the burial service seemed to excite his strongest sympathy. His friends said he was surly—he insisted he was nervous ; they thought him a lucky dog, but he protested that he was "the most unfortunate man in the world." Cold as he was, and wretched as he declared himself to be, he was not wholly unsusceptible of attachments. He revered the memory of Hoyle, as he was himself an admirable and imperturbable whist-player, and he chuckled with delight at a fretful and impatient adversary. He adored King Herod for his massacre of the innocents ; and if he hated one thing more than another, it was a child. However, he could hardly be said to hate anything in particular, because he disliked everything in general ; but perhaps his greatest antipathies were cabs, old women, doors that would not shut, musical amateurs, and omnibus cads. He subscribed to the "Society for the Suppression of Vice" for the pleasure of putting a stop to any harmless amusements; and he contributed largely towards the support of two itinerant methodist parsons, in the amiable hope that if circumstances rendered any people happy in this world, they might perchance be rendered miserable by fears for the next.

Mr. Dumps had a nephew who had been married about a

year, and who was somewhat of a favourite with his uncle, because he was an admirable subject to exercise his misery-creating powers upon. Mr. Charles Kitterbell was a small, sharp, spare man, with a very large head, and a broad, good-humoured countenance. He looked like a faded giant, with the head and face partially restored ; and he had a cast in his eye which rendered it quite impossible for any one with whom he conversed to know where he was looking. His eyes appeared fixed on the wall, and he was staring you out of countenance ; in short, there was no catching his eye, and perhaps it is a merciful dispensation of Providence that such eyes are not catching. In addition to these characteristics, it may be added that Mr. Charles Kitterbell was one of the most credulous and matter-of-fact little personages that ever took *to* himself a wife, and *for* himself a house in Great Russell Street, Bedford Square. (Uncle Dumps always dropped the "Bedford Square," and inserted in lieu thereof the dreadful words "Tottenham Court Road.")

"No, but, uncle, 'pon my life you must—you must promise to be godfather," said Mr. Kitterbell, as he sat in conversation with his respected relative one morning.

"I cannot, indeed I cannot," returned Dumps.

"Well, but why not ? Jemima will think it very unkind. It's very little trouble."

"As to the trouble," rejoined the most unhappy man in existence, "I don't mind that ; but my nerves are in that state—I cannot go through the ceremony. You know I don't like going out.—For God's sake, Charles, don't fidget with that stool so ; you'll drive me mad." Mr. Kitterbell, quite regardless of his uncle's nerves, had occupied himself for some ten minutes in describing a circle on the floor with one leg of the office-stool on which he was seated, keeping the other three up in the air, and holding fast on by the desk.

"I beg your pardon, uncle," said Kitterbell, quite abashed, suddenly releasing his hold of the desk, and bringing the three wandering legs back to the floor, with a force sufficient to drive them through it.

"But come, don't refuse. If it's a boy, you know, we must have two godfathers."

"*If* it's a boy !" said Dumps ; "why can't you say at once whether it *is* a boy or not ?"

"I should be very happy to tell you, but it's impossible I

can undertake to say whether it's a girl or a boy, if the child isn't born yet."

"Not born yet!" echoed Dumps, with a gleam of hope lighting up his lugubrious visage. "Oh, well, it *may* be a girl, and then you won't want me; or if it is a boy, it *may* die before it is christened."

"I hope not," said the father that expected to be, looking very grave.

"I hope not," acquiesced Dumps, evidently pleased with the subject. He was beginning to get happy. "*I* hope not, but distressing cases frequently occur during the first two or three days of a child's life; fits, I am told, are exceedingly common, and alarming convulsions are almost matters of course."

"Lord, uncle!" ejaculated little Kitterbell, gasping for breath.

"Yes; my landlady was confined—let me see—last Tuesday: an uncommonly fine boy. On the Thursday night the nurse was sitting with him upon her knee before the fire, and he was as well as possible. Suddenly he became black in the face, and alarmingly spasmodic. The medical man was instantly sent for, and every remedy was tried, but——"

"How frightful!" interrupted the horror-stricken Kitterbell.

"The child died, of course. However, your child *may* not die; and if it should be a boy, and should *live* to be christened, why I suppose I must be one of the sponsors." Dumps was evidently good-natured on the faith of his anticipations.

"Thank you, uncle," said his agitated nephew, grasping his hand as warmly as if he had done him some essential service. "Perhaps I had better not tell Mrs. K. what you have mentioned."

"Why, if she's low-spirited, perhaps you had better not mention the melancholy case to her," returned Dumps, who of course had invented the whole story; "though perhaps it would be but doing your duty as a husband to prepare her for the *worst*."

A day or two afterwards, as Dumps was perusing a morning paper at the chop-house which he regularly frequented, the following paragraph met his eyes :—

"*Births.*—On Saturday, the 18th inst., in Great Russell Street, the lady of Charles Kitterbell, Esq., of a son."

"It *is* a boy!" he exclaimed, dashing down the paper, to the astonishment of the waiters. "It *is* a boy!" But he speedily regained his composure as his eye rested on a paragraph quoting the number of infant deaths from the bills of mortality.

Six weeks passed away, and as no communication had been received from the Kitterbells, Dumps was beginning to flatter himself that the child was dead, when the following note painfully resolved his doubts:—

> "*Great Russell Street,*
> "*Monday morning.*

"DEAR UNCLE,—You will be delighted to hear that my dear Jemima has left her room, and that your future godson is getting on capitally. He was very thin at first, but he is getting much larger, and nurse says he is filling out every day. He cries a good deal, and is a very singular colour, which made Jemima and me rather uncomfortable; but as nurse says it's natural, and as of course we know nothing about these things yet, we are quite satisfied with what nurse says. We think he will be a sharp child; and nurse says she's sure he will, because he never goes to sleep. You will readily believe that we are all very happy, only we're a little worn out for want of rest, as he keeps us awake all night; but this we must expect, nurse says, for the first six or eight months. He has been vaccinated, but in consequence of the operation being rather awkwardly performed, some small particles of glass were introduced into the arm with the matter. Perhaps this may in some degree account for his being rather fractious; at least, so nurse says. We propose to have him christened at twelve o'clock on Friday, at Saint George's church, in Hart Street, by the name of Frederick Charles William. Pray don't be later than a quarter before twelve. We shall have a very few friends in the evening, when of course we shall see you. I am sorry to say that the dear boy appears rather restless and uneasy to-day: the cause, I fear, is fever

> "Believe me, dear Uncle,
> "Yours affectionately,
> "CHARLES KITTERBELL.

"P.S.—I open this note to say that we have just discovered the cause of little Frederick's restlessness. It is not fever, as

I apprehended, but a small pin, which nurse accidentally stuck in his leg yesterday evening. We have taken it out, and he appears more composed, though he still sobs a good deal."

It is almost unnecessary to say that the perusal of the above interesting statement was no great relief to the mind of the hypochondriacal Dumps. It was impossible to recede, however, and so he put the best face—that is to say, an uncommonly miserable one—upon the matter ; and purchased a handsome silver mug for the infant Kitterbell, upon which he ordered the initials "F. C. W. K.," with the customary untrained grape-vine-looking flourishes, and a large full stop, to be engraved forthwith.

Monday was a fine day, Tuesday was delightful, Wednesday was equal to either, and Thursday was finer than ever ; four successive fine days in London ! Hackney-coachmen became revolutionary, and crossing-sweepers began to doubt the existence of a First Cause. The *Morning Herald* informed its readers that an old woman in Camden Town had been heard to say that the fineness of the season was "unprecedented in the memory of the oldest inhabitant ; " and Islington clerks, with large families and small salaries, left off their black gaiters, disdained to carry their once green cotton umbrellas, and walked to town in the conscious pride of white stockings and cleanly brushed Bluchers. Dumps beheld all this with an eye of supreme contempt—his triumph was at hand. He knew that if it had been fine for four weeks instead of four days, it would rain when he went out ; he was lugubriously happy in the conviction that Friday would be a wretched day—and so it was. "I knew how it would be," said Dumps, as he turned round opposite the Mansion House at half-past eleven o'clock on the Friday morning. "I knew how it would be. *I* am concerned, and that's enough ; "— and certainly the appearance of the day was sufficient to depress the spirits of a much more buoyant-hearted individual than himself. It had rained, without a moment's cessation, since eight o'clock ; everybody that passed up Cheapside, and down Cheapside, looked wet, cold, and dirty. All sorts of forgotten and long-concealed umbrellas had been put into requisition. Cabs whisked about, with the "fare" as carefully boxed up behind two glazed calico curtains as any mysterious picture in any one of Mrs. Radcliffe's castles ;

omnibus horses smoked like steam-engines ; nobody thought of "standing up" under doorways or arches ; they were painfully convinced it was a hopeless case ; and so everybody went hastily along, jumbling and jostling, and swearing and perspiring, and slipping about, like amateur skaters behind wooden chairs on the Serpentine on a frosty Sunday.

Dumps paused ; he could not think of walking, being rather smart for the christening. If he took a cab he was sure to be spilt, and a hackney-coach was too expensive for his economical ideas. An omnibus was waiting at the opposite corner—it was a desperate case—he had never heard of an omnibus upsetting or running away, and if the cad did knock him down, he could "pull him up" in return.

"Now, sir !" cried the young gentleman who officiated as "cad" to the "Lads of the Village," which was the name of the machine just noticed. Dumps crossed.

"This vay, sir !" shouted the driver of the "Hark-away," pulling up his vehicle immediately across the door of the opposition—"This vay, sir—he's full." Dumps hesitated, whereupon the "Lads of the Village" commenced pouring out a torrent of abuse against the "Hark-away ;" but the conductor of the "Admiral Napier" settled the contest in a most satisfactory manner for all parties by seizing Dumps round the waist, and thrusting him into the middle of his vehicle, which had just come up and only wanted the sixteenth inside.

"All right," said the "Admiral," and off the thing thundered, like a fire-engine at full gallop, with the kidnapped customer inside, standing in the position of a half doubled-up bootjack, and falling about with every jerk of the machine, first on the one side, and then on the other, like a "Jack-in-the-green," on May-day, setting to the lady with a brass ladle.

"For Heaven's sake, where am I to sit?" inquired the miserable man of an old gentleman, into whose stomach he had just fallen for the fourth time.

"Anywhere but on my *chest*, sir," replied the old gentleman in a surly tone.

"Perhaps the *box* would suit the gentleman better," suggested a very damp lawyer's clerk, in a pink shirt, and a smirking countenance.

After a great deal of struggling and falling about, Dumps at last managed to squeeze himself into a seat, which, in addition to the slight disadvantage of being between a

The Bloomsbury Christening

window that would not shut, and a door that must be open, placed him in close contact with a passenger, who had been walking about all the morning without an umbrella, and who looked as if he had spent the day in a full water-butt—only wetter.

"Don't bang the door so," said Dumps to the conductor, as he shut it after letting out four of the passengers; "I am very nervous—it destroys me."

"Did any gen'lm'n say anythink?" replied the cad, thrusting in his head, and trying to look as if he didn't understand the request.

"I told you not to bang the door so!" repeated Dumps, with an expression of countenance like the knave of clubs, in convulsions.

"Oh! vy, it's rather a sing'ler circumstance about this here door, sir, that it von't shut without banging," replied the conductor; and he opened the door very wide, and shut it again with a terrific bang, in proof of the assertion.

"I beg your pardon, sir," said a little prim, wheezing old gentleman, sitting opposite Dumps, "I beg your pardon; but have you ever observed, when you have been in an omnibus on a wet day, that four people out of five always come in with large cotton umbrellas, without a handle at the top, or the brass spike at the bottom?"

"Why, sir," returned Dumps, as he heard the clock strike twelve, "it never struck me before; but now you mention it, I——Hollo! hollo!" shouted the persecuted individual, as the omnibus dashed past Drury Lane, where he had directed to be set down—"Where is the cad?"

"I think he's on the box, sir," said the young gentleman before noticed in the pink shirt, which looked like a white one ruled with red ink.

"I want to be set down!" said Dumps in a faint voice, overcome by his previous efforts.

"I think these cads want to be *set down*," returned the attorney's clerk, chuckling at his sally.

"Hollo!" cried Dumps again.

"Hollo!" echoed the passengers. The omnibus passed St. Giles's church.

"Hold hard!" said the conductor; "I'm blowed if we ha'n't forgot the gen'lm'n as vas to be set down at Doory Lane.—Now, sir, make haste, if you please," he added. opening the door, and assisting Dumps out with as much coolness as if it was "all right." Dumps's indignation was for once getting the better of his cynical equanimity. "Drury Lane!" he gasped, with the voice of a boy in a cold bath for the first time.

"Doory Lane, sir?—yes, sir,—third turning on the right-hand side, sir."

Dumps's passion was paramount: he clutched his umbrella, and was striding off with the firm determination of not paying the fare. The cad, by a remarkable coincidence, happened to entertain a directly contrary opinion, and Heaven knows how far the altercation would have proceeded, if it had not been most ably and satisfactorily brought to a close by the driver.

"Hollo!" said that respectable person, standing up on the box, and leaning with one hand on the roof of the omnibus. "Hollo, Tom! tell the gentleman if so be as he feels aggrieved, we will take him up to the Edge-er (Edgeware) Road for nothing, and set him down at Doory Lane when we comes back. He can't reject that, anyhow."

The argument was irresistible: Dumps paid the disputed sixpence, and in a quarter of an hour was on the staircase of No. 14, Great Russell Street.

Everything indicated that preparations were making for the reception of "a few friends" in the evening. Two dozen extra tumblers, and four ditto wine-glasses—looking anything but transparent, with little bits of straw in them—were on the slab in the passage, just arrived. There was a great smell of nutmeg, port wine, and almonds, on the staircase : the covers were taken off the stair-carpet, and the figure of Venus on the first landing looked as if she were ashamed of the composition-candle in her right hand, which contrasted beautifully with the lamp-blacked drapery of the goddess of love. The female servant (who looked very warm and bustling) ushered Dumps into a front drawing-room, very prettily furnished, with a plentiful sprinkling of little baskets, paper table-mats, china watchmen, pink and gold albums, and rainbow-bound little books on the different tables.

"Ah, uncle!" said Mr. Kitterbell, "how d'ye do? Allow me—Jemima, my dear—my uncle. I think you've seen Jemima before, sir?"

"Have had the *pleasure*," returned big Dumps, his tone and look making it doubtful whether in his life he had ever experienced the sensation.

"I'm sure," said Mrs. Kitterbell, with a languid smile, and a slight cough. "I'm sure—hem—any friend—of Charles's —hem—much less a relation, is—— "

"I knew you'd say so, my love," said little Kitterbell, who, while he appeared to be gazing on the opposite houses, was looking at his wife with a most affectionate air : "Bless you!" The last two words were accompanied with a simper, and a squeeze of the hand, which stirred up all Uncle Dumps's bile.

"Jane, tell nurse to bring down baby," said Mrs. Kitterbell, addressing the servant. Mrs. Kitterbell was a tall, thin young lady, with very light hair, and a particularly white face—one of those young women who almost invariably, though one hardly knows why, recall to one's mind the idea of a cold fillet of veal. Out went the servant, and in came the nurse, with a remarkably small parcel in her arms, packed up in a blue mantle trimmed with white fur.—This was the baby.

"Now, uncle," said Mr. Kitterbell, lifting up that part of the mantle which covered the infant's face, with an air of great triumph, "*who* do you think he's like?"

"He! he! Yes, who?" said Mrs. K., putting her arm through her husband's, and looking up into Dumps's face with an expression of as much interest as she was capable of displaying.

"Good God, how small he is!" cried the amiable uncle, starting back with well-feigned surprise ; "*remarkably* small indeed."

"Do you think so?" inquired poor little Kitterbell, rather alarmed. "He's a monster to what he was—ain't he, nurse?"

"He's a dear," said the nurse, squeezing the child, and evading the question—not because she scrupled to disguise the fact, but because she couldn't afford to throw away the chance of Dumps's half-crown.

"Well, but who is he like?" inquired little Kitterbell.

Dumps looked at the little pink heap before him, and only thought at the moment of the best mode of mortifying the youthful parents.

"I really don't know *who* he's like," he answered, very well knowing the reply expected of him.

"Don't you think he's like *me?*" inquired his nephew with a knowing air.

T

"Oh, *decidedly* not!" returned Dumps, with an emphasis not to be misunderstood. "Decidedly not like you.—Oh, certainly not."

"Like Jemima?" asked Kitterbell, faintly.

"Oh, dear no; not in the least. I'm no judge, of course, in such cases; but I really think he's more like one of those little carved representations that one sometimes sees blowing a trumpet on a tombstone!" The nurse stooped down over the child, and with great difficulty prevented an explosion of mirth. Pa and ma looked almost as miserable as their amiable uncle.

"Well!" said the disappointed little father, "you'll be better able to tell what he's like by-and-bye. You shall see him this evening with his mantle off."

"Thank you," said Dumps, feeling particularly grateful.

"Now, my love," said Kitterbell to his wife, "it's time we were off. We're to meet the other godfather and the god-mother at the church, uncle,—Mr. and Mrs. Wilson from over the way—uncommonly nice people. My love, are you well wrapped up?"

"Yes, dear."

"Are you sure you won't have another shawl?" inquired the anxious husband.

"No, sweet," returned the charming mother, accepting Dumps's proffered arm; and the little party entered the hackney-coach that was to take them to the church; Dumps amusing Mrs. Kitterbell by expatiating largely on the danger of measles, thrush, teeth-cutting, and other interesting dis-eases to which children are subject.

The ceremony (which occupied about five minutes) passed off without anything particular occurring. The clergyman had to dine some distance from town, and had two church-ings, three christenings, and a funeral to perform in some-thing less than an hour. The godfathers and godmother, therefore, promised to renounce the devil and all his works —"and all that sort of thing"—as little Kitterbell said— "in less than no time;" and with the exception of Dumps nearly letting the child fall into the font when he handed it to the clergyman, the whole affair went off in the usual business-like and matter-of-course manner, and Dumps re-entered the Bank-gates at two o'clock with a heavy heart, and the painful conviction that he was regularly booked for an evening party.

Evening came—and so did Dumps's pumps, black silk stockings, and white cravat which he had ordered to be forwarded, per boy, from Pentonville. The depressed god-father dressed himself at a friend's counting-house, from whence, with his spirits fifty degrees below proof, he sallied forth—as the weather had cleared up, and the evening was tolerably fine—to walk to Great Russell Street. Slowly he paced up Cheapside, Newgate Street, down Snow Hill, and up Holborn ditto, looking as grim as the figure-head of a man-of-war, and finding out fresh causes of misery at every step. As he was crossing the corner of Hatton Garden, a man, apparently intoxicated, rushed against him, and would have knocked him down, had he not been providentially caught by a very genteel young man, who happened to be close to him at the time. The shock so disarranged Dumps's nerves, as well as his dress, that he could hardly stand. The gentleman took his arm, and in the kindest manner walked with him as far as Furnival's Inn. Dumps, for about the first time in his life, felt grateful and polite; and he and the gentlemanly-looking young man parted with mutual ex-pressions of goodwill.

"There are at least some well-disposed men in the world," ruminated the misanthropical Dumps, as he proceeded to-wards his destination.

Rat—tat—ta-ra-ra-ra-ra-rat—knocked a hackney-coachman at Kitterbell's door, in imitation of a gentleman's servant, just as Dumps reached it; and out came an old lady in a large toque, and an old gentleman in a blue coat, and three female copies of the old lady in pink dresses, and shoes to match.

"It's a large party," sighed the unhappy godfather, wiping the perspiration from his forehead, and leaning against the area-railings. It was some time before the miserable man could muster up courage to knock at the door, and when he did, the smart appearance of a neighbouring greengrocer (who had been hired to wait for seven and sixpence, and whose calves alone were worth double the money), the lamp in the passage, and the Venus on the landing, added to the hum of many voices, and the sound of a harp and two violins, painfully convinced him that his surmises were but too well founded.

"How are you?" said little Kitterbell, in a greater bustle than ever, bolting out of the little back parlour with a corkscrew in his hand, and various particles of sawdust, looking like so many inverted commas, on his inexpressibles.

"Good God!" said Dumps, turning into the aforesaid parlour to put his shoes on, which he had brought in his coat-pocket, and still more appalled by the sight of seven fresh-drawn corks, and a corresponding number of decanters. "How many people are there up-stairs?"

"Oh, not above thirty-five. We've had the carpet taken up in the back drawing-room, and the piano and the card-tables are in the front. Jemima thought we'd better have a regular sit-down supper in the front parlour, because of the speechifying, and all that. But, Lord! uncle, what's the matter?" continued the excited little man, as Dumps stood with one shoe on, rummaging his pockets with the most frightful distortion of visage. "What have you lost? Your pocket-book?"

"No," returned Dumps, diving first into one pocket and then into the other, and speaking in a voice like Desdemona with the pillow over her mouth.

"Your card-case? snuff-box? the key of your lodgings?" continued Kitterbell, pouring question on question with the rapidity of lightning.

"No! no!" ejaculated Dumps, still diving eagerly into his empty pockets.

"Not—not—the *mug* you spoke of this morning?"

"Yes, the *mug!*" replied Dumps, sinking into a chair.

"How *could* you have done it?" inquired Kitterbell. "Are you sure you brought it out?"

"Yes! yes! I see it all!" said Dumps, starting up as the idea flashed across his mind; "miserable dog that I am— I was born to suffer. I see it all: it was the gentlemanly-looking young man!"

"Mr. Dumps!" shouted the greengrocer in a stentorian voice, as he ushered the somewhat recovered godfather into the drawing-room half an hour after the above declaration. "Mr. Dumps!"—everybody looked at the door, and in came Dumps, feeling about as much out of place as a salmon might be supposed to be on a gravel-walk.

"Happy to see you again," said Mrs. Kitterbell, quite unconscious of the unfortunate man's confusion and misery; "you must allow me to introduce you to a few of our friends:—my mamma, Mr. Dumps—my papa and sisters." Dumps seized the hand of the mother as warmly as if she was his own parent, bowed *to* the young ladies, and *against* a gentleman behind him, and took no notice whatever of the father, who had been bowing incessantly for three minutes and a quarter.

"Uncle," said little Kitterbell, after Dumps had been introduced to a select dozen or two, "you must let me lead you to the other end of the room, to introduce you to my friend Danton. Such a splendid fellow!—I'm sure you'll like him—this way."—Dumps followed as tractably as a tame bear.

Mr. Danton was a young man of about five-and-twenty, with a considerable stock of impudence, and a very small share of ideas: he was a great favourite, especially with young ladies of from sixteen to twenty-six years of age, both inclusive. He could imitate the French-horn to admiration, sang comic songs most inimitably, and had the most insinuating way of saying impertinent nothings to his doting female admirers. He had acquired, somehow or other, the reputation of being a great wit, and, accordingly, whenever he opened his mouth, everybody who knew him laughed very heartily.

The introduction took place in due form. Mr. Danton bowed, and twirled a lady's handkerchief, which he held in his hand, in a most comic way. Everybody smiled.

"Very warm," said Dumps, feeling it necessary to say something.

"Yes. It was warmer yesterday," returned the brilliant Mr. Danton.—A general laugh.

"I have great pleasure in congratulating you on your first appearance in the character of a father, sir," he continued, addressing Dumps—"godfather, I mean."—The young ladies were convulsed, and the gentlemen in ecstasies.

A general hum of admiration interrupted the conversation, and announced the entrance of nurse with the baby. An universal rush of the young ladies immediately took place. (Girls are always *so* fond of babies in company.)

"Oh, you dear!" said one.

"How sweet!" cried another, in a low tone of the most enthusiastic admiration.

"Heavenly!" added a third.

"Oh! what dear little arms!" said a fourth, holding up an arm and fist about the size and shape of the leg of a fowl cleanly picked.

" Did you ever !"—said a little coquette with a large bustle, who looked like a French lithograph, appealing to a gentleman in three waistcoats—"Did you ever!"

"Never, in my life," returned her admirer, pulling up his collar.

"Oh! *do* let me take it, nurse!" cried another young lady. "The love!"

" Can it open its eyes, nurse?" inquired another, affecting the utmost innocence.—Suffice it to say, that the single ladies unanimously voted him an angel, and that the married ones, *nem. con.*, agreed that he was decidedly the finest baby they had ever beheld—except their own.

The quadrilles were resumed with great spirit. Mr. Danton was universally admitted to be beyond himself; several young ladies enchanted the company and gained admirers by singing "We met"—"I saw her at the Fancy Fair"—and other equally sentimental and interesting ballads. "The young men," as Mrs. Kitterbell said, "made themselves very agreeable;" the girls did not lose their opportunity; and the evening promised to go off excellently. Dumps didn't mind it : he had devised a plan for himself—a little bit of fun in his own way—and he was almost happy! He played a rubber and lost every point. Mr. Danton said he could not have lost every point, because he made a point of losing : everybody laughed tremendously. Dumps retorted with a better joke, and nobody smiled, with the exception of the host, who seemed to consider it his duty to laugh till he was black in the face, at everything. There was only one drawback—the musicians did not play with quite as much spirit as could have been wished. The cause, however, was satisfactorily explained; for it appeared, on the testimony of a gentleman who had come up from Gravesend in the afternoon, that they had been engaged on board a steamer all day, and had played almost without cessation all the way to Gravesend, and all the way back again.

The "sit-down supper" was excellent; there were four barley-sugar temples on the table, which would have looked beautiful if they had not melted away when the supper began ; and a water-mill, whose only fault was that instead of going round, it ran over the table-cloth. Then there were fowls, and tongue, and trifle, and sweets, and lobster salad, and potted beef—and everything. And little Kitterbell kept calling out for clean plates, and the clean plates did not

Out-and-Out Young Gentlemen
(*p. 504*)

come: and then the gentlemen who wanted the plates said they didn't mind, they'd take a lady's; and then Mrs. Kitterbell applauded their gallantry, and the greengrocer ran about till he thought his seven and sixpence was very hardly earned; and the young ladies didn't eat much for fear it shouldn't look romantic, and the married ladies eat as much as possible, for fear they shouldn't have enough; and a great deal of wine was drunk, and everybody talked and laughed considerably.

"Hush! hush!" said Mr. Kitterbell, rising and looking very important. "My love (this was addressed to his wife at the other end of the table), take care of Mrs. Maxwell, and your mamma, and the rest of the married ladies; the gentlemen will persuade the young ladies to fill their glasses, I am sure."

"Ladies and gentlemen," said long Dumps, in a very sepulchral voice and rueful accent, rising from his chair like the ghost in Don Juan, "will you have the kindness to charge your glasses?. I am desirous of proposing a toast."

A dead silence ensued, and the glasses were filled—everybody looked serious.

"Ladies and gentlemen," slowly continued the ominous Dumps, "I"—(here Mr. Danton imitated two notes from the French-horn, in a very loud key, which electrified the nervous toast-proposer, and convulsed his audience).

"Order! order!" said little Kitterbell, endeavouring to suppress his laughter.

"Order!" said the gentlemen.

"Danton, be quiet," said a particular friend on the opposite side of the table.

"Ladies and gentlemen," resumed Dumps, somewhat recovered, and not much disconcerted, for he was always a pretty good hand at a speech—"In accordance with what is, I believe, the established usage on these occasions, I, as one of the godfathers of Master Frederick Charles William Kitterbell—(here the speaker's voice faltered, for he remembered the mug)—venture to rise to propose a toast. I need hardly say that it is the health and prosperity of that young gentleman, the particular event of whose early life we are here met to celebrate—(applause). Ladies and gentlemen, it is impossible to suppose that our friends here, whose sincere well-wishers we all are, can pass through life without some trials, con-

siderable suffering, severe affliction, and heavy losses!"—Here
the arch-traitor paused, and slowly drew forth a long, white
pocket-handkerchief—his example was followed by several
ladies. "That these trials may be long spared them is my
most earnest prayer, my most fervent wish (a distinct sob
from the grandmother). I hope and trust, ladies and gentlemen, that the infant whose christening we have this evening
met to celebrate, may not be removed from the arms of his
parents by premature decay (several cambrics were in requisition): that his young and now *apparently* healthy form
may not be wasted by lingering disease. (Here Dumps cast
a sardonic glance around, for a great sensation was manifest
among the married ladies.) You, I am sure, will concur with
me in wishing that he may live to be a comfort and a blessing to his parents. ('Hear, hear!' and an audible sob from
Mr. Kitterbell.) But should he not be what we could wish
—should he forget in after times the duty which he owes to
them—should they unhappily experience that distracting
truth, 'how sharper than a serpent's tooth it is to have a
thankless child'"—Here Mrs. Kitterbell, with her handkerchief to her eyes, and accompanied by several ladies, rushed
from the room, and went into violent hysterics in the passage,
leaving her better half in almost as bad a condition, and a
general impression in Dumps's favour; for people like sentiment, after all.

It need hardly be added, that this occurrence quite put
a stop to the harmony of the evening. Vinegar, hartshorn,
and cold water, were now as much in request as negus, rout-
cakes, and *bon-bons* had been a short time before. Mrs.
Kitterbell was immediately conveyed to her apartment, the
musicians were silenced, flirting ceased, and the company
slowly departed. Dumps left the house at the commencement
of the bustle, and walked home with a light step, and (for
him) a cheerful heart. His landlady, who slept in the next
room, has offered to make oath that she heard him laugh,
in his peculiar manner, after he had locked his door. The
assertion, however, is so improbable, and bears on the face of
it such strong evidence of untruth, that it has never obtained
credence to this hour.

The family of Mr. Kitterbell has considerably increased
since the period to which we have referred; he has now two
sons and a daughter; and as he expects, at no distant period,
to have another addition to his blooming progeny, he is

anxious to secure an eligible godfather for the occasion.   He is determined, however, to impose upon him two conditions. He must bind himself, by a solemn obligation, not to make any speech after supper; and it is indispensable that he should be in no way connected with " the most miserable man in the world."

CHAPTER XII

THE DRUNKARD'S DEATH

WE will be bold to say, that there is scarcely a man in the constant habit of walking, day after day, through any of the crowded thoroughfares of London, who cannot recollect among the people whom he "knows by sight," to use a familiar phrase, some being of abject and wretched appearance whom he remembers to have seen in a very different condition, whom he has observed sinking lower and lower, by almost imperceptible degrees, and the shabbiness and utter destitution of whose appearance, at last, strike forcibly and painfully upon him, as he passes by. Is there any man who has mixed much with society, or whose avocations have caused him to mingle, at one time or other, with a great number of people, who cannot call to mind the time when some shabby, miserable wretch, in rags and filth. who shuffles past him now in all the squalor of disease and poverty, was a respectable tradesman, or clerk, or a man following some thriving pursuit, with good prospects, and decent means?—or cannot any of our readers call to mind from among the list of their *quondam* acquaintance. some fallen and degraded man, who lingers about the pavement in hungry misery—from whom every one turns coldly away, and who preserves himself from sheer starvation. nobody knows how? Alas! such cases are of too frequent occurrence to be rare items in any man's experience : and but too often arise from one cause—drunkenness—that fierce rage for the slow, sure poison, that oversteps every other consideration ; that casts aside wife, children, friends, happiness, and station ; and hurries its victims madly on to degradation and death.

Some of these men have been impelled, by misfortune and misery, to the vice that has degraded them. The ruin of worldly expectations, the death of those they loved, the sorrow that slowly consumes, but will not break the heart, has driven them wild ; and they present the hideous spectacle of madmen, slowly dying by their own hands. But by far the greater part have wilfully, and with open eyes, plunged into the gulf from which the man who once enters it never rises more, but into which he sinks deeper and deeper down, until recovery is hopeless.

Such a man as this once stood by the bedside of his dying wife, while his children knelt around, and mingled low bursts of grief with their innocent prayers. The room was scantily and meanly furnished ; and it needed but a glance at the pale form from which the light of life was fast passing away, to know that grief, and want, and anxious care, had been busy at the heart for many a weary year. An elderly woman, with her face bathed in tears, was supporting the head of the dying woman—her daughter—on her arm. But it was not towards her that the wan face turned ; it was not her hand that the cold and trembling fingers clasped ; they pressed the husband's arm ; the eyes so soon to be closed in death rested on his face, and the man shook beneath their gaze. His dress was slovenly and disordered, his face inflamed, his eyes blood-shot and heavy. He had been summoned from some wild debauch to the bed of sorrow and death.

A shaded lamp by the bedside cast a dim light on the figures around, and left the remainder of the room in thick, deep shadow. The silence of night prevailed without the house, and the stillness of death was in the chamber. A watch hung over the mantel-shelf ; its low ticking was the only sound that broke the profound quiet, but it was a solemn one, for well they knew, who heard it, that before it had recorded the passing of another hour, it would beat the knell of a departed spirit.

It is a dreadful thing to wait and watch for the approach of death; to know that hope is gone, and recovery impossible; and to sit and count the dreary hours through long, long nights—such nights as only watchers by the bed of sickness know. It chills the blood to hear the dearest secrets of the heart—the pent-up, hidden secrets of many years—poured forth by the unconscious helpless being before you; and to think how little the reserve and cunning of a whole life will avail, when fever and delirium tear off the mask at last. Strange tales have been told in the wanderings of dying men ; tales so full of guilt and crime, that those who stood by the sick person's couch have fled in horror and affright, lest they should be scared to madness by what they heard and saw ; and many a wretch has died alone, raving of deeds the very name of which has driven the boldest man away.

But no such ravings were to be heard at the bedside by which the children knelt. Their half-stifled sobs and moanings alone broke the silence of the lonely chamber. And when at last the mother's grasp relaxed, and, turning one look from the children to the father, she vainly strove to speak, and fell backward on the pillow, all was so calm and tranquil that she seemed to sink to sleep. They leant over her; they called upon her name, softly at first, and then in the loud and piercing tones of desperation. But there was no reply. They listened for her breath, but no sound came. They felt for the palpitation of the heart, but no faint throb responded to the touch. That heart was broken, and she was dead!

The husband sunk into a chair by the bedside, and clasped his hands upon his burning forehead. He gazed from child to child, but when a weeping eye met his, he quailed beneath its look. No word of comfort was whispered in his ear, no look of kindness lighted on his face. All shrunk from and avoided him; and when at last he staggered from the room, no one sought to follow or console the widower.

The time had been when many a friend would have crowded round him in his affliction, and many a heartfelt condolence would have met him in his grief. Where were they now? One by one, friends, relations, the commonest acquaintance even, had fallen off from and deserted the drunkard. His wife alone had clung to him in good and evil, in sickness and poverty, and how had he rewarded her? He had reeled from the tavern to her bedside in time to see her die.

He rushed from the house, and walked swiftly through the streets. Remorse, fear, shame, all crowded on his mind. Stupefied with drink, and bewildered with the scene he had just witnessed, he re-entered the tavern he had quitted shortly before. Glass succeeded glass. His blood mounted, and his brain whirled round. Death! Every one must die, and why not *she?* She was too good for him; her relations had often told him so. Curses on them! Had they not deserted her, and left her to whine away the time at home? Well—she was dead, and happy perhaps. It was better as it was. Another glass—one more! Hurrah! It was a merry life while it lasted; and he would make the most of it.

Time went on; the three children who were left to him, grew up and were children no longer. The father remained the same—poorer, shabbier, and more dissolute-looking, but the same confirmed and irreclaimable drunkard. The boys had, long ago, run wild in the streets, and left him ; the girl alone remained, but she worked hard, and words or blows could always procure him something for the tavern. So he went on in the old course, and a merry life he led.

One night, as early as ten o'clock—for the girl had been sick for many days, and there was, consequently, little to spend at the public-house—he bent his steps homeward, bethinking himself that if he would have her able to earn money, it would be as well to apply to the parish surgeon, or, at all events, to take the trouble of inquiring what ailed her, which he had not yet thought it worth while to do. It was a wet December night ; the wind blew piercing cold, and the rain poured heavily down. He begged a few halfpence from a passer-by, and having bought a small loaf (for it was his interest to keep the girl alive, if he could), he shuffled onwards as fast as the wind and rain would let him.

At the back of Fleet Street, and lying between it and the water-side, are several mean and narrow courts, which form a portion of Whitefriars: it was to one of these that he directed his steps.

The alley into which he turned might, for filth and misery, have competed with the darkest corner of this ancient sanctuary in its dirtiest and most lawless time. The houses, varying from two stories in height to four, were stained with every indescribable hue that long exposure to the weather, damp, and rottenness can impart to tenements composed originally of the roughest and coarsest materials. The windows were patched with paper, and stuffed with the foulest rags ; the doors were falling from their hinges ; poles with lines on which to dry clothes, projected from every case-ment, and sounds of quarrelling or drunkenness issued from every room.

The solitary oil lamp in the centre of the court had been blown out, either by the violence of the wind or the act of some inhabitant who had excellent reasons for objecting to his residence being rendered too conspicuous ; and the only light which fell upon the broken and uneven pavement, was derived from the miserable candles that here and there twinkled in the rooms of such of the more fortunate residents as could afford to indulge in so expensive a luxury. A gutter ran down the centre of the alley—all the sluggish odours of which had been called forth by the rain; and as the wind whistled through the old houses, the doors and shutters creaked upon their hinges, and the windows shook in their frames, with a violence which every moment seemed to threaten the destruction of the whole place.

The man whom we have followed into this den, walked on in the darkness, sometimes stumbling into the main gutter, and at others into some branch repositories of garbage which had been formed by the rain, until he reached the last house in the court. The door, or rather what was left of it, stood ajar, for the convenience of the numerous lodgers; and he proceeded to grope his way up the old and broken stair, to the attic story.

He was within a step or two of his room-door, when it opened, and a girl, whose miserable and emaciated appearance was only to be equalled by that of the candle which she shaded with her hand, peeped anxiously out.

"Is that you, father?" said the girl.

"Who else should it be?" replied the man gruffly. "What are you trembling at? It's little enough that I've had to drink to-day, for there's no drink without money, and no money without work. What the devil's the matter with the girl?"

"I am not well, father—not at all well," said the girl, bursting into tears.

"Ah!" replied the man, in the tone of a person who is compelled to admit a very unpleasant fact, to which he would rather remain blind, if he could. "You must get better somehow, for we must have money. You must go to the parish doctor, and make him give you some medicine. They're paid for it, damn 'em. What are you standing before the door for? Let me come in, can't you?"

"Father," whispered the girl, shutting the door behind her, and placing herself before it, "William has come back."

"Who?" said the man, with a start.

"Hush!" replied the girl, "William; brother William."

"And what does he want?" said the man, with an effort at composure—"money? meat? drink? He's come to the wrong shop for that, if he does. Give me the candle—give me the candle, fool—I ain't going to hurt him." He snatched the candle from her hand, and walked into the room.

Sitting on an old box, with his head resting on his hand, and his eyes fixed on a wretched cinder fire that was smouldering on the hearth, was a young man of about two-and-twenty, miserably clad in an old coarse jacket and trousers. He started up when his father entered.

"Fasten the door, Mary," said the young man hastily— "Fasten the door. You look as if you didn't know me, father. It's long enough since you drove me from home; you may well forget me."

"And what do you want here, now?" said the father, seating himself on a stool, on the other side of the fireplace. "What do you want here, now?"

"Shelter," replied the son. "I'm in trouble: that's enough. If I'm caught I shall swing; that's certain. Caught I shall be, unless I stop here; that's *as* certain. And there's an end of it."

"You mean to say, you've been robbing, or murdering, then?" said the father.

"Yes, I do," replied the son. "Does it surprise you, father?" He looked steadily in the man's face, but he withdrew his eyes, and bent them on the ground.

"Where's your brothers?" he said, after a long pause.

"Where they'll never trouble you," replied his son: "John's gone to America, and Henry's dead."

"Dead!" said the father, with a shudder, which even he could not repress.

"Dead," replied the young man. "He died in my arms —shot like a dog, by a gamekeeper. He staggered back, I caught him, and his blood trickled down my hands. It poured out from his side like water. He was weak, and it blinded him, but he threw himself down on his knees, on the grass, and prayed to God, that if his mother was in heaven, He would hear her prayers for pardon for her youngest son. 'I was her favourite boy, Will,' he said, 'and I am glad to think, now, that when she was dying, though I was a very young child then, and my little heart was almost bursting, I knelt down at the foot of the bed, and thanked God for having made me so fond of her as to have never once done anything to bring the tears into her eyes. O Will, why was she taken away, and father left?' There's his dying words, father," said the young man; "make the best you can of 'em. You struck him across the face, in a drunken fit, the morning we ran away; and here's the end of it."

The girl wept aloud; and the father, sinking his head upon his knees, rocked himself to and fro.

"If I am taken," said the young man, "I shall be carried back into the country, and hung for that man's murder. They cannot trace me here, without your assistance, father. For aught I know, you may give me up to justice; but unless you do, here I stop, until I can venture to escape abroad."

For two whole days, all three remained in the wretched room, without stirring out. On the third evening, however, the girl was worse than she had been yet, and the few scraps of food they had were gone. It was indispensably necessary that somebody should go out; and as the girl was too weak and ill, the father went, just at nightfall.

He got some medicine for the girl, and a trifle in the way of pecuniary assistance. On his way back, he earned six-pence by holding a horse; and he turned homewards with enough money to supply their most pressing wants for two or three days to come. He had to pass the public-house. He lingered for an instant, walked past it, turned back again, lingered once more, and finally slunk in. Two men whom he had not observed, were on the watch. They were on the point of giving up their search in despair, when his loitering attracted their attention; and when he entered the public-house, they followed him.

"You'll drink with me, master," said one of them, proffering him a glass of liquor.

"And me too," said the other, replenishing the glass as soon as it was drained of its contents.

The man thought of his hungry children, and his son's danger. But they were nothing to the drunkard. He *did* drink; and his reason left him.

"A wet night, Warden," whispered one of the men in his ear, as he at length turned to go away, after spending in liquor one-half of the money on which, perhaps, his daughter's life depended.

"The right sort of night for our friends in hiding, Master Warden," whispered the other.

"Sit down here," said the one who had spoken first, drawing him into a corner. "We have been looking arter the young un. We came to tell him it's all right now, but we couldn't find him 'cause we hadn't got the precise direction. But that ain't strange, for I don't think he know'd it himself, when he come to London, did he?"

"No, he didn't," replied the father.

The two men exchanged glances.

"There's a vessel down at the docks, to sail at midnight, when it's high water," resumed the first speaker, "and we'll put him on board. His passage is taken in another name, and what's better than that, it's paid for. It's lucky we met you."

"Very," said the second.

"Capital luck," said the first, with a wink to his companion.

"Great," replied the second, with a slight nod of intelligence.

"Another glass here; quick"—said the first speaker. And in five minutes more, the father had unconsciously yielded up his own son into the hangman's hands.

Slowly and heavily the time dragged along, as the brother and sister, in their miserable hiding-place, listened in anxious suspense to the slightest sound. At length, a heavy footstep was heard upon the stair; it approached nearer; it reached the landing; and the father staggered into the room.

The girl saw that he was intoxicated, and advanced with the candle in her hand to meet him; she stopped short, gave a loud scream, and fell senseless on the ground. She had caught sight of the shadow of a man reflected on the floor. They both rushed in, and in another instant the young man was a prisoner, and handcuffed.

"Very quietly done," said one of the men to his companion, "thanks to the old man. Lift up the girl, Tom—come, come, it's no use crying, young woman. It's all over now, and can't be helped."

The young man stooped for an instant over the girl, and then turned fiercely round upon his father, who had reeled against the wall, and was gazing on the group with drunken stupidity.

"Listen to me, father," he said, in a tone that made the drunkard's flesh creep. "My brother's blood, and mine, is on your head: I never had kind look, or word, or care, from you, and alive or dead, I never will forgive you. Die when you will, or how, I will be with you. I speak as a dead man now, and I warn you, father, that as surely as you must one day stand before your Maker, so surely shall your children be there, hand in hand, to cry for judgment against you." He raised his manacled hands in a threatening attitude, fixed his eyes on his shrinking parent, and slowly left the room;

and neither father nor sister ever beheld him more, on this side of the grave.

When the dim and misty light of a winter's morning penetrated into the narrow court, and struggled through the begrimed window of the wretched room, Warden awoke from his heavy sleep, and found himself alone. He rose, and looked round him; the old flock mattress on the floor was undisturbed; everything was just as he remembered to have seen it last: and there were no signs of any one, save himself, having occupied the room during the night. He inquired of the other lodgers, and of the neighbours; but his daughter had not been seen or heard of. He rambled through the streets, and scrutinised each wretched face among the crowds that thronged them, with anxious eyes. But his search was fruitless, and he returned to his garret when night came on, desolate and weary.

For many days he occupied himself in the same manner, but no trace of his daughter did he meet with, and no word of her reached his ears. At length he gave up the pursuit as hopeless. He had long thought of the probability of her leaving him, and endeavouring to gain her bread in quiet, elsewhere. She had left him at last to starve alone. He ground his teeth, and cursed her!

He begged his bread from door to door. Every halfpenny he could wring from the pity or credulity of those to whom he addressed himself, was spent in the old way. A year passed over his head; the roof of a jail was the only one that had sheltered him for many months. He slept under archways, and in brickfields—anywhere, where there was some warmth or shelter from the cold and rain. But in the last stage of poverty, disease, and houseless want, he was a drunkard still.

At last, one bitter night, he sunk down on a door-step faint and ill. The premature decay of vice and profligacy had worn him to the bone. His cheeks were hollow and livid; his eyes were sunken, and their sight was dim. His legs trembled beneath his weight, and a cold shiver ran through every limb.

And now the long-forgotten scenes of a misspent life crowded thick and fast upon him. He thought of the time when he had a home—a happy, cheerful home—and of those who peopled it, and flocked about him then, until the forms of his elder children seemed to rise from the grave, and stand about him—so plain, so clear, and so distinct they were that he could touch and feel them. Looks that he had long forgotten were fixed upon him once more ; voices long since hushed in death sounded in his ears like the music of village bells. But it was only for an instant. The rain beat heavily upon him; and cold and hunger were gnawing at his heart again.

He rose, and dragged his feeble limbs a few paces further. The street was silent and empty ; the few passengers who passed by, at that late hour, hurried quickly on, and his tremulous voice was lost in the violence of the storm. Again that heavy chill struck through his frame, and his blood seemed to stagnate beneath it. He coiled himself up in a projecting doorway, and tried to sleep.

But sleep had fled from his dull and glazed eyes. His mind wandered strangely, but he was awake, and conscious. The well-known shout of drunken mirth sounded in his ear, the glass was at his lips, the board was covered with choice rich food—they were before him : he could see them all, he had but to reach out his hand, and take them—and, though the illusion was reality itself, he knew that he was sitting alone in the deserted street, watching the rain-drops as they pattered on the stones ; that death was coming upon him by inches—and that there were none to care for or help him.

Suddenly he started up, in the extremity of terror. He had heard his own voice shouting in the night air, he knew not what, or why. Hark ! A groan !—another ! His senses were leaving him : half-formed and incoherent words burst from his lips ; and his hands sought to tear and lacerate his flesh. He was going mad, and he shrieked for help till his voice failed him.

He raised his head, and looked up the long dismal street. He recollected that outcasts like himself, condemned to wander day and night in those dreadful streets, had sometimes gone distracted with their own loneliness. He remembered to have heard many years before that a homeless wretch had once been found in a solitary corner, sharpening a rusty knife to plunge into his own heart, preferring death to that endless, weary, wandering to and fro. In an instant his resolve was taken, his limbs received new life ; he ran quickly from the spot, and paused not for breath until he reached the river-side.

He crept softly down the steep stone stairs that lead from

the commencement of Waterloo Bridge, down to the water's level. He crouched into a corner, and held his breath, as the patrol passed. Never did prisoner's heart throb with the hope of liberty and life half so eagerly as did that of the wretched man at the prospect of death. · The watch passed close to him, but he remained unobserved ; and after waiting till the sound of footsteps had died away in the distance, he cautiously descended, and stood beneath the gloomy arch that forms the landing-place from the river.

The tide was in, and the water flowed at his feet. The rain had ceased, the wind was lulled, and all was, for the moment, still and quiet—so quiet, that the slightest sound on the opposite bank, even the rippling of the water against the barges that were moored there, was distinctly audible to his ear. The stream stole languidly and sluggishly on. Strange and fantastic forms rose to the surface, and beckoned him to approach ; dark gleaming eyes peered from the water, and seemed to mock his hesitation, while hollow murmurs from behind urged him onwards. He retreated a few paces, took a short run, desperate leap, and plunged into the river.

Not five seconds had passed when he rose to the water's surface—but what a change had taken place in that short time, in all his thoughts and feelings ! Life—life in any form, poverty, misery, starvation—anything but death. He fought and struggled with the water that closed over his head, and screamed in agonies of terror. The curse of his own son rang in his ears. The shore—but one foot of dry ground—he could almost touch the step. One hand's breadth nearer, and he was saved—but the tide bore him onward, under the dark arches of the bridge, and he sank to the bottom.

Again he rose, and struggled for life. For one instant—for one brief instant—the buildings on the river's banks, the lights on the bridge through which the current had borne him, the black water, and the fast-flying clouds, were distinctly visible—once more he sunk, and once again he rose. Bright flames of fire shot up from earth to heaven, and reeled before his eyes, while the water thundered in his ears, and stunned him with its furious roar.

A week afterwards the body was washed ashore, some miles down the river, a swollen and disfigured mass. Unrecognised and unpitied, it was borne to the grave ; and there it has long since mouldered away !

Sketches of Young Gentlemen

TO THE YOUNG LADIES

OF THE

United Kingdom of Great Britain and Ireland;

ALSO

THE YOUNG LADIES

OF

The Principality of Wales,

AND LIKEWISE

THE YOUNG LADIES

RESIDENT IN THE ISLES OF

Guernsey, Jersey, Alderney, and Sark,

THE HUMBLE DEDICATION OF THEIR DEVOTED ADMIRER,

SHEWETH,—

THAT your Dedicator has perused, with feelings of virtuous indignation, a work purporting to be "Sketches of Young Ladies;" written by Quiz, illustrated by Phiz, and published in one volume, square twelvemo.

THAT after an attentive and vigilant perusal of the said work, your Dedicator is humbly of opinion that so many libels, upon your Honourable sex, were never contained in any previously published work, in twelvemo or any other mo.

THAT in the title page and preface to the said work, your Honourable sex are described and classified as animals; and although your Dedicator is not at present prepared to deny that you *are* animals, still he humbly submits that it is not polite to call you so.

THAT in the aforesaid preface, your Honourable sex are also described as Troglodites, which, being a hard word, may, for aught your Honourable sex or your Dedicator can say to the contrary, be an injurious and disrespectful appellation.

THAT the author of the said work applied himself to his task in malice prepense and with wickedness aforethought ; a fact which, your Dedicator contends, is sufficiently demonstrated by his assuming the name of Quiz, which, your Dedicator submits, denotes a foregone conclusion, and implies an intention of quizzing.

THAT in the execution of his evil design, the said Quiz, or author of the said work, must have betrayed some trust or confidence reposed in him by some members of your Honourable sex, otherwise he never could have acquired so much information relative to the manners and customs of your Honourable sex in general.

THAT actuated by these considerations, and further moved by various slanders and insinuations respecting your Honourable sex contained in the said work, square twelvemo, entitled "Sketches of Young Ladies," your Dedicator ventures to produce another work, square twelvemo, entitled "Sketches of Young Gentlemen," of which he now solicits your acceptance and approval.

THAT as the Young Ladies are the best companions of the Young Gentlemen, so the Young Gentlemen should be the best companions of the Young Ladies ; and extending the comparison from animals (to quote the disrespectful language of the said Quiz) to inanimate objects, your Dedicator humbly suggests, that such of your Honourable sex as purchased the bane should possess themselves of the antidote, and that those of your Honourable sex who were not rash enough to take the first, should lose no time in swallowing the last,— prevention being in all cases better than cure, as we are informed upon the authority, not only of general acknowledgment, but also of traditionary wisdom.

THAT with reference to the said bane and antidote, your Dedicator has no further remarks to make, than are comprised in the printed directions issued with Doctor Morison's pills ; namely, that whenever your Honourable sex take twenty-five of Number 1, you will be pleased to take fifty of Number 2, without delay.

And your Dedicator shall ever pray, &c.

SKETCHES OF
YOUNG GENTLEMEN

THE BASHFUL YOUNG GENTLEMAN

WE found ourself seated at a small dinner party the other day, opposite a stranger of such singular appearance and manner, that he irresistibly attracted our attention.

This was a fresh coloured young gentleman, with as good a promise of light whisker as one might wish to see, and possessed of a very velvet-like soft-looking countenance. We do not use the latter term invidiously, but merely to denote a pair of smooth, plump, highly-coloured cheeks of capacious dimensions, and a mouth rather remarkable for the fresh hue of the lips than for any marked or striking expression it presented. His whole face was suffused with a crimson blush, and bore that downcast, timid, retiring look, which betokens a man ill at ease with himself.

There was nothing in these symptoms to attract more than a passing remark, but our attention had been originally drawn to the bashful young gentleman, on his first appearance in the drawing-room above-stairs, into which he was no sooner introduced, than making his way towards us who were standing in a window, and wholly neglecting several persons who warmly accosted him, he seized our hand with visible emotion, and pressed it with a convulsive grasp for a good couple of minutes, after which he dived in a nervous manner across the room, oversetting in his way a fine little girl of six years and a quarter old—and shrouding himself behind some hangings, was seen no more, until the eagle eye of the hostess detecting him in his concealment, on the announcement of dinner, he was requested to pair off with a lively single lady of two or three and thirty.

This most flattering salutation from a perfect stranger, would have gratified us not a little as a token of his having held us in high respect, and for that reason been desirous of our acquaintance, if we had not suspected from the first, that the young gentleman, in making a desperate effort to get through the ceremony of introduction, had, in the bewilderment of his ideas, shaken hands with us at random. This impression was fully confirmed by the subsequent behaviour of the bashful young gentleman in question, which we noted particularly, with the view of ascertaining whether we were right in our conjecture.

The young gentleman seated himself at table with evident misgivings, and turning sharp round to pay attention to some observation of his loquacious neighbour, overset his bread. There was nothing very bad in this, and if he had had the presence of mind to let it go, and say nothing about it, nobody but the man who had laid the cloth would have been a bit the wiser; but the young gentleman in various semi-successful attempts to prevent its fall, played with it a little, as gentlemen in the streets may be seen to do with their hats on a windy day, and then giving the roll a smart rap in his anxiety to catch it, knocked it with great adroitness into a tureen of white soup at some distance, to the unspeakable terror and disturbance of a very amiable bald gentleman, who was dispensing the contents. We thought the bashful young gentleman would have gone off in an apoplectic fit, consequent upon the violent rush of blood to his face at the occurrence of this catastrophe.

From this moment we perceived, in the phraseology of the fancy, that it was "all up" with the bashful young gentleman, and so indeed it was. Several benevolent persons endeavoured to relieve his embarrassment by taking wine with him, but finding that it only augmented his sufferings, and that after mingling sherry, champagne, hock, and moselle together, he applied the greater part of the mixture externally, instead of internally, they gradually dropped off, and left him to the exclusive care of the talkative lady, who not noting the wildness of his eye, firmly believed she had secured a listener. He broke a glass or two in the course of the meal, and disappeared shortly afterwards; it is inferred

that he went away in some confusion, inasmuch as he left
the house in another gentleman's coat, and the footman's
hat.

This little incident led us to reflect upon the most
prominent characteristics of bashful young gentlemen in the
abstract; and as this portable volume will be the great text-
book of young ladies in all future generations, we record
them here for their guidance and behoof.

If the bashful young gentleman, in turning a street corner,
chance to stumble suddenly upon two or three young ladies
of his acquaintance, nothing can exceed his confusion and
agitation. His first impulse is to make a great variety of
bows, and dart past them, which he does until, observing
that they wish to stop, but are uncertain whether to do so or
not, he makes several feints of returning, which causes them
to do the same; and at length, after a great quantity of unnecessary dodging and falling up against the other passengers,
he returns and shakes hands most affectionately with all of
them, in doing which he knocks out of their grasp sundry
little parcels, which he hastily picks up, and returns very
muddy and disordered. The chances are that the bashful
young gentleman then observes it is very fine weather, and
being reminded that it has only just left off raining for the
first time these three days, he blushes very much, and smiles
as if he had said a very good thing. The young lady who
was most anxious to speak, here inquires, with an air of
great commiseration, how his dear sister Harriet is to-day;
to which the young gentleman, without the slightest consideration, replies with many thanks, that she is remarkably
well. "Well, Mr. Hopkins!" cries the young lady, "why,
we heard she was bled yesterday evening, and have been
perfectly miserable about her." "Oh, ah," says the young
gentleman, "so she was. Oh, she's very ill, very ill indeed."
The young gentleman then shakes his head, and looks very
desponding (he has been smiling perpetually up to this time),
and after a short pause, gives his glove a great wrench at the
wrist, and says, with a strong emphasis on the adjective,
"*Good* morning, *good* morning." And making a great number of bows in acknowledgment of several little messages to
his sister, walks backward a few paces, and comes with great
violence against a lamp-post, knocking his hat off in the
contact, which in his mental confusion and bodily pain he is
going to walk away without, until a great roar from a carter

attracts his attention, when he picks it up, and tries to smile cheerfully to the young ladies, who are looking back, and who, he has the satisfaction of seeing, are all laughing heartily.

At a quadrille party, the bashful young gentleman always remains as near the entrance of the room as possible, from which position he smiles at the people he knows as they come in, and sometimes steps forward to shake hands with more intimate friends: a process which on each repetition seems to turn him a deeper scarlet than before. He declines dancing the first set or two, observing, in a faint voice, that he would rather wait a little ; but at length is absolutely compelled to allow himself to be introduced to a partner, when he is led, in a great heat and blushing furiously, across the room to a spot where half-a-dozen unknown ladies are congregated together.

"Miss Lambert, let me introduce Mr. Hopkins for the next quadrille." Miss Lambert inclines her head graciously. Mr. Hopkins bows, and his fair conductress disappears, leaving Mr. Hopkins, as he too well knows, to make himself agreeable. The young lady more than half expects that the bashful young gentleman will say something, and the bashful young gentleman feeling this, seriously thinks whether he has got anything to say, which, upon mature reflection, he is rather disposed to conclude he has not, since nothing occurs to him. Meanwhile, the young lady, after several inspections of her *bouquet*, all made in the expectation that the bashful young gentleman is going to talk, whispers her mamma, who is sitting next her, which whisper the bashful young gentleman immediately suspects (and possibly with very good reason) must be about *him*. In this comfortable condition he remains until it is time to "stand up," when murmuring a "Will you allow me ? " he gives the young lady his arm, and after inquiring where she will stand, and receiving a reply that she has no choice, conducts her to the remotest corner of the quadrille, and making one attempt at conversation, which turns out a desperate failure, preserves a profound silence until it is all over, when he walks her twice round the room, deposits her in her old seat. and retires in confusion.

A married bashful gentleman—for these bashful gentlemen *do* get married sometimes ; how it is ever brought about is a mystery to us—a married bashful gentleman either causes his wife to appear bold by contrast, or merges her proper importance in his own insignificance. Bashful young gentlemen should be cured or avoided. They are never hopeless, and never will be, while female beauty and attractions retain their influence, as any young lady will find, who may think it worth while on this confident assurance to take a patient in hand.

THE OUT-AND-OUT YOUNG GENTLEMAN

OUT-AND-OUT young gentlemen may be divided into two classes—those who have something to do, and those who have nothing. I shall commence with the former, because that species come more frequently under the notice of young ladies, whom it is our province to warn and to instruct.

The out-and-out young gentleman is usually no great dresser, his instructions to his tailor being all comprehended in the one general direction to "make that what's-a-name a regular bang-up sort of thing." For some years past, the favourite costume of the out-and-out young gentleman has been a rough pilot coat, with two gilt hooks and eyes to the velvet collar; buttons somewhat larger than crown-pieces; a black or fancy neckerchief, loosely tied; a wide-brimmed hat, with a low crown; tightish inexpressibles, and iron-shod boots. Out of doors he sometimes carries a large ash stick, but only on special occasions, for he prefers keeping his hands in his coat pockets. He smokes at all hours, of course, and swears considerably.

The out-and-out young gentleman is employed in a city counting-house or solicitor's office, in which he does as little as he possibly can: his chief places of resort are the streets, the taverns, and the theatres. In the streets at evening time, out-and-out young gentlemen have a pleasant custom of walking six or eight abreast, thus driving females and other inoffensive persons into the road, which never fails to afford them the highest satisfaction, especially if there be any immediate danger of their being run over, which enhances the fun of the thing materially. In all places of public resort, the out-and-outers are careful to select each a seat to himself, upon which he lies at full length, and (if the weather be very dirty, but not in any other case) he lies with his knees up, and the soles of his boots planted firmly on the cushion, so that if any low fellow should ask him to make room for a lady, he takes ample revenge upon her dress, without going at all out of his way to do it. He always sits with his hat on, and flourishes his stick in the air while the play is proceeding, with a dignified contempt of the performance; if it be possible for one or two out-and-out young gentlemen to get up a little crowding in the passages, they are quite in their element, squeezing, pushing, whooping, and shouting in the most humorous manner possible. If they can only succeed in irritating the gentleman who has a family of daughters under his charge, they are like to die with laughing, and boast of it among their companions for a week afterwards, adding, that one or two of them were "devilish fine girls," and that they really thought the youngest would have fainted, which was the only thing wanted to render the joke complete.

If the out-and-out young gentleman have a mother and sisters, of course he treats them with becoming contempt, inasmuch as they (poor things!) having no notion of life or gaiety, are far too weak-spirited and moping for him. Sometimes, however, on a birth-day or at Christmas-time, he cannot very well help accompanying them to a party at some old friend's, with which view he comes home when they have been dressed an hour or two, smelling very strongly of tobacco and spirits, and after exchanging his rough coat for some more suitable attire (in which, however, he loses nothing of the out-and-outer), gets into the coach and grumbles all the way at his own good nature: his bitter reflections aggravated by the recollection that Tom Smith has taken the chair at a little impromptu dinner at a fighting man's, and that a s t-to was to take place on a dining-table, between the fighting man and his brother-in-law, which is probably "coming off" at that very instant.

As the out-and-out young gentleman is by no means at his ease in ladies' society, he shrinks into a corner of the drawing-room when they reach the friend's, and unless one of his sisters is kind enough to talk to him, remains there without being much troubled by the attentions of other people, until he espies, lingering outside the door, another gentleman, whom he at once knows, by his air and manner (for there is a kind of free-masonry in the craft), to be a brother out-and-outer, and towards whom he accordingly makes his way. Conversation being soon opened by some casual remark, the second out-and-outer confidentially informs the first, that he is one of the rough sort and hates that kind of thing, only he couldn't very well be off coming; to

U

which the other replies, that that's just his case—"and I'll tell you what," continues the out-and-outer in a whisper, "I should like a glass of warm brandy and water just now," —"Or a pint of stout and a pipe," suggests the other out-and-outer.

The discovery is at once made that they are sympathetic souls; each of them says at the same moment, that he sees the other understands what's what: and they become fast friends at once, more especially when it appears that the second out-and-outer is no other than a gentleman, long favourably known to his familiars as "Mr. Warmint Blake," who upon divers occasions has distinguished himself in a manner that would not have disgraced the fighting man, and who—having been a pretty long time about town—had the honour of once shaking hands with the celebrated Mr. Thurtell himself.

At supper, these gentlemen greatly distinguish themselves, brightening up very much when the ladies leave the table, and proclaiming aloud their intention of beginning to spend the evening—a process which is generally understood to be satisfactorily performed, when a great deal of wine is drunk and a great deal of noise made, both of which feats the out-and-out young gentlemen execute to perfection. Having protracted their sitting until long after the host and the other guests have adjourned to the drawing-room, and finding that they have drained the decanters empty, they follow them thither with complexions rather heightened, and faces rather bloated with wine; and the agitated lady of the house whispers her friends as they waltz together, to the great terror of the whole room, that "both Mr. Blake and Mr. Dummins are very nice sort of young men in their way, only they are eccentric persons, and unfortunately *rather too wild!*"

The remaining class of out-and-out young gentlemen is composed of persons who, having no money of their own and a soul above earning any, enjoy similar pleasures, nobody knows how. These respectable gentlemen, without aiming quite so much at the out-and-out in external appearance, are distinguished by all the same amiable and attractive characteristics, in an equal or perhaps greater degree, and now and then find their way into society, through the medium of the other class of out-and-out young gentlemen, who will sometimes carry them home, and who usually pay their tavern bills. As they are equally gentlemanly, clever, witty, intelligent, wise, and well-bred, we need scarcely have recommended them to the peculiar consideration of the young ladies, if it were not that some of the gentle creatures whom we hold in such high respect, are perhaps a little too apt to confound a great many heavier terms with the light word eccentricity, which we beg them henceforth to take in a strictly Johnsonian sense, without any liberality or latitude of construction.

THE VERY FRIENDLY YOUNG GENTLEMAN

We know—and all people know—so many specimens of this class, that in selecting the few heads our limits enable us to take from a great number, we have been induced to give the very friendly young gentleman the preference over many others, to whose claims upon a more cursory view of the question we had felt disposed to assign the priority.

The very friendly young gentleman is very friendly to everybody, but he attaches himself particularly to two, or at most to three families : regulating his choice by their dinners, their circle of acquaintance, or some other criterion in which he has an immediate interest. He is of any age between twenty and forty, unmarried of course, must be fond of children, and is expected to make himself generally useful if possible. Let us illustrate our meaning by an example, which is the shortest mode and the clearest.

We encountered one day, by chance, an old friend of whom we had lost sight for some years, and who—expressing a strong anxiety to renew our former intimacy—urged us to dine with him on an early day, that we might talk over old times. We readily assented, adding, that we hoped we should be alone. "Oh, certainly, certainly," said our friend, "not a soul with us but Mincin." "And who is Mincin?" was our natural inquiry. "O don't mind him," replied our friend, "he's a most particular friend of mine, and a very friendly fellow you will find him ; " and so he left us.

We thought no more about Mincin until we duly presented ourselves at the house next day, when, after a hearty welcome, our friend motioned towards a gentleman who had been previously showing his teeth by the fireplace, and gave us to understand that it was Mr. Mincin, of whom he had spoken. It required no great penetration on our part to discover at once that Mr. Mincin was in every respect a very friendly young gentleman.

"I am delighted," said Mincin, hastily advancing, and pressing our hand warmly between both of his, "I am delighted, I am sure, to make your acquaintance—(here he smiled)—very much delighted indeed—(here he exhibited a little emotion)—I assure you that I have looked forward to it anxiously for a very long time:" here he released our hands, and rubbing his own, observed that the day was severe, but that he was delighted to perceive from our appearance that it agreed with us wonderfully; and then went on to observe that, notwithstanding the coldness of the weather, he had that morning seen in the paper an exceedingly curious paragraph, to the effect that there was now in the garden of Mr. Wilkins of Chichester, a pumpkin, measuring four feet in height, and eleven feet seven inches in circumference, which he looked upon as a very extraordinary piece of intelligence. We ventured to remark, that we had a dim recollection of having once or twice before observed a similar paragraph in the public prints, upon which Mr. Mincin took us confidentially by the button, and said, Exactly, exactly, to be sure, we were very right, and he wondered what the editors meant by putting in such things. Who the deuce, he should like to know, did they suppose cared about them? that struck him as being the best of it.

The lady of the house appeared shortly afterwards, and Mr. Mincin's friendliness, as will readily be supposed, suffered no diminution in consequence; he exerted much strength and skill in wheeling a large easy-chair up to the fire, and the lady being seated in it, carefully closed the door, stirred the fire, and looked to the windows to see that they admitted no air; having satisfied himself upon all these points, he expressed himself quite easy in his mind, and begged to know how she found herself to-day. Upon the lady's replying very well, Mr. Mincin (who it appeared was a medical gentleman) offered some general remarks upon the nature and treatment of colds in the head, which occupied us agreeably until dinner-time. During the meal, he devoted himself to complimenting everybody, not forgetting himself, so that we were an uncommonly agreeable quartette.

"I'll tell you what, Capper," said Mr. Mincin to our host, as he closed the room-door after the lady had retired, "you have very great reason to be fond of your wife. Sweet woman, Mrs. Capper, sir!" "Nay, Mincin—I beg," interposed the host, as we were about to reply that Mrs. Capper unquestionably was particularly sweet. "Pray, Mincin, don't." "Why not?" exclaimed Mr. Mincin, "why not? Why should you feel any delicacy before your old friend—*our* old friend, if I may be allowed to call you so, sir; why should you, I ask?" We of course wished to know why he should also, upon which our friend admitted that Mrs. Capper *was* a very sweet woman, at which admission Mr. Mincin cried "Bravo!" and begged to propose Mrs. Capper with heartfelt enthusiasm, whereupon our host said, "Thank you, Mincin," with deep feeling; and gave us, in a low voice, to understand that Mincin had saved Mrs. Capper's cousin's life no less than fourteen times in a year and a half, which he considered no common circumstance—an opinion to which we most cordially subscribed.

Now that we three were left to entertain ourselves with conversation, Mr. Mincin's extreme friendliness became every moment more apparent; he was so amazingly friendly, indeed, that it was impossible to talk about anything in which he had not the chief concern. We happened to allude to some affairs in which our friend and we had been mutually engaged nearly fourteen years before, when Mr. Mincin was all at once reminded of a joke which our friend had made on that day four years, which he positively must insist upon telling—and which he did tell accordingly, with many pleasant recollections of what he said, and what Mrs. Capper said, and how he well remembered that they had been to the play with orders on the very night previous, and had seen Romeo and Juliet, and the pantomime, and how Mrs. Capper being faint had been led into the lobby, where she smiled, said it was nothing after all, and went back again, with many other interesting and absorbing particulars: after which the friendly young gentleman went on to assure us, that our friend had experienced a marvellously prophetic opinion of that same pantomime, which was of such an admirable kind, that two morning papers took the same view next day: to this our friend replied, with a little triumph, that in that instance he had some reason to think he had been correct, which gave the friendly young gentleman occasion to believe that our friend was always correct; and so we went on, until our friend, filling a bumper, said he must drink one glass to his dear friend Mincin, than whom he would say no man saved the lives of his acquaintances more, or had a more friendly heart. Finally, our friend having emptied his glass, said, "God bless you, Mincin,"—and Mr. Mincin and he shook hands across the table with much affection and earnestness.

But great as the friendly young gentleman is, in a limited scene like this. he plays the same part on a larger scale with increased *éclat*. Mr. Mincin is invited to an evening party with his dear friends the Martins, where he meets his dear friends the Cappers, and his dear friends the Watsons, and a hundred other dear friends too numerous to mention. He is as much at home with the Martins as with the Cappers; but how exquisitely he balances his attentions, and divides them among his dear friends! If he flirts with one of the Miss Watsons, he has one little Martin on the sofa pulling his hair, and the other little Martin on the carpet riding on his foot. He carries Mrs. Watson down to supper on one arm. and Miss Martin on the other, and takes wine so judiciously, and in such exact order, that it is impossible for the most punctilious old lady to consider herself neglected. If any young lady, being prevailed upon to sing, become nervous afterwards, Mr. Mincin leads her tenderly into the next room, and restores her with port wine, which she must take medicinally. If any gentleman be standing by the piano during the progress of the ballad, Mr. Mincin seizes him by the arm at one point of the melody, and softly beating time the while with his head, expresses in dumb show his intense perception of the delicacy of the passage. If anybody's self-love is to be flattered, Mr. Mincin is at hand. If anybody's overweening vanity is to be pampered, Mr. Mincin will surfeit it. What wonder that people of all stations and ages recognise Mr. Mincin's friendliness; that he is universally allowed to be handsome as amiable; that mothers think him an oracle, daughters a dear, brothers a beau, and fathers a wonder! And who would not have the reputation of the very friendly young gentleman?

THE MILITARY YOUNG GENTLEMAN

WE are rather at a loss to imagine how it has come to pass that military young gentlemen have obtained so much favour in the eyes of the young ladies of this kingdom. We cannot think so lightly of them as to suppose that the mere circumstance of a man's wearing a red coat ensures him a ready passport to their regard; and even if this were the case, it would be no satisfactory explanation of the circumstance, because, although the analogy may in some degree hold good in the case of mail coachmen and guards, still general postmen wear red coats, and *they* are not to our knowledge better received than other men; nor are firemen either, who wear (or used to wear) not only red coats, but very resplendent and massive badges besides—much larger than epaulettes. Neither do the twopenny post-office boys, if the result of our inquiries be correct, find any peculiar favour in woman's eyes, although they wear very bright red jackets, and have the additional advantage of constantly appearing in public on horseback, which last circumstance may be naturally supposed to be greatly in their favour.

We have sometimes thought that this phenomenon may take its rise in the conventional behaviour of captains and colonels and other gentlemen in red coats on the stage, where they are invariably represented as fine swaggering fellows, talking of nothing but charming girls, their king and country, their honour, and their debts, and crowing over the inferior classes of the community, whom they occasionally treat with a little gentlemanly swindling, no less to the improvement and pleasure of the audience, than to the satisfaction and approval of the choice spirits who consort with them. But we will not devote these pages to our speculations upon the subject, inasmuch as our business at the present moment is not so much with the young ladies who are bewitched by her Majesty's livery as with the young gentlemen whose heads are turned by it. For "heads" we had

Military Young Gentlemen

written "brains;" but upon consideration, we think the former the more appropriate word of the two.

These young gentlemen may be divided into two classes—young gentlemen who are actually in the army, and young gentlemen who, having an intense and enthusiastic admiration for all things appertaining to a military life, are compelled by adverse fortune or adverse relations to wear out their existence in some ignoble counting-house. We will take this latter description of military young gentlemen first.

The whole heart and soul of the military young gentleman are concentrated in his favourite topic. There is nothing that he is so learned upon as uniforms ; he will tell you, without faltering for an instant, what the habiliments of any one regiment are turned up with, what regiment wear stripes down the outside and inside of the leg, and how many buttons the Tenth had on their coats ; he knows to a fraction how many yards and odd inches of gold lace it takes to make an ensign in the Guards ; is deeply read in the comparative merits of different bands, and the apparelling of trumpeters ; and is very luminous indeed in descanting upon " crack regiments," and the " crack " gentlemen who compose them, of whose mightiness and grandeur he is never tired of telling.

We were suggesting to a military young gentleman only the other day, after he had related to us several dazzling instances of the profusion of half-a-dozen honourable ensign somebodies or nobodies in the articles of kid gloves and polished boots, that possibly " cracked " regiments would be an improvement upon "crack," as being a more expressive and appropriate designation, when he suddenly interrupted us by pulling out his watch, and observing that he must hurry off to the Park in a cab, or he would be too late to hear the band play. Not wishing to interfere with so important an engagement, and being in fact already slightly overwhelmed by the anecdotes of the honourable ensigns afore-mentioned, we made no attempt to detain the military young gentleman, but parted company with ready good-will.

Some three or four hours afterwards, we chanced to be walking down Whitehall, on the Admiralty side of the way, when, as we drew near to one of the little stone places in which a couple of horse soldiers mount guard in the day-time, we were attracted by the motionless appearance and eager gaze of a young gentleman, who was devouring both man and horse with his eyes, so eagerly, that he seemed deaf and blind to all that was passing around him. We were not much surprised at the discovery that it was our friend, the military young gentleman, but we *were* a little astonished when we returned from a walk to South Lambeth to find him still there, looking on with the same intensity as before. As it was a very windy day, we felt bound to awaken the young gentleman from his reverie, when he inquired of us with great enthusiasm, whether "that was not a glorious spectacle," and proceeded to give us a detailed account of the weight of every article of the spectacle's trappings, from the man's gloves to the horse's shoes.

We have made it a practice since, to take the Horse Guards in our daily walk, and we find it is the custom of military young gentlemen to plant themselves opposite the sentries, and contemplate them at leisure, in periods varying from fifteen minutes to fifty, and averaging twenty-five. We were much struck a day or two since, by the behaviour of a very promising young butcher who (evincing an interest in the service, which cannot be too strongly commended or encouraged), after a prolonged inspection of the sentry, proceeded to handle his boots with great curiosity, and as much composure and indifference as if the man were wax-work.

But the really military young gentleman is waiting all this time, and at the very moment that an apology rises to our lips, he emerges from the barrack gate (he is quartered in a garrison town), and takes the way towards the high street. He wears his undress uniform, which somewhat mars the glory of his outward man; but still how great, how grand, he is! What a happy mixture of ease and ferocity in his gait and carriage, and how lightly he carries that dreadful sword under his arm, making no more ado about it than if it were a silk umbrella! The lion is sleeping: only think if an enemy were in sight, how soon he'd whip it out of the scabbard, and what a terrible fellow he would be!

But he walks on, thinking of nothing less than blood and slaughter; and now he comes in sight of three other military young gentlemen, arm-in-arm, who are bearing down towards him, clanking their iron heels on the pavement, and clashing their swords with a noise, which should cause all peaceful men to quail at heart. They stop to talk. See how the flaxen-haired young gentleman with the weak legs—he who has his pocket-handkerchief thrust into the breast of his coat —glares upon the faint-hearted civilians who linger to look upon his glory; how the next young gentleman elevates his head in the air, and majestically places his arms a-kimbo, while the third stands with his legs very wide apart, and clasps his hands behind him. Well may we inquire—not in familiar jest, but in respectful earnest—if you call that nothing. Oh! if some encroaching foreign power—the Emperor of Russia, for instance, or any of those deep fellows, could only see those military young gentlemen as they move on together towards the billiard-room over the way, wouldn't he tremble a little!

And then, at the Theatre at night, when the performances are by command of Colonel Fitz-Sordust and the officers of the garrison—what a splendid sight it is! How sternly the defenders of their country look round the house as if in mute assurance to the audience, that they may make themselves comfortable regarding any foreign invasion, for they (the military young gentlemen) are keeping a sharp look-out, and are ready for anything. And what a contrast between them, and that stage-box full of grey-headed officers with tokens of many battles about them, who have nothing at all in common with the military young gentlemen, and who— but for an old-fashioned kind of manly dignity in their looks and bearing—might be common hard-working soldiers for anything they take the pains to announce to the contrary!

Ah! here is a family just come in who recognise the flaxen-headed young gentleman; and the flaxen-headed young gentleman recognises them too, only he doesn't care to show it just now. Very well done indeed! He talks louder to the little group of military young gentlemen who are standing by him, and coughs to induce some ladies in the next box but one to look round, in order that their faces may undergo the same ordeal of criticism to which they have subjected, in not a wholly inaudible tone, the majority of the female portion of the audience. Oh! a gentleman in the same box looks round as if he were disposed to resent this as an impertinence; and the flaxen-headed young gentleman sees his friends at once, and hurries away to them with the most charming cordiality.

Three young ladies, one young man, and the mamma of the party, receive the military young gentleman with great warmth and politeness, and in five minutes afterwards the military young gentleman, stimulated by the mamma, introduces the two other military young gentlemen with whom he was walking in the morning, who take their seats behind the young ladies and commence conversation; whereat the mamma bestows a triumphant bow upon a rival mamma, who has not succeeded in decoying any military young gentlemen, and prepares to consider her visitors from that moment three of the most elegant and superior young gentlemen in the whole world.

THE POLITICAL YOUNG GENTLEMAN

ONCE upon a time—*not* in the days when pigs drank wine, but in a more recent period of our history—it was customary to banish politics when ladies were present. If this usage still prevailed, we should have had no chapter for political young gentlemen, for ladies would have neither known nor cared what kind of monster a political young gentleman was. But as this good custom in common with many others has " gone out," and left no word when it is likely to be home again ; as political young ladies are by no means rare, and political young gentlemen the very reverse of scarce, we are bound in the strict discharge of our most responsible duty not to neglect this natural division of our subject.

If the political young gentleman be resident in a country town (and there *are* political young gentlemen in country towns sometimes), he is wholly absorbed in his politics ; as a pair of purple spectacles communicate the same uniform tint to all objects near and remote, so the political glasses, with which the young gentleman assists his mental vision, give to everything the hue and tinge of party feeling. The political young gentleman would as soon think of being struck with the beauty of a young lady in the opposite interest, as he would dream of marrying his sister to the opposite member.

If the political young gentleman be a Conservative, he has usually some vague ideas about Ireland and the Pope which he cannot very clearly explain, but which he knows are the right sort of thing, and not to be very easily got over by the other side. He has also some choice sentences regarding church and state, culled from the banners in use at the last election, with which he intersperses his conversation at intervals with surprising effect. But his great topic is the constitution, upon which he will declaim, by the hour together, with much heat and fury ; not that he has any particular information on the subject, but because he knows that the constitution is somehow church and state, and church and state somehow the constitution, and that the fellows on the other side say it isn't, which is quite a sufficient reason for him to say it is, and to stick to it.

Perhaps his greatest topic of all, though, is the people. If a fight takes place in a populous town, in which many noses are broken, and a few windows, the young gentleman throws down the newspaper with a triumphant air, and exclaims, "Here's your precious people!" if half-a-dozen boys run across the course at race time, when it ought to be kept clear, the young gentleman looks indignantly round, and begs you to observe the conduct of the people; if the gallery demand a hornpipe between the play and the after-piece, the same young gentleman cries "No" and "Shame" till he is hoarse, and then inquires with a sneer what you think of popular moderation *now;* in short, the people form a never-failing theme for him; and when the attorney, on the side of his candidate, dwells upon it with great power of eloquence at election time, as he never fails to do, the young gentleman and his friends, and the body they head, cheer with great violence against *the other people*, with whom, of course, they have no possible connexion. In much the same manner the audience at a theatre never fail to be highly amused with any jokes at the expense of the public—always laughing heartily at some other public, and never at themselves.

If the political young gentleman be a Radical, he is usually a very profound person indeed, having great store of theo-retical questions to put to you, with an infinite variety of possible cases and logical deductions therefrom. If he be of the utilitarian school, too, which is more than probable, he is particularly pleasant company, having many ingenious remarks to offer upon the voluntary principle and various cheerful disquisitions connected with the population of the country, the position of Great Britain in the scale of nations, and the balance of power. Then he is exceedingly well versed in all doctrines of political economy as laid down in the newspapers, and knows a great many parliamentary speeches by heart; nay, he has a small stock of aphorisms, none of them exceeding a couple of lines in length, which will settle the toughest question and leave you nothing to say. He gives all the young ladies to understand, that Miss Martineau is the greatest woman that ever lived; and when they praise the good looks of Mr. Hawkins the new member, says he's very well for a representative, all things considered, but he wants a little calling to account, and he is more than half afraid it will be necessary to bring him down on his knees for that vote on the miscellaneous estimates. At this, the young ladies express much wonderment, and say surely a Member of Parliament is not to be brought upon his knees so easily; in reply to which the political young gentleman smiles sternly, and throws out dark hints regarding the speedy arrival of that day when Members of Parliament will be paid salaries, and required to render weekly accounts of their proceedings, at which the young ladies utter many expressions of astonishment and incredulity, while their lady-mothers regard the prophecy as little else than blasphemous.

It is extremely improving and interesting to hear two political young gentlemen, of diverse opinions, discuss some great question across a dinner-table; such as whether, if the public were admitted to Westminster Abbey for nothing, they would or would not convey small chisels and hammers in their pockets, and immediately set about chipping all the noses off the statues; or whether, if they once got into the Tower for a shilling, they would not insist upon trying the crown on their own heads, and loading and firing off all the small arms in the armoury, to the great discomposure of Whitechapel and the Minories. Upon these, and many other momentous questions which agitate the public mind in these desperate days, they will discourse with great vehemence and irritation for a considerable time together, both leaving off precisely where they began, and each thoroughly persuaded that he has got the better of the other.

In society, at assemblies, balls, and playhouses, these political young gentlemen are perpetually on the watch for a political allusion, or anything which can be tortured or construed into being one; when, thrusting themselves into the very smallest openings for their favourite discourse, they fall upon the unhappy company tooth and nail. They have recently had many favourable opportunities of opening in churches, but as there the clergyman has it all his own way, and must not be contradicted, whatever politics he preaches, they are fain to hold their tongues until they reach the outer door, though at the imminent risk of bursting in the effort.

As such discussions can please nobody but the talkative parties concerned, we hope they will henceforth take the hint and discontinue them, otherwise we now give them warning, that the ladies have our advice to discountenance such talkers altogether.

THE DOMESTIC YOUNG GENTLEMAN

LET us make a slight sketch of our amiable friend, Mr. Felix Nixon. We are strongly disposed to think, that if we put him in this place, he will answer our purpose without another word of comment.

Felix, then, is a young gentleman who lives at home with his mother, just within the twopenny-post office circle of three miles from St. Martin-le-Grand. He wears India-rubber goloshes when the weather is at all damp, and always has a silk handkerchief neatly folded up in the right-hand pocket of his great-coat, to tie over his mouth when he goes home at night; moreover, being rather near-sighted, he carries spectacles for particular occasions, and has a weakish tremulous voice, of which he makes great use, for he talks as much as any old lady breathing.

The two chief subjects of Felix's discourse, are himself and his mother, both of whom would appear to be very wonderful and interesting persons. As Felix and his mother are seldom apart in body, so Felix and his mother are scarcely ever separate in spirit. If you ask Felix how he finds himself to-day, he prefaces his reply with a long and minute bulletin of his mother's state of health; and the good lady in her turn, edifies her acquaintance with a circumstantial and alarming account, how he sneezed four times and coughed once after being out in the rain the other night, but having his feet promptly put into hot water, and his head into a flannel-something, which we will not describe more particularly than by this delicate allusion, was happily brought round by the next morning, and enabled to go to business as usual.

Our friend is not a very adventurous or hot-headed person, but he has passed through many dangers, as his mother can testify : there is one great story in particular, concerning a hackney coachman who wanted to overcharge him one night for bringing them home from the play, upon which Felix gave the aforesaid coachman a look which his mother thought

The Domestic Young Gentleman

would have crushed him to the earth, but which did not crush him quite, for he continued to demand another sixpence, notwithstanding that Felix took out his pocket-book, and, with the aid of a flat candle, pointed out the fare in print, which the coachman obstinately disregarding, he shut the street-door with a slam which his mother shudders to think of; and then, roused to the most appalling pitch of passion by the coachman knocking a double knock to show that he was by no means convinced, he broke with uncontrollable force from his parent and the servant girl, and running into the street without his hat, actually shook his fist at the coachman, and came back again with a face as white, Mrs. Nixon says, looking about her for a simile, as white as that ceiling. She never will forget his fury that night, Never!

To this account Felix listens with a solemn face, occasionally looking at you to see how it affects you, and when his mother has made an end of it, adds that he looked at every coachman he met for three weeks afterwards, in hopes that he might see the scoundrel; whereupon Mrs. Nixon, with an exclamation of terror, requests to know what he would have done to him if he *had* seen him, at which Felix smiling darkly and clenching his right fist, she exclaims, " Goodness gracious!" with a distracted air, and insists upon extorting a promise that he never will on any account do anything so rash, which her dutiful son—it being something more than three years since the offence was committed—reluctantly concedes, and his mother, shaking her head prophetically, fears with a sigh that his spirit will lead him into something violent yet. The discourse then, by an easy transition, turns upon the spirit which glows within the bosom of Felix, upon which point Felix himself becomes eloquent, and relates a thrilling anecdote of the time when he used to sit up till two o'clock in the morning reading French, and how his mother used to say, "Felix, you will make yourself ill. I know you will;" and how *he* used to say, "Mother, I don't care—I will do it;" and how at last his mother privately procured a doctor to come and see him, who declared, the moment he felt his pulse, that if he had gone on reading one night more—only one night more—he must have put a blister on each temple, and another between his shoulders; and who, as it was, sat down upon the instant, and writing a prescription for a blue pill, said it must be taken immediately, or he wouldn't answer for the consequences. The recital of these and many other moving perils of the like nature, constantly harrows up the feelings of Mr. Nixon's friends.

Mrs. Nixon has a tolerably extensive circle of female acquaintance, being a good-humoured talkative, bustling little body, and to the unmarried girls among them she is constantly vaunting the virtues of her son, hinting that she will be a very happy person who wins him, but that they must mind their P's and Q's, for ho is very particular, and terribly severe upon young ladies. At this last caution the young ladies resident in the same row, who happen to be spending the evening there, put their pocket-handkerchiefs before their mouths, and are troubled with a short cough ; just then Felix knocks at the door, and his mother drawing the tea-table nearer the fire, calls out to him as he takes off his boots in the back parlour that he needn't mind coming in in his slippers, for there are only the two Miss Greys and Miss Thompson, and she is quite sure they will excuse *him*, and nodding to the two Miss Greys, she adds, in a whisper, that Julia Thompson is a great favourite with Felix, at which intelligence the short cough comes again, and Miss Thompson in particular is greatly troubled with it, till Felix coming in, very faint for want of his tea, changes the subject of discourse, and enables her to laugh out boldly and tell Amelia Grey not to be so foolish. Here they all three laugh, and Mrs. Nixon says they are giddy girls ; in which stage of the proceedings, Felix, who has by this time re-freshened himself with the grateful herb that "cheers but not inebriates," removes his cup from his countenance and says with a knowing smile, that all girls are ; whereat his admiring mamma pats him on the back and tells him not to be sly, which calls forth a general laugh from the young ladies, and another smile from Felix, who thinking he looks very sly indeed, is perfectly satisfied.

Tea being over, the young ladies resume their work, and Felix insists upon holding a skein of silk while Miss Thompson winds it on a card. This process having been performed to the satisfaction of all parties, he brings down his flute in compliance with a request from the youngest Miss Grey, and plays divers tunes out of a very small music-book till supper-time, when he is very facetious and talkative indeed. Finally, after half a tumblerful of warm sherry and water, he gallantly puts on his goloshes over his slippers, and telling Miss Thompson's servant to run on first and get the door open, escorts that young lady to her house, five doors off: the Miss Greys who live in the next house but one stopping to peep with merry faces from their own door till he comes back again, when they call out "Very well, Mr. Felix," and trip into the passage with a laugh more musical than any flute that was ever played.

Felix is rather prim in his appearance, and perhaps a little priggish about his books and flute, and so forth, which have all their peculiar corners of peculiar shelves in his bedroom : indeed all his female acquaintance (and they are good judges) have long ago set him down as a thorough old bachelor. He is a favourite with them however, in a certain way, as an honest, inoffensive, kind-hearted creature; and as his peculiarities harm nobody, not even himself, we are induced to hope that many who are not personally acquainted with him will take our good word in his behalf, and be content to leave him to a long continuance of his harmless existence.

THE CENSORIOUS YOUNG GENTLEMAN

THERE is an amiable kind of young gentleman going about in society, upon whom, after much experience of him, and considerable turning over of the subject in our mind, we feel it our duty to affix the above appellation. Young ladies mildly call him a "sarcastic" young gentleman, or a "severe" young gentleman. We, who know better, beg to acquaint them with the fact, that he is merely a censorious young gentleman, and nothing else.

The censorious young gentleman has the reputation among his familiars of a remarkably clever person, which he maintains by receiving all intelligence and expressing all opinions with a dubious sneer, accompanied with a half smile, expressive of anything you please but good-humour. This sets people about thinking what on earth the censorious young gentleman means, and they speedily arrive at the conclusion that he means something very deep indeed; for they reason in this way—"This young gentleman looks so very knowing that he must mean something, and as I am by no means a dull individual, what a very deep meaning he must have if *I* can't find it out!" It is extraordinary how soon a censorious young gentleman may make a reputation in his own small circle if he bear this in his mind, and regulate his proceedings accordingly.

As young ladies are generally—not curious, but laudably desirous to acquire information, the censorious young gentleman is much talked about among them, and many surmises are hazarded regarding him. "I wonder," exclaims the eldest Miss Greenwood, laying down her work to turn up the lamp, "I wonder whether Mr. Fairfax will ever be married." "Bless me, dear," cries Miss Marshall, "what ever made you think of him?" "Really, I hardly know," replies Miss Greenwood; "he is such a very mysterious person, that I often wonder about him." "Well, to tell you the truth," replies Miss Marshall, "and so do I." Here two other young ladies profess that they are constantly doing the like, and all present appear in the same condition except one young lady, who, not scrupling to state that she considers Mr. Fairfax "a horror," draws down all the opposition of the others, which having been expressed in a great many ejaculatory passages, such as "Well, did I ever!"—and "Lor, Emily, dear!" ma takes up the subject, and gravely states, that she must say she does not think Mr. Fairfax by any means a horror, but rather takes him to be a young man of very great ability; "and I am quite sure," adds the worthy lady, "he always means a great deal more than he says."

The door opens at this point of the discourse, and who of all people alive walks into the room, but the very Mr. Fairfax, who has been the subject of conversation! "Well, it really is curious," cries ma, "we were at that very moment talking about you." "You did me great honour," replies Mr. Fairfax; "may I venture to ask what you were saying?" "Why, if you must know," returns the eldest girl, "we were remarking what a very mysterious man you are." "Aye, aye!" observes Mr. Fairfax, "Indeed!" Now Mr. Fairfax says this aye, aye, and indeed, which are slight words enough in themselves, with so very unfathomable an air, and accompanies them with such a very equivocal smile, that ma and the young ladies are more than ever convinced that he means an immensity, and so tell him he is a very dangerous man, and seems to be always thinking ill of somebody, which is precisely the sort of character the censorious young gentleman is most desirous to establish; wherefore he says, "Oh, dear, no," in a tone, obviously intended to mean, "You have me there," and which gives them to understand that they have hit the right nail on the very centre of its head.

When the conversation ranges from the mystery overhanging the censorious young gentleman's behaviour, to the general topics of the day, he sustains his character to admiration. He considers the new tragedy well enough *for* a new tragedy, but Lord bless us—well, no matter; he could say a great deal on that point, but he would rather not, lest he should be thought ill-natured, as he knows he would be. "But is not Mr. So-and-So's performance truly charming?" inquires a young lady. "Charming!" replies the censorious young gentleman. "Oh, dear, yes, certainly; very charming—oh, very charming indeed." After this, he stirs the fire, smiling contemptuously all the while: and a modest young gentleman, who has been a silent listener, thinks what a great thing it must be to have such a critical judgment. Of music, pictures, books, and poetry, the censorious young gentleman has an equally fine conception. As to men and women, he can tell all about them at a glance. "Now let us hear your opinion of young Mrs. Barker," says some great believer in the powers of Mr. Fairfax, "but don't be too severe." "I never am severe," replies the censorious young gentleman. "Well, never mind that now. She is very lady-like, is she not?" "Lady-like!" repeats the censorious young gentleman (for he always repeats when he is at a loss for anything to say). "Did you observe her manner? Bless my heart and soul, Mrs. Thompson, did you observe her manner?—that's all I ask." "I thought I had done so," rejoins the poor lady, much perplexed; "I did not observe it very closely perhaps." "Oh, not very closely," rejoins the censorious young gentleman, triumphantly. "Very good; then *I* did. Let us talk no more about her." The censorious young gentleman purses up his lips, and nods his head sagely, as he says this; and it is forthwith whispered about, that Mr. Fairfax (who, though he is a little prejudiced, must be admitted to be a very excellent judge) has observed something exceedingly odd in Mrs. Barker's manner.

THE FUNNY YOUNG GENTLEMAN

As one funny young gentleman will serve as a sample of all funny young gentlemen, we purpose merely to note down the conduct and behaviour of an individual specimen of this class, whom we happened to meet at an annual family Christmas party in the course of this very last Christmas that ever came.

We were all seated round a blazing fire which crackled pleasantly as the guests talked merrily and the urn steamed cheerily—for, being an old fashioned party, there was an urn, and a teapot besides—when there came a postman's knock at the door, so violent and sudden, that it startled the whole circle, and actually caused two or three very interesting and most unaffected young ladies to scream aloud and to exhibit many afflicting symptoms of terror and distress, until they had been several times assured by their respective adorers, that they were in no danger. We were about to remark that it was surely beyond post-time, and must have been a runaway knock, when our host, who had hitherto been paralysed with wonder, sank into a chair in a perfect ecstasy of laughter, and offered to lay twenty pounds that it was that droll dog Griggins. He had no sooner said this, than the majority of the company and all the children of the house burst into a roar of laughter too, as if some inimitable joke flashed upon them simultaneously, and gave vent to various exclamations of—To be sure it must be Griggins, and How like him that was, and What spirits he was always in! with many other commendatory remarks of the like nature.

Not having the happiness to know Griggins, we became extremely desirous to see so pleasant a fellow, the more especially as a stout gentleman with a powdered head, who was sitting with his breeches buckles almost touching the hob, whispered us he was a wit of the first water, when the door opened, and Mr. Griggins being announced, presented himself, amidst another shout of laughter and a loud clapping

of hands from the younger branches. This welcome he acknowledged by sundry contortions of countenance, imitative
of the clown in one of the new pantomimes, which were so
extremely successful, that one stout gentleman rolled upon
an ottoman in a paroxysm of delight, protesting, with many
gasps, that if somebody didn't make that fellow Griggins
leave off, he would be the death of him, he knew. At this
the company only laughed more boisterously than before, and
as we always like to accommodate our tone and spirit if
possible to the humour of any society in which we find ourself, we laughed with the rest, and exclaimed, "Oh! capital,
capital!" as loud as any of them.

When he had quite exhausted all beholders, Mr. Griggins
received the welcomes and congratulations of the circle, and
went through the needful introductions with much ease and
many puns. This ceremony over, he avowed his intention
of sitting in somebody's lap unless the young ladies made
room for him on the sofa, which being done, after a great
deal of tittering and pleasantry, he squeezed himself among
them, and likened his condition to that of love among the
roses. At this novel jest we all roared once more. "You
should consider yourself highly honoured, sir," said we.
"Sir," replied Mr. Griggins, "you do me proud." Here
everybody laughed again; and the stout gentleman by the
fire whispered in our ear that Griggins was making a dead
set at us.

The tea-things having been removed, we all sat down to
a round game, and here Mr. Griggins shone forth with
peculiar brilliancy, abstracting other people's fish, and looking over their hands in the most comical manner. He made
one most excellent joke in snuffing a candle, which was
neither more nor less than setting fire to the hair of a pale
young gentleman who sat next him, and afterwards begging
his pardon with considerable humour. As the young gentleman could not see the joke, however, possibly in consequence
of its being on the top of his own head, it did not go off
quite as well as it might have done; indeed, the young
gentleman was heard to murmur some general references
to "impertinence," and a "rascal," and to state the number
of his lodgings in an angry tone—a turn of the conversation
which might have been productive of slaughterous consequences, if a young lady, betrothed to the young gentleman,
had not used her immediate influence to bring about a

The Funny Young Gentleman

reconciliation: emphatically declaring in an agitated whisper, intended for his peculiar edification but audible to the whole table, that if he went on in that way, she never would think of him otherwise than as a friend, though as that she must always regard him. At this terrible threat the young gentle-man became calm, and the young lady, overcome by the revulsion of feeling, instantaneously fainted.

Mr. Griggins's spirits were slightly depressed for a short period by this unlooked-for result of such a harmless pleasantry, but being promptly elevated by the attentions of the host and several glasses of wine, he soon recovered, and became even more vivacious than before, insomuch that the stout gentleman previously referred to, assured us that although he had known him since he was *that* high (some-thing smaller than a nutmeg-grater), he had never beheld him in such excellent cue.

When the round game and several games at blind man's buff which followed it were all over, and we were going down to supper, the inexhaustible Mr. Griggins produced a small sprig of mistletoe from his waistcoat pocket, and commenced a general kissing of the assembled females, which occasioned great commotion and much excitement. We observed that several young gentlemen—including the young gentleman with the pale countenance—were greatly scandal-ised at this indecorous proceeding, and talked very big among themselves in corners; and we observed too, that several young ladies when remonstrated with by the aforesaid young gentlemen, called each other to witness how they had struggled, and protested vehemently that it was very rude, and that they were surprised at Mrs. Brown's allowing it, and that they couldn't bear it, and had no patience with such impertinence. But such is the gentle and forgiving nature of woman, that although we looked very narrowly for it, we could not detect the slightest harshness in the subsequent treatment of Mr. Griggins. Indeed, upon the whole, it struck us that among the ladies he seemed rather more popular than before!

To recount all the drollery of Mr. Griggins at supper, would fill such a tiny volume as this [1], to the very bottom of the outside cover. How he drank out of other people's glasses, and ate of other people's bread, how he frightened into screaming convulsions a little boy who was sitting up

[1] [In its original form.]

to supper in a high chair, by sinking below the table and suddenly reappearing with a mask on ; how the hostess was really surprised that anybody could find a pleasure in tormenting children, and how the host frowned at the hostess, and felt convinced that Mr. Griggins had done it with the very best intentions ; how Mr. Griggins explained, and how everybody's good-humour was restored but the child's ;—to tell these and a hundred other things ever so briefly, would occupy more of our room and our readers' patience, than either they or we can conveniently spare.   Therefore we change the subject, merely observing that we have offered no description of the funny young gentleman's personal appearance, believing that almost every society has a Griggins of its own, and leaving all readers to supply the deficiency, according to the particular circumstances of their particular case.

THE THEATRICAL YOUNG GENTLEMAN

ALL gentlemen who love the drama—and there are few gentlemen who are not attached to the most intellectual and rational of all our amusements—do not come within this definition. As we have no mean relish for theatrical entertainments ourself, we are disinterestedly anxious that this should be perfectly understood.

The theatrical young gentleman has early and important information on all theatrical topics. "Well," says he, abruptly, when you meet him in the street, "here's a pretty to-do. Flimkins has thrown up his part in the melodrama at the Surrey."—"And what's to be done?" you inquire with as much gravity as you can counterfeit. "Ah, that's the point," replies the theatrical young gentleman, looking very serious; "Boozle declines it; positively declines it. From all I am told, I should say it was decidedly in Boozle's line, and that he would be very likely to make a great hit in it; but he objects on the ground of Flimkins having been put up in the part first, and says no earthly power shall induce him to take the character. It's a fine part, too—excellent business, I'm told. He has to kill six people in the course of the piece, and to fight over a bridge in red fire, which is as safe a card, you know, as can be. Don't mention it; but I hear that the last scene, when he is first poisoned, and then stabbed, by Mrs. Flimkins as Vengedora, will be the greatest thing that has been done these many years." With this piece of news, and laying his finger on his lips as a caution for you not to excite the town with it, the theatrical young gentleman hurries away.

The theatrical young gentleman, from often frequenting the different theatrical establishments, has pet and familiar names for them all. Thus Covent Garden is the garden, Drury Lane the lane, the Victoria the vic, and the Olympic the pic. Actresses, too, are always designated by their surnames only, as Taylor, Nisbett, Faucit, Honey; that talented and lady-like girl Sheriff, that clever little creature

Horton, and so on.   In the same manner he prefixes Christian names when he mentions the actors, as Charley Young, Jemmy Buckstone, Fred. Yates, Paul Bedford. When he is at a loss for a Christian name, the word "old" applied indiscriminately answers quite as well : as old Charley Matthews at Vestris's, old Harley, and old Braham. He has a great knowledge of the private proceedings of actresses, especially of their getting married, and can tell you in a breath half-a-dozen who have changed their names without avowing it.   Whenever an alteration of this kind is made in the playbills, he will remind you that he let you into the secret six months ago.

The theatrical young gentleman has a great reverence for all that is connected with the stage department of the different theatres. He would, at any time, prefer going a street or two out of his way, to omitting to pass a stage-entrance, into which he always looks with a curious and searching eye. If he can only identify a popular actor in the street, he is in a perfect transport of delight ; and no sooner meets him than he hurries back, and walks a few paces in front of him, so that he can turn round from time to time, and have a good stare at his features. He looks upon a theatrical-fund dinner as one of the most enchanting festivities ever known ; and thinks that to be a member of the Garrick Club, and see so many actors in their plain clothes, must be one of the highest gratifications the world can bestow.

The theatrical young gentleman is a constant half-price visitor at one or other of the theatres, and has an infinite relish for all pieces which display the fullest resources of the establishment. He likes to place implicit reliance upon the play-bills when he goes to see a show-piece, and works himself up to such a pitch of enthusiasm, as not only to believe (if the bills say so) that there are three hundred and seventy-five people on the stage at one time in the last scene, but is highly indignant with you, unless you believe it also. He considers that if the stage be opened from the foot-lights to the back wall, in any new play, the piece is a triumph of dramatic writing, and applauds accordingly. He has a great notion of trap-doors too ; and thinks any character going down or coming up a trap (no matter whether he be an angel or a demon—they both do it occasionally) one of the most interesting feats in the whole range of scenic illusion.

Besides these acquirements, he 'has several veracious accounts to communicate of the private manners and customs of different actors, which, during the pauses of a quadrille, he usually communicates to his partner, or imparts to his neighbour at a supper table. Thus he is advised that Mr. Liston always had a footman in gorgeous livery waiting at the side-scene with a brandy bottle and tumbler, to administer half a pint or so of spirit to him every time he came off, without which assistance he must infallibly have fainted. He knows for a fact that, after an arduous part, Mr. George Bennett is put between two feather beds, to absorb the perspiration; and is credibly informed that Mr. Baker has, for many years, submitted to a course of lukewarm toast-and-water, to qualify him to sustain his favourite characters. He looks upon Mr. Fitz Ball as the principal dramatic genius and poet of the day; but holds that there are great writers extant besides him, in proof whereof he refers you to various dramas and melo-dramas recently produced, of which he takes in all the sixpenny and threepenny editions as fast as they appear.

The theatrical young gentleman is a great advocate for violence of emotion and redundancy of action. If a father has to curse a child upon the stage, he likes to see it done in the thorough-going style, with no mistake about it: to which end it is essential that the child should follow the father on her knees, and be knocked violently over on her face by the old gentleman as he goes into a small cottage, and shuts the door behind him. He likes to see a blessing invoked upon the young lady, when the old gentleman repents, with equal earnestness, and accompanied by the usual conventional forms, which consist of the old gentleman looking anxiously up into the clouds, as if to see whether it rains, and then spreading an imaginary tablecloth in the air over the young lady's head—soft music playing all the while. Upon these, and other points of a similar kind, the theatrical young gentleman is a great critic indeed. He is likewise very acute in judging of natural expressions of the passions. and knows precisely the frown, wink, nod, or leer, which stands for any one of them, or the means by which it may be converted into any other: as jealousy, with a good stamp of the right foot, becomes anger; or wildness, with the hands clasped before the throat, instead of tearing the wig, is passionate love. If you venture to express a doubt of the accuracy of any of these portraitures, the theatrical young gentleman assures you, with a haughty smile, that it always has been done in that way, and he supposes they are not going to change it at this time of day to please you ; to which, of course, you meekly reply that you suppose not.

There are innumerable disquisitions of this nature, in which the theatrical young gentleman is very profound, especially to ladies whom he is most in the habit of entertaining with them ; but as we have no space to recapitulate them at greater length, we must rest content with calling the attention of the young ladies in general to the theatrical young gentlemen of their own acquaintance.

THE POETICAL YOUNG GENTLEMAN

TIME was, and not very long ago either, when a singular epidemic raged among the young gentlemen, vast numbers of whom, under the influence of the malady, tore off their neckerchiefs, turned down their shirt collars, and exhibited themselves in the open streets with bare throats and dejected countenances, before the eyes of an astonished public. These were poetical young gentlemen. The custom was gradually found to be inconvenient, as involving the necessity of too much clean linen and too large washing bills, and these outward symptoms have consequently passed away; but we are disposed to think, notwithstanding, that the number of poetical young gentlemen is considerably on the increase.

We know a poetical young gentleman—a very poetical young gentleman. We do not mean to say that he is troubled with the gift of poesy in any remarkable degree, but his countenance is of a plaintive and melancholy cast, his manner is abstracted and bespeaks affliction of soul: he seldom has his hair cut, and often talks about being an outcast and wanting a kindred spirit; from which, as well as from many general observations in which he is wont to indulge, concerning mysterious impulses, and yearnings of the heart, and the supremacy of intellect gilding all earthly things with the glowing magic of immortal verse, it is clear to all his friends that he has been stricken poetical.

The favourite attitude of the poetical young gentleman is lounging on a sofa with his eyes fixed upon the ceiling, or sitting bolt upright in a high-backed chair, staring with very round eyes at the opposite wall. When he is in one of these positions, his mother, who is a worthy affectionate old soul, will give you a nudge to bespeak your attention without disturbing the abstracted one, and whisper with a shake of the head, that John's imagination is at some extraordinary work or other, you may take her word for it. Hereupon John looks more fiercely intent upon vacancy than before, and suddenly snatching a pencil from his pocket, puts down three words, and a cross on the back of a card, sighs deeply, paces once or twice across the room, inflicts a most unmerciful slap upon his head, and walks moodily up to his dormitory.

The poetical young gentleman is apt to acquire peculiar notions of things too, which plain ordinary people, unblessed with a poetical obliquity of vision, would suppose to be rather distorted. For instance, when the sickening murder and mangling of a wretched woman was affording delicious food wherewithal to gorge the insatiable curiosity of the public, our friend the poetical young gentleman was in ecstasies— not of disgust, but admiration. "Heavens!" cried the poetical young gentleman, "how grand; how great!" We ventured deferentially to inquire upon whom these epithets were bestowed: our humble thoughts oscillating between the police officer who found the criminal, and the lock-keeper who found the head. "Upon whom!" exclaimed the poetical young gentleman in a frenzy of poetry, "Upon whom should they be bestowed but upon the murderer!"—and thereupon it came out, in a fine torrent of eloquence, that the murderer was a great spirit, a bold creature full of daring and nerve, a man of dauntless heart and determined courage, and withal a great casuist and able reasoner, as was fully demonstrated in his philosophical colloquies with the great and noble of the land. We held our peace, and meekly signified our in-disposition to controvert these opinions—firstly, because we were no match at quotation for the poetical young gentleman; and secondly, because we felt it would be of little use our entering into any disputation, if we were: being perfectly convinced that the respectable and immoral hero in question is not the first and will not be the last hanged gentleman upon whom false sympathy or diseased curiosity will be plentifully expended.

This was a stern mystic flight of the poetical young gentleman. In his milder and softer moments he occasionally lays down his neckcloth, and pens stanzas, which sometimes find their way into a Lady's Magazine, or the "Poets' Corner" of some country newspaper; or which, in default of either vent for his genius, adorn the rainbow leaves of a lady's album. These are generally written upon some such occasions as contemplating the Bank of England by midnight, or beholding Saint Paul's in a snow-storm; and when these gloomy objects fail to afford him inspiration, he pours forth his soul in a touching address to a violet, or a plaintive

The Poetical Young Gentleman

lament that he is no longer a child, but has gradually grown up.

The poetical young gentleman is fond of quoting passages from his favourite authors, who are all of the gloomy and desponding school. He has a great deal to say, too, about the world, and is much given to opining, especially if he has taken anything strong to drink, that there is nothing in it worth living for. He gives you to understand, however, that for the sake of society, he means to bear his part in the tiresome play, manfully resisting the gratification of his own strong desire to make a premature exit; and consoles himself with the reflection, that immortality has some chosen nook for himself and the other great spirits whom earth has chafed and wearied.

When the poetical young gentleman makes use of adjectives, they are all superlatives. Everything is of the grandest. greatest, noblest, mightiest, loftiest ; or the lowest, meanest. obscurest, vilest, and most pitiful. He knows no medium. for enthusiasm is the soul of poetry ; and who so enthusiastic as a poetical young gentleman ? " Mr. Milkwash," says a young lady as she unlocks her album to receive the young gentleman's original impromptu contribution, " how very silent you are ! I think you must be in love." " Love ! " cries the poetical young gentleman, starting from his seat by the fire and terrifying the cat who scampers off at full speed, " Love ! that burning consuming passion ; that ardour of the soul, that fierce glowing of the heart. Love ! The withering, blighting influence of hope misplaced and affection slighted. Love, did you say ! Ha ! ha ! ha ! "

With this, the poetical young gentleman laughs a laugh belonging only to poets and Mr. O. Smith of the Adelphi Theatre, and sits down, pen in hand, to throw off a page or two of verse in the biting, semi-atheistical demoniac style, which, like the poetical young gentleman himself, is full of sound and fury, signifying nothing.

THE "THROWING-OFF" YOUNG GENTLEMAN

THERE is a certain kind of impostor—a bragging, vaunting, puffing young gentleman—against whom we are desirous to warn that fairer part of the creation, to whom we more peculiarly devote these our labours. And we are particularly induced to lay especial stress upon this division of our subject, by a little dialogue we held some short time ago, with an esteemed young lady of our acquaintance, touching a most gross specimen of this class of men. We had been urging all the absurdities of his conduct and conversation, and dwelling upon the impossibilities he constantly recounted—to which indeed we had not scrupled to prefix a certain hard little word of one syllable and three letters—when our fair friend, unable to maintain the contest any longer, reluctantly cried, "Well; he certainly has a habit of throwing-off, but then—" What then? Throw him off yourself, said we. And so she did, but not at our instance, for other reasons appeared, and it might have been better if she had done so at first.

The throwing-off young gentleman has so often a father possessed of vast property in some remote district of Ireland, that we look with some suspicion upon all young gentlemen who volunteer this description of themselves. The deceased grandfather of the throwing-off young gentleman was a man of immense possessions, and untold wealth ; the throwing-off young gentleman remembers, as well as if it were only yesterday, the deceased baronet's library, with its long rows of scarce and valuable books in superbly embossed bindings, arranged in cases, reaching from the lofty ceiling to the oaken floor ; and the fine antique chairs and tables, and the noble old castle of Ballykillbabaloo, with its splendid prospect of hill and dale, and wood, and rich wild scenery, and the fine hunting stables and the spacious court-yards, "and—and—everything upon the same magnificent scale," says the throwing-off young gentleman, "princely ; quite princely.

Ah ! " And he sighs as if mourning over the fallen fortunes of his noble house.

The throwing-off young gentleman is a universal genius ; at walking, running, rowing, swimming, and skating, he is unrivalled ; at all games of chance or skill, at hunting, shooting, fishing, riding, driving, or amateur theatricals, no one can touch him—that is *could* not, because he gives you carefully to understand, lest there should be any opportunity of testing his skill, that he is quite out of practice just now, and has been for some years. If you mention any beautiful girl of your common acquaintance in his hearing, the throwing-off young gentleman starts, smiles, and begs you not to mind him, for it was quite involuntary : people do say indeed that they were once engaged, but no—although she is a very fine girl, he was so situated at that time that he couldn't possibly encourage the—" but it's of no use talking about it ! " he adds, interrupting himself. " She has got over it now, and I firmly hope and trust is happy." With this benevolent aspiration he nods his head in a mysterious manner, and whistling the first part of some popular air, thinks perhaps it will be better to change the subject.

There is another great characteristic of the throwing-off young gentleman, which is, that he "happens to be acquainted" with a most extraordinary variety of people in all parts of the world. Thus in all disputed questions, when the throwing-off young gentleman has no argument to bring forward, he invariably happens to be acquainted with some distant person, intimately connected with the subject, whose testimony decides the point against you, to the great—may we say it—to the great admiration of three young ladies out of every four, who consider the throwing-off young gentleman a very highly-connected young man, and a most charming person.

Sometimes the throwing-off young gentleman happens to look in upon a little family circle of young ladies who are quietly spending the evening together, and then indeed is he at the very height and summit of his glory ; for it is to be observed that he by no means shines to equal advantage in the presence of men as in the society of over-credulous young ladies, which is his proper element. It is delightful to hear the number of pretty things the throwing-off young gentleman gives utterance to during tea, and still more so to observe the ease with which, from long practice and study, he delicately blends one compliment to a lady with two for himself. "Did you ever see a more lovely blue than this flower, Mr. Caveton?" asks a young lady who, truth to tell, is rather smitten with the throwing-off young gentleman. "Never," he replies, bending over the object of admiration, "never but in your eyes." "Oh, Mr. Caveton," cries the young lady, blushing of course. "Indeed I speak the truth," replies the throwing-off young gentleman, "I never saw any approach to them. I used to think my cousin's blue eyes lovely, but they grow dim and colourless beside yours." "Oh! a beautiful cousin, Mr. Caveton!" replies the young lady, with that perfect artlessness which is the distinguishing characteristic of all young ladies; "an affair, of course." "No; indeed, indeed you wrong me," rejoins the throwing-off young gentleman with great energy. "I fervently hope that her attachment towards me may be nothing but the natural result of our close intimacy in childhood, and that in change of scene and among new faces she may soon overcome it. I love her! Think not so meanly of me, Miss Lowfield, I beseech, as to suppose that title, lands, riches, and beauty, can influence *my* choice. The heart, the heart, Miss Lowfield." Here the throwing-off young gentleman sinks his voice to a still lower whisper; and the young lady duly proclaims to all the other young ladies when they go up-stairs, to put their bonnets on, that Mr. Caveton's relations are all immensely rich, and that he is hopelessly beloved by title, lands, riches, and beauty.

We have seen a throwing-off young gentleman who, to our certain knowledge, was innocent of a note of music, and scarcely able to recognise a tune by ear, volunteer a Spanish air upon the guitar when he had previously satisfied himself that there was not such an instrument within a mile of the house.

We have heard another throwing-off young gentleman, after striking a note or two upon the piano, and accompanying it correctly (by dint of laborious practice) with his voice, assure a circle of wondering listeners that so acute was his ear that he was wholly unable to sing out of tune, let him try as he would. We have lived to witness the unmasking of another throwing-off young gentleman, who went out a-visiting in a military cap with a gold band and tassel, and who, after passing successfully for a captain, and being lauded to the skies for his red whiskers, his bravery, his soldierly bearing and his pride, turned out to be the dishonest son of an honest linen-draper in a small country town, and whom, if it were not for this fortunate exposure, we should not yet despair of encountering as the fortunate husband of some rich heiress. Ladies, ladies, the throwing-off young gentlemen are often swindlers, and always fools. So pray you avoid them.

THE YOUNG LADIES' YOUNG GENTLEMAN

THIS young gentleman has several titles. Some young ladies consider him "a nice young man," others "a fine young man," others "quite a lady's man," others "a handsome man," others "a remarkably good-looking young man." With some young ladies he is "a perfect angel," and with others "quite a love." He is likewise a charming creature, a duck, and a dear.

The young ladies' young gentleman has usually a fresh colour and very white teeth, which latter articles, of course, he displays on every possible opportunity. He has brown or black hair, and whiskers of the same, if possible; but a slight tinge of red, or the hue which is vulgarly known as *sandy*, is not considered an objection. If his head and face be large, his nose prominent, and his figure square, he is an uncommonly fine young man, and worshipped accordingly. Should his whiskers meet beneath his chin, so much the better, though this is not absolutely insisted on; but he must wear an under-waistcoat, and smile constantly.

There was a great party got up by some party-loving friends of ours last summer, to go and dine in Epping Forest. As we hold that such wild expeditions should never be indulged in, save by people of the smallest means, who have no dinner at home, we should indubitably have excused ourself from attending, if we had not recollected that the projectors of the excursion were always accompanied on such occasions by a choice sample of the young ladies' young gentleman, whom we were very anxious to have an opportunity of meeting. This determined us, and we went.

We were to make for Chigwell in four glass coaches, each with a trifling company of six or eight inside, and a little boy belonging to the projectors on the box—and to start from the residence of the projectors, Woburn Place, Russell Square, at half-past ten precisely. We arrived at the place of rendezvous at the appointed time, and found the glass coaches and the little boys quite ready, and divers young ladies and young gentlemen looking anxiously over the breakfast-parlour blinds, who appeared by no means so much gratified by our approach as we might have expected, but evidently wished we had been somebody else. Observing that our arrival in lieu of the unknown occasioned some disappointment, we ventured to inquire who was yet to come, when we found, from the hasty reply of a dozen voices, that it was no other than the young ladies' young gentleman.

"I cannot imagine," said the mamma, "what has become of Mr. Balim—always so punctual, always so pleasant and agreeable. I am sure I can-*not* think." As these last words were uttered in that measured, emphatic manner which painfully announces that the speaker has not quite made up his or her mind what to say, but is determined to talk on nevertheless, the eldest daughter took up the subject, and hoped no accident had happened to Mr. Balim, upon which there was a general chorus of "Dear Mr. Balim!" and one young lady, more adventurous than the rest, proposed that an express should be straightway sent to dear Mr. Balim's lodgings. This, however, the papa resolutely opposed, observing, in what a short young lady behind us termed "quite a bearish way," that if Mr. Balim didn't choose to come, he might stop at home. At this all the daughters raised a murmur of "Oh, pa!" except one sprightly little girl of eight or ten years old, who, taking advantage of a pause in the discourse, remarked that perhaps Mr. Balim might have been married that morning—for which impertinent suggestion she was summarily ejected from the room by her eldest sister.

We were all in a state of great mortification and uneasiness, when one of the little boys, running into the room as airily as little boys usually run who have an unlimited allowance of animal food in the holidays, and keep their hands constantly forced down to the bottoms of very deep trouser-pockets when they take exercise, joyfully announced that Mr. Balim was at that moment coming up the street in a hackney-cab; and the intelligence was confirmed beyond all doubt a minute afterwards by the entry of Mr. Balim himself, who was received with repeated cries of "Where have you been, you naughty creature?" whereunto the naughty creature replied that he had been in bed in consequence of a late party the night before, and had only just risen. The acknowledgment awakened a variety of agonizing fears that he had taken no breakfast; which appearing after a slight cross-examination to be the real state of the case, breakfast for one was immediately ordered, notwithstanding Mr. Balim's repeated protestations that he couldn't think of it. He did think of it though, and thought better of it too, for he made a remarkably good meal when it came, and was assiduously served by a select knot of young ladies. It was quite delightful to see how he ate and drank, while one pair of fair hands poured out his coffee, and another put in the sugar, and another the milk; the rest of the company ever and anon casting angry glances at their watches, and the glass coaches,—and the little boys looking on in an agony of apprehension lest it should begin to rain before we set out; it might have rained all day, after we were once too far to turn back again, and welcome for aught they cared.

However, the cavalcade moved at length, every coachman being accommodated with a hamper between his legs something larger than a wheelbarrow; and the company being packed as closely as they possibly could in the carriages, "according," as one married lady observed, "to the immemorial custom, which was half the diversion of gipsy parties." Thinking it very likely it might be (we have never been able to discover the other half), we submitted to be stowed away with a cheerful aspect, and were fortunate enough to occupy one corner of a coach in which were one old lady, four young ladies, and the renowned Mr. Balim, the young ladies' young gentleman.

We were no sooner fairly off than the young ladies' young gentleman hummed a fragment of an air, which induced a young lady to inquire whether he had danced to that the night before. "By Heaven, then, I did," replied the young gentleman, "and with a lovely heiress; a superb creature, with twenty thousand pounds." "You seem rather struck," observed another young lady. "'Gad, she was a sweet creature," returned the young gentleman, arranging his hair. "Of course *she* was struck too?" inquired the first young lady. "How can you ask, love?" interposed the second; "could she fail to be?" "Well, honestly I think she was," observed the young gentleman. At this point of the dialogue, the young lady who had spoken first, and who sat on the young gentleman's right, struck him a severe blow on the arm with a rosebud, and said he was a vain man—whereupon the young gentleman insisted on having the rosebud, and the

The Young Ladies' Young Gentleman

young lady appealing for help to the other young ladies, a charming struggle ensued, terminating in the victory of the young gentleman, and the capture of the rosebud. This little skirmish over, the married lady, who was the mother of the rosebud, smiled sweetly upon the young gentleman, and accused him of being a flirt; the young gentleman pleading not guilty, a most interesting discussion took place upon the important point whether the young gentleman was a flirt or not, which being an agreeable conversation of a light kind, lasted a considerable time. At length, a short silence occurring, the young ladies on either side of the young gentleman fell suddenly fast asleep; and the young gentleman, winking upon us to preserve silence, won a pair of gloves from each, thereby causing them to wake with equal suddenness and to scream very loud. The lively conversation to which this pleasantry gave rise, lasted for the remainder of the ride, and would have eked out a much longer one.

We dined rather more comfortably than people usually do under such circumstances, nothing having been left behind but the corkscrew and the bread. The married gentlemen were unusually thirsty, which they attributed to the heat of the weather; the little boys ate to inconvenience; mammas were very jovial, and their daughters very fascinating; and the attendants being well-behaved men, got exceedingly drunk at a respectful distance.

We had our eye on Mr. Balim at dinner-time, and perceived that he flourished wonderfully, being still surrounded by a little group of young ladies, who listened to him as an oracle, while he ate from their plates and drank from their glasses in a manner truly captivating from its excessive playfulness. His conversation, too, was exceedingly brilliant. In fact, one elderly lady assured us, that in the course of a little lively *badinage* on the subject of ladies' dresses, he had evinced as much knowledge as if he had been born and bred a milliner.

As such of the fat people who did not happen to fall asleep after dinner entered upon a most vigorous game at ball, we slipped away alone into a thicker part of the wood, hoping to fall in with Mr. Balim, the greater part of the young people having dropped off in twos and threes, and the young ladies' young gentleman among them.   Nor were we disappointed, for we had not walked far, when, peeping through the trees, we discovered him before us, and truly it was a pleasant thing to contemplate his greatness.

The young ladies' young gentleman was seated upon the ground, at the feet of a few young ladies who were reclining on a bank ; he was so profusely decked with scarfs, ribands, flowers, and other pretty spoils, that he looked like a lamb —or perhaps a calf would be a better simile—adorned for the sacrifice. One young lady supported a parasol over his interesting head, another held his hat, and a third his neck-cloth, which in romantic fashion he had thrown off ; the young gentleman himself, with his hand upon his breast, and his face moulded into an expression of the most honeyed sweet-ness, was warbling forth some choice specimens of vocal music in praise of female loveliness, in a style so exquisitely perfect. that we burst into an involuntary shout of laughter, and made a hasty retreat.

What charming fellows these young ladies' young gentle-men are ! Ducks, dears, loves, angels, are all terms inade-quate to express their merit. They are such amazingly, uncommonly, wonderfully, nice men.

CONCLUSION

As we have placed before the young ladies so many specimens of young gentlemen, and have also in the dedication of
this volume given them to understand how much we reverence
and admire their numerous virtues and perfections; as we
have given them such strong reasons to treat us with confidence, and to banish, in our case, all that reserve and distrust
of the male sex which, as a point of general behaviour, they
cannot do better than preserve and maintain—we say, as we
have done all this, we feel that now, when we have arrived
at the close of our task, they may naturally press upon us
the inquiry, what particular description of young gentlemen
we can conscientiously recommend.

Here we are at a loss. We look over our list, and can
neither recommend the bashful young gentleman, nor the
out-and-out young gentleman, nor the very friendly young
gentleman, nor the military young gentleman, nor the
political young gentleman, nor the domestic young gentleman, nor the censorious young gentleman, nor the funny
young gentleman, nor the theatrical young gentleman, nor
the poetical young gentleman, nor the throwing-off young
gentleman, nor the young ladies' young gentleman.

As there are some good points about many of them, which
still are not sufficiently numerous to render any one among
them eligible, as a whole, our respectful advice to the young
ladies is, to seek for a young gentleman who unites in himself the best qualities of all, and the worst weaknesses of none.
and to lead him forthwith to the hymeneal altar, whether
he will or no. And to the young lady who secures him,
we beg to tender one short fragment of matrimonial advice,
selected from many sound passages of a similar tendency, to
be found in a letter written by Dean Swift to a young lady
on her marriage.

"The grand affair of your life will be to gain and preserve
the esteem of your husband. Neither good-nature nor virtue
will suffer him to *esteem* you against his judgment; and

although he is not capable of using you ill, yet you will in time grow a thing indifferent and perhaps contemptible; unless you can supply the loss of youth and beauty with more durable qualities. You have but a very few years to be young and handsome in the eyes of the world; and as few months to be so in the eyes of a husband who is not a fool; for I hope you do not still dream of charms and raptures, which marriage ever did, and ever will, put a sudden end to."

From the anxiety we express for the proper behaviour of the fortunate lady after marriage, it may possibly be inferred that the young gentleman to whom we have so delicately alluded, is no other than ourself. Without in any way committing ourself upon this point, we have merely to observe that we are ready to receive sealed offers containing a full specification of age, temper, appearance, and condition; but we beg it to be distinctly understood that we do not pledge ourself to accept the highest bidder.

These offers may be forwarded to the Publishers, Messrs. Chapman and Hall, London; to whom all pieces of plate and other testimonials of approbation from the young ladies generally, are respectfully requested to be addressed.

Sketches of Young Couples

An Urgent Remonstrance, &c.

TO THE GENTLEMEN OF ENGLAND,

(BEING BACHELORS OR WIDOWERS,)

THE REMONSTRANCE OF THEIR FAITHFUL FELLOW-SUBJECT,

SHEWETH,—

THAT Her Most Gracious Majesty, Victoria, by the Grace of God of the United Kingdom of Great Britain and Ireland Queen, Defender of the Faith, did, on the 23rd day of November last past, declare and pronounce to Her Most Honourable Privy Council, Her Majesty's Most Gracious intention of entering into the bonds of wedlock.

THAT Her Most Gracious Majesty, in so making known Her Most Gracious intention to Her Most Honourable Privy Council as aforesaid, did use and employ the words—"It is my intention to ally myself in marriage with Prince Albert of Saxe Coburg and Gotha."

THAT the present is Bissextile, or Leap Year, in which it is held and considered lawful for any lady to offer and submit proposals of marriage to any gentleman, and to enforce and insist upon acceptance of the same, under pain of a certain fine or penalty; to wit, one silk or satin dress of the first quality, to be chosen by the lady and paid (or owed) for, by the gentleman.

THAT these and other the horrors and dangers with which the said Bissextile, or Leap Year, threatens the gentlemen of England on every occasion of its periodical return, have been greatly aggravated and augmented by the terms of Her Majesty's said Most Gracious communication, which have filled the heads of divers young ladies in this Realm with certain new ideas destructive to the peace of mankind, that never entered their imagination before.

THAT a case has occurred in Camberwell, in which a young

lady informed her Papa that " she intended to ally herself in marriage" with Mr. Smith of Stepney; and that another, and a very distressing case, has occurred at Tottenham, in which a young lady not only stated her intention of allying herself in marriage with her cousin John, but, taking violent possession of her said cousin, actually married him.

THAT similar outrages are of constant occurrence, not only in the capital and its neighbourhood, but throughout the kingdom, and that unless the excited female populace be speedily checked and restrained in their lawless proceedings, most deplorable results must ensue therefrom; among which may be anticipated a most alarming increase in the population of the country, with which no efforts of the agricultural or manufacturing interest can possibly keep pace.

THAT there is strong reason to suspect the existence of a most extensive plot, conspiracy, or design, secretly contrived by vast numbers of single ladies in the United Kingdom of Great Britain and Ireland, and now extending its ramifications in every quarter of the land; the object and intent of which plainly appears to be the holding and solemnising of an enormous and unprecedented number of marriages, on the day on which the nuptials of Her said Most Gracious Majesty are performed.

THAT such plot, conspiracy, or design, strongly savours of Popery, as tending to the discomfiture of the Clergy of the Established Church, by entailing upon them great mental and physical exhaustion; and that such Popish plots are fomented and encouraged by Her Majesty's Ministers, which clearly appears—not only from Her Majesty's principal Secretary of State for Foreign Affairs traitorously getting married while holding office under the Crown; but from Mr. O'Connell having been heard to declare and avow that, if he had a daughter to marry, she should be married on the same day as Her said Most Gracious Majesty.

THAT such arch plots, conspiracies, and designs, besides being fraught with danger to the Established Church, and (consequently) to the State, cannot fail to bring ruin and bankruptcy upon a large class of Her Majesty's subjects; as a great and sudden increase in the number of married men occasioning the comparative desertion (for a time) of Taverns, Hotels, Billiard-rooms, and Gaming-Houses, will deprive the Proprietors of their accustomed profits and returns. And in further proof of the depth and baseness of such designs, it

Departure of the Young Couple

may be here observed, that all proprietors of Taverns, Hotels, Billiard-rooms, and Gaming-Houses, are (especially the last) solemnly devoted to the Protestant religion.

For all these reasons, and many others of no less gravity and import, an urgent appeal is made to the gentlemen of England (being bachelors or widowers) to take immediate steps for convening a Public meeting; To consider of the best and surest means of averting the dangers with which they are threatened by the recurrence of Bissextile, or Leap Year, and the additional sensation created among single ladies by the terms of Her Majesty's Most Gracious Declaration; To take measures, without delay, for resisting the said single Ladies, and counteracting their evil designs; And to pray Her Majesty to dismiss her present Ministers, and to summon to her Councils those distinguished Gentlemen in various Honourable Professions who, by insulting on all occasions the only Lady in England who can be insulted with safety, have given a sufficient guarantee to Her Majesty's Loving Subjects that they, at least, are qualified to make war with women, and are already expert in the use of those weapons which are common to the lowest and most abandoned of the sex.

SKETCHES OF YOUNG COUPLES

THE YOUNG COUPLE

THERE is to be a wedding this morning at the corner house in the terrace. The pastry-cook's people have been there half-a-dozen times already; all day yesterday there was a great stir and bustle, and they were up this morning as soon as it was light. Miss Emma Fielding is going to be married to young Mr. Harvey.

Heaven alone can tell in what bright colours this marriage is painted upon the mind of the little housemaid at number six, who has hardly slept a wink all night with thinking of it, and now stands on the unswept door-steps leaning upon her broom, and looking wistfully towards the enchanted house. Nothing short of omniscience can divine what visions of the baker, or the green-grocer, or the smart and most insinuating butterman, are flitting across her mind—what thoughts of how she would dress on such an occasion, if she were a lady—of how she would dress, if she were only a bride —of how cook would dress, being bridesmaid, conjointly with her sister "in place" at Fulham, and how the clergyman, deeming them so many ladies, would be quite humbled and respectful. What day-dreams of hope and happiness—of life being one perpetual holiday, with no master and no mistress to grant or withhold it—of every Sunday being a Sunday out —of pure freedom as to curls and ringlets, and no obligation to hide fine heads of hair in caps—what pictures of happiness, vast and immense to her, but utterly ridiculous to us, bewilder the brain of the little housemaid at number six, all called into existence by the wedding at the corner!

We smile at such things, and so we should, though perhaps for a better reason than commonly presents itself. It should be pleasant to us to know that there are notions of happiness so moderate and limited, since upon those who entertain them, happiness and lightness of heart are very easily bestowed.

But the little housemaid is awakened from her reverie, for forth from the door of the magical corner house there runs towards her, all fluttering in smart new dress and streaming ribands, her friend Jane Adams, who comes all out of breath to redeem a solemn promise of taking her in, under cover of the confusion, to see the breakfast table spread forth in state, and—sight of sights !—her young mistress ready dressed for church.

And there, in good truth, when they have stolen up-stairs on tiptoe and edged themselves in at the chamber-door— there is Miss Emma " looking like the sweetest picter," in a white chip bonnet and orange flower, and all other elegancies becoming a bride, (with the make, shape, and quality of every article of which the girl is perfectly familiar in one moment, and never forgets to her dying day)—and there is Miss Emma's mamma in tears, and Miss Emma's papa comforting her, and saying how that of course she has been long looking forward to this, and how happy she ought to be— and there too is Miss Emma's sister with her arms round her neck, and the other bridesmaid all smiles and tears, quieting the children, who would cry more but that they are so finely dressed, and yet sob for fear sister Emma should be taken away—and it is all so affecting, that the two servant-girls cry more than anybody ; and Jane Adams, sitting down upon the stairs, when they have crept away, declares that her legs tremble so that she don't know what to do, and that she will say for Miss Emma, that she never had a hasty word from her, and that she does hope and pray she may be happy.

But Jane soon comes round again, and then surely there never was anything like the breakfast table, glittering with plate and china, and set out with flowers and sweets, and long-necked bottles, in the most sumptuous and dazzling manner. In the centre, too, is the mighty charm, the cake, glistening with frosted sugar, and garnished beautiful. They agree that there ought to be a little Cupid under one of the barley-sugar temples, or at least two hearts and an arrow ; but, with this exception, there is nothing to wish for, and a table could not be handsomer. As they arrive at this conclusion, who should come in but Mr. John! to whom Jane says that it's only Anne from number six; and John says *he* knows, for he's often winked his eye down the area, which causes Anne to blush and look confused. She is going away, indeed; when Mr. John will have it that she must drink a glass of wine, and he says never mind it's being early in the morning, it won't hurt her: so they shut the door and pour out the wine; and Anne drinking Jane's health, and adding, "and here's wishing you yours, Mr. John," drinks it in a great many sips,—Mr. John all the time making jokes appropriate to the occasion. At last Mr. John, who has waxed bolder by degrees, pleads the usage at weddings, and claims the privilege of a kiss, which he obtains after a great scuffle; and footsteps being now heard on the stairs, they disperse suddenly.

By this time a carriage has driven up to convey the bride to church, and Anne of number six prolonging the process of "cleaning her door," has the satisfaction of beholding the bride and bridesmaids, and the papa and mamma, hurry into the same and drive rapidly off. Nor is this all, for soon other carriages begin to arrive with a posse of company all beautifully dressed, at whom she could stand and gaze for ever; but having something else to do, is compelled to take one last long look and shut the street-door.

And now the company have gone down to breakfast, and tears have given place to smiles, for all the corks are out of the long-necked bottles, and their contents are disappearing rapidly. Miss Emma's papa is at the top of the table; Miss Emma's mamma at the bottom; and beside the latter are Miss Emma herself and her husband,—admitted on all hands to be the handsomest and most interesting young couple ever known. All down both sides of the table, too, are various young ladies, beautiful to see, and various young gentlemen who seem to think so; and there, in a post of honour, is an unmarried aunt of Miss Emma's, reported to possess unheard-of riches, and to have expressed vast testamentary intentions respecting her favourite niece and new nephew. This lady has been very liberal and generous already, as the jewels worn by the bride abundantly testify, but that is nothing to what she means to do, or even to what she has done, for she put herself in close communication with the dress-maker three months ago, and prepared a wardrobe (with some articles worked by her own hands) fit for a Princess. People

Y

may call her an old maid, and so she may be, but she is neither cross nor ugly for all that; on the contrary, she is very cheerful and pleasant-looking, and very kind and tender-hearted: which is no matter of surprise except to those who yield to popular prejudices without thinking why, and will never grow wiser and never know better.

Of all the company though, none are more pleasant to behold or better pleased with themselves than two young children, who, in honour of the day, have seats among the guests. Of these, one is a little fellow of six or eight years old, brother to the bride,—and the other a girl of the same age, or something younger, whom he calls "his wife." The real bride and bridegroom are not more devoted than they: he all love and attention, and she all blushes and fondness, toying with a little bouquet which he gave her this morning, and placing the scattered rose-leaves in her bosom with nature's own coquettishness. They have dreamt of each other in their quiet dreams, these children, and their little hearts have been nearly broken when the absent one has been dispraised in jest. When will there come in after-life a passion so earnest, generous, and true as theirs; what, even in its gentlest realities, can have the grace and charm that hover round such fairy lovers!

By this time the merriment and happiness of the feast have gained their height; certain ominous looks begin to be exchanged between the bridesmaids, and somehow it gets whispered about that the carriage which is to take the young couple into the country has arrived. Such members of the party as are most disposed to prolong its enjoyments, affect to consider this a false alarm, but it turns out too true, being speedily confirmed, first by the retirement of the bride and a select file of intimates who are to prepare her for the journey, and secondly by the withdrawal of the ladies generally. To this there ensues a particularly awkward pause, in which everybody essays to be facetious, and nobody succeeds; at length the bridegroom makes a mysterious disappearance in obedience to some equally mysterious signal; and the table is deserted.

Now, for at least six weeks last past it has been solemnly devised and settled that the young couple should go away in secret; but they no sooner appear without the door than the drawing-room windows are blocked up with ladies waving their handkerchiefs and kissing their hands, and the dining-room panes with gentlemen's faces beaming farewell in every queer variety of its expression. The hall and steps are crowded with servants in white favours, mixed up with particular friends and relations who have darted out to say good b'ye; and foremost in the group are the tiny lovers arm in arm, thinking, with fluttering hearts, what happiness it would be to dash away together in that gallant coach, and never part again.

The bride has barely time for one hurried glance at her old home, when the steps rattle, the door slams, the horses clatter on the pavement, and they have left it far away.

A knot of women servants still remain clustered in the hall, whispering among themselves, and there of course is Anne from number six, who has made another escape on some plea or other, and been an admiring witness of the departure. There are two points on which Anne expatiates over and over again, without the smallest appearance of fatigue or intending to leave off; one is, that she "never see in all her life such a—oh such a angel of a gentleman as Mr. Harvey"—and the other, that she "can't tell how it is, but it don't seem a bit like a work-a-day, or a Sunday neither —it's all so unsettled and unregular."

THE FORMAL COUPLE

THE formal couple are the most prim, cold, immovable, and unsatisfactory people on the face of the earth. Their faces, voices, dress, house, furniture, walk, and manner, are all the essence of formality, unrelieved by one redeeming touch of frankness, heartiness, or nature.

Everything with the formal couple resolves itself into a matter of form. They don't call upon you on your account, but their own; not to see how you are, but to show how they are: it is not a ceremony to do honour to you, but to themselves,—not due to your position, but to theirs. If one of a friend's children die, the formal couple are as sure and punctual in sending to the house as the undertaker; if a friend's family be increased, the monthly nurse is not more attentive than they. The formal couple, in fact, joyfully seize all occasions of testifying their good-breeding and precise observance of the little usages of society; and for you, who are the means to this end, they care as much as a man does for the tailor who has enabled him to cut a figure, or a woman for the milliner who has assisted her to a conquest.

Having an extensive connexion among that kind of people who make acquaintances and eschew friends, the formal gentleman attends from time to time a great many funerals, to which he is formally invited, and to which he formally goes, as returning a call for the last time. Here his deportment is of the most faultless description; he knows the exact pitch of voice it is proper to assume, the sombre look he ought to wear, the melancholy tread which should be his gait for the day. He is perfectly acquainted with all the dreary courtesies to be observed in a mourning-coach; knows when to sigh, and when to hide his nose in the white handkerchief; and looks into the grave and shakes his head when the ceremony is concluded, with the sad formality of a mute.

"What kind of funeral was it?" says the formal lady, when he returns home. "Oh!" replies the formal gentleman, "there never was such a gross and disgusting impropriety; there were no feathers." "No feathers!" cries the lady, as if on wings of black feathers dead people fly to Heaven, and, lacking them, they must of necessity go elsewhere. Her husband shakes his head; and further adds, that they had seed-cake instead of plum-cake, and that it was all white wine. "All white wine!" exclaims his wife. "Nothing but sherry and madeira," says the husband. "What! no port?" "Not a drop." No port, no plums, and no feathers! "You will recollect, my dear," says the formal lady, in a voice of stately reproof, "that when we first met this poor man who is now dead and gone, and he took that very strange course of addressing me at dinner without being previously introduced, I ventured to express my opinion that the family were quite ignorant of etiquette, and very imperfectly acquainted with the decencies of life. You have now had a good opportunity of judging for yourself, and all I have to say is, that I trust you will never go to a funeral *there* again." "My dear," replies the formal gentleman, "I never will." So the informal deceased is cut in his grave; and the formal couple, when they tell the story of the funeral, shake their heads, and wonder what some people's feelings *are* made of, and what their notions of propriety *can* be!

If the formal couple have a family (which they sometimes have), they are not children, but little, pale, sour, sharp-nosed men and women; and so exquisitely brought up, that they might be very old dwarfs for anything that appeareth to the contrary. Indeed, they are so acquainted with forms and conventionalities, and conduct themselves with such strict decorum, that to see the little girl break a looking-glass in some wild outbreak, or the little boy kick his parents, would be to any visitor an unspeakable relief and consolation.

The formal couple are always sticklers for what is rigidly proper, and have a great readiness in detecting hidden impropriety of speech or thought, which by less scrupulous people would be wholly unsuspected. Thus, if they pay a visit to the theatre, they sit all night in a perfect agony lest anything improper or immoral should proceed from the stage; and if anything should happen to be said which admits of a double construction, they never fail to take it up directly, and to express by their looks the great outrage which their feelings have sustained. Perhaps this is their chief reason for absenting themselves almost entirely from places of public amusement. They go sometimes to the Exhibition of the Royal Academy ;—but that is often more shocking than the stage itself, and the formal lady thinks that it really is high time Mr. Etty was prosecuted and made a public example of.

We made one at a christening party not long since, where there were amongst the guests a formal couple, who suffered the acutest torture from certain jokes, incidental to such an occasion, cut—and very likely dried also—by one of the godfathers ; a red-faced elderly gentleman, who, being highly popular with the rest of the company, had it all his own way, and was in great spirits. It was at supper-time that this gentleman came out in full force. We—being of a grave and quiet demeanour—had been chosen to escort the formal lady down-stairs, and, sitting beside her, had a favourable opportunity of observing her emotions.

We have a shrewd suspicion that, in the very beginning, and in the first blush—literally the first blush—of the matter, the formal lady had not felt quite certain whether the being present at such a ceremony, and encouraging, as it were, the public exhibition of a baby, was not an act involving some degree of indelicacy and impropriety; but certain we are, that when that baby's health was drunk, and allusions were made, by a grey-headed gentleman proposing it, to the time when he had dandled in his arms the young Christian's mother,—certain we are that then the formal lady took the alarm, and recoiled from the old gentleman as from a hoary profligate. Still she bore it ; she fanned herself with an indignant air, but still she bore it. A comic song was sung, involving a confession from some imaginary gentleman that he had kissed a female, and yet the formal lady bore it. But when at last, the health of the godfather before-mentioned being drunk, the godfather rose to return thanks, and in the course of his observations darkly hinted at babies yet unborn, and even contemplated the possibility of the subject of that festival having brothers and sisters, the formal lady could endure no more, but, bowing slightly round, and sweeping haughtily past the offender, left the room in tears, under the protection of the formal gentleman.

THE LOVING COUPLE

THERE cannot be a better practical illustration of the wise saw and ancient instance, that there may be too much of a good thing, than is presented by a loving couple. Undoubtedly it is meet and proper that two persons joined together in holy matrimony should be loving, and unquestionably it is pleasant to know and see that they are so; but there is a time for all things, and the couple who happen to be always in a loving state before company, are well-nigh intolerable.

And in taking up this position we would have it distinctly understood that we do not seek alone the sympathy of bachelors, in whose objection to loving couples we recognise interested motives and personal considerations. We grant that to that unfortunate class of society there may be something very irritating, tantalising, and provoking, in being compelled to witness those gentle endearments and chaste interchanges which to loving couples are quite the ordinary business of life. But while we recognise the natural character of the prejudice to which these unhappy men are subject, we can neither receive their biassed evidence, nor address ourself to their inflamed and angered minds. Dispassionate experience is our only guide; and in these moral essays we seek no less to reform hymeneal offenders than to hold out a timely warning to all rising couples, and even to those who have not yet set forth upon their pilgrimage towards the matrimonial altar.

Let all couples, present or to come, therefore profit by the example of Mr. and Mrs. Leaver, themselves a loving couple in the first degree.

Mr. and Mrs. Leaver are pronounced by Mrs. Starling, a widow lady who lost her husband when she was young, and lost herself about the same time—for by her own count she has never since grown five years older—to be a perfect model of wedded felicity. "You would suppose," says the romantic lady, "that they were lovers only just now engaged. Never was such happiness! They are so tender, so affectionate, so attached to each other, so enamoured, that positively nothing can be more charming!"

"Augusta, my soul," says Mr. Leaver. "Augustus, my life," replies Mrs. Leaver. "Sing some little ballad, darling," quoth Mr. Leaver. "I couldn't, indeed, dearest," returns Mrs. Leaver. "Do, my dove," says Mr. Leaver. "I couldn't possibly, my love," replies Mrs. Leaver; "and it's very naughty of you to ask me." "Naughty, darling!" cries Mr. Leaver. "Yes, very naughty, and very cruel," returns Mrs. Leaver, "for you know I have a sore throat, and that to sing would give me great pain. You're a monster, and I hate you. Go away!" Mrs. Leaver has said "go away," because Mr. Leaver has tapped her under the chin: Mr. Leaver not doing as he is bid, but on the contrary, sitting down beside her, Mrs. Leaver slaps Mr. Leaver; and Mr. Leaver in return slaps Mrs. Leaver, and it being now time for all persons present to look the other way, they look the other way, and hear a still small sound as of kissing, at which Mrs. Starling is thoroughly enraptured, and whispers her neighbour that if all married couples were like that, what a heaven this earth would be!

The loving couple are at home when this occurs, and maybe only three or four friends are present, but, unaccustomed to reserve upon this interesting point, they are pretty much the same abroad. Indeed upon some occasions, such as a pic-nic or a water-party, their lovingness is even more developed, as we had an opportunity last summer of observing in person.

There was a great water-party made up to go to Twickenham and dine, and afterwards dance in an empty villa by the river-side, hired expressly for the purpose. Mr. and Mrs. Leaver were of the company; and it was our fortune to have a seat in the same boat, which was an eight-oared galley, manned by amateurs, with a blue striped awning of the same pattern as their Guernsey shirts, and a dingy red flag of the same shade as the whiskers of the stroke oar. A coxswain being appointed, and all other matters adjusted, the eight gentlemen threw themselves into strong paroxysms, and pulled up with the tide, stimulated by the compassionate remarks of the ladies, who one and all exclaimed, that it seemed an immense exertion—as indeed it did. At first we raced the other boat, which came alongside in gallant style; but this being found an unpleasant amusement, as giving rise to a great quantity of splashing, and rendering the cold pies and other viands very moist, it was unanimously voted down, and we were suffered to shoot a-head, while the second boat followed ingloriously in our wake.

It was at this time that we first recognised Mr. Leaver. There were two firemen-watermen in the boat, lying by until somebody was exhausted; and one of them, who had taken upon himself the direction of affairs, was heard to cry in a gruff voice, "Pull away, number two—give it her, number two—take a longer reach, number two—now, number two, sir, think you're winning a boat." The greater part of the company had no doubt begun to wonder which of the striped Guernseys it might be that stood in need of such encouragement, when a stifled shriek from Mrs. Leaver confirmed the doubtful and informed the ignorant; and Mr. Leaver, still further disguised in a straw hat and no neckcloth, was observed to be in a fearful perspiration, and failing visibly. Nor was the general consternation diminished at this instant by the same gentleman (in the performance of an accidental aquatic feat, termed "catching a crab") plunging suddenly backward, and displaying nothing of himself to the company, but two violently struggling legs. Mrs. Leaver shrieked again several times, and cried piteously—"Is he dead? Tell me the worst. Is he dead?"

Now, a moment's reflection might have convinced the loving wife, that unless her husband were endowed with some most surprising powers of muscular action, he never could be dead while he kicked so hard; but still Mrs. Leaver cried, "Is he dead? is he dead?" and still everybody else cried—"No, no, no," until such time as Mr. Leaver was replaced in a sitting posture, and his oar (which had been going through all kinds of wrong-headed performances on its own account) was once more put in his hand, by the exertions of the two firemen-watermen. Mrs. Leaver then exclaimed, "Augustus, my child, come to me;" and Mr. Leaver said, "Augusta, my love, compose yourself, I am not injured." But Mrs. Leaver cried again more piteously than before, "Augustus, my child, come to me;" and now the company generally, who seemed to be apprehensive that if Mr. Leaver remained where he was, he might contribute more than his proper share towards the drowning of the party, disinterestedly took part with Mrs. Leaver, and said he really ought to go, and that he was not strong enough

for such violent exercise, and ought never to have undertaken it. Reluctantly, Mr. Leaver went, and laid himself
down at Mrs. Leaver's feet, and Mrs. Leaver stooping over
him, said, "Oh Augustus, how could you terrify me so?"
and Mr. Leaver said, "Augusta, my sweet, I never meant
to terrify you;" and Mrs. Leaver said, "You are faint, my
dear;" and Mr. Leaver said, "I am rather so, my love;"
and they were very loving indeed under Mrs. Leaver's veil,
until at length Mr. Leaver came forth again, and pleasantly
asked if he had not heard something said about bottled stout
and sandwiches.

Mrs. Starling, who was one of the party, was perfectly
delighted with this scene, and frequently murmured half-
aside, "What a loving couple you are!" or "How delightful
it is to see man and wife so happy together!" To us she
was quite poetical, (for we are a kind of cousins,) observing
that hearts beating in unison like that made life a paradise
of sweets; and that when kindred creatures were drawn
together by sympathies so fine and delicate, what more than
mortal happiness did not our souls partake! To all this we
answered "Certainly," or "Very true," or merely sighed, as
the case might be. At every new act of the loving couple,
the widow's admiration broke out afresh; and when Mrs.
Leaver would not permit Mr. Leaver to keep his hat off, lest
the sun should strike to his head, and give him a brain fever,
Mrs. Starling actually shed tears, and said it reminded her
of Adam and Eve.

The loving couple were thus loving all the way to Twickenham, but when we arrived there (by which time the amateur
crew looked very thirsty and vicious) they were more playful
than ever, for Mrs. Leaver threw stones at Mr. Leaver, and
Mr. Leaver ran after Mrs. Leaver on the grass, in a most
innocent and enchanting manner. At dinner, too, Mr. Leaver
would steal Mrs. Leaver's tongue, and Mrs. Leaver *would*
retaliate upon Mr. Leaver's fowl; and when Mrs. Leaver was
going to take some lobster salad, Mr. Leaver wouldn't let
her have any, saying that it made her ill, and she was
always sorry for it afterwards, which afforded Mrs. Leaver
an opportunity of pretending to be cross, and showing many
other prettinesses. But this was merely the smiling surface
of their loves, not the mighty depths of the stream, down
to which the company, to say the truth, dived rather unexpectedly, from the following accident. It chanced that

Mr. Leaver took upon himself to propose the bachelors who had first originated the notion of that entertainment, in doing which, he affected to regret that he was no longer of their body himself, and pretended grievously to lament his fallen state. This Mrs. Leaver's feelings could not brook, even in jest, and consequently, exclaiming aloud, "He loves me not, he loves me not!" she fell in ⌂ very pitiable state into the arms of Mrs. Starling, and, directly becoming insensible, was conveyed by that lady and her husband into another room. Presently Mr. Leaver came running back to know if there was a medical gentleman in company, and as there was, (in what company is there not?) both Mr. Leaver and the medical gentleman hurried away together.

The medical gentleman was the first who returned, and among his intimate friends he was observed to laugh and wink, and look as unmedical as might be; but when Mr. Leaver came back he was very solemn, and in answer to all inquiries, shook his head, and remarked that Augusta was far too sensitive to be trifled with—an opinion which the widow subsequently confirmed. Finding that she was in no imminent peril, however, the rest of the party betook themselves to dancing on the green, and very merry and happy they were, and a vast quantity of flirtation there was; the last circumstance being no doubt attributable, partly to the fineness of the weather, and partly to the locality, which is well known to be favourable to all harmless recreations.

In the bustle of the scene, Mr. and Mrs. Leaver stole down to the boat, and disposed themselves under the awning, Mrs. Leaver reclining her head upon Mr. Leaver's shoulder, and Mr. Leaver grasping her hand with great fervour, and looking in her face from time to time with a melancholy and sympathetic aspect. The widow sat apart, feigning to be occupied with a book, but stealthily observing them from behind her fan; and the two firemen-watermen, smoking their pipes on the bank hard by, nudged each other, and grinned in enjoyment of the joke. Very few of the party missed the loving couple; and the few who did, heartily congratulated each other on their disappearance.

THE CONTRADICTORY COUPLE

ONE would suppose that two people who are to pass their whole lives together, and must necessarily be very often alone with each other, could find little pleasure in mutual contradiction ; and yet what is more common than a contradictory couple ?

The contradictory couple agree in nothing but contradiction. They return home from Mrs. Bluebottle's dinner-party, each in an opposite corner of the coach, and do not exchange a syllable until they have been seated for at least twenty minutes by the fireside at home, when the gentleman, raising his eyes from the stove, all at once breaks silence :

"What a very extraordinary thing it is," says he, "that you *will* contradict, Charlotte !" "*I* contradict !" cries the lady, "but that's just like you." "What's like me ?" says the gentleman sharply. "Saying that I contradict you," replies the lady. "Do you mean to say that you do *not* contradict me ?" retorts the gentleman ; "do you mean to say that you have not been contradicting me the whole of this day ? Do you mean to tell me now, that you have not ?" "I mean to tell you nothing of the kind," replies the lady quietly ; "when you are wrong, of course I shall contradict you."

During this dialogue the gentleman has been taking his brandy-and-water on one side of the fire, and the lady, with her dressing-case on the table, has been curling her hair on the other. She now lets down her back hair, and proceeds to brush it ; preserving at the same time an air of conscious rectitude and suffering virtue, which is intended to exasperate the gentleman—and does so.

"I do believe," he says, taking the spoon out of his glass, and tossing it on the table, "that of all the obstinate, positive, wrong-headed creatures that were ever born, you are the most so, Charlotte." "Certainly, certainly, have it your own way, pray. You see how much *I* contradict you," re-

The Loving Couple
(*p.* 567)

joins the lady. "Of course, you didn't contradict me at dinner-time—oh no, not you!" says the gentleman. "Yes, I did," says the lady. "Oh, you did," cries the gentleman; "you admit that?" "If you call that contradiction, I do," the lady answers; "and I say again, Edward, that when I know you are wrong, I will contradict you. I am not your slave." "Not my slave!" repeats the gentleman bitterly; "and you still mean to say that in the Blackburns' new house there are not more than fourteen doors, including the door of the wine-cellar!" "I mean to say," retorts the lady, beating time with her hair-brush on the palm of her hand, "that in that house there are fourteen doors and no more." "Well then—" cries the gentleman, rising in despair, and pacing the room with rapid strides. "By G—, this is enough to destroy a man's intellect, and drive him mad!"

By-and-bye the gentleman comes-to a little, and passing his hand gloomily across his forehead, reseats himself in his former chair. There is a long silence, and this time the lady begins. "I appealed to Mr. Jenkins, who sat next to me on the sofa in the drawing-room during tea—" "Morgan, you mean," interrupts the gentleman. "I do not mean anything of the kind," answers the lady. "Now, by all that is aggravating and impossible to bear," cries the gentleman, clenching his hands and looking upwards in agony, "she is going to insist upon it that Morgan is Jenkins!" "Do you take me for a perfect fool?" exclaims the lady; "do you suppose I don't know the one from the other? Do you suppose I don't know that the man in the blue coat was Mr. Jenkins?" "Jenkins in a blue coat!" cries the gentleman with a groan; "Jenkins in a blue coat! a man who would suffer death rather than wear anything but brown!" "Do you dare to charge me with telling an untruth?" demands the lady, bursting into tears. "I charge you, ma'am," retorts the gentleman, starting up, "with being a monster of contradiction, a monster of aggravation, a—a—a—Jenkins in a blue coat!—what have I done that I should be doomed to hear such statements!"

Expressing himself with great scorn and anguish, the gentleman takes up his candle and stalks off to bed, where feigning to be fast asleep when the lady comes up-stairs drowned in tears, murmuring lamentations over her hard fate and indistinct intentions of consulting her brothers, he undergoes the secret torture of hearing her exclaim between whiles, " I know there are only fourteen doors in the house, I know it was Mr. Jenkins, I know he had a blue coat on, and I would say it as positively as I do now, if they were the last words I had to speak ! "

If the contradictory couple are blessed with children, they are not the less contradictory on that account. Master James and Miss Charlotte present themselves after dinner, and being in perfect good humour, and finding their parents in the same amiable state, augur from these appearances half a glass of wine a-piece and other extraordinary indulgences. But unfortunately Master James, growing talkative upon such prospects, asks his mamma how tall Mrs. Parsons is, and whether she is not six feet high ; to which his mamma replies, " Yes, she should think she was, for Mrs. Parsons is a very tall lady indeed ; quite a giantess." " For Heaven's sake, Charlotte," cries her husband, " do not tell the child such preposterous nonsense. Six feet high ! " " Well," replies the lady, " surely I may be permitted to have an opinion ; my opinion is, that she is six feet high—at least six feet." " Now you know, Charlotte," retorts the gentleman sternly, " that that is *not* your opinion—that you have no such idea—and that you only say this for the sake of contradiction." " You are exceedingly polite," his wife replies ; " to be wrong about such a paltry question as anybody's height, would be no great crime ; but I say again, that I believe Mrs. Parsons to be six feet—more than six feet ; nay, I believe you know her to be full six feet, and only say she is not, because I say she is." This taunt disposes the gentleman to become violent, but he checks himself, and is content to mutter, in a haughty tone, " Six feet —ha ! ha ! Mrs. Parsons six feet ! " and the lady answers, " Yes, six feet. I am sure I am glad you are amused, and I'll say it again—six feet." Thus the subject gradually drops off, and the contradiction begins to be forgotten, when Master James, with some undefined notion of making himself agreeable, and putting things to rights again, unfortunately asks his mamma what the moon's made of ; which gives her occasion to say that he had better not ask her, for she is always wrong and never can be right ; that he only exposes her to contradiction by asking any question of her : and that he had better ask his papa, who is infallible, and never can be wrong. Papa, smarting under this attack, gives a terrible pull at the bell, and says, that if the conversation is to proceed in this way, the children had better be removed. Removed they are, after a few tears and many struggles; and Pa having looked at Ma sideways for a minute or two, with a baleful eye, draws his pocket-handkerchief over his face, and composes himself for his after-dinner nap.

The friends of the contradictory couple often deplore their frequent disputes, though they rather make light of them at the same time: observing, that there is no doubt they are very much attached to each other, and that they never quarrel except about trifles. But neither the friends of the contradictory couple, nor the contradictory couple themselves, reflect, that as the most stupendous objects in nature are but vast collections of minute particles, so the slightest and least considered trifles make up the sum of human happiness or misery.

THE COUPLE WHO DOTE UPON THEIR CHILDREN

THE couple who dote upon their children have usually a great many of them : six or eight at least. The children are either the healthiest in all the world, or the most unfortunate in existence. In either case, they are equally the theme of their doting parents, and equally a source of mental anguish and irritation to their doting parents' friends.

The couple who dote upon their children recognise no dates but those connected with their births, accidents, illnesses, or remarkable deeds. They keep a mental almanack with a vast number of Innocents'-days, all in red letters. They recollect the last coronation, because on that day little Tom fell down the kitchen stairs ; the anniversary of the Gunpowder Plot, because it was on the fifth of November that Ned asked whether wooden legs were made in heaven and cocked hats grew in gardens. Mrs. Whiffler will never cease to recollect the last day of the old year as long as she lives, for it was on that day that the baby had the four red spots on its nose which they took for measles : nor Christmas Day, for twenty-one days after Christmas Day the twins were born ; nor Good Friday, for it was on a Good Friday that she was frightened by the donkey-cart when she was in the family way with Georgiana. The movable feasts have no motion for Mr. and Mrs. Whiffler, but remain pinned down tight and fast to the shoulders of some small child, from whom they can never be separated any more. Time was made, according to their creed, not for slaves but for girls and boys ; the restless sands in his glass are but little children at play.

As we have already intimated, the children of this couple can know no medium. They are either prodigies of good health or prodigies of bad health ; whatever they are, they must be prodigies. Mr. Whiffler must have to describe at his office such excruciating agonies constantly undergone by his eldest boy, as nobody else's eldest boy ever underwent ; or he must be able to declare that there never was a child endowed with such amazing health, such an indomitable constitution, and such a cast-iron frame, as his child. His children must be, in some respect or other, above and beyond the children of all other people. To such an extent is this feeling pushed, that we were once slightly acquainted with a lady and gentleman who carried their heads so high and became so proud after their youngest child fell out of a two-pair-of-stairs window without hurting himself much, that the greater part of their friends were obliged to forego their acquaintance. But perhaps this may be an extreme case, and one not justly entitled to be considered as a precedent of general application.

If a friend happen to dine in a friendly way with one of these couples who dote upon their children, it is nearly impossible for him to divert the conversation from their favourite topic. Everything reminds Mr. Whiffler of Ned, or Mrs. Whiffler of Mary Anne, or of the time before Ned was born, or the time before Mary Anne was thought of. The slightest remark, however harmless in itself, will awaken slumbering recollections of the twins. It is impossible to steer clear of them. They will come uppermost, let the poor man do what he may. Ned has been known to be lost sight of for half an hour, Dick has been forgotten, the name of Mary Anne has not been mentioned, but the twins will out. Nothing can keep down the twins.

"It's a very extraordinary thing, Saunders," says Mr. Whiffler to the visitor, "but—you have seen our little babies, the—the—twins?" The friend's heart sinks within him as he answers, "Oh, yes—often." "Your talking of the Pyramids," says Mr. Whiffler, quite as a matter of course, "reminds me of the twins. It's a very extraordinary thing about those babies—what colour should you say their eyes were?" "Upon my word," the friend stammers, "I hardly know how to answer"—the fact being, that except as the friend does not remember to have heard of any departure from the ordinary course of nature in the instance of these twins, they might have no eyes at all for aught he has observed to the contrary. "You wouldn't say they were red, I suppose?" says Mr. Whiffler. The friend hesitates, and rather thinks they are ; but inferring from the expression of Mr. Whiffler's face that red is not the colour, smiles with some confidence, and says, "No, no! very different from that." "What should you say to blue?" says Mr. Whiffler. The friend glances at him, and observing a different expression in his face, ventures to say, "I should say they *were* blue—a decided blue." "To be sure !" cries Mr. Whiffler, triumphantly, " I knew you would! But what should you say if I was to tell you that the boy's eyes are blue and the girl's hazel, eh?" "Impossible !" exclaims the friend, not at all knowing why it should be impossible. "A fact, notwithstanding," cries Mr. Whiffler; "and let me tell you, Saunders, *that's* not a common thing in twins, or a circumstance that'll happen every day."

In this dialogue Mrs. Whiffler, as being deeply responsible for the twins, their charms and singularities, has taken no share; but she now relates, in broken English, a witticism of little Dick's bearing upon the subject just discussed, which delights Mr. Whiffler beyond measure, and causes him to declare that he would have sworn that was Dick's if he had heard it anywhere. Then he requests that Mrs. Whiffler will tell Saunders what Tom said about mad bulls; and Mrs. Whiffler relating the anecdote, a discussion ensues upon the different character of Tom's wit and Dick's wit, from which it appears that Dick's humour is of a lively turn, while Tom's style is the dry and caustic. This discussion being enlivened by various illustrations, lasts a long time, and is only stopped by Mrs. Whiffler instructing the footman to ring the nursery bell, as the children were promised that they should come down and taste the pudding.

The friend turns pale when this order is given, and paler still when it is followed up by a great pattering on the staircase, (not unlike the sound of rain upon a skylight,) a violent bursting open of the dining-room door, and the tumultuous appearance of six small children, closely succeeded by a strong nursery-maid with a twin in each arm. As the whole eight are screaming, shouting, or kicking—some influenced by a ravenous appetite, some by a horror of the stranger, and some by a conflict of the two feelings—a pretty long space elapses before all their heads can be ranged round the table and anything like order restored; in bringing about which happy state of things both the nurse and footman are severely scratched. At length Mrs. Whiffler is heard to say, "Mr. Saunders, shall I give you some pudding?" A breathless silence ensues, and sixteen small eyes are fixed upon the guest in expectation of his reply. A wild shout of joy proclaims that he has said " No, thank you." Spoons are waved in the air, legs appear above the table-cloth in uncontrollable ecstasy, and eighty short fingers dabble in damson syrup.

While the pudding is being disposed of, Mr. and Mrs. Whiffler look on with beaming countenances, and Mr. Whiffler nudging his friend Saunders, begs him to take notice of Tom's eyes, or Dick's chin, or Ned's nose, or Mary Anne's hair, or Emily's figure, or little Bob's calves, or Fanny's mouth, or Carry's head, as the case may be. What-ever the attention of Mr. Saunders is called to, Mr. Saunders admires of course; though he is rather confused about the sex of the youngest branches and looks at the wrong chil-dren, turning to a girl when Mr. Whiffler directs his atten-tion to a boy, and falling into raptures with a boy when he ought to be enchanted with a girl. Then the dessert comes, and there is a vast deal of scrambling after fruit, and sudden spirting forth of juice out of tight oranges into infant eyes, and much screeching and wailing in consequence. At length it becomes time for Mrs. Whiffler to retire, and all the children are by force of arms compelled to kiss and love Mr. Saunders before going up-stairs, except Tom, who, lying on his back in the hall, proclaims that Mr. Saunders "is a naughty beast;" and Dick, who having drunk his father's wine when he was looking another way, is found to be intoxicated and is carried out, very limp and helpless.

Mr. Whiffler and his friend are left alone together, but Mr. Whiffler's thoughts are still with his family, if his family are not with him. "Saunders," says he, after a short silence, "if you please, we'll drink Mrs. Whiffler and the chil-dren." Mr. Saunders feels this to be a reproach against him-self for not proposing the same sentiment, and drinks it in some confusion. "Ah!" Mr. Whiffler sighs, "these children, Saunders, make one quite an old man." Mr. Saunders thinks that if they were his, they would make him a very old man; but he says nothing. "And yet," pursues Mr. Whiffler, "what can equal domestic happiness? what can equal the engaging ways of children! Saunders, why don't *you* get married?" Now, this is an embarrassing question, because Mr. Saunders has been thinking that if he had at any time entertained matrimonial designs, the revelation of that day would surely have routed them for ever. "I am glad, however," says Mr. Whiffler, "that you *are* a bachelor,—glad on one account, Saunders; a selfish one, I admit. Will you do Mrs. Whiffler and myself a favour?" Mr. Saunders is surprised—evidently surprised; but he replies, "with the greatest pleasure." "Then, will you, Saunders," says Mr. Whiffler, in an impressive manner, "will you cement and consolidate our friendship by coming into the family (so to speak) as a godfather?" "I shall be proud and delighted," replies Mr. Saunders: "which of the children is it? really, I thought they were all christened; or—" "Saunders," Mr. Whiffler interposes, "they *are* all christened; you are right. The fact is, that Mrs. Whiffler is—in short, we expect another." "Not a ninth!" cries the friend, all aghast at the idea. "Yes, Saunders," rejoins Mr. Whiffler, solemnly, "a ninth. Did we drink Mrs. Whiffler's health? Let us drink it again, Saunders, and wish her well over it!"

Doctor Johnson used to tell a story of a man who had but one idea, which was a wrong one. The couple who dote upon their children are in the same predicament: at home or abroad, at all times, and in all places, their thoughts are bound up in this one subject, and have no sphere beyond. They relate the clever things their offspring say or do, and weary every company with their prolixity and absurdity. Mr. Whiffler takes a friend by the button at a street corner on a windy day to tell him a *bon mot* of his youngest boy's; and Mrs. Whiffler, calling to see a sick acquaintance, entertains her with a cheerful account of all her own past sufferings and present expectations. In such cases the sins of the fathers indeed descend upon the children; for people soon come to regard them as predestined little bores. The couple who dote upon their children cannot be said to be actuated by a general love for these engaging little people (which would be a great excuse); for they are apt to underrate and entertain a jealousy of any children but their own. If they examined their own hearts, they would, perhaps, find at the bottom of all this, more self-love and egotism than they think of. Self-love and egotism are bad qualities, of which the unrestrained exhibition, though it may be sometimes amusing, never fails to be wearisome and unpleasant. Couples who dote upon their children, therefore, are best avoided.

The Couple who dote upon their Children
(*p. 575*)

THE COOL COUPLE

THERE is an old-fashioned weather-glass representing a house with two doorways, in one of which is the figure of a gentleman, in the other the figure of a lady. When the weather is to be fine the lady comes out and the gentleman goes in; when wet, the gentleman comes out and the lady goes in. They never seek each other's society, are never elevated and depressed by the same cause, and have nothing in common. They are the model of a cool couple, except that there is something of politeness and consideration about the behaviour of the gentleman in the weather-glass, in which neither of the cool couple can be said to participate.

The cool couple are seldom alone together, and when they are, nothing can exceed their apathy and dulness: the gentleman being for the most part drowsy, and the lady silent. If they enter into conversation, it is usually of an ironical or recriminatory nature. Thus, when the gentleman has indulged in a very long yawn and settled himself more snugly in his easy-chair, the lady will perhaps remark, "Well, I am sure, Charles! I hope you're comfortable." To which the gentleman replies, "Oh yes, he's quite comfortable—quite." "There are not many married men, I hope," returns the lady, "who seek comfort in such selfish gratifications as you do." "Nor many wives who seek comfort in such selfish gratifications as *you* do, I hope," retorts the gentleman. "Whose fault is that?" demands the lady. The gentleman becoming more sleepy, returns no answer. "Whose fault is that?" the lady repeats. The gentleman still returning no answer, she goes on to say that she believes there never was in all this world anybody so attached to her home, so thoroughly domestic, so unwilling to seek a moment's gratification or pleasure beyond her own fireside as she. God knows that before she was married she never thought or dreamt of such a thing; and she remembers that her poor papa used to say again and again, almost every day of his life, "Oh, my dear Louisa, if

you only marry a man who understands you, and takes the
trouble to consider your happiness and accommodate himself a very little to your disposition, what a treasure he will
find in you!" She supposes her papa knew what her disposition was—he had known her long enough—he ought to
have been acquainted with it, but what can she do? If
her home is always dull and lonely, and her husband is
always absent and finds no pleasure in her society, she is
naturally sometimes driven (seldom enough, she is sure) to
seek a little recreation elsewhere; she is not expected to
pine and mope to death, she hopes. "Then come, Louisa,"
says the gentleman, waking up as suddenly as he fell
asleep, "stop at home this evening, and so will I." "I
should be sorry to suppose, Charles, that you took a pleasure
in aggravating me," replies the lady; "but you know as
well as I do that I am particularly engaged to Mrs. Mortimer, and that it would be an act of the grossest rudeness
and ill-breeding, after accepting a seat in her box and preventing her from inviting anybody else, not to go." "Ah!
there it is!" says the gentleman, shrugging his shoulders,
"I knew that perfectly well. I knew you couldn't devote
an evening to your own home. Now all I have to say,
Louisa, is this—recollect that *I* was quite willing to stay
at home, and that it's no fault of *mine* we are not oftener
together."

With that the gentleman goes away to keep an old
appointment at his club, and the lady hurries off to dress for
Mrs. Mortimer's; and neither thinks of the other until by
some odd chance they find themselves alone again.

But it must not be supposed that the cool couple are
habitually a quarrelsome one. Quite the contrary. These
differences are only occasions for a little self-excuse,—nothing
more. In general they are as easy and careless, and dispute
as seldom, as any common acquaintances may; for it is
neither worth their while to put each other out of the way,
nor to ruffle themselves.

When they meet in society, the cool couple are the best-
bred people in existence. The lady is seated in a corner
among a little knot of lady friends, one of whom exclaims,
"Why, I vow and declare there is your husband, my dear!"
"Whose?—mine?" she says, carelessly. "Aye, yours, and
coming this way too." "How very odd!" says the lady, in
a languid tone, "I thought he had been at Dover." The

gentleman coming up, and speaking to all the other ladies and nodding slightly to his wife, it turns out that he has been at Dover, and has just now returned. "What a strange creature you are!" cries his wife; "and what on earth brought you here, I wonder?" "I came to look after you, *of course*," rejoins her husband. This is so pleasant a jest that the lady is mightily amused, as are all the other ladies similarly situated who are within hearing; and while they are enjoying it to the full, the gentleman nods again, turns upon his heel, and saunters away.

There are times, however, when his company is not so agreeable, though equally unexpected; such as when the lady has invited one or two particular friends to tea and scandal, and he happens to come home in the very midst of their diversion. It is a hundred chances to one that he remains in the house half an hour, but the lady is rather disturbed by the intrusion, notwithstanding, and reasons within herself,—"I am sure I never interfere with him, and why should he interfere with me? It can scarcely be accidental; it never happens that I have a particular reason for not wishing him to come home, but he always comes. It's very provoking and tiresome; and I am sure when he leaves me so much alone for his own pleasure, the least he could do would be to do as much for mine." Observing what passes in her mind, the gentleman, who has come home for his own accommodation, makes a merit of it with himself; arrives at the conclusion that it is the very last place in which he can hope to be comfortable; and determines, as he takes up his hat and cane, never to be so virtuous again.

Thus a great many cool couples go on until they are cold couples, and the grave has closed over their folly and indifference. Loss of name, station, character, life itself, has ensued from causes as slight as these, before now; and when gossips tell such tales, and aggravate their deformities, they elevate their hands and eyebrows, and call each other to witness what a cool couple Mr. and Mrs. So-and-So always were, even in the best of times.

THE PLAUSIBLE COUPLE

THE plausible couple have many titles. They are "a delightful couple," an "affectionate couple," "a most agreeable couple," "a good-hearted couple," and "the best-natured couple in existence." The truth is, that the plausible couple are people of the world ; and either the way of pleasing the world has grown much easier than it was in the days of the old man and his ass, or the old man was but a bad hand at it, and knew very little of the trade.

"But is it really possible to please the world?" says some doubting reader. It is indeed. Nay, it is not only very possible, but very easy. The ways are crooked, and sometimes foul and low. What then? A man need but crawl upon his hands and knees, know when to close his eyes and when his ears, when to stoop and when to stand upright ; and if by the world is meant that atom of it in which he moves himself, he shall please it, never fear.

Now, it will be readily seen, that if a plausible man or woman have an easy means of pleasing the world by an adaptation of self to all its twistings and twinings, a plausible man *and* woman, or, in other words, a plausible couple, playing into each other's hands, and acting in concert, have a manifest advantage. Hence it is that plausible couples scarcely ever fail of success on a pretty large scale ; and hence it is that if the reader, laying down this unwieldy volume at the next full stop, will have the goodness to review his or her circle of acquaintance, and to search particularly for some man and wife with a large connexion and a good name, not easily referable to their abilities or their wealth, he or she (that is, the male or female reader) will certainly find that gentleman or lady, on a very short reflection, to be a plausible couple.

The plausible couple are the most ecstatic people living : the most sensitive people—to merit—on the face of the earth. Nothing clever or virtuous escapes them. They have microscopic eyes for such endowments, and can find them anywhere. The plausible couple never fawn—oh no! They don't even scruple to tell their friends of their faults. One is too generous, another too candid; a third has a tendency to think all people like himself, and to regard mankind as a company of angels; a fourth is kind-hearted to a fault. "We never flatter, my dear Mrs. Jackson," say the plausible couple; "we speak our minds. Neither you nor Mr. Jackson have faults enough. It may sound strangely, but it is true. You have not faults enough. You know our way,—we must speak out, and always do. Quarrel with us for saying so, if you will; but we repeat it,—you have not faults enough!"

The plausible couple are no less plausible to each other than to third parties. They are always loving and harmonious. The plausible gentleman calls his wife "darling," and the plausible lady addresses him as "dearest." If it be Mr. and Mrs. Bobtail Widger, Mrs. Widger is "Lavinia, darling," and Mr. Widger is "Bobtail, dearest." Speaking of each other, they observe the same tender form. Mrs. Widger relates what "Bobtail" said, and Mr. Widger recounts what "darling" thought and did.

If you sit next to the plausible lady at a dinner-table, she takes the earliest opportunity of expressing her belief that you are acquainted with the Clickits; she is sure she has heard the Clickits speak of you—she must not tell you in what terms, or you will take her for a flatterer. You admit a knowledge of the Clickits; the plausible lady immediately launches out in their praise. She quite loves the Clickits. Were there ever such true-hearted, hospitable, excellent people—such a gentle, interesting little woman as Mrs. Clickit, or such a frank, unaffected creature as Mr. Clickit? were there ever two people, in short, so little spoiled by the world as they are? "As who, darling?" cries Mr. Widger, from the opposite side of the table. "The Clickits, dearest," replies Mrs. Widger. "Indeed you are right, darling," Mr. Widger rejoins; "the Clickits are a very high-minded, worthy, estimable couple." Mrs. Widger remarking that Bobtail always grows quite eloquent upon this subject, Mr. Widger admits that he feels very strongly whenever such people as the Clickits and some other friends of his (here he glances at the host and hostess) are mentioned; for they are an honour to human nature, and do one good to think of.

"*You* know the Clickits, Mrs. Jackson?" he says, address-ing the lady of the house. "No, indeed; we have not that pleasure," she replies. "You astonish me!" exclaims Mr. Widger: "not know the Clickits! why, you are the very people of all others who ought to be their bosom friends. You are kindred beings; you are one and the same thing:—not know the Clickits! Now *will* you know the Clickits? Will you make a point of knowing them? Will you meet them in a friendly way at our house one evening, and be acquainted with them?" Mrs. Jackson will be quite delighted; nothing would give her more pleasure. "Then, Lavinia, my darling," says Mr. Widger, "mind you don't lose sight of that; now, pray take care that Mr. and Mrs. Jackson know the Clickits without loss of time. Such people ought not to be strangers to each other." Mrs. Widger books both families as the centre of attraction for her next party; and Mr. Widger, going on to expatiate upon the virtues of the Clickits, adds to their other moral qualities, that they keep one of the neatest phaetons in town, and have two thousand a year.

As the plausible couple never laud the merits of any absent person, without dexterously contriving that their praises shall reflect upon somebody who is present, so they never depreciate anything or anybody, without turning their depreciation to the same account. Their friend, Mr. Slum-mery, say they, is unquestionably a clever painter, and would no doubt be very popular, and sell his pictures at a very high price, if that cruel Mr. Fithers had not forestalled him in his department of art, and made it thoroughly and com-pletely his own;—Fithers, it is to be observed, being present and within hearing, and Slummery elsewhere. Is Mrs. Tabblewick really as beautiful as people say? Why, there indeed you ask them a very puzzling question, because there is no doubt that she is a very charming woman, and they have long known her intimately. She is no doubt beautiful, very beautiful; they once thought her the most beautiful woman ever seen; still if you press them for an honest answer, they are bound to say that this was before they had ever seen our lovely friend on the sofa, (the sofa is hard by, and our lovely friend can't help hearing the whispers in which this is said;) since that time, perhaps, they have been hardly fair judges; Mrs. Tabblewick is no doubt extremely handsome,—very like our friend, in fact, in the form of the features,—but in point of expression, and soul, and figure, and air altogether—oh dear!

But while the plausible couple depreciate, they are still careful to preserve their character for amiability and kind feeling; indeed the depreciation itself is often made to grow out of their excessive sympathy and good will. The plausible lady calls on a lady who dotes upon her children, and is sitting with a little girl upon her knee, enraptured by her artless replies, and protesting that there is nothing she delights in so much as conversing with these fairies; when the other lady inquires if she has seen young Mrs. Finching lately, and whether the baby has turned out a finer one than it promised to be. "Oh dear!" cries the plausible lady, "you can-not think how often Bobtail and I have talked about poor Mrs. Finching—she is such a dear soul, and was so anxious that the baby should be a fine child—and, very naturally, because she was very much here at one time, and there is, you know, a natural emulation among mothers—that it is impossible to tell you how much we have felt for her." "Is it weak or plain, or what?" inquires the other. "Weak or plain, my love," returns the plausible lady, "it's a fright—a perfect little fright; you ne-ver saw such a miserable creature in all your days. Positively you must not let her see one of these beautiful dears again, or you'll break her heart, you will indeed. —Heaven bless this child, see how she is looking in my face! can you conceive anything prettier than that? If poor Mrs. Finching could only hope —but that's impossible—and the gifts of Providence, you know—What *did* I do with my pocket-handkerchief!"

What prompts the mother, who dotes upon her children, to comment to her lord that evening on the plausible lady's engaging qualities and feeling heart, and what is it that procures Mr. and Mrs. Bobtail Widger an immediate invitation to dinner?

THE NICE LITTLE COUPLE

A CUSTOM once prevailed in old-fashioned circles, that when a lady or gentleman was unable to sing a song, he or she should enliven the company with a story. As we find ourself in the predicament of not being able to describe (to our own satisfaction) nice little couples in the abstract, we purpose telling in this place a little story about a nice little couple of our acquaintance.

Mr. and Mrs. Chirrup are the nice little couple in question. Mr. Chirrup has the smartness, and something of the brisk, quick manner of a small bird. Mrs. Chirrup is the prettiest of all little women, and has the prettiest little figure conceivable. She has the neatest little foot, and the softest little voice, and the pleasantest little smile, and the tidiest little curls, and the brightest little eyes, and the quietest little manner, and is, in short, altogether one of the most engaging of all little women, dead or alive. She is a condensation of all the domestic virtues,—a pocket edition of the young man's best companion,—a little woman at a very high pressure, with an amazing quantity of goodness and usefulness in an exceedingly small space. Little as she is, Mrs. Chirrup might furnish forth matter for the moral equipment of a score of housewives, six feet high in their stockings—if, in the presence of ladies, we máy be allowed the expression—and of corresponding robustness.

Nobody knows all this better than Mr. Chirrup, though he rather takes on that he don't. Accordingly he is very proud of his better-half, and evidently considers himself, as all other people consider him, rather fortunate in having her to wife. We say evidently, because Mr. Chirrup is a warm-hearted little fellow; and if you catch his eye when he has been slyly glancing at Mrs. Chirrup in company, there is a certain complacent twinkle in it, accompanied, perhaps, by a half-expressed toss of the head, which as clearly indicates what has been passing in his mind as if he had put it into words. and shouted it out through a speaking-trumpet.

Moreover, Mr. Chirrup hás a particularly mild and bird-like manner of calling Mrs. Chirrup "my dear;" and—for he is of a jocose turn—of cutting little witticisms upon her, and making her the subject of various harmless pleasantries, which nobody enjoys more thoroughly than Mrs. Chirrup herself. Mr. Chirrup, too, now and then affects to deplore his bachelor-days, and to bemoan (with a marvellously contented and smirking face) the loss of his freedom, and the sorrow of his heart at having been taken captive by Mrs. Chirrup—all of which circumstances combine to show the secret triumph and satisfaction of Mr. Chirrup's soul.

We have already had occasion to observe that Mrs. Chirrup is an incomparable housewife. In all the arts of domestic arrangement and management, in all the mysteries of con· fectionery-making, pickling, and preserving, never was such a thorough adept as that nice little body. She is, besides, a cunning worker in muslin and fine linen, and a special hand at marketing to the very best advantage. But if there be one branch of housekeeping in which she excels to an utterly unparalleled and unprecedented extent, it is in the important one of carving. A roast goose is universally allowed to be the great stumbling-block in the way of young aspirants to perfection in this department of science; many promising carvers, beginning with legs of mutton, and preserving a good reputation through fillets of veal, sirloins of beef, quarters of lamb, fowls, and even ducks, have sunk before a roast goose, and lost caste and character for ever. To Mrs. Chirrup the resolving a goose into its smallest component parts is a pleasant pastime—a practical joke—a thing to be done in a minute or so, without the smallest interruption to the conversation of the time. No handing the dish over to an unfortunate man upon her right or left, no wild sharpening of the knife, no hacking and sawing at an unruly joint, no noise, no splash, no heat, no leaving off in despair; all is confidence and cheerfulness. The dish is set upon the table. the cover is removed; for an instant, and only an instant, you observe that Mrs. Chirrup's attention is distracted; she smiles, but heareth not. You proceed with your story; meanwhile the glittering knife is slowly upraised, both Mrs. Chirrup's wrists are slightly but not ungracefully agitated, she com· presses her lips for an instant, then breaks into a smile, and all is over. The legs of the bird slide gently down into a pool of gravy, the wings seem to melt from the body, the

z

breast separates into a row of juicy slices, the smaller and more complicated parts of his anatomy are perfectly developed, a cavern of stuffing is revealed, and the goose is gone!

To dine with Mr. and Mrs. Chirrup is one of the pleasantest things in the world. Mr. Chirrup has a bachelor friend, who lived with him in his own days of single blessedness, and to whom he is mightily attached. Contrary to the usual custom, this bachelor friend is no less a friend of Mrs. Chirrup's, and, consequently, whenever you dine with Mr. and Mrs. Chirrup, you meet the bachelor friend. It would put any reasonably-conditioned mortal into good-humour to observe the entire unanimity which subsists between these three; but there is a quiet welcome dimpling in Mrs. Chirrup's face, a bustling hospitality oozing as it were out of the waistcoat-pockets of Mr. Chirrup, and a patronising enjoyment of their cordiality and satisfaction on the part of the bachelor friend, which is quite delightful. On these occasions Mr. Chirrup usually takes an opportunity of rallying the friend on being single, and the friend retorts on Mr. Chirrup for being married, at which moments some single young ladies present are like to die of laughter; and we have more than once observed them bestow looks upon the friend, which convinces us that his position is by no means a safe one, as, indeed, we hold no bachelor's to be who visits married friends and cracks jokes on wedlock, for certain it is that such men walk among traps and nets and pitfalls innumerable, and often find themselves down upon their knees at the altar rails, taking M. or N. for their wedded wives, before they know anything about the matter.

However, this is no business of Mr. Chirrup's, who talks, and laughs, and drinks his wine, and laughs again, and talks more, until it is time to repair to the drawing-room, where, coffee served and over, Mrs. Chirrup prepares for a round game, by sorting the nicest possible little fish into the nicest possible little pools, and calling Mr. Chirrup to assist her, which Mr. Chirrup does. As they stand side by side, you find that Mr. Chirrup is the least possible shadow of a shade taller than Mrs. Chirrup, and that they are the neatest and best-matched little couple that can be, which the chances are ten to one against your observing with such effect at any other time, unless you see them in the street arm-in-arm, or meet them some rainy day trotting along under a very

The nice little Couple

small umbrella. The round game (at which Mr. Chirrup is the merriest of the party) being done and over, in course of time a nice little tray appears, on which is a nice little supper; and when that is finished likewise, and you have said "Good night," you find yourself repeating a dozen times, as you ride home, that there never was such a nice little couple as Mr. and Mrs. Chirrup.

Whether it is that pleasant qualities, being packed more closely in small bodies than in large, come more readily to hand than when they are diffused over a wider space, and have to be gathered together for use, we don't know, but as a general rule,—strengthened like all other rules by its exceptions,—we hold that little people are sprightly and good-natured. The more sprightly and good-natured people we have, the better; therefore, let us wish well to all nice little couples, and hope that they may increase and multiply.

THE EGOTISTICAL COUPLE

EGOTISM in couples is of two kinds.—It is our purpose to show this by two examples.

The egotistical couple may be young, old, middle-aged, well to do, or ill to do; they may have a small family, a large family, or no family at all. There is no outward sign by which an egotistical couple may be known and avoided. They come upon you unawares; there is no guarding against them. No man can of himself be forewarned or forearmed against an egotistical couple.

The egotistical couple have undergone every calamity, and experienced every pleasurable and painful sensation of which our nature is susceptible. You cannot by possibility tell the egotistical couple anything they don't know, or describe to them anything they have not felt. They have been everything but dead. Sometimes we are tempted to wish they had been even that, but only in our uncharitable moments, which are few and far between.

We happened the other day, in the course of a morning call, to encounter an egotistical couple, nor were we suffered to remain long in ignorance of the fact, for our very first inquiry of the lady of the house brought them into active and vigorous operation. The inquiry was of course touching the lady's health, and the answer happened to be, that she had not been very well. "Oh, my dear!" said the egotistica. lady, "don't talk of not being well. We have been in *such* a state since we saw you last!"—The lady of the house happening to remark that her lord had not been well either, the egotistical gentleman struck in: "Never let Briggs complain of not being well—never let Briggs complain, my dear Mrs. Briggs, after what I have undergone within these six weeks. He doesn't know what it is to be ill, he hasn't the least idea of it; not the faintest conception."—"My dear," interposed his wife smiling, "you talk as if it were almost a crime in Mr. Briggs not to have been as ill as we have been.

instead of feeling thankful to Providence that both he and
our dear Mrs. Briggs are in such blissful ignorance of real
suffering."—"My love," returned the egotistical gentleman,
in a low and pious voice, "you mistake me ;—I feel grateful
—very grateful. I trust our friends may never purchase
their experience as dearly as we have bought ours; I hope
they never may!"

Having put down Mrs. Briggs upon this theme, and
settled the question thus, the egotistical gentleman turned
to us, and, after a few preliminary remarks, all tending towards and leading up to the point he had in his mind,
inquired if we happened to be acquainted with the Dowager
Lady Snorflerer. On our replying in the negative, he presumed we had often met Lord Slang, or beyond all doubt,
that we were on intimate terms with Sir Chipkins Glogwog.
Finding that we were equally unable to lay claim to either
of these distinctions, he expressed great astonishment, and
turning to his wife with a retrospective smile, inquired who
it was that had told that capital story about the mashed
potatoes. "Who, my dear?" returned the egotistical lady,
"why Sir Chipkins, of course ; how can you ask! Don't
you remember his applying it to our cook, and saying that
you and I were so like the Prince and Princess, that he
could almost have sworn we were they?" "To be sure,
I remember that," said the egotistical gentleman, "but are you
quite certain that didn't apply to the other anecdote about
the Emperor of Austria and the pump?" "Upon my word
then, I think it did," replied his wife. "To be sure it did,"
said the egotistical gentleman, "it was Slang's story, I remember now, perfectly." However, it turned out, a few
seconds afterwards, that the egotistical gentleman's memory
was rather treacherous, as he began to have a misgiving that
the story had been told by the Dowager Lady Snorflerer the
very last time they dined there; but there appearing, on
further consideration, strong circumstantial evidence tending
to show that this couldn't be, inasmuch as the Dowager
Lady Snorflerer had been, on the occasion in question,
wholly engrossed by the egotistical lady, the egotistical
gentleman recanted this opinion ; and after laying the story
at the doors of a great many great people, happily left it at
last with the Duke of Scuttlewig :—observing that it was
not extraordinary he had forgotten his Grace hitherto, as it
often happened that the names of those with whom we were

upon the most familiar footing were the very last to present themselves to our thoughts.

It not only appeared that the egotistical couple knew everybody, but that scarcely any event of importance or notoriety had occurred for many years with which they had not been in some way or other connected. Thus we learned that when the well-known attempt upon the life of George the Third was made by Hatfield in Drury Lane theatre, the egotistical gentleman's grandfather sat upon his right hand and was the first man who collared him; and that the egotistical lady's aunt, sitting within a few boxes of the royal party, was the only person in the audience who heard his Majesty exclaim, "Charlotte Charlotte, don't be frightened don't be frightened; they're letting off squibs they're letting off squibs." When the fire broke out, which ended in the destruction of the two houses of parliament, the egotistical couple, being at the time at a drawing-room window on Blackheath, then and there simultaneously exclaimed, to the astonishment of a whole party—"It's the House of Lords!" Nor was this a solitary instance of their peculiar discernment, for chancing to be (as by a comparison of dates and circumstances they afterwards found) in the same omnibus with Mr. Greenacre, when he carried his victim's head about town in a blue bag, they both remarked a singular twitching in the muscles of his countenance; and walking down Fish Street Hill, a few weeks since, the egotistical gentleman said to his lady—slightly casting up his eyes to the top of the Monument—"There's a boy up there, my dear, reading a Bible. It's very strange. I don't like it.— In five seconds afterwards, Sir," says the egotistical gentleman, bringing his hands together with one violent clap— "the lad was over!"

Diversifying these topics by the introduction of many others of the same kind, and entertaining us between whiles with a minute account of what weather and diet agreed with them, and what weather and diet disagreed with them, and at what time they usually got up, and at what time went to bed, with many other particulars of their domestic economy too numerous to mention; the egotistical couple at length took their leave, and afforded us an opportunity of doing the same.

Mr. and Mrs. Sliverstone are an egotistical couple of another class, for all the lady's egotism is about her husband.

and all the gentleman's about his wife. For example :—
Mr. Sliverstone is a clerical gentleman, and occasionally
writes sermons, as clerical gentlemen do. If you happen to
obtain admission at the street-door while he is so engaged,
Mrs. Sliverstone appears on tip-toe, and speaking in a solemn
whisper, as if there were at least three or four particular
friends up-stairs, all upon the point of death, implores you
to be very silent, for Mr. Sliverstone is composing, and she
need not say how very important it is that he should not be
disturbed. Unwilling to interrupt anything so serious, you
hasten to withdraw, with many apologies; but this Mrs.
Sliverstone will by no means allow, observing, that she
knows you would like to see him, as it is very natural you
should, and that she is determined to make a trial for you,
as you are a great favourite. So you are led up-stairs—still
on tip-toe—to the door of a little back room, in which, as
the lady informs you in a whisper, Mr. Sliverstone always
writes. No answer being returned to a couple of soft taps,
the lady opens the door, and there, sure enough, is Mr.
Sliverstone, with dishevelled hair, powdering away with
pen, ink, and paper, at a rate which, if he has any power of
sustaining it, would settle the longest sermon in no time.
At first he is too much absorbed to be roused by this intrusion; but presently looking up, says faintly, "Ah!" and
pointing to his desk with a weary and languid smile, extends
his hand, and hopes you'll forgive him. Then Mrs. Sliverstone sits down beside him, and taking his hand in hers,
tells you how that Mr. Sliverstone has been shut up there
ever since nine o'clock in the morning, (it is by this time
twelve at noon,) and how she knows it cannot be good for
his health, and is very uneasy about it. Unto this Mr.
Sliverstone replies firmly, that "It must be done;" which
agonizes Mrs. Sliverstone still more, and she goes on to tell
you that such were Mr. Sliverstone's labours last week—
what with the buryings, marryings, churchings, christenings,
and all together,—that when he was going up the pulpit
stairs on Sunday evening, he was obliged to hold on by the
rails, or he would certainly have fallen over into his own
pew. Mr. Sliverstone, who has been listening and smiling
meekly, says, "Not quite so bad as that, not quite so bad!"
he admits though, on cross-examination, that he *was* very
near falling upon the verger who was following him up to
bolt the door; but adds, that it was his duty as a Christian

to fall upon him, if need were, and that he, Mr. Sliverstone, (and possibly the verger too) ought to glory in it.

This sentiment communicates new impulse to Mrs. Sliverstone, who launches into new praises of Mr. Sliverstone's worth and excellence, to which he listens in the same meek silence, save when he puts in a word of self-denial relative to some question of fact, as—" Not seventy-two christenings that week, my dear. Only seventy-one, only seventy-one." At length his lady has quite concluded, and then he says, Why should he repine, why should he give way, why should he suffer his heart to sink within him ? Is it he alone who toils and suffers ? What has she gone through, he should like to know? What does she go through every day for him and for society ?

With such an exordium Mr. Sliverstone launches out into glowing praises of the conduct of Mrs. Sliverstone in the production of eight young children, and the subsequent rearing and fostering of the same ; and thus the husband magnifies the wife, and the wife the husband.

This would be well enough if Mr. and Mrs. Sliverstone kept it to themselves, or even to themselves and a friend or two ; but they do not. The more hearers they have, the more egotistical the couple become, and the more anxious they are to make believers in their merits. Perhaps this is the worst kind of egotism. It has not even the poor excuse of being spontaneous, but is the result of a deliberate system and malice aforethought. Mere empty-headed conceit excites our pity, but ostentatious hypocrisy awakens our disgust.

THE COUPLE WHO CODDLE THEMSELVES

MRS. MERRYWINKLE's maiden name was Chopper. She was the only child of Mr. and Mrs. Chopper. Her father died when she was, as the play-books express it, "yet an infant;" and so old Mrs. Chopper, when her daughter married, made the house of her son-in-law her home from that time henceforth, and set up her staff of rest with Mr. and Mrs. Merrywinkle.

Mr. and Mrs. Merrywinkle are a couple who coddle themselves; and the venerable Mrs. Chopper is an aider and abettor in the same.

Mr. Merrywinkle is a rather lean and long-necked gentleman, middle-aged and middle-sized, and usually troubled with a cold in the head. Mrs. Merrywinkle is a delicate looking lady, with very light hair, and is exceedingly subject to the same unpleasant disorder. The venerable Mrs. Chopper—who is strictly entitled to the appellation, her daughter not being very young, otherwise than by courtesy, at the time of her marriage, which was some years ago—is a mysterious old lady who lurks behind a pair of spectacles, and is afflicted with a chronic disease, respecting which she has taken a vast deal of medical advice, and referred to a vast number of medical books, without meeting any definition of symptoms that at all suits her, or enables her to say, "That's my complaint." Indeed, the absence of authentic information upon the subject of this complaint would seem to be Mrs. Chopper's greatest ill, as in all other respects she is an uncommonly hale and hearty gentlewoman.

Both Mr. and Mrs. Chopper wear an extraordinary quantity of flannel, and have a habit of putting their feet in hot water to an unnatural extent. They likewise indulge in chamomile tea and such-like compounds, and rub themselves on the slightest provocation with camphorated spirits and other lotions applicable to mumps, sore-throat, rheumatism, or lumbago.

Mr. Merrywinkle's leaving home to go to business on a damp or wet morning is a very elaborate affair. He puts on wash-leather socks over his stockings, and India-rubber shoes above his boots, and wears under his waistcoat a cuirass of hare-skin. Besides these precautions, he winds a thick shawl round his throat, and blocks up his mouth with a large silk handkerchief. Thus accoutred, and furnished besides with a great-coat and umbrella, he braves the dangers of the streets; travelling in severe weather at a gentle trot, the better to preserve the circulation, and bringing his mouth to the surface to take breath, but very seldom, and with the utmost caution. His office-door opened, he shoots past his clerk at the same pace, and diving into his own private room, closes the door, examines the window-fastenings, and gradually unrobes himself: hanging his pocket-handkerchief on the fender to air, and determining to write to the newspapers about the fog, which, he says, "has really got to that pitch that it is quite unbearable."

In this last opinion Mrs. Merrywinkle and her respected mother fully concur; for though not present, their thoughts and tongues are occupied with the same subject, which is their constant theme all day. If anybody happens to call, Mrs. Merrywinkle opines that they must assuredly be mad, and her first salutation is, "Why, what in the name of goodness can bring you out in such weather? You know you *must* catch your death." This assurance is corroborated by Mrs. Chopper, who adds, in further confirmation, a dismal legend concerning an individual of her acquaintance who, making a call under precisely parallel circumstances, and being then in the best health and spirits, expired in forty-eight hours afterwards, of a complication of inflammatory disorders. The visitor, rendered not altogether comfortable perhaps by this and other precedents, inquires very affectionately after Mr. Merrywinkle, but by so doing brings about no change of the subject; for Mr. Merrywinkle's name is inseparably connected with his complaints, and his complaints are inseparably connected with Mrs. Merrywinkle's; and when these are done with, Mrs. Chopper, who has been biding her time, cuts in with the chronic disorder—a subject upon which the amiable old lady never leaves off speaking until she is left alone, and very often not then.

But Mr. Merrywinkle comes home to dinner. He is received by Mrs. Merrywinkle and Mrs. Chopper, who, on his remarking that he thinks his feet are damp, turn pale as ashes and drag him up-stairs, imploring him to have them rubbed directly with a dry coarse towel. Rubbed they are, one by Mrs. Merrywinkle and one by Mrs. Chopper, until the friction causes Mr. Merrywinkle to make horrible faces, and look as if he had been smelling very powerful onions; when they desist, and the patient, provided for his better security with thick worsted stockings and list slippers, is borne down-stairs to dinner. Now the dinner is always a good one, the appetites of the diners being delicate, and requiring a little of what Mrs. Merrywinkle calls "tittivation;" the secret of which is understood to lie in good cookery and tasteful spices, and which process is so successfully performed in the present instance, that both Mr. and Mrs. Merrywinkle eat a remarkably good dinner, and even the afflicted Mrs. Chopper wields her knife and fork with much of the spirit and elasticity of youth. But Mr. Merrywinkle, in his desire to gratify his appetite, is not unmindful of his health, for he has a bottle of carbonate of soda with which to qualify his porter, and a little pair of scales in which to weigh it out. Neither in his anxiety to take care of his body is he unmindful of the welfare of his immortal part, as he always prays that for what he is going to receive he may be made truly thankful; and in order that he may be as thankful as possible, eats and drinks to the utmost.

Either from eating and drinking so much, or from being the victim of this constitutional infirmity, among others, Mr. Merrywinkle, after two or three glasses of wine, falls fast asleep; and he has scarcely closed his eyes, when Mrs. Merrywinkle and Mrs. Chopper fall asleep likewise. It is on awakening at tea-time that their most alarming symptoms prevail; for then Mr. Merrywinkle feels as if his temples were tightly bound round with the chain of the street-door, and Mrs. Merrywinkle as if she had made a hearty dinner of half-hundredweights, and Mrs. Chopper as if cold water were running down her back, and oyster-knives with sharp points were plunging of their own accord into her ribs. Symptoms like these are enough to make people peevish, and no wonder that they remain so until supper-time, doing little more than doze and complain, unless Mr. Merrywinkle calls out very loudly to a servant "to keep that draught out," or rushes into the passage to flourish his fist in the countenance of the twopenny-postman, for daring to give such a knock as he had just performed at the door of a private gentleman with nerves.

Supper, coming after dinner, should consist of some gentle provocative ; and therefore the tittivating art is again in requisition, and again done honour to by Mr. and Mrs. Merrywinkle, still comforted and abetted by Mrs. Chopper. After supper, it is ten to one but the last-named old lady becomes worse, and is led off to bed with the chronic complaint in full vigour. Mr. and Mrs. Merrywinkle, having administered to her a warm cordial, which is something of the strongest, then repair to their own room, where Mr. Merrywinkle, with his legs and feet in hot water, super-intends the mulling of some wine which he is to drink at the very moment he plunges into bed, while Mrs. Merry-winkle, in garments whose nature is unknown to and un-imagined by all but married men, takes four small pills with a spasmodic look between each, and finally comes to some-thing hot and fragrant out of another little saucepan, which serves as her composing-draught for the night.

There is another kind of couple who coddle themselves, and who do so at a cheaper rate and on more spare diet, because they are niggardly and parsimonious ; for which reason they are kind enough to coddle their visitors too. It is unnecessary to describe them, for our readers may rest assured of the accuracy of these general principles :—that all couples who coddle themselves are selfish and slothful,— that they charge upon every wind that blows, every rain that falls, and every vapour that hangs in the air, the evils which arise from their own imprudence or the gloom which is engendered in their own tempers,—and that all men and women, in couples or otherwise, who fall into exclusive habits of self-indulgence, and forget their natural sympathy and close connexion with everybody and everything in the world around them, not only neglect the first duty of life, but, by a happy retributive justice, deprive themselves of its truest and best enjoyment.

THE OLD COUPLE

THEY are grandfather and grandmother to a dozen grown people and have great-grandchildren besides; their bodies are bent, their hair is grey, their step tottering and infirm. Is this the lightsome pair whose wedding was so merry, and have the young couple indeed grown old so soon!

It seems but yesterday—and yet what a host of cares and griefs are crowded into the intervening time which, reckoned by them, lengthens out into a century! How many new associations have wreathed themselves about their hearts since then! The old time is gone, and a new time has come for others—not for them. They are but the rusting link that feebly joins the two, and is silently loosening its hold and dropping asunder.

It seems but yesterday—and yet three of their children have sunk into the grave, and the tree that shades it has grown quite old. One was an infant—they wept for him; the next a girl, a slight young thing too delicate for earth—her loss was hard indeed to bear. The third, a man. That was the worst of all, but even that grief is softened now.

It seems but yesterday—and yet how the gay and laughing faces of that bright morning have changed and vanished from above ground! Faint likenesses of some remain about them yet, but they are very faint and scarcely to be traced. The rest are only seen in dreams, and even they are unlike what they were, in eyes so old and dim.

One or two dresses from the bridal wardrobe are yet preserved. They are of a quaint and antique fashion, and seldom seen except in pictures. White has turned yellow, and brighter hues have faded. Do you wonder, child? The wrinkled face was once as smooth as yours, the eyes as bright, the shrivelled skin as fair and delicate. It is the work of hands that have been dust these many years.

Where are the fairy lovers of that happy day, whose annual return comes upon the old man and his wife like the echo of some village bell which has long been silent? Let yonder peevish bachelor, racked by rheumatic pains, and quarrelling with the world, let him answer to the question. He recollects something of a favourite playmate; her name was Lucy—so they tell him. He is not sure whether she was married, or went abroad, or died. It is a long while ago, and he don't remember.

Is nothing as it used to be; does no one feel, or think, or act, as in days of yore? Yes. There is an aged woman who once lived servant with the old lady's father, and is sheltered in an alms-house not far off. She is still attached to the family, and loves them all; she nursed the children in her lap, and tended in their sickness those who are no more. Her old mistress has still something of youth in her eyes; the young ladies are like what she was but not quite so handsome, nor are the gentlemen as stately as Mr. Harvey used to be. She has seen a great deal of trouble; her husband and her son died long ago; but she has got over that, and is happy now—quite happy.

If ever her attachment to her old protectors were disturbed by fresher cares and hopes, it has long since resumed its former current. It has filled the void in the poor creature's heart, and replaced the love of kindred. Death has not left her alone, and this, with a roof above her head, and a warm hearth to sit by, makes her cheerful and contented. Does she remember the marriage of great-grandmamma? Aye, that she does, as well—as if it was only yesterday. You wouldn't think it to look at her now, and perhaps she ought not to say so of herself, but she was as smart a young girl then as you'd wish to see. She recollects she took a friend of hers up-stairs to see Miss Emma dressed for church; her name was—ah! she forgets the name, but she remembers that she was a very pretty girl, and that she married not long afterwards, and lived—it has quite passed out of her mind where she lived, but she knows she had a bad husband who used her ill, and that she died in Lambeth workhouse. Dear, dear, in Lambeth workhouse!

And the old couple—have they no comfort or enjoyment of existence? See them among their grandchildren and great-grandchildren; how garrulous they are, how they compare one with another, and insist on likenesses which no one else can see; how gently the old lady lectures the girls on points of breeding and decorum, and points the moral by

The Couple who coddle themselves

(p. 596)

anecdotes of herself in her young days—how the old gentleman chuckles over boyish feats and roguish tricks, and tells
long stories of a "barring-out" achieved at the school he
went to: which was very wrong, he tells the boys, and never
to be imitated of course, but which he cannot help letting
them know was very pleasant too—especially when he kissed
the master's niece. This last, however, is a point on which
the old lady is very tender, for she considers it a shocking
and indelicate thing to talk about, and always says so whenever it is mentioned, never failing to observe that he ought
to be very penitent for having been so sinful. So the old
gentleman gets no further, and what the schoolmaster's niece
said afterwards (which he is always going to tell) is lost to
posterity.

The old gentleman is eighty years old to-day—"Eighty
years old, Crofts, and never had a headache," he tells the
barber who shaves him (the barber being a young fellow,
and very subject to that complaint). "That's a great age,
Crofts," says the old gentleman. "I don't think it's sich a
wery great age, Sir," replied the barber. "Crofts," rejoins
the old gentleman, "you're talking nonsense to me. Eighty
not a great age?" "It's a wery great age, Sir, for a gentleman to be as healthy and active as you are," returns the
barber; "but my grandfather, Sir, he was ninety-four."
"You don't mean that, Crofts?" says the old gentleman.
"I do indeed, Sir," retorts the barber, "and as wiggerous
as Julius Cæsar, my grandfather was." The old gentleman
muses a little time, and then says, "What did he die of,
Crofts?" "He died accidentally, Sir," returns the barber:
"he didn't mean to do it. He always would go a-running
about the streets—walking never satisfied *his* spirit—and he
run against a post and died of a hurt in his chest." The
old gentleman says no more until the shaving is concluded,
and then he gives Crofts half-a-crown to drink his health.
He is a little doubtful of the barber's veracity afterwards, and
telling the anecdote to the old lady, affects to make very
light of it—though to be sure (he adds) there was old
Parr, and in some parts of England, ninety-five or so is a
common age, quite a common age.

This morning the old couple are cheerful but serious,
recalling old times as well as they can remember them,
and dwelling upon many passages in their past lives which
the day brings to mind. The old lady reads aloud, in a

tremulous voice, out of a great Bible, and the old gentleman with his hand to his ear, listens with profound respect. When the book is closed, they sit silent for a short space, and afterwards resume their conversation, with a reference perhaps to their dead children, as a subject not unsuited to that they have just left. By degrees they are led to consider which of those who survive are the most like those dearly-remembered objects, and so they fall into a less solemn strain, and become cheerful again.

How many people in all, grandchildren, great-grandchildren, and one or two intimate friends of the family, dine together to-day at the eldest son's to congratulate the old couple, and wish them many happy returns, is a calculation beyond our powers: but this we know, that the old couple no sooner present themselves, very sprucely and carefully attired, than there is a violent shouting and rushing forward of the younger branches with all manner of presents, such as pocket-books, pencil-cases, pen-wipers, watch-papers, pin-cushions, sleeve-buckles, worked-slippers, watch-guards, and even a nutmeg-grater: the latter article being presented by a very chubby and very little boy, who exhibits it in great triumph as an extraordinary variety. The old couple's emotion at these tokens of remembrance occasions quite a pathetic scene, of which the chief ingredients are a vast quantity of kissing and hugging, and repeated wipings of small eyes and noses with small square pocket-handkerchiefs, which don't come at all easily out of small pockets. Even the peevish bachelor is moved, and he says, as he presents the old gentleman with a queer sort of antique ring from his own finger, that he'll be de'ed if he doesn't think he looks younger than he did ten years ago.

But the great time is after dinner, when the dessert and wine are on the table, which is pushed back to make plenty of room, and they are all gathered in a large circle round the fire, for it is then—the glasses being filled, and everybody ready to drink the toast—that two great-grandchildren rush out at a given signal, and presently return, dragging in old Jane Adams leaning upon her crutched stick, and trembling with age and pleasure. Who so popular as poor old Jane, nurse and story-teller in ordinary to two generations; and who so happy as she, striving to bend her stiff limbs into a curtsey, while tears of pleasure steal down her withered cheeks!

The old couple sit side by side, and the old time seems like yesterday indeed. Looking back upon the path they have travelled, its dust and ashes disappear; the flowers that withered long ago, show brightly again upon its borders, and they grow young once more in the youth of those about them.

CONCLUSION

WE have taken for the subjects of the foregoing moral essays, twelve samples of married couples, carefully selected from a large stock on hand, open to the inspection of all comers. These samples are intended for the benefit of the rising generation of both sexes, and, for their more easy and pleasant information, have been separately ticketed and labelled in the manner they have seen.

We have purposely excluded from consideration the couple in which the lady reigns paramount and supreme, holding such cases to be of a very unnatural kind, and like hideous births and other monstrous deformities, only to be discreetly and sparingly exhibited.

And here our self-imposed task would have ended, but that to those young ladies and gentlemen who are yet revolving singly round the church, awaiting the advent of that time when the mysterious laws of attraction shall draw them towards it in couples, we are desirous of addressing a few last words.

Before marriage and afterwards, let them learn to centre all their hopes of real and lasting happiness in their own fireside; let them cherish the faith that in home, and all the English virtues which the love of home engenders. lies the only true source of domestic felicity; let them believe that round the household gods, contentment and tranquillity cluster in their gentlest and most graceful forms; and that many weary hunters of happiness through the noisy world, have learnt this truth too late, and found a cheerful spirit and a quiet mind only at home at last.

How much may depend on the education of daughters and the conduct of mothers; how much of the brightest part of our old national character may be perpetuated by their wisdom or frittered away by their folly—how much of it may have been lost already, and how much more in danger of vanishing every day—are questions too weighty for discussion here, but well deserving a little serious consideration from all young couples nevertheless.

To that one young couple on whose bright destiny the thoughts of nations are fixed, may the youth of England look, and not in vain, for an example. From that one young couple, blessed and favoured as they are, may they learn that even the glare and glitter of a court, the splendour of a palace, and the pomp and glory of a throne, yield in their power of conferring happiness, to domestic worth and virtue. From that one young couple may they learn that the crown of a great empire, costly and jewelled though it be, gives place in the estimation of a Queen to the plain gold ring that links her woman's nature to that of tens of thousands of her humble subjects, and guards in her woman's heart one secret store of tenderness, whose proudest boast shall be that it knows no Royalty save Nature's own, and no pride of birth but being the child of heaven !

So shall the highest young couple in the land for once hear the truth, when men throw up their caps, and cry with loving shouts—

GOD BLESS THEM.

The Mudfog and other Sketches

THE MUDFOG AND OTHER SKETCHES

PUBLIC LIFE OF MR. TULRUMBLE

ONCE MAYOR OF MUDFOG

Mudfog is a pleasant town—a remarkably pleasant town—
situated in a charming hollow by the side of a river, from
which river Mudfog derives an agreeable scent of pitch, tar.
coals, and rope-yarn, a roving population in oilskin hats, a
pretty steady influx of drunken bargemen, and a great many
other maritime advantages. There is a good deal of water
about Mudfog, and yet it is not exactly the sort of town for
a watering-place, either. Water is a perverse sort of element
at the best of times, and in Mudfog it is particularly so.
In winter, it comes oozing down the streets and tumbling
over the fields,—nay, rushes into the very cellars and kitchens
of the houses, with a lavish prodigality that might well be
dispensed with; but in the hot summer weather it *will* dry
up, and turn green: and, although green is a very good
colour in its way, especially in grass, still it certainly is not
becoming to water; and it cannot be denied that the beauty
of Mudfog is rather impaired, even by this trifling circumstance. Mudfog is a healthy place—very healthy;—damp,
perhaps, but none the worse for that. It's quite a mistake
to suppose that damp is unwholesome: plants thrive best in
damp situations, and why shouldn't men? The inhabitants
of Mudfog are unanimous in asserting that there exists not
a finer race of people on the face of the earth; here we have
an indisputable and veracious contradiction of the vulgar

error at once.   So, admitting Mudfog to be damp, we distinctly state that it is salubrious.

The town of Mudfog is extremely picturesque. Limehouse and Ratcliff Highway are both something like it, but they give you a very faint idea of Mudfog.   There are a great many more public-houses in Mudfog—more than in Ratcliff Highway and Limehouse put together.   The public buildings, too, are very imposing.   We consider the town-hall one of the finest specimens of shed architecture, extant : it is a combination of the pig-sty and tea-garden-box orders ; and the simplicity of its design is of surpassing beauty.   The idea of placing a large window on one side of the door, and a small one on the other, is particularly happy.   There is a fine old Doric beauty, too, about the padlock and scraper, which is strictly in keeping with the general effect.

In this room do the mayor and corporation of Mudfog assemble together in solemn council for the public weal. Seated on the massive wooden benches, which, with the table in the centre, form the only furniture of the whitewashed apartment, the sage men of Mudfog spend hour after hour in grave deliberation.   Here they settle at what hour of the night the public-houses shall be closed, at what hour of the morning they shall be permitted to open, how soon it shall be lawful for people to eat their dinner on church-days, and other great political questions ; and sometimes, long after silence has fallen on the town, and the distant lights from the shops and houses have ceased to twinkle, like far-off stars, to the sight of the boatmen on the river, the illumination in the two unequal-sized windows of the town-hall warns the inhabitants of Mudfog that its little body of legislators, like a larger and better-known body of the same genus, a great deal more noisy, and not a whit more profound, are patriotically dozing away in company, far into the night, for their country's good.

Among this knot of sage and learned men, no one was so eminently distinguished, during many years, for the quiet modesty of his appearance and demeanour, as Nicholas Tulrumble, the well-known coal-dealer.   However exciting the subject of discussion, however animated the tone of the debate, or however warm the personalities exchanged, (and even in Mudfog we get personal sometimes,) Nicholas Tulrumble was always the same.   To say truth, Nicholas, being an industrious man, and always up betimes, was apt to fall

The old Couple
(*p. 600*)

asleep when a debate began, and to remain asleep till it was over, when he would wake up very much refreshed, and give his vote with the greatest complacency. The fact was, that Nicholas Tulrumble, knowing that everybody there had made up his mind beforehand, considered the talking as just a long botheration about nothing at all; and to the present hour it remains a question, whether, on this point at all events, Nicholas Tulrumble was not pretty near right.

Time, which strews a man's head with silver, sometimes fills his pockets with gold. As he gradually performed one good office for Nicholas Tulrumble, he was obliging enough not to omit the other. Nicholas began life in a wooden tenement of four feet square, with a capital of two and ninepence, and a stock in trade of three bushels and a half of coals, exclusive of the large lump which hung, by way of sign-board, outside. Then he enlarged the shed, and kept a truck; then he left the shed, and the truck too, and started a donkey and a Mrs. Tulrumble; then he moved again and set up a cart; the cart was soon afterwards exchanged for a waggon; and so he went on like his great predecessor Whittington—only without a cat for a partner —increasing in wealth and fame, until at last he gave up business altogether, and retired with Mrs. Tulrumble and family to Mudfog Hall, which he had himself erected, on something which he attempted to delude himself into the belief was a hill, about a quarter of a mile distant from the town of Mudfog.

About this time it began to be murmured in Mudfog that Nicholas Tulrumble was growing vain and haughty: that prosperity and success had corrupted the simplicity of his manners, and tainted the natural goodness of his heart: in short, that he was setting up for a public character, and a great gentleman, and affected to look down upon his old companions with compassion and contempt. Whether these reports were at the time well-founded or not, certain it is that Mrs. Tulrumble very shortly afterwards started a four-wheel chaise, driven by a tall postilion in a yellow cap,—that Mr. Tulrumble junior took to smoking cigars, and calling the footman a "feller,"—and that Mr. Tulrumble, from that time forth, was no more seen in his old seat in the chimney-corner of the Lighterman's Arms at night. This looked bad; but, more than this, it began to be observed that Mr. Nicholas Tulrumble attended the corporation meetings more frequently than heretofore; and he no longer went to sleep as he had done for so many years, but propped his eyelids open with his two forefingers; that he read the newspapers by himself at home; and that he was in the habit of indulging abroad in distant and mysterious allusions to "masses of people," and "the property of the country," and "productive power," and "the monied interest:" all of which denoted and proved that Nicholas Tulrumble was either mad, or worse; and it puzzled the good people of Mudfog amazingly.

At length, about the middle of the month of October, Mr. Tulrumble and family went up to London; the middle of October being, as Mrs. Tulrumble informed her acquaintance in Mudfog, the very height of the fashionable season.

Somehow or other, just about this time, despite the health-preserving air of Mudfog, the Mayor died. It was a most extraordinary circumstance; he had lived in Mudfog for eighty-five years. The corporation didn't understand it at all; indeed it was with great difficulty that one old gentleman, who was a great stickler for forms, was dissuaded from proposing a vote of censure on such unaccountable conduct. Strange as it was, however, die he did, without taking the slightest notice of the corporation; and the corporation were imperatively called upon to elect his successor. So they met for the purpose; and being very full of Nicholas Tulrumble just then, and Nicholas Tulrumble being a very important man, they elected him, and wrote off to London by the very next post to acquaint Nicholas Tulrumble with his new elevation.

Now, it being November time, and Mr. Nicholas Tulrumble being in the capital, it fell out that he was present at the Lord Mayor's show and dinner, at sight of the glory and splendour whereof he, Mr. Tulrumble, was greatly mortified, inasmuch as the reflection would force itself on his mind, that, had he been born in London instead of in Mudfog, he might have been a Lord Mayor too, and have patronized the judges, and been affable to the Lord Chancellor, and friendly with the Premier, and coldly condescending to the Secretary to the Treasury, and have dined with a flag behind his back, and done a great many other acts and deeds which unto Lord Mayors of London peculiarly appertain. The more he thought of the Lord Mayor, the more enviable a personage he seemed. To be a King was all very well; but what was the King to the Lord Mayor! When the King made a speech, everybody knew it was somebody else's writing: whereas here was the Lord Mayor, talking away for half an hour—all out of his own head—amidst the enthusiastic applause of the whole company, while it was notorious that the King might talk to his parliament till he was black in the face without getting so much as a single cheer. As all these reflections passed through the mind of Mr. Nicholas Tulrumble, the Lord Mayor of London appeared to him the greatest sovereign on the face of the earth, beating the Emperor of Russia all to nothing, and leaving the Great Mogul immeasurably behind.

Mr. Nicholas Tulrumble was pondering over these things, and inwardly cursing the fate which had pitched his coal-shed in Mudfog, when the letter of the corporation was put into his hand. A crimson flush mantled over his face as he read it, for visions of brightness were already dancing before his imagination.

"My dear," said Mr. Tulrumble to his wife, "they have elected me Mayor of Mudfog."

"Lor-a-mussy!" said Mrs. Tulrumble: "why, what's become of old Sniggs?"

"The late Mr. Sniggs, Mrs. Tulrumble," said Mr. Tulrumble sharply, for he by no means approved of the notion of unceremoniously designating a gentleman who filled the high office of Mayor, as "Old Sniggs,"—"The late Mr. Sniggs, Mrs. Tulrumble, is dead."

The communication was very unexpected; but Mrs. Tulrumble only ejaculated "Lor-a-mussy!" once again, as if a Mayor were a mere ordinary Christian, at which Mr. Tulrumble frowned gloomily.

"What a pity 'tan't in London, ain't it?" said Mrs. Tulrumble, after a short pause; "what a pity 'tan't in London, where you might have had a show."

"I *might* have a show in Mudfog, if I thought proper, I apprehend," said Mr. Tulrumble mysteriously.

"Lor! so you might, I declare," replied Mrs. Tulrumble.

"And a good one too," said Mr. Tulrumble.

"Delightful!" exclaimed Mrs. Tulrumble.

"One which would rather astonish the ignorant people down there," said Mr. Tulrumble.

"It would kill them with envy," said Mrs. Tulrumble.

So it was agreed that his Majesty's lieges in Mudfog should be astonished with splendour, and slaughtered with envy, and

A a

that such a show should take place as had never been seen in that town, or in any other town before,—no, not even in London itself.

On the very next day after the receipt of the letter, down came the tall postilion in a post-chaise,—not upon one of the horses, but inside—actually inside the chaise,—and, driving up to the very door of the town-hall, where the corporation were assembled, delivered a letter, written by the Lord knows who, and signed by Nicholas Tulrumble, in which Nicholas said, all through four sides of closely-written, gilt-edged, hot-pressed, Bath post letter paper, that he responded to the call of his fellow-townsmen with feelings of heartfelt delight; that he accepted the arduous office which their confidence had imposed upon him; that they would never find him shrinking from the discharge of his duty; that he would endeavour to execute his functions with all that dignity which their magnitude and importance demanded; and a great deal more to the same effect. But even this was not all. The tall postilion produced from his right-hand top-boot a damp copy of that afternoon's number of the county paper; and there, in large type, running the whole length of the very first column, was a long address from Nicholas Tulrumble to the inhabitants of Mudfog, in which he said that he cheerfully complied with their requisition, and, in short, as if to prevent any mistake about the matter, told them over again what a grand fellow he meant to be, in very much the same terms as those in which he had already told them all about the matter in his letter.

The corporation stared at one another very hard at all this, and then looked as if for explanation to the tall postilion, but as the tall postilion was intently contemplating the gold tassel on the top of his yellow cap, and could have afforded no explanation whatever, even if his thoughts had been entirely disengaged, they contented themselves with coughing very dubiously, and looking very grave. The tall postilion then delivered another letter, in which Nicholas Tulrumble informed the corporation that he intended repairing to the town-hall, in grand state and gorgeous procession, on the Monday afternoon next ensuing. At this the corporation looked still more solemn; but as the epistle wound up with a formal invitation to the whole body to dine with the Mayor on that day, at Mudfog Hall, Mudfog Hill, Mudfog, they began to see the fun of the thing directly, and sent back their compliments, and they'd be sure to come.

Now there happened to be in Mudfog, as somehow or other there does happen to be, in almost every town in the British dominions, and perhaps in foreign dominions too—we think it very likely, but, being no great traveller, cannot distinctly say—there happened to be, in Mudfog, a merry-tempered, pleasant-faced, good-for-nothing sort of vagabond, with an invincible dislike to manual labour, and an unconquerable attachment to strong beer and spirits, whom everybody knew, and nobody, except his wife, took the trouble to quarrel with, who inherited from his ancestors the appellation of Edward Twigger, and rejoiced in the *sobriquet* of Bottle-nosed Ned. He was drunk upon the average once a day, and penitent upon an equally fair calculation once a month; and when he was penitent he was invariably in the very last stage of maudlin intoxication. He was a ragged, roving, roaring kind of fellow, with a burly form, a sharp wit, and a ready head, and could turn his hand to anything when he chose to do it. He was by no means opposed to hard labour on principle, for he would work away at a cricket-match by the day together, —running, and catching, and batting, and bowling, and revelling in toil which would exhaust a galley-slave. He would have been invaluable to a fire-office; never was a man with such a natural taste for pumping engines, running up ladders, and throwing furniture out of two-pair-of-stairs' windows : nor was this the only element in which he was at home; he was a humane society in himself, a portable drag, an animated life-preserver, and had saved more people in his time from drowning than the Plymouth life-boat, or Captain Manby's apparatus. With all these qualifications, notwithstanding his dissipation, Bottle-nosed Ned was a general favourite; and the authorities of Mudfog, remembering his numerous services to the population, allowed him in return to get drunk in his own way, without the fear of stocks, fine, or imprisonment. He had a general licence, and he showed his sense of the compliment by making the most of it.

We have been thus particular in describing the character and avocations of Bottle-nosed Ned, because it enables us to introduce a fact politely, without hauling it into the reader's presence with indecent haste by the head and shoulders, and brings us very naturally to relate, that on the very same evening on which Mr. Nicholas Tulrumble and family returned to Mudfog, Mr. Tulrumble's new secretary, just imported from London, with a pale face and light whiskers, thrust his head down to the very bottom of his neckcloth-tie, in at the tap-room door of the Lighterman's Arms, and inquiring whether one Ned Twigger was luxuriating within, announced himself as the bearer of a message from Nicholas Tulrumble, Esquire, requiring Mr. Twigger's immediate attendance at the hall on private and particular business. It being by no means Mr. Twigger's interest to affront the Mayor, he rose from the fireplace with a slight sigh, and followed the light-whiskered secretary through the dirt and wet of Mudfog streets, up to Mudfog Hall, without further ado.

Mr. Nicholas Tulrumble was seated in a small cavern with a skylight, which he called his library, sketching out a plan of the procession on a large sheet of paper; and into the cavern the secretary ushered Ned Twigger.

"Well, Twigger!" said Nicholas Tulrumble, condescendingly.

There was a time when Twigger would have replied, "Well, Nick!" but that was in the days of the truck, and a couple of years before the donkey; so he only bowed.

"I want you to go into training, Twigger," said Mr. Tulrumble.

"What for, sir?" inquired Ned, with a stare.

"Hush, hush, Twigger!" said the Mayor. "Shut the door, Mr. Jennings. Look here, Twigger."

As the Mayor said this, he unlocked a high closet, and disclosed a complete suit of brass armour of gigantic dimensions.

"I want you to wear this next Monday, Twigger," said the Mayor.

"Bless your heart and soul, sir!" replied Ned, "you might as well ask me to wear a seventy-four pounder, or a cast-iron boiler."

"Nonsense, Twigger, nonsense!" said the Mayor.

"I couldn't stand under it, sir," said Twigger; "it would make mashed potatoes of me if I attempted it."

"Pooh, pooh, Twigger!" returned the Mayor. "I tell you I have seen it done with my own eyes, in London, and the man wasn't half such a man as you are, either."

"I should as soon have thought of a man's wearing the case of an eight-day clock to save his linen," said Twigger, casting a look of apprehension at the brass suit.

"It's the easiest thing in the world," rejoined the Mayor.

"It's nothing," said Mr. Jennings

"When you're used to it," added Ned.

"You do it by degrees," said the Mayor. "You would begin with one piece to-morrow, and two the next day, and so on, till you had got it all on. Mr. Jennings, give Twigger a glass of rum. Just try the breast-plate, Twigger. Stay; take another glass of rum first. Help me to lift it, Mr. Jennings. Stand firm, Twigger! There!—it isn't half as heavy as it looks, is it?"

Twigger was a good strong, stout fellow; so, after a great deal of staggering, he managed to keep himself up, under the breast-plate, and even contrived, with the aid of another glass of rum, to walk about in it, and the gauntlets into the bargain. He made a trial of the helmet, but was not equally successful, inasmuch as he tipped over instantly,—an accident which Mr. Tulrumble clearly demonstrated to be occasioned by his not having a counteracting weight of brass on his legs.

"Now, wear that with grace and propriety on Monday next," said Tulrumble, "and I'll make your fortune."

"I'll try what I can do, sir," said Twigger.

"It must be kept a profound secret," said Tulrumble.

"Of course, sir," replied Twigger.

"And you must be sober," said Tulrumble; "perfectly sober."

Mr. Twigger at once solemnly pledged himself to be as sober as a judge, and Nicholas Tulrumble was satisfied, although, had we been Nicholas, we should certainly have exacted some promise of a more specific nature; inasmuch as, having attended the Mudfog assizes in the evening more than once, we can solemnly testify to having seen judges with very strong symptoms of dinner under their wigs. However, that's neither here nor there.

The next day, and the day following, and the day after that, Ned Twigger was securely locked up in the small cavern with the skylight, hard at work at the armour. With every additional piece he could manage to stand upright in, he had an additional glass of rum; and at last, after many partial suffocations, he contrived to get on the whole suit, and to stagger up and down the room in it, like an intoxicated effigy from Westminster Abbey.

Never was man so delighted as Nicholas Tulrumble; never was woman so charmed as Nicholas Tulrumble's wife. Here was a sight for the common people of Mudfog! A live man in brass armour! Why, they would go wild with wonder!

The day—*the* Monday—arrived.

If the morning had been made to order, it couldn't have been better adapted to the purpose. They never showed a better fog in London on Lord Mayor's day, than enwrapped the town of Mudfog on that eventful occasion. It had risen slowly and surely from the green and stagnant water with the first light of morning, until it reached a little above the lamp-post tops; and there it had stopped, with a sleepy, sluggish obstinacy, which bade defiance to the sun, who had got up very blood-shot about the eyes, as if he had been at a drinking-party over-night, and was doing his day's work with the worst possible grace. The thick damp mist hung over the town like a huge gauze curtain. All was dim and dismal. The church steeples had bidden a temporary adieu to the world below; and every object of lesser importance—houses, barns, hedges, trees, and barges—had all taken the veil.

The church-clock struck one. A cracked trumpet from the front garden of Mudfog Hall produced a feeble flourish, as if some asthmatic person had coughed into it accidentally; the gate flew open, and out came a gentleman, on a moist-sugar coloured charger, intended to represent a herald, but bearing a much stronger resemblance to a court-card on horseback. This was one of the Circus people, who always came down to Mudfog at that time of the year, and who had been engaged by Nicholas Tulrumble expressly for the occasion. There was the horse, whisking his tail about, balancing himself on his hind-legs, and flourishing away with his fore-feet, in a manner which would have gone to the hearts and souls of any reasonable crowd. But a Mudfog crowd never was a reasonable one, and in all probability never will be. Instead of scattering the very fog with their shouts, as they ought most indubitably to have done, and were fully intended to do by Nicholas Tulrumble, they no sooner recognized the herald, than they began to growl forth the most unqualified disapprobation at the bare notion of his riding like any other man. If he had come out on his head indeed, or jumping through a hoop, or flying through a red-hot drum, or even standing on one leg with his other foot in his mouth, they might have had something to say to him; but for a professional gentleman to sit astride in the saddle, with his feet in the stirrups, was rather too good a joke. So the herald was a decided failure, and the crowd hooted with great energy, as he pranced ingloriously away.

On the procession came. We are afraid to say how many supernumeraries there were, in striped shirts and black velvet caps, to imitate the London watermen, or how many base imitations of running-footmen, or how many banners, which, owing to the heaviness of the atmosphere, could by no means be prevailed on to display their inscriptions : still less do we feel disposed to relate how the men who played the wind instruments, looking up into the sky (we mean the fog) with musical fervour, walked through pools of water and hillocks of mud, till they covered the powdered heads of the running-footmen aforesaid with splashes, that looked curious, but not ornamental; or how the barrel-organ performer put on the wrong stop, and played one tune while the band played another; or how the horses, being used to the arena, and not to the streets, would stand still and dance, instead of going on and prancing;—all of which are matters which might be dilated upon to great advantage, but which we have not the least intention of dilating upon, notwithstanding.

Oh! it was a grand and beautiful sight to behold a corporation in glass coaches, provided at the sole cost and charge of Nicholas Tulrumble, coming rolling along, like a funeral out of mourning, and to watch the attempts the corporation made to look great and solemn, when Nicholas Tulrumble himself, in the four-wheel chaise, with the tall postilion, rolled out after them, with Mr. Jennings on one side to look like a chaplain, and a supernumerary on the other, with an old life-guardsman's sabre, to imitate the sword-bearer; and to see the tears rolling down the faces of the mob as they screamed with merriment. This was beautiful! and so was the appearance of Mrs. Tulrumble and son, as they bowed with grave dignity out of their coach-window to all the dirty faces that were laughing around them : but it is not even with this that we have to do, but with the sudden stopping of the procession at another blast of the trumpet, whereat, and whereupon, a profound silence ensued, and all eyes were turned towards Mudfog Hall, in the confident anticipation of some new wonder.

"They won't laugh now, Mr. Jennings," said Nicholas Tulrumble.

"I think not, sir," said Mr. Jennings.

"See how eager they look," said Nicholas Tulrumble. "Aha! the laugh will be on our side now; eh, Mr. Jennings?"

" No doubt of that, sir," replied Mr. Jennings; and Nicholas Tulrumble, in a state of pleasurable excitement, stood up in the four-wheel chaise, and telegraphed gratification to the Mayoress behind.

While all this was going forward, Ned Twigger had descended into the kitchen of Mudfog Hall for the purpose of indulging the servants with a private view of the curiosity that was to burst upon the town; and, somehow or other, the footman was so companionable, and the housemaid so kind, and the cook so friendly, that he could not resist the offer of the first-mentioned to sit down and take something—just to drink success to master in.

So down Ned Twigger sat himself in his brass livery on the top of the kitchen-table; and in a mug of something strong, paid for by the unconscious Nicholas Tulrumble, and provided by the companionable footman, drank success to the Mayor and his procession; and, as Ned laid by his helmet to imbibe the something strong, the companionable footman put it on his own head, to the immeasurable and unrecordable delight of the cook and housemaid. The companionable footman was very facetious to Ned, and Ned was very gallant to the cook and housemaid by turns. They were all very cosy and comfortable; and the something strong went briskly round.

At last Ned Twigger was loudly called for by the procession people: and, having had his helmet fixed on, in a very complicated manner, by the companionable footman, and the kind housemaid, and the friendly cook, he walked gravely forth, and appeared before the multitude.

The crowd roared—it was not with wonder, it was not with surprise; it was most decidedly and unquestionably with laughter.

"What!" said Mr. Tulrumble, starting up in the four-wheel chaise. "Laughing? If they laugh at a man in real brass armour, they'd laugh when their own fathers were dying. Why doesn't he go into his place, Mr. Jennings? What's he rolling down towards us for? he has no business here!"

"I am afraid, sir——" faltered Mr. Jennings.

"Afraid of what, sir?" said Nicholas Tulrumble, looking up into the secretary's face.

"I am afraid he's drunk, sir," replied Mr. Jennings.

Nicholas Tulrumble took one look at the extraordinary figure that was bearing down upon them; and then, clasping his secretary by the arm, uttered an audible groan in anguish of spirit.

It is a melancholy fact that Mr. Twigger having full licence to demand a single glass of rum on the putting on of every piece of the armour, got, by some means or other, rather out of his calculation in the hurry and confusion of preparation, and drank about four glasses to a piece instead of one, not to mention the something strong which went on the top of it. Whether the brass armour checked the natural flow of perspiration, and thus prevented the spirit from evaporating, we are not scientific enough to know; but, whatever the cause was, Mr. Twigger no sooner found himself outside the gate of Mudfog Hall, than he also found himself in a very considerable state of intoxication; and hence his extraordinary style of progressing. This was bad enough, but, as if fate and fortune had conspired against Nicholas Tulrumble, Mr. Twigger, not having been penitent for a good calendar month, took it into his head to be most especially and particularly sentimental, just when his repentance could have been most conveniently dispensed with. Immense tears were rolling down his cheeks, and he was vainly endeavouring to conceal his grief by applying to his eyes a blue cotton pocket-handkerchief with white spots,—an article not strictly in keeping with a suit of armour some three hundred years old, or thereabouts.

"Twigger, you villain!" said Nicholas Tulrumble, quite forgetting his dignity, "go back."

"Never," said Ned, "I'm a miserable wretch. I'll never leave you."

The by-standers of course received this declaration with acclamations of "That's right, Ned; don't!"

"I don't intend it," said Ned, with all the obstinacy of a very tipsy man. "I'm very unhappy. I'm the wretched father of an unfortunate family; but I am very faithful, sir. I'll never leave you." Having reiterated this obliging promise, Ned proceeded in broken words to harangue the crowd upon the number of years he had lived in Mudfog, the excessive respectability of his character, and other topics of the like nature.

"Here! will anybody lead him away?" said Nicholas; "if they'll call on me afterwards, I'll reward them well."

Two or three men stepped forward, with the view of bearing Ned off, when the secretary interposed.

"Take care! take care!" said Mr. Jennings. "I beg your pardon, sir; but they'd better not go too near him, because, if he falls over, he'll certainly crush somebody."

At this hint the crowd retired on all sides to a very respectful distance, and left Ned, like the Duke of Devonshire, in a little circle of his own.

"But, Mr. Jennings," said Nicholas Tulrumble, "he'll be suffocated."

"I'm very sorry for it, sir," replied Mr. Jennings; "but nobody can get that armour off, without his own assistance. I'm quite certain of it from the way he put it on."

Here Ned wept dolefully, and shook his helmeted head, in a manner that might have touched a heart of stone; but the crowd had not hearts of stone, and they laughed heartily.

"Dear me, Mr. Jennings," said Nicholas, turning pale at the possibility of Ned's being smothered in his antique costume—"Dear me, Mr. Jennings, can nothing be done with him?"

"Nothing at all," replied Ned, "nothing at all. Gentlemen, I'm an unhappy wretch. I'm a body, gentlemen, in a brass coffin." At this poetical idea of his own conjuring up, Ned cried so much that the people began to get sympathetic, and to ask what Nicholas Tulrumble meant by putting a man into such a machine as that; and one individual in a hairy waistcoat like the top of a trunk, who had previously expressed his opinion that if Ned hadn't been a poor man, Nicholas wouldn't have dared do it, hinted at the propriety of breaking the four-wheel chaise, or Nicholas's head, or both, which last compound proposition the crowd seemed to consider a very good notion.

It was not acted upon, however, for it had hardly been broached, when Ned Twigger's wife made her appearance abruptly in the little circle before noticed, and Ned no sooner caught a glimpse of her face and form, than from the mere force of habit he set off towards his home just as fast as his legs could carry him; and that was not very quick in the present instance either, for, however ready they might have been to carry *him*, they couldn't get on very well under the brass armour. So Mrs. Twigger had plenty of time to denounce Nicholas Tulrumble to his face: to express her opinion that he was a decided monster; and to intimate that, if her ill-used husband sustained any personal damage from the brass armour, she would have the law of Nicholas

Tulrumble for manslaughter. When she had said all this with due vehemence, she posted after Ned, who was dragging himself along as best he could, and deploring his unhappiness in most dismal tones.

What a wailing and screaming Ned's children raised when he got home at last! Mrs. Twigger tried to undo the armour, first in one place and then in another, but she couldn't manage it; so she tumbled Ned into bed, helmet, armour, gauntlets, and all. Such a creaking as the bedstead made, under Ned's weight in his new suit! It didn't break down though; and there Ned lay, like the anonymous vessel in the Bay of Biscay, till next day, drinking barley-water, and looking miserable: and every time he groaned, his good lady said it served him right, which was all the consolation Ned Twigger got.

Nicholas Tulrumble and the gorgeous procession went on together to the town hall, amid the hisses and groans of all the spectators, who had suddenly taken it into their heads to consider poor Ned a martyr. Nicholas was formally installed in his new office, in acknowledgment of which ceremony he delivered himself of a speech, composed by the secretary, which was very long, and no doubt very good, only the noise of the people outside prevented anybody from hearing it, but Nicholas Tulrumble himself. After which, the procession got back to Mudfog Hall any how it could; and Nicholas and the corporation sat down to dinner.

But the dinner was flat, and Nicholas was disappointed. They were such dull sleepy old fellows, that corporation. Nicholas made quite as long speeches as the Lord Mayor of London had done, nay, he said the very same things that the Lord Mayor of London had said, and the deuce a cheer the corporation gave him. There was only one man in the party who was thoroughly awake; and he was insolent, and called him Nick. Nick! What would be the consequence, thought Nicholas, of anybody presuming to call the Lord Mayor of London "Nick!" He should like to know what the sword-bearer would say to that; or the recorder, or the toast-master, or any other of the great officers of the city. They'd nick him.

But these were not the worst of Nicholas Tulrumble's doings. If they had been, he might have remained a Mayor to this day, and have talked till he lost his voice. He contracted a relish for statistics, and got philosophical; and the statistics and the philosophy together led him into an act which increased his unpopularity and hastened his downfall.

At the very end of the Mudfog High Street, and abutting on the river-side, stands the Jolly Boatmen, an old-fashioned low-roofed, bay-windowed house, with a bar, kitchen, and tap-room all in one, and a large fireplace with a kettle to correspond, round which the working men have congregated time out of mind on a winter's night, refreshed by draughts of good strong beer, and cheered by the sounds of a fiddle and tambourine : the Jolly Boatmen having been duly licensed by the Mayor and corporation, to scrape the fiddle and thumb the tambourine from time whereof the memory of the oldest inhabitants goeth not to the contrary. Now Nicholas Tulrumble had been reading pamphlets on crime, and parliamentary reports,—or had made the secretary read them to him, which is the same thing in effect,—and he at once perceived that this fiddle and tambourine must have done more to demoralize Mudfog, than any other operating causes that ingenuity could imagine. So he read up for the subject, and determined to come out on the corporation with a burst, the very next time the licence was applied for.

The licensing day came, and the red-faced landlord of the Jolly Boatmen walked into the town-hall, looking as jolly as need be, having actually put on an extra fiddle for that night, to commemorate the anniversary of the Jolly Boatmen's music licence. It was applied for in due form, and was just about to be granted as a matter of course, when up rose Nicholas Tulrumble, and drowned the astonished corporation in a torrent of eloquence. He descanted in glowing terms upon the increasing depravity of his native town of Mudfog, and the excesses committed by its population. Then, he related how shocked he had been, to see barrels of beer sliding down into the cellar of the Jolly Boatmen week after week ; and how he had sat at a window opposite the Jolly Boatmen for two days together, to count the people who went in for beer between the hours of twelve and one o'clock alone—which, by-the-bye, was the time at which the great majority of the Mudfog people dined. Then he went on to state, how the number of people who came out with beer-jugs averaged twenty-one in five minutes, which, being multiplied by twelve, gave two hundred and fifty-two people with beer-jugs in an hour, and multiplied again by fifteen (the number of hours during which the house was open daily) yielded three thousand seven hundred and eighty people with beer-jugs per day, or twenty-six thousand four hundred and sixty people with beer-jugs, per week. Then he proceeded to show that a tambourine and moral degrada- tion were synonymous terms, and a fiddle and vicious propensities wholly inseparable. All these arguments he strengthened and demonstrated by frequent references to a large book with a blue cover, and sundry quotations from the Middlesex magistrates; and in the end, the corporation, who were posed with the figures, and sleepy with the speech, and sadly in want of dinner into the bargain, yielded the palm to Nicholas Tulrumble, and refused the music licence to the Jolly Boatmen.

But although Nicholas triumphed, his triumph was short. He carried on the war against beer-jugs and fiddles, forgetting the time when he was glad to drink out of the one, and to dance to the other, till the people hated, and his old friends shunned him. He grew tired of the lonely magnificence of Mudfog Hall, and his heart yearned towards the Lighter- man's Arms. He wished he had never set up as a public man, and sighed for the good old times of the coal-shop, and the chimney corner.

At length old Nicholas, being thoroughly miserable, took heart of grace, paid the secretary a quarter's wages in advance, and packed him off to London by the next coach. Having taken this step, he put his hat on his head, and his pride in his pocket, and walked down to the old room at the Lighterman's Arms. There were only two of the old fellows there, and they looked coldly on Nicholas as he proffered his hand.

"Are you going to put down pipes, Mr. Tulrumble?" said one.

"Or trace the progress of crime to 'bacca?" growled another.

"Neither," replied Nicholas Tulrumble, shaking hands with them both, whether they would or not. "I've come down to say that I'm very sorry for having made a fool of myself, and that I hope you'll give me up the old chair again."

The old fellows opened their eyes, and three or four more old fellows opened the door, to whom Nicholas, with tears in his eyes, thrust out his hand too, and told the same story. They raised a shout of joy, that made the bells in the ancient church-tower vibrate again, and wheeling the old chair into the warm corner, thrust old Nicholas down into it, and ordered in the very largest-sized bowl of hot punch, with an unlimited number of pipes, directly.

The next day the Jolly Boatmen got the licence, and the next night old Nicholas and Ned Twigger's wife led off a dance to the music of the fiddle and tambourine, the tone of which seemed mightily improved by a little rest, for they never had played so merrily before. Ned Twigger was in the very height of his glory, and he danced hornpipes, and balanced chairs on his chin, and straws on his nose, till the whole company, including the corporation, were in raptures of admiration at the brilliancy of his acquirements.

Mr. Tulrumble, junior, couldn't make up his mind to be anything but magnificent, so he went up to London and drew bills on his father; and when he had overdrawn, and got into debt, he grew penitent and came home again.

As to old Nicholas, he kept his word, and having had six weeks of public life, never tried it any more. He went to sleep in the town-hall at the very next meeting; and, in full proof of his sincerity, has requested us to write this faithful narrative. We wish it could have the effect of reminding the Tulrumbles of another sphere, that puffed-up conceit is not dignity, and that snarling at the little pleasures they were once glad to enjoy, because they would rather forget the times when they were of lower station, renders them objects of contempt and ridicule.

This is the first time we have published any of our gleanings from this particular source. Perhaps, at some future period, we may venture to open the chronicles of Mudfog.

FULL REPORT OF THE FIRST MEETING OF THE MUDFOG ASSOCIATION

FOR THE ADVANCEMENT OF EVERYTHING

WE have made the most unparalleled and extraordinary exertions to place before our readers a complete and accurate account of the proceedings at the late grand meeting of the Mudfog Association, holden in the town of Mudfog; it affords us great happiness to lay the result before them, in the shape of various communications received from our able, talented, and graphic correspondent, expressly sent down for the purpose, who has immortalized us, himself, Mudfog, and the association, all at one and the same time. We have been, indeed, for some days unable to determine who will transmit the greatest name to posterity; ourselves, who sent our correspondent down; our correspondent, who wrote an account of the matter; or the association, who gave our correspondent something to write about. We rather incline to the opinion that we are the greatest man of the party, inasmuch as the notion of an exclusive and authentic report originated with us; this may be prejudice: it may arise from a prepossession on our part in our own favour. Be it so. We have no doubt that every gentleman concerned in this mighty assemblage is troubled with the same complaint in a greater or less degree; and it is a consolation to us to know that we have at least this feeling in common with the great scientific stars, the brilliant and extraordinary luminaries, whose speculations we record.

We give our correspondent's letters in the order in which they reached us. Any attempt at amalgamating them into one beautiful whole, would only destroy that glowing tone, that dash of wildness, and rich vein of picturesque interest, which pervade them throughout.

" Mudfog, Monday night, seven o'clock.

"We are in a state of great excitement here. Nothing is spoken of, but the approaching meeting of the association. The inn-doors are thronged with waiters anxiously looking for the expected arrivals ; and the numerous bills which are wafered up in the windows of private houses, intimating that there are beds to let within, give the streets a very animated and cheerful appearance, the wafers being of a great variety of colours, and the monotony of printed inscriptions being relieved by every possible size and style of hand-writing. It is confidently rumoured that Professors Snore, Doze, and Wheezy have engaged three beds and a sitting-room at the Pig and Tinder-box. I give you the rumour as it has reached me ; but I cannot, as yet, vouch for its accuracy. The moment I have been enabled to obtain any certain information upon this interesting point, you may depend upon receiving it."

" Half-past seven.

"I have just returned from a personal interview with the landlord of the Pig and Tinder-box. He speaks confidently of the probability of Professors Snore, Doze, and Wheezy taking up their residence at his house during the sitting of the association, but denies that the beds have been yet engaged ; in which representation he is confirmed by the chambermaid—a girl of artless manners, and interesting appearance. The boots denies that it is at all likely that Professors Snore, Doze, and Wheezy will put up here ; but I have reason to believe that this man has been suborned by the proprietor of the Original Pig, which is the opposition hotel. Amidst such conflicting testimony it is difficult to arrive at the real truth ; but you may depend upon receiving authentic information upon this point the moment the fact is ascertained. The excitement still continues. A boy fell through the window of the pastrycook's shop at the corner of the High Street about half an hour ago, which has occasioned much confusion. The general impression is that it was an accident. Pray heaven it may prove so !"

" Tuesday, noon.

"At an early hour this morning the bells of all the churches struck seven o'clock ; the effect of which, in the present lively state of the town, was extremely singular. While I was at breakfast, a yellow gig, drawn by a dark grey horse, with a patch of white over his right eyelid, proceeded at a rapid pace in the direction of the Original Pig stables; it is currently reported that this gentleman has arrived here for the purpose of attending the association, and, from what I have heard, I consider it extremely probable, although nothing decisive is yet known regarding him. You may conceive the anxiety with which we are all looking forward to the arrival of the four o'clock coach this afternoon.

"Notwithstanding the excited state of the populace, no outrage has yet been committed, owing to the admirable discipline and discretion of the police, who are nowhere to be seen. A barrel-organ is playing opposite my window, and groups of people, offering fish and vegetables for sale, parade the streets. With these exceptions everything is quiet, and I trust will continue so."

Five o'clock.

"It is now ascertained, beyond all doubt, that Professors Snore, Doze, and Wheezy will *not* repair to the Pig and Tinder-box, but have actually engaged apartments at the Original Pig. This intelligence is *exclusive*; and I leave you and your readers to draw their own inferences from it. Why Professor Wheezy, of all people in the world, should repair to the Original Pig in preference to the Pig and Tinder-box, it is not easy to conceive. The professor is a man who should be above all such petty feelings. Some people here openly impute treachery, and a distinct breach of faith to Professors Snore and Doze; while others, again, are disposed to acquit them of any culpability in the transaction, and to insinuate that the blame rests solely with Professor Wheezy. I own that I incline to the latter opinion; and although it gives me great pain to speak in terms of censure or disapprobation of a man of such transcendent genius and acquirements, still I am bound to say that, if my suspicions be well founded, and if all the reports which have reached my ears be true, I really do not well know what to make of the matter.

"Mr. Slug, so celebrated for his statistical researches, arrived this afternoon by the four o'clock stage. His complexion is a dark purple, and he has a habit of sighing constantly. He looked extremely well, and appeared in high health and spirits. Mr. Woodensconce also came down in the same conveyance. The distinguished gentleman was

fast asleep on his arrival, and I am informed by the guard
that he had been so the whole way. He was, no doubt,
preparing for his approaching fatigues ; but what gigantic
visions must those be that flit through the brain of such
a man when his body is in a state of torpidity !

"The influx of visitors increases every moment. I am
told (I know not how truly) that two post-chaises have
arrived at the Original Pig within the last half-hour, and
I myself observed a wheelbarrow, containing three carpet
bags and a bundle, entering the yard of the Pig and Tinder-
box no longer ago than five minutes since. The people are
still quietly pursuing their ordinary occupations ; but there
is a wildness in their eyes, and an unwonted rigidity in the
muscles of their countenances, which shows to the observant
spectator that their expectations are strained to the very
utmost pitch. I fear, unless some very extraordinary
arrivals take place to-night, that consequences may arise from
this popular ferment, which every man of sense and feeling
would deplore."

" *Twenty minutes past six.*

"I have just heard that the boy who fell through the
pastrycook's window last night has died of the fright. He
was suddenly called upon to pay three and sixpence for the
damage done, and his constitution, it seems, was not strong
enough to bear up against the shock. The inquest, it is
said, will be held to-morrow."

" *Three-quarters past seven.*

"Professors Muff and Nogo have just driven up to the
hotel door ; they at once ordered dinner with great condescension. We are all very much delighted with the
urbanity of their manners, and the ease with which they
adapt themselves to the forms and ceremonies of ordinary
life. Immediately on their arrival they sent for the head
waiter, and privately requested him to purchase a live dog,
—as cheap a one as he could meet with,—and to send him
up after dinner, with a pie-board, a knife and fork, and a
clean plate. It is conjectured that some experiments will
be tried upon the dog to-night ; if any particulars should
transpire, I will forward them by express."

" *Half-past eight.*

"The animal has been procured. He is a pug-dog, of
rather intelligent appearance, in good condition, and with

very short legs. He has been tied to a curtain-peg in a dark room, and is howling dreadfully."

" Ten minutes to nine.

"The dog has just been rung for. With an instinct which would appear almost the result of reason, the sagacious animal seized the waiter by the calf of the leg when he approached to take him, and made a desperate, though ineffectual resistance. I have not been able to procure admission to the apartment occupied by the scientific gentlemen ; but, judging from the sounds which reached my ears when I stood upon the landing-place outside the door, just now, I should be disposed to say that the dog had retreated growling beneath some article of furniture, and was keeping the professors at bay. This conjecture is confirmed by the testimony of the ostler, who, after peeping through the key-hole, assures me that he distinctly saw Professor Nogo on his knees, holding forth a small bottle of prussic acid, to which the animal, who was crouched beneath an arm-chair, obstinately declined to smell. You cannot imagine the feverish state of irritation we are in, lest the interests of science should be sacrificed to the prejudices of a brute creature, who is not endowed with sufficient sense to foresee the incalculable benefits which the whole human race may derive from so very slight a concession on his part."

" Nine o'clock.

"The dog's tail and ears have been sent down-stairs to be washed ; from which circumstance we infer that the animal is no more. His forelegs have been delivered to the boots to be brushed, which strengthens the supposition."

" Half after ten.

" My feelings are so overpowered by what has taken place in the course of the last hour and a half, that I have scarcely strength to detail the rapid succession of events which have quite bewildered all those who are cognizant of their occurrence. It appears that the pug-dog mentioned in my last was surreptitiously obtained,—stolen, in fact,—by some person attached to the stable department, from an unmarried lady resident in this town. Frantic on discovering the loss of her favourite, the lady rushed distractedly into the street, calling in the most heart-rending and pathetic manner upon the passengers to restore her, her Augustus,—for so the deceased was named, in affectionate remembrance of a former lover of his mistress, to whom he bore a striking personal resemblance, which renders the circumstances additionally affecting. I am not yet in a condition to inform you what circumstance induced the bereaved lady to direct her steps to the hotel which had witnessed the last struggles of her *protégé*. I can only state that she arrived there, at the very instant when his detached members were passing through the passage on a small tray. Her shrieks still reverberate in my ears! I grieve to say that the expressive features of Professor Muff were much scratched and lacerated by the injured lady; and that Professor Nogo, besides sustaining several severe bites, has lost some handfuls of hair from the same cause. It must be some consolation to these gentlemen to know that their ardent attachment to scientific pursuits has alone occasioned these unpleasant consequences; for which the sympathy of a grateful country will sufficiently reward them. The unfortunate lady remains at the Pig and Tinder-box, and up to this time is reported in a very precarious state.

"I need scarcely tell you that this unlooked-for catastrophe has cast a damp and gloom upon us in the midst of our exhilaration; natural in any case, but greatly enhanced in this, by the amiable qualities of the deceased animal, who appears to have been much and deservedly respected by the whole of his acquaintance."

" Twelve o'clock.

"I take the last opportunity before sealing my parcel to inform you that the boy who fell through the pastrycook's window is not dead, as was universally believed, but alive and well. The report appears to have had its origin in his mysterious disappearance. He was found half an hour since on the premises of a sweet-stuff maker, where a raffle had been announced for a second-hand seal-skin cap and a tambourine; and where—a sufficient number of members not having been obtained at first—he had patiently waited until the list was completed. This fortunate discovery has in some degree restored our gaiety and cheerfulness. It is proposed to get up a subscription for him without delay.

"Everybody is nervously anxious to see what to-morrow will bring forth. If any one should arrive in the course of the night, I have left strict directions to be called immediately. I should have sat up, indeed, but the agitating events of this day have been too much for me.

"No news yet of either of the Professors Snore, Doze, or Wheezy. It is very strange!"

"Wednesday afternoon.

"All is now over; and, upon one point at least, I am at length enabled to set the minds of your readers at rest. The three professors arrived at ten minutes after two o'clock, and, instead of taking up their quarters at the Original Pig. as it was universally understood in the course of yesterday that they would assuredly have done, drove straight to the Pig and Tinder-box, where they threw off the mask at once, and openly announced their intention of remaining. Professor Wheezy *may* reconcile this very extraordinary conduct with *his* notions of fair and equitable dealing, but I would recommend Professor Wheezy to be cautious how he presumes too far upon his well-earned reputation. How such a man as Professor Snore, or, which is still more extraordinary, such an individual as Professor Doze, can quietly allow himself to be mixed up with such proceedings as these, you will naturally inquire. Upon this head, rumour is silent; I have my speculations, but forbear to give utterance to them just now."

"Four o'clock.

"The town is filling fast; eighteenpence has been offered for a bed and refused. Several gentlemen were under the necessity last night of sleeping in the brick fields, and on the steps of doors, for which they were taken before the magistrates in a body this morning, and committed to prison as vagrants for various terms. One of these persons I understand to be a highly-respectable tinker, of great practical skill, who had forwarded a paper to the President of Section D. Mechanical Science, on the construction of pipkins with copper bottoms and safety-valves, of which report speaks highly. The incarceration of this gentleman is greatly to be regretted, as his absence will preclude any discussion on the subject.

"The bills are being taken down in all directions, and lodgings are being secured on almost any terms. I have heard of fifteen shillings a week for two rooms, exclusive of coals and attendance, but I can scarcely believe it. The excitement is dreadful. I was informed this morning that the civil authorities, apprehensive of some outbreak of popular feeling, had commanded a recruiting sergeant and two corporals to be under arms; and that, with the view of not irritating the people unnecessarily by their presence, they had been requested to take up their position before daybreak in a turnpike, distant about a quarter of a mile from the town. The vigour and promptness of these measures cannot be too highly extolled.

"Intelligence has just been brought me, that an elderly female, in a state of inebriety, has declared in the open street her intention to 'do' for Mr. Slug. Some statistical returns compiled by that gentleman, relative to the consumption of raw spirituous liquors in this place, are supposed to be the cause of the wretch's animosity. It is added that this declaration was loudly cheered by a crowd of persons who had assembled on the spot; and that one man had the boldness to designate Mr. Slug aloud by the opprobrious epithet of 'Stick-in-the-mud!' It is earnestly to be hoped that now, when the moment has arrived for their interference, the magistrates will not shrink from the exercise of that power which is vested in them by the constitution of our common country."

"Half-past ten.

"The disturbance, I am happy to inform you, has been completely quelled, and the ringleader taken into custody. She had a pail of cold water thrown over her, previous to being locked up, and expresses great contrition and uneasiness. We are all in a fever of anticipation about to-morrow; but now that we are within a few hours of the meeting of the association, and at last enjoy the proud consciousness of having its illustrious members amongst us, I trust and hope everything may go off peaceably. I shall send you a full report of to-morrow's proceedings by the night coach."

"Eleven o'clock.

"I open my letter to say that nothing whatever has occurred since I folded it up."

"Thursday.

"The sun rose this morning at the usual hour. I did not observe anything particular in the aspect of the glorious planet, except that he appeared to me (it might have been a delusion of my heightened fancy) to shine with more than common brilliancy, and to shed a refulgent lustre upon the town, such as I had never observed before. This is the more extraordinary, as the sky was perfectly cloudless, and the atmosphere peculiarly fine. At half-past nine o'clock the general committee assembled, with the last year's president in the chair. The report of the council was read ; and one passage, which stated that the council had corresponded with no less than three thousand five hundred and seventy-one persons, (all of whom paid their own postage,) on no fewer than seven thousand two hundred and forty-three topics, was received with a degree of enthusiasm which no efforts could suppress. The various committees and sections having been appointed, and the more formal business transacted, the great proceedings of the meeting commenced at eleven o'clock precisely. I had the happiness of occupying a most eligible position at that time, in

"SECTION A.—ZOOLOGY AND BOTANY.

GREAT ROOM, PIG AND TINDER-BOX.

*President—*Professor Snore. *Vice-Presidents—*Professors Doze and Wheezy.

"The scene at this moment was particularly striking. The sun streamed through the windows of the apartments, and tinted the whole scene with its brilliant rays, bringing out in strong relief the noble visages of the professors and scientific gentlemen, who, some with bald heads, some with red heads, some with brown heads, some with grey heads, some with black heads, some with block heads, presented a *coup d'œil* which no eye-witness will readily forget. In front of these gentlemen were papers and inkstands ; and round the room, on elevated benches extending as far as the forms could reach, were assembled a brilliant concourse of those lovely and elegant women for which Mudfog is justly acknowledged to be without a rival in the whole world. The contrast between their fair faces and the dark coats and trousers of the scientific gentlemen I shall never cease to remember while Memory holds her seat.

"Time having been allowed for a slight confusion, occasioned by the falling down of the greater part of the platforms, to subside, the president called on one of the secretaries to read a communication entitled, 'Some remarks on the industrious fleas, with considerations on the importance of establishing infant-schools among that numerous class of society ; of directing their industry to useful and practical ends ; and of applying the surplus fruits thereof, towards providing for them a comfortable and respectable maintenance in their old age.'

"The author stated that, having long turned his attention to the moral and social condition of these interesting animals, he had been induced to visit an exhibition in Regent Street, London, commonly known by the designation of 'The Industrious Fleas.' He had there seen many fleas, occupied certainly in various pursuits and avocations, but occupied, he was bound to add, in a manner which no man of well-regulated mind could fail to regard with sorrow and regret. One flea, reduced to the level of a beast of burden, was drawing about a miniature gig, containing a particularly small effigy of His Grace the Duke of Wellington; while another was staggering beneath the weight of a golden model of his great adversary Napoleon Bonaparte. Some, brought up as mountebanks and ballet-dancers, were performing a figure-dance (he regretted to observe that, of the fleas so employed, several were females); others were in training, in a small card-board box, for pedestrians,—mere sporting characters—and two were actually engaged in the cold-blooded and barbarous occupation of duelling ; a pursuit from which humanity recoiled with horror and disgust. He suggested that measures should be immediately taken to employ the labour of these fleas as part and parcel of the productive power of the country, which might easily be done by the establishment among them of infant schools and houses of industry, in which a system of virtuous education, based upon sound principles, should be observed, and moral precepts strictly inculcated. He proposed that every flea who presumed to exhibit, for hire, music, or dancing, or any species of theatrical entertainment, without a licence, should be considered a vagabond, and treated accordingly ; in which respect he only placed him upon a level with the rest of mankind. He would further suggest that their labour should be placed under the control and regulation of the state, who should set apart from the profits, a fund for the support of superannuated or disabled fleas, their widows and orphans. With this view, he proposed that liberal premiums should be offered for the three best designs for a general almshouse ; from which—as insect architecture was well known to be in a very advanced and perfect state—we might possibly derive many valuable hints for the improvement of our metropolitan universities, national galleries, and other public edifices.

"THE PRESIDENT wished to be informed how the ingenious gentleman proposed to open a communication with fleas generally, in the first instance, so that they might be thoroughly imbued with a sense of the advantages they must necessarily derive from changing their mode of life, and applying themselves to honest labour. This appeared to him the only difficulty.

"THE AUTHOR submitted that this difficulty was easily overcome, or rather that there was no difficulty at all in the case. Obviously the course to be pursued, if her Majesty's government could be prevailed upon to take up the plan, would be, to secure at a remunerative salary the individual to whom he had alluded as presiding over the exhibition in Regent Street at the period of his visit. That gentleman would at once be able to put himself in communication with the mass of the fleas, and to instruct them in pursuance of some general plan of education, to be sanctioned by Parliament, until such time as the more intelligent among them were advanced enough to officiate as teachers to the rest.

"The President and several members of the section highly complimented the author of the paper last read, on his most ingenious and important treatise. It was determined that the subject should be recommended to the immediate consideration of the council.

"MR. WIGSBY produced a cauliflower somewhat larger than a chaise-umbrella, which had been raised by no other artificial means than the simple application of highly carbonated soda-water as manure. He explained that by scooping out the head, which would afford a new and delicious species of nourishment for the poor, a parachute, in principle something similar to that constructed by M. Garnerin, was at once obtained; the stalk of course being kept downwards. He added that he was perfectly willing to make a descent from a height of not less than three miles and a quarter; and had in fact already proposed the same to the proprietors of Vauxhall Gardens, who in the handsomest manner at once consented to his wishes, and appointed an early day next summer for the undertaking; merely stipulating that the rim of the cauliflower should be previously broken in three or four places to ensure the safety of the descent.

"THE PRESIDENT congratulated the public on the *grand gala* in store for them, and warmly eulogised the proprietors of the establishment alluded to, for their love of science, and regard for the safety of human life, both of which did them the highest honour.

"A MEMBER wished to know how many thousand additional lamps the royal property would be illuminated with, on the night after the descent.

"MR. WIGSBY replied that the point was not yet finally decided; but he believed it was proposed, over and above the ordinary illuminations, to exhibit in various devices eight millions and a half of additional lamps.

"The Member expressed himself much gratified with this announcement.

"MR. BLUNDERUM delighted the section with a most interesting and valuable paper 'on the last moments of the learned pig,' which produced a very strong impression on the assembly, the account being compiled from the personal recollections of his favourite attendant. The account stated in the most emphatic terms that the animal's name was not Toby, but Solomon; and distinctly proved that he could have no near relatives in the profession, as many designing persons had falsely stated, inasmuch as his father, mother, brothers and sisters, had all fallen victims to the butcher at different times. An uncle of his indeed, had with very great labour been traced to a sty in Somers Town; but as he was in a very infirm state at the time, being afflicted with measles, and shortly afterwards disappeared, there appeared too much reason to conjecture that he had been converted into sausages. The disorder of the learned pig was originally a severe cold, which, being aggravated by excessive trough indulgence, finally settled upon the lungs, and terminated in a general decay of the constitution. A melancholy instance of a presentiment entertained by the animal of his approaching dissolution was recorded. After gratifying a numerous and fashionable company with his performances, in which no falling off whatever was visible, he fixed his eyes on the biographer, and, turning to the watch which lay on the floor, and on which he was accustomed to point out the hour, deliberately passed his snout twice round the dial. In precisely four-and-twenty hours from that time he had ceased to exist!

"PROFESSOR WHEEZY inquired whether, previous to his

demise, the animal had expressed, by signs or otherwise, any wishes regarding the disposal of his little property.

"MR. BLUNDERUM replied that, when the biographer took up the pack of cards at the conclusion of the performance, the animal grunted several times in a significant manner, and nodding his head as he was accustomed to do when gratified. From these gestures it was understood that he wished the attendant to keep the cards, which he had ever since done. He had not expressed any wish relative to his watch, which had accordingly been pawned by the same individual.

"THE PRESIDENT wished to know whether any Member of the section had ever seen or conversed with the pig-faced lady, who was reported to have worn a black velvet mask, and to have taken her meals from a golden trough.

"After some hesitation a Member replied that the pig-faced lady was his mother-in-law, and that he trusted the President would not violate the sanctity of private life.

"THE PRESIDENT begged pardon. He had considered the pig-faced lady a public character. Would the honourable member object to state, with a view to the advancement of science, whether she was in any way connected with the learned pig?

"The Member replied in the same low tone that, as the question appeared to involve a suspicion that the learned pig might be his half-brother, he must decline answering it.

"SECTION B.—ANATOMY AND MEDICINE.

COACH-HOUSE, PIG AND TINDER-BOX.

President – Dr. Toorell.   *Vice Presidents*—Professors Muff and Nogo.

"DR. KUTANKUMAGEN (of Moscow) read to the section a report of a case which had occurred within his own practice, strikingly illustrative of the power of medicine, as exemplified in his successful treatment of a virulent disorder. He had been called in to visit the patient on the 1st of April, 1837. He was then labouring under symptoms peculiarly alarming to any medical man. His frame was stout and muscular, his step firm and elastic, his cheeks plump and red, his voice loud, his appetite good, his pulse full and round. He was in the constant habit of eating three meals *per diem*, and of drinking at least one bottle of wine, and one glass of spirituous liquors diluted with water, in the course of the four-and-twenty hours. He laughed constantly, and in so hearty a manner that it was terrible to hear him. By dint of powerful medicine, low diet, and bleeding, the symptoms in the course of three days perceptibly decreased. A rigid perseverance in the same course of treatment for only one week, accompanied with small doses of water-gruel, weak broth, and barley-water, led to their entire disappearance. In the course of a month he was sufficiently recovered to be carried down-stairs by two nurses, and to enjoy an airing in a close carriage, supported by soft pillows. At the present moment he was restored so far as to walk about, with the slight assistance of a crutch and a boy. It would perhaps be gratifying to the section to learn that he ate little, drank little, slept little, and was never heard to laugh by any accident whatever.

"Dr. W. R. Fee, in complimenting the honourable member upon the triumphant cure he had effected, begged to ask whether the patient still bled freely?

"Dr. Kutankumagen replied in the affirmative.

"Dr. W. R. Fee.—And you found that he bled freely during the whole course of the disorder?

"Dr. Kutankumagen.—Oh dear, yes; most freely.

"Dr. Neeshawts supposed that if the patient had not submitted to be bled with great readiness and perseverance, so extraordinary a cure could never, in fact, have been accomplished. Dr. Kutankumagen rejoined, certainly not.

"Mr. Knight Bell (M.R.C.S.) exhibited a wax preparation of the interior of a gentleman who in early life had inadvertently swallowed a door-key. It was a curious fact that a medical student of dissipated habits, being present at the *post mortem* examination, found means to escape unobserved from the room, with that portion of the coats of the stomach upon which an exact model of the instrument was distinctly impressed, with which he hastened to a locksmith of doubtful character, who made a new key from the pattern so shown to him. With this key the medical student entered the house of the deceased gentleman, and committed a burglary to a large amount, for which he was subsequently tried and executed.

"The President wished to know what became of the original key after the lapse of years. Mr. Knight Bell replied that the gentleman was always much accustomed to punch, and it was supposed the acid had gradually devoured it.

"DR. NEESHAWTS and several of the members were of opinion that the key must have lain very cold and heavy upon the gentleman's stomach.

"MR. KNIGHT BELL believed it did at first. It was worthy of remark, perhaps, that for some years the gentleman was troubled with a night-mare, under the influence of which he always imagined himself a wine-cellar door.

"PROFESSOR MUFF related a very extraordinary and convincing proof of the wonderful efficacy of the system of infinitesimal doses, which the section were doubtless aware was based upon the theory that the very minutest amount of any given drug, properly dispersed through the human frame, would be productive of precisely the same result as a very large dose administered in the usual manner. Thus, the fortieth part of a grain of calomel was supposed to be equal to a five-grain calomel pill, and so on in proportion throughout the whole range of medicine. He had tried the experiment in a curious manner upon a publican who had been brought into the hospital with a broken head, and was cured upon the infinitesimal system in the incredibly short space of three months. This man was a hard drinker. He (Professor Muff) had dispersed three drops of rum through a bucket of water, and requested the man to drink the whole. What was the result? Before he had drunk a quart, he was in a state of beastly intoxication; and five other men were made dead drunk with the remainder.

"THE PRESIDENT wished to know whether an infinitesimal dose of soda-water would have recovered them? Professor Muff replied that the twenty-fifth part of a teaspoonful, properly administered to each patient, would have sobered him immediately. The President remarked that this was a most important discovery, and he hoped the Lord Mayor and Court of Aldermen would patronize it immediately.

"A MEMBER begged to be informed whether it would be possible to administer—say, the twentieth part of a grain of bread and cheese to all grown-up paupers, and the fortieth part to children, with the same satisfying effect as their present allowance.

"PROFESSOR MUFF was willing to stake his professional reputation on the perfect adequacy of such a quantity of food to the support of human life—in workhouses; the addition of the fifteenth part of a grain of pudding twice a week would render it a high diet.

"Professor Nogo called the attention of the section to a very extraordinary case of animal magnetism. A private watchman, being merely looked at by the operator from the opposite side of a wide street, was at once observed to be in a very drowsy and languid state. He was followed to his box, and being once slightly rubbed on the palms of the hands, fell into a sound sleep, in which he continued without intermission for ten hours.

"Section C.—Statistics.

HAY-LOFT, ORIGINAL PIG.

President—Mr. Woodensconce.   *Vice-Presidents*—Mr. Ledbrain and Mr. Timbered.

"Mr. Slug stated to the section the result of some calculations he had made with great difficulty and labour, regarding the state of infant education among the middle classes of London.   He found that, within a circle of three miles from the Elephant and Castle, the following were the names and numbers of children's books principally in circulation :—

"Jack the Giant-killer	7,943
Ditto and Bean-stalk	8,621
Ditto and Eleven Brothers	2,845
Ditto and Jill	1,998
Total	21,407

" He found that the proportion of Robinson Crusoes to Philip Quarlls was as four and a half to one ; and that the preponderance of Valentine and Orsons over Goody Two Shoeses was as three and an eighth of the former to half a one of the latter ; a comparison of Seven Champions with Simple Simons gave the same result.   The ignorance that prevailed was lamentable.   One child, on being asked whether he would rather be Saint George of England or a respectable tallow-chandler, instantly replied, 'Taint George of Ingling.'   Another, a little boy of eight years old, was found to be firmly impressed with a belief in the existence of dragons, and openly stated that it was his intention when he grew up, to rush forth sword in hand for the deliverance of captive princesses, and the promiscuous slaughter of giants. Not one child among the number interrogated had ever heard of Mungo Park,—some inquiring whether he was at all connected with the black man that swept the crossing; and others whether he was in any way related to the Regent's Park. They had not the slightest conception of the commonest principles of mathematics, and considered Sindbad the Sailor the most enterprising voyager that the world had ever produced.

" A MEMBER strongly deprecating the use of all the other books mentioned, suggested that Jack and Jill might perhaps be exempted from the general censure, inasmuch as the hero and heroine, in the very outset of the tale, were depicted as going *up* a hill to fetch a pail of water, which was a laborious and useful occupation,—supposing the family linen was being washed, for instance.

" MR. SLUG feared that the moral effect of this passage was more than counterbalanced by another in a subsequent part of the poem, in which very gross allusion was made to the mode in which the heroine was personally chastised by her mother

"'For laughing at Jack's disaster;'

besides, the whole work had this one great fault, *it was not true*.

" THE PRESIDENT complimented the honourable member on the excellent distinction he had drawn. Several other members, too, dwelt upon the immense and urgent necessity of storing the minds of children with nothing but facts and figures; which process the President very forcibly remarked, had made them (the section) the men they were.

" MR. SLUG then stated some curious calculations respecting the dogs'-meat barrows of London. He found that the total number of small carts and barrows engaged in dispensing provision to the cats and dogs of the metropolis was one thousand seven hundred and forty-three. The average number of skewers delivered daily with the provender, by each dogs'-meat cart or barrow, was thirty-six. Now, multiplying the number of skewers so delivered by the number of barrows, a total of sixty-two thousand seven hundred and forty-eight skewers daily would be obtained. Allowing that, of these sixty-two thousand seven hundred and forty-eight skewers, the odd two thousand seven hundred and forty-eight were accidentally devoured with the meat, by the most voracious of the animals supplied, it followed that sixty thousand skewers per day, or the enormous number of twenty-one millions nine hundred thousand skewers annually, were wasted in the kennels and dustholes of London ; which, if collected and warehoused, would in ten years' time afford a mass of timber more than sufficient for the construction of a first-rate vessel of war for the use of her Majesty's navy, to be called ' The Royal Skewer,' and to become under that name the terror of all the enemies of this island.

"Mr. X. LEDBRAIN read a very ingenious communication, from which it appeared that the total number of legs belonging to the manufacturing population of one great town in Yorkshire was, in round numbers, forty thousand, while the total number of chair and stool legs in their houses was only thirty thousand, which, upon the very favourable average of three legs to a seat, yielded only ten thousand seats in all. From this calculation it would appear,—not taking wooden or cork legs into the account, but allowing two legs to every person,—that ten thousand individuals (one-half of the whole population) were either destitute of any rest for their legs at all, or passed the whole of their leisure time in sitting upon boxes.

"SECTION D.—MECHANICAL SCIENCE.

COACH-HOUSE, ORIGINAL PIG.

President—Mr. Carter.   *Vice-Presidents*—Mr. Truck and Mr. Waghorn.

"PROFESSOR QUEERSPECK exhibited an elegant model of a portable railway, neatly mounted in a green case, for the waistcoat pocket.   By attaching this beautiful instrument to his boots, any Bank or public-office clerk could transport himself from his place of residence to his place of business, at the easy rate of sixty-five miles an hour, which, to gentlemen of sedentary pursuits, would be an incalculable advantage.

"THE PRESIDENT was desirous of knowing whether it was necessary to have a level surface on which the gentleman was to run.

"PROFESSOR QUEERSPECK explained that City gentlemen would run in trains, being handcuffed together to prevent confusion or unpleasantness.   For instance, trains would start every morning at eight, nine, and ten o'clock, from Camden Town, Islington, Camberwell, Hackney, and various other places in which City gentlemen are accustomed to reside.   It would be necessary to have a level, but he had provided for this difficulty by proposing that the best line that the circumstances would admit of, should be taken through the sewers which undermine the streets of the metropolis, and which, well lighted by jets from the gas pipes which run immediately above them, would form a pleasant and commodious arcade, especially in winter-time, when the inconvenient custom of carrying umbrellas, now so general, could be wholly dispensed with. In reply to another question, Professor Queerspeck stated that no substitute for the purposes to which these arcades were at present devoted had yet occurred to him, but that he hoped no fanciful objection on this head would be allowed to interfere with so great an undertaking.

"Mr. Jobba produced a forcing-machine on a novel plan, for bringing joint-stock railway shares prematurely to a premium. The instrument was in the form of an elegant gilt weather-glass, of most dazzling appearance, and was worked behind, by strings, after the manner of a pantomime trick, the strings being always pulled by the directors of the company to which the machine belonged. The quicksilver was so ingeniously placed, that when the acting directors held shares in their pockets, figures denoting very small expenses and very large returns appeared upon the glass ; but the moment the directors parted with these pieces of paper, the estimate of needful expenditure suddenly increased itself to an immense extent, while the statements of certain profits became reduced in the same proportion. Mr. Jobba stated that the machine had been in constant requisition for some months past, and he had never once known it to fail.

"A Member expressed his opinion that it was extremely neat and pretty. He wished to know whether it was not liable to accidental derangement? Mr. Jobba said that the whole machine was undoubtedly liable to be blown up, but that was the only objection to it.

"Professor Nogo arrived from the anatomical section to exhibit a model of a safety fire-escape, which could be fixed at any time, in less than half an hour, and by means of which, the youngest or most infirm persons (successfully resisting the progress of the flames until it was quite ready) could be preserved if they merely balanced themselves for a few minutes on the sill of their bedroom window, and got into the escape without falling into the street. The Professor stated that the number of boys who had been rescued in the daytime by this machine from houses which were not on fire, was almost incredible.   Not a conflagration had occurred in the whole of London for many months past to which the escape had not been carried on the very next day, and put in action before a concourse of persons.

"THE PRESIDENT inquired whether there was not some difficulty in ascertaining which was the top of the machine, and which the bottom, in cases of pressing emergency.

"PROFESSOR NOGO explained that of course it could not be expected to act quite as well when there was a fire, as when there was not a fire; but in the former case he thought it would be of equal service whether the top were up or down."

With the last section our correspondent concludes his most able and faithful Report, which will never cease to reflect credit upon him for his scientific attainments, and upon us for our enterprising spirit.   It is needless to take a review of the subjects which have been discussed; of the mode in which they have been examined; of the great truths which they have elicited.   They are now before the world, and we leave them to read, to consider, and to profit.

The place of meeting for next year has undergone discussion, and has at length been decided, regard being had to, and evidence being taken upon, the goodness of its wines, the supply of its markets, the hospitality of its inhabitants, and the quality of its hotels.   We hope at this next meeting our correspondent may again be present, and that we may be once more the means of placing his communications before the world.   Until that period we have been prevailed upon to allow this number of our Miscellany to be retailed to the public, or wholesaled to the trade, without any advance upon our usual price.

We have only to add, that the committees are now broken up, and that Mudfog is once again restored to its accustomed tranquillity,—that Professors and Members have had balls, and *soirées*, and suppers, and great mutual complimentations, and have at length dispersed to their several homes,—whither all good wishes and joys attend them, until next year!

Signed   Boz.

FULL REPORT OF THE SECOND MEETING OF THE MUDFOG ASSOCIATION

FOR THE ADVANCEMENT OF EVERYTHING

In October last, we did ourselves the immortal credit of recording, at an enormous expense, and by dint of exertions unparalleled in the history of periodical publication, the proceedings of the Mudfog Association for the Advancement of Everything, which in that month held its first great half-yearly meeting, to the wonder and delight of the whole empire. We announced at the conclusion of that extraordinary and most remarkable Report, that when the Second Meeting of the Society should take place, we should be found again at our post, renewing our gigantic and spirited endeavours, and once more making the world ring with the accuracy, authenticity, immeasurable superiority, and intense remarkability of our account of its proceedings. In redemption of this pledge, we caused to be dispatched per steam to Oldcastle (at which place this second meeting of the Society was held on the 20th instant), the same superhumanly-endowed gentleman who furnished the former report, and who,—gifted by nature with transcendent abilities, and furnished by us with a body of assistants scarcely inferior to himself,—has forwarded a series of letters which, for faithfulness of description, power of language, fervour of thought, happiness of expression, and importance of subject-matter, have no equal in the epistolary literature of any age or country. We give this gentleman's correspondence entire, and in the order in which it reached our office.

> "*Saloon of Steamer, Thursday night, half-past eight.*

"When I left New Burlington Street this evening in the hackney cabriolet, number four thousand two hundred and eighty-five, I experienced sensations as novel as they were oppressive. A sense of the importance of the task I had undertaken, a consciousness that I was leaving London, and, stranger still, going somewhere else, a feeling of loneliness and a sensation of jolting, quite bewildered my thoughts, and for a time rendered me even insensible to the presence of my carpet-bag and hat-box. I shall ever feel grateful to the driver of a Blackwall omnibus who, by thrusting the pole of his vehicle through the small door of the cabriolet, awakened me from a tumult of imaginings that are wholly indescribable. But of such materials is our imperfect nature composed!

"I am happy to say that I am the first passenger on board, and shall thus be enabled to give you an account of all that happens in the order of its occurrence. The chimney is smoking a good deal, and so are the crew; and the captain, I am informed, is very drunk in a little house upon deck, something like a black turnpike. I should infer from all I hear that he has got the steam up.

"You will readily guess with what feelings I have just made the discovery that my berth is in the same closet with those engaged by Professor Woodensconce, Mr. Slug, and Professor Grime. Professor Woodensconce has taken the shelf above me, and Mr. Slug and Professor Grime the two shelves opposite. Their luggage has already arrived. On Mr. Slug's bed is a long tin tube of about three inches in diameter, carefully closed at both ends. What can this contain? Some powerful instrument of a new construction, doubtless.

" Ten minutes past nine.

"Nobody has yet arrived, nor has anything fresh come in my way except several joints of beef and mutton, from which I conclude that a good plain dinner has been provided for to-morrow. There is a singular smell below, which gave me some uneasiness at first; but as the steward says it is always there, and never goes away, I am quite comfortable again. I learn from this man that the different sections will be distributed at the Black Boy and Stomach-ache, and the Boot-jack and Countenance. If this intelligence be true (and I have no reason to doubt it), your readers will draw such conclusions as their different opinions may suggest.

"I write down these remarks as they occur to me, or as the facts come to my knowledge, in order that my first impressions may lose nothing of their original vividness. I shall dispatch them in small packets as opportunities arise."

" Half-past nine.

"Some dark object has just appeared upon the wharf. I think it is a travelling carriage."

" A quarter to ten.

"No, it isn't."

" Half-past ten.

"The passengers are pouring in every instant. Four omnibuses full have just arrived upon the wharf, and all is bustle and activity. The noise and confusion are very great. Cloths are laid in the cabins, and the steward is placing blue plates-full of knobs of cheese at equal distances down the centre of the tables. He drops a great many knobs; but, being used to it, picks them up again with great dexterity, and, after wiping them on his sleeve, throws them back into the plates. He is a young man of exceedingly prepossessing appearance—either dirty or a mulatto, but I think the former.

"An interesting old gentleman, who came to the wharf in an omnibus, has just quarrelled violently with the porters, and is staggering towards the vessel with a large trunk in his arms. I trust and hope that he may reach it in safety; but the board he has to cross is narrow and slippery. Was that a splash? Gracious powers!

"I have just returned from the deck. The trunk is standing upon the extreme brink of the wharf, but the old gentleman is nowhere to be seen. The watchman is not sure whether he went down or not, but promises to drag for him the first thing to-morrow morning. May his humane efforts prove successful!

"Professor Nogo has this moment arrived with his night-cap on under his hat. He has ordered a glass of cold brandy and water, with a hard biscuit and a bason, and has gone straight to bed. What can this mean?

"The three other scientific gentlemen to whom I have already alluded have come on board, and have all tried their beds, with the exception of Professor Woodensconce, who sleeps in one of the top ones, and can't get into it. Mr. Slug, who sleeps in the other top one, is unable to get out of his, and is to have his supper handed up by a boy. I have had the honour to introduce myself to these gentlemen, and we have amicably arranged the order in which we shall retire to rest; which it is necessary to agree upon, because, although the cabin is very comfortable, there is not room for more than one gentleman to be out of bed at a time, and even he must take his boots off in the passage.

"As I anticipated, the knobs of cheese were provided for the passengers' supper, and are now in course of consumption. Your readers will be surprised to hear that Professor Woodensconce has abstained from cheese for eight years, although he takes butter in considerable quantities. Professor Grime having lost several teeth, is unable, I observe, to eat his crusts without previously soaking them in his bottled porter. How interesting are these peculiarities!"

"*Half-past eleven.*

"Professors Woodensconce and Grime, with a degree of good humour that delights us all, have just arranged to toss for a bottle of mulled port. There has been some discussion whether the payment should be decided by the first toss or the best out of three. Eventually the latter course has been determined on. Deeply do I wish that both gentlemen could win; but that being impossible, I own that my personal aspirations (I speak as an individual, and do not compromise either you or your readers by this expression of feeling) are with Professor Woodensconce. I have backed that gentleman to the amount of eighteenpence."

"*Twenty minutes to twelve.*

"Professor Grime has inadvertently tossed his half-crown out of one of the cabin-windows, and it has been arranged that the steward shall toss for him. Bets are offered on any side to any amount, but there are no takers.

"Professor Woodensconce has just called 'woman;' but the coin having lodged in a beam, is a long time coming down again. The interest and suspense of this one moment are beyond anything that can be imagined."

"*Twelve o'clock.*

"The mulled port is smoking on the table before me, and Professor Grime has won. Tossing is a game of chance; but on every ground, whether of public or private character, intellectual endowments, or scientific attainments, I cannot help expressing my opinion that Professor Woodensconce *ought* to have come off victorious. There is an exultation about Professor Grime incompatible, I fear, with true greatness."

Ned Twigger in the Kitchen of Mudfog Hall

(p. 618)

" A quarter past twelve.

"Professor Grime continues to exult, and to boast of his victory in no very measured terms, observing that he always does win, and that he knew it would be a 'head' before-hand, with many other remarks of a similar nature. Surely this gentleman is not so lost to every feeling of decency and propriety as not to feel and know the superiority of Professor Woodensconce? Is Professor Grime insane? or does he wish to be reminded in plain language of his true position in society, and the precise level of his acquirements and abilities? Professor Grime will do well to look to this."

" One o'clock.

"I am writing in bed. The small cabin is illuminated by the feeble light of a flickering lamp suspended from the ceiling; Professor Grime is lying on the opposite shelf on the broad of his back, with his mouth wide open. The scene is indescribably solemn. The rippling of the tide, the noise of the sailors' feet overhead, the gruff voices on the river, the dogs on the shore, the snoring of the passengers, and a constant creaking of every plank in the vessel, are the only sounds that meet the ear. With these exceptions, all is profound silence.

"My curiosity has been within the last moment very much excited. Mr. Slug, who lies above Professor Grime, has cautiously withdrawn the curtains of his berth, and, after looking anxiously out, as if to satisfy himself that his companions are asleep, has taken up the tin tube of which I have before spoken, and is regarding it with great interest. What rare mechanical combination can be contained in that mysterious case? It is evidently a profound secret to all."

" A quarter past one.

"The behaviour of Mr. Slug grows more and more mysterious. He has unscrewed the top of the tube, and now renews his observations upon his companions, evidently to make sure that he is wholly unobserved. He is clearly on the eve of some great experiment. Pray heaven that it be not a dangerous one; but the interests of science must be promoted, and I am prepared for the worst."

" Five minutes later.

"He has produced a large pair of scissors, and drawn a roll of some substance, not unlike parchment in appearance.

from the tin case. The experiment is about to begin. I must strain my eyes to the utmost, in the attempt to follow its minutest operation."

" Twenty minutes before two.

"I have at length been enabled to ascertain that the tin tube contains a few yards of some celebrated plaster, recommended—as I discover on regarding the label attentively through my eye-glass — as a preservative against sea-sickness. Mr. Slug has cut it up into small portions, and is now sticking it over himself in every direction."

" Three o'clock.

"Precisely a quarter of an hour ago we weighed anchor, and the machinery was suddenly put in motion with a noise so appalling, that Professor Woodensconce (who had ascended to his berth by means of a platform of carpet-bags arranged by himself on geometrical principles) darted from his shelf head foremost, and, gaining his feet with all the rapidity of extreme terror, ran wildly into the ladies' cabin, under the impression that we were sinking, and uttering loud cries for aid. I am assured that the scene which ensued baffles all description. There were one hundred and forty-seven ladies in their respective berths at the time.

"Mr. Slug has remarked, as an additional instance of the extreme ingenuity of the steam-engine as applied to purposes of navigation, that in whatever part of the vessel a passenger's berth may be situated, the machinery always appears to be exactly under his pillow. He intends stating this very beautiful, though simple discovery, to the association."

" Half-past three.

"We are still in smooth water ; that is to say, in as smooth water as a steam-vessel ever can be, for, as Professor Woodensconce (who has just woke up) learnedly remarks, another great point of ingenuity about a steamer is, that it always carries a little storm with it. You can scarcely conceive how exciting the jerking pulsation of the ship becomes. It is a matter of positive difficulty to get to sleep."

" Friday afternoon, six o'clock.

"I regret to inform you that Mr. Slug's plaster has proved of no avail. He is in great agony, but has applied several large additional pieces notwithstanding. How affecting is this extreme devotion to science and pursuit of knowledge under the most trying circumstances!

"We were extremely happy this morning, and the breakfast was one of the most animated description. Nothing unpleasant occurred until noon, with the exception of Doctor Foxey's brown silk umbrella and white hat becoming entangled in the machinery while he was explaining to a knot of ladies the construction of the steam-engine. I fear the gravy soup for lunch was injudicious. We lost a great many passengers almost immediately afterwards."

"Half-past six.

"I am again in bed. Anything so heart-rending as Mr. Slug's sufferings it has never yet been my lot to witness."

"Seven o'clock.

"A messenger has just come down for a clean pocket-handkerchief from Professor Woodensconce's bag, that unfortunate gentleman being quite unable to leave the deck, and imploring constantly to be thrown overboard. From this man I understand that Professor Nogo, though in a state of utter exhaustion, clings feebly to the hard biscuit and cold brandy and water, under the impression that they will yet restore him. Such is the triumph of mind over matter.

"Professor Grime is in bed, to all appearance quite well; but he *will* eat, and it is disagreeable to see him. Has this gentleman no sympathy with the sufferings of his fellow-creatures? If he has, on what principle can he call for mutton-chops—and smile?"

"Black Boy and Stomach-ache,
Oldcastle, Saturday noon.

"You will be happy to learn that I have at length arrived here in safety. The town is excessively crowded, and all the private lodgings and hotels are filled with *savans* of both sexes. The tremendous assemblage of intellect that one encounters in every street is in the last degree overwhelming.

"Notwithstanding the throng of people here, I have been fortunate enough to meet with very comfortable accommodation on very reasonable terms, having secured a sofa in the first-floor passage at one guinea per night, which includes permission to take my meals in the bar, on condition that I walk about the streets at all other times, to make room for other gentlemen similarly situated. I have been over the outhouses intended to be devoted to the reception of the various sections, both here and at the Boot-jack and Countenance, and am much delighted with the arrangements. Nothing can exceed the fresh appearance of the saw-dust with which the floors are sprinkled. The forms are of unplaned deal, and the general effect, as you can well imagine, is extremely beautiful."

" Half-past nine.

"The number and rapidity of the arrivals are quite bewildering. Within the last ten minutes a stage-coach has driven up to the door, filled inside and out with distinguished characters, comprising Mr. Muddlebranes, Mr. Drawley, Professor Muff, Mr. X. Misty, Mr. X. X. Misty, Mr.' Purblind, Professor Rummun, The Honourable and Reverend Mr. Long Eers, Professor John Ketch, Sir William Joltered, Doctor Buffer, Mr. Smith (of London), Mr. Brown (of Edinburgh), Sir Hookham Snivey, and Professor Pumpkinskull. The ten last-named gentlemen were wet through, and looked extremely intelligent."

" Sunday, two o'clock, p.m.

"The Honourable and Reverend Mr. Long Eers, accompanied by Sir William Joltered, walked and drove this morning. They accomplished the former feat in boots, and the latter in a hired fly. This has naturally given rise to much discussion.

"I have just learnt that an interview has taken place at the Boot-jack and Countenance between Sowster, the active and intelligent beadle of this place, and Professor Pumpkinskull, who, as your readers are doubtless aware, is an influential member of the council. I forbear to communicate any of the rumours to which this very extraordinary proceeding has given rise until I have seen Sowster, and endeavoured to ascertain the truth from him."

" Half-past six.

" I engaged a donkey-chaise shortly after writing the above, and proceeded at a brisk trot in the direction of Sowster's residence, passing through a beautiful expanse of country, with red brick buildings on either side, and stopping in the market-place to observe the spot where Mr. Kwakley's hat was blown off yesterday. It is an uneven piece of paving, but has certainly no appearance which would lead one to suppose that any such event had recently occurred there. From this point I proceeded—passing the gas-works and tallow-melter's—to a lane which had been pointed out to me as the beadle's place of residence ; and before I had driven a dozen yards further, I had the good fortune to meet Sowster himself advancing towards me.

"Sowster is a fat man, with a more enlarged development of that peculiar conformation of countenance which is vulgarly termed a double chin than I remember to have ever seen before. He has also a very red nose, which he attributes to a habit of early rising—so red, indeed, that but for this explanation I should have supposed it to proceed from occasional inebriety. He informed me that he did not feel himself at liberty to relate what had passed between himself and Professor Pumpkinskull, but had no objection to state that it was connected with a matter of police regulation, and added with peculiar significance 'Never wos sitch times !'

"You will easily believe that this intelligence gave mo considerable surprise, not wholly unmixed with anxiety, and that I lost no time in waiting on Professor Pumpkinskull, and stating the object of my visit. After a few moments' reflection, the Professor, who, I am bound to say, behaved with the utmost politeness, openly avowed (I mark the passage in italics) *that he had requested Sowster to attend on the Monday morning at the Boot-jack and Countenance, to keep off the boys ; and that he had further desired that the under-beadle might be stationed, with the same object, at the Black Boy and Stomach-ache!*

"Now I leave this unconstitutional proceeding to your comments and the consideration of your readers. I have yet to learn that a beadle, without the precincts of a church, churchyard, or workhouse, and acting otherwise than under the express orders of churchwardens and overseers in council assembled, to enforce the law against people who come upon the parish, and other offenders, has any lawful authority whatever over the rising youth of this country. I have yet to learn that a beadle can be called out by any civilian to exercise a domination and despotism over the boys of Britain. I have yet to learn that a beadle will be permitted by the commissioners of poor law regulation to wear out the soles and heels of his boots in illegal interference with the liberties of people not proved poor or otherwise criminal. I have yet to learn that a beadle has power to stop up the Queen's highway at his will and pleasure, or that the whole width of the street is not free and open to any man, boy, or woman in existence, up to the very walls of the houses—aye, be they Black Boys and Stomach-aches, or Boot-jacks and Countenances, I care not."

" Nine o'clock.

"I have procured a local artist to make a faithful sketch of the tyrant Sowster, which, as he has acquired this infamous

The Tyrant Sowster.

celebrity, you will no doubt wish to have engraved for the purpose of presenting a copy with every copy of your next number. I enclose it. The under-beadle has consented to write his life, but it is to be strictly anonymous.

"The accompanying likeness is of course from the life, and

complete in every respect. Even if I had been totally ignorant of the man's real character, and it had been placed before me without remark, I should have shuddered involuntarily. There is an intense malignity of expression in the features, and a baleful ferocity of purpose in the ruffian's eye, which appals and sickens. His whole air is rampant with cruelty, nor is the stomach less characteristic of his demoniac propensities."

"*Monday.*

"The great day has at length arrived. I have neither eyes, nor ears, nor pens, nor ink, nor paper, for anything but the wonderful proceedings that have astounded my senses. Let me collect my energies and proceed to the account.

"Section A.—Zoology and Botany.

FRONT PARLOUR, BLACK BOY AND STOMACH-ACHE.

President Sir William Joltered. *Vice-Presidents*—Mr. Muddlebranes and Mr. Drawley.

"Mr. X. X. Misty communicated some remarks on the disappearance of dancing-bears from the streets of London, with observations on the exhibition of monkeys as connected with barrel-organs. The writer had observed, with feelings of the utmost pain and regret, that some years ago a sudden and unaccountable change in the public taste took place with reference to itinerant bears, who, being discountenanced by the populace, gradually fell off one by one from the streets of the metropolis, until not one remained to create a taste for natural history in the breasts of the poor and uninstructed. One bear, indeed,—a brown and ragged animal,—had lingered about the haunts of his former triumphs, with a worn and dejected visage and feeble limbs, and had essayed to wield his quarter-staff for the amusement of the multitude; but hunger, and an utter want of any due recompense for his abilities, had at length driven him from the field, and it was only too probable that he had fallen a sacrifice to the rising taste for grease. He regretted to add that a similar, and no less lamentable, change had taken place with reference to monkeys. These delightful animals had formerly been almost as plentiful as the organs on the tops of which they were accustomed to sit; the proportion in the year 1829 (it appeared by the parliamentary return) being as one monkey to three organs. Owing, however, to an altered taste in musical instruments, and the substitution, in a great measure, of narrow boxes of music for organs, which left the monkeys nothing to sit upon, this source of public amusement was wholly dried up. Considering it a matter of the deepest importance, in connection with national education, that the people should not lose such opportunities of making themselves acquainted with the manners and customs of two most interesting species of animals, the author submitted that some measures should be immediately taken for the restoration of these pleasing and truly intellectual amusements.

"THE PRESIDENT inquired by what means the honourable member proposed to attain this most desirable end?

"THE AUTHOR submitted that it could be most fully and satisfactorily accomplished, if her Majesty's Government would cause to be brought over to England, and maintained at the public expense, and for the public amusement, such a number of bears as would enable every quarter of the town to be visited—say at least by three bears a week. No difficulty whatever need be experienced in providing a fitting place for the reception of these animals, as a commodious bear-garden could be erected in the immediate neighbourhood of both Houses of Parliament; obviously the most proper and eligible spot for such an establishment.

"PROFESSOR MULL doubted very much whether any correct ideas of natural history were propagated by the means to which the honourable member had so ably adverted. On the contrary, he believed that they had been the means of diffusing very incorrect and imperfect notions on the subject. He spoke from personal observation and personal experience, when he said that many children of great abilities had been induced to believe, from what they had observed in the streets, at and before the period to which the honourable gentleman had referred, that all monkeys were born in red coats and spangles, and that their hats and feathers also came by nature. He wished to know distinctly whether the honourable gentleman attributed the want of encouragement the bears had met with to the decline of public taste in that respect, or to a want of ability on the part of the bears themselves?

"MR. X. X. MISTY replied that he could not bring himself to believe but that there must be a great deal of floating talent among the bears and monkeys generally; which, in the absence of any proper encouragement, was dispersed in other directions.

"PROFESSOR PUMPKINSKULL wished to take that opportunity of calling the attention of the section to a most important and serious point. The author of the treatise just read had alluded to the prevalent taste for bears'-grease as a means of promoting the growth of hair, which undoubtedly was diffused to a very great and (as it appeared to him) very alarming extent. No gentleman attending that section could fail to be aware of the fact that the youth of the present age evinced, by their behaviour in the streets, and at all places of public resort, a considerable lack of that gallantry and gentlemanly feeling which, in more ignorant times, had been thought becoming. He wished to know whether it were possible that a constant outward application of bears'-grease by the young gentlemen about town had imperceptibly infused into those unhappy persons something of the nature and quality of the bear. He shuddered as he threw out the remark; but if this theory, on inquiry, should prove to be well founded, it would at once explain a great deal of unpleasant eccentricity of behaviour, which, without some such discovery, was wholly unaccountable.

"THE PRESIDENT highly complimented the learned gentleman on his most valuable suggestion, which produced the greatest effect upon the assembly; and remarked that only a week previous he had seen some young gentlemen at a theatre eyeing a box of ladies with a fierce intensity, which nothing but the influence of some brutish appetite could possibly explain. It was dreadful to reflect that our youth were so rapidly verging into a generation of bears.

" After a scene of scientific enthusiasm it was resolved that this important question should be immediately submitted to the consideration of the council.

"THE PRESIDENT wished to know whether any gentleman could inform the section what had become of the dancing-dogs?

"A MEMBER replied, after some hesitation, that on the day after three glee-singers had been committed to prison as criminals by a late most zealous police-magistrate of the metropolis, the dogs had abandoned their professional duties, and dispersed themselves in different quarters of the town to gain a livelihood by less dangerous means. He was given to understand that since that period they had supported themselves by lying in wait for and robbing blind men's poodles.

" MR. FLUMMERY exhibited a twig, claiming to be a veritable branch of that noble tree known to naturalists as the SHAK-SPEARE, which has taken root in every land and climate, and gathered under the shade of its broad green boughs the great family of mankind. The learned gentleman remarked that the twig had been undoubtedly called by other names in its time ; but that it had been pointed out to him by an old lady in Warwickshire, where the great tree had grown, as a shoot of the genuine SHAKSPEARE, by which name he begged to introduce it to his countrymen.

" THE PRESIDENT wished to know what botanical definition the honourable gentleman could afford of the curiosity.

" MR. FLUMMERY expressed his opinion that it was A DECIDED PLANT.

"SECTION B.—DISPLAY OF MODELS AND MECHANICAL SCIENCE.

LARGE ROOM, BOOT-JACK AND COUNTENANCE.

President—Mr. Mallett.   *Vice-Presidents*—Messrs. Leaver and Scroo.

" MR. CRINKLES exhibited a most beautiful and delicate machine, of little larger size than an ordinary snuff-box, manufactured entirely by himself, and composed exclusively of steel, by the aid of which more pockets could be picked in one hour than by the present slow and tedious process in four-and-twenty. The inventor remarked that it had been put into active operation in Fleet Street, the Strand, and other thoroughfares, and had never been once known to fail.

" After some slight delay, occasioned by the various members of the section buttoning their pockets,

" THE PRESIDENT narrowly inspected the invention, and declared that he had never seen a machine of more beautiful or exquisite construction. Would the inventor be good enough to inform the section whether he had taken any and what means for bringing it into general operation ?

" MR. CRINKLES stated that, after encountering some pre-liminary difficulties, he had succeeded in putting himself in communication with Mr. Fogle Hunter, and other gentlemen connected with the swell mob, who had awarded the inven-tion the very highest and most unqualified approbation. He regretted to say, however, that these distinguished prac-titioners, in common with a gentleman of the name of

Gimlet-eyed Tommy, and other members of a secondary grade of the profession whom he was understood to represent, entertained an insuperable objection to its being brought into general use, on the ground that it would have the inevitable effect of almost entirely superseding manual labour, and throwing a great number of highly-deserving persons out of employment.

"THE PRESIDENT hoped that no such fanciful objections would be allowed to stand in the way of such a great public improvement.

"MR. CRINKLES hoped so too; but he feared that if the gentlemen of the swell mob persevered in their objection, nothing could be done.

"PROFESSOR GRIME suggested that surely, in that case, her Majesty's Government might be prevailed upon to take it up.

"MR. CRINKLES said that if the objection were found to be insuperable he should apply to parliament, which he thought could not fail to recognise the utility of the invention.

"THE PRESIDENT observed that, up to this time parliament had certainly got on very well without it; but, as they did their business on a very large scale, he had no doubt they would gladly adopt the improvement. His only fear was that the machine might be worn out by constant working.

"MR. COPPERNOSE called the attention of the section to a proposition of great magnitude and interest, illustrated by a vast number of models, and stated with much clearness and perspicuity in a treatise entitled 'Practical Suggestions on the necessity of providing some harmless and wholesome relaxation for the young noblemen of England.' His proposition was, that a space of ground of not less than ten miles in length and four in breadth should be purchased by a new company, to be incorporated by Act of Parliament, and inclosed by a brick wall of not less than twelve feet in height. He proposed that it should be laid out with highway roads, turnpikes, bridges, miniature villages, and every object that could conduce to the comfort and glory of Four-in-hand Clubs, so that they might be fairly presumed to require no drive beyond it. This delightful retreat would be fitted up with most commodious and extensive stables, for the convenience of such of the nobility and gentry as had a taste for ostlering, and with houses of entertainment furnished in the most expensive and handsome style. It would be further provided with whole streets of door-knockers and bell-handles of extra size, so constructed that they could be easily wrenched off at night, and regularly screwed on again, by attendants provided for the purpose, every day. There would also be gas lamps of real glass, which could be broken at a comparatively small expense per dozen, and a broad and handsome foot pavement for gentlemen to drive their cabriolets upon when they were humorously disposed—for the full enjoyment of which feat live pedestrians would be procured from the workhouse at a very small charge per head. The place being inclosed, and carefully screened from the intrusion of the public, there would be no objection to gentlemen laying aside any article of their costume that was considered to interfere with a pleasant frolic, or, indeed, to their walking about without any costume at all, if they liked that better. In short, every facility of enjoyment would be afforded that the most gentle-manly person could possibly desire. But as even these advantages would be incomplete unless there were some means provided of enabling the nobility and gentry to display their prowess when they sallied forth after dinner, and as some inconvenience might be experienced in the event of their being reduced to the necessity of pummelling each other, the inventor had turned his attention to the construc-tion of an entirely new police force, composed exclusively of automaton figures, which, with the assistance of the ingenious Signor Gagliardi, of Windmill Street, in the Haymarket, he had succeeded in making with such nicety, that a policeman, cab-driver, or old woman, made upon the principle of the models exhibited, would walk about until knocked down like any real man ; nay, more, if set upon and beaten by six or eight noblemen or gentlemen, after it was down, the figure would utter divers groans, mingled with entreaties for mercy, thus rendering the illusion complete, and the enjoyment perfect. But the invention did not stop even here ; for station-houses would be built, containing good beds for noblemen and gentlemen during the night, and in the morning they would repair to a commodious police office, where a pantomimic investigation would take place before the automaton magistrates,—quite equal to life,—who would fine them in so many counters, with which they would be previously provided for the purpose. This office would be furnished with an inclined plane, for the convenience of any nobleman or gentleman who might wish to bring in his horse as a witness; and the prisoners would be at perfect liberty, as they were now, to interrupt the complainants as much as they pleased, and to make any remarks that they thought proper. The charge for these amusements would amount to very little more than they already cost, and the inventor submitted that the public would be much benefited and comforted by the proposed arrangement.

"PROFESSOR NOGO wished to be informed what amount of automaton police force it was proposed to raise in the first instance.

"MR. COPPERNOSE replied, that it was proposed to begin with seven divisions of police of a score each, lettered from A to G inclusive. It was proposed that not more than half this number should be placed on active duty, and that the remainder should be kept on shelves in the police office ready to be called out at a moment's notice.

"THE PRESIDENT, awarding the utmost merit to the ingenious gentleman who had originated the idea, doubted whether the automaton police would quite answer the purpose. He feared that noblemen and gentlemen would perhaps require the excitement of thrashing living subjects.

"MR. COPPERNOSE submitted that as the usual odds in such cases were ten noblemen or gentlemen to one policeman or cab-driver, it could make very little difference in point of excitement whether the policeman or cab-driver were a man or a block. The great advantage would be, that a policeman's limbs might be all knocked off, and yet he would be in a condition to do duty next day. He might even give his evidence next morning with his head in his hand, and give it equally well.

"PROFESSOR MUFF.—Will you allow me to ask you, sir, of what materials it is intended that the magistrates' heads shall be composed?

"MR. COPPERNOSE.—The magistrates will have wooden heads, of course, and they will be made of the toughest and thickest materials that can possibly be obtained.

"PROFESSOR MUFF.—I am quite satisfied. This is a great invention.

"PROFESSOR NOGO.—I see but one objection to it. It appears to me that the magistrates ought to talk.

"MR. COPPERNOSE no sooner heard this suggestion than he touched a small spring in each of the two models of magistrates which were placed upon the table; one of the figures immediately began to exclaim with great volubility that he was sorry to see gentlemen in such a situation, and the other to express a fear that the policeman was intoxicated.

"The section, as with one accord, declared with a shout of applause that the invention was complete; and the President, much excited, retired with Mr. Coppernose to lay it before the council.   On his return,

"MR. TICKLE displayed his newly-invented spectacles, which enabled the wearer to discern, in very bright colours, objects at a great distance, and rendered him wholly blind to those immediately before him.   It was, he said, a most valuable and useful invention, based strictly upon the principle of the human eye.

"THE PRESIDENT required some information upon this point.   He had yet to learn that the human eye was remarkable for the peculiarities of which the honourable gentleman had spoken.

"MR. TICKLE was rather astonished to hear this, when the President could not fail to be aware that a large number of most excellent persons and great statesmen could see, with the naked eye, most marvellous horrors on West India plantations, while they could discern nothing whatever in the interior of Manchester cotton mills.   He must know, too, with what quickness of perception most people could discover their neighbour's faults, and how very blind they were to their own.   If the President differed from the great majority of men in this respect, his eye was a defective one, and it was to assist his vision that these glasses were made.

"MR. BLANK exhibited a model of a fashionable annual, composed of copper-plates, gold leaf, and silk boards, and worked entirely by milk and water.

"MR. PROSEE, after examining the machine, declared it to be so ingeniously composed, that he was wholly unable to discover how it went on at all.

"MR. BLANK.—Nobody can, and that is the beauty of it.

"SECTION C.—ANATOMY AND MEDICINE.

BAR ROOM, BLACK BOY AND STOMACH-ACHE.

President—Dr. Soemup. *Vice-Presidents*—Messrs. Pessell and Mortair.

"DR. GRUMMIDGE stated to the section a most interesting case of monomania, and described the course of treatment he had pursued with perfect success. The patient was a married lady in the middle rank of life, who, having seen another lady at an evening party in a full suit of pearls, was suddenly seized with a desire to possess a similar equipment, although her husband's finances were by no means equal to the necessary outlay. Finding her wish ungratified, she fell sick, and the symptoms soon became so alarming, that he (Dr. Grummidge) was called in. At this period the prominent tokens of the disorder were sullenness, a total indisposition to perform domestic dutiou, great peevishness, and extreme languor, except when pearls were mentioned, at which times the pulse quickened, the eyes grew brighter, the pupils dilated, and the patient, after various incoherent exclamations, burst into a passion of tears, and exclaimed that nobody cared for her, and that she wished herself dead. Finding that the patient's appetite was affected in the presence of company, he began by ordering a total abstinence from all stimulants, and forbidding any sustenance but weak gruel; he then took twenty ounces of blood, applied a blister under each ear, one upon the chest, and another on the back : having done which, and administered five grains of calomel, he left the patient to her repose. The next day she was somewhat low, but decidedly better, and all appearances of irritation were removed. The next day she improved still further, and on the next again. On the fourth there was some appearance of a return of the old symptoms, which no sooner developed themselves, than he administered another dose of calomel, and left strict orders that, unless a decidedly favourable change occurred within two hours, the patient's head should be immediately shaved to the very last curl. From that moment she began to mend, and, in less than four-and-twenty hours was perfectly restored. She did not now betray the least emotion at the sight or mention of pearls or any other ornaments. She was cheerful and good-humoured, and a most beneficial change had been effected in her whole temperament and condition.

"MR. PIPKIN (M.R.C.S.) read a short but most interesting communication in which he sought to prove the complete belief of Sir William Courtenay, otherwise Thom, recently shot at Canterbury, in the Homœopathic system. The section would bear in mind that one of the Homœopathic doctrines was, that infinitesimal doses of any medicine which would occasion the disease under which the patient laboured, supposing him to be in a healthy state, would cure it. Now, it was a remarkable circumstance—proved in the evidence— that the deceased Thom employed a woman to follow him about all day with a pail of water, assuring her that one drop (a purely homœopathic remedy, the section would observe), placed upon his tongue, after death, would restore him. What was the obvious inference? That Thom, who was marching and countermarching in osier beds, and other swampy places, was impressed with a presentiment that he should be drowned; in which case, had his instructions been complied with, he could not fail to have been brought to life again instantly by his own prescription. As it was, if this woman, or any other person, had administered an infinitesimal dose of lead and gunpowder immediately after he fell, he would have recovered forthwith. But unhappily the woman concerned did not possess the power of reasoning by analogy, or carrying out a principle, and thus the unfortunate gentle-man had been sacrificed to the ignorance of the peasantry.

"SECTION D.—STATISTICS.

OUT-HOUSE, BLACK BOY AND STOMACH-ACHE

President—Mr. Slug. *Vice-Presidents*—Messrs. Noakes and Styles.

"MR. KWAKLEY stated the result of some most ingenious statistical inquiries relative to the difference between the value of the qualification of several members of Parliament as published to the world, and its real nature and amount. After reminding the section that every member of Parliament for a town or borough was supposed to possess a clear freehold estate of three hundred pounds per annum, the honourable gentleman excited great amusement and laughter by stating the exact amount of freehold property possessed by a column of legislators, in which he had included himself. It appeared from this table, that the amount of such income possessed by each was o pounds, o shillings, and o pence, yielding an average of the same. (Great laughter.) It was

George Cruikshank

Automaton Police Office, and the real Offenders

(p. 660)

From the model exhibited before Section B of the Mudfog Association

pretty well known that there were accommodating gentlemen in the habit of furnishing new members with temporary qualifications, to the ownership of which they swore solemnly —of course as a mere matter of form. He argued from these *data* that it was wholly unnecessary for members of Parliament to possess any property at all, especially as when they had none the public could get them so much cheaper.

"SUPPLEMENTARY SECTION, E.—UMBUGOLOGY AND DITCHWATERISICS.

President—Mr. Grub. *Vice-Presidents*—Messrs. Dull and Dummy.

" A paper was read by the secretary descriptive of a bay pony with one eye, which had been seen by the author standing in a butcher's cart at the corner of Newgate Market. The communication described the author of the paper as having, in the prosecution of a mercantile pursuit, betaken himself one Saturday morning last summer from Somers Town to Cheapside; in the course of which expedition he had beheld the extraordinary appearance above described. The pony had one distinct eye, and it had been pointed out to him by his friend Captain Blunderbore, of the Horse Marines, who assisted the author in his search, that whenever he winked this eye he whisked his tail (possibly to drive the flies off), but that he always winked and whisked at the same time. The animal was lean, spavined, and tottering; and the author proposed to constitute it of the family of *Fitfordogsmeataurious.* It certainly did occur to him that there was no case on record of a pony with one clearly-defined and distinct organ of vision, winking and whisking at the same moment.

" Mr. Q. J. SNUFFLETOFFLE had heard of a pony winking his eye, and likewise of a pony whisking his tail, but whether they were two ponies or the same pony he could not undertake positively to say. At all events, he was acquainted with no authenticated instance of a simultaneous winking and whisking, and he really could not but doubt the existence of such a marvellous pony in opposition to all those natural laws by which ponies were governed. Referring, however, to the mere question of his one organ of vision, might he suggest the possibility of this pony having been literally half asleep at the time he was seen, and having closed only one eye.

"THE PRESIDENT observed that, whether the pony was half asleep or fast asleep, there could be no doubt that the association was wide awake, and therefore that they had better get the business over, and go to dinner. He had certainly never seen anything analogous to this pony, but he was not prepared to doubt its existence; for he had seen many queerer ponies in his time, though he did not pretend to have seen any more remarkable donkeys than the other gentlemen around him.

"PROFESSOR JOHN KETCH was then called upon to exhibit the skull of the late Mr. Greenacre, which he produced from a blue bag, remarking, on being invited to make any observations that occurred to him, 'that he'd pound it as that 'ere 'spectable section had never seed a more gamerer cove nor he vos.'

"A most animated discussion upon this interesting relic ensued; and, some difference of opinion arising respecting the real character of the deceased gentleman, Mr. Blubb delivered a lecture upon the cranium before him, clearly showing that Mr. Greenacre possessed the organ of destructiveness to a most unusual extent, with a most remarkable development of the organ of carveativeness. Sir Hookham Snivey was proceeding to combat this opinion, when Professor Ketch suddenly interrupted the proceedings by exclaiming, with great excitement of manner, 'Walker!'

"THE PRESIDENT begged to call the learned gentleman to order.

"PROFESSOR KETCH.—'Order be blowed! you've got the wrong un, I tell you. It ain't no 'ed at all; it's a coker-nut as my brother-in-law has been a-carvin', to hornament his new baked tatur-stall wots a-comin' down 'ere vile the 'sociation's in the town. Hand over, vill you?'

"With these words, Professor Ketch hastily repossessed himself of the cocoa-nut, and drew forth the skull, in mistake for which he had exhibited it. A most interesting conversation ensued; but as there appeared some doubt ultimately whether the skull was Mr. Greenacre's, or a hospital patient's, or a pauper's, or a man's, or a woman's, or a monkey's, no particular result was obtained."

"I cannot," says our talented correspondent in conclusion, "I cannot close my account of these gigantic researches and sublime and noble triumphs without repeating a *bon mot* of

Professor Woodensconce's, which shows how the greatest minds may occasionally unbend when truth can be presented to listening ears, clothed in an attractive and playful form. I was standing by, when, after a week of feasting and feeding, that learned gentleman, accompanied by the whole body of wonderful men, entered the hall yesterday, where a sumptuous dinner was prepared ; where the richest wines sparkled on the board, and fat bucks—propitiatory sacrifices to learning—sent forth their savoury odours. 'Ah !' said Professor Woodensconce, rubbing his hands, 'this is what we meet for ; this is what inspires us ; this is what keeps us together. and beckons us onward : this is the *spread* of science, and a glorious spread it is.'"

THE PANTOMIME OF LIFE

Before we plunge headlong into this paper, let us at once confess to a fondness for pantomimes—to a gentle sympathy with clowns and pantaloons—to an unqualified admiration of harlequins and columbines—to a chaste delight in every action of their brief existence, varied and many-coloured as those actions are, and inconsistent though they occasionally be with those rigid and formal rules of propriety which regulate the proceedings of meaner and less comprehensive minds. We revel in pantomimes—not because they dazzle one's eyes with tinsel and gold leaf; not because they present to us, once again, the well-beloved chalked faces and goggle eyes of our childhood; not even because, like Christmas-day, and Twelfth-night, and Shrove-Tuesday, and one's own birthday, they come to us but once a year;—our attachment is founded on a graver and a very different reason. A pantomime is to us a mirror of life; nay more, we maintain that it is so to audiences generally, although they are not aware of it, and that this very circumstance is the secret cause of their amusement and delight.

Let us take a slight example. The scene is a street: an elderly gentleman, with a large face and strongly marked features, appears. His countenance beams with a sunny smile, and a perpetual dimple is on his broad, red cheek. He is evidently an opulent elderly gentleman, comfortable in circumstances, and well-to-do in the world. He is not unmindful of the adornment of his person, for he is richly, not to say gaudily, dressed; and that he indulges to a reasonable extent in the pleasures of the table may be inferred from the joyous and oily manner in which he rubs his stomach, by way of informing the audience that he is going home to dinner. In the fulness of his heart, in the fancied security of wealth, in the possession and enjoyment of all the good things of life, the elderly gentleman suddenly loses his footing and stumbles. How the audience roar! He is set upon by a noisy and officious crowd, who buffet and cuff him unmercifully. They scream with delight!

Every time the elderly gentleman struggles to get up, his
relentless persecutors knock him down again. The spectators are convulsed with merriment! And when at last
the elderly gentleman does get up, and staggers away,
despoiled of hat, wig, and clothing, himself battered to
pieces, and his watch and money gone, they are exhausted
with laughter, and express their merriment and admiration
in rounds of applause.

Is this like life? Change the scene to any real street;—
to the Stock Exchange, or the City banker's; the merchant's
counting-house, or even the tradesman's shop. See any one
of these men fall,—the more suddenly, and the nearer the
zenith of his pride and riches, the better. What a wild hallo
is raised over his prostrate carcase by the shouting mob;
how they whoop and yell as he lies humbled beneath them!
Mark how eagerly they set upon him when he is down; and
how they mock and deride him as he slinks away. Why, it
is the pantomime to the very letter.

Of all the pantomimic *dramatis personae*, we consider the
pantaloon the most worthless and debauched. Independent
of the dislike one naturally feels at seeing a gentleman of
his years engaged in pursuits highly unbecoming his gravity
and time of life, we cannot conceal from ourselves the fact
that he is a treacherous, worldly-minded old villain, constantly enticing his younger companion, the clown, into acts
of fraud or petty larceny, and generally standing aside to
watch the result of the enterprise. If it be successful, he
never forgets to return for his share of the spoil; but if it
turn out a failure, he generally retires with remarkable
caution and expedition, and keeps carefully aloof until the
affair has blown over. His amorous propensities, too, are
eminently disagreeable; and his mode of addressing ladies
in the open street at noon-day is downright improper, being
usually neither more nor less than a perceptible tickling of
the aforesaid ladies in the waist, after committing which, he
starts back, manifestly ashamed (as well he may be) of his
own indecorum and temerity; continuing, nevertheless, to
ogle and beckon to them from a distance in a very unpleasant and immoral manner.

Is there any man who cannot count a dozen pantaloons in
his own social circle? Is there any man who has not seen
them swarming at the west end of the town on a sunshiny
day or a summer's evening, going through the last-named

pantomimic feats with as much liquorish energy, and as total an absence of reserve, as if they were on the very stage itself? We can tell upon our fingers a dozen pantaloons of our acquaintance at this moment—capital pantaloons, who have been performing all kinds of strange freaks, to the great amusement of their friends and acquaintance, for years past : and who to this day are making such comical and ineffectual attempts to be young and dissolute, that all beholders are like to die with laughter.

Take that old gentleman who has just emerged from the *Café de l'Europe* in the Haymarket, where he has been dining at the expense of the young man upon town with whom he shakes hands as they part at the door of the tavern. The affected warmth of that shake of the hand, the courteous nod, the obvious recollection of the dinner, the savoury flavour of which still hangs upon his lips, are all characteristics of his great prototype. He hobbles away humming an opera tune, and twirling his cane to and fro, with affected careless-ness. Suddenly he stops—'tis at the milliner's window. He peeps through one of the large panes of glass ; and, his view of the ladies within being obstructed by the India shawls, directs his attentions to the young girl with the band-box in her hand, who is gazing in at the window also. See ! he draws beside her. He coughs ; she turns away from him. He draws near her again ; she disregards him. He gleefully chucks her under the chin, and, retreating a few steps, nods and beckons with fantastic grimaces, while the girl bestows a contemptuous and supercilious look upon his wrinkled visage. She turns away with a flounce, and the old gentleman trots after her with a toothless chuckle. The pantaloon to the life !

But the close resemblance which the clowns of the stage bear to those of every-day life is perfectly extraordinary. Some people talk with a sigh of the decline of pantomime, and murmur in low and dismal tones the name of Grimaldi. We mean no disparagement to the worthy and excellent old man when we say that this is downright nonsense. Clowns that beat Grimaldi all to nothing turn up every day, and nobody patronizes them—more's the pity !

"I know who you mean," says some dirty-faced patron of Mr. Osbaldistone's, laying down the Miscellany when he has got thus far, and bestowing upon vacancy a most knowing glance ; "you mean C. J. Smith as did Guy Fawkes, and

George Barnwell at the Garden." The dirty-faced gentleman has hardly uttered the words, when he is interrupted
by a young gentleman in no shirt-collar and a Petersham
coat. "No, no," says the young gentleman; "he means
Brown, King, and Gibson, at the 'Delphi." Now, with great
deference both to the first-named gentleman with the dirty
face, and the last-named gentleman in the non-existing shirt-
collar, we do *not* mean either the performer who so grotesquely
burlesqued the Popish conspirator, or the three unchangeables
who have been dancing the same dance under different imposing titles, and doing the same thing under various high-
sounding names for some five or six years last past. We
have no sooner made this avowal, than the public, who have
hitherto been silent witnesses of the dispute, inquire what
on earth it is we *do* mean ; and, with becoming respect, we
proceed to tell them.

It is very well known to all playgoers and pantomime-seers,
that the scenes in which a theatrical clown is at the very
height of his glory are those which are described in the play-
bills as "Cheesemonger's shop and Crockery warehouse," or
"Tailor's shop, and Mrs. Queertable's boarding-house," or
places bearing some such title, where the great fun of the
thing consists in the hero's taking lodgings which he has not
the slightest intention of paying for, or obtaining goods under
false pretences, or abstracting the stock-in-trade of the respectable shopkeeper next door, or robbing warehouse porters as
they pass under his window, or, to shorten the catalogue,
in his swindling everybody he possibly can, it only remaining
to be observed that, the more extensive the swindling is, and
the more barefaced the impudence of the swindler, the greater
the rapture and ecstasy of the audience. Now it is a most
remarkable fact that precisely this sort of thing occurs in real
life day after day, and nobody sees the humour of it. Let
us illustrate our position by detailing the plot of this portion
of the pantomime—not of the theatre, but of life.

The Honourable Captain Fitz-Whisker Fiercy, attended by
his livery servant Do'em—a most respectable servant to look
at, who has grown grey in the service of the captain's family
—views, treats for, and ultimately obtains possession of, the
unfurnished house, such a number, such a street. All the
tradesmen in the neighbourhood are in agonies of competition
for the captain's custom ; the captain is a good-natured, kind-
hearted, easy man, and, to avoid being the cause of disap-

pointment to any, he most handsomely gives orders to all. Hampers of wine, baskets of provisions, cart-loads of furniture, boxes of jewellery, supplies of luxuries of the costliest description, flock to the house of the Honourable Captain Fitz-Whisker Fiercy, where they are received with the utmost readiness by the highly respectable Do'em ; while the captain himself struts and swaggers about with that compound air of conscious superiority and general blood-thirstiness which a military captain should always, and does most times, wear, to the admiration and terror of plebeian men. But the tradesmen's backs are no sooner turned, than the captain, with all the eccentricity of a mighty mind, and assisted by the faithful Do'em, whose devoted fidelity is not the least touching part of his character, disposes of everything to great advantage ; for, although the articles fetch small sums, still they are sold considerably above cost price, the cost to the captain having been nothing at all. After various manœuvres, the imposture is discovered, Fitz-Fiercy and Do'em are recognized as confederates, and the police office to which they are both taken is thronged with their dupes.

Who can fail to recognize in this, the exact counterpart of the best portion of a theatrical pantomime—Fitz-Whisker Fiercy by the clown ; Do'em by the pantaloon ; and supernumeraries by the tradesmen ? The best of the joke, too, is that the very coal-merchant who is loudest in his complaints against the person who defrauded him, is the identical man who sat in the centre of the very front row of the pit last night and laughed the most boisterously at this very same thing,—and not so well done either. Talk of Grimaldi, we say again ! Did Grimaldi, in his best days, ever do anything in this way equal to Da Costa ?

The mention of this latter justly celebrated clown reminds us of his last piece of humour, the fraudulently obtaining certain stamped acceptances from a young gentleman in the army. We had scarcely laid down our pen to contemplate for a few moments this admirable actor's performance of that exquisite practical joke, than a new branch of our subject flashed suddenly upon us. So we take it up again at once.

All people who have been behind the scenes, and most people who have been before them, know that in the representation of a pantomime, a good many men are sent upon the stage for the express purpose of being cheated, or knocked down, or both. Now, down to a moment ago, we had never

been able to understand for what possible purpose a great
number of odd, lazy, large-headed men, whom one is in the
habit of meeting here, and there, and everywhere, could
ever have been created. We see it all, now. They are the
supernumeraries in the pantomime of life; the men who
have been thrust into it, with no other view than to be
constantly tumbling over each other, and running their
heads against all sorts of strange things. We sat opposite
to one of these men at a supper-table, only last week. Now
we think of it, he was exactly like the gentlemen with the
pasteboard heads and faces, who do the corresponding business
in the theatrical pantomimes; there was the same broad
stolid simper—the same dull leaden eye—the same unmeaning, vacant stare; and whatever was said, or whatever was
done, he always came in at precisely the wrong place, or
jostled against something that he had not the slightest
business with. We looked at the man across the table again
and again, and could not satisfy ourselves what race of
beings to class him with. How very odd that this never
occurred to us before!

We will frankly own that we have been much troubled with
the harlequin. We see harlequins of so many kinds in the
real living pantomime, that we hardly know which to select
as the proper fellow of him of the theatres. At one time we
were disposed to think that the harlequin was neither more
nor less than a young man of family and independent property,
who had run away with an opera-dancer, and was fooling his
life and his means away in light and trivial amusements.
On reflection, however, we remembered that harlequins are
occasionally guilty of witty and even clever acts, and we
are rather disposed to acquit our young men of family and
independent property, generally speaking, of any such mis-
demeanours. On a more mature consideration of the subject,
we have arrived at the conclusion that the harlequins of life
are just ordinary men, to be found in no particular walk or
degree, on whom a certain station, or particular conjunction
of circumstances, confers the magic wand. And this brings
us to a few words on the pantomime of public and political
life, which we shall say at once, and then conclude—merely
premising in this place that we decline any reference whatever
to the columbine, being in no wise satisfied of the nature of
her connection with her parti-coloured lover, and not feeling
by any means clear that we should be justified in introducing

her to the virtuous and respectable ladies who peruse our lucubrations.

We take it that the commencement of a Session of Parliament is neither more nor less than the drawing up of the curtain for a grand comic pantomime, and that his Majesty's most gracious speech on the opening thereof may be not inaptly compared to the clown's opening speech of "Here we are!" "My lords and gentlemen, here we are!" appears, to our mind at least, to be a very good abstract of the point and meaning of the propitiatory address of the ministry. When we remember how frequently this speech is made, immediately after *the change* too, the parallel is quite perfect, and still more singular.

Perhaps the cast of our political pantomime never was richer than at this day. We are particularly strong in clowns. At no former time, we should say, have we had such astonishing tumblers, or performers so ready to go through the whole of their feats for the amusement of an admiring throng. Their extreme readiness to exhibit, indeed, has given rise to some ill-natured reflections; it having been objected that by exhibiting gratuitously through the country when the theatre is closed, they reduce themselves to the level of mountebanks, and thereby tend to degrade the respectability of the profession. Certainly Grimaldi never did this sort of thing; and though Brown, King, and Gibson have gone to the Surrey in vacation time, and Mr. C. J. Smith has ruralised at Sadler's Wells, we find no theatrical precedent for a general tumbling through the country, except in the gentleman, name unknown, who threw summersets on behalf of the late Mr. Richardson, and who is no authority either, because he had never been on the regular boards.

But laying aside this question, which after all is a mere matter of taste, we may reflect with pride and gratification of heart on the proficiency of our clowns as exhibited in the season. Night after night will they twist and tumble about, till two, three, and four o'clock in the morning; playing the strangest antics, and giving each other the funniest slaps on the face that can possibly be imagined, without evincing the smallest tokens of fatigue. The strange noises, the confusion, the shouting and roaring, amid which all this is done, too, would put to shame the most turbulent sixpenny gallery that ever yelled through a boxing-night.

It is especially curious to behold one of these clowns

compelled to go through the most surprising contortions by the irresistible influence of the wand of office, which his leader or harlequin holds above his head. Acted upon by this wonderful charm he will become perfectly motionless, moving neither hand, foot, nor finger, and will even lose the faculty of speech at an instant's notice; or on the other hand, he will become all life and animation if required, pouring forth a torrent of words without sense or meaning, throwing him-self into the wildest and most fantastic contortions, and even grovelling on the earth and licking up the dust. These exhibitions are more curious than pleasing; indeed, they are rather disgusting than otherwise, except to the admirers of such things, with whom we confess we have no fellow-feeling.

Strange tricks—very strange tricks—are also performed by the harlequin who holds for the time being the magic wand which we have just mentioned. The mere waving it before a man's eyes will dispossess his brains of all the notions pre-viously stored there, and fill it with an entirely new set of ideas; one gentle tap on the back will alter the colour of a man's coat completely; and there are some expert performers who, having this wand held first on one side and then on the other, will change from side to side, turning their coats at every evolution, with so much rapidity and dexterity, that the quickest eye can scarcely detect their motions. Occasionally, the genius who confers the wand, wrests it from the hand of the temporary possessor, and consigns it to some new per-former; on which occasions all the characters change sides, and then the race and the hard knocks begin anew.

We might have extended this chapter to a much greater length—we might have carried the comparison into the liberal professions—we might have shown, as was in fact our original purpose, that each is in itself a little pantomime with scenes and characters of its own, complete; but as we fear we have been quite lengthy enough already, we shall leave this chapter just where it is. A gentleman, not altogether unknown as a dramatic poet, wrote thus a year or two ago—

"All the world's a stage,
And all the men and women merely players:"

and we, tracking out his footsteps at the scarcely-worth-mentioning little distance of a few millions of leagues behind, venture to add, by way of new reading, that he meant a Pantomime. and that we are all actors in The Pantomime of Life.

SOME PARTICULARS CONCERNING A LION

WE have a great respect for lions in the abstract. In common with most other people, we have heard and read of many instances of their bravery and generosity. We have duly admired that heroic self-denial and charming philanthropy which prompts them never to eat people except when they are hungry, and we have been deeply impressed with a becoming sense of the politeness they are said to display towards unmarried ladies of a certain state. All natural histories teem with anecdotes illustrative of their excellent qualities ; and one old spelling-book in particular recounts a touching instance of an old lion, of high moral dignity and stern principle, who felt it his imperative duty to devour a young man who had contracted a habit of swearing, as a striking example to the rising generation.

All this is extremely pleasant to reflect upon, and, indeed, says a very great deal in favour of lions as a mass. We are bound to state, however, that such individual lions as we have happened to fall in with have not put forth any very striking characteristics, and have not acted up to the chivalrous character assigned them by their chroniclers. We never saw a lion in what is called his natural state, certainly ; that is to say, we have never met a lion out walking in a forest, or crouching in his lair under a tropical sun, waiting till his dinner should happen to come by, hot from the baker's. But we have seen some under the influence of captivity, and the pressure of misfortune ; and we must say that they appeared to us very apathetic, heavy-headed fellows.

The lion at the Zoological Gardens, for instance. He is all very well ; he has an undeniable mane, and looks very fierce ; but, Lord bless us ! what of that ? The lions of the fashionable world look just as ferocious, and are the most harmless creatures breathing. A box-lobby lion or a Regent Street animal will put on a most terrible aspect, and roar fearfully, if you affront him ; but he will never bite, and, if you offer to attack him manfully, will fairly turn tail and sneak off. Doubtless these creatures roam about sometimes in herds, and if they meet any especially meek-looking and peaceably-disposed fellow, will endeavour to frighten him ; but the faintest show of a vigorous resistance is sufficient to scare them even then. These are pleasant characteristics, whereas we make it matter of distinct charge against the Zoological lion and his brethren at the fairs, that they are sleepy, dreamy, sluggish quadrupeds.

We do not remember to have ever seen one of them per· fectly awake, except at feeding-time. In every respect we uphold the biped lions against their four-footed namesakes, and we boldly challenge controversy upon the subject.

With these opinions it may be easily imagined that our curiosity and interest were very much excited the other day, when a lady of our acquaintance called on us and resolutely declined to accept our refusal of her invitation to an even· ing party ; "for," said she, "I have got a lion coming." We at once retracted our plea of a prior engagement, and became as anxious to go, as we had previously been to stay away.

We went early, and posted ourselves in an eligible part of the drawing-room, from whence we could hope to obtain a full view of the interesting animal. Two or three hours passed, the quadrilles began, the room filled ; but no lion appeared. The lady of the house became inconsolable,—for it is one of the peculiar privileges of these lions to make solemn appointments and never keep them,—when all of a sudden there came a tremendous double rap at the street-door, and the master of the house, after gliding out (un-observed as he flattered himself) to peep over the banisters, came into the room, rubbing his hands together with great glee, and cried out in a very important voice, "My dear, Mr. —— (naming the lion) has this moment arrived."

Upon this, all eyes were turned towards the door, and we observed several young ladies, who had been laughing and conversing previously with great gaiety and good humour, grow extremely quiet and sentimental ; while some young gentlemen, who had been cutting great figures in the face-tious and small-talk way, suddenly sank very obviously in the estimation of the company, and were looked upon with great coldness and indifference. Even the young man who had been ordered from the music shop to play the pianoforte was visibly affected, and struck several false notes in the excess of his excitement.

All this time there was a great talking outside, more than once accompanied by a loud laugh, and a cry of "Oh! capital! excellent!" from which we inferred that the lion was jocose, and that these exclamations were occasioned by the transports of his keeper and our host. Nor were we deceived; for when the lion at last appeared, we overheard his keeper, who was a little prim man, whisper to several gentlemen of his acquaintance, with uplifted hands, and every expression of half-suppressed admiration, that —— (naming the lion again) was in *such* cue to-night!

The lion was a literary one. Of course there were a vast number of people present who had admired his roarings, and were anxious to be introduced to him; and very pleasant it was to see them brought up for the purpose, and to observe the patient dignity with which he received all their patting and caressing. This brought forcibly to our mind what we had so often witnessed at country fairs, where the other lions are compelled to go through as many forms of courtesy as they chance to be acquainted with, just as often as admiring parties happen to drop in upon them.

While the lion was exhibiting in this way, his keeper was not idle, for he mingled among the crowd, and spread his praises most industriously. To one gentleman he whispered some very choice thing that the noble animal had said in the very act of coming up-stairs, which, of course, rendered the mental effort still more astonishing; to another he murmured a hasty account of a grand dinner that had taken place the day before, where twenty-seven gentlemen had got up all at once to demand an extra cheer for the lion; and to the ladies he made sundry promises of interceding to procure the majestic brute's sign-manual for their albums. Then there were little private consultations in different corners, relative to the personal appearance and stature of the lion; whether he was shorter than they had expected to see him, or taller, or thinner, or fatter, or younger, or older; whether he was like his portrait, or unlike it; and whether the particular shade of his eyes was black, or blue, or hazel, or green, or yellow, or mixture. At all these consultations the keeper assisted; and, in short, the lion was the sole and single subject of discussion till they sat him down to whist, and then the people relapsed into their old topics of conversation—themselves and each other.

We must confess that we looked forward with no slight impatience to the announcement of supper; for if you wish to see a tame lion under particularly favourable circumstances, feeding-time is the period of all others to pitch upon. We were therefore very much delighted to observe a sensation among the guests, which we well knew how to interpret, and immediately afterwards to behold the lion escorting the lady of the house down-stairs. We offered our arm to an elderly female of our acquaintance, who—dear old soul! —is the very best person that ever lived, to lead down to any meal; for, be the room ever so small, or the party ever so large, she is sure, by some intuitive perception of the eligible, to push and pull herself and conductor close to the best dishes on the table;—we say we offered our arm to this elderly female, and, descending the stairs shortly after the lion, were fortunate enough to obtain a seat nearly opposite him.

Of course the keeper was there already. He had planted himself at precisely that distance from his charge which afforded him a decent pretext for raising his voice, when he addressed him, to so loud a key as could not fail to attract the attention of the whole company, and immediately began to apply himself seriously to the task of bringing the lion out, and putting him through the whole of his manœuvres. Such flashes of wit as he elicited from the lion! First of all, they began to make puns upon a salt-cellar, and then upon the breast of a fowl, and then upon the trifle; but the best jokes of all were decidedly on the lobster salad, upon which latter subject the lion came out most vigorously, and, in the opinion of the most competent authorities, quite outshone himself. This is a very excellent mode of shining in society, and is founded, we humbly conceive, upon the classic model of the dialogues between Mr. Punch and his friend the proprietor, wherein the latter takes all the up-hill work, and is content to pioneer to the jokes and repartees of Mr. P. himself, who never fails to gain great credit and excite much laughter thereby. Whatever it be founded on, however, we recommend it to all lions, present and to come; for in this instance it succeeded to admiration, and perfectly dazzled the whole body of hearers.

When the salt-cellar, and the fowl's breast, and the trifle, and the lobster salad were all exhausted, and could not afford standing-room for another solitary witticism, the keeper performed that very dangerous feat which is still done with some of the caravan lions, although in one instance it terminated fatally, of putting his head in the animal's mouth, and placing himself entirely at its mercy. Boswell frequently presents a melancholy instance of the lamentable results of this achievement, and other keepers and jackals have been terribly lacerated for their daring. It is due to our lion to state that he condescended to be trifled with in the most gentle manner, and finally went home with the showman in a hack cab: perfectly peaceable, but slightly fuddled.

Being in a contemplative mood, we were led to make some reflections upon the character and conduct of this genus of lions as we walked homewards, and we were not long in arriving at the conclusion that our former impression in their favour was very much strengthened and confirmed by what we had recently seen. While the other lions receive company and compliments in a sullen, moody, not to say snarling manner, these appear flattered by the attentions that are paid them ; while those conceal themselves to the utmost of their power from the vulgar gaze, these court the popular eye, and, unlike their brethren, whom nothing short of compulsion will move to exertion, are ever ready to display their acquirements to the wondering throng. We have known bears of undoubted ability who, when the expectations of a large audience have been wound up to the utmost pitch, have peremptorily refused to dance ; well-taught monkeys, who have unaccountably objected to exhibit on the slack wire ; and elephants of unquestioned genius, who have suddenly declined to turn the barrel-organ ; but we never once knew or heard of a biped lion, literary or otherwise,—and we state it as a fact which is highly creditable to the whole species,—who, occasion offering, did not seize with avidity on any opportunity which was afforded him, of performing to his heart's content on the first violin.

MR. ROBERT BOLTON

THE "GENTLEMAN CONNECTED WITH THE PRESS"

In the parlour of the Green Dragon, a public-house in the immediate neighbourhood of Westminster Bridge, everybody talks politics, every evening, the great political authority being Mr. Robert Bolton, an individual who defines himself as "a gentleman connected with the press," which is a definition of peculiar indefiniteness. Mr. Robert Bolton's regular circle of admirers and listeners are an undertaker, a green-grocer, a hairdresser, a baker, a large stomach surmounted by a man's head, and placed on the top of two particularly short legs, and a thin man in black, name, profession, and pursuit unknown, who always sits in the same position. always displays the same long, vacant face, and never opens his lips, surrounded as he is by most enthusiastic conversation, except to puff forth a volume of tobacco smoke, or give vent to a very snappy, loud, and shrill *hem!* The conversation sometimes turns upon literature, Mr. Bolton being a literary character, and always upon such news of the day as is exclusively possessed by that talented individual. I found myself (of course, accidentally) in the Green Dragon the other evening, and, being somewhat amused by the following conversation, preserved it.

"Can you lend me a ten-pound note till Christmas?" inquired the hairdresser of the stomach.

"Where's your security, Mr. Clip?"

"My stock in trade,—there's enough of it, I'm thinking, Mr. Thicknesse. Some fifty wigs, two poles, half-a-dozen head blocks, and a dead Bruin."

"No, I won't, then," growled out Thicknesse. "I lends nothing on the security of the whigs or the Poles either. As for whigs, they're cheats; as for the Poles, they've got no cash. I never have nothing to do with blockheads, unless I can't avoid it (ironically), and a dead bear's about as much use to me as I could be to a dead bear."

"Well, then," urged the other, "there's a book as belonged to Pope, Byron's Poems, valued at forty pounds, because it's got Pope's identical scratch on the back ; what do you think of that for security?"

"Well, to be sure!" cried the baker. "But how d'ye mean, Mr. Clip?"

"Mean! why, that it's got the *hottergruff* of Pope.

> 'Steal not this book, for fear of hangman's rope ;
> For it belongs to Alexander Pope.'

All that's written on the inside of the binding of the book ; so, as my son says, we're *bound* to believe it."

"Well, sir," observed the undertaker, deferentially, and in a half-whisper, leaning over the table, and knocking over the hairdresser's grog as he spoke, "that argument's very easy upset."

"Perhaps, sir," said Clip, a little flurried, "you'll pay for the first upset afore you thinks of another."

"Now," said the undertaker, bowing amicably to the hair-dresser, "I *think*, I says I *think*—you'll excuse me, Mr. Clip, I *think*, you see, that won't go down with the present company —unfortunately, my master had the honour of making the coffin of that ere Lord's housemaid, not no more nor twenty year ago. Don't think I'm proud on it, gentlemen ; others might be ; but I hate rank of any sort. I've no more respect for a Lord's footman than I have for any respectable trades-man in this room. I may say no more nor I have for Mr. Clip! (bowing). Therefore, that ere Lord must have been born long after Pope died. And it's a logical interferance to defer, that they neither of them lived at the same time. So what I mean is this here, that Pope never had no book. never seed, felt, never smelt no book (triumphantly) as belonged to that ere Lord. And, gentlemen, when I con-sider how patiently you have 'eared the ideas what I have expressed, I feel bound, as the best way to reward you for the kindness you have exhibited, to sit down without saying anything more—partickler as I perceive a worthier visitor nor myself is just entered. I am not in the habit of paying compliments, gentlemen ; when I do, therefore, I hope I strikes with double force."

"Ah, Mr. Murgatroyd! what's all this about striking with double force?" said the object of the above remark, as he entered. "I never excuse a man's getting into a rage during winter, even when he's seated so close to the fire as you are. It is very injudicious to put yourself into such a perspiration. What is the cause of this extreme physical and mental excitement, sir?"

Such was the very philosophical address of Mr. Robert Bolton, a shorthand-writer, as he termed himself—a bit of equivoque passing current among his fraternity, which must give the uninitiated a vast idea of the establishment of the ministerial organ, while to the initiated it signifies that no one paper can lay claim to the enjoyment of their services. Mr. Bolton was a young man, with a somewhat sickly and very dissipated expression of countenance. His habiliments were composed of an exquisite union of gentility, slovenliness, assumption, simplicity, *newness*, and old age. Half of him was dressed for the winter, the other half for the summer. His hat was of the newest cut, the D'Orsay; his trousers had been white, but the inroads of mud and ink, etc., had given them a piebald appearance; round his throat he wore a very high black cravat, of the most tyrannical stiffness; while his *tout ensemble* was hidden beneath the enormous folds of an old brown poodle-collared great-coat, which was closely buttoned up to the aforesaid cravat. His fingers peeped through the ends of his black kid gloves, and two of the toes of each foot took a similar view of society through the extremities of his high-lows. Sacred to the bare walls of his garret be the mysteries of his interior dress! He was a short, spare man, of a somewhat inferior deportment. Everybody seemed influenced by his entry into the room, and his salutation of each member partook of the patronizing. The hairdresser made way for him between himself and the stomach. A minute afterwards he had taken possession of his pint and pipe. A pause in the conversation took place. Everybody was waiting, anxious for his first observation.

"Horrid murder in Westminster this morning," observed Mr. Bolton.

Everybody changed their positions. All eyes were fixed upon the man of paragraphs.

"A baker murdered his son by boiling him in a copper," said Mr. Bolton.

"Good heavens!" exclaimed everybody, in simultaneous horror.

"Boiled him, gentlemen!" added Mr. Bolton, with the most effective emphasis; "*boiled* him!"

" And the particulars, Mr. B.," inquired the hairdresser, "the particulars?"

Mr. Bolton took a very long draught of porter, and some two or three dozen whiffs of tobacco, doubtless to instil into the commercial capacities of the company the superiority of a gentleman connected with the press, and then said—

"The man was a baker, gentlemen. (Every one looked at the baker present, who stared at Bolton.) His victim, being his son, also was necessarily the son of a baker. The wretched murderer had a wife, whom he was frequently in the habit, while in an intoxicated state, of kicking, pummelling, flinging mugs at, knocking down, and half-killing while in bed, by inserting in her mouth a considerable portion of a sheet or blanket."

The speaker took another draught, everybody looked at everybody else, and exclaimed, "Horrid!"

" It appears in evidence, gentlemen," continued Mr. Bolton, "that, on the evening of yesterday, Sawyer the baker came home in a reprehensible state of beer. Mrs. S., connubially considerate, carried him in that condition up-stairs into his chamber, and consigned him to their mutual couch. In a minute or two she lay sleeping beside the man whom the morrow's dawn beheld a murderer! (Entire silence informed the reporter that his picture had attained the awful effect he desired.) The son came home about an hour afterwards, opened the door, and went up to bed. Scarcely (gentlemen, conceive his feelings of alarm), scarcely had he taken off his indescribables, when shrieks (to his experienced ear *maternal* shrieks) scared the silence of surrounding night. He put his indescribables on again, and ran down-stairs. He opened the door of the parental bed-chamber. His father was dancing upon his mother. What must have been his feelings! In the agony of the minute he rushed at his male parent as he was about to plunge a knife into the side of his female. The mother shrieked. The father caught the son (who had wrested the knife from the paternal grasp) up in his arms, carried him down-stairs, shoved him into a copper of boiling water among some linen, closed the lid, and jumped upon the top of it, in which position he was found with a ferocious countenance by the mother, who arrived in the melancholy wash-house just as he had so settled himself.

" 'Where's my boy?' shrieked the mother.

" 'In that copper, boiling,' coolly replied the benign father.

"Struck by the awful intelligence, the mother rushed from the house, and alarmed the neighbourhood. The police entered a minute afterwards. The father, having bolted the wash-house door, had bolted himself. They dragged the lifeless body of the boiled baker from the cauldron, and, with a promptitude commendable in men of their station, they immediately carried it to the station-house. Subsequently, the baker was apprehended while seated on the top of a lamp-post in Parliament Street, lighting his pipe."

The whole horrible ideality of the Mysteries of Udolpho, condensed into the pithy effect of a ten-line paragraph, could not possibly have so affected the narrator's auditory. Silence, the purest and most noble of all kinds of applause, bore ample testimony to the barbarity of the baker, as well as to Bolton's knack of narration ; and it was only broken after some minutes had elapsed by interjectional expressions of the intense indignation of every man present. The baker wondered how a British baker could so disgrace himself and the highly honourable calling to which he belonged ; and the others indulged in a variety of wonderments connected with the subject ; among which not the least wonderment was that which was awakened by the genius and information of Mr. Robert Bolton, who, after a glowing eulogium on himself, and his unspeakable influence with the daily press, was proceeding, with a most solemn countenance, to hear the pros and cons of the Pope autograph question, when I took up my hat, and left.

FAMILIAR EPISTLE FROM A PARENT
TO A CHILD

AGED TWO YEARS AND TWO MONTHS

My Child,

To recount with what trouble I have brought you up —with what an anxious eye I have regarded your progress,— how late and how often I have sat up at night working for you,—and how many thousand letters I have received from, and written to your various relations and friends, many of whom have been of a querulous and irritable turn,—to dwell on the anxiety and tenderness with which I have (as far as I possessed the power) inspected and chosen your food ; rejecting the indigestible and heavy matter which some injudicious but well-meaning old ladies would have had you swallow, and retaining only those light and pleasant articles which I deemed calculated to keep you free from all gross humours, and to render you an agreeable child, and one who might be popular with society in general,—to dilate on the steadiness with which I have prevented your annoying any company by talking politics—always assuring you that you would thank me for it yourself some day when you grew older,—to expatiate, in short, upon my own assiduity as a parent, is beside my present purpose, though I cannot but contemplate your fair appearance—your robust health, and unimpeded circulation (which I take to be the great secret of your good looks) without the liveliest satisfaction and delight.

It is a trite observation, and one which, young as you are, I have no doubt you have often heard repeated, that we have fallen upon strange times, and live in days of constant shiftings and changes. I had a melancholy instance of this only a week or two since. I was returning from Manchester to London by the Mail Train, when I suddenly fell into another train—a mixed train—of reflection, occasioned by the dejected and disconsolate demeanour of the Post Office Guard. We were stopping at some station where they take in water, when he dismounted slowly from the little box in which he sits in ghastly mockery of his old condition with pistol and blunderbuss beside him, ready to shoot the first highway-man (or railwayman) who shall attempt to stop the horses, which now travel (when they travel at all) *inside* and in a portable stable invented for the purpose,—he dismounted, I say, slowly and sadly, from his post, and looking mournfully about him as if in dismal recollection of the old roadside public-house—the blazing fire—the glass of foaming ale—the buxom handmaid and admiring hangers-on of tap-room and stable, all honoured by his notice ; and, retiring a little apart, stood leaning against a signal-post, surveying the engine with a look of combined affliction and disgust which no words can describe. His scarlet coat and golden lace were tarnished with ignoble smoke ; flakes of soot had fallen on his bright green shawl—his pride in days of yore —the steam condensed in the tunnel from which we had just emerged, shone upon his hat like rain. His eye be-tokened that he was thinking of the coachman ; and as it wandered to his own seat and his own fast-fading garb, it was plain to see that he felt his office and himself had alike no business there, and were nothing but an elaborate practical joke.

As we whirled away, I was led insensibly into an anticipa-tion of those days to come, when mail-coach guards shall no longer be judges of horse-flesh—when a mail-coach guard shall never even have seen a horse—when stations shall have superseded stables, and corn shall have given place to coke. " In those dawning times," thought I, " exhibition-rooms shall teem with portraits of her Majesty's favourite engine, with boilers after Nature by future Landseers. Some Amburgh, yet unborn, shall break wild horses by his magic power ; and in the dress of a mail-coach guard exhibit his TRAINED ANIMALS in a mock mail-coach. Then shall wondering crowds observe how that, with the exception of his whip, it is all his eye ; and crowned heads shall see them fed on oats, and stand alone unmoved and undismayed, while courtiers flee affrighted when the coursers neigh ! "

Such, my child, were the reflections from which I was only awakened then, as I am now, by the necessity of attending to matters of present though minor importance. I offer no apology to you for the digression, for it brings me very naturally to the subject of change, which is the very subject of which I desire to treat.

In fact, my child, you have changed hands. Henceforth I resign you to the guardianship and protection of one of my most intimate and valued friends, Mr. Ainsworth, with whom, and with you, my best wishes and warmest feelings will ever remain. I reap no gain or profit by parting from you, nor will any conveyance of your property be required, for, in this respect, you have always been literally "Bentley's" Miscellany, and never mine.

Unlike the driver of the old Manchester mail, I regard this altered state of things with feelings of unmingled pleasure and satisfaction. Unlike the guard of the new Manchester mail, *your* guard is at home in his new place, and has roystering highwaymen and gallant desperadoes ever within call. And if I might compare you, my child, to an engine; (not a Tory engine, nor a Whig engine, but a brisk and rapid locomotive;) your friends and patrons to passengers; and he who now stands towards you *in loco parentis* as the skilful engineer and supervisor of the whole, I would humbly crave leave to postpone the departure of the train on its new and auspicious course for one brief instant, while, with hat in hand, I approach side by side with the friend who travelled with me on the old road, and presume to solicit favour and kindness in behalf of him and his new charge, both for their sakes and that of the old coachman,

Boz.

THE END